FIFA WORLD CUP

GERMANY
2006

9 June – 9 July 2006

WORLD

CUP

SOCCER

GERMANY 2006

Michael Lewis

Moyer Bell

Kingston, Rhode Island & Lancaster, England

To Debbie and Rob, two of my biggest supporters

Published by Moyer Bell

Fourth Revised Edition

LIBRARY OF CONGRESS

CATALOGING IN PUBLICATION DATA

Lewis, Michael, 1952-
World Cup Soccer / Michael Lewis 4th ed.

p. cm.
Includes bibliographical references and appendices
1. World Cup (Soccer) 1. Title

GV943.49.L48	2006
796.334'668-dc20	93-4585
ISBN: 1-55921-358-2	CIP

Printed in the United States of America
Distributed in North America by Acorn Alliance,
549 Old North Road, Kingston, Rhode Island 02881,
401-783-5480, www.moyerbellbooks.com and
in the United Kingdom, Eire, and Europe by
Gazelle Book Services Ltd.,
White Cross Mills, High Town,
Lancaster LA1 1RN England,
1-44-1524-68765, www.gazellebooks.co.uk

Contents

CONTENTS

Foreword

July 12, 1998—The day we became legends in soccer history—not just within the borders of France, but throughout the entire world.   The day I joined players like Pele, Maradona and Beckenbauer in the pantheon of football champions. The day my country and I defeated Brazil three-nil on soccer's grandest stage, on our native soil.

The day I was crowned a World Cup champion.

Not a day goes by now—whether in Monaco, Milan, Miami or Manhattan—when I am not reminded of that life-altering day. Family, friends, journalists, supporters, even total strangers all love to talk about our run in 1998. Some want to congratulate me. Some simply say "thank you" for bringing the joy of our first World Cup home to France. But most ask the same thing: "What is it like? What is it like to win a World Cup?"

No matter how many times I'm asked that question, it still remains difficult to answer. "There is nothing in the world like it" and "it is impossible to put into words" are common responses I have given. But those replies don't do the whole experience justice. So let me try something different. Let me take you through that unforgettable summer day in July. With police cars riding alongside us and police helicopters flying overhead, our bus left the team hotel three hours before kickoff, and what I saw on the way to the stadium in Saint-Denis was just incredible. The streets were all painted blue, white and red. Hundreds of men, women, and children lined the avenues near the hotel waving French flags wildly, wearing our team jerseys proudly, and throwing blue, white and red confetti.

Once more people realized the French National Team was in this police escort, the entire country stopped in its tracks. Cars pulled over and honked as the bus drove by. Police helicopters were joined in the skies by news helicopters. On the highway, some people parked their cars in the middle of the road and danced as we passed them. Others even decided to turn the highway into a soccer field and started kicking a ball around in traffic. What normally was a 30-minute drive from Clairefontaine to the stadium ended up taking two hours!

And the frenzy did not stop once we finally arrived at the field. Our locker room was littered with faxes and letters—sent by everyone from famous rock stars, to celebrities and even the Pope—all wishing us "bon chance."

All of this simply added to the immense pressure we felt before the match. France had never even played in a World Cup final before—much less win one—but our team had a quiet air of confidence about us. We knew we had been playing our best football to date and felt that if we kept our form, there was not a team in the world that could beat us.

Not even Brazil.

Leaving the locker room, I could hear the hum of the crowd echoing through the tunnel, the noise intensifying as we approached the pitch. The fans were over-whelmingly in our favor and Zinedine Zidane's first goal in the 27th made the stadium explode. With the Brazilians on their heels, I connected with Zidane off a corner kick to make it 2-0 right before halftime. And then Emmanuel Petitâ ™s late second half strike sealed the deal.

We were World Cup champions.

Here is where things get a little fuzzy. I don't recall the exact thoughts racing through my mind once the final whistle blew, but I do remember looking around at my teammates and thinking about all we had been through together. The '98 tournament was the climax in a campaign that began four years earlier after the 1994 World Cup. We were a new generation of French footballers that possessed big appetites for winning and the motivation to accomplish greatness. All the pain, hard work and sacrifice we endured over that time developed a brotherly bond among us, and being able to share the moment of winning the World Cup with these team-mates was the ultimate reward.

When it was my turn to hold the trophy, I felt as though I was touching the Holy Grail. I took it and held it high over my head for all the world to see. While the feeling was indescribable, I can tell you this: those emotions are why you play, why you compete, why you dream. To be a part of that moment, on that day.

This summer at the 2006 World Cup, another team will be fortunate enough to experience that moment and the ecstasy that comes along with it. They will have their moment. And they will have their day. *Bon Chance.*

This summer at the 2006 World Cup, another team—which has been researched and detailed by Michael Lewis in this book—will be fortunate enough to experience that moment and the ecstasy that comes along with it. They will have their moment. And they will have their day. *Bon Chance.*

Youri Djorkaeff (as told to Eric Tosi)
Forward, French National Team

Introduction

Michael Lewis

Here it is less than 90 days before the greatest show on earth and already I have World Cup fever.

Yes, I contracted it when I was researching and writing this book.

But I get it every four years at about this time, even before I penned my first World Cup book. Let's face it. There isn't any other sporting event on earth like the World Cup. Sure, there are the Olympics, but it is so over hyped by TV that it is easy to get turned off by it before it begins.

Even though Germany 2006 will be my sixth World Cup—I might be considered an old veteran at covering the competition—it certainly hasn't become old hat to me.

Psst. I'll let you in a little secret. I live for the World Cup. That's right. Nothing against all the other soccer events I have covered or watch, but the World Cup gives me life in more ways than you can imagine. Now don't get me wrong—covering Major League Soccer and other domestic-oriented leagues and events are my bread-and-butter. The World Cup is my endless dessert tray. There is so much from which to choose—Black Forest cake, French cheese cake and American apple pie, among other delectable delights.

What draws me and others to watch every four years? Perhaps it is the unpredictability of the competition. After all, who thought that Cameroon would stun defending champion Argentina at the Italia '90 opener or that Senegal would do the same to France in Korea in 2002?

Or that the U.S., after such a poor showing at France '98 stunned Portugal in its first game and went on a rather inexplicable run to the quarterfinals before losing to Germany, 1-0, on what many thought was a handball in the penalty area. Even German native Franz Beckenbauer who is ahead of Germany's World Cup Organizing Committee felt his countrymen were lucky.

"I saw the replay," he told the audience at a World Cup dinner in Manhattan on Feb. 23, 2006. "Now it's too late, but it was a hand ball.

"Thank God the referee didn't see."

I have been blessed because I am only one of a handful of reporters who witnessed in the stadium live all three England-Argentina encounters. I marveled at Diego Maradona's chicanery and magnificence only minutes apart in 1986 were entertained by Michael Owens' great individual effort in 1998 and realized the simple things of life just by surviving of what could have been a life-and-death mixed zone encounter with David Beckham in 2002.

Of course, my World Cup experience is extremely personal as well.

In 1986 as one of a few American journalists to venture down to Mexico (remember, the U.S. got bounced from qualifying exactly a year to the day of the start of the competition), I paid my own way down as a free-lance journalist. I got my credentials through Soccer America and my credentials said Berling Communications, named after the owners of the publication. However, all the journalists thought I was from Germany.

In 1990, my World Cup tenure with the New York Daily News began. Our headquarters was an apartment in Florence, Italy for the first three weeks before claiming Rome as our new point of attack. Beyond the grandeur of a Renaissance city, interestingly, my most nagging memory of Florence was when we ran out of toilet paper and our landlord did not re stock (we left for the press center and/or games before stores opened and returned after they closed. So I had to be resourceful and borrowed toilet paper from the press center every day. After all, we didn't want to get, ahem, wiped out.

In 1994, I had no headquarters as I bounced around the country and wound up visiting nine of the 10 venues. I had the rare opportunity of being in three cities in one day on July 3. I flew out of Chicago for the Romania-Argentina second-round match in the Rose Bowl in Pasadena, Calif. and wound up in San Francisco hours after that game for the July 4 encounter between the U.S. and Brazil.

In 1998, Paris was our headquarters and my most shining moment again did not come during a match, but afterwards. The hotel I was supposed to stay at in Marseille did not have room for me, even though I had a voucher. I wound up sleeping on a couch in the hotel lobby with my computer bag's handle wrapped around my arm (that must have been one pretty sight). I got on a train—and no, I had not showered (that must have been one stinky odor) and stood virtually the entire way to Paris before completing the quick switch of my life, getting a shower, new clothes, lunch and scurried out for a trip to another train station for a journey to Nantes for the U.S.-Yugoslavia match. My roommates, who were out eating lunch during my cameo appearance, didn't even realize I came and went. After learning of my quick change, they nicknamed me "The wind."

In 2002, because the tournament was in two countries, we had to split up. New York Daily News columnist Filip Bondy got Korea and I got Japan. I had some great games to cover, but I do regret not covering the U.S., although—and please, please, don't repeat this to coach Bruce Arena or anyone from U.S. Soccer—I have never seen the United States win a game at the World Cup (they'll have me banned from all U.S. games). Or tie one for that matter. I am 0-7. But remember, that's between you and me. Perhaps the streak will be broken this June.

My most memorable and harrowing 2002 experience came in the mixed zone area—where journalists can act like animals while trying to interview players one-on-one after the match—after England avenged its 1998 elimination with a rather lackluster 1-0 win. David Beckham converted the lone goal, on a penalty. I positioned myself next to a BBC radio I knew because England PR officials would bring the players out to him. A surge of journalists raced toward us and bent the wooden barrier toward Beckham. It seemed to be only a matter of time before we would topple on him and end his World Cup—and perhaps his life—prematurely. But Japanese security, always on the ball, made the save of the tournament. A number of personnel got on their knees and kept the barrier propped up while we got Beckham's words of wisdom for our stories—and lived to tell about it.

I have to let you in on another secret as well. Since 1990, I have covered every Cup with Filip. We have split coverage of the knockout-round matches and historically, even if a game looked like a dog on paper, it would turn into a memorable encounter for yours truly. For example, Filip took Argentina-Brazil. Well, I "got stuck" with the Netherlands-Germany The better match? Germany's win over the Dutch with the infamous spitting incident. Filip grabbed Germany-Czechoslovakia, and I "got stuck" with England-Cameroon, which almost finished as an upset of epic proportions before the English managed to eke out an extra-time win. And so on it has gone. Just please don't tell him about it because he will do the exact opposite, perhaps not unlike what George Costanza did during several Seinfield episodes.

But you know, I don't care what game I cover. It's what you get out of it and when you're at the World Cup, there is always something new and different to take in or wonder about, whether it's a fabulous goal, an historic moment or the color and rapid fans. That's the absolute beauty of the event.

I just can't wait for it to start. Just blame it on my World Cup fever.

Michael Lewis
March 12, 2006

The Basics

For those unfamiliar with all the terms of soccer (a.k.a. futbol and calico), the following might help to acquaint you with the language of the game.

backpass—Usually a pass from a defender to the goalkeeper.

capped—An international appearance by a player.

CONCACAF—Confederation of North, Central American and Caribbean Association Football—the governing body of soccer in the Western Hemisphere—excluding South America. The United States is a member of CONCACAF and must play its World Cup qualifying games through this organization.

corner kick—A kick given to the attacking team when the defending side knocks or clears the ball over the end or goal line. The kick is taken from the corner on the side in which the ball went out of bounds.

deadball—When the ball is not in play while on the field, usually on free kicks and corner kicks.

Euro 2004—Another way to describe the European Championship in Portugal.

field (size)—At the World Cup and international level, field size generally runs from 110 to 120 yards in length and from 75 to 85 yards in width.

FIFA—Federation Internationale de Football Association, the sport's governing body, which is headquartered in Zurich, Switzerland.

forward—A player who usually performs exclusively in an attacking role.

France '98—Another way to describe the 1998 World Cup in France.

fullback—A defender, usually one of four players who are in front of the goalkeeper.

GAA—Goals against average for goalkeepers.

game (length)—A soccer game is ninety minutes. If it is tied in the knockout rounds of the World Cup, then a pair of sudden-death fifteen minute overtimes are played.

Germany 2006—Another way to describe the 2006 World Cup in Germany

hand ball—When a player, other than the goalkeeper, touches the ball on purpose. If the ball hits the player's hand by chance, it is up to the referee to call it.

hat trick—When a player scores three goals in one game.

header—When a player hits the ball with his head.

Italia '90—Another way to describe the 1990 World Cup in Italy.

MLS—Major League Soccer, the First Division league in the United States that kicked off in 1996.

N minute—The measurement of time in a soccer game, particularly at the international level. If a goal is scored fifteen seconds into the match, it is officially listed as the first minute.

North American Soccer League—A defunct First Division league in the United States in which Pelé starred for three years. It lasted seventeen seasons (1968-84).

officials—They also are known as game officials: the referee and linesmen. In recent years, FIFA has preferred to use referee's assistants for linesmen.

offside—This is soccer's most controversial rule because it is a bang-bang play for game officials, happening in a matter of seconds, in which a quick decision must be made. A player is considered offside—on the attacking side of the field—when he is beyond the final defender (not the goalkeeper) when the ball is first played, not when he receives it.

penalty kick—When a player is fouled in the penalty area (an 18 by 44 yard box in front of the goal), his team is given a free kick from 12 yards.

players (how many)—-There are eleven players on a soccer team, ten field players and a goalkeeper. A game is abandoned if a team can only field six players.

red card—An automatic ejection by the referee for a violent foul or an accumulation of fouls. Think of it as a red light as in stop, you cannot play any-more in this game.

striker—Another way to describe a forward, particularly someone who is a prolific goalscorer.

sweeper—The free safety of soccer. He usually doesn't have to cover anyone and is the last line of defense in front of the goalkeeper.

throw-in—It is the only time a field player is allowed to use his hands (an overhead throw using both hands) because he throws the ball into play after an opposing player knocks it out of bounds over the sidelines.

trap—The method in which a player stops the ball, usually with his chest or foot.

UEFA—Union of European Football Associations, the governing body of European soccer.

UNAM—Universidad Nacional Autonoma de Mexico, a successful First Division club in Mexico that plays in Mexico City. Its nickname is "Los Pumas."

USA '94—Another way to describe the 1994 World Cup.

USL—United Soccer Leagues, the umbrella for a series of organized minor leagues with a men's league at three levels and a women's league called the W-League.

USSF—United States Soccer Federation, the U.S.'s governing body for soc-cer. Its headquarters are in Chicago. It is better known as U.S. Soccer

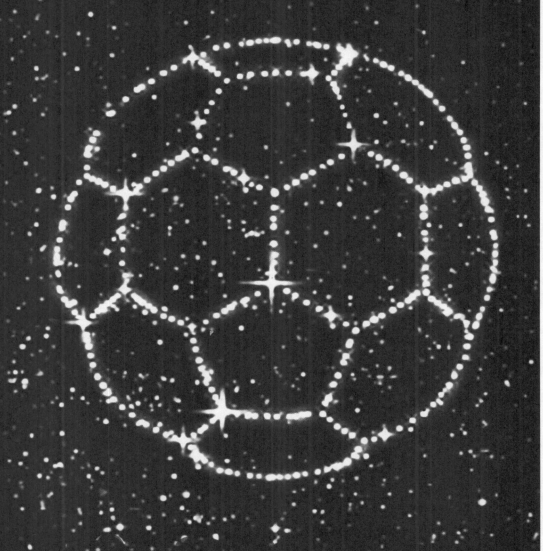

WORLD CUP SOCCER

2006
Germany

The Mystique

Imagine, if you will, the World Series, Super Bowl and the Olympics all rolled into one, and you begin to understand the magnitude of what will occur in Germany this summer. The World Cup is expected to leave scores of countries and at a standstill for a month and international soccer fans trying to find various excuses to get out of work to watch their favorite team on TV, awaiting the latest news from across the Atlantic.

England's Gordon Banks clears a head shot by Dumitrache of Romania with Mullery and Labone near by.

Beginning June 9, and for thirty days thereafter, thirty-two teams representing their countries, including the United States, will play a total of sixty-four games in twelve stadiums in as many cities in Germany in what is undoubtedly the world's greatest sporting spectacle. These games are expected to be watched in person or on television by nearly a cumulative audience of thirty-seven billion people—-including several million in the United States—and reach a climax when the two best soccer teams in the world face off at refurbished Olympic Stadium in Berlin on July 9.

The object of desire? The 14-karat gold FIFA World Cup trophy.

But numbers tell only part of the story. The World Cup is about passion, nationalism, beauty, history and controversy. It is about a month-long celebration of soccer that occurs only once every four years.

It is truly the greatest show on earth.

The World Cup has transformed kings into coaches and players into stars and even legends. King Carol of Romania hand-picked his squad for the very first World Cup in 1930 and made sure the players did not lose their jobs back home because of the 3-month round-trip Trans-Atlantic boat trip and stay in Uruguay.

In 1958, a seventeen-year-old Brazilian named Edison Arantes do Nascimento, otherwise known as Pele to the rest of the planet, made his international debut, leading his country to the first of three unprecedented world championships in four tries.

In 1982, Paolo Rossi went from pariah to hero in a matter of weeks, wiping away the stigma of a betting scandal by scoring six goals to lead Italy to the championship.

In 1986, Argentina's Diego Maradona's Hand of God—-he knocked the ball into the net with his hand—-and feet of a god—-an incredible sixty-yard jaunt through the English midfield and defense en route to a goal—forever etched his name into soccer history.

In 1950, the United States staged one of the greatest upsets in sporting annals by stunning heavily favored England, 1-0, as the fans of Belo Horizonte, Brazil, took these unknown warriors onto their shoulders in a post-match victory celebration.

In 1966, the Jules Rimet Trophy, the original World Cup trophy, was stolen while it was on exhibit at a stamp show in England. During a massive police and public hunt for the trophy, a dog by the name of Pickles unearthed the trophy under some shrubs in London. Pickles and his owner collected a $10,000 reward (In 1983, the trophy again was stolen by thieves in Rio de Janeiro in Brazil and was never recovered; it was believed to have been melted down).

In 1990, thirty-eight year-old Roger Milla was coaxed out of retirement, and, as a super-sub, helped a carefree Cameroon side to

global fame, thanks to an opening-match upset of the defending champion Argentines and to an amazing, unforgettable, heart-breaking 3-2 extra-time loss to England in the quarterfinals.

Columbia's Carlos Valderrama blocks a pass by Romania's Gheorge Hagi in 1994.

In 1998, France, one of the founders of FIFA—Federation International de Football Association, the sport's governing body—and of the World Cup, finally culminated its sixty-eight year quest in dramatic fashion by capturing the sport's biggest prize. Millions of Frenchmen and women—yes, many observers before the World Cup felt they lacked passion—thronged Champs-Elysees that summer night of July 12—the biggest celebration in France since Liberation Day in 1944.

And as recently as 2002, Ronaldo performed a self-resurrection of epic proportions by leading Brazil to an unprecedented and incredible fifth world championship. Ronaldo became the first player to score at least eight goals in a tournament since German striker Gerd (Der Bomber) Mueller found the back of the net ten times in 1970, while burying the ghosts of 1998 behind him.

The World Cup has all the festivity of Carnival, a joyous event that allows people and fans to put aside everyday cares. In 1978, for instance, Argentines forgot about 300 percent inflation and severe political problems to celebrate their first title. Fans moved en masse out into the streets of Buenos Aires and other major cities for an all-night party. Argentina again is among the final 32 teams and is considered a favorite to make the quarterfinals, if not the semifinals or even championship game.

And certainly no World Cup would be complete without Brazil, the only country that has qualified for all eighteen editions, and its enthusiastic supporters. Those fans, who can easily be detected by their yellow shirts, put on a show of their own, as they samba before, during and after games—-win, lose or draw.

Not surprisingly, Brazil again is the favorite to repeat and win an amazing sixth world championship. Coach Carlos Alberto Parreira, who guided the South Americans to the USA '94, crown, is back to accomplish what only one other man has achieved—winning two World Cup titles (coach Vittorio Pozzo directed the Italians to back-to-back championships in 1934 and 1938).

In 1982, however, nobody could upstage the Italians, who celebrated their country's third title by diving into the Trevi Fountain in Rome, which, no doubt will be duplicated should they again emerge victorious. There is something of a tradition of winners at the World Cup: Only seven countries—-Brazil (5), Italy (3), Germany (3), Argentina (2), Uruguay (2), England (1) and France (1)—-have won championships.

Like soccer in general, the World Cup does stir passions, only a bit more so.

In 1970, Honduras and El Salvador went to war over a qualification match. In 1978, a West Berlin carpenter leapt out of a second-story window shouting, "I don't want to live anymore," after Austria eliminated West Germany, while at a Frankfurt cafe, a nun tried to strangle a man who cheered the Austrians. In 1982, when Brazil was upset by Italy in the quarterfinals, three people committed suicide in Rio de Janeiro and a bar customer in Sao Paulo was shot and killed over an argument about the game. In 1990, seventeen year-old Xia Qianli strangled his father in Zhejang, China, because he was not allowed to watch the opening ceremony. And in 1994, one fan,

Brazilian Enzio de Souza, who, with a Brazilian flag around his neck, drove his motorcycle from South American to the Rose Bowl in Pasadena, Calif. in time for the semifinal. And yet another fan in Albania was so confident that Argentina would beat Bulgaria in an opening round game that he put up his wife in a bet with a friend (his wife disappeared with the winner and the fan complained to the police).

Snow was the surprise weather condition during a qualifying match in Munich, West Germany, for the 1966 competition.

What causes such extreme behavior? Soccer is the only organized sport in many countries. National honor is at stake. And sometimes a country's culture and way of life are put on the line.

Perhaps this passion had its seeds at the very first tournament in Montevideo, Uruguay, in 1930. In that final, two different balls were used in the championship match between Uruguay-Argentina. With a ball made in Argentina, the visitors grabbed a 2-1 halftime lead. The Uruguayans, using their ball in the second half, rallied for a 4-2 victory. When news of the defeat reached Buenos Aires, an angry mob attacked the Uruguayan Consulate with bricks and stones.

Some seventy-six years and eighteen World Cups later, the tournament is alive and kicking in the 21st century. In fact, the 1994 World Cup gave soccer in the U.S. a much-needed boost at the professional level. Two years after the cup, Major League Soccer, the first First Division league in this country since the North American Soccer League folded in 1984, was born. The new league has given many players a chance to develop their skills and make a name for themselves. The list includes Landon Donovan and DaMarcus Beasley, a pair of twenty-four year-olds who are in their prime.

Each World Cup has its own unique flavor and atmosphere, and Germany 2006 will be no different.

In 1994, the U.S.-hosted cup made history by becoming the first competition to hold soccer in a domed-stadium with grass. France '98 was expanded to thirty-two countries for the first time. The previous four World Cups had twenty-four teams each. In the opening round, each team—including the eight seeded teams who once enjoyed playing all their games at the same venue—played at three different stadiums.

Like France, the 2002 version had each team play at a different venue in the opening round. However, there were a number of innovations that made this World Cup unique. For the first time a World Cup was held in two countries, thanks to FIFA's controversial awarding of the Cup in 1996. What made matters (and traveling) more challenging was that these countries did not border on each other, but were separated by the East Sea and Sea of Japan.

For Germany 2006, it was back to normalcy as one country took over the daunting chores of running the greatest show on earth as the venues were pared down to a dozen—Berlin, Cologne, Dortmund, Frankfurt, Gelsenkirchen, Hamburg, Hannover, Kaiserslautern, Leipzig, Munich, Nuremburg and Stuttgart.

Due to the events of Sept. 11, 2001 this World Cup is expected to be the heaviest guarded and most secure.

All twelve stadiums will be no-fly zones during the tournament and Germany was expected to ask NATO to provide AWACS surveillance aircraft to patrol its airspace. More measures and precautions are likely to be made—public and secret—before the Cup begins.

The spectacle kicks off at Olympic Stadium in Munich on June 9, when host Germany and Costa Rica tussle.

Then, for the next month, the eyes of the world will be on Germany. That's when each of the thirty-two countries plays three games in the first round, which has four teams in eight groups. The top sixteen—two in each group—advance to the second round. The survivors then move onto to the knockout competition: the second round, quarterfinals, semifinals and championship match.

A very young Pelé at his first World Cup in 1958

The big question is: Who will play in that final in Berlin on July 9?

If you go by tradition and history, it would be wise to pick an Italy, Germany, France or England to win in Europe. When teams play off continent or out of their hemisphere, they usually have to battle new time zones (sleeping habits), food and culture (many teams bring their own chef), among other challenges.

The early favorites are defending champion Brazil, which brings back several key players from its 2002 side that captured the 2005 FIFA Confederations Cup, a World Cup rehearsal in Germany. This just might be the last hurrah for the twenty-nine-year-old Ronaldo, who has indicated that Germany 2006 would be his World Cup finale. And if Ronaldo's aging and ailing knees get the best of him, the Brazilians have an endless list of wannabe heroes ready to

Escobar's memory lives on

On a field in Flushing Meadow Park in New York City on July 4, 2006, Miguel Cuellar will address several hundred young, budding soccer players and their parents about a good and decent man he once knew.

He will tell them about the man's character, about what type of a soccer player he was, about how he lived, and just as importantly, how he died.

Cuellar then will ask for a moment of silence for his fallen comrade, Andres Escobar.

Tuesday, July 2, 2006 will be the twelfth anniversary of Escobar's death. The Colombian defender was gunned down outside a Medellin, Colombia, nightclub just days after accidentally scoring an own goal in the World Cup. Escobar, who was 27, was shot twelve times as one of the gunmen shouted, "Goal! Goal!"

FIFA president Sepp Blatter called it "the saddest day I have ever witnessed in football."

Escobar's only crime was that he was guilty of trying too hard to stop an American offensive foray into the Colombian penalty area on June 21, 1994. U.S. midfielder John Harkes had sent a low drive from the left wing intended for midfielder Earnie Stewart. But the ball never got there.

Escobar, in a sliding attempt to clear the ball out of harm's way, accidentally pushed the ball into his own net for the Americans' first goal of what was to become a 2-1 upset.

The U.S. eventually went on to the second round. The Colombians went home in disgrace after they were eliminated several days later, and Escobar wound up paying the ultimate price.

That is where Cuellar came in. Cuellar, a fifty-three year-old sales manager for Duggan's Distillers and the soccer director of Flushing Meadow Park in Queens, had started a youth soccer club—

make history. Their gallery includes strikers Adriano, who has filled the nets in the defensive-tough Serie A in Italy the past several years, and Robinho, who performs for Real Madrid in Spain.

Germany is far from the team that many countries feared in the eighties and nineties. There are no superstars in the mold of a Juergen Klinsmann or Lothar Matthaeus, save for midfielder Michael Ballack. Klinsmann is now coach of the team and he has shaken up the traditional Germans with innovative coaching techniques and the controversial fact that he lives in Orange County in southern California, which has left himself wide open for criticism if Germany stumbles. Thanks to the combination of playing at home and a great German soccer tradition of a never-say-die attitude, however, the hosts must be respected.

England, a team that has so much promise, but usually finds a

the New York Inter Soccer Institute—earlier in 1994.

On July 2 of that year he had awakened early to listen to radio programs from his native Colombia. He was expecting to hear folk songs. What he heard was shocking—the details of Escobar's death. Cuellar was so shaken he woke his wife. Later in the day, he decided to rename his fledgling club the Andres Escobar Soccer Institute.

The Institute has 130 players on recreational and competitive teams. The boys and girls range in age from four to fifteen. The players wear the green and white of Escobar's old club, Nacional.

"He was a gentleman inside and outside the field," Cuellar said. "That's what we want to tell the kids.

"Soccer is only a game to enjoy. You have to learn to win, lose or draw. Some people can't deal with losing a game."

Escobar's cousin, Ernesto Bencosmo, a seventeen year-old defender who is a convert from baseball, has played with the club

for several years.

"He was a good player," Bencosmo said. "I didn't think there was any reason for his death because many players have scored goals for the opposing team.

"I like to play soccer. I like to defend. I like to play where my cousin played. Having the club named after my cousin meant a lot of me. It made me play more and play better."

Bencosmo said he would would love to play professional soccer someday.

"As long as it's a professional career, it doesn't matter where I play—the U.S. or Colombia," said Bencosmo, whose favorite players are former Colombian World Cup captain and former Colorado Rapids midfielder Carlos Valderrama and Rapids defender Mike Petke. "I'd love to play in MLS. I love the uniforms."

Cuellar is proud of Bencosmo's progress on and off the field.

"When he joined us, he didn't know anything about soccer," he said. "He will way to shoot itself in the proverbial foot, is considered a favorite in many quarters. There are, however, a number of obstacles and headaches, internal and external. Striker Michael Owen, who enjoyed a spectacular Cup debut as an eighteen year-old at France '98, is recovering from a broken foot suffered this winter. David Beckham attracts attention whether he is making a politically incorrect foul or getting red-carded or just showing up with his wife, the former Victoria Adams (aka Posh Spice). Coach Sven-Goran Eriksson, a Swede whose affair with the English Football Association secretary, was fodder for British tabloids, announced he was stepping down as coach after the Cup—with two more years remaining on his contract

make it as a soccer player. He's an A student."

Several years ago, a rather eerie scenario took place during an indoor tournament. Ernesto Bencosmo scored an own goal, just like his cousin.

"We had to talk to him," Cuellar said. "We told him that every player makes mistakes and scores own goals. If he does it again, we will have to talk to him."

Cuellar is expecting several hundred people to show up at Flushing Meadow Park on July 4th, after a mass given by a local priest and Cuellar's speech, a special under-eleven boys game will be held between the Institute and Bolanos Soccer School. Both clubs participate in the MetroKids Interregional Soccer League (1,700 players and growing), which is also operated by Cuellar.

In his talk, Cuellar will tell the players and their parents the story of Andres Escobar.

"I will say, 'Remember who Andres Escobar was, as a player and a person,'" Cuellar said. "We would like to have kids play and act like Andres Escobar did in and

outside the field. We will tell the kids that you don't have to be a good player, but a good man outside the field.

"He is still in our minds and hearts."

The Escobar Institute has branched out to Colombia (in four cities) and to London.

The club's goals are simple. "Even if they don't become soccer players, they can get an education," Cuellar said, "and learn how to be a better man, a better person in life and to be a winner."

Cuellar is gratified when he sees the institute's graduates move on to college.

"One of the fathers came up to me and tells me his son is going to North Carolina on a scholarship," he said. "That touched my heart. It tells me that my time isn't wasted.

"One day we're going to see one of the kids from the Andres Escobar Institute in MLS."

Cuellar understands his role in the soccer universe. He will continue to develop players and educate them and their parents about Escobar.

"Every year," he said, "until I can't do it."

after he revealed some revelations about the English game to a fake sheikh during a scam by a British newspaper.

Off a bitterly disappointing and embarrassing first-round elimination in Korea four years ago in which they failed to win a game (a World Cup first for defending champions), the French certainly have something to prove that 2002 was a fluke. They struggled through most of qualifying and did not find themselves until Zidane Zinedine, who had declared his international retirement a few years prior, put on the boots for France again.

Outside of Brazil, which won the whole thing in 1958, Argentina is the only other South American team that reached the championship game in a Euro-based World Cup (the Argentines lost to Germany, 1-0, on a late penalty kick in 1990). Big things were expected of Argentina in 2002, but the team was shown the door in Japan after an abysmal opening-round showing.

South Korea and Japan will be out to prove that their 2002 showing in their home countries was not an aberration or a fluke mainly due to the fact they were hosts. Korea, which had never won a World Cup match previously, reached the semifinals. Japan, which qualified for its first tournament at France '98, made it to the second round. Saudi Arabia, which has shown some promise in the past, and Iran, which bested the U.S. in 1998, are the two other Asian representatives who aren't expected to go far.

Africa certainly has a new look. Instead of the usual suspects of

Portugal star Eusebio, in the 2-1 victory over the Soviet Union and goalkeeper Lev Yashin in the 1966 Cup.

perennial powerhouses Cameroon and Nigeria, touted by many experts and observers as possibly the first African countries to win it all, come teams with literally no Cup experience. Angola, Ivory Coast, Ghana and Togo are all WC newcomers. It remains to be seen whether they can pull off an upset for the ages or two.

Tunisia, which has been around the World Cup block three times before, is considered a weak side and not given much of a chance to get out of its group in one piece. Incredibly, South Africa, named host of the 2010 World Cup in 2004, failed to qualify for Germany. The South Africans became only the second nation not to participate in the World Cup before it hosted one.

It's been more than a generation since Australia last performed on the world stage. In fact, the only time the Aussies played in the Cup was in 1974, when it was hosted by Germany. The Aussies survived a home-and-home playoff with Uruguay.

Trinidad & Tobago also had to overcome a long-range playoff series with Bahrain to book its place, suffering through sixteen years of angst for not qualifying in 1990, before finally making it to soccer's promised land for the very first time.

Outside of Brazil and Argentina, not much is expected of South American sides Paraguay and Ecuador.

Europe runs the gamut of having some quality sides to others that are expectded to struggle.

Two of the best and most respected teams find themselves in Group E, which happens to be the Americans' group.

The Czech Republic, second ranked in FIFA's poll, might not have ever won a Cup, but it was a surprise side at Euro 2004 in Portugal and considered a dangerous side with the likes of one-time player of the year Pavel Nedved, who came out of international retirement to help his nation qualify.

Three-time champion Italy, obviously must get respect due to its steel chain of a defense. The Italians can be a slow-starting side that has been known to pick up steam. However, Italy has underachieved in the eyes of many observers in recent major international competitions, was ousted in the 2002 second round by Korea and failed to get out of the group stages at Euro 2004.

The Dutch are back for the first time since 1998, when they fin-

Chapter One : The Mystique

ished fourth in France. For a country its size (sixteen million), the Netherlands has produced some of the best soccer players in the world. This year's team certainly is no exception with Manchester United striker Ruud Van Nistelrooy and teammate and goalkeeper Edwin Van der Sar and captain Phillip Cocu leading the way. Like the Italians, the Dutch have a history of not reaching their potential in this competition.

And while on the subject, Portugal will be out for some retribution after an absolutely awful 2002 performance in which it was sent packing home after a poor first round. The Portuguese, who were boosted by a talented generation of players, reached the final of Euro 2004 (which it hosted), but lost to an upstart Greece (The Greeks, incidentally, failed to qualify for the Cup).

And then there's Spain, forever underachievers. Despite producing one quality player after another through the years, the Spanish have major problems getting out of the second round or quarterfinals. Except for their most ardent supporters, it will be difficult to convince anyone else the Spanish can break this confounding pattern.

Despite not having a full professional league, Sweden keeps reaching the World Cup (this is the Swedes' eleventh appearance) with a third-place finish at USA '94 its most recent Cup glory.

Poland will be attempting to rediscover lost glory, when it was

Geoff Hurst gives England an undisputed victory with this shot that completes his hat trick in the 1966 final against Germany.

an international force in the seventies and eighties, capturing Olympic gold medals and reaching the Cup semifinals.

The Ukraine, led by the fabulous Andriy Shevchenko, was the first Euro side to qualify, and is expected to reach the second round from Group C. Likewise for Switzerland, which meets up with qualifying opponent France again in Group H with weaker Korea and Togo as the other rivals.

Serbia & Montenegro, part of the former Yugoslavia, qualified for the very first time via the playoffs and is considered a long shot to get out of the first round alive because it has found itself in this tournament's version of the "Group of Death." That's Group C, which includes Argentina, the Netherlands and Ivory Coast.

Success at the World Cup can be defined in many ways. It doesn't always mean taking a victory lap while parading with the FIFA World Cup trophy around the stadium.

Sometimes it means overachieving or finishing well above expectations.

Korea and Japan certainly fell into that category in 2002. Senegal stunned defending champion France four years ago and made it all the way to the quarterfinals.

Croatia enjoyed a third-place finish as the surprise team at France '98 as striker Davor Suker, who finished with a Cup-high six goals. The Croatians, who finished out of the money in 2002, will be hard-pressed to duplicate its success of eight years ago this time around.

Costa Rica, making its third appearance, wound up as first-round wonders in 1990. The Central Americans defeated the more experienced Scotland and Sweden (losing to Brazil, but then again, no one is perfect) and became the first CONCACAF team to reach the second round of a Euro-based World Cup before Czechoslovakia handed them their heads in a second-round defeat.

Mexico, which will compete in its thirteenth tournament, duplicated Costa Rica's feat at France '98, but lost to Germany in the second round, 2-1, after grabbing the lead in that encounter.

Not every country has a chance to win it all or as a recognizable player who can make a difference in a match. Tunisia and Saudi Arabia should have their roles reduced to that of a spoiler in the opening round, trying to pull off an upset for the ages and perhaps somehow sneak into the second round.

At the time this chapter was being written, at least one familiar face was missing from the World Cup line-up—Bora Milutinovic, the former coach of the U.S. National Team and MetroStars (MLS), who hadn't hooked with with a National Team, despite guiding five countries in as many tournaments. Bora, has coached Mexico (1986), Costa Rica (1990), the United States (1994), Nigeria (1998) and China (2002). All but the Chinese reached at least the second round.

In the 1930 final, Jose Nasazzi of Uruguay (left) and Nolo Ferreira of Argentina shake hands with the Belgian referee Jean Langenus looking on.

But don't count Bora out because the World Cup coach mortality rate is high, even for ones in the tournament. In fact, only months before the 1990 Cup, Bora was hired by Costa Rica and he continued to forge his reputation as a miracle worker. The Costa Ricans became the very first CONCACAF team to win two first-round games and reach the second round in a European World Cup.

Getting out of the first round won't be an easy task for the U.S.

After a disastrous display and dismal last-place finish at France '98, the Americans rebounded spectacularly in Korea, reaching the quarterfinals before falling to World Cup runner-up Germany in a 1-0 result in which many observers felt the U.S. had deserved to win.

So, the U.S. won't be able to sneak up or surprise anyone this time. In fact, most countries would rather not play with the U.S. because the Americans have one of the most respected sides in the world. In fact, they have been ranked as high as fifth in the monthly FIFA rankings, an accomplishment that coach Bruce Arena has downplayed.

But Arena has built a resourceful, gritty and confident side, led by veteran goalkeeper Kasey Keller, who was called on to make several big saves during qualifying, Donovan, a midfielder-forward who has a knack of raising his level of play and becoming an impact performer in key matches, and Beasley, whose speed and vision have turned him into an impact player despite his size (5'-8", one hundred forty-five lbs.).

One of the Americans' biggest hurdles could be injuries at key positions before or during the Cup. Take, for instance what transpired during the months leading up to the tournament. The U.S. found itself with several defensive and/or holding midfielders sidelined due to an injury. The disabled list included Chris Armas, Claudio Reyna and Pablo Mastroeni. Arena needs two of those three players healthy come June or his options will be quite thin.

To move onto the second round, the U.S. probably will have to accrue at least four points—a victory (three points) and a draw (one point). And even that might not be enough if goal differential is needed to decide who moves on and who goes home.

But let's be realistic on accruing four points. The U.S. need to play the highly touted Czech Republic or Italy to at least a draw and then defeat Ghana.

One thing is certain. American soccer fans and their counterparts back here in the states certainly will have an easier time following their favorite team as opposed to waking up in the middle of the night and coping with some serious sleep deprivation to watch games from Korea and Japan four years ago. Most of the games will be televised in the afternoon or morning (for west coast fans),

Whether you are fortunate to watch it live in person or on TV, the World Cup once again promises to be some show.

The Cup Runneth Over—
A History of the World Cup

Even before FIFA was formed, there were thoughts of organizing a world championship. FIFA (Federation Internationale de Football Association) was formed in 1904, and several members, including Frenchmen Henri Delaunay and Jules Rimet, the organization's president, pushed for a competition. After several false starts—World War I interrupted the organization's plans, for example—it was voted in 1919 to establish a world championship. Noticing the success of the 1924 and 1928 soccer championships in the Olympics, FIFA officials were spurred into organizing a world championship, not just for amateurs, but for professionals as well. After securing its second consecutive Olympic title in 1928, Uruguay was selected as the site for the first world championship—which was to be called the World Cup—in honor of the 100th anniversary of the country's birth. Soccer—inter-

(Sir) Stanley Mathews was the most famous player of his time and the most intrepid, retiring in his fifties

HOW IT BEGAN

This is one of the two of the most coveted trophies in the world—the Jules Rimet Trophy retired in 1970 by Brazil after they became the first country to win three World Cups.

national soccer—would never be the same.

It has been hidden under a bed, stolen twice and melted down.

The World Cup trophy, the most sought after award in all of sport, has enjoyed a well-traveled and intriguing existence.

On Sunday, June 30, 2002, the second incarnation of the trophy wound up in the hands of the Brazilian side for a record fifth time since World Cup competition began in 1930.

The first, the Jules Rimet Trophy, was retired after the 1970 World Cup by Brazil, which captured its third title. Since then the FIFA World Cup trophy has been the big prize, every country's object of desire. The original trophy was produced for the 1930 competition in Uruguay. FIFA commissioned French sculptor Abel Lafleur, who created a statuette some thirty centimeters high and weighing four kilograms as a winged goddess of victory with her arms raised supporting an octagonal cup. The statue was made of solid gold and at the time cost some 50,000 French francs, which is the equivalent of $35,000 today.

During the final years of World War II, FIFA Vice President Ottorino Barassi of Italy hid it in a shoe box under his bed to safeguard it against the raids of Germans retreating from his country. FIFA eventually renamed the cup the Jules Rimet Trophy, after the man who made the most significant contribution to the founding of the World Cup.

On March 20, 1966, several months before the next competition in England, the trophy was stolen while on display at a stamp exhibition in the Central Hall of Westminster in England. The authorities, including Scotland Yard, were baffled, fearing the trophy had been melted down. But Pickles, a white-and-black dog of undetermined pedigree, saved the day as the unlikely hero. Pickles found the trophy buried near a tree in a London garden.

Pickles' owner collected an award valued between $15,000 and $20,000, including a year's supply of dog food. The thief, who demanded a $50,000 ransom for the cup, was given a two year jail term. Pickles, alas, did not meet a fate deserved for a hero. He reportedly strangled himself on his leash while chasing a cat within a year of his heroics, before he could enjoy all his just rewards.

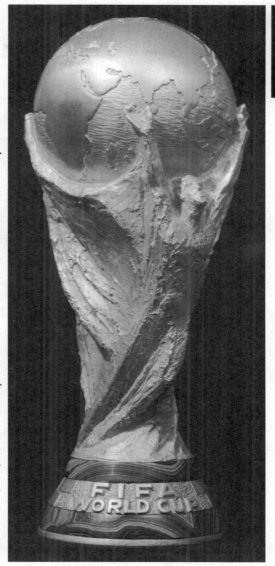

The FIFA World Cup Trophy is up for grabs every four years.

In 1970, the Brazilian Soccer Confederation became the permanent home to the Jules Rimet Trophy when the Brazilians became the first team to win the cup three times (they are also the first to win it five times, earning the Cup in 1994 and 2002)—until the night of December 20, 1983. Thieves broke into the confederation offices and stole the gold cup. It was never recovered, and authorities feared it was melted down. Three men were arrested in connection with its theft, but were released the next day because of insufficient evidence (one of those arrested, Antonio Carlos Aranha, was found dead on

December 30, 1989, with seven bullet wounds from a pistol).

"It was terrible," Pedro T. Natal said. "Everybody was sick about this . . . I had a feeling in my skin the robber was not Brazilian. He has no feeling of patriotism."

In stepped Kodak Brazil of Sao Paulo to save the day. "When we heard about the robbery, we were sick," said Natal, then Kodak Brazil Communication Director. "We decided to do something about it. This is the most important display of Brazilian culture. Certainly there was a tremendous loss in Brazil when the cup was stolen. We wanted to do something that would restore to the Brazilian people the most important symbol of the country's primary sport. This is a donation to the people of Brazil."

FIFA held a special competition for its design, and fifty-three models were presented to trophy manufacturers of seven countries. The design of the Italian firm, Bertoni, the work of Milanese sculptor Silvio Gazzaniga was chosen. The cup, 18-karat solid gold, weighs eleven pounds (4970 grams), stands fourteen inches (thirty-six centimeters) high, and cost $20,000 to produce. "The lines go from a base rising in a sphere and covering the world," Gazzaniga said. "From the body of the sculpture, two figures stand out—two athletes in a moving celebration of victory."

The trophy's base was banded by two rings of Malachite, which is a green gemstone. It contains enough space for the names of seventeen victorious countries to be engraved upon it. With the names of six countries already inscribed on the base—West Germany (1974), Argentina (1978), Italy (1982), Argentina (1986), West Germany (1990), and Brazil (1994)—there is enough room until the 2038 World Cup.

1930
URUGUAY
TRIUMPHANT
AT HOME

The first World Cup competition was hardly the moneymaking bonanza of today's tournament. In fact, it was difficult just to get countries to show up at this invitational tournament. Imagine a country giving up an opportunity to play in the cup today.

While organizers would have preferred sixteen countries, thirteen teams agreed to participate in the first cup. Because of the long voyage across the Atlantic, only four European squads—France, Belgium, Romania, and Yugoslavia—made the round trip, which was expected to take up to three months to complete. The rest of the field came from the United States, Mexico, and South America.

There were other problems. It rained for much of the competition in Montevideo (all games were played in the Uruguayan capital, unlike today's event which is held at several venues), leaving the playing fields in less than perfect shape. Work on the new, 100,000-capacity Centenary Stadium fell behind schedule. At the start of the tournament, it was not ready, but with builders working twenty-four hours a day, it was ready for Uruguay's opening match against Peru on July 18.

The tournament kicked off on July 13, 1930 as 1,000 curious souls at Pocitos Stadium watched France defeat Mexico, 4–1. The game included a number of firsts. Frenchman Lucien Laurent scored the first goal of the tournament nineteen minutes into the match—the only goal he would score in the competition. Mexicans Manuel and Felip Rosas became the first brothers to play in the Cup. Despite losing their goalkeeper—Alex Thepot had his jaw broken in the 10th minute and there were no substitutes in those days, so midfielder Augustin Chantrel took his place between the posts—the French prevailed as Andre Maschinot scored a goal in each half and Marcel Langiller added another. An interesting footnote to the game: Alex Villaplane, who was the French captain, was executed by a firing squad in 1944 for collaborating with the Germans during World War II.

Argentina took the silver medal to Uruguay's gold in the 1928 Olympics, and were the winners of the South American championship. The Argentinians got out of the opening round, defeating France, 1–0, Mexico, 6–3, and Chile, 3–1, but they seemed to be involved in a series of incidents that demonstrated the growing pains of the fledgling tournament. For example, while the Argentines clung to a 1–0 lead against France, referee Almeilda Rego of Brazil signaled the end of the game six minutes prematurely. Argentine fans ran onto the field to congratulate their team while the French protested. Rego discovered the error of his ways; the crowd on the field was cleared by mounted policemen and the match completed. Or take, for instance, Argentina's victory over Mexico. Argentine captain Nolo Ferreira could not play because he had to return home to take an important college examination. Guillermo Stabile took his place and recorded the first hat trick in World Cup history. The Rosas brothers were at it again, each scoring a goal for yet another first.

Group 2 was short and sweet with only three nations— Yugoslavia, Brazil and Bolivia. Defying logic and odds, the European team qualified for the semifinals, winning both its matches, 2–1 over Brazil and 4–0 over Bolivia. Ivan Beck led the Slavs, scoring one goal in the first game, two in the second. The Brazilians blanked Bolivia.

Not surprisingly, Uruguay was considered the favorite to win the first trophy, thanks to its Olympic superiority. The hosts got off on the right foot in Group 3 with a 1–0 win over Peru, followed by a 4–0 rout of Romania, whose team was picked by King Carol. Because of the extended trip, the king promised the players they would still have their jobs when they returned home. While as many as 93,000 fans would watch Uruguay perform at one game, the local population was not as excited about the other matches. A crowd of 300—an all-time World Cup low—turned out to watch Romania defeat Peru, 3–1, at Pocitos Stadium on July 14, three days before 800 witnessed the Yugoslavia-Bolivia encounter at Central Park.

Group 4 produced the most surprising of all results. The U.S. team, nicknamed "the shot-putters" by the French because of the tremendous bulk of several players, was made up of a number of former professional English players. The Americans, however, emerged victorious with 3–0 wins over Belgium and Paraguay. (To truly appreciate the Americans' accomplishment, they would win only one other World Cup match in eight attempts and would score only eight more goals before the 1994 competition). Bert Patenaude was credited with two goals in the Paraguay match, although U.S. soccer officials claimed that Patenaude had scored the third goal, which would have made him the first player to register a hat trick in Cup history. Depending on the source, the third goal was eitherawarded as an own goal—Paraguay accidentally knocked the ball into its own net—or U.S. Captain Thomas Florie was awarded the goal.

The Americans had their collective heads handed to them by Argentina in the semifinals, dropping a 6–1 decision as Stabile and Carlos Peucelle finished with two goals apiece. Uruguay prevailed over Yugoslavia by the same score, with Pedro Cea converting a hat trick.

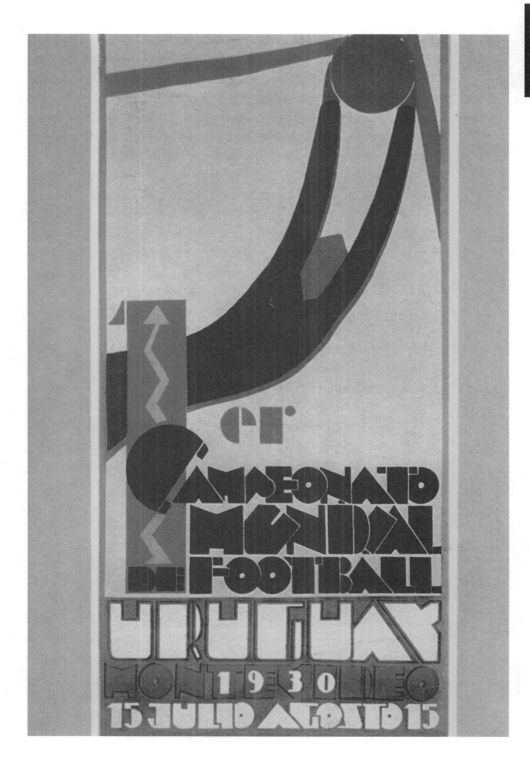

FINAL

1930

So, the two best teams in the world qualified for the championship match, which was not without controversy. Each side wanted to use its ball. In a Solomon-esque gesture, referee Jean Langenus allowed Argentina to use its ball in the opening half, the Uruguayans theirs in the second. And guess what happened? The Argentines, with their ball, took a 2–1 halftime lead on goals by Pablo Dorado and Stabile that were sandwiched around a score by Peucelle. Using their ball in the second half, the Uruguayans rallied with three unanswered goals—by Cea in the 57th minute, Santos Iriarte in the 68th, and the one-armed Hector Castro in the 89th.

The mood of the competing nations' capitals showed varying reactions. There was dancing in the Montevideo streets as the next day was declared a national holiday. In Buenos Aires, angry Argentines vented their anger by throwing bricks and stones at the Uruguayan embassy. The World Cup was born.

Uruguay 4, Argentina 2
Centenary Stadium
Montevideo, Uruguay
July 30,1930

Uruguay: Ballesteros, Nasazzi, Mascheroni, Andrade, Fernandez, Gestido, Dorado, Scarone, Castro, Cea, Iriarte

Argentina: Botasso, Della Torre, Paternoster, J. Evaristo, Monti, Suarez, Peucelle, Varallo, Stabile, Ferreyra, M. Evaristo

Goals: Dorado (U) 12, Peucelle (A) 20, Stabile (A) 37, Cea (U) 57, Iriarte (U) 68, Castro (U) 89

Referee: Langenus (Belgium)

Attendance: 93,000

1934

VIVA ITALIA AT

HOME

Two years before the tournament, Italy, under the reign of terror of Benito Mussolini, was awarded the World Cup, which was seen as a perfect platform to spew his Fascist propaganda. In contrast to the first Cup, which had mostly South American countries participating, this was European-dominated, as twelve teams came from the continent. The only exceptions were the U.S., Egypt, Brazil, and

Argentina. Uruguay was a no-show, becoming the only champion that failed to try to defend its crown.

The first round was an elimination competition. Italy, with four Argentine stars on its squad, rolled past the U.S., 7–1, as Angelo Schiavio struck three times, only days after the Americans defeated Mexico, 4–2, in a special qualifier in Rome. The Italians should have saved some of those goals, because they scored only five goals in their remaining four games. Czechoslovakia edged Romania, 2–1 (it was not known whether King Carol picked this team), on a pair of second-half goals. Germany romped past Belgium, 5–2, on Edmund Conen's hat trick, and Austria ousted France, 3–2, scoring the go-ahead goal by Anton Schall, who was blatantly offside on the play. It was not a good tournament for non-European sides, as Spain beat Brazil, 3–1, Sweden nipped Argentina, 3–2 and Hungary downed Egypt, 4–2. It would be Egypt's last appearance until 1990.

The quarterfinals, which then were called the second round, saw Germany, Austria, Czechoslovakia and Italy emerge victorious, although the Italians needed a replay to get past the Spanish. A day after playing to a 1–1 tie, Italy defeated Spain, 1–0, on Giuseppe Meazza's first-half goal.

Oldrich Nejedly proved to be a one-man show for Czechoslovakia, scoring all the goals in a 3–1 semifinal victory over Germany. The Italians, who suffered a 4–2 loss to Austria in Turin less than four months before the Cup, avenged the defeat with a 1–0 win during a downpour in Milan. Enrique Guaita scored for the winners in the 19th minute.

In a rare World Cup occurrence, both teams were captained by their goalkeepers—the Italians by Giampiero Combi, who was play-ing in his 47th and last international, the Czechs by Frantisek Planicka. Both teams attacked, but it took seventy minutes before anyone found the back of the net. Antonin Puc took a corner kick that bounded back to him and scored from a difficult angle for a 1–0 Czech advantage. But the Italians equalized with ten minutes remain-ing in regulation as Raimundo Orsi raced through the defense, faked a shot with his left foot and fired a shot with his right. Five minutes into the first extra period, Schiavio drove a shot barely under the crossbar for a 2–1 lead and eventually the title.

FINAL, 1934

Italy 2, Czechoslovakia 1
PNF Stadium
Rome, Italy
June 10, 1934

Italy: Combi, Monzeglio, Allemandi, Ferraris IV, Monti, Bertolini, Guaita, Meazza, Schiavio, Ferrari, Orsi

Czechoslovakia: Planicka, Zenisek, Ctyroky, Kostalek, Cambal, Krcil, Funek, Svoboda, Sobotka, Nejedly, Puc

Goals: Puc (C) 70, Orsi (I) 80, Schiavio (I) 95

Referee: Eklind (Sweden)

Attendance: 55,000

1938

ITALY WINS

AGAIN—IN

FRANCE

Believing the World Cup would alternate between continents, Argentina applied to host the 1938 tournament. FIFA, however, remembering the problems in Uruguay and the travel headaches, decided to keep the Cup in Europe, despite the possibility of war on the horizon. France was selected as the venue, and an angry Argentina decided not to participate in the qualifying competition. Brazil and Cuba showed up, and the rest of field consisted of European teams.

Only two years after Hitler's pro-Nazi propaganda of the 1936 Berlin Olympics, the Germans were hoping to use this World Cup to show how dominant their soccer team could be. Neighboring Switzerland, however, had other ideas, playing Germany to a surprising 1–1 draw in the tournament opener in the knockout competition. In the subsequent replay, the Swiss eliminated the Germans, 4–2, as Andre Abegglen III broke a 2–2 tie late in the match, scoring twice in three minutes. Cuba, which qualified only because Mexico dropped out, and Romania played to a 3–3 draw. That forced another playoff, as the Cubans prevailed, 2–1, despite the benching of goalkeeper Beinto Carvajeles, who enjoyed a spectacular first game. His replacement, Juan Ayra, was just as good and Carlos Maquina scored the game-winner in the 80th minute.

There were more close calls. The Netherlands held the Czechs, 1934 runners-up, to a scoreless tie in regulation, but succumbed in extra time, 3–0. Defending champion Italy sweated out a 2–1 extra-

time victory over Norway, as Silvio Piola scored. Then there was Brazil's 6–5 overtime triumph over Poland, the only match in World Cup history in which players on opposing sides scored four goals. Leonidas da Silva, considered the father of modern Brazilian soccer, accomplished that feat for the Brazilians, while Ernst Willimowski duplicated it for the Poles. Leonidas scored early in the first extra session and Romeo gave the Brazilians some breathing room before Willimowski scored his fourth, but it was too late, in one of the most remarkable soccer games of all-time. The rest of the first round fell into place: France 3, Belgium 1; and Hungary 6, Dutch East Indies 0.

In the second round, the defending champs, Italy, prevailed over the hosts, France, 3–1, as Piola struck twice. Sweden had few problems with dispatching Cuba, 8–0, as Gustav Wetterstrom found the back of the next four times. Hungary blanked the Swiss, 2–0, as Gyula Zsengeller scored in each half, and Brazil and Czechoslovakia played to a 1–1 tie, forcing another playoff. Of course, it was a minor miracle that either of those two teams was standing after that encounter—now called the Battle of Bordeaux—a physical affair that left Oldrich Nejedly with a broken leg and goalkeeper Frantisek Planicka playing part of the game with a broken arm. In the replay two days later, Brazil stopped the Czechs, 2–1, as the Brazilians used six new players. There were no incidents.

Two days later, Brazil had to face the Italians, who recorded a 2–1 semifinal win behind Luigi Colaussi and Meazza (penalty kick). Hungary had few problems with Sweden in the other semifinal, as Zsengeller connected for a hat trick in a 5–1 victory.

The site of the championship match was Colombes Stadium—which had been the venue for the track and field drama of the "Chariots of Fire" Olympics in 1924.

The teams traded early goals—by Italy's Colaussi in the 5th minute and by Hungary's Pal Titkos two minutes later. But Piola, who was named player of the tournament, scored in the 16th minute, and the Italians were on their way, extending the margin to 3–1 at half on Colaussi's second goal. Hungary sliced the lead to a goal midway through the second half, but Piola put home an insurance goal eight minutes from time as Italy became the first country to win the World Cup twice.

Unfortunately, Italy would have to wait some twelve years to defend its title because of World War II, although no one knew it at the time.

Italy 4, Hungary 2
Colombes Stadium
Paris, France
June 19, 1938
>   Italy: Olivieri, Foni, Rava, Seratoni, Andreolo, Locatelli, Biavati, Meazza, Piola, Ferrari, Colaussi
>   Hungary: Szabo, Polgar, Biro, Szalay, Szucs, Lazar, Sas, Vincze, Sarosi, Szengeller, Titkos
>   Goals: Colaussi (I) 5, Titkos (H) 7, Piola (I) 16, Colaussi (I) 35, Sarosi (H) 70, Piola (I) 82
>   Referee: Capdeville (France)
>   Attendance: 55,000

1950

URUGUAY'S

SURPRISE IN

BRAZIL

The 1950 tournament—set for Brazil and a spanking new Maracana Stadium (200,000 capacity)—seemed cursed from the outset. Only thirty-one countries entered the qualifying competition. Turkey, for example, qualified after Austria withdrew, but the Turks decided to drop out. India followed the same route after its group rival, Burma, withdrew. Four South American sides had walk-overs in the qualifying round. Bolivia and Chile made it into the tournament without playing a match after Argentina withdrew. Likewise for Uruguay and Paraguay, after Ecuador and Peru decided not to play.

Despite that, the World Cup produced some of the most dramatic wins in the history of the competition. Instead of a single-elimination, teams would play three matches apiece in the first round. Mahayana Stadium was not completed by the start of the opener. But 81,649 fans showed up to watch a 21-gun salute, fireworks, and 5,000 pigeons released and a smashing 4–0 victory by Brazil over Mexico behind Ademir's two goals. It turned out to be an inauspicious start for Mexican goalkeeper Antonio Carbajal, who would go on to play in a record five World Cups. Brazil won the group, playing Switzerland to a 2–2 draw and shutting down Yugoslavia, 2–0.

In the second pool, England, playing in its first World Cup, was considered among the favorites, but could win only one game—2–0 over Chile. The English met their match against an unlikely group of American amateur players who posted a 1–0 victory in a small mining town in Belo Horizonte. Joe Gaetjens scored the game-winner off a header in the 37th minute. They held on for one of the most incredible results in sports history. Stunned, the English dropped a 1–0 decision to Spain as Zarra scored, and returned home in disgrace. Spain, meanwhile, won the group with a perfect 3–0 mark, rallying from a 1–0 deficit in the final ten minutes for a 3–1 victory over the U.S., as Brunet Basora scored twice. The Spanish also stopped Chile, 2–0, as Basora and Zarra had goals.

Sweden barely got past Italy in the three team third pool. The Swedes edged the Italians, 3–2, and tied Paraguay, 2–2. Italy downed the South Americans, 2–0, but did not advance because the Swedes had scored more goals (5 to 4) than Italy did.

Uruguay, meanwhile, could not have had an easier route to the final round, having to play only Bolivia (because France had dropped out after the final pools had been set). The Uruguayans, behind Juan Schiaffino's four goals, romped to an 8–0 victory.

The final round was among the most confusing in Cup history. Four teams—Brazil, Sweden, Spain and Uruguay—played in a round-robin competition, leaving no true championship game. Fortunately, the success of Brazil and Uruguay ensured there would be an equivalent of one. In front of a crowd of 138,886 at Maracana, the Brazilians, behind Ademir's four goals, leveled Sweden, 7–1. After Spain held Uruguay to a 2–2 tie, the hosts went on the warpath again, rolling over Spain, 6–1, as Ademir and Chico connected twice. Oscar Miguez scored two goals as Uruguay squeaked past Sweden, 3–2, and Sweden downed Spain, 3–1, in a rather meaningless affair, to set up the ultimate confrontation—Uruguay vs. Brazil.

As luck would have it, the last game of the final round turned out to be for the championship. Because of the standings, the Brazilians (2–0–0, 4 points) needed but a tie, the Uruguayans (1–1–0; 3 points) a victory.

A World Cup record crowd of 199,854 (172,772 were paid) showed up at Maracana, anticipating a festive match and post-game

FINAL, 1950

celebration. The Brazilians were considered 1–10 favorites to take home the trophy for the first time, with bonuses of $20,000 in the offing (remember, this was 1950). But then again, the Uruguayans had other ideas to spoil the party.

The Brazilians attacked from the outset, but could not score in the opening half. Then, two minutes into the second half, Ademir set up Carnosa Friaca for a 1–0 lead. But a miscommunication occurred. Brazilian coach Flavio Costa gave instructions for Jair to drop back to defense, but word never reached him. Uruguay took advantage of the gaps on defense and Schiaffino converted a pass by Alcide Ghiggia in the 66th minute. If the score remained that way, Brazil still would have won the title. Incredibly, Brazil continued to attack instead of defend. Ghiggia himself scored with eleven minutes left to give the Uruguayans a 2–1 lead before a stunned crowd.

For Uruguay, it would be its last great World Cup glory. For Brazil, it would mean an eight-year wait to take a victory lap with the coveted Jules Rimet Trophy.

Uruguay 2, Brazil 1
Maracana Stadium
Rio de Janeiro, Brazil
July 16, 1950

Uruguay: Maspoli, Gonzales, Tejera, Gambetta, Varela, Andrade, Ghiggia, Perez, Miguez, Schiaffino, Moran

Brazil: Barbosa, Augusto, Juvenal, Bauer, Danilo, Bigode, Friaca, Ziznho, Ademir, Jair, Chico

Goals: Friaca (B) 47, Schiaffino (U) 66, Ghiggia (U) 79

Referee: Reader (England)

Attendance: 199,854

1954

GERMANS RULE,

OVERCOMING

SWISS CHEESE

DEFENSE

The 1954 World Cup will forever be remembered for the great comeback by West Germany, which calculated its way to the final in Switzerland. It also will be remembered as the highest-scoring Cup in history. The sixteen finalists produced 140 goals in twenty-six games, an average of 5.38 per match (the next best average came in the 1938 competition at 4.66 per match). Victorious teams scored seven or more goals on six occasions, including an amazing 7–5

victory by Austria over the hosts.

The opening match gave very little indication of what was to come as Yugoslavia got past France, 1–0, as a young forward by the name of Milos Milutinovic tallied in the 15th minute. He is the older brother of Bora Milutinovic, who coached the U.S. in the 1994 World Cup. As it turned out, Pool 1 was a defensive battle, as thirteen goals were scored in four matches. Brazil and Yugoslavia advanced to the quarterfinals. The Brazilians routed Mexico, 5–0, and tied Yugoslavia, 1–1.

Pool 2 produced some of the most intriguing results in the history of the Cup. Favored Hungary, the Magic Magyars who were the dominant national soccer team in the fifties, crushed South Korea, 9–0, as Sandor Kocsis had a hat trick and Ferenc Puskas chipped in with two goals. The Hungarians also rolled over the Germans, 8–3, (Kocsis had four goals in this one, but Puskas sustained an injury that would sideline him until the final), but scores can be deceiving. German coach Sepp Herberger realized that if his side lost to Hungary it would avoid playing the highly touted Brazilians in the quarterfinals. Instead, the Germans would have to meet Turkey or South Korea in a special playoff, and the winner of that encounter would play Yugoslavia in the next round. So, Herberger, after a 4–1 win over Turkey, revamped his lineup and lost by five goals. Turkey went on to beat South Korea, 7–0, setting up a playoff. Herberger restored his regulars and the West Germans romped past Turkey, 7–3, as Maximillian Morlock led the way with three goals and the Walter brothers—Olaf and Fritz—each had a goal.

Every match in the third pool was decided by a shutout with Uruguay and Austria finishing on top.

In the fourth pool, England, still smarting from a 7–1 pasting by Hungary before the tournament, and Italy qualified for the quarterfinals. The English started off slow with a 4–4 overtime draw with Austria, but rebounded with a 2–0 win over the Swiss. Italy struggled with a 2–1 loss to the hosts, but rebounded with a 4–1 victory over Belgium, setting up a special playoff with the Swiss, who beat the Italians for the second time in a week.

The quarterfinals produced some of the highest scoring and

most brutal games in Cup history. Austria and the Swiss started things off with a World Cup record twelve goals as the Austrians managed to walk away with a 7–5 win. The Swiss bolted to a 3–0 advantage in the opening twenty-three minutes, but Austria answered back with five consecutive goals. The Austrians tied it with three goals in as many minutes behind Theodor Wagner, who scored two of his three goals, and Alfred Koerner who scored one of his two goals during that span. They continued their onslaught as captain Ernst Ocwirk gave the Austrians the lead to stay, 4–3, as Wagner, Koerner, and Erich Probst added insurance goals.

The next two matches were of the garden variety, as far as this tournament was concerned: Uruguay over England, 4–2, as Schiaffino scored, and Germany—its strategy worked—over Yugoslavia, 2–0, on an own goal and a score by Helmut Rahn. Then there was Hungary's 4–2 victory over Brazil in what turned into the most disgraceful match in World Cup history. It became known as the battle of Berne. The game was chippy from the opening whistle and turned into a physical tussle as Brazilian Nilton Santos and Jozsef Bozsik of Hungary were sent off for fighting; they needed police to escort them off the field. After the final whistle, the battle continued en route to the locker rooms. One version had the Brazilians hiding and attacking the Hungarians in the tunnel.

Even without the injured Puskas, Hungary managed to over-come Uruguay in one semifinal, 4–2, in extra time, as Kocsis scored off a pair of headers in the second extra period. Germany, meanwhile, dispatched Austria, 6–1, as the Walter brothers struck not once, but twice apiece.

The final was a rematch of the first round game, yet it wasn't because the West Germans used completely different players in this encounter at Wankdorf Stadium in Berne on July 4. Puskas, although he was not fully fit, insisted on playing for Hungary. The decision looked good early on as the Hungarians grabbed a 2-0 lead in the opening eight minutes when Puskas put in a rebound of Kocsis' shot in the 6th minute and Zoltan Czibor made it 2–0 only two minutes later.

The Germans, however, refused to give up. Maximillian Morlock cut the lead in half in the 10th minute and Rahn equalized in the 18th minute for a 2–2 tie. The score remained that way until the 84th, when Rahn struck again. He picked up a so-so clearance by Mihaly Lantos, bolted into the penalty area, and fired the ball past goalkeeper Gyula Groscis. It appeared that Hungary had tied it on a Puskas goal with only two minutes left, but linesman Mervyn Griffiths of Wales ruled it was offside. Two minutes later, the Hungarians had suffered their first loss in thirty internationals, dating back to May 1950, and the Germans were world champions.

West Germany 3, Hungary 2
Wankdorf Stadium
Berne, Switzerland
July 4, 1954
> West Germany: Turek, Posipal, Liebrich, Kohlmeyer, Eckel, Mai, Rahn, Morlock, O. Walter, F. Walter, Schaeffer
> Hungary: Grosics, Buzansky, Lorant, Lantos, Bozsik, Zakarias, Czibor, Kocsis, Hidegkuti, Puskas, Toth
> Goals: Puskas (H) 4, Czibor (H) 8, Morlock (WG) 10, Rahn (WG) 18, Rahn (WG) 84
> Referee: Ling (England)
> Attendance: 60,000

The 1958 World Cup can be summed up in one word—Pelé. The scary thing about it was that he missed the first two games and still managed to score six goals. Even scarier was that he was only seventeen years old, with a glorious career in front of him that would make him a household word in virtually every country in the world.

> 1958
> BRAZILIANS
> STORM
> SWEDEN

Brazil's triumph in Sweden was noteworthy for several reasons. Brazil became the only team to win out of its hemisphere, finally establishing itself as one of the great soccer countries, and started an incredible run of three world championships in four tries—an accomplishment that will be difficult to equal or surpass.

Using an innovative and attack-minded 4–2–4 lineup, the Brazilians were tough to beat. They started off with a 3–0 triumph over Austria as Altafini Mazzola scored once in each half and Nilton Santos four minutes into the second half. England, however, managed to shut down the vaunted attack in a scoreless tie, setting up a must-win situation with the Soviet Union. Brazil made several tactical changes, inserting Zito, Garrincha, and Pelé into the lineup. While Pelé did not score, he and the other two additions opened up the Soviet defense for Vava, who found the back of the net twice in a 2–0 triumph as Brazil reached the quarterfinals along with the English, who played in three ties. As for the other groups:

Defending champion West Germany stumbled to a 1–0–2 mark in the first pool, defeating Argentina, 4–1, but tying Czechoslovakia and Northern Ireland by 2–2 results, and advanced with Northern Ireland. The Irish had to edge the Czechs in a special playoff, 2–1—as Peter McParland scored with ten minutes remaining in extra time. France, behind the awesome firepower of Just Fontaine, who hit for the hat trick in a 7–3 thumping of Paraguay, added two more in a 3–2 loss to Yugoslavia (also advanced from Pool 2) and scored what proved to be the decisive goal in a 2–1 win over Scotland.

The host Swedes, who won the Olympic gold medal ten years earlier in London, were a pleasant surprise in Group 3. Buoyed by their Italian exports—Nils Liedholm (A.C. Milan), Kurt Hamrin (Padova), Arne Selmonsson (Lazio), Nacka Skoglund (Inter Milan), and Bengt Gustavsson (Atalanta), they went undefeated in pool 3. They blanked Mexico, 3–0, as Ange Simonsson twice beat goalkeeper Antonio Carbajal, playing in his third consecutive tournament; edged Hungary, 2–1, behind Hamrin's two scores; and played Wales to a scoreless tie. By then, Sweden had qualified for the quarterfinals, although the Welsh needed a 2–1 comeback win in a special playoff against the Hungarians—as Ivor Allchurch and Terence Medwin scored in the final half—to move on. The Hungarians were a mere shadow of themselves as a team because of the 1956 uprising. Many of their stars had either retired or jumped ship—Puskas to Spain, for example. Only Gyula Groscis, defender Jozsef Bozsik, and forward Nandor Hidegkuti returned from that great 1954 team.

Helmut Rahn, who was recalled to the team after falling out of favor with coach Sepp Herberger, scored in the first half of Germany's 1–0 triumph over Yugoslavia. The Germans were followed into the semifinals by Sweden—Hamrin and Simonsson scored in a 2–0 win over the Soviet Union—and the French, who were led by

Fontaine, who connected two more times in a 4–0 victory over Northern Ireland.

It was in the quarterfinals that Pelé started to make this a virtual one-man show. He scored his first World Cup goal—he later called it "the most important goal of my career"—in the 73rd minute to lead Brazil to a 1–0 victory over a tough Welsh side. Five days later, the seventeen-year-old showed his performance against the Welsh was no mistake, scoring three times within a twenty-minute span in the second half to turn a 2–1 advantage into a 5–2 victory over the French (Fontaine had a goal in that one). The Brazilians' opponent was to be Sweden, which bested West Germany, 3–1, in the other semifinal encounter. After the Germans were reduced to ten players when Erich Juskowiak was ejected for a retaliation foul, the Swedes scored twice behind Gunnar Gren and Hamrin.

A day after Fontaine (France) completed one of the finest individual performances in the World Cup—four goals in a 6–3 triumph over West Germany in the consolation match to give him a record thirteen goals that still stands today—Pelé and Brazil put the exclamation point on this memorable tournament.

FINAL, 1958

The Swedes took a 1–0 lead four minutes into the match as Nils Liedholm scored. Brazil found itself behind for the first time in the tournament, and many soccer observers felt they would self-destruct. If anything, it spurred them on. Only five minutes later, Vava equalized off a fine cross from Garrincha. The players duplicated the feat in the 32nd minute as Brazil grabbed a 2–1 halftime lead.

Pelé ? He owned the second half. In the 55th minute, he scored a goal worthy of highlight films. He trapped the ball with his chest, bolted around his marker, and volleyed the ball into the net past goalkeeper Karl-Oskar Svensson. Mario Zagallo was able to follow up his own cross on a corner kick in amidst the defensive chaos in the 68th minute for a 4–1 margin. Simonsson cut the lead in half in the 80th minute. Then, most appropriately, Pelé put the finishing touches on the World Cup by heading home the final goal as time was running out.

It was just the start of an amazing run for Brazil.

Brazil 5, Sweden 2
Rasunda Stadium

Stockholm, Sweden
June 29, 1958

> Brazil: Gilmar, D. Santos, N. Santos, Zito, Bellini, Orlando, Garrincha, Didi, Vava, Pelé , Zagallo
>
> Sweden: Svensson, Bergmark, Axbom, Boerjesson, Gustavsson, Parling, Hamrin, Gren, Simonsson, Liedholm, Skoglund
>
> Goals: Liedholm (S) 3, Vava (B) 9, Vava (B) 32, Pelé (B) 55, Zagallo (B) 68, Simonsson (S) 80, Pelé (B) 90
>
> Referee: Guigue (France)
>
> Attendance: 49,737

Pelé continued to prove his World Cup success was no fluke with Santos and the Brazilian National Team. But the Brazilians demonstrated how great they really were by winning their second straight tournament, without the Black Pearl, who suffered a pulled muscle in their second match. That result was a scoreless tie against Czechoslovakia after Mario Zagallo and Pelé scored in a 2–0 Group 3 victory over Mexico and goalkeeper Antonio Carbajal, playing in his fourth consecutive Cup. Like a fairy tale come to life, Pelé replacement, Amarildo—his full name, Amarildo Tavares de Silveira—stepped to the forefront. Trailing 1–0 in the second half to Spain, Amarildo took the match into his own hands—actually, it was his feet—scoring in the 71st and 90th minutes for a 2–1 victory to clinch a spot in the quarterfinals.

The rest of the Cup seemed like a set-up: who was going to meet Brazil in the final?

Group 1's nominations—this was the first time FIFA used the word "group" to signify opening-round matches—included the Soviet Union (gold medal in 1956) and Yugoslavia (silver medals in 1952 and 1956), who enjoyed great success at the two most recent Olympics.

West Germany and Chile emerged as the top two countries from Group 2, but not before the hosts took on Italy in what turned into the battle of Santiago. Tempers started to boil over before the opening kickoff as Italian journalists criticized the living and playing conditions in Chile. Referee Ken Aston threw out Italian Giorgio Ferrini

1962
NO PELÉ ,
BUT BRAZIL'S
OK IN CHILE

for a retaliation foul, but it was the call Aston did not make that made this a game to forget. About five minutes before halftime, Leonel Sanchez, after he was taken down by Humberto Maschio, broke the Italian's nose with a punch that everyone in the stadium and those watching on TV had seen—everyone but Aston. Sanchez was not ejected. And, oh, yes, Chile went on to record a 2–0 victory.

From Group 4 came Hungary and England, which defeated a disappointing Argentina, 3–1, on goals by Ronald Flowers, Bobby Charlton and Jimmy Greaves. Chile should have been a home-field advantage for the Argentines.

Sanchez, who scored two goals in Chile's opening victory over Switzerland, proved that he could play some soccer, too, connecting for the first goal in a 2–1 victory over the Soviets in the quarterfinals (Eladio Rojas had the other goal). Yugoslavia avenged a pair of defeats to West Germany in the two previous quarterfinals with a 1–0 win behind Peter Radakovic's goal in the 87th minute. The Czechs outlasted Hungary thanks to an early score by Adolf Scherer. Brazil? No problem, as the South Americans bounced the English with a 3–1 win as Garrincha, in the middle of another outstanding tournament, scored twice, and Vava once.

The Brazilians continued their sterling play in the semifinals, disposing of Chile, 4–2, as Garrincha struck twice in the opening half and Vava duplicated the feat in the final forty-five minutes. Garrincha was ejected for kicking Rojas, worrying Brazilian officials that the talented winger might have to sit out the final.

In a 3–1 victory over Yugoslavia, the Czechs scored three times in the second half—Scherer had two and Josef Kadraba one to set up another confrontration between the Group 3 rivals.

The Brazilians scored an important victory a couple of days before the final was played, when FIFA officials determined that Garrincha could play. The six other players who were sent off during the Cup were hit with a one-match ban. Garrincha received but a reprimand. As it turned out, he had a relatively quiet match, but there were others who stepped up to fill the breach.

FINAL, 1962

First, however, the Czechs struck in the 15th minute on a goal by Masopust, who converted a long pass from Schrer. The Brazilians weren't jolted. After all, in four of the last six final matches, the even-

tual winner had to rally from a 1–0 deficit. They equalized only two minutes later as Amarildo scored from a difficult angle. The score remained that way until the 68th minute, when Zito headed in an Amarildo cross. Vava then took advantage of a mistake by goalkeeper Viliam Schroif, who fumbled a cross from Djalma Santos in the penalty area with thirteen minutes left and scored.

In perhaps the ultimate display of teamwork, no Brazilian player scored more than four goals—Garrincha and Vava finished with four apiece. Amarildo chipped in with three, and Zagalo, Pelé and Zito had one each.

The Czechs themselves made history by becoming the first European team to play in a World Cup championship game in the Americas. They were followed by Italy (1970), Netherlands (1978), West Germany (1986), and Italy (1994).

Brazil 3, Czechoslovakia 1
Estadio Nacional
Santiago, Chile
June 17, 1962
> Brazil: Gilmar, D. Santos, N. Santos, Zito, Mauro, Zozimo, Garrincha, Didi, Vava, Amarildo, Zagallo
> Czechoslovakia: Schroif, Tichy, Novak, Pluskal, Popluhar, Masopust, Posichal, Scherer, Kvasniak, Kadraba, Jelinek
> Goals: Masopust (C) 15, Amarildo (B) 17, Zito (B) 68, Vava (B) 77
> Referee: Latishev (Soviet Union)
> Attendance: 68,679

1966
HOST
ENGLAND
OVERCOMES
CONTROVERAY

Finally, after sixteen years of trying, England ruled the World Cup roost, winning at the crown jewel of soccer—Wembley Stadium.

In contrast to the controversial and exciting eventual final, the Cup hardly got off to an auspicious start as England played Uruguay to a scoreless tie in a Group 1 match at Wembley. Still, those two teams qualified for the quarterfinals. The English, coached by Alf Ramsey, who was soon to be knighted Sir Alf Ramsey for his World Cup success, had assembled one of their greatest teams. That side included captain and defender Bobby Moore, midfielder and schemer Bobby Charlton (his brother, Jack Charlton coached Ireland in the 1994 World Cup), a crafty winger in Alan Ball, forward Geoff Hurst, and a sure-handed goalkeeper in Gordon Banks.

After the draw, England began to build its momentum, as Bobby Charlton and Roger Hunt scored in a 2–0 triumph over Mexico—no, Mexico's Carbajal was not in the nets for this encounter, Gonzalez Calderon was. (Carbajal played in the 0–0 draw with Uruguay to make it five consecutive World Cups). The hosts added another 2–0 victory as Hunt found the back of the net twice.

The eventual finalists, Germany, sparked by the overall play of sweeper Franz Beckenbauer, won Group 2 by goal differential over Argentina after both sides played to a scoreless tie. In their first match, the West Germans got off on the right foot with a 5–0 triumph over Switzerland—Beckenbauer and Helmut Haller led the way with two goals apiece, and Siegfried Held had 1. Uwe Seeler, performing in his third World Cup, sealed the 2–1 victory over Spain with a goal with only six minutes remaining.

Two-time defending champion Brazil really could never get going in Group 3. The Brazilians defeated Bulgaria, 2–0, in their first Group 3 match, but it was a pyrrhic victory because defender Zhechev put Pelé on the sidelines for the next encounter with Hungary with a leg injury. Without Pelé , Hungary beat Brazil, 3–1. Pélé returned against Portugal, but he was brought down by two vicious tackles early on to set the tone of the match. Eusebio, the Portuguese star who had only one goal in the first two matches, created the first goal and scored the last two in a 3–1 win. Portugal booked a spot in the quarterfinals, Brazil, incredibly, did not.

It was in Group 4, however, in which the most intriguing result was produced. The Soviet Union had little trouble advancing, blanking newcomer North Korea, 3–0, and Italy, 1–0, and edging Chile, 2–1. The quest for second place came down to North Korea and the heavily favored Italians. The Korean forwards proved to be too quick for the slow Italian defense. Italy was reduced to ten players because Giacomo Bulgarelli injured his knee (substitutions were allowed in 1970) in the 34th minute. Only four minutes before halftime, the Koreans took advantage of the defensive liabilities as Pak Dooik scored. They made the lead hold up for one of the greatest upsets in history.

The North Koreans were ready to make it two straight stunners in the quarterfinals, rolling to a 3–0 lead over Portugal twenty-two minutes into the match. Pak Seung-zin, Dong-woon and Seung-kook scored for the Asians, but Eusebio took charge to slice the margin to 3–2 at the half with goals in the 27th and 42nd minutes, the later a penalty kick (he finished the tournament with four penalty kicks). Eusebio equalized from point-blank range in the 55th minute, and the Koreans were never the same. Three minutes later he struck again from the penalty spot for a 4–3 advantage after he was fouled follow-ing a brilliant individual run. And as if to show he wasn't selfish, Eusebio's corner kick set up Augusto's goal, an insurance score in the 78th minute in a 5–3 win.

The other quarterfinals were anticlimactic. England got past Argentina on Hurst's goal in the 78th minute in a match that was held up for several minutes because Argentine Antonio Rattin refused to leave the field after he was ejected. Four players—Held, Beckenbauer, Seeler, and Haller—tallied in West Germany's 4–0 win over Uruguay, and the Soviets outlasted Hungary, 2–1.

The West Germans grabbed a 2–0 lead behind Haller and Beckenbauer to reach the finals with a 2–1 victory over the Soviet Union, and England overcame Portugal and Eusebio (he converted yet another penalty kick, and had another penalty in the 2–1 triumph over the Soviets in the consolation match) in a 2–1 win as Bobby Charlton scored in each half before a packed house at Wembley.

FINAL, 1966

The final was a match that had everything—lead changes, last-minute heroics, and controversial goals. In the end, England had emerged with a 4–2 extra-time victory and its trophy, although the West Germans weren't entirely convinced of that, especially after what transpired in overtime.

Haller gave the Germans a 1–0 lead in the 13th minute, but Hurst countered six minutes later. The score remained tied at 1–1 until Martin Peters lifted the English to a 2–1 edge in the 78th minute. As time was running out, Wolfgang Weber put one past goal-keeper Gordon Banks for a 2–2 deadlock.

Eleven minutes into the first extra session, Hurst scored one of the most controversial goals in history, firing a shot that bounded off

the crossbar and into the goal. Did the goal cross the line or didn't it? Linesman Tofik Bakhramov of the Soviet Union said yes, much to the chagrin of the Germans. Hurst added an insurance tally in the final minute to become the only player to score three goals in a championship game.

> **England 4, West Germany 2 (OT)**
> **Wembley Stadium**
> **London, England**
> **July 30, 1966**
>> England: Banks, Cohen, Wilson, Stiles, J. Charlton, Moore, Ball, Hurst, B. Charlton, Hunt, Peters
>> West Germany: Tilkowski, Hottges, Schnellinger, Beckenbauer, Schulz, Weber, Haller, Seeler, Held, Overath, Emmerich
>> Goals: Haller (WG) 12, Hurst (E) 18, Peters (E) 78, Weber (WG) 90, Hurst (E) 101, Hurst (E) 120
>> Referee: Dienst (Switzerland)
>> Attendance: 96,924

1970
BRAZIL'S
MEXICAN
HAT(TRICK)
DANCE

Returning to their own backyard, the revitalized Brazilians dominated the tournament, winning all six matches while outscoring their opponents, 19–6, to complete their amazing run by becoming the first nation to win three World Cups, retiring the Jules Rimet Trophy.

Pelé, allowed to play without the close marking, took center stage once again in the world spotlight. He finished with 'only' four goals, but his presence in the lineup opened things up for his teammates, particularly Jairzinho, who scored seven goals.

In what was becoming an unwanted tradition, the opening match of the Cup was another boring, scoreless tie. This time Mexico and the Soviet Union were the guilty parties. As it turned out, both teams made it out of Group 1, which was no mean feat for the Mexicans, who entered the tournament having only won World Cup game in seventeen tries (1–13–3). The Mexicans' 4–0 triumph over El Salvador was marred by a controversial officiating decision that led to the first goal. As time was running out in the first half, referee Ali

Kandil of Egypt whistled a foul on a Mexican player. But Mexico's Gutierrez Padilla took the kick and passed to Huerta Valdiva, who scored. Kandil incredibly allowed the goal to stand. El Salvador goalkeeper Monzon Magana refused to take the ball from the back of the net, and Kandil had to bring it to the center spot.

Italy and Uruguay barely got out of Group 2 in one piece. The Italians (1–0–2) could win only once—a tough Israeli team played them to a 0–0 draw—and Uruguay squeaked past Sweden on goal differential.

Brazil and England had it a lot easier in Group 3. The Brazilians romped past Czechoslovakia, 4–1, on three second-half goals, two by Jairzinho and one by Pelé. The play of the match turned out not to be a goal. Noticing that Czech goalkeeper Ivo Viktor was out of the nets late in the first half, Pelé, some sixty yards away, lobbed the ball towards the unattended goal. The ball bounced only inches wide of the post. In a match better-suited for the later rounds, Brazil edged England, 1–0, on Jairzinho's goal in the 59th minute. But like their opening match, this encounter is better remembered for a goal that Pelé did not score as goalkeeper Gordon Banks produced one of the greatest saves in soccer history. Standing at the far post, Banks managed to leap toward the opposite corner of the net knock away Pelé's head shot. The Brazilians then defeated Romania, 3–2, as Pelé struck twice and Jairzinho once to make it three games in a row, but the Europeans exposed some weaknesses in the Brazilian defense.

Group 4 was dominated by Gerd Mueller and the West Germans, who stormed to three consecutive victories. Mueller was lethal from the opening match, scoring with twelve minutes left to give the Germans a 2–1 comeback victory over Morocco, which had taken a 1–0 halftime lead on a score by Houmane Jarir. Incidentally, Morocco did not have a full complement of players for the start of the second half and had no one in goal—goalkeeper Allal Ben Kassu was in the locker room—for about a minute. The Moroccan coach complained that referee Laurens Van Ravens of the Netherlands did not notify his players in the locker room that the second half was to begin. The Germans proved they did not need any outside help as Mueller registered a hat trick in a 5–2 triumph over Bulgaria. Mueller finished off his incredible opening round—a record seven goals in three matches—with yet another three-goal performance in a 3–1 win over Peru, which had a goal from Nene Cubillas (four first-round goals).

In a rematch of the 1966 championship game, it took Mueller some 108 minutes to connect against England in the quarterfinals, scoring the game-winner in a 3–2 victory. The English were forced to play Peter Bonetti in the nets after Banks woke up with an upset stomach the day of the match. Alan Mullery struck first for the English in the 31st minute, and Martin Peters made it 2–0. But the Germans, who had become adept at comebacks (see the 1954 final), staged another memorable one. Coach Helmut Schoen started the wheels turning by inserting Juergen Grabowski into the match for Reinhard Libuda in the second half against the tiring English. Beckenbauer cut the lead to one with a shot from the edge of the penalty area and Seeler leveled the score at 2–2, heading the ball past Bonetti. Mueller, who had been relatively silent for most of the match, came to life in extra time, volleying in a Johannes Loehr feed from point-blank range for the win.

Uruguay got past the Soviets behind substitute Victor Esparrago's goal with time running out in extra time in a 1–0 win. The Brazilians continued to roll, besting Peru and Cubillas (his fifth goal), 4–2, as Tostao was the hero this time with two goals. Rivellino and Jairzinho also scored.

The match was the Brazilians' fifth consecutive at Jaslisco Stadium in Guadalajara, where they were seeded, and they felt right at home. In fact, Uruguay complained to FIFA about an unfair home-field advantage, but the governing body did not take it seriously. They were just following the schedule. The Brazilians had forged a reputation as being a strong second-half team, scoring goals to break close games open, and this match was no exception. After the teams traded goals in the opening forty-five minutes, Clodoaldo for Brazil, Luis Cubilla for Uruguay, the Brazilians took command. Jairzinho scored in the 76th minute and Rivellino added an insurance tally off a Pelé pass in the 89th.

The Italians earned a place in the final the hard way; they earned it in a wild, 4–3 victory over the Germans that included five goals in thrity minutes of overtime. They struck in the seventh minute as Roberto Boninsegna put home a rebound. Germany tied it as Karl-Heinz Schnellinger knocked in a cross seven minutes from time. Mueller, again silent in regulation took advantage of a defensive

FINAL, 1970

error for a 2–1 German lead five minutes into overtime. Italy, however, came back as Giovanni Rivera put in a free kick and Luigi Riva scored for a 3–2 advantage after the first extra period. With ten minutes remaining in the second session, Mueller struck again—his 10th goal of the Cup—for a 3–3 tie. Barely a minute later, however, Boninsegna set up Rivera, who scored for a 4–3 lead and eventually the win as the Italians had qualified for their first final since 1938.

It was Brazil's first game other than Guadalajara, but nothing could stop the South Americans in Azteca Stadium.

Predictably, the halftime score was 1–1. Pelé, most appropriately, scored Brazil's 100th World Cup goal after eighteen minutes, heading in a Rivellino feed. He also became only the second player to score goals in two championship matches (he did it in 1958), emulating former teammate Vava's feat in 1958 and 1962. The Italians equalized in the 37th minute as Boninsegna took advantage of a defensive error.

The Brazilians revved things up in the second half as Gerson put Brazil into the lead in the 65th minute. Five minutes later Jairzinho made Cup history with a goal and a 3–1 lead as he became the first player to score in every match in every round including the final. Brazilian Captain Carlos Alberto closed out the scoring four minutes from time, firing home a bullet of a shot on an overlap from his right fullback position as his teammates retired the Jules Rimet Trophy to their confederation offices as the first country to win the Cup three times. Brazilian coach Mario Zagallo also made history, becoming the first participant to win as a player (1958) and coach.

It was the last time Brazil would reach the finals of the World Cup until 1994.

Brazil 4, Italy 1
Azteca Stadium
Mexico City, Mexico
June 30, 1970
   Brazil: Felix, Alberto, Everaldo, Clodoaldo, Brito, Piazza, Jairzinho, Gerson, Tostao, Pelé, Rivellino
   Italy: Albertosi, Burgnich, Facchetti, Bertini (Juliano, 73), Rosato, Cera, Domenghini, Mazzola, Boninsegna

(Rivera, 84), De Sisti, Riva

Goals: Pelé (B) 18, Boninsegna (I) 37, Gerson (B) 65,
   Jainzinho (B) 70, Alberto (B) 86

Referee: Gloeckner (East Germany)

Attendance: 107,412

1974
WEST GERMANS
ARE THE BEST
AT HOME

After two close calls, West Germany finally had the opportunity
to win the Cup, even if there was a new trophy. With the Jules Rimet
Trophy retired, a new trophy was unveiled—the FIFA World Cup.
There were only a handful of players leftover from the 1966 and 1970
teams—Franz Beckenbauer, goalkeeper Sepp Maier, Gerd Mueller,
and Juergen Grabowski. But the Germans would be a tough side to
beat.

They started out slowly, showing very little in a 1–0 victory
over Chile as defender Paul Breitner scored. They improved with a
3–0 triumph over Australia behind goals by Wolfgang Overath,
Bernhard Cullman and Mueller. But in the most political of battles on
the field, the West Germans could not overcome their Eastern counterparts, dropping a 1–0 decision in the first meeting between those
two rivals, in Hamburg. Not surprisingly, tight security surrounded
the match and only 3,000 East German fans were allowed to cross the
border because officials feared few fans would return to their
Communist homeland. The West Germans already were assured of a
spot in the quarterfinals, but the East Germans needed a point—a
draw—to advance. They got more than they bargained for, a 1–0
victory, as Juergen Sparwasser scored the lone goal in the 80th
minute.

Defending champion Brazil could never find the magic of its
triumph four years earlier. Perhaps it was because the great Pélé had
retired from international soccer. Perhaps it was because a talented
generation of players, including Tostao and Gerson, could not be
replaced so quickly. Or perhaps it was because they played a more
defensive instead of creative style. In the opening match of the World
Cup, the Brazilians wound up with a scoreless draw with Yugoslavia.
They added yet another 0–0 tie against Scotland—which has never
qualified for the second round of a World Cup in seven tries—before
securing a place in the quarterfinals with a 3–0 win over Zaire.

Brazil, which finished in a second-place tie with Scotland, advanced because it had a better goal differential (3 to 2).

While two stalwarts struggled early on, there was a new light—the extremely talented Netherlands. Led by Johan Cruyff, Johan Neeskens, Rudi Krol, Wim Rijsbergen, and Robbie Rensenbrink, the Dutch, who were participating in their first Cup since 1934, played a style called Total Football, or Total Soccer. That meant any player could become an attacker or a defender. En route to the Group 3 crown, the Dutch showed the world what the style was all about. They stopped a vicious Uruguayan side, 2–0, as Johnny Rep scored a goal in each half. They were held to a scoreless tie by a defensive-minded Swedish team that also would qualify for the quarterfinals and they took Bulgaria apart, 4–1, as Cruyff dominated the match. Neeskens converted two penalty kicks and Rep and Theodorus de Jong added goals.

In Group 4, Poland and Argentina qualifed, leaving Italy out in the cold after reaching the finals in 1970. The Poles, in the midst of Olympic domination behind the likes of Grzegorz Lato, Kaz Deyna, and Robert Gadocha, won the group, edging Argentina, 3–2, as Lato struck twice, routing Haiti, 7–0, as Andrezej Szarmach netted a hat trick and Lato added two more, and getting past Italy, 2–1, behind Smarzach and Deyna. The Italians had their problems. In their first match, Haitian forward Manny Sanon, who would go on to play for the San Diego Sockers (North American Soccer League), predicted he would score two goals against the slow Italian defense. He connected a minute into the second half to break goalkeeper Dino Zoff's international goalless streak at 1,142 minutes. Sanon was only half right, not scoring again in a 3–1 Italian victory. Italy, however, could never get it together, playing Argentina to a 1–1 draw and losing to Poland. The Haitians, playing in their first Cup, also had their problems. Defender Ernst Jean-Joseph was discovered to have taken illegal drugs and was thrown out of the Cup. He returned home in disgrace, although he went on to play for the Chicago Sting (NASL).

Instead of a single-elimination in the quarterfinals, the eight remaining countries were placed in two groups of four teams apiece. The winners of each group would advance to the final, changing the strategy of teams from winning outright to accruing points. It all but

Fußball-Weltmeisterschaft 1974
FIFA World Cup 1974
Coupe du Monde de la FIFA 1974
Copa Mundial de la FIFA 1974

13. 6. – 7. 7. 1974
Hamburg   Düsseldorf   Frankfurt
West · Berlin Gelsenkirchen Stuttgart
Hannover   Dortmund   München

killed the drama of the knockout rounds. The Netherlands dominated Group A, winning its three matches. Cruyff masterminded the 4–0 demolition of Argentina with two goals, with Krol and Rep adding one apiece. Cruyff was marked out of the East German encounter by Konrad Weise, as the scoring responsibilities fell to Neeskens and Rensenbrink in a 2–0 triumph. Needing but a tie against Brazil, the Dutch recorded a 2–0 victory as Neeskens and Cruyff scored.

West Germany, whose second-place finish to the East Germans, meant an easier group, also won their three matches. The Germans shut down Yugoslavia, 2–0, behind Breitner and Mueller. They rallied from a 1–0 deficit against Sweden and registered a 4–2 win as Overath, Reiner Bonhof, Grabowski, and Uli Hoeness shared the scoring load. And they stopped the Poles, 1–0, on a muddy field as Mueller tallied, to set up a classic confrontation between two European sides in the final.

FINAL, 1974

The game did not get off to a promising start as the game officials noticed that the corner flags were missing so the opening kickoff was delayed until the flags were placed at their proper spots. With the match barely a minute old, referee Jack Taylor of England awarded the Dutch a penalty kick when Cruyff had been brought down in the penalty area after the Dutch has strung together nearly a dozen passes. Neeskens converted for a 1–0 lead. The Germans equalized on a penalty of their own in the 25th minute. Bernd Holzenbein was fouled by Wim Jansen, and Breitner converted. Mueller scored the game-winner with two minutes remaining in the first half, putting in a Bonhof pass. It was Mueller's fourth goal of the Cup and 14th of his World Cup career, surpassing the total of thirteen held by Frenchman Just Fontaine.

It also was the last goal of the match. In the second half, the Germans managed to shut down the great Cruyff, who was given a yellow card in his frustration to the close marking. And thanks to injuries to Rensenbrink and Rijsbergen, the Germans held on for their second title. The championship completed a unique hat trick for Overath. He was on the squad that finished second in 1966 and third in 1970.

West Germany 2, Netherlands 1
Olympic Stadium
Munich, West Germany
July 7, 1974

> West Germany: Maier, Beckenbauer, Vogts, Breitner, Schwarzenbeck, Overath, Bonhof, Hoeness, Grabowski, Mueller, Holzenbein
>
> Netherlands: Jongbloed, Suurbier, Rijsbergen (De Jong, 58), Krol, Haan, Jansen, Van Hanegem, Neeskens, Rep, Cruyff, Rensenbrink (R. Van de Kerkhof, 46)
>
> Goals: Neeskens (N) 1, Breitner (WG) 25 PK, Mueller (WG) 43
>
> Referee: Taylor (England)
>
> Attendance: 77,833

Despite political unrest and raging inflation, the 1978 World Cup still was held in Argentina. The Argentines did not disappoint their faithful, orchestrating a changing of the guard in South American soccer as Brazil continued to win, but could not win the big games.

1978 ARGENTINES ENJOY HOME COOKING

The Netherlands continued their artistry on the field, but again walked frustrated away with second-place medals. The Dutch would be remembered as the best second-place team never to win a World Cup.

The Argentines had some talent themselves. They were so loaded with Mario Kempes, Osvaldo Ardiles, and Daniel Passarella, they decided to leave off a talented 17-year-old by the name of Diego Maradona.

The Argentines won their first two matches—2–1 over Hungary as Ricardo Bertoni broke a 1–1 tie with seven minutes left—and 2–1 over France as Passarella and Leopoldo Luque scored. They met their match in a 1–0 loss to Italy for the Group 1 title—Roberto Bettega tallied in the 67th minute—but it was to be the last time the hosts would lose.

With soccer lightweights Tunisia and Mexico in Group 2, Poland and West Germany had few problems reaching the next round—that round-robin second round. In fact, the two sides played in the tournament opener. On paper, it looked like a superb match up between the defending champions and third-place finishers. On the field, it was yet another dreary scoreless tie. The crowd booed the fourth consecutive scoreless tie that opened a World Cup. The Germans, missing Franz Beckenbauer who decided to keep playing with the New York Cosmos (NASL), did post a 6–0 victory over Mexico, but played Tunisia to a 0–0 draw. Poland, with most of its 1974 squad intact, rebounded with a 1–0 win over Tunisia and a 3–1 triumph over Mexico.

Brazil, with Rivellino as the only surviving member of the 1970 championship team, did not demonstrate the flair that made it the most imposing soccer team in the world. The Brazilians reached the next round on points—a 1–1 tie with Sweden, a scoreless draw with Spain and a 1–0 win over Austria, which won Group 3—and not by merit.

The Dutch, who did not have Cruyff this time to drive opposing defenses crazy, still were a formidable bunch. They started out slowly with a 1–1–1 record, which was good enough to advance behind a 2–0–1 Peruvian side led by Nene Cubillas, who became the first player to score five or more goals in two separate Cups. Robbie Rensenbrink converted two penalties in the 3–0 win over Iran, which was followed by a 0–0 draw with Peru and a 3–2 loss to Scotland.

The Netherlands survived Group A (the second round) with a 2–0–1 mark. The Dutch treated themselves to a 5–1 triumph over Austria as Rep struck twice. They played West Germany to a 2–2 tie. The Germans already had drawn Italy, 0–0 and edged Italy, 2–1, as Ernie Brandts, making amends for a 19th-minute own goal, and Arend Haan scored in the second half to rally from a 1–0 halftime deficit. Haan's goal was considered to be the goal of the tournament as he beat Dino Zoff from thirty yards. Argentina barely got past Brazil on goal differential (8 to 5). The hosts blanked Poland, 2–0, and played Brazil to a scoreless tie. The Brazilians downed Peru, 3–0. Entering the final day of the group competition, both sides were tied in points, but Brazil enjoyed a better goal differential, 3 to 2. Brazil beat Poland, 3–1, as Roberto scored twice. Argentina, realizing it needed a big victory, routed Peru, 6–0, as Kempes and Luque had two goals apiece. The six-goal margin was enough to boost the

Argentines into the final, sparking speculation that Peru laid down or was paid off. It was never proved, although a number of theories have surfaced through the years.

The championship game, which was televised in ninety countries, including the United States, pitted two countries—Argentina and the Netherlands—neither had won the World Cup crown, the first time since 1958 this situation had occurred.

FINAL, 1978

The Argentines came out and attacked, while the Dutch employed physical tactics. The ploy worked for the hosts as Mario Kempes scored in the 37th minute. Dick Nanninga, who had boasted to the media before the match that he would score a goal as a substitute in the final, did so. He replaced Rep in the 58th minute, and equalized after Rene van de Kerkhof beat an offside trap with nine minutes remaining in regulation. Rensenbrink hit the post in the final minutes. Kempes turned out to be the hero. After beating three players, he lifted the Argentines into a 2–1 lead with his sixth goal of the tournament in the last minute of the first fifteen minute overtime. Bertoni added an insurance tally six minutes from time.

Argentina 3, Netherlands 1 (OT)
Estadio Antonio Liberti Monumental
Buenos Aires, Argentina
June 25, 1978

> Argentina: Fillol, Olguin, Galvan, Passarella, Taratini, Ardiles (Larrosa, 65), Gallego, Kempes, Luque, Bertoni, Ortiz (Houseman, 77)
> Netherlands: Jongbloed, Jansen (Suurbier, 72), Brandts, Krol, Poortvliet, Haan, Neeskeens, W. van de Kerkhof, R. Van de Kerkhof, Rep (Nanninga, 58), Resenbrink
> Goals: Kempes (A) 37, Nanninga (N) 81, Kempes (A) 104, Bertoni (A) 114
> Referee: Gonella (Italy)
> Attendance: 77,260

1982

ITALIANS

REIGN IN

SPAIN

There were changes afoot in FIFA and the World Cup. FIFA president Dr. Joao Havelange, who was elected with strong support by Third World countries in 1974, kept his promise by expanding the tournament from sixteen to twenty-four teams. The idea was to open up the Cup to the lesser soccer countries of the world. Because of that, a number of countries that might not have gotten to the world stage would have an opportunity to show what they could do. Cameroon was impressive in the opening round, as was Algeria, which stunned Germany.

The 1982 World Cup, however, belonged to Italy—which started off as 14–1 long shots to win the trophy—although you would have not known the Italians were title contenders due their slow start in Group 1. The Italians wound up playing three first-round ties, scoring two goals and allowing as many. They showed absolutely nothing in a 0–0 draw with Poland, a 1–1 tie with Peru and a 1–1 result with Cameroon, which missed out on advancing to the second round because Italy had scored one more goal than the Africans.

The West Germans had their problems in Group 2, too, losing to the Algerians, 2–1 as Rabah Madjer and Lakhdar Belloumi, the African Player of the Year, scored for the winners, Karl-Heinz Rummenigge for the losers. The Germans rebounded with a 4–1 triumph over Chile with Rummenigge netting a hat trick, setting up a disgraceful match with Austria. Germany needed a victory and Austria, at the worst, needed to lose by only a goal. After Horst Hrubesch scored in the 10th minute, both sides were content to knock the ball around midfield. Algeria finished unbeaten with two victories, but did not advance because of goal differential (Austria had plus 2, Algeria 0). Defending champion Argentina, playing in Group 3, never found its rhythm to be consistent. Bolstered by the latest superstar pretender to Pelé's throne—Diego Maradona—the Argentines stumbled in the World Cup opener as Belgium recorded a 1–0 win on Erwin Vandenbergh's second-half goal. Argentina did rebound in the first round with a 4–1 victory over Hungary and a 2–0 win over El Salvador. It seemed that everyone fed on Cup newcomer El Salvador. For example, Hungary rolled to a 10–1 victory as second-half substitute Laszlo Kiss recorded a hat trick, the best performance by a sub in World Cup history.

England surprisingly ruled Group 4, which included France. In fact, the English took care of the French in their first match, 3–1, as Bryan Robson scored the quickest goal in Cup history—27 seconds into the match. He added another in the second half, and Paul Mariner also tallied. England finished at 3–0, defeating Czechoslovakia, 2–0, and edging Kuwait, 1–0. France, which took second at 1–1–1, played one of the more unusual matches in Cup history against Kuwait, a 4–1 victory. The commotion came with the game all but decided and with the French leading 3–1 with fifteen minutes left. Alain Giresse put in a free kick to give his team a 4–1 advantage, or so he thought. The Kuwaitis claimed they had heard a whistle and stopped in their tracks. Prince Fahid, the country's Football Association president, walked from the stands onto the field to protest and argue the decision, which was reversed. France did get an official fourth goal as Maxime Bossis scored in the final minute.

Even though it was host, Spain struggled in Group five to reach the next round, tying Honduras, 1–1, edging Yugoslavia, 2–1, and losing to group leader Northern Ireland, 1–0. Criticism was so severe that one Spanish newspaper refused to publish the team's lineup after one match.

In Group 6, it looked like Brazil had rediscovered the magic it had during its three world championship run, outscoring the opposition, 10–2, en route to three impressive victories. The Brazilians started it off with a 2–1 win over the Soviet Union, with Socrates and Eder scoring. They continued it with a 4–1 thumping of Scotland, as Zico, Oscar, Eder, and Falcao found the back of the net. And they completed it with a 4–0 romp past World Cup newcomers New Zealand, 4–0, as Zico tallied, twice, and Falcao and Serginho once each.

In a new twist to the later rounds, four second-round groups were used to determine the four semifinalists.

In Group A, Poland prevailed, blanking Belgium 3–0, and playing the Soviets to a scoreless draw after the Soviet Union bested Belgium, 1–0. In Group B, the West Germans emerged on top, playing England to a scoreless draw, but edging Spain, 2–1, on goals by Pierre Littbarski and Klaus Fischer. England and Spain eliminated themselves with a 0–0 tie. Group C brought together Italy, Argentina and Brazil. Italy got past the defending champs, 2–1, as Marco Tardelli and Antonio Cabrini scored in the second half. Maradona, who was closely marked by the Italians, vented his frustration and

anger in a 3–1 loss to Brazil several days later. He kicked Batista's groin in the waning minutes and was subsequently ejected by referee Mario Rubio Vazquez of Mexico. Brazil, meanwhile, was brilliant as ever, getting goals from Zico, Serginho, and Junior to set up a memorable encounter with Italy. Paolo Rossi, who had recently come back from a two-year suspension because of his involvement in a game-fixing scandal, was blanked during the opening round. But he could not have picked a better place to break out of scoring slump. He was brilliant, scoring three times—in the fifth, 25th and 75th minutes to give the Italians leads each time against Brazil, which had goals from Socrates and Falcao. The victory boosted the Italians into the semifinals.

In Group D, France advanced on the basis of its 1–0 win over Austria and 4–1 triumph over Northern Ireland. Austria tied Northern Ireland, 2–2.

Rossi was as hot as the weather—100 degrees at Nou Camp Stadium in Barcelona, striking twice in the Italians' 2–0 semifinal win over Poland. And as well as Rossi and his teammates played, their game was anticlimatic compared to the tussle between West Germany and France. The West Germans managed to outlast their rivals, 5–4, in penalty kicks after playing to a 3–3 tie after extra-time in what many observers called the greatest World Cup game ever. The Germans took a 1–0 lead in the 18th minute on Littbarski's goal, but the French tied in on Michel Platini's penalty kick nine minutes later. In the 57th minute, the game turned on a controversial play. Racing toward the German penalty area, Patrick Battiston was knocked down by goalkeeper Toni Schumacher. Battison was so badly injured, he was replaced. Schumacher, who should have received a yellow card at the very least, and perhaps a red card, did not and remained in the game. So, the Germans were able to play at even strength into extra-time. The French scored twice behind Marius Tresor and Alain Giresse. It appeared the Germans were dead, but they somehow rallied as substitute Karl-Heinz Rummenigge, who had been bothered by a leg injury and Klaus Fischer scored. That set up penalty kicks. With the tie-breaker score at 4–4, Schumacher saved Jean-Luc Bossis' try and Horst Hrubesch converted the game-winner.

FINAL, 1982   Unless you were a West German fan, the entire world knew what was going to happen at Santiago Bernabeu Stadium in Madrid on July 11—an Italian victory to end a storybook tournament. It appeared the horse-drawn carriage would turn into a pumpkin in the 25th minute, as Italian Antonio Cabrini became the first player to miss a penalty kick in a World Cup final.

The score was 0–0 at the half, and the Germans felt they still had a chance—or so they thought. Rossi found the back of the net one last time with his sixth goal of the tournament, heading the ball past Schumacher in the 57th minute. Marco Tardelli doubled the lead eleven minutes later, scoring from the edge of the penalty area, and Alessandro Altobelli, who came in for Francesco Graziani, made it 3–0 in the 81st minute. Paul Breitner scored two minutes later to became only the third player to score in two finals—Brazil's Vava and Pélé had accomplished the feat. It was too little and too late to deny this team their destiny.

Italy 3, West Germany 1
Santiago Bernabeu Stadium
Madrid, Spain
July 11, 1982

> Italy: Zoff, Scirea, Gentile, Cabrini, Collovati, Bergomi, Tardelli, Oriali, Conti, Rossi, Graziani (Altobelli, 8, Causio, 89)
> West Germany: Schumacher, Stielike, Katz, Briegel, K.H. Foerster, B. Foerster, Breitner, Dremmler (Hrubesch, 61), Littbarski, Fischer, Rummenigge (Mueller, 69)
> Goals: Rossi (I) 57, Tardelli (I) 68, Altobelli (I) 81, Breitner (WG) 83
> Referee: Coehlo (Brazil)
> Attendance: 90,080

Diego Maradona dominated this tournament from start to finish, and although he did not score a goal in the championship game, he managed to set up the game-winner with a brilliant, yet simple pass in the waning minutes.

The tournament originally was scheduled to be played in

1986
DIEGO AND
THE RGEN-
TINES PUT ON
A SHOW
IN MEXICO

Colombia, but with the World Cup expanded from sixteen to twenty-four teams and mounting financial problems at home, Colombia admitted that it did not have enough money or stadiums to organize properly such an enormous event. So, only three years before the kickoff—countries usually need six years to organize this Herculean effort—Mexico was awarded the cup, becoming the first country to host the World Cup twice.

To complicate matters, only eight months before the Cup, a massive earthquake hit Mexico and Mexico City, killing 25,000 people and destroying or damaging thousands of structures. Despite this horrible disaster, Mexico rebuilt itself and the show went on, and what a show Maradona put on.

Even though the Cup started with yet another tie—a 1–1 draw between defending champion Italy and Bulgaria—it wasn't a bad game. In fact, the Bulgarian team, which was stuck in a traffic jam on the way to Azteca Stadium, managed to tie the match on a goal by Nasko Sirakov with five minutes left after Alessandro Altobelli scored in the 43rd minute. Altobelli, incidentally, scored the final goal for Italy in the 1982 Cup.

Maradona showed his brilliance from Argentina's opening match, a 3–1 win over South Korea. He was punished with several fouls by the Asians, but every time he was knocked down within striking distance, Maradona got even. Maradona's free kick rebounded off the Korean wall to himself, and he passed to Jorge Valdano, who scored. After another foul in the 17th minute, his free kick set up Oscar Ruggeri, who headed it home. And finally, his cross set up Valdano for an easy goal barely a minute into the second half. In Argentina's 1–1 tie with Italy, Maradona set up his team's lone goal on a magnificent long ball to Valdano. As if he realized he wasn't going to be needed in the 2–0 victory over Bulgaria, Maradona had a relatively silent game. He was saving his best for later.

Mexico, which underwent intensive training preparation and several world-wide tours a year before the competition under Yugoslav coach Bora Milutinovic, had some promising results at Azteca. The Mexicans defeated Belgium, destined to be in the Final Four, 2–1, scoring all their goals in the first half—by Fernando Quirarte and Hugo Sanchez. They also got past a tough Iraqi side,

CHAPTER
2

1–0, on Quirarte's goal. Sandwiched between those two matches was an intriguing affair with Paraguay, a 1–1 draw, but it was one of the most exciting ties fans had ever seen. The Mexicans, who committed forty-five of the game's seventy-seven fouls, had taken a 1–0 half-time lead on a goal by Luis Flores. The Paraguayans equalized with six minutes left as former Cosmos forward J.C. Romero—now known as Romerito—headed in a goal. With barely a minute remaining, the hosts were given a chance to win when Sanchez appeared to have been taken down outside the penalty area, but referee George Courtney of England awarded a penalty. Sanchez, who had been appearing in soft drink commercial converting a penalty to the cheers of the crowd, took this one in reality and goalkeeper Roberto Fernandez knocked the ball off the post. A stunned Sanchez was jeered by the crowd.

France and the Soviet Union had the best of play and results in Group C. They tied, 1–1. The French, under the midfield leadership of Michel Platini, disposed of Canada, playing in its first World Cup under former Vancouver Whitecaps coach Tony Waiters, 1–0, and Hungary, 3–0. The Soviets, made up of players from mostly Dynamo Kiev, routed Hungary, 6–0, and blanked Canada, 2–0.

Brazil, based in Guadalajara in Group D, the site of its previous success in 1970, scored only five goals in three matches, but did not allow any. The Brazilians edged Spain, 1–0, on a goal by Socrates, who was a medical doctor when he wasn't playing soccer. The match was not without its controversies. The Brazilian national anthem wasn't played. Instead, "Song of the Flag," a patriotic tune played at political gatherings, was used. Then, in the 58th minute, it appeared that the Spanish had scored a goal when Michel's shot that hit the crossbar bounced into the goal, but referee Chris Bambridge of Australia did not signal a goal. Careca provided the only score in the second half, in a 1–0 win over Algeria, one of the Brazilians' most low-key performances. Their offense woke up against Northern Ireland, as Careca struck twice in a 3–0 victory on June 12. It turned out to be an emotional match for Northern Ireland goalkeeper Pat Jennings, who was celebrating his 41st birthday and final international game. After the match ended, both teams allowed Jennings to walk off the field by himself as he disappeared into the tunnel. The Brazilian players signed the game ball and gave it to the veteran keeper.

Group E, with World Cup veterans West Germany, Uruguay and Scotland and promising newcomer Denmark, was rightfully called the Group of Death. After the dust had cleared, the new kids on the block, Denmark, had won all three of its matches. Germany finished second at 1–1–1 a course, incidentally, that would avoid Argentina until the final. The Germans rallied on a late goal by Klaus Allofs to tie Uruguay, 1–1, got past Scotland, 2–1, on another second-half goal by Allofs and dropped a 2–1 decision to Denmark. The free-wheeling Danes—their nickname was Danish Dynamite—might have shot their wad in the opening round. They blanked Scotland, 1–0, rolled over Uruguay, 6–1, as Preben Elkjaer-Larsen recorded a hat trick and beat Germany. In one of the more forgettable matches of the Cup, Scotland and Uruguay played to a scoreless tie after Uruguayan Jose Batista was red-carded fifty-three seconds into the match after he fouled Gordon Strachan. The South Americans, who needed a tie to advance, had their game reduced to time-wasting tactics and brutal tackling.

Then there was Group F—the Group of Sleep—because the first four matches in Monterrey produced a total of two goals. For example: Morocco 0, Poland 0; Portugal 1, England 0; England 0, Morocco 0; Poland 1, Portugal 0. It was so bad that one player pleaded with fans to stay away from the stadiums. England, considered one of the world's powers, entered its vital, final match against Poland without two key players—injury-prone captain Bryan Robson with a dislocated shoulder and midfielder Ray Wilkins, who was ejected after throwing the ball at referee Gabriel Gonzalez for showing his disgust at a decision. Finally, on the final day of the group competition, at least two teams woke up as England posted a 3–0 win over Poland and Morocco defeated Portugal, 3–1, behind two goals by Abdelrazak Khairi to become the first African and Third World country to win a group.

The second round produced some memorable performances. Manuel Negrete scored on a brilliant volley—newspapers called it the butterfly goal—and set up another in Mexico's 2–0 win over Bulgaria, which managed to advance without winning a match. In one of the great individual performances in a losing effort, Igor

Belanov recorded a hat trick in Belgium's 4–3 victory over the Soviet Union in extra time. Stephane Demol and Nico Claesen scored for the Belgians in OT, while Belanov netted his third. The Brazilians, who finally rediscovered their game, rolled past Poland, 4–0. Platini continued to show his magic, scoring one goal in France's 2–0 victory over a rather listless Italy, which did not use 1982 hero Paolo Rossi for a minute. The claim was that he was out-of-shape. But wasn't that the case four years earlier?

In the first World Cup meeting between those two South American rivals since the 1930 championship game, Argentina edged Uruguay, 1–0, on a goal by Pedro Pasculi in a tight, defensive match that was played during a thunderstorm. Morocco showed that its first-round performance was no fluke, playing the West Germans tough, but the Europeans prevailed, 1–0, on Lothar Matthaeus' free-kick goal in the waning minutes. The Danes, who won over the crowd with their attack-minded performances in the first round, self-destructed against Spain, which scored four times in the second half as Emilio Butragueno—nicknamed the Vulture—finished with four goals in a 5–1 win. The beginning of the end for the Danes turned out to be an ill-advised pass in the penalty area in the 43rd minute by Jesper Olsen, who had scored earlier. Butragueno intercepted and scored. Gary Lineker scored twice and Peter Beardsley, who once played for the Vancouver Whitecaps (NASL), scored once in England's 3–0 win over Paraguay.

As if to top the previous round's results, three of the four quarterfinals turned out to be classics. It started with the France-Brazil match, which ended in a 1–1 draw after regulation (the second half was end-to-end action) and extra time. Careca had given the Brazilians the lead, but Platini equalized. It came down to penalty kicks, as Platini and Brazil's Julio Cesar missed theirs, setting up Luis Fernandez to become the hero by converting his. The Mexicans, playing far away from the friendly confines of Azteca and in the heat of Monterrey, managed to play West Germany even through 120 scoreless minutes. But nerves got to the hosts in penalties, as the Germans prevailed, 4–1, with Allofs, Andreas Brehme, Matthaeus, and Pierre Littbarski recording their chances. Belgium also outlasted Spain, 5–4, in penalties, after playing to a 1–1 draw.

Back at Azteca, England and Argentina played for the first time since the Falkland Wars in 1982. But Maradona made certain no one would remember the Falklands in a 2–1 victory. Six minutes into the second half, Maradona had tried to play the ball into the penalty area, but English midfielder Steve Hodge out-battled the Argentine for the ball and lifted a backpass to goalkeeper Peter Shilton. Maradona and the keeper arrived at the same time and the Argentine knocked the ball into the net with his left hand. Despite protests by the English, referee Ali Bennaceur of Tunisia pointed to the center spot. Maradona later claimed "the hand of God" scored that goal. As if to make amends, Maradona embarked on an amazing journey four minutes later. He took possession of the ball ten yards in Argentine territory. He performed an 180-degree turn that left Peter Reid and Peter Beardsley standing in their tracks. He then raced down the right side into English territory past Ray Wilkins. Terry Fenwick tried to pull him down at the top of the penalty area, but Maradona shrugged him off. Shilton came out of the goal, committed himself and fell to the turf, eight yards out. Terry Butcher tried a last-ditch effort with a sliding tackle under Maradona, who pushed the ball into the unattended net. Total time: ten seconds. Number of touches: nine. Even his opponents were astonished by the performance. "Today he scored one of the most brilliant goals you'll ever see," England coach Bobby Robson said. "That first goal was dubious, the second goal a miracle. It was a fantastic goal. It's marvelous for football that every now and then the world produces a player like Maradona. I didn't like his second goal, but I did admire it."

It would be difficult to surpass his one-man show in the quarterfinals, but Maradona did his best in the semifinals, scoring twice in a 2–0 victory over Belgium at Azteca. Though it was only a thirty-yard jaunt, his second goal was reminiscent of his goal against England, as he raced around three defenders. In a rematch of the 1982 semifinals, West Germany took on France in Guadalajara, but the result was anticlimatic. It lacked the excitement of the Germans' comeback victory in OT. Brehme scored in the first half and Rudi Voeller tallied off a counterattack in a 2–0 German win that was known for the winners' tenacious defense that shut down Platini and held his teammates in check with tactical precision.

FINAL

1986

In front of the second largest crowd for a final, Argentina managed to overcome the Germans, who battled back from a two-goal deficit with seventeen minutes left.

The Argentines struck first, as Jorge Burruchaga's free kick set up Jose Luis Brown with a header goal in the 22nd minute. They doubled their lead on Valdano's goal in the 55th minute. Trailing by two goals, the Germans were forced to open up their attack. It took a while, but they found the back of the net. First, Karl-Heinz Rummenigge headed home a corner kick by Brehme in the 73rd minute; it was the third consecutive tournament in which he had scored. The Germans equalized some eight minutes later off another Brehme corner as Thomas Berthold headed the ball to second-half substitute Rudi Voeller, who scored.

As the match appeared to be heading for overtime, Maradona, who had been effectively marked out of the match, noticed Burruchaga alone at midfield. He blooped an innocent-looking pass to his teammate, who beat goalkeeper Toni Schumacher with seven minutes remaining. The Argentines held on for a 3–2 triumph, and Maradona was crowned player of the tournament.

Argentina 3, West Germany 2
Azteca Stadium
Mexico City, Mexico
June 29, 1986
>   Argentina: Pumpido, Cuciuffo, Olarticoechea, Ruggeri,
>   Brown, Batista, Burruchaga (Trobbiani, 89), Giusti,
>   Enrique, Maradona, Valdano
>   West Germany: Schumacher, Jackos, K.H. Foerster,
>   Bethold, Briegel, Eder, Brehme, Matthaeus,
>   Rummenigge, Magath (Hoeness, 61), Allofs (Voeller, 46)
>   Goals: Brown (A) 22, Valdano (A) 55, Rummenigge (WG)
>   73, Voeller (WG) 81, Burruchaga (A) 83
>   Referee: Filho (Brazil)
>   Attendance: 114,590

Except for a handful of golden moments, the tournament

brought out, on many occasions, the worst soccer had to offer—brutal defensive plays, gamesmanship and a new philosophy. You've heard of win at all costs? Coaches tried not to lose at all costs, many times content to play for a tie and take a chance with penalty kicks in the elimination rounds. The play was so conservative that this tournement turned into the lowest-scoring World Cup ever—averaging 2.21 goals per match. The previous low was 2.53 in Mexico four years prior.

1990
GERMANY
GETS
REVENGE
IN ITALY

CHAPTER
2

Through this mess emerged several encouraging signs, including a Cameroon team that showed the entire world how to play the game, a Cinderella performance by Italy's Salvatore Schillaci and another solid showing by the eventual champions, West Germany. The Germans, who enjoyed a sterling first-round performance, seemed to wear down a bit as the tournament progressed because of the opposition's conservative tactics.

The defending champion Argentines, led by an ailing Diego Maradona, were transformed into anti-heroes and became the masters of the-not lose-at-all-costs school. The fact they were able to reach the championship match without a superb performance—coach Carlos Bilardo masterfully used twenty players in and out of the lineup due to injuries and yellow and red card suspensions—was disturbing indeed, to top soccer officials. One of the most disturbing images that emerged from the Cup was a disbelieving Maradona, with his hands extended out from his side, trying to convince the referee that a foul should have been called on an opposing player.

Fans got an inkling of what was to come in the opener in Milan by an aggressive Cameroon side that played open soccer while on attack, but a physical game when on defense. Cameroon players fouled Maradona thirteen times in that encounter, as he never could regain the brilliance he had shown in Mexico. Only five minutes after Kana Biyik was ejected in the 60th minute in the scoreless game, his brother Francois Omam Biyik headed the ball past goalkeeper Nery Pumpido. With two minutes remaining, Ben Massing was red-carded as Cameroon finished the match with nine players.

It went from bad to worse in Argentina's 2–0 victory over the Soviet Union. Pedro Troglio and Jorge Burruchaga scored, but the real story transpired around the Argentine goal as the defending champions lost Pumpido to a fractured leg after colliding with Julio Olarticoechea. Sergio Goycochea, a relative unknown on the international scene who was destined for glory, replaced him. Several minutes later, it appeared the Soviets were about to score the first goal, but Maradona—the man who gave the world "The Hand of God" goal only four years prior—did a variation, knocking a certain goal by Oleg Kuznetsov out of harm's way with his hand. Referee Erik Fredriksson, who stood ten feet from the incident, did not call anything. Argentina qualified for the second round after it played Romania to a 1–1 draw.

Cameroon, on the other hand, defeated Romania, 2–1, as 38-year-old substitute Roger Milla scored twice in the second half. Milla, who performed in the 1982 World Cup as a spritely 30-year-old, was coaxed out of semi-retirement to play for his country. When he tallied in the 76th minute, Milla became the oldest player to score in the Cup. To top off this crazy group, the Soviet Union, which already had been eliminated, romped to a 4–0 win over Cameroon, as the Africans became the first group winner to finish with a negative goal total (three goals for, five against).

Italy's tough defense gave it a lock on the Group A title. The hosts scored but four goals—two by Schillaci—but, more important, did not allow a goal. Although the Italians played some attractive soccer against Austria, they could not solve the defense, so Schillaci was inserted in place of Andrea Carnevale late in the game. Four minutes later, he scored the lone goal of the match. It looked like the Christians against the Lions when the Italians took on the United States, which suffered a humiliating 5–1 loss to Czechoslovakia in its first World Cup appearance in forty years. The Americans, however, turned the Roman fans against the home team, playing a conservative match in a 1–0 Italian victory as Giuseppe Giannini scored. The hosts wrapped up a perfect opening round with a 2–0 win over the Czechs as Schillaci made good use of his first start with a goal. Roberto Baggio chipped in a goal.

The Americans' showing against the Czechs was nothing short of a disaster as the Europeans uncovered virtually every weakness of the U.S. team. Tomas Skuhravy, who would have a field day against teams from the Western Hemisphere, led the way with two goals. After

ITALIA 90

an encouraging performance against Italy, the U.S. had one more chance to redeem itself, but managed to drop a 2–1 decision to Austria, despite enjoying a one-man advantage for most of the game.

Brazil, which deployed more of a defensive-oriented style, enjoyed similar results as the Italians in Group C, winning all three matches, scoring four goals and surrendering but one. Careca connected twice in a 2–1 victory over Sweden before the Brazilians recorded 1–0 wins over Costa Rica and Scotland as Muller scored both goals. The surprise team of the group was first-time qualifier Costa Rica, coached by Bora Milutinovic, who was hired some ninety days before the start of the competition. The Costa Ricans managed a 2–1–0 mark, upending Cup veterans Sweden, 2–1, and Scotland, 1–0, to reach the next round. The Scots, incredibly, have never advanced to the second round in seven appearances.

West Germany could have registered a perfect record in Group D had it not been for an 11th-hour lapse in its third match against Colombia. The Germans started off with a 4–1 triumph over Yugoslavia as captain Lothar Matthaeus netted two goals and Juergen Klinsmann and Rudi Voeller one apiece, and they continued their overwhelming performance with a 5–1 victory over the United Arab Emirates as Voeller led the way with two goals, followed by Klinsmann, Matthaeus and Uwe Bein. They scored in the 89th minute on a Pierre Littbarski goal, but the Colombians countered two minutes into injury time as Freddy Rincon scored off a superb pass by Carlos Valderrama, the man with the human fright wig who now plays for the Colorado Rapids (Major League Soccer).

Spain prevailed in Group E, as it played Uruguay to a scoreless tie, recorded a 3–1 win over South Korea, thanks to a Michel hat trick, and then edged Belgium, 2–1 as Michel converted a penalty and Alberto Gorriz scored a goal. Perhaps the most dramatic moment of this group came in the worst match of the first round—Uruguay's 1–0 victory over South Korea. Uruguay, which needed a victory to gain the second round, scored on a goal by sub Daniel Fonseca two minutes into injury time.

Group F was playfully called the "Hooligans Group" because of the rowdy and rambunctious fans of England and the Netherlands. It was too bad their energy was not transferred to the soccer field as only seven goals were scored in six matches. The only result that was not a tie turned out to be England's 1–0 victory over Egypt, making its first World Cup appearance in more than two generations—fifty-six years. The win broke a logjam. Had England not won, all four teams would have been tied. As it was, Ireland, under coach Jack Charlton of England, finished second without winning a match, recording three ties—1–1 with the English, 0–0 with Egypt and 1–1 with the Netherlands. The Dutch, picked by many to win the World Cup crown behind the firepower of Marco van Basten, the European Player of the Year, and Ruud Gullit, were disappointing and hardly looked like potential champions, playing a 1–1 tie with Egypt and a scoreless draw with England.

The second round—also called the round of sixteen by FIFA—produced a couple of surprises or two. Milla magic continued for Cameroon as he came off the bench to score two more goals. The game-winner came in overtime as Colombian goalkeeper Rene Higuita, nicknamed the Merry Wanderer because of his forays into the offensive end, was caught some ten yards out of his goal, and Milla had an easy goal and Cameroon an unlikely 2–1 win. Skuhravy continued to feast off of Western Hemisphere teams as he hit for a hat trick—all headers—in a 4–1 triumph over Costa Rica. The Brazilians dominated the Argentines, who scored on virtually their only clear chance of the match—Maradona had set up Claudio Caniggia—en route to a 1–0 win. In one of the most intense matches in Cup history, West Germany bested the Netherlands 2–1, in an encounter that should have been played in the semifinals or final. Dutch defender Frank Rijkaard was ejected for spitting at Rudi Voeller, who also was given his marching orders for running into the goalkeeper. Klinsmann and Andreas Brehme scored for the winners, as the Dutch returned home dazed, frustrated and embarrassed. The luck of the Irish continued for Ireland, which played its fourth consecutive tie, a 0–0 result with Romania. But the Irish prevailed in penalties, 5–4. Schillaci's fairy tale continued in Italy's 2–0 victory over Uruguay, which had been whistled for thirty-six fouls. England edged Belgium, 1–0, on David Platt's goal some thirty seconds from the end of extra time and a penalty-kick tie-breaker, and Yugoslavia squeaked past Spain, 2–1, on Dragan Stojkovic's goal in extra time.

All four quarterfinals were decided by a goal or by tie-breakers. The best of the lot was England's 3–2 comeback win over Cameroon, whose lack of subtlety on defense caught up with the Africans. Gary Lineker was the man of the match, recording two penalty kicks, the last in overtime. Milla did not score as a substitute this time, but he did set up both of Cameroon's goals.

The others? The Argentines continued to use mirrors as they got past the Yugoslavs on penalties, 3–2, after 120 minutes of scoreless soccer. The Yugoslavians had a player ejected, but it was they who played as though they had a man advantage. Schillaci—who else?—scored in the first half for Italy in its 1–0 triumph over Ireland, a day after the Irish visited the Pope. Germany shut down Skuhravy, and Matthaeus converted a penalty kick for a 1–0 win.

It looked as if the Italians would play the Germans in the final, but the Argentines had other plans in the semifinals. Italy made a tactical mistake. They scored too early as Schillaci connected for his fifth goal in the 17th minute. That woke up the Argentines, who would have been content to stay in their shell and play for a tie-breaker. Forced to play soccer, Argentina equalized in the 67th minute, with Caniggia heading home a cross from Olarticoechea. The goal snapped goalkeeper Walter Zenga's goalless streak of 517 minutes, a World Cup record. Goycochea turned out to be the real hero for the Argentines, who prevailed on penalties, 4–3, as he saved attempts by Roberto Donadoni and Aldo Serena. West Germany, meanwhile, outlasted the English, 4–3, on penalty kicks after playing to a 1–1 tie in regulation and extra time after Brehme scored for the winners, Lineker for England.

FINAL, 1990

Andreas Brehme converted a penalty kick in the 84th minute to lead West Germany to its third World Cup title after a 1–0 victory over Argentina at Olympic Stadium in Rome. Oh, you want more? Well, as said before, the less said the better.

The Argentines, with several players sidelined with injuries and suspensions, were no doubt the less talented side. They had four regulars on the sidelines. Midfielder Ricardo Giusti missed the match because of a red card and midfielders Sergio Batista, Olarticoechea, and Caniggia due to yellow-card accumulations. So, not surprisingly, they tried to play for a tie-breaker using negative, defensive soccer. "It was just too bad the Argentines didn't participate," German coach Franz Beckenbauer said. "They wanted to destroy. They were too weak. It is too bad that happened in a final game."

The Germans played down to the level of their opponents and could never get their game going. At least they tried to play. The Argentines got within striking distance of the goal in the 38th minute after Guido Buchwald, who did a masterful job of shadowing Maradona, tripped Jose Basualdo twenty yards out on the right side. Maradona's free kick sailed over the goal and goalkeeper Bodo Illgner, who only touched the ball when a teammate passed it back. That was the extent of the Argentine attack.

Referee Edgardo Codesal of Mexico red-carded Pedro Monson—the first player ejected in a championship match—for tripping Juergen Klinsmann in the 65th minute. The Argentines, down to ten players, went further into their shell, if that was indeed possible. But the Germans continued to push up and were rewarded in the 84th minute when defender Roberto Sensisi tripped Voeller in the penalty area. Brehme converted the ensuing penalty, beating Goycochea to the lower left post. Before the match was over, Argentine forward Gustavo Dezotti joined Monzon on the sidelines, getting red-carded for grabbing defender Juergen Kohler by the neck in the 87th minute. That set up a disgraceful display by the Argentines, who continued to argue with Codesal after the final whistle. IThe Argentines' exit was an appropriate way to end the most negative of all World Cups.

West Germany 1, Argentina 0
Stadio Olympico
Rome, Italy
July 8, 1990
West Germany: Illgner, Berthold (Reuter, 75), Kohler, Augenthaler, Buchwald, Brehme, Haessler, Matthaeus, Littbarski, Klinsmann, Voeller
Argentina: Goycoechea, Ruggeri (Monzon, 46), Simon, Serrizuela, Lorenzo, Basualdo,Troglio, Burruchaga (Calderon, 53), Sensini, Dezotti, Maradona
Goal: Brehme (WG) 84 PK
Referee: Codesal (Mexico)
Attendance: 73,603

1994

A PERFECT

FINISH TO AN

IMPERFECT

WORLD CUP

In contrast to the ultra-defensive, foul-ridden Italia '90, USA '94 Cup was a delight. A record attendance of 3,587,538 watched the 52 matches, nearly a million more than the previous high. Thanks to a number of FIFA directives to referees, players were punished for fouls from behind. Thus, games were more exciting and there were fewer ties. Moreover, there were fewer ties (three) in the knockout rounds.

To top it off, Brazil became the first country to win four World Cup titles, even if the July 17 championship match against Italy was a feat considerably short of most of the 51 previous contests.

It would be unfair to compare the 1994 champions to the great Brazilian sides of yesteryear—1958, 1962 and 1970.

Those teams had a player named Pelé and a generation of soccer superstars that might not ever be duplicated by any country. The 1994 team, as coach Carlos Alberto Parreira liked to say, played modern football, not fantasy football.

"Soccer is no longer the same," he said. "There are no super-stars on this team. This team has to be more arranged. We don't have five or six players who can make the game."

Still, there was little doubt that the best team won the World Cup, a glorious event that was marred by the assassination of Colombian defender Andres Escobar, yet another drug scandal involving the notorious and forever humiliated Diego Maradona, and a soulless final.

The Brazilians finished the month-long extravaganza unde-feated at 5-0-2 (even though they were crowned champions, the final game officially goes into the record books as a scoreless tie), outscoring their opposition, 11-2.

"We are the most balanced team, the most efficient team," Parreira said. "We have not been threatened by any of the teams in any of the games. I don't remember a team reaching the finals in such a way.

"Again, Brazil is No. 1 in the world. Our mission has been accomplished."

The title broke a 24-year drought during which Brazil not only failed to reach the World Cup final, but the semifinals as well. Not surprisingly, as favorites they were under constant scrutiny and criticism from an unforgiving and unsatisfied media.

"Not many people believed in us," forward Bebeto said. "The players believed we could win. It was a well-deserved title because Brazil was the best team throughout the competition. Every team that played us changed their way of playing. Everyone went to the back (defense). Italy was proof of that."

Incredible as it may sound, Brazil won without a credible midfield. Dunga, the team captain, was a hard worker, but not in the class of the great Brazilian schemers of the past. The attack usually went from the backline—which had an endless pool of talent—to a most lethal scoring duo up front—Romario and Bebeto.

How deep was the defense?

The backline wound up with the sixth, seventh and eighth players on the depth chart due to injuries and suspensions, and they did the job. For example, Branco replaced the suspended Leonardo. All he did was score the game-winning goal on a spectacular free kick against the Netherlands in the quarterfinals. Cafu replaced an ailing Jorginho in the final and was one of the offensive forces of the match, overlapping and creating a number of opportunities from the right wing.

As for the front line, there were strong rumors that Brazil's dynamic duo did not get along.

"There are a lot of stories that are going around that aren't true," said Bebeto, the World Cup's MVP who finished with five goals. "To say we don't get along is false and a lie."

But they could not be any more different. Romario was a tabloid's dream. He was mercurial, arrogant, controversial and had a reputation for not working hard. Bebeto wasn't as noisy. His headlines usually came from his scoring feats thanks to his skill and hard work. As Romario aptly put it, "Bebeto likes to stay at home. I'm a street cat."

Bebeto, who did not have as spectacular a World Cup as his running mate, finished with three goals.

"The only thing we have in common is that we score goals," Romario said. "Bebeto is a far more free-flowing player than I am. Bebeto is always concentrated for ninety minutes. My strength is that sometimes people think I'm just sleeping."

CHAPTER

2

The man who masterminded Brazil's path to glory—Parreira—had been in the World Cup twice before as a head coach of Kuwait (1982) and United Arab Emirates (1990), as well as directing Saudi Arabia national team in the 1984 Olympics (he also was assistant coach of the Brazilian team on two occasions).

Parreira combined the free-flowing Brazilian game with European tactics, which further inflamed his critics.

"When you see us playing, you see a team completely different from a normal Brazilian team," Romario said. "We have a much better brand of soccer. Our physical strength and our unity has overcome what we might not have technically.

"For years people have said the yellow jersey is pretty, but it doesn't have a heart beating inside. After the World Cup, they might say the yellow jersey is pretty, but there are eleven hearts beating inside."

Before, during and after USA '94, Parreira found himself under a barrage of criticism—his mother even made lineup suggestions on Brazilian national TV—that never subsided.

Still, he never wavered from his course and he never gloated to the media after Brazil earned the trophy.

"We Brazilians have yet to admire the honest work done by Parreira," Romario said. "Many sections of the Brazilian media should be very thankful for what he's done the past three years. To put up with what he's had to put up with, particularly someone like me, many people wouldn't put up with it."

In fact, each of the Final Four teams considered it an achievement to get that far. For Bulgaria, which finished a surprising fourth, it was a complete turnaround of its fortunes in five previous appearances. The Bulgarians entered the tournament with a 16-game winless streak in World Cup play, needing a last-second goal by Emil Kostadinov to upend France, 2-1, to advance to USA '94.

Not many observers gave a talented Swedish side a chance to go far in the tournament. The Swedes had talent, but there were better sides—Germany and Argentina, at least on paper—before the Cup began. The Swedes, behind goalkeeper Thomas Ravelli and forwards Tomas Brolin and Kennet Andersson, enjoyed a fun ride. They upended Bulgaria in a rather entertaining third-place match, 4-0.

Italy, on the other hand, was considered a possible Final Four

candidate thanks to Roberto Baggio, nicknamed the Divine Ponytail for obvious reasons. Heard of the luck of the Irish? Well, USA '94 turned into the luck of the Italians. Coach Arrigo Sacchi, who eventually resigned as national coach midway through France '98 qualifying, managed to piece together a competitive side despite a number of suspensions and injuries all the way to the championship game.

And for Brazil, of course, it was a grand opportunity to exorcise the ghosts of World Cups of the past 24 years.

FIRST ROUND

The Brazilians started out with a pair of shutouts in Stanford Stadium, blanking Russia, 2-0, as Romario and Rai found the back of the net, doing the same to a disorganized Cameroon squad, 3-0. Romario, Bebeto and Marcio Santos connected for goals. By the time they flew to the Pontiac Silverdome to meet seemingly eternal foe Sweden, the Brazilians had already clinched the Group B tie. As if both sides knew they were going to meet again in the not too distant future, they played a so-so scoreless tie under the roof. Andersson scored in the first half and Romario equalized in the final half.

Sweden's path to the second round wasn't as smooth. The Swedes squandered an early lead, then needed a goal by Martin Dahlin in the 75th minute to tie Cameroon, 2-2. Roger Ljung, with his first international goal in five years, gave them a 1-0 lead eight minutes into the match, but the Africans came back behind David Embe (31st minute) and Francois Oman-Biyik (47th).

Russia, playing in its first Cup since the breakup of the Soviet Union, received some consolation in its final game, a 6-1 drubbing of Cameroon as forward Oleg Salenko put on a scoring show never seen at a World Cup. He scored a record five goals (the previous mark was four, held by nine players, most recently by Spain's Emilio Butragueno), striking in the 16th (penalty kick), 41st (free kick), 45th (penalty kick), 73rd (breakaway) and 75th minutes (breakaway) against Cameroon's backup goalkeeper. Its regular keeper, Joseph-Antoine Bell, quit the team after playing in the first two games over major disagreements with the Cameroon Soccer Federation about bonuses and match payment. As a footnote, 42-year-old Roger Milla became the oldest player to score in a Cup, tallying as a substitute.

The U.S. had been drawn into a difficult group—Switzerland, Romania and Colombia in Group A—and was not given much of a chance of advancing to the second round. But the Americans responded and surprised many of their detractors and critics. They managed to tie the Swiss, 1-1, at the Pontiac Silverdome on July 18, the first indoor match in World Cup history (the game was played on movable modules of grass, instead of artificial turf) on a marvelous 30-yard free kick that was turned into a goal by Eric Wynalda in the waning seconds of the first half that equalized a goal by Georges Bregy only six minutes prior.

Four days later at the Rose Bowl, the U.S. pulled off one of the great upsets in Cup history, upending heavily favored Colombia, 2-1, after taking a 2-goal lead. Colombia had trouble penetrating the U.S. defensive zone, particularly in the final third. The Americans, looking for holes in the Colombian defense, finally found one in the 35th minute when midfielder John Harkes crossed the ball from the left wing to Ernie Stewart. But the ball never got to Stewart as defender Andres Escobar redirected it into his own net for a 1-0 U.S. advantage. Stewart did score in the 52nd minute before Adolfo Valencia cut the deficit in half in the 90th minute.

The Americans had an opportunity to finish first instead of third and get a wildcard berth in its group with a tie with Romania. It was the difference between playing Argentina in Stanford on July 3 or Brazil at Stanford on July 4. The U.S. wound up with Brazil after a 1-0 loss to Romania as Dan Pestrescu scored off a free kick to the near post for which goalkeeper Tony Meola was not lined up properly. Romania, even though it dropped a 4-1 decision to the Swiss (Stephane Chapuisat, Adrian Knup and Bregy scored), won the group with the Swiss finishing ahead of the U.S. on goal differential.

Of course, it could have been worse. Consider Colombia, which humiliated Argentina during qualifying, 5-0. The South Americans boasted one of the most talented sides in the world, including master playmaker Carlos Valderrama and strikers Fredy Rincon and Faustino Asprilla. However, they never lived up to their promise. After losing to both the U.S. and Romania (a 3-1 decision highlighted by two goals from Florin Raducioiu and one by Gheorge Hagi), they recorded a rather meaningless 2-0 win over Switzerland (Herman Gavira and Harold Lorenzo had the goals).

Several days after the team returned home, Escobar was gunned down outside a nightclub in Medellin. Escobar, who was 27-years-old, was shot twelve times on July 2 as one of the gunmen shouted, "Goal! Goal!" each time he fired. FIFA general secretary Sepp Blatter called it "the saddest day I have ever witnessed in football, in a World Cup or any other competition. If something happens by accident, you can say it was the will of God. But when people deliberately shoot and kill somebody because he made a mistake in the game, something is wrong."

Germany, which was considered to be one of the tournament favorites, really did not find its rhythm. Observers cited age—many players were 30 or beyond (the average age of the team was 29, third highest of the 24 teams and behind only Belgium's 29 years, 5 months and Ireland's 29 years, 1 month)—and internal problems and squabbling. Still, the Germans were good enough to upend Bolivia in the Cup opener on June 17 as Juergen Klinsmann scored the first of his five goals in a 1-0 win in Chicago. Only three minutes after he entered the match, Bolivian midfielder Marco Etcheverry was red-carded for fouling sweeper Lothar Matthaeus from behind, effectively ending his participation in the Cup.

Later that day, South Korea gave an indication of what the Cup was to become, scoring twice in the waning minutes to tie favored Spain, 2-2, in the Cotton Bowl. The Spanish, who had captain and sweeper Miguel Angel Nadal red-carded in the 26th minute, took a 2-0 bulge with a pair of goals by Julio Salinas and Antonio Goikoetxea within five minutes early in the second half. But the South Koreans never relented, connecting twice in the waning minutes (Myung-bo Hong in the 85th and Jung-won Seo in the final minute).

The Germans, however, could not get into the swing of things. They needed a Klinsmann header to tie Spain in Chicago, 1-1, after Goikoetxea scored. They also held on for dear life against the Koreans several days later, 3-2, after taking a lead on two goals by Klinsmann and a third by Karlheinz Riedle.

Group D had the most interesting story lines. There was free-attacking and unpredictable (offensively and defensively) Nigeria, which would make history two years later by becoming the first African country to earn a soccer gold medal. There was Bulgaria, which was ready to turn its own personal World Cup history around.

And there was Argentina and a svelte Diego Maradona, who would make history—in the most notorious way—while playing in his fourth and final World Cup.

Eric Wynalda (11) scored a spectacular goal off a free kick in the 1-1 tie with Switzerland
[photo: Stephen Slade]

They all finished with 2-1 records, meaning that someone had to absorb the rest of the losses. That someone was Greece, on which the other three sides beat up. Poor Greece, coached by former U.S. national coach Alkis Panagoulias, was no match for its three opponents as it lost all its opening-round matches, scoring no goals while surrendering ten.

Nigeria won the group on goal differential (plus four to plus three to its opponents). Bulgaria took second on the strength of its 2-0 win over Argentina, which advanced to the second round as a wild card team.

Nigeria blanked Bulgaria, which gave little indication it would reach the Final Four by a 3-0 decision in Dallas as Rashidi Yekini, Daniel Amokachi and Emmanuel Amunike found the back of the net. The Africans demonstrated how many problems they experienced while holding the lead, taking a 1-0 advantage on a Samson Siasia goal in the 8th minute.

However, the Argentines, with Maradona in the midfield and Gabriel Batistuta teaming with Claudio Caniggia up front, rallied as Caniggia struck in the 22nd and 29th minutes en route to a 2-1 victory. The Nigerians clinched the group title with a 2-0 victory over Greece in Foxboro as Finidi George and Amokachi scored.

After that opening loss, the Bulgarians gathered themselves and rolled to a 4-0 win over hapless Greece for their very first World Cup win in eighteen tries. They needed to beat the Argentines, who romped past the Greeks, 4-0 (Batistuta collected a hat trick and Maradona added a goal). A Bulgarian win seemed unlikely until a set of drug tests from Argentina's win over Nigeria came up. Maradona was tested twice and both results were positive.

This wasn't an isolated incident. Maradona had been banned from playing for fifteen months in 1991 for cocaine use. This time, stimulants, including diet pills, were found in Maradona's system. There was a reason why people were questioning how slim and fit Maradona appeared entering the tournament. For the record, the cocktail included five banned substances—the drugs ephedrine and norepinephrine and three of their derivatives.

In typical Maradona fashion, he blamed everyone but himself. "I don't know, maybe we were careless, but I swear I did not drug myself to play. With my abilities, I don't need to drug myself. They (FIFA) have retired me from soccer. I don't think I want another revenge; my soul is broken. I don't understand. It hurts. They cut my legs off when I had a chance to recover." Maradona eventually was slapped with another suspension.

Stunned, Argentina lost to Bulgaria, 2-0, as Hristo Stoichkov and Nasko Sirakov, whose late goal gave the Eastern Europeans a 1-1 draw with defending champion Italy in the opener of the 1986 World Cup, scored for the Europeans.

On paper, Group E was considered the Group of Death with Italy, Ireland, Mexico and Norway vying for at least two and maybe three spots in the next round. Every game was close or ended in a tie, prompting some observers to rename it the Group of Sleep.

The Italians hardly looked like a team that would wind up in the championship game, but they had a history of starting slowly and picking up steam (see 1982). In their first game, they dropped a 1-0 decision to Ireland before a pro-Irish crowd at Giants Stadium. Baggio, voted everyone's top soccer player in the universe in 1993, was virtually nonexistent.

To remedy this situation, Sacchi decide to shake up his lineup for the Norway match, replacing defender Mauro Tassotti with Antonio Benarrivo, midfielder Roberto Donadoni with Nicola Berti and forward Alberigo Evani with Pierluigi Casiraghi.

As it turned out, Sacchi's most important switches came during the match. It happened with the game only twenty-one minutes old when goalkeeper Gianluca Pagliuca handled the ball outside the penalty area and was expelled for doing so. Luca Marchegiani replaced him in goal, but a field player needed to be taken off. Incredibly, Sacchi selected Baggio.

There were more troubles. Only three minutes into the second half, captain and veteran sweeper Franco Baresi limped off with a knee injury that later would need arthroscopic surgery. It was presumed he would be out of the Cup. Through all this misery, a miracle occurred. The other Baggio—Dino (no relation)—provided the scoring, off a header in the 69th minute. They held the predictable Norwegians at bay en route to a 1-0 triumph.

Italy needed at least a draw with Mexico in its third and final match to advance. Daniele Massaro scored three minutes into the second half before the Mexicans equalized on Marcelino Bernal's goal. Italy (1-1-1) barely made the next round as a wild card, the third place team in the group.

All four teams finished at 1-1-1, but Mexico, on the strength of its 2-1 victory over Ireland (Luis Garcia scored twice) won the group with the most goals (three), followed by Ireland (two goals), which was given the nod over Italy thanks to its win. Norway, which had beaten group winner Mexico, 1-0, was left out in the cold.

The Group F standings were just like Group D. Three countries—The Netherlands, Saudi Arabia and Belgium—finished at 2-1 apiece with winless Morocco (0-3) bringing up the rear.

The Netherlands, which had a frustrated Ruud Gullit quit only weeks before the opening kickoff, bested the Arab teams by identical 2-1 scores, but could not get past eternal rival Belgium, which registered a 1-0 win on Philippe Albert's goal and some superb late goalkeeping by Michel Preud'homme in Orlando. The Belgians also defeated Morocco, 1-0, but were upset by Saudi Arabia in Washington, D.C., 1-0, on Saeed Owiran's 5th minute score. The

Saudis, who were making their Cup debut, also edged Morocco, 2-1, at Giants Stadium.

Saudi Arabia, however, did not fare as well in the second round, losing to Sweden, 3-1, as Andersson scored twice in the second half after Dahlin found the net in the opening forty-five minutes.

Spain made relatively easy work of the Swiss, registering a 3-0 shutout in Washington, D.C. on goals by Fernando Hierro, taking advantage of a poor clearance in the 15th minute, Enrique in the 74th and Aitor on a penalty kick in the 87th.

In Orlando, the Netherlands took advantage of a mistake by Irish goalkeeper Packy Bonner to record a 2-0 victory. After Dennis Bergkamp tallied eleven minutes into the match, Bonner made one of those blunders that fans and sportswriters remember forever. In the 41st minute, Bonner managed to get in front of a 30-yard shot by midfielder Wim Jonk, but the ball slipped through his hands and into the goal.

So did some referees. The Germans appeared to have gotten their act together against Belgium, connecting three times in the opening half before holding off their foes in a 3-2 triumph in Chicago that had more than its share of controversy. Rudi Voeller, who had to be coaxed out of international soccer retirement by Coach Berti Vogts, led the way with two goals, and added one. But it was a goal the Belgians did not have an opportunity to score that left a bad taste in everyone's mouth. Swiss referee Kurt Roethlisberger admitted he made a mistake for not calling a foul and penalty kick in the 70th minute. Several days later, FIFA sent Roethlisberger packing.

With the U.S. reaching the second round, there was a collective sigh of relief that the host team reached that round, keeping the string going for each of the fifteen World Cups. Advancing to the quarter-finals, however, was to be an entirely different story as the Americans took on the favored Brazilians at Stanford Stadium on July 4. Not surprisingly, having the match played on the 218th anniversary of the birth of the country helped to hype the match to non-soccer fans. The television rating was a decent 9.3.

Unfortunately, the U.S., which played without midfielder John Harkes (yellow card suspension), did not live up to its hype. Coach Bora Milutinovic decided to play a defensive match, even after the Americans enjoyed a one man advantage. With two minutes remain-

ing in the first half, U.S. midfielder Tab Ramos took a vicious elbow to his head from defender Leonardo which fractured his skull. Leonardo was given a red card and eventually was suspended from the Cup.

Despite enjoying the one man advantage over the final forty-five minutes, the U.S. was content with playing its same defensive game. Bebeto finally beat the U.S. defense in the 74th minute, beating Alexi Lalas and Meola as Brazil held on for a 1-0 win.

In one of the ugliest games of the Cup, Bulgaria outlasted Mexico in penalty kicks, 3-1, after playing to a 1-1 tie after 120 minutes of regulation and overtime at Giants Stadium. The game was marred by two red cards and ten yellow cards.

Stoichkov had given the Bulgarians a lead in the 7th minute, but Alberto Garcia Aspe equalized for Mexico on a penalty kick in the 17th. The score remained that way until another set of penalties.

Bulgarian goalkeeper Borislav Mikhailov came up big in the tie-breaker, saving attempts by Bernal and Jorge Rodriguez. Bontcho Guentchev, who played a total of seventeen minutes in the tournament, Daniel Borimirov and Iordan Letchkov connected for the winners.

Against a tough and up-and-coming Nigerian side, Italy managed to pull out a win in Foxboro. With the Africans clinging to a 1-0 lead on a 26th minute score by Emmanuel Amunike and a

Russia's Oleg Salenko (9) enjoyed a dream game against Cameroon connecting for a World Cup record five goals.
[photo: Daniel Molz]

player advantage (Italy's Gianfranco Zola was red-carded for taking a dive in the penalty area), and only two minutes remaining in regulation, Roberto connected off a counterattack. He added a penalty kick after he was taken down in the box ten minutes into extratime (overtime), and Italy had a rather improbable 2-1 triumph.

The most entertaining match of the round of sixteen was Romania's 3-2 win over Argentina at the Rose Bowl. Dumitrescu found the back of the net in the 11th and 18th minutes and set up a goal by Gheorge Hagi in the 58th minute that gave Romania a 3-1 lead. Argentina, playing without the suspended Maradona, certainly made a game of it. Batistuta converted a penalty kick in the 16th minute and Abel Balbo struck on a rebound in the 75th.

In recent Cup history, the best games of the tournament usually wound up being the quarterfinals, and 1994 followed suit.

In what many observers called the game of the tournament, Brazil managed to prevail over The Netherlands, 3-2. The halftime score was 0-0, but if you witnessed the match, you had a pretty good inkling the game was going to bust open in the final forty-five minutes.

Brazil and the Netherlands combined for five goals in twenty-nine minutes, including a dramatic and marvelous game winner by Brazilian defender Branco, who was only playing because teammate Leonardo was suspended.

The Brazilians grabbed a 2-0 advantage behind goals by Romario (52nd minute) and Bebeto (63rd)—a controversial goal the Dutch claimed was offside (the ball floated over the head of Romario, who appeared to be in an offside position) that Bebeto celebrated with his famous cradle rock with teammates, commemorating the birth of his son.

The Dutch, however, refused to give up and continued to go forward. They equalized as Dennis Bergkamp (64th) and Aron Winter (77th) found the back of the net. Finally, Branco fired home a brilliant 25-yard free kick in the 81st minute to break the score. Brazil managed to hold on to win.

There were so many twists and turns for Italy that fans, media and other interested observers began to compare the 1994

version to the Italian side that captured the title in 1982, when Paolo Rossi, fresh off a two-year ban because of a goal-fixing scandal, went from pariah to hero in a matter of weeks.

This time, in his place was Baggio, who connected in a 2-1 quarterfinal victory over Spain in extremely humid conditions in Foxboro. Dino Baggio lifted the Italians into the lead in the 26th minute, but Jose Luis Caminero countered in the 59th minute, when his shot deflected off Benarrivo and past Pagliucia. Pagliuca did stop Julio Salinas with six minutes left in regulation, knocking the ball away with the tip of his shoe. This left the heroics up to Roberto Baggio, who connected with only two minutes remaining in regulation.

Germany, nicknamed Team Semifinal for reaching the Final Four in eight of the past ten World Cups, was favored to get past Bulgaria at Giants Stadium. After the Germans grabbed a 1-0 lead, the Bulgarians struck for a pair of goals within a 148 second span late in the match to pull off an incredible 2-1 upset. Actually, it appeared the Germans would make it nine of eleven as they enjoyed a 1-0 edge, thanks to a Matthaeus penalty kick in the 49th minute. The Germans give up a late lead to a supposed inferior side?

But the Bulgarians never gave up, although some luck was involved. In the 74th minute, Andreas Moeller's long-range shot bounced off the post. Moeller put in the rebound, but was called offside.

Stoichkov connected on a free kick in the 76th minute in which goalkeeper Bobo Illgner never moved and Letchkov headed home a feed by Zlatko Iankov barely three minutes later.

Hristo Stoichkov (8) struck in five consecutive games for Bulgaria [photo: J. Brett Whitesell]

The strangest game of this quartet was Sweden's win over Romania in penalty kicks at Stanford after playing to a 2-2 draw. The Swedes prevailed in penalties, 5-4. There was no scoring for the opening seventy-eighth minutes. Then the floodgates opened as the teams combined for four goals over the final 12 minutes of regulation and the first twenty-five minutes of extratime. Brolin powered in a 15-yard free kick in the 79th, but Raducioiu equalized with a minute remaining in regulation, knocking in Hagi's free kick that rebounded off the defensive wall. Raducioiu gave Romania a 2-1 advantage, scoring from the edge of the box eleven minutes into the first extra-time period. After Sweden's Stefan Schwarz was given his marching orders for his second yellow card of the match, the Swedes pulled even on Andersson's header in the 115th minute, with five minutes to spare. In the end, it was left to the goalkeepers to sort this one out. Ravelli, the Swedish keeper emerged as the hero, stopping Miodrag Belodrdici after teammate and substitute Henrik Larsson converted the go-ahead attempt.

That win was a spot in the semifinals.

The Italians' victory over Spain came at a price. Defender Mauro Tassotti broke the nose of Spanish forward Luis Enrique with an elbow to the face. He was cited for infractions during the match, but after watching tapes of the incident, FIFA officials slapped Tassotti with an eight-game suspension, the longest ever in World Cup history.

SEMIFINALS

Roberto Mussi replaced Tassotti and the Italians recorded a 2-1 semifinal over Bulgaria, winning the more conventional way. This time Roberto Baggio pulled off his scoring heroics early, striking in the 20th and 25th minutes to book a date in the final.

The Bulgarians? They thought the French referee, Joel Quiniou, had it in for them. They claimed Italian defender Alessandro Costacurta should have been called for a handball and that a penalty kick should have been awarded after Letchkov was tackled in the penalty area.

Later that day, Brazil took on Sweden for a second time— remember, they tied, 1-1, in their first round encounter. While the final score, 1-0, did not indicate the South Americans' dominance, they had little trouble with the Swedes in one of the most lopsided

FINAL, 1994

games in Cup history. The Brazilians outshot Sweden in the first half 15-1 and an amazing 26-3 for the game. Romario headed home a cross by Jorginho at the far post in the 80th minute and Brazil was heading for its first final in twenty-four years.

Two tired teams tried to slug it out. The Brazilians had better chances—quantity and quality—but had nothing to show for it. The game turned out to be one of the most anticlimatic matches in World Cup history, even if Brazil became the first team to win the Cup four times, its first championship since 1970.

When the Brazilians tried to attack, they could not find the back of the net. Part of that was due to the fine play of defenders Paolo Maldini and Franco Baresi, the sweeper, who was hobbled by a knee injury, and the fact that Italy packed the back with as many as eight players before a crowd of 94,194.

The two countries battled and cramped up through 120 minutes of scoreless soccer—ninety minutes in regulation and another thirty in extratime—so sport's most unthinkable way to decide a match—the penalty kick tie-breaker—was required.

Brazilian goalkeeper Claudio Taffarel, unemployed during the World Cup after completing a stint with Reggiana (Italy), had to make only twelve saves in six games entering the match. Ironically, he wound up as one of the heroes of the tie-breaker. "There's a lot of luck involved," he said. "Penalty kicks are like a lottery and nobody likes to arrive at a penalty-kick decision."

Baresi, a surprise starter despite his knee injury, took the first kick and blasted it into the stands. Brazil's Marcio Santos returned the favor seconds later as goalkeeper Gianluca Pagliuca blocked his try.

Demetrio Albertini nailed one into the upper right corner and Romario equalized, barely hitting the left post. Alberico Evani fired one into the middle of the net with Taffarel diving to his right, but Branco slotted his try into the lower right corner for a 2-2 tie. Daniele Massaro, hero of A.C. Milan's European Cup triumph over Barcelona and Romario only two months earlier, had his attempt blocked by Taffarel. Dunga, the Brazilian captain, powered his shot to the right side for a 3-2 edge.

Next up was Roberto Baggio, who carried Italy into the final with five goals in three games but had been doubtful for the match due to a hamstring injury. Baggio sailed his attempt into the stands, incredibly ending the match on an anticlimatic note.

"I usually place my (penalty) kicks, but I had no energy left, so I just hit it as hard as I could," Baggio said.

Stunned, Baggio stood in front of the penalty spot with his hands on his hips. Luca Bucci, the third-string goalkeeper, came over to console his teammate, as Brazilian players danced at midfield, hugging each other and draping themselves in their country's flag.

They took a victory lap around the entire field. During a special ceremony, the FIFA World Cup trophy was handed to Dunga, and the real party began.

Brazil 0, Italy 0
Brazil wins on penalty kicks, 3-2
Rose Bowl
Pasadena, CA
July 17, 1994

> Italy—Gianluca Pagliuca; Roberto Mussi (Luigi Apolloni, 35), Franco Baresi, Antonio Benarrivo, Paulo Maldini; Demetrio Albertini, Dino Baggio (Alberigo Evani, 95), Nicola Berti, Roberto Donadoni; Roberto Baggio, Daniele Massaro.
>
> Brazil—Claudio Taffarel; Jorginho (Cafu, 21), Branco, Aldair, Marcio Santos; Mazinho, Mauro Silva, Dunga, Zinho (Viola, 106); Bebeto, Romario.
>
> Scoring—None.
>
> Penalty kicks—Italy 2 (Baresi NG, Albertini G, Evani G, Massaro,NG, R.Baggio NG); Brazil 3 (Marcio Santos NG, Romario G, Branco G, Dunga G).
>
> Yellow Cards—Mazinho (B) 4, Apolloni (I) 42, Albertini (I) 43), Cafu (B) 87.
>
> Red Cards—None.
>
> Referee— Puhl (Hungary). Linesmen—Zarate (Paraguay), Fanei (Iran).
>
> Attendance: 94,194.

Entering France '98, French coach Aime Jacquet and his team had more than their share of doubters and critics, considering Jacquet had searched in vain for more than three years for a forward who could score consistently at the international level. History says that virtually all World Cup champions have someone who can put the ball in the net on a regular basis.

France wrote some history of its own during that June and July. By capturing the 16th World Cup with a stunning 3-0 victory over defending champion Brazil on July 12, 1998, France became only the seventh country to win soccer's most prestigious prize, joining Brazil, Italy, Germany, Argentina, Uruguay and England in an exclusive club.

France became the first country to win at home since Argentina pulled off that feat in 1978. What made the victory even more amazing was that it was accomplished by a team that relied on teamwork more than great stars. There was no question that Zinedine Zidane was the focal point, but it was the team defense, particularly the fabulous back four. The midfield could possess the ball for long periods of time, and despite a team-wide inability to shoot the ball past the opposing goalkeeper, France rose to the ocassion. The team's ability to overcome its faults and play as a team stood as the French's greatest triumph. That, plus the inclusion of players from former colonies and the sons of immigrants made this a lesson for the rest of the world that so many players with diverse backgrounds not only can play together, but they can excel as well. Much had been said of the ethnic mixture of the team, although Jacquet downplayed that factor, saying he saw only soccer players, not someone's heritage.

The defense included Ghananian-born Marcel Desailly and Lilian Thuram, of Guadeloupean heritage. The midfield boasted such diverse backgrounds as New Caledonia (Christian Karembeu), Senegal (Patrick Viera), the Basque region (Didier Deschamps), a player of Algerian descent (Zidane) and even French (Emmanuel Petit). The forward line had French-born Thierry Henry and Argentine-born David Trezeguet.

The French triumph climaxed a thirty-three day tournament that won't rank with Mexico '70, considered the greatest World Cup ever, or even Spain '82, but probably right behind the latter along with

Mexico '86. As good as USA '94 was, there was little question that France '98 topped it.

There were many factors and heroes. While France isn't considered a great soccer country, it was accessible from the rest of Europe and from parts of the rest of the world. Thousands of fans poured in from neighboring countries to cheer on their heroes or just bask in the glory and madness that is considered the World Cup.

There was some madness off the field. Newly elected FIFA President Sepp Blatter, like a little boy with a game in which he can change the rules any time he wanted, did exactly that, admonishing referees for not awarding enough red cards one day and publicly criticizing them the next. It confused the hell out of the men in the middle, action that should have been taken many months before the opening kickoff at St.-Denis on June 10.

Referees always seemed to be in the middle of things as the players, many of whom apparently went to acting school in their spare time, fell, stumbled and showed varying degrees of pain on their faces, doing their damnedest to feign injury to get a free kick for their side or a yellow or red card for an opposing player. Some of these players were so well schooled, they even deceived referees on several occasions. Just ask Blanc.

Beyond France, the most surprising side was Croatia, which finished third after losing to France in the semifinals, 2-1, and then bested the Netherlands by the same score. Davor Suker finished as the leading scorer of the tournament with six goals, beating opposing goalkeepers in six of his seven matches. Argentine goalkeeper Carlos Roa, hero of the second-round shootout victory over England, holds the distinction of keeping Suker off the scoreboard.

There were other heroes and emerging stars as well. Michael Owen, only eighteen years old, scored what was arguably the goal of the tournament on an amazing 50-yard run in that Argentine match. Dennis Bergkamp, who at times gave new meaning to the term invisible man, might argue with that as he scored a marvelous goal of his own, taking in a 50-yard cross-field pass from Frank DeBoer, dribbling around a defender and beating Roa with two minutes to spare for a Dutch 2-1 victory in the quarterfinals.

The Nigerians entertained fans before their defense, or lack

thereof, betrayed them. Denmark, which played so conservatively in the first round, upended the Nigerians in the second round, 4-1, and gave the Brazilians a run for their money losing in a pleasing quarterfinal confrontation, 3-2.

The French National Team after the final [photo: J. Brett Whitesell

England midfielder David Beckham, fiancé of the Spice Girls' Posh Spice, was red-carded for a silly foul on Argentine midfielder Diego Simeone early in the second half of a tied match. Argentina went on to win in a shootout as England, forced to change its attacking tactics, circled the wagons and prayed for a miracle. Ariel Ortega headbutted goalkeeper Edwin Van Der Sar and seeing red for it.

The Germans did not play up to expectations. For an unprecedented second consecutive World Cup and for the first time the event had been held in Europe since World War II, they finished out of the Final Four.

The Italians' defense wasn't up to par with some of their recent vintage and except for Christian Vieri and an occasional Roberto Baggio, had severe problems finding the back of the net.

The most disappointing side to Americans was the woefully underachieving U.S. team.

To the rest of the world, Brazil was a big disappointment. While good enough to win its group with a 2-1 record and advance to the final with unlike-Brazil victories, the Brazilians did not live up to the pre-tournament hype of four-time winner and defending champions.

Something was missing. Perhaps it was the high expectations and the low realizations of the Brazilians' 21-year-old superstar Ronaldo. On paper, it appeared he had a fine World Cup, scoring four goals and helping to set up three others. But when counted the most—the championship game—Ronaldo failed spectacularly. He was hardly a factor and his teammates weren't too far behind.

Brazil escaped Le Stade de France with a 2-1 victory over Scotland on June 10, kicking off France '98 with a mediocre performance. Cesar Sampaio scored with the match only four minutes old, but the Scots equalized on John Collins' 38th minute penalty kick.

The Brazilians managed to secure the win on a goal by Scottish defender Tommy Boyd, who accidentally knocked the ball into his goal from four yards during a scramble in the penalty area in the 73rd minute. Defender Cafu, the last Brazilian to touch the ball was so elated that he did a flip in the air.

"It's the worst moment of my life," Boyd said. "But I couldn't do anything about it."

"You could see the way they reacted after they scored the goal," Scotland coach Craig Brown said. "They seemed to be relieved and delighted because they realized it was a difficult game. They were fortunate to have won the game."

FIRST ROUND

Group A—Still, Brazil had few problems securing passage to the second round with a 3-0 victory over Morocco. As expected, that left it to the three other teams to battle for second place.

One of the most dramatic and controversial opening-round finishes came in the waning minutes of the Brazil-Norway encounter on a hot and steamy night in Marseille. With the Norwegians facing a 1-0 deficit in the final ten minutes and desperately needing a win to advance, they got their wish, but not without astonishment by the fans and international media. First, Tore Andre Flo put in the equalizer in the 83rd minute and then Kjetil Rekdal fired home a penalty kick in the 88th minute.

American referee Esse Baharmast ruled that Brazilian defender Goncalves had fouled Flo, although very few, if any spectators at Le Stade Velodrome, seemed to have witnessed the same play. Baharmast was vilified in the international media, until replays from Swedish television showed that Goncalves had taken down his opponent by his shirt from an angle that wasn't captured on live TV.

Group B—Italy, behind a hot Vieri (a goal in each of the three matches), went undefeated, tying Chile, 2-2, on a controversial penalty kick by Roberto Baggio in the 84th minute, and defeated disappointing Cameroon, 3-0, and Austria, 2-1. Chile reached the second round the hard way—tying all three of its matches. In fact, the Chileans seemed to be the most snakebit of all teams, losing a 1-0 lead to Austria two minutes into stoppage as Ivica Vastic scored. Many observers wondered where the referee found all that extra time to add on.

Croatia's Davor Suker struck six times to lead all goalscorers at France '98 [photo: J. Brett Whitesell]

Group C—The French started their amazing rollercoaster ride on a high note at Le Stade Velodrome in soccer-mad Marseille, rolling to a 3-0 triumph over an inferior South African side that really had no chance. In their next match, at the new Le Stade de France in St.-Denis in suburban Paris, the French cruised to another relatively easy win, a 4-0 romp over Saudi Arabia. That victory, however, came at great cost, when the team's midfield general, Zidane, stomped on midfielder Fuad Amin. His punishment? A red card and a two-game suspension. They also lost forward Christophe Dugarry to a leg injury until he came on in the waning minutes of the Final.

No one realized at the time, but incredibly the game would mark the last time a French forward—Trezeguet found the back of the net in the 69th minute—would score a goal in the tournament.

The resilient French continued on their personal Tour de France, outlasting Denmark, 2-1, in Lyon, in their final opening-round encounter to become only one of two sides (Argentina was the other) in the thirty-two team tournament to finish the first round unbeaten and untied.

The Danes managed to reach the second round on the strength of a 1-0 win over Saudi Arabia and a 1-1 draw with South Africa.

The only real history the Saudis produced was firing coach Carlos Alberto Parreira, the former New York/New Jersey MetroStars coach who guided Brazil to the world championship in 1994, after only two games and with one match remaining.

Group D—this competition's Group of Death—turned out to be the death of the quadrennially underachieving Spanish side, which failed to advance as coach Javier Clemente verbally sparred with the media. Goalkeeper Andoni Zubizaretta, whom many critics claimed was over his head in this Cup, found a way to make the worst mistake at the very worst time. Take, for instance, Spain's 3-2 loss to Nigeria. The Nigerians played a free-wheeling game, sometimes allowing gaping holes in their midfield and defense. But Nigeria took advantage of Spain's defensive deficiencies as Zubizaretta gave away one goal when he batted in Garba Lawal's shot from a severe angle in the 73rd minute. It was difficult to stop the game-winner—a marvelous 25-yard drive by Sunday Oliseh twelve minutes from time. To celebrate the win, coach Bora Milutinovic attended the post-match press conference in traditional Nigerian garb. By the time Spain recovered its soccer senses—a 6-1 drubbing of Bulgaria in its final match—it already had been eliminated.

Nigeria, Olympic gold medalists two years prior, won the group, edging Bulgaria, 1-0, but losing to previously punchless Paraguay (two scoreless ties) and outspoken goalkeeper Jose Luis Chilavert, 3-1, in the final match.

Group E—Mexico went down to the final seconds literally in one of the most thrilling opening-round matches. Rallying from a two goal deficit, Mexico managed to tie the favored Netherlands, 2-2, in the last game of the group to stay alive. The heroics were provided by Luis Hernandez. He who found the back of the net four minutes into stoppage time.

Both teams wound up tied for the lead with identical 1-0-2 records and five points, but the Dutch got top honors because of

CHAPTER
2

CHAPTER 2

superior goal differential (five to two). Belgium didn't lose, but didn't win either, playing to draws in all three matches. South Korea, which had never won a Cup match in forty-four years, finished 0-2-1 as Coach Cha Bum-kun was fired.

Group F—Germany and Yugoslavia advanced easily earning wins over inferior teams from the U.S. and Iran. The Americans' situation turned into a mess. Only twenty-one seconds into their opener against Germany, Claudio Reyna was upended by defensive midfielder Jens Jeremies. He was never the same player. The aging German side found holes in the U.S. defense recording a 2-0 victory on goals by Andreas Moeller and Juergen Klinsmann.

The U.S. still had a chance to advance, but it needed to defeat Iran in what was called "The Mother of All Games." In a game that gave a new meaning to the phrase political football, it was only the second time these two countries met in the sports area since the hostage crisis in 1979. Iran proved to be the superior side, taking a two goal lead as the U.S. produced the wrong type of hat trick, hitting

These Players Were The Stars Of Stars

Between all the refereeing gaffes and mistaken red cards, flops and flips and other errors, there were a number of exceptional players at France '98. Here's one writer's choice of a starting eleven:
Jose Luis Chilavert (Paraguay), goalkeeper—Unlike many of his contemporaries, he lived up to his hype and then some, directing the Paraguayan backline and coming up with the big save when it counted.
Honorable mention to **Fabien Barthez** (France) and **Carlos Roa** (Argentina) overcame a shaky start and made several big saves .
Lilian Thuram (France), right fullback—Scoring a pair of timely goals against Croatia in the semifinals finally put him in the spotlight after a fine defensive

performance in his other matches. Honorable mention to **Cafu** (Brazil).
Marcel Desailly (France), central defender—The best player in the tournament. He anchored a fabulous backline that could play elegantly, physically and offensively (God knows the French needed all the goals they could get). Honorable mention to **Carlos Gammara** (Paraguay).
Frank DeBoer (Netherlands), central defender—Lost in the Dutch's football was a beautiful defender who not only defended well, but sent an incredible 50-yard pass in the air crossfield to Dennis Bergkamp for the game-winning goal. Honorable mention to **Laurent Blanc** (France).
Bixente Lizarazu (France), left full-

each post and the crossbar en route to a 2-1 victory. Brian McBride had the lone U.S. score.

By the time the Americans took on Yugoslavia, they were a mentally beaten side with many veteran players complaining how they were misused or benched. Yugoslavia forged out a 1-0 win and moved on. Several days later Steve Sampson resigned as U.S. coach.

"This World Cup was a mess. It was a shambles," midfielder Tab Ramos said. "I think it's unfair we couldn't show the progress we made in the last four years."

In what turned into the match that decided the group title, Germany played Yugoslavia to a 2-2 draw on Oliver Bierhoff's goal in the 78th minute.

Group G—The one place you didn't want to be was in any city the English team was in, because their unruly and self-destructive fans probably weren't too far behind. Like clockwork, English fans rioted in Marseille before their team blanked Tunisia in the first encounter, 2-0, a game that marked the World Cup debut of Michael Owen as

back—On a team which boasts Laurent Blanc, Lilian Thuram and Marcel Desailly, it is easy to get lost in the shuffle. But Lizarazu was a steady and solid influence on the left side. Honorable mention to **Paolo Maldini** (Italy).

Edgar Davids (Netherlands), midfielder—He and coach Guus Hiddink buried the hatchet (and not in each others' backs), letting skill win out over personality conflicts. Davids ran his team as well, if not better, than virtually every other playmaking midfielder. Honorable mention to **Dunga** (Brazil).

Zinedine Zidane (France), midfielder—He didn't have much of a first round, thanks to that two-game red-card suspension. It took him all the way to the semifinal before he began to rediscover his playmaking skills. He literally rose to the

occasion on those two header goals in the finale. Honorable mention to **Ronald DeBoer** (Netherlands), a solid midfielder who is Frank's twin brother.

Rivaldo (Brazil), midfielder—He was practically nowhere to be found in the championship match, but it would be unfair to penalize such a fine player. Rivaldo was the motor of the Brazilian side, whether it was bringing the ball down or setting up Ronaldo. Honorable mention to **Emmanuel Petit** (France), who saved his best for the last match.

Davor Suker (Croatia), forward—He won the scoring title, achieving something few players have accomplished in Cup history—scoring in six out of a possible seven matches. In fact, Suker found the back of the net in his last four games, including all four in the knockout rounds, substitute. Owen came on as a sub to score in a 2-1 loss to Romania. England rebounded with a 2-0 victory over Colombia.

Group H—Argentina had a relatively easy time of it playing three countries making their World Cup debut. The South Americans shut out Japan, 1-0, Jamaica, 5-0, and Croatia, 1-0. That was Croatia's last loss until France in the semifinals. The Croatians, playing in the Cup for the first time since the breakup of Yugoslavia, started their amazing run behind striker Suker with wins over Jamaica, 3-1, and Japan, 1-0. Jamaica, the minnows of this competition and one of the smallest countries to participate in a Cup, acquitted itself quite well, edging Japan, 2-1.

SECOND
ROUND

After a rocky first-round, Brazil got on track with a solid 4-1 effort against Chile as Sampaio collected a pair of first-half goals and Ronaldo added two more in the final forty-five minutes in Paris.

Vieri connected for his Cup-leading fifth goal in the 18th minute in Italy's 1-0 triumph over Norway in Marseille. That early goal forced defensive-minded Norway to push up, allowing Italy to

yet another rare feat. His only "clean sheet" was against Argentina.

Marcelo Salas (Chile), forward—What a joy to watch. Not only does this 21-year-old have talent, but he works his tail off, along with his other front-running mate, Ivan Zamarano. He finished with four goals in as many matches. Who knows how many goals he could have scored had Chile been a better side? Gabriel Batistuta? Dennis Bergkamp? Christian Vieri? Give this author Marcelo Salas any day of the week. Honorable mention to **Ronaldo**, whose statistics looked impressive enough (four goals, three assists), but who underachieved, particularly when it counted the most—the championship match.

Michael Owen (England), forward—He's only 18-years-old, with a storybook career ahead of him. The first chapter of the fairy tale has already been written, scoring

twice for England, including that spectacular goal off a 50-yard run through Argentine territory. It was the goal of the tournament, although Dennis Bergkamp might give you an argument on his score against Argentina. Honorable mention to **Luis Hernandez** (Mexico), who scored one of the most dramatic goals of the tournament to tie the Dutch and send the Mexicans into the second round, a first for Mexico in Europe.

Aime Jacquet (France), coach—Through injuries, red-card suspensions and the inconsistent performance of his forwards, Jacquet moved players in and out of the lineup with the skill of a magician. He got the most out of his talent and it paid off big in the end. Of course, he still couldn't get more than a handful of goals from his frontline, but then again, no one is perfect.

counterattack.

The French survived a close call against Paraguay and world-class goalkeeper Jose Luis Chilavert in Lens, as Laurent Blanc snuck up from his central defender position and scored the game winner in the 114th minute for a 1-0 win, only six minutes from the dreaded penalty-kick shootout.

The Nigerians' defensive deficiencies were exposed as they finally met their match against Denmark. The Danes grabbed a 2-0 bulge after twelve minutes behind Peter Moeller and Michael Laudrup and never looked back in a 4-1 triumph at St.-Denis.

Argentina managed to get past England in Lyon, 4-3 in penalty kicks after playing to a 2-2 tie after 120 minutes. In their first Cup encounter

Brian McBride (20) scored the lone American goal at France '98
[photo: J. Brett Whitesell]

since Diego Maradona's "hand of God" goal in 1986, it came down to the quick hands of Argentine goalkeeper Roa, who made a pair of saves in the penalty kick shootout. The teams traded dubious penalties; then it got interesting. First, Michael Owen's incredible 50-yard jaunt through the Argentine defense created one of the greatest goals of World Cup history. Then, the Argentines got even on instructions from the bench on a free kick taken by Juan Sebastian Veron. The ball was shuffled to Javier Zanetti, who scored. The game took a turn early in the second half as Beckham kicked Diego Simeone while he was on the ground. Simeone supposedly saw stars, Beckham a red card.

Germany again pulled off one of their miraculous comebacks, this time against Mexico, overcoming a 1-0 deficit with a pair of second-half goals en route to a 2-1 win in Montpellier. Bierhoff's six-yard header with four minutes remaining climaxed the rally. The Mexicans could have put this match away in the 62nd minute but they missed two golden opportunities by Jesus Arellano and Hernandez.

In Toulouse, the Netherlands barely got past Yugoslavia, 2-1, on a goal by Edgar Davids two minutes into injury time.

In a battle of Eastern European countries, Croatia continued its winning ways, edging a tough Romanian side, 1-0. But this encounter wasn't without its own controversy. As time was running out in the opening half, Suker fired in a penalty. When the referee had him retake it because of encroachment, Suker converted that one as well.

QUARTER

FINALS

Zidane returned in the quarterfinals against Italy in St.-Denis, but he did not look entirely fit and never was a factor as the hosts again survived a close one, winning on penalties, 4-3, after playing to a scoreless tie.

With the match only ninety-two seconds old, Denmark served notice to Brazil it wasn't going to roll over and die, defending champions or not. The Danes scored on a quick free kick to silence the mostly partisan, yellow-clad Brazilian crowd at La Beaujoire in Nantes. For a good portion of the next eighty-eight minutes, they made life as miserable as they could for the Brazilians, but not before a six-yard header by defender Marc Rieper rattled off the crossbar with sixty-seven seconds remaining in regulation. By then, Brazil had secured a 3-2 lead on Rivaldo's second goal, in the 59th minute (he also tallied in the 25th minute). Bebeto had a goal in the 10th minute.

One of the most memorable moments did not result in a score, but only a red face and a bruised ego for Brazilian defender Roberto Carlos, who tried a little flair when he attempted to clear a cross out of the penalty area with a bicycle kick. He failed to time his kick properly and missed the ball. Fortunately for Brazil, nothing came out of the embarrassing play.

In Lyon, Croatia surprisingly stopped Germany, 3-0, as the Germans suffered their worst defeat since an 8-3 pasting by Hungary in 1954 (or by the Allied Powers back in 1945). The Germans, who had never failed to reach a Final Four in any of the previous World

Cups in Europe, were eliminated in the quarterfinals for the second consecutive time. The Germans had Christian Woerns sent off before halftime as the Croatians struck behind Robert Jarni (45th minute), Goran Vlaovic (80th) and Suker (85th).

On two plays early and late in the Netherlands-Argentina encounter, Dutch forward Dennis Bergkamp lived up to the strikers' reputation of being invisible for eighty-nine minutes and then literally striking in the final minute to win this July 4 firecracker of a match in Marseille, 2-1. In the 12th minute, his diving header set up Patrick Kluivert's goal. The Argentines seemingly had an advantage when Dutch defender Arthur Numan was red-carded in the 77th minute. But Ariel Ortega, who wears Diego Maradona's number 10 (now that must explain his brilliance and madness) was himself ejected for head-butting goalkeeper Edwin Van Der Sar in the penalty area eleven minutes later. Bergkamp trapped a 50-yard cross-field pass from defender Frank De Boer, took a couple of steps around defenders and placed a 12-yard shot past goalkeeper Carlos Roa on the right side.

Compared to their confrontation at USA '94, there wasn't much to write home about in the opening forty-five minutes of the Brazil-Netherlands encounter in Marseille. But the game got better and better in this clash of soccer titans. Many soccer observers and members of the media felt this was the real final. Ronaldo gave Brazil a 1-0 edge

Brazil's Ronaldo in the semifinals against the Netherlands [photo: Daniel Motz]

SEMIFINALS

only seconds into the second half and Kluivert, who spent most of the tournament either sitting out a red-card suspension or firing more errant shots from within the penalty area at the net, drew the Dutch even with three minutes left in regulation. Extra time was up and down before Brazil's much-maligned goalkeeper, Claudio Taffarel, emerged as the hero, stopping two Dutch shots in the tie-breaker.

Back again at St.-Denis for the semifinals, Suker drew first blood for Croatia only twenty-five seconds into the game, which woke up the French. They retaliated barely sixty-six seconds later when defender Lilian Thuram, who had not scored once in thirty-eight previous international appearances, scored. The storybook finish continued in the 70th minute when Thuram struck for his second goal of the match, six minutes before Blanc was sent off for an alleged foul on Croatian defender Slaven Bilic. The French, however, held on for a 2-1 win.

THIRD PLACE
MATCH

As third-place World Cup matches go, the only real drama at the July 11 encounter between Croatia and the Netherlands was whether striker Suker would get his sixth goal.

He did—to break a three-way tie for the scoring lead in Croatia's 2-1 victory at Parc des Princes in Paris. Ronaldo, who had four goals, was the only player in the July 12 World Cup final between Brazil and France who had a realistic shot of tying or surpassing the Croatian for the scoring title.

Even though there was little at stake, the partisan French crowd got into the match, hooting Bilic with boos, hisses or whistles every time he touched the ball, as well as during pre-game introduction and the bronze-medal ceremony afterward, for his great acting on an alleged foul that led to the banishment of Blanc.

Few fans, however, booed Suker, whose goal in the 40th minute had a double meaning. Not only did it boost him past Vieri and Batistuta in the scoring race, it also broke a 1-1 tie. Bilic started the counter up the right wing. The ball eventually came to Zvonimir Boban in the middle and he shuffled a short pass to Suker on the left side. He took a step into the penalty area and curled a shot into the lower left corner past keeper Edwin Van Der Sar. As though he realized he had clinched the title, Suker raised his arms triumphantly and then crossed himself.

"Suker's goal was a masterpiece," Croatian defender Igor Stimac said. "I hope he winds up as the best goal scorer in the World Cup." Suker unselfishly turned playmaker on Croatia's first goal in the 13th minute, starting the counterattack to Zvonimir Boban, who raced down the left wing. He crossed the ball into the middle to Robert Jarni, who then shuffled a short pass to Robert Prosinecki. Prosinecki, who was mysteriously benched in the semifinal loss, then went through three defenders before tucking in an 8-yard shot.

Only seven minutes later, the Dutch equalized on a great individual effort by Boudewijn Zenden, who bolted down the right wing, suddenly made a turn toward the middle of the field and with Jarni on his back, rifled home a 24-yard blast past goalkeeper Drazen Ladic for one of the Cup's most spectacular goals.

Call it the ultimate French kiss. After French National Team captain Didier Deschamps was handed the FIFA World Cup trophy, he kissed it and held it triumphantly over his head. He then handed it to Zidane, who planted one of his own on the precious 18-karat gold cup. No one would have blamed Zidane had he kissed it a second time to symbolize each of the goals scored in France's stunning 3-0 victory over heavily favored defending champion Brazil at Le Stade de France in St.-Denis on July 12.

In the most surprising World Cup championship victory since West Germany upset the Magic Magyars of Hungary for the 1954 title, the French were world champions of soccer, thanks not only to Zidane's legendary goal scoring heroics, but the unrelenting hard work of his teammates and several timely and sometimes spectacular saves by goalkeeper Fabien Barthez as well.

By the time forward Emmanuel Petit scored three minutes into stoppage time, France had secured its place in history, becoming only the seventh country to win a world title, along with four-time champion Brazil, Germany, Italy, Argentina, Uruguay and England.

The victory touched off the wildest celebration in France this side of the end of World War II. Hundreds of thousands of people poured out onto streets of Paris, mobbing the Champs-Elysees to celebrate the stupefying result.

"All of France was behind us," French coach Aime Jacquet said. "Everybody saw today that France was able to play with pride, heart and determination. We've been working for this for two years. We fully deserve it."

It wasn't an easy climb to the top of international soccer's mountain. The French had no world-class scoring threat up front. Their defense wound up decimated, starting the match without their second-best defender, Laurent Blanc (red-card suspension), and finishing without their top backline player, Marcel Desailly (67th minute ejection).

The first fifteen minutes gave an indication of what was to come as the Brazilians played at half speed while the French attacked from both flanks. The South Americans, with an ailing Ronaldo (left ankle), seemed content bringing the ball up through defender Cafu and midfielder Leonardo on the right wing, ignoring their stars, defender Roberto Carlos and playmaking midfielder Rivaldo.

The French broke through in the 27th minute after Carlos tried to knock defender Lilian Thuram's ball over the right touchline. The ball rolled over the end line for a corner kick. Petit's corner kick inswinger found Zidane, who leaped over Leonardo and headed the ball from six yards into the lower corner past goalkeeper Claudio Taffarel.

Two minutes into stoppage time, Zidane struck again with a virtual duplicate of the goal on the left side. This time Youri Djorkaeff provided the corner as Zidane headed the ball home from seven yards.

"The French were better," Brazilian coach Mario Zagallo said. "We lost the game in the first half. We were only able to put together two attacks."

The question on everyone's mind was whether Ronaldo should have played. Only hours before the match, Ronaldo was taken to a hospital, reportedly for tests on his left ankle. He was cleared to play forty-five minutes before the game. Depending on what report you believed, Ronaldo had either an ankle injury, convulsions, or came down with a stomach ailment on the day of the game. There were reports that Ronaldo had vomited and that there were arguments in the locker room about whether Ronaldo should play.

There were rumors and accusations that Nike had pressured Ronaldo and Zagallo to play the superstar. Nike, which has a ten year sponsorship deal for a reported $200 million with the Brazilian

Soccer Confederation, said in a statement that it "wants to emphasize that the report of such involvement is absolutely false."

That statement was released by Nike's Italian branch in Rome after receiving a directive from the company's headquarters in the U.S. Ronaldo, who had signed an eleven year, $125 million deal with Inter Milan, was the major focus of Nike's ad campaign at France '98.

Ronaldo admitted he was tired of all his outside activities. He was found sprawled on the floor trembling—mentally and physically—by roommate and defender Roberto Carlos in their hotel room five hours before the 9:00 P.M. kickoff, according to inside sources. Ronaldo was taken to a hospital for tests.

"There's too much pressure," Ronaldo said. "I need to change my life. I need a better life."

Whatever the ailment, the 21-year-old superstar striker hardly played up to his stature as the world's greatest soccer player as the French inflicted on the Brazilians their worst loss in World Cup history. Remember, four-time champion Brazil had lost but twelve times in the Cup entering the confrontation.

A pair of timely leaps transformed midfielder Zinedine Zidane into a French national hero
[photo: A. Bibard]

"I knew he was hurt," Brazilian coach Mario Zagallo said. "I knew I was taking a gamble. Ronaldo should not have played." Zagallo originally unveiled a lineup with temperamental forward Edmundo in the place of Ronaldo. "Psychologically, everyone became distraught and overwhelmed," Zagallo said. "When it seeped through into the team, the motivation went down."

Always in the world spotlight, an ineffective Ronaldo was an invisible man. He had only one serious chance, a three-yard shot from a severe angle on the right side that French goalkeeper Fabien Barthez saved in the 56th minute.

Zagallo, who had been either a coach or a player in Brazil's four championships, got into an argument with a Brazilian reporter. "I'm explaining something," Zagallo angrily said. "I don't want to go down to your level. You (Brazil) owe me a lot. I have character and dignity. What about you?"

Then Zagallo stormed out of the press conference, probably the most forceful thing anyone associated with the team did all night.

France 3, Brazil 0
Le Stade de France
St.-Denis, France
July 12, 1998

Brazil—Claudio Taffarel, Cafu, Aldair, Junior Baiano, Roberto Carlos, Cesar Sampaio (Edmundo, 74), Dunga, Rivaldo, Leonardo (Denilson, 46), Bebeto, Ronaldo.

France—Fabien Barthez, Frank Lebouef, Lilian Thuram, Didier Deschamps, Marcel Desailly, Youri Djorkaeff (Patrick Vieira, 75), Stephane Guivarc'h (Christoph Dugarry, 66), Zinedine Zidane, Bixente Lizarazu, Emmanuel Petit, Christian Karembeu (Alain Boghossian, 57).

Goals—Zidane (F) 27, Zidane (F) 46, Petit (F) 92nd.

Yellow cards —Baiano (F) 34, Deschamps (F) 38, Desailly (F) 47, Karembeau (F) 47, Desailly (F) 68.

Red cards— Desailly (France) 68.

Attendance: 80,000

For the first time, a World Cup was played out of Europe and the Americas. And for the first time, a World Cup was hosted not by one, but by two countries—South Korea and Japan. The tournament territory had a number of surprises and upsets.

Unheralded sides such as Senegal, Korea, Turkey and even the U.S. pulled off surprise after surprise. In fact, the highly unlikely duo

Fabien Barthez knocked out Ronaldo and Brazil helping France to win [photo: J. Brett Whitesell]

115

of Korea and Turkey actually made it all the way to the semifinals. The Koreans, who entered the tournament never having won in 14 matches (0-10-4), went 3-0-2 before stumbling in their final two matches with a 0-2 mark.

After the dust had settled, however, a familiar name emerged at the top of the international soccer hill—Brazil, which recorded its penta—that's fifth in Portuguese—World Cup title. No other country—Germany and Italy—have more than three crowns to its credit.

While the Cup was a success logistically, it brought up the stark reality that some of the best players and teams in the world entered the tournament fatigued.

France blamed its first-round elimination due to tired legs. The French, who captured Euro 2000 as well, became the first defending World Cup champion to be ousted in the opening round since Brazil in 1966 and the first ever not to score a goal. Co-favorites Argentina and Portugal, who also had tired players, crashed out in the opening round as well. Besides their league, many players have to perform in European club competitions, such as the grueling Champions League, and various domestic cups.

FIFA confirmed that too much soccer had put players at an increased risk of injury and burnout. Jiri Dvorak, FIFA's chief medical officer at the tournament, said there had been an increase in the number of players getting injured in matches in "non-contact situations"—injuries like strained muscles when no tackles are involved. "Professional footballers are definitely playing too many games," he said. "If there is not sufficient time to recover or they don't recover completely, there can be an accumulation of injuries that can lead to one major injury. Some players are playing between 80-to-90 games a season. That is too much."

Former German great Franz Beckenbauer, the only man to captain (1974) and coach (1990) World Cup champions, felt the players played too many games in Europe. "Billions of viewers around the world are switching on television to watch the World Cup and what are they seeing—tired stars," he said. "All the best players play in Europe and they have to play too many matches. FIFA has to do something. It has to react."

The Cup got off to a rousing and stunning start as debutantes

Senegal set the tone for the most unpredictable of first rounds with a 1-0 Group A victory over defending champion France on a 30th-minute goal by Pape Bouba Diop. The French, forced to play their first two matches without ailing playmaker Zinedine Zidane, never recovered from this loss. They became the first defending champ since Brazil in 1966 to fail to get out of the first round in one piece and the first champion ever not to score in defense of its title. They wound up playing Uruguay to a scoreless tie and lost to Denmark, 2-0, even with Zidane in the lineup.

Incredibly, the Senegalese took advantage of the French failings, qualifying for the second round by drawing its next two encounters, 1-1 with the Danes and a wild 3-3 tie with Uruguay. The Africans enjoyed a 3-0 halftime advantage in that encounter behind a pair of first-half goals by Diop. But the Uruguayans rallied for three second-half goals, including a penalty by Alvaro Recoba in the 88th minute.

The Danes, as expected, also moved on as Jon Dahl Tomasson scored in all three games. He struck late in each half of the 2-1 win over Uruguay, converted a penalty against Senegal and put in the insurance goal in the 67th minute vs. beleaguered France.

For years classic notorious underachievers, Spain got off to a strong start, scoring three goals in each of its first-round Group B triumphs, emerging victorious by a collective 9-4 score. The Spanish began with a 3-1 thrashing of Slovenia as Raul scored in the 44th minute and Juan Carlos Valeron and Fernando Hierro added late goals. They continued with a 3-1 win over Paraguay, scoring all of their goals in the second half—two by Fernando Moreintes and a late penalty by Hierro—after surrendering a 10th-minute own goal by defender Carles Puyol. They completed their perfect slate with a hard-fought 3-2 decision over South Africa as Raul connected early in each half. Gaizka Mendietta added a goal in the final minute of the opening half.

Paraguay also reached the second round for the second consecutive Cup with a 1-1-1 mark. Paraguay lost a 2-0 lead early in the second half as the South Africans drew even, 2-2, on Quinton Fortune's dramatic 90th-minute penalty. After the Spain loss, the

South Americans rebounded with a 3-1 result over self-destructing Slovenia as Nelson Cuevas struck twice in the second half. The Slovenians, making their first Cup appearance, sent star midfielder Zlatko Zahovic home after a row with coach Srecko Katanec. Katanec found himself in a rather embarrassing situation in a 1-0 loss to South Africa—the Africans' first World Cup win—as he was ejected and wound up watching the second half from the stands.

Critics claimed that this was an inferior Brazilian side and that the South Americans had a relatively easy time in Group C. But at the World Cup, a victory is a victory and few teams give back goals or wins. Like Spain, the Brazilians were a perfect 3-0, although they were not without some controversies. In their 2-1 win over Turkey, Rivaldo connected on a penalty shot three minutes from time after he was involved in a controversial red card on Hakan Unsal. Unsal kicked the ball at Rivaldo's legs while he was waiting to take a corner kick. Rivaldo crumpled to the ground clutching his face in apparent agony. It turned out to be a stupid move by both players. Rivaldo was fined $6,390 by FIFA for his bad acting. Brazil rolled over China and coach Bora Milutinovic as the four R's each had a goal—Roberto Carlos, Ronaldo, Ronaldinho and Rivaldo. The Brazilians closed out the group with one of the most open matches of the Cup, a 5-2 triumph over Costa Rica. Ronaldo connected twice in the opening 13 minutes, but defender Edmilson stole the spotlight with a spectacular goal. Despite its penchant of talking back to the referees, Turkey got down to playing and managed to book a spot in the second round, surviving a 1-1 draw with Costa Rica Winston Parks equalized in the 86th minute for the Central Americans, who almost won it several minutes later, and registered a solid 3-0 win over China as Sas Hasan, Korkmaz Bulent and Davala Umit, sporting a Mohawk hair-do, tallied.

In perhaps one of the most surprising first-round finishes in Cup history, two teams who had won a combined four games in ten past Cup appearances wound up one-two in Group D—Korea and the United States. Spurred on by their enthusiastic fans in and out of the stadiums and a work ethic rarely seen at these levels, the Koreans not only qualified for the second round, but didn't lose a match. Only thirty-six minutes into their opener against heavily favored Portugal, the Americans found themselves with an unbelievable 3-0 lead,

taking advantage of Portuguese defensive mistakes and some luck. John O'Brien put in a rebound of a corner kick that goalkeeper Vitor Baia should have caught instead of punching out. Jorge Costa gave them a gift, an own goal in the 29th minute, and Brian McBride's header gave the U.S. a three-goal bulge. Portugal rallied for two second-half goals, but goalkeeper Brad Friedel stopped any further serious threats. Friedel came up big in a 1-1 draw with Korea, which solved the big keeper with an Ahn Jung-hwan goal in the 78th minute. The Koreans essentially laid siege to the American goal in the second half after Clint Mathis connected on a textbook goal in the 24th minute as he trapped an O'Brien cross with his right foot and scored with his left foot.

The U.S. could thank Korea for reaching second round. The Americans needed a tie with Poland to advance, but any thoughts of that was squelched as the Poles grabbed a 2-0 lead five minutes into the match in what turned into a 3-1 U.S. loss. The Americans, however, still advanced as Korea managed to pull off a 1-0 win over Portugal on Park Ji-sung's 70th-minute goal. Had the Portuguese managed a draw—Sergio Conceicao hit the goalpost in the 84th minute—they would have moved on. The Koreans had started their rather improbable run to the semifinals with a 2-0 victory over Poland as Hwang Sun-hong and Yoo Sang-chul scored. Lost in the shuffle of Portugal and its golden generation being denied World Cup glory was a magnificent performance by Pauleta, who hit for a hat-trick in a 4-0 demolition of Poland in the rain.

Just a day after Senegal dispatched France, Germany conjured up a surprising result, rolling to an easy 8-0 Group E romp over Saudi Arabia. The Germans did just about everything they wanted to do against the Saudis, the only team in the tournament that did not have a player performing in a European league. Miroslav Klose headed in three goals in that rout. As it turned out, Germany would score a total of six more goals in five matches through the semifinals. The Germans didn't get out of this group unscathed, though, as Ireland, pulling three top defenders in favor of three attackers in the final minutes, pulled out a dramatic 1-1 tie on Robbie Keane's goal two minutes into stoppage time. As it turned out, it was this Keane who turned out to be Ireland's hero—he scored the first goal in the 3-0 victory over the Saudis that clinched a second-round berth. Team captain and midfielder Roy Keane was sent home after a major blow-up with coach Mick McCarthy in front of the team. The Germans, however, managed to overcome a horrible and nightmarish performance by Spanish referee Antonio Lopez, who, for some reason, handed out a Cup record 16 yellow cards and two red cards. One of those expulsions—to midfielder Carsten Ramelow—put the Germans at a man disadvantage, but their famed resolve helped them survive a potential disaster. Midfielder Marco Bode scored with a man down and Klose, off yet another header, helped Germany to a well-deserved 2-0 result. Cameroon, the 2000 Olympic gold-medal champions, proved to be a major disappointment. The two-time defending African Nations Cup champs finished with a 1-1-1 record, but was sent packing. Ireland had better goal differential (plus three to minus one) because Cameroon could only beat Saudi Arabia, 1-0, on a goal by Samuel Eto'o.

The Group of Death proved deadly for one pre-tournament favorite—Argentina, which could score only twice in three Group F matches. Coach Marcelo Bielsa, owed thousands of dollars by the Argentine Football Federation, made a number of curious decisions. Perhaps the most bewildering was starting 33-year-old Gabriel Batistuta, who experienced a miserable club season for Roma and using 26-year-old Hernan Crespo, a striker in his prime who played well for Lazio, as a substitute. Batistuta scored the lone goal in the 1-0 win over Nigeria, but never found the back of the net again in the 1-0 loss to England and 1-1 draw with Sweden. In fact, it was Crespo that connected in the 88th minute against the Swedes, but it was too little and too late. The Swedes surprisingly showed some offensive oomph, forcing a deserved tie with England behind a strong second half and a goal by Niclas Alexandersson. They went on to edge Nigeria, 2-1, on a pair of goals by striker Henrik Larrson, the last a penalty that broke a 1-1 deadlock in the 62nd minute. Anders Svensson's goal in the 59th minute held the Argentines at bay until Crespo struck. After a horrible second-half vs. Sweden, the English avenged their second-round exit at France '98 with a 1-0 triumph over the Argentines. Ironically, the hero of this match was David Beckham, who converted a penalty kick in the 44th minute as England won in the Sapporo Dome. Beckham was the pariah of France '98 for England as he was sent off for a foolish red card against the Argentines, who prevailed to oust their archrivals in the second-round encounter. In this Cup, the English went on to play Nigeria to a meek, nondescript, 0-0 draw to clinch a second-round berth.

Italy was supposed to dominate Group G. Instead, Mexico outplayed its opposition en route to a 2-0-1 mark. Trained by coach and former L.A. Aztec Javier Aguirre not to be intimidated by European opposition, the Mexicans showed some unique character. They outlasted Croatia, which finished a surprising third at France '98, by a 1-0 score thanks to a 60th-minute penalty by Cuauhtemoc Blanco. The also rallied from an early 1-0 deficit to upend Ecuador, 2-1, as Jared Borgetti and Gerardo Torrado tallied. That set up a confrontation with the Italians, who had more than their share of problems. They recorded a 2-0 win over Ecuador behind a pair of second-half goals by Christian Vieri. The Italians' next game was in many respects a microcosm of their tournament. During the second half, Croatia benched veterans and thirtysomethings Robert Prosinecki and Davor Suker, France '98's leading scorer, for younger legs. The strategy worked as Ivica Olic and Milan Rapaic solved the vaunted Italian backline for scores in the 73rd and 76th minutes, respectively. Italy, however, could not equalize, though it was no fault of its own. Two goals were called back—on an offside ruling another on a foul. A loss to Mexico would have put the Italians out of the tournament. The Mexicans dominated the match and were rewarded on a Borgetti goal in the 34th minute. But second-half substitute Alessandro Del Piero scored in the 85th minute and stopped a disgraceful early exit and embarrassing return home by the Italians, who might have been pelted by rotten vegetables by their fans after the way they performed.

SECOND

ROUND

Like the Koreans, the Japanese continued the tradition of a host team never missing the second round. They began their journey with a 2-2 Group H draw with Belgium. Junichi Inamato, who had given the hosts a 2-1 lead in the 68th minute, had a goal called back due to a questionable call by the referee with only minutes remaining in regulation. The Japanese didn't complain, at least not publicly. They bounced back with a pair of solid wins. The first was a 1-0 victory over Russia as Inamoto, a holding midfielder playing in the shadow of Hidetoshi Nakata and Shinji Ono, again was the scoring hero. They clinched a spot in the next round with a 2-0 triumph over Tunisia as Hiroaki Morishima and Nakata found the back of the net in the second half. The plodding Belgians, whose shining star was Marc Wilmots (three goals), actually surprised observers by finishing unbeaten at 1-0-2 and moving forward. They somehow managed to tie lowly Tunisia, 1-0, but erupted for three goals in a wild 3-2 win over Russia.

After getting off to a strong start against the Saudis, the Germans were getting by each game by the skin of their teeth. It looked like their match with Paraguay was heading for extra time, but Oliver Neuville connected two minutes from time in regulation for a 1-0 victory in Seogwipo, Korea.

The English finally found their bearings, grabbing a surprising 3-0 halftime lead en route to the same final score against Denmark. In rapid succession, Michael Owen, David Beckham and Emile Heskey scored to stun just about everyone at Big Swan Stadium in Niigata, Japan. "The third goal killed the game," England coach Sven-Goran Eriksson said. "To have that in your head going to the locker room is not easy."

Senegal and Sweden battled through the heat of an Oita, Japan afternoon before Henri Camara found the back of the net in the 104th minute for a 2-1 Senagalese triumph to decide one of the best games and celebrate one of the most dramatic finishes of the tournament. Camara was hoisted on his teammates' shoulders as they took a victory lap. A few times the players stopped in one of the corners of the stadium and did a shuffling dance to the delight of their supporters called "Boul Falle," which roughly means "It's not my matter. I'm free."

Keane went from goat to hero as time was running out in regulation, connecting on a penalty kick to force extra time against Spain, which tried to hold the lead on an 8th minute goal by Fernando Morientes in Suwon, Korea. After an added thirty minutes of scoreless soccer, Spanish goalkeeper Iker Casillas, only playing because No. 1 keeper, Santiago Canizares, injured himself in a senseless bathroom accident before the tournament, made two key saves in the penalty-kick tie-breaker as Spain prevailed, 3-2.

In the first confrontation of CONCACAF teams in any World Cup, the United States surprised Mexico on neutral ground in Jeonju, Korea 2-0. The Americans advanced to the quarterfinals for only the second time in Cup history and the first time since the very first Cup in 1930, as Brian McBride scored in the 8th minute and Landon Donovan added an insurance goal in the 65th.

The Brazilians found Belgium difficult to break down in Kobe, Japan as the South Americans finally found the back of the net in the 67th minute on a Rivaldo goal. Ronaldo gave the winners some breathing room in the 87th minute en route to a 2-0 win.

Turkey discovered a way to silence the loud and enthusiastic Japanese fans in Miyagi, Japan. They scored first—on a Davala header in the 12th minute and held on for a 1-0 triumph. Japanese defender Koji Nakata cost his team the game, knocking the ball over the end line for a corner kick in the 12th minute when he could have kicked it just about anywhere else. Ergun Penbe swung the ball into the box and midfielder Davala headed the ball off his Mohawk from six yards past goalkeeper Seigo Narazaki. "Some people have under-estimated us," Turkey coach Senol Gunes said. "We know how we are in Europe (Euro 2000). We want to find out our right place in the world." Knowing they bumped out one of the host sides, the Turkish players did their best to win support for the quarterfinals and beyond. They went to each of the four corners of the stadium, held their hands together, bowed to the crowd and applauded them. "We will represent Japan right now," said Gunes, continuing the public relations gesture. "Their players should not be sad. We will continue to represent Japan in the latter stages of the tournament."

Once again, the vaunted Italian defense could not hold a lead and once again the never-say-die Korean side refused to say die as the hosts recorded a stunning extra-time victory on a goal by Ahn Jung Hwan with four minutes remaining, in Daejeon, Korea. Christian Vieri had given Italy an 18th-minute edge, but Seol Ky Hyeon managed to equalize with two minutes remaining in regulation. Once again, the Italians complained that two goals were called back, and they were correct. But it was the way they whined about it that turned off a lot of fans and observers.

Like it or not, England goalkeeper David Seaman forever will be haunted by a 32-yard free kick from Brazilian midfielder Ronaldinho that broke a 1-1 tie in the 50th minute and the English's hearts as well. Seaman did not move before it was too late on Ronaldinho's majestic shot, which he thought was a cross. That brought up memories of Seaman allowing Nayim's 45-yard lob in the final seconds for Real Zaragoza in a 2-1 victory over Arsenal in the 1995 European Cup Winners Cup final. Seven minutes later, Ronaldinho was red-carded for a mysterious and controversial foul on defender Danny Mills, leaving the English a man up for the final 33 minutes. But they never made anything out of it. The Brazilians held the ball for long periods of time and the English, for some reason, never felt an urgency to push up.

Turkey outlasted Senegal, 1-0, on a golden goal by substitute Ilhan Mansiz three minutes into extra time in Osaka, Japan to reach the semifinals for the first time. The Africans played as though they had little energy left from their amazing run as the Turks easily had more serious goal-scoring opportunities. However, every time they got the ball in the penalty area, the Turks could not get a decent shot on goal. Either the ball would somehow jump over a players' foot or a poorly timed pass would result. Finally, Mansiz, who came on for the popular Hasan Sukur, put this mediocre, labored affair to rest.

All good things have to end sometime and for the U.S., its incredible Cup journey was stopped by a fierce German side that would not allow them to score in Ulsan, Korea. The Americans outplayed their foes, but luck was not on their side as goalkeeper Oliver Kahn found a way to stop their shots after Michael Ballack's header had given the Germans the lead in the 39th minute. Tony Sanneh might have had the best American chance, but his late header barely missed the left corner. More than anything, in sharp contrast to the great debacle at France '98, the Americans left this tournament with a new profound respect from the rest of the world, much more self-confidence and their heads held up high.

Riding the wave of its enthusiastic crowd, Korea nudged by Spain in penalties, 5-3, after playing 120 minutes of scoreless soccer in Gwangju, Korea. Keeper Lee Woon Jae proved to be the hero, saving Joaquin's effort before Hong Myung Bo, in his 137th interna-

QUARTER
FINALS

tional game, converted the game-winner. "It's been a while since I've taken a penalty like that so I did feel the pressure going up for the shot," Hong said. "I'm glad I struck it well." Joaquin experienced a miserable day in more ways than one. He thought he had set up the game-winner to Fernando Morientes, but linesman Michael Ragoonath of Trinidad & Tobago ruled that the ball was out of bounds while the replays clearly showed it was on the line. The Spanish had another goal called back due to a foul and packed for home shaking their heads thinking they were robbed.

SEMIFINALS

Germany ended South Korea's dream with a 1-0 victory in front of 65,256 screaming enthusiastic fans in Seoul. It wasn't the prettiest of games or goals—Ballack put in the game-winner off his own rebound in the 75th minute—but the three-time champion Germans didn't complain. They reached the Cup finals for the seventh time. Ironically, Ballack would miss the championship game after incurring his second yellow card after taking down Lee Young Pyo just outside his penalty area only four minutes prior. Goalkeeper Oliver Kahn continued to be at the top of his game, catching or punching away everything kicked his way. Hard-working and never-say-die Korea, the first Asian team to reach the semifinals, simply ran out of steam after five end-to-end matches. Even after the match, the Koreans' fans chanted, "Dae-han-min-guk! (Republic of Korea). It was estimated that thirteen million of the nation's thirty million people watched the match on TV, including seven million who witnessed it on big screens at public gatherings.

Ronaldo shook off a left thigh injury to score the lone goal in a 1-0 victory over Turkey in Saitama, Japan. Before he tallied, the game was essentially a goalkeeper's duel with Turkey's Rustu Recber and Brazil's Marcos trading big save for big save. But Ronaldo connected for his sixth goal on a brilliant strike in the 49th minute, After defender Lucio chested Hasan Sas's left-wing cross to Marcos, the goalkeeper passed to Gilberto Silva, who raced down the left side. Silva fed Ronaldo. He ran through four players—Faith Akyel, Alpay Ozalan, Ergun Penbe and Bulent Korkmaz—before placing a fifteen yard toe shot that a diving Recber managed to get a hand on, but could not stop from nestling into the lower right corner. So, Brazil booked a place in the World Cup final for the third consecutive time, equaling a record held by Germany (1982, 1986 and 1990).

Four years ago, his performance and health were shrouded in a cloak of mystery as a forlorn Brazil went down to defeat in the World Cup final in Saint Denis, France. But on June 30th, a jubilant Ronaldo was only shrouded in the green, yellow and blue Brazilian flag, celebrating his country's latest Cup triumph. No one had greater reason to celebrate as Ronaldo, after a virtuoso performance, accounted for both goals in a 2-0 victory over Germany as Brazil paraded around with the World Cup trophy an unprecedented fifth time. No other country has more than three. (Germany and Italy have three each.)

"I don't feel in debt to anyone but a weight has been lifted from my conscience," Ronaldo said. "I'm free. All this celebrating could have happened four years ago but destiny was that we would have to wait until 2002.

"I don't want to think about the future now. I'm just trying to think how I'm going to celebrate."

Ronaldo's descent into soccer hell only made his resurrection that much sweeter. He was the center of controversy on whether he should have played in Brazil's loss to the French at France '98. News reports revealed that he had seizures before the match.

In January, 2002 the Brazilian newspaper Lance reported that Ronaldo had taken eight injections of the painkiller Xylocaine to alleviate pain in his right knee, which caused a fit before the final. The injections entered the bloodstream, which raised his heart rate and sent him into convulsions.

"I want to point out, hopefully for the last time, that some statements are totally false and offend not only myself, but also the National Team's medical staff," Ronaldo said in early 2002. "It is time to close this chapter of the past and think only about the future. That is on the pitch." Those knee and leg muscle ailments kept him shelved for the most of the past 2 1/2 years.

His comeback was a deliberate one. Ronaldo scored his first goal in two years for his Italian club, Inter in a 3-1 win over Brescia on Dec. 9. "A goal after two years was so important," he said. "I have dreamt of this. It's a moment of few words and great happiness."

A pulled muscle kept Ronaldo sidelined for most of the winter.

CHAPTER

2

FINAL

2002

He finally played an international match for Brazil, lasting the first half in a 1-0 victory over Yugoslavia on March 27. He didn't score, but was just happy to put on the yellow jersey of his country.

"I have a lot of things to thank God for," he said on June 30. "My big victory, as I have said before, was to play football again, to run again and to score goals again. This conquest today, our fifth world title, has crowned my struggle, my recovery.

"More than anything, it's a victory for the whole group. I must never forget how marvelous the rest of the group was. The whole team ran and battled and helped each other. No individual conquest can beat what the group achieved."

In the early going, it was the Germans, and not the Brazilians, who forced the issue. The Germans had several free kicks around the penalty area and corner kicks as well, but could never convert. When it seemed Germany would have a free shot, the pass or shot would not reach its intended target or teammate or a Brazilian defender would get in the way to block it.

It took a while, but the Brazilians started to find minute holes in the vaunted German defense. Ronaldo mostly was the recipient, but he failed to take advantage of three superb opportunities in the opening half. While zeroing in on the net, Ronaldo toe-poked a slow shot from seven yards, wide left of goalkeeper Oliver Kahn in the 19th minute. He chested down a pass and found himself in point-blank range in front of Kahn, who managed to get his left hand on the ball before falling on it in the 30th minute. Ronaldo was at it again a minute into stoppage time in the opening half. Rivaldo's pass found his teammate at the penalty spot. Ronaldo turned on Thomas Linke and fired a shot that Kahn blocked with his right foot.

Kleberson got into the act in the 45th minute, banging a 24-yard shot off the crossbar while Kahn was diving in that direction.

The Germans seemed to get a second wind with two close encounters in the first five minutes of the second half. First, Jens Jeremies powered a header toward the Brazilian goal sixty-five seconds into the half, but Edmilson blocked the shot with his right foot. Three minutes later, Oliver Neuville hammered a thirty-five yard free kick off the right post.

The game was not without some comedic moments. Edmilson

had ripped his shirt in the 61st minute, so he went to the sidelines for a new shirt. But he had problems putting it on, much to the laughter of the 69,029 and referee Pierluigi Collina, who even had to crack a smile.

When he finally found his mark, it took Ronaldo only 12 minutes to turn the game and Germany's World Cup upside down. He took advantage of a rare blunder by Kahn, regarded as the best goal-keeper in the world, in the 67th minute. Ronaldo displaced Dietmar Hamann of the ball outside the penalty area to give Brazil possession. Rivaldo then sent in a long drive that Kahn fumbled as an onrushing Ronaldo stuffed home the rebound.

As if to prove the first one was not a mistake, the 25-year-old striker whipped in a 16-yard bullet in the 79th minute off a nifty dummy by Rivaldo, who allowed Kleberson's right-wing pass to go through his legs to Ronaldo at the top of the penalty area.

So, the manchild, "The Phenomenon," now can be called a legend. The goal was his eighth of the tournament, the most since Germany's Gerd Mueller collected 10 in 1970. It was also his 12th career Cup score, tying the great Pele for third place on the all-time list, behind only Mueller (14) and France's Just Fontaine (13).

Ronaldo dedicated those goals to his family and Dr. Gerard Saillant, who operated on his knee. "It was thanks to him I am able to celebrate two goals in the World Cup final after 2 1/2 years of suffering and sorrow," he said.

It was Kahn's turn and time for some suffering and sorrow. Ironically, like Ronaldo, Kahn played a pretty decent Cup before faltering in the finale. And like Ronaldo in 1998, Kahn was named the tournament's top player, despite the championship match mishap.

"Of course it's bitter when you make a mistake in the final, I think it was the only mistake in the tournament - it's ten times as bitter," Kahn said. "There's no consolation. I made my only mistake out of seven games and it was brutally punished.

"But we must not let one unlucky goal destroy our memories of this World Cup. We have put German football back where it belongs which is extremely important for the four years to come."

Brazil 2, Germany 0
International Stadium
Yokohama, Japan
June 30, 2002

Germany: Oliver Kahn, Thomas Linke, Carsten Ramelow, Christoph Metzelder, Torsten Frings, Bernd Schneider, Jens Jeremies (Gerald Asamoah, 77), Deitmar Hamann, Marco Bode (Christian Ziege, 84), Oliver Neuville, Miroslav Klose (Oliver Bierhoff, 73).

Brazil: Marcos, Edmilson, Lucio, Junior Roque Junior, Cafu, Kleberson, Gilberto, Roberto Carlos, Ronaldinho (Juninho Paulista, 85), Rivaldo, Ronaldo (Denilson 90).

Goals: Ronaldo (Brazil) 67, Ronaldo (Brazil) 79

Yellow cards: Junior (Brazil) 6, Klose (Germany) 9

Attendance: 69,029.

Referee: Pierluigi Collina (Italy).

Qualifying—
Getting there was half the fun

Unlike other years where there was a clear-cut match that kicked off qualifying, as three matches were played on Saturday, Sept. 6, 2003 (South America was allowed to start early because of its endless 18-game schedule for each country).

However, the Argentina-Chile match at River Plate Stadium in Buenos Aires, Argentina kicked off two hours before the Ecuador-Venezuela encounter in Quito, so that game gets the honor of the very first qualifier.

The honor of the first goal went to Argentina's Cristian Gonzalez, who found the back of the net and beat Chile goalkeeper Nelson Tapia in the 32nd minute. Argentine midfielder Juan Veron was awarded the first yellow card in the 22nd minute and teammate Walter Samuel and Chile's Cristian Alvarez were slapped with the first red cards in the 87th minute of what turned into a 2-2 draw before 35,372 spectators.

In the other matches of the day, Ecuador blanked Venezuela. 2-0, at Estadio Olimpico Atahualpa in Quito in front of a crowd of 14,997 and Peru rolled to a 4-1 victory over Paraguay in front of 42,557 at Estadio Nacional Jose Diaz later that night.

The Haitian national team thought it was safe and far from the chaos that was enveloping its homeland in Feb. 2004, but players learned they could not escape the violence's devastating effects. Three hours before Haiti met Turks and Caicos in a qualifier in Hialeah, Fla. on Saturday, Feb. 21, 2004 midfielder Peter Germain discovered his home in Saint-Marc, Haiti had been burned to the ground during fighting.

"When I first heard the news I cried a lot. Immediately after I had to think about the game," Germain said after a 2-0 victory that clinched the total-goal series, 7-0. "That was very important. I will have plenty of time to reflect on what is happening back home."

Germain said his family and friends left town and were safe. "Despite the tragedy, my motivation was to be sure that I played a very good game, to be sure my country qualifies," he added. "My main focus was on that. The tragedy had to take second place."

When he became coach, Fernando Clavijo, who currently directs the Colorado Rapids (MLS), realized he would encounter challenges directing a team that hails from the world's second poorest nation. "It never crossed my mind it would be like this," he said. "It's incredible."

After the match, seven players returned home to their families, but they had be back before the team left for the next Sunday's friendly in Nicaragua. "It is so hard," Clavijo said. "If my wife is at home in Haiti, and I have two kids, I will go. I don't care how bad it is. We cannot kidnap them and keep them here."

Clavijo's responsibilities went beyond coaching. "If I do not do the visas today or tomorrow, they most likely won't be done properly," he said. "I'm prepared for everything."

Home financial support has ceased and unpaid training expenses reportedly were at least $200,000. "The biggest challenge is to anticipate what is going to happen the next day," said Clavijo, who is owed salary. "Forget about next month. Every day something new happens.

"The thing that keeps me going is the players. We have a great group. They have touched me. I feel when I look at them that we have an opportunity to do something wonderful here."

Unfortunately, it did not work out. Haiti, which played in the 1974 WC in West Germany, did not get out of the second round. The Haitians were eliminated by Jamaica in June of that year, tying the first encounter at home, 1-1, but losing away, 3-0.

Regardless what he does or doesn't do, England midfielder and captain David Beckham will make headlines. It just depends how intense the situation or headlines are.

He certainly got his money's worth when he admitted he took a yellow card on purpose in a 2-0 victory over Wales on Oct. 9, 2004 because he knew he was going to miss the next game—vs. Azerbaijan—with a broken rib he incurred minutes prior. Beckham,

CHAPTER

3

who already had a yellow card from a previous match, said he thought he was being "clever" when he intentionally and recklessly fouled Welsh defender Ben Thatcher in the 83rd minute at Old Trafford in Manchester, England (Beckham had scored seven minutes prior).

"It was deliberate," Beckham said. "I am sure some people think that I have not got the brains to be that clever, but I do have the brains."

He added: "I knew straight away I had broken my ribs. I have done it before. I knew I will be out for a few weeks, so I thought: 'Let's get the yellow card out of the way."

Not surprisingly, it raised a firestorm, not just in the British game, but internationally.

"Where are we going when football's ambassadors do not show fair play?" FIFA president Sepp Blatter told Sky Sports television. "David Beckham is a role model for young children, an ambassador of football and an ambassador of fair play. . . . We are concerned at the attitude, the possible bad attitude, of the player."

Geoff Hurst, whose hat-trick boosted England to its one and only World Cup championship in 1966, also took a swipe at Beckham. "It saddens me," he told the Associated Press. "I would argue that it brings the country into disrepute. I can't possibly imagine that happening in our time."

Beckham eventually apologized for his mental blunder. "I now know that was wrong and apologize to the Football Association, the England manager, my teammates and all England fans for this," he said. "I know that as captain you are in a privileged position and must always abide by FIFA's code of fair play, something which I have always done throughout my career. On this occasion I made a mistake."

Not to outdo himself, almost a day to the first infraction, Beckham became the first English player to be sent off twice and the first captain to be red-carded in the 1-0 qualifying triumph over Austria at Old Trafford on Oct. 8, 2005, which clinched a WC berth. Beckham was given his marching orders in the 59th minute after getting slapped with two yellow cards within a minute for a pair of fouls on midfielder Andreas Ibertsberger. The first yellow was awarded to Beckham for raising his arm in a challenge, the second for challenging and making contact with the Austrian player. "I thought the first yellow was harsh and the second even harsher," Beckham told AP. "I saw the referee's reaction when he looked at the linesman and I knew what was going to happen. Everyone who has seen it on television has said it was harsh (but) I don't think the referee will change his mind."

A SHIRT TALE,
OR IN THIS
CASE, NONE

Even before it played a minute in qualifying, Cameroon was docked six points after the team broke a pledge to FIFA that it would not wear its controversial one piece uniform during the African Nations Cup qualifiers.

Cameroon was fined $154,000 in April, 2004 by FIFA, which wanted the African side to wear regulation shirts and shorts.

At the 2002 African Nations Cup in Mali, the team wore sleeveless shirts, which eventually were banned by soccer's world governing body. For the 2004 Nations Cup quarterfinals, Cameroon wore an athletics style uniform. The uniforms featured red claw marks down the sides.

"FIFA had shown leniency at the time for Cameroon's attire in the group round of the competition after the (Cameroon) soccer association had given assurances that the team would wear authorized playing kit in the knockout phases," the FIFA statement said. "Despite this agreement, Cameroon subsequently wore the same equipment in the quarterfinals. Cameroon eventually got the six points back, but of course, did not reach Germany.

THE NEVER-
ENDING
COACHING
CAROUSEL --
PART I

Being a National Team coach is not safe at any speed, even after leading a country into soccer's promised land. In fact, eight countries that qualified—a quarter of the 32 finalists—changed coaches at least once during the road to Germany.

⊕ Argentina coach Marcelo Bielsa stunned everyone by resigning out of the blue on Sept. 15, 2004, less than a month after directing his country's team to its first Olympic gold medal at the Athens Summer Games. Bielsa, an eccentric coach who usually would not look at the person who asked him a question during

CHAPTER

3

press conferences, said he had run out of energy after six years on the job. "I realized the amount of energy which is absorbed by the various tasks which are involved in being coach of the team . . . and that I didn't have this energy any more," Bielsa said. Bielsa was spared the axe after Argentina grossly under-achieved at the 2002 WC as the South Americans were elimi-nated in the opening round. Bielsa had a 42-10-16 record and had his team in second-place in SA qualifying (the top four teams made Germany). Jose Pekerman eventually was named his replacement.

⊕ Steve Sampson, who directed the U.S. to a 32nd and last-place finish in France, was fired by Costa Rica on June 21, 2004 after a pair of embarrassing draws to CONCACAF minnows Cuba, 1-1 and 2-2. Colombian Jorge Luis Pinto replaced him. "Football deals with results, and Mr. Sampson's have not been favorable," the Costa Rican Football Federation said. Sampson, who had been coaching since 2002, had an 11-7-4 record. Pinto, however, couldn't get Costa Rica on the right track, so he was fired on April 1, 2005 and replaced by Alexandre Guimaraes. Guimaraes, who left in November, 2002, had directed the Central American side to its second World Cup appearance in 2002.

⊕ After only one qualifier, Angola bounced Brazilain Ismael Kurtz on Oct. 17, 2003, after a stunning 3-1 defeat by lowly Chad. Luis Goncalves Oliveira, who coached the country's Olympic team, was promoted to the top spot. "Maybe a chance is what is needed for the players and supporters," Kurtz told **Reuters**. "We can still qualify for the next round. We can beat them by five goals in the return match." Angola rebounded and eventually qualified for the World Cup.

⊕ With its first World Cup berth in sight, Trinidad & Tobago fired Bertille St. Clair on April 1, 2005 and replaced him with veteran Dutch coach Leo Beenhakker. St. Clair, who felt people held it against him because he came from Tobago, forged a 19-13-6 record. T&T technical director Lincoln Phillips told the Express newspaper the plans for a new coach had been in the making for some time and were the result of poor qualifying performances.

"We have looked at it for quite some time, and you always have to make contingency plans," said Phillips, who said that the players had an input into the coaching selection. "I didn't make the decision alone," he added. "Myself, the technical committee, the players . . . the players were heavily involved in the style of coaching. They felt comfortable with a Dutch coach, and two Dutch coaches were offered, both of them were called, and Beenhakker was the one that everyone agreed on. They had the final decision of who would be the coach." The strategy worked. Beenbakker guided T&T into soccer's promised land.

⊕ Ghana finally reached its first World Cup, but the Africans did it the hard way, using four coaches. Ghana started with Ralf Zumdick in the preliminary round, then tried Marinao Barretto and Sam Arday before settling on Ratomir Dujkovic. Dujkovic, by the way, started the Cup competition with Rwanda.

⊕ Saudi Arabia has a notorious reputation of getting rid of coaches quickly, very quickly. Only minutes after his team was eliminated from the Asian Cup by Iraq, 2-1, on July 25, 2004, Dutchman Gerard van der Lem was sacked. He became the 13th coach to be fired by the Saudis in the past decade. Van der Lem guided Saudi Arabia to a 19-game unbeaten streak after its horrendous showing at the 2002 WC. The Saudis have been known to be quick with the trigger. Brazilian Carlos Alberto Parreira was fired two games into the opening round after losing both games and Czech Milan Macala was given the pink slip after a 4-1 loss to Japan in the first match of the 2000 Asian Cup.

⊕ And just because you directed your team to the World Cup doesn't necessarily mean you will get an opportunity to coach the side in soccer's promised land. Argentine Gabriel Calderon was shown the door on Dec. 31, 2005, six months before the kick-off. The Saudi Football Federation said it was "dissatisfied" with Calderon's preparations and replaced him with Brazilian Marcos Paqueta. The Saudis had finished fourth in the West Asian Games in Qatar in December, losing to Iraq in the semifinals and Iran in the third-place match.

⊕ The same went for Dutch Jo Bonfrere, who directed Korea into

CHAPTER

3

the World Cup, but had to resign amid criticism due to his team's poor performances in the summer of 2005. Bonfrere had coached Nigeria to the Olympic gold medal in 1996. Korea, which enjoyed its best WC showing in 2002, reaching the semi-finals and finishing fourth, had higher expectations. Bonfrere, however, said it wasn't fair to compare his team to the 2002 side, which received much more support because Korea was co-hosts with Japan. He also criticized the Korea Football Federation for demanding wins, although it did not guarantee enough time for pre-game training. "No coach in the world can bring a team together in two days," Bonfrere said. "The media and fans had too much expectation." "Coach Bonfrere has decided it would be difficult for him to continue being a coach under current circumstances . . . and the technical committee members agreed with him on this," association committee chairman Lee Hoi-Taek said. Bonfrere, incidentally, took over from Portuguese coach Humberto Coelho, who also was forced to quit due to criticism of the team's poor performance in April 2004, after 15 months on the job. Coelho, who led Portugal to the Euro 2000 semifinals, had a mutual parting of the ways. Bonfrere was preceded by Park Sung-Hwa as caretaker coach for 66 days before he resigned following a 2-0 win over Vietnam. Park reportedly felt he had fulfilled his duties.

For every team that reaches the World Cup, it seems there are five coaches who get sacked. Here's a sampling of the quick and deadly coaching mentality during qualifying:

THE NEVER-ENDING COACHING CAROUSE;— PART II

⊕ Benin and Malawi had the honor—or is it dishonor?—of using the most coaches—five each. Benin began with former Ghana star Cecil Jones Attuquayefio. Then came Wabi Gomez, two Frenchmen, Herve Revilli and Serge Devez, and finally Benin native Edme Codjo. Malawi started with John Kaputa and Kinnah Phiri sharing the job. They were replaced by Alan Gillet, Yasin Osman and Michael Hennigan. Here's a sobering thought: Only three of the 30 African countries participating in the qualifying process stuck with the same coach the entire way—Cape Verde Island (Alexandre Alhinho), Zambia (Kalusha Bwalya) and Botswana (Vesselin Jelusic).

⊕ Former MetroStars and U.S. national coach Bora Milutinovic, the only man to have directed five countries to the World Cup, has quit as coach of the Honduran National Team on July 1, 2004. Honduran Football Federation president Rafael Callejas told reporters that Bora, as he is known throughout the world was disillusioned at the constant criticism of his work from the media and local coaches. Bora had been the coach since September, 2003. "He's decided to abandon the Honduran team," Callejas told Reuters after returning from Mexico, where he spent two days trying to convince Milutinovic to stay on. Bora had a statement for reporters, which Callejas read: "The atmosphere created with the commentaries and declarations of coaches, directors and the Honduran media is not favorable for me to do my job." Bora's resignation was stunning because he never resigned during a World Cup qualifying campaign. He usually completed the term of his contract or was fired (Mexico in 1997). The criticism came from everyone, including the Catholic church. According to **Reuters**, Cardinal Oscar Andres Rodriguez said that Bora's salary—reportedly between $30,000 and $60,000 a month—was a slap in the face for the country's poor majority. Honduras stumbled in early friendlies under Bora but bounced back to defeat the Netherlands Antilles in the aggregate goal series in the second round, 6-2, to reach the CONCACAF semifinals. Bora coached Mexico at the 1986 World Cup, Costa Rica in 1990, the U.S. in 1994, Nigeria in 1998 and China in 2002. China is the only team that failed to reach at least the second round. In contrast, Honduras has qualified for the World Cup once—in 1982.

⊕ Macedonia used three coaches during the preliminary round.— Dragan Kanatlarovski, who was replaced in March, 2005, Slobodan Santrac, who resigned on Aug. 23, 2005 after a 1-3 record, and former Macedonia international Boban Babunski, who was named a caretaker coach for the final two meaningless matches.

⊕ Georgy Yartsev decided to get out before the axe fell as he resigned as Russian coach in April, 2005. Yartsev decided to quit after new Russian Football Union president Vitaly Mutko had hinted that he was going to sack the coach with the team third in European Group 3. Lokomotiv Moscow coachYuri Syomin was named his successor several weeks later.

⊕ Belgium failed to qualify for the World Cup for the first time in seven consecutive attempts, dating back to 1978. Not surprisingly, Aime Anthuenis was shown the door in October, 2005.

⊕ It looked like it was a bad marriage from the start for Bolivia coach Nelson Acosta and the National Team. Acosta, who was born in Uruguay and who holds Chilean citizenship, repeatedly criticized the state of the game in Bolivia. He resigned on April 7, 2004. Acosta's woes weren't helped by the fact his laptop computer—which had plans for earlier qualifiers against Argentina and Venezuela—was stolen when burglars ransacked his house. Bolivian Football Federation officials said that Acosta's contract had stipulated an $80,000 payoff if the coach was fired, a figure that the federation could not afford. Both sides eventually settled on a $25,000 payoff. Ramiro Blacut succeeded him.

⊕ Uruguay also stumbled to a bad start as Jorge Fossati replaced Juan Carrasco, although his start was far from memorable—two straight defeats. Carrasco was given a pink slip when Uruguay was stunned by lowly Venezuela, 3-0. Carrasco needed a police escort to the bus. Venezuela is the only South American country never to have reached the World Cup.

⊕ In the department of what have you done for us lately, Francisco Maturana was dismissed as Colombia coach after three consecutive qualifying defeats (Brazil, Bolivia and Venezuela) in favor of Reinaldo Rueda. Remember, Maturana is a national hero for guiding Colombia to the World Cup in 2002.

⊕ Mali, which reached the 2004 Olympic tournament, gave Alain Moizan the boot after tying once in three matches, while losing to the Congo and Liberia, not exactly African powers. "Everyone knows that we should have been looking for nine points in the three matches and we only got one point," Mali Football Federation president Tidiani Niambele said. "So already the results are not good enough."

- With less than a month remaining before a key qualifier against Kuwait, former Colorado Rapids coach and Englishman Bob Houghton was fired by Uzbekistan on July 25, 2005. Houghton, 58, who most recently was the China national coach, succeeded Ravshan Haydarov, who was a caretaker coach for German Hans Jurgen Gede, who was fired after a 2-1 loss to South Korea on March 30.
- Guatemala gave the axe to Ramon Maradiaga on Oct. 4, 2005, after the team failed to qualify. The Central Americans were edged out by Trinidad & Tobago for fourth place in CONCA-CAF, which allowed the Caribbean side to meet Bahrain in a home-and-home playoff to determine which country would reach Germany.
- Now, this was a rarity—a coach resigning in the wake of criticism from a country's prime minister. That's what Thailand coach Carlos Roberto Carvalho of Brazil did after prime minister Thaksin Shinawatra criticized the team after a 4-1 loss to North Korea in June, 2004. He said the players weren't putting their hearts in the game. Carvalho said he didn't resign because of the North Korea defeat. "But as a professional coach, when the host is not happy, I would rather give them the chance to find another option," he was quoted by AP. Chatchai Paholpaet replaced him.
- Zimbabwe coach Sunday Marimo quit on May 29 after he heard plans to hire a foreign technical adviser to assist him during qualifying. His resignation came a week before Zimbabwe's first group match at Gabon. Marimo, according to **Reuters**, said he was not prepared to work with a foreign adviser unless he was a high-profile coach from countries such as Brazil, England or Germany. Marimo also was angry that the federation wanted to replace both his assistant coaches as well.
- Former England captain Bryan Robson thought he had the Nigeria job in 2003, but his appointment was rejected by sports minister Musa Mohammed, who said that soccer federation's process was flawed.

Of course, not everyone lost their jobs.

⊕ Consider the curious case and comments by Mexican coach Ricardo LaVolpe. In July 2004, he told reporters that he had more than enough of the pressure-cooker of a job. "I'm out," he said. "If I coach the team for another year, that'll be it. It's good enough for me." At last look, LaVolpe was still coach of Mexico.

⊕ And then there was Ukraine coach Oleg Blokhin, who was allowed to return to his job as national coach by the Appeal court in Kiev, Ukraine on March 25, 2005. Blokhin resigned earlier that month, claiming he could not combine the post with his day job—as a member of Ukrainian parliament. The court, however, ruled, that he could combine the two positions. Blokhin directed Ukraine into the WC, the first Euro side to qualify.

⊕ Here's a first: a coach's firing was delayed because the government had not yet approved the soccer federation's decision to fire him. Frenchman Guy Stephan was bounced as Senegal coach in March after the country's quarterfinal ousting from the African Nations Cup and amid accusations of his lack of discipline and control of the team's top players. The decision, however, needed to be approved by the sports ministry, which co-signed the coach's contract and paid for part of his salary. Stephan had a 7-4-3 record.

SOMETIMES THE COACHING CAROUSEL STOPS

CHAPTER 3

How crazy are Brazilian fans about their National Team? Well, the March 25, 2005 practice session in Goiana, Brazil will explain it all. An estimated crowd of 25,000 turned up to watch the South Americans prepare for their qualifier at the very same stadium against Peru the next day. To get into training, fans had to donate nonperishable food items, of which more than 2,200 pounds were donated. MLS would love to get crowds like that for actual games, let alone practices.

SOME BRAZILIAN NUTS

There were at least four tragedies in which fans were killed.

⊕ On Sept. 4, 2004, an Albanian man, Gramoz Palushi, was stabbed to death after a qualifier between Albania and Euro 2004 champion Greece. Palushi, who was 20, died during fight-

DEATH IN THE STANDS

ing that broke out between Greek fans and Albanian immigrants, hours after Albania stunned Greece, 2-1, in Tirana, Albania.

⊕ On Oct. 10, 2004, four people were killed and eight others injured during a stampede at the end of a qualifier between host Togo and Mali in Lome. Because of a power outage, the lights at the game went out as fans in one section of Kegue Stadium panicked and ran for the exits. Togo won the match, 1-0. Togo president Gnassingbe Eyadema ordered an investigation and said that the government would financially assist the families of the dead and those who were injured. It was not mentioned in the AP report how much money would be given to the families.

⊕ On March 27, 2005, Mali experienced some problems at its home stadium when at least 19 fans were injured when Mali's 2-1 loss to Togo in Bamako. Mali was abandoned in the final minute after the crowd invaded the field. "It was the worst incident I have experienced, but I was not scared," Mali forward Frederic Kanoute told **Reuters**. "I felt more upset than scared. It was just sad because it is a bad image for African soccer again."

⊕ On March 26, 2005, five Iranian fans were trampled to death and 40 others were injured at a qualifier against Japan in Tehran, Iran, according to state IRNA news agency of Iran. The fans died as the crowd, reported to be 100,000, left Tehran's Azadi stadium. Iran won the Asian zone match, 2-1.

⊕ Kenya was ordered by FIFA to play its Sept. 3, 2005 qualifier against Tunisia behind closed doors after a fan was killed during crowd trouble in a June, 2005 game against Morocco. Before the match, the crowd forced down stadium gates, which left a 15-year-old fan dead and 15 fans injured. The Kenya Football Federation also was fined $19,440 by FIFA. Tunisia won, 2-0.

Turkey was slapped with one of the most severe punishments ever handed to a European country on Feb. 7, 2006, being forced to play their Euro 2008 home qualifying matches behind closed doors in a neutral country, some 300 miles from its border, for the violence that marred its WC playoff game against Switzerland in Istanbul on Nov.

16, 2005. The Turks also were fined $154,200.

Although the teams ended their total goals series at 4-4, Turkey was eliminated on the away goals rule as players and officials from teams were involved in a brawl in the players' tunnel. But FIFA felt the hosts were mostly to blame. The Swiss players left the field under a hail of missiles and objects thrown from the stands while defender Stephane Grichting was taken to hospital covered in blood after the tunnel fight.

According to the AP: "Swiss player Benjamin Huggel was seen kicking Turkish assistant coach Mehmet Ozdilek in the back of the legs as the two teams left the field. Turkey's Alpay Ozalan tried to kick Huggel in retaliation, but instead made contact with another Swiss player in front of him. Huggel then grabbed Alpay around the neck and fell to the ground, with the other players, coaches and security guards piling on." A host of fines and suspensions were handed out:

CHAPTER

3

SANCTIONS,

FINES, SUSPEN-

SIONS AND

STUFF FROM

THE POLICE

BLOTTER

- ⊕ Six-match suspensions to Turkish players Ozalan and Emre Belozoglu and fines of $11,470 each and a two-match ban and a $3,823 fine to Serkan Balci and a 12-month ban and $11,470 fine to Ozdilek.

- ⊕ A six-game suspension to Huggel that will start in the World Cup and an $11,470 fine and a two-match ban to the team physiotherapist, Stephan Meyer. "In the truest sense of the word, fair play was trampled underfoot," Blatter said. "This is unworthy of football. Football should promote understanding among peoples. This didn't happen here."

In other dubious offenses throughout qualifying:

- ⊕ FIFA banned the stadium in Zenica, Bosnia for two matches after Spanish player Juan Valeron was hit by object thrown from the crowd in qualifier in August, 2004. The match ended in a 1-1 tie. Bosnia was scheduled to play Serbia and Montenegro in Zenica on Oct. 9, 2004, but moved the European Group 7 match to Sarajevo's Kosevo stadium.

- ⊕ Stupid red card. Most red cards mean a one or two game suspension. Costa Rica defender Douglas Sequeira was suspended by FIFA for three qualfiiers after fouling U.S. defender Steve Cherundolo in the Americans' 3-0 victory on June 4, 2005.

Sequeira was given the heave-ho in second-half injury time, of all times, after kneeing the right fullback in his stomach.

⊕ Costa Rica was fined $17,000 and was forced to play its CONCACAF final-round match against Panama at Saprissa Stadium on March 26, 2005 behind closed doors after fans rioted following a 2-1 loss to Mexico on Feb. 9, 2005. Costa Rican fans threw coins and batteries onto the field at Saprissa.

⊕ Guatemala coach Ramon Maradiaga of Honduras threw four players from Guatemalan club side Coban Imperial off the team on June 21, 2004, only four days before its CONCACAF match with Surinam. Coban Imperial captured the Guatemalan championship several days prior and the four players celebrated the win when they should have reported for international training. The four were goalkeeper Miguel Angel Klee, defender Nelson Morales, midfielder Hetzon Pereira and forward Walter Estrada, who was the league's leading scorer (14 goals).

⊕ The June 5, 2005 qualifier in Angola against Algeria was postponed until Aug. 17 because of an outbreak of the Marburg virus that killed nearly 300 people in the north of the country. The Angolan Football Federation criticized the decision, saying there was a great distance between the capital of Luanda and the northern province of Uige, the area of the virus outbreak. The game eventually was moved back to June 5 as Angola prevailed, 2-1, in front of 27,000 spectators.

⊕ Costa Rica forward Froylan Ledezma was suspended for one year for abandoning his National Team before its away qualifier in Trinidad & Tobago. Ledezma walked off of the team in San Jose, Costa Rica without the permission of coach Jorge Luis Pinto, after he was told he was not in the starting lineup of its 2005 game in Port of Spain, according to the Costa Rica Football Federation's disciplinary tribunal

⊕ Zambian striker Collins Mbesuma sought police protection after angry fans threatened him in a Lusaka bar in August, 2005. Mbesuma, who played for Portsmouth (English Premiership), returned to his native country to play in a World Cup qualifier vs. Senegal in Chililabombwe, was accused of drinking by fans rather than training for the game. Mbesuma was held by police through the afternoon to keep him away from the mob before they escorted him to training camp. Mbesuma scored six qualifying goals.

- Latvia captain Vitalijs Astafevs claimed that players and team officials were offered bribes to throw the Auu. 17, 2005 qualifier with Russia (the match was a 1-1 draw). Latvian and Russian team officials denied his allegations, which were published in the Lavian newspaper Sporta Avize. Astafjevs, who scored Latvia's lone goal, wouldn't say how much money was offered, but he called the amount "impressive." Astafjevs told the newspaper: "It was a bribe from the Russian side. They offered us money to lose the game." Russian Football Union president Vitaly Mutko was quoted by Tass, calling the allegations "absolute rubbish."

- Bulgaria coach Hristo Stoitchkov, the mainstay of his country's fourth-place finish at USA '94 and who played for the Chicago Fire, has never been known to keep his mouth shut. After Bulgaria dropped a 3-0 defeat to Sweden on Aug. 17, 2005, Stoitchkov accused UEFA president Lennart Johansson as influencing the match's outcome. Stoitchkov strongly suggested to the media that Johansson, a Swede, left the game early, claiming it was proof the UEFA president was "only interested in how to make more money." Johansson said he wanted to beat the crowd because his wife needs crutches to walk. In a letter to Blatter, Bulgarian Football Union president Ivan Slavkov said: "Please accept my personal apologies for the inadequate behavior of Mr. Hristo Stoitchkov." It was not known whether Stoitchkov took his foot out of his mouth long enough to issue an apology of his own.

- More than 100 Croatian fans were deported from Malta on Sept. 9 when violence during and after a qualifier in Valletta, Malta injured 14 policemen. Problems began after underdog Malta equalized at 1-1. Fans threw seats toward Malta fans in the VIP area as one hit government minister Censu Galea in the head. He needed four stitches. Many Croatian supporters covered their faces with the red and white soccer shirts during the melee.

CHAPTER

3

⊕ Although it had nothing to do directly with anything that went on in the field, Venezuela averted a WC and international ban when the country's football federation held elections and ended a dispute. FIFA had threatened to suspend Venezuela from international matches unless the federation held elections for a new president on March 19, 2005. Rafael Esquivel was re-elected president by 26 of the 34 federation members (made up of the country's soccer clubs and associations).

STILL NEAR
THE BOTTOM

In 2002, a Dutch filmmaker decided to determine the world's worst National Team, so he financed a trip that took then 202nd-ranked Montserrat halfway around the world to Bhutan the day of the World Cup final between Brazil and Germany. Bhutan prevailed, 2-0.

Four years later Montserrat still is having problems in CONCA-CAF, which will never be confused with Europe. Montserrat, which had its island population decimated (from 11,000 to 4,500) due to several volcanic eruptions the past decade, was trounced by host Bermuda, 13-0, in its first qualifier for the 2006 Cup. For the record, John Barry Nusum and Damon Ming each had a hat-trick for the winners. At that time of that match, Montserrat was ranked 205th and Bermuda was 179th.

AFTER SIXTEEN
BITTERSWEET
YEARS,
TRINIDAD IS IN

Carnival had arrived several months early in Trinidad & Tobago in November, 2005. In virtually every city and town, the country had come to a standstill. People left their jobs to celebrate into the night of Nov. 16 and into the wee hours of the next morning. That's when Picaro Airport outside Port of Spain became a sea of red. Thousands of red-clad people waving the red, white and black flag of Trinidad, mobbed the international airport, waiting to greet their heroes on their triumphant return home the following day.

"It was something that I can find no words to describe," said FIFA vice president Jack Warner, who is also a special consultant to the Trinidad & Tobago Football Federation "There was something for which there is no superlatives. . . . It was a torrent of national affection and adulation that was unparalleled and unsurpassed."

What seemed to be an impossible dream turned into stunning reality as the Soca Warriors had qualified for its first World Cup.

After 35 years and 10 failed attempts at trying, Trinidad finally reached soccer's promised land, booking a spot for Germany, overcoming Bahrain, 2-1, in the aggregate goals series to become the smallest country ever—1.3 million people—to qualify for the world's greatest sporting showcase.

Team captain and striker Dwight Yorke, who had endured five sometimes torturous qualifying campaigns called it ". . . the icing on the cake" of a professional career that has spanned nearly two decades.

"It is history, it is unbelievable," he told **Reuters**. "It's a fantastic achievement for our small nation with such a small population. And it is great for me personally to have come back from retirement to play again and to be going to the World Cup now I am 34.

"To be honest, I don't know how to describe my feelings and I don't know what to say."

Government officials did. They declared a national public holiday for celebration.

This time the government did it after the National Team had accomplished something. In 1989, officials declared the day after Trinidad's qualifier vs. the U.S. for Italia '90 a holiday. There was one slight problem: Trinidad hadn't qualified.

It raised expectations to a ridiculously unfair level and turned Nov. 19, 1989, a day that lives in Trinidad football infamy, as what many felt was the best opportunity to reach the World Cup had slithered through the National Team's grasp. Trinidad needed only a tie to clinch a spot at Italia '90, the young United States side a victory. The Americans won, 1-0. Despite its enthusiasm, the crowd went home disappointed and empty-handed. The Americans secured a 1-0 victory on a goal by Paul Caligiuri that boosted them into World Cup heaven and Trinidad into a living hell.

"My memories of that day will never die," Warner said, "because I couldn't believe that Trinidad & Tobago, needing only one point, which they had in the dressing room and gave it away on the field.

"For many years I was devastated, The country, I think, won't be ever able to replicate the whole momentum and atmosphere for that match," Warner said during qualifying.

For 16 bittersweet years Trinidad & Tobago had longed to get another taste at World Cup glory.

After accruing only one point in its first three games in the six-team CONCACAF final group competition (10 matches), it appeared the streak would continue for at least another four years.

But some changes were made. Veteran Dutch coach Leo Beenhakker was brought in to replace Bertille St Clair as coach and slowly but surely Trinidad made progress. Trying to catch confederation powers U.S., Mexico and Costa Rica might have been out of the question. But securing fourth place, which ensured a playoff with the fifth-place Asian side, certainly was within reason.

The Caribbean side barely clinched the fourth place spot. The Soca Warriors (4-1-5, 13 points) defeated Mexico on the final day of the competition on Oct. 12, 2-1, edging out Guatemala (3-2-5, 11) for the opportunity to play Bahrain, the fifth-place Asian team, for one of 32 spots in Germany.

Getting there certainly wasn't without its trials and tribulations.

In the first leg of the home-and-home, aggregate goal series on Nov. 12, 2005 Trinidad squandered home-field advantage, allowing Bahrain to leave Crawford Stadium with a 1-1 draw. With away goals worth twice the amount, Trinidad had to find a way to score in Manama a half a world away four days later.

Ironically, Trinidad's day in the qualifying sun came only three days shy of the 16th anniversary of its devastating loss to the U.S. An unmarked Dennis Lawrence, a 6-foot-7 defender who plays for Wrexham in Coca Cola League Two (fourth division in England's professional pecking order), headed in a Yorke corner kick from seven yards to the lower right of goalkeeper Ali Hassan in the 49th minute.

Still, the Soca Warriors had to sweat this one out as goalkeeper Kelvin Jack wound up in the middle of the spotlight and controversy on each occasion. Jack almost gave the hosts a gift goal in the 40th minute, when he misjudged an air ball and let it bounce over his head toward an empty net, but defender Marvin Andrews headed it out of harm's way with forward Hussain Ali Ahmed on his back.

Bahrain claimed it had scored a goal only seconds into stoppage time as Ahmed blocked Jack's punt and kicked the ball into the net. Referee Oscar Ruiz ruled that Ahmed had fouled Jack, although replays showed he hadn't touched him.

And only seconds before the final whistle, Jack was forced to tip Talal Yousef's long-range blast over the crossbar.

For Yorke, it was an emotional win. He had retired from international football, only to be enticed to come back by St. Clair. "My decision to come out of international retirement was correct - very much so - and I am glad I did but I give a lot of credit to Bertille St Clair, who was my first coach and mentor, someone I look up to immensely," said Yorke, who had played in that 1989 loss to the U.S. "He talked me into coming back and making one last effort to represent my country and take my country to the World Cup".

CHAPTER

3

It couldn't get any worse for defender Pierre Wome. Not only did he miss a penalty kick in the fifth minute of injury time that cost Cameroon a chance to reach Germany on Oct. 8, 2005, he said he could have been killed by irate fans. Had Wome converted his PK against Egypt, Cameroon would have won, 2-1, and qualified. Instead, the 1-1 tie allowed Ivory Coast to capture the African Group 3 title.

THE WORST
KIND OF MISS

Referee Komlan Coulibaly awarded Cameroon a PK, but Wome fired the ball off the left post and it bounced away for a goal kick. Seconds later, Coulibaly blew the final whistle.

The National Team needed military intervention to get the players out of the stadium, where they waited two hours. The fans went crazy, rioting in Yaounde, setting fire to cars.

Ironically, Wome connected on the penalty that boosted Cameroon to the 2000 Olympic gold medal. He was the toast of the country then. In 2005, many soccer fans wanted to make Wome and his family toast. Wome quickly was taken out of the country to his Italian club, Inter Milan.

In fact, Wome's family was forced to live under police protection after his miss. "It could have ended very badly indeed," he told reporters. "They wanted to and could have killed me. Even though I am a tough lad and I have never been afraid of death, my concern was about the safety of my relatives."

Wome said that some fans had mistakenly attacked cars they thought belonged to him after post-match riots.

Depending on your point of view or who you believed, Wome asked to take the kick or did not want to. Forward Samuel Eto'o, the two-time African Footballer of the year, has revealed that he did not take the PK because Wome asked to instead.

"Why didn't I take the penalty? I went to take it but Wome came up to me and said he was really confident of scoring," Eto'o was quoted by Spanish sports daily Sport. "You have to accept that these things happen in football sometimes. . . . It is very hard to have had everything in your own hands and throw it all away in the final seconds," Eto'o said.

Wome disputed the Eto'o version. "I'm very angry with Eto'o because what he said isn't true," he said. "We did not talk on the pitch but I took into account that he and the captain didn't feel up to it so I went to take it myself given that I was on the list of penalty takers."

Ironically, Eto'o was involved in another penalty kick failure that eliminated Cameroon from yet another major competition. Eto'o converted his first attempt, but sent his second try over the crossbar as Ivory Coast moved onto the semifinals of the African Nations Cup in Cairo, Egypt on Feb. 5, 2006. Wome, by the way, was not included on Cameroon roster for the Nations Cup.

LOTHAR'S REVENGE?

Well, well, well. It's funny how things can go full circle.

Five years after he played for the MetroStars in MLS, Lothar Matthaeus found himself empowered with a task that would influence the United States' World Cup fortunes this June. His primary job at the Dec. 9 World Cup draw in Leipzig was to pick the countries out of a brandy sifter for Pot 4—which includes CONCACAF and Asian teams—that would begin the machinations of the Americans' cup fate.

It was just a coincidence that FIFA selected the captain of Germany's 1990 world championship team to pick the group that included the CONCACAF and Asian teams.

"I love to influence football and soccer in any part of the world," Matthaeus said.

MLS and MetroStars fans in particular, might remember Matthaeus's outspoken and controversial ways during his days with the club in 2000.

In fact, Matthaeus was quite diplomatic when he spoke about the U.S. "It doesn't matter what ball I pick," he said. "I would be delighted—since I played football in the U.S.—if the U.S. had a tournament as successful as they had in 2002. It would give U.S. football some big stimulus."

Matthaeus, who agreed to coach Brazilian club team Atletico Paranaense in January, 2006, must have mellowed a bit in the past five years. After Hungary managed to scrape out an unlikely and ugly qualifying victory in Iceland last June, Matthaeus actually apologized to the Icelandic people.

But controversy follows Matthaeus around forever. After the event, television channel Sky Italia reportedly accused him of picking up a ball for Group E—Italy's Group E—before he put it back into the bowl to pull out another.

Sky Italia claimed that prepared hot and cold balls allowed Matthaeus to know which team he was picking, as he pulled out the United States, at the time No. 7 in FIFA's rankings, for the group.

"The Italians are mad if they think that," Matthaeus told the Bild. "I had no idea which ball corresponded to which team. That is utter nonsense."

Besides coaching Matthaeus found himself in the spotlight as the program's spokesman as FIFA unveiled a new award—for the best young player (sponsored by Gillette) at the draw.

There was no such honor in the previous 17 Cups, although FIFA showed a video of promising young players took center stage from past tournaments.

On the screen above the press conference podium flashed goal-scoring feats of Belgian's Enzo Scifo (1986), followed by Yugoslavia's Robert Prosinecki (1990), Holland's Marc Overmars (1994) and England's Michael Owen (1998). Then the U.S.'s Landon Donovan (2002) suddenly appeared, scoring a goal in the stunning 3-2 triumph over Portugal.

"Pressure is getting more and more [difficult] at a big tournament," Matthaeus said. "People expect more. Thirty years ago it wasn't a big deal if a player made a mistake."

"Why a new award?" FIFA spokesman Andreas Herren said. "There is a special group of young players who have yet to establish themselves freely. The World Cup is a platform to emerge."

There was little question Donovan emerged in 2002, striking twice to help the Americans to a surprising quarterfinal finish before they met their match against the Germans, although many members of the German media felt the U.S. outplayed their side in the 1-0 loss.

"Donovan was the best young player of the World Cup," Matthaeus said.

For all you number crunchers out here, are some intriguing numbers to ponder and consider, according to FIFA:

- A total of 847 qualifiers were needed to determine the 32 finalists for Germany. Europe led the way with 282 games.
- Some 194 countries participated.
- Trinidad & Tobago played the most games (20), while Australia needed only nine.
- Home teams compiled a 410-219-183 record, winning half of the time.
- Ten teams finished the competition unbeaten—Croatia, Cuba, France, Israel, Morocco, the Netherlands, Portugal, Saudi Arabia, Serbia and Montenegro and Spain. However, Cuba, Israel and Morocco did not qualify.
- Of the qualifiers, Sweden had the oldest team (27 years, three months), while Togo had the youngest (22 years, four months).
- A total of 2,464 goals were scored, an average of 2.91 per match. Oceania led the way at 4.31 goals per match, while South America was the low at 2.59.
- Costa Rica and Portugal had the most goals by substitutes—nine each, as the U.S.'s Eddie Johnson took individual honors with four goals off the bench.
- Mexico striker Jared Borgetti led everyone with 14 goals.
- Guatemala forward Carlos Ruiz, who also performs for F.C. Dallas finished with a world-high seven yellow cards.
- A total of 18,657,843 spectators watched the matches, for an average of 22,028. South America led all continental regions with an average of 33,750. Next, surprise, surprise was not Europe, but Africa at 26,290. Asia was third at 21,162, followed by Europe (20,657), CONCAAF (14,802) and Oceania (7,009).

- U.S. referee Kevin Stott tied for the most games worked in the middle with nine.
- MacDonald Taylor of the Virgin Islands (46 years, seven months) was the oldest player of the competition playing against St. Kitts and Nevis in a 7-0 loss on March 31, 2004, while Johny Saelua of American Samoa, who came in as a substitute in a 10-0 loss to Fiji in Oceania qualifying on May 15, 2004, was the youngest (15 years, nine months).

CHAPTER

3

The U.S. Challenge
America's Qualifying Ordeal

[photo: Linda Cuttone]

Once CONCACAF doormats, the U.S. has enjoyed a role reversal over the past eighteen years, emerging as a regional powerhouse and respected side to qualify for the World Cup. The bar had been raised so high with four consecutive trips to the tournament that observers and the media expected the Americans to clinch a berth with several games to spare, instead of relying on the 11th-hour dramatics.

The U.S. enjoyed its easiest trip to the cup, losing only twice and one of those setbacks came after the Americans had booked a spot. The U.S.'s record was an impressive 12-2-4. The Americans were invincible at home, registering a 8-0-1, its lone blemish a meaningless 1-1 draw with Jamaica after they already had clinched a final round berth.

Of course, that's looking back with 20-20 hindsight. There still were enough intriguing scenarios, nail-biting finishes and a few bizarre incidents with which to contend.

Due to their superior World Cup history, the Americans were spared from competing in the opening round—an aggregate goals series—as they awaited the winner of the Grenada-Guyana series.

At the World Cup qualifying draw in Frankfurt, Germany on

Dec. 5, 2003, Arena admitted he did not know much on either team. "In all fairness, I don't," he said. "We've never played against them, but we will have the opportunity to scout their games in February and March. We're going to prepare for those countries like we prepare for anybody; treat them with the right respect and have our team prepared to play, and if we do that properly, I believe we'll be successful."

After a resounding 5-0 home triumph on Feb. 18, 2004, Grenada was all but assured of being the Americans' opponents. The Caribbean side wrapped things up with a 3-1 road win on March 31.

Any American soccer fan who flocked to Columbus Crew Stadium in Columbus, Ohio between the heavily favored United States and Grenada on June 13 might have expected the hosts to score at will against the minnows from the Caribbean.

Well, they received quite a rude awakening. From the opening kickoff to the final whistle, the U.S. dominated the game at every level, but the Americans had tremendous difficulty penetrating Grenada's steel curtain in the penalty area en route to a 3-0 victory.

In this total goal series, every goal was important. Grenada's strategy entering the match was keep the score as low as possible so the 138th ranked team in the world had a fighting chance against the ninth-ranked side in the return leg in St. George's, Grenada a week later.

In fact, it wasn't until three minutes into stoppage time at the end of the match that the Americans could breathe easier on defender Greg Vanney's first international goal in twenty-nine appearances, a 20-yard effort. "A two-goal lead is tough," he said. "You think you're comfortable and you're really not. Three goals make it a lot easier."

The American domination was absurd. They outshot the visitors, 34-6. They totaled seventeen corner kicks to Grenada's one, while forcing goalkeeper Kellon Baptiste to make eleven saves.

The Grenadans packed their penalty area with so many players that the game resembled pinball rather than soccer, balls were ricocheting off their defenders so much. So, the longer the game went, the better chance Grenada had in the next encounter. "We knew the first goal would be tough, whether it was in the first minute or the 45th minute," said DaMarcus Beasley, who scored twice. "After we

CHAPTER
4

got that first one, the second and third were going to come. We didn't panic."

    Arena downplayed the U.S.'s inability to score. "We weren't expecting to walk into halftime of any World Cup qualifying game and think that we will have five goals," he said. "That doesn't happen. Tactically, I think the guys did the right things.

    "We basically choreographed the game. If there was any criticism, it's that we were sloppy. We had five, six seven opportunities to score goals today."

DaMarcus Beasley [photo: Linda Cuttone]

157

Arena said he was not worried about the U.S. expending so much energy in the first half, but not walking away with goals. "No, because the fitter team is our team," he said. "All along, we knew over ninety minutes that their fitness was going to be a question. However, it's a little bit easier when they just sit back and aren't running as much. After thirty-five minutes, you could see that they were basically done."

Even in the waning minutes before a paltry crowd of 9,137 the Grenadans still had as many as seven players in their own penalty area to defend against three U.S. attackers.

"Give them credit," Arena said. "They played with a lot of heart and emotion. They were difficult to break down."

Beasley gave the U.S. some comfort a minute into stoppage time in the first half, heading home a Claudio Reyna right-wing cross from four yards. "It was a big relief," Beasley said. "If it was 0-0 at halftime, there would have been some things to do. We knew the first goal was going to be tough, whether we got in the first minute of 45th minute. After that the second was going to come. Bruce said to keep fighting and don't panic. Keep crossing into the box. Something will happen."

It did—in the 71st minute when Beasley connected again, running some fifty yards before Landon Donovan shuffled him the ball to score from thirteen yards. It was only Beasley's seventh international goal in thirty-four matches.

Grenada coach Ali Bebellotte tried some gamesmanship before the match, wanting to switch players at the last minute--forward Everett Watts for Nigel Bishop. Arena protested and a minor controversy delayed the start of the match by several minutes. The match commissioner ruled in Grenada's favor.

Still, that didn't stop Arena from voicing his opinion afterwards. "Why do you submit lineups?" he asked. "So we can look at the lineups and make four-five changes? "I think that's a good lesson for CONCACAF. I have a hard time believing that is acceptable."

Ironically, Bishop came in as a sub for Watts in the 52nd minute.

Now the pressure was on Grenada, which had to produce a four-goal margin of victory at home. It was among the longest of long-shots. The last time the U.S. lost a qualifier by more than three goals was a 5-1 defeat to Mexico in 1980.

"That will be a difficult task," Bebellotte said, "but we hope at least we can win. A development for Grenada soccer is if we get a win over the U.S. If we get four, we'll accept it."

Exactly a week later, the U.S. punched its ticket to the semifinal round. Arena had warned about strange things happening on the road while his team is on the road to Germany. And his team's 3-2 victory in Grenada certainly fit the bill. After a pre-match rain on the Caribbean island made the field wet and the players' footing and passing unpredictable and sometimes unreliable, the U.S. secured a berth in the CONCACAF semifinal qualifying round. The Americans won the total goals series, 6-2.

The water-logged field at Grenada's National Cricket Stadium made sure passes stopped yards from their destination, allowing defenders on both sides to obtain possession of the ball, only to lose it for the same reason.

"I think we may have scored more goals," Arena said. "It was in great shape yesterday, but then the rains came. They did a terrific job of getting the field ready, but the showers came before the kickoff and made it difficult. I thought the field conditions made it difficult for both teams. These games tend to be games of mistakes. You need to be alert for ninety minutes."

Donovan certainly was alert when it counted, scoring the first goal—his very first qualifying goal—and setting up the second before 15,267 spectators. "The first goal is always important," he said. "You don't want to give them a chance and scoring early makes them open up a lot."

Donovan scored from the center of the penalty area in the sixth minute on a perfect pass from Reyna, who dropped the ball back to the forward from the end line after being played into the area from Josh Wolff. Donovan slotted the ball past two defenders and Baptiste.

Only six minutes later, Grenada snapped the U.S.'s shutout streak at 393 minutes (over six games) with a penalty kick from Jason Roberts past keeper Kasey Keller after Pablo Mastroeni was whistled for a foul in the penalty area moments earlier.

Donovan turned goal maker in the 19th minute as the then San Jose Earthquakes star collected Brian McBride's header off the cross bar and directed it to Wolff, who scored from four yards.

The teams exchanged goals in the second half only 60 seconds apart with Beasley connecting on his team-leading fourth goal of the year through the legs of Baptiste in the 77th minute on an assist from second-half sub Earnie Stewart. Stewart was making his 100th international appearance. That was followed by a close finish from Grenada's Ricky Charles after Grenada captain Anthony Modeste had fired in a low cross from the right flank.

"I give the team from Grenada a lot of credit," Arena said. "They fought hard and did a terrific job. . . . It was a good experience for our young players. We're pleased. It's the type of game that helped us get ready for the next round."

The Americans' next challenge was getting through the four-team, six-game round-robin semifinal round. The top two teams in their Group A would advance to the six-team final round in 2005. The U.S. obviously was an immense favorite to move on against the likes of Panama, El Salvador and Jamaica.

But it wasn't always easy. In fact, the U.S. was fortunate to walk away with a point at The Office, the nickname for the National Stadium of Jamaica in Kingston, on Aug. 18, scoring in the final minute to secure a 1-1 draw and stave off a major upset. Brian Ching performed the late-match heroics with a dramatic 89th-minute equalizer.

"I told the team at halftime that I thought the second half would go in our favor, but giving up the early goal obviously put us under pressure," Arena said. "The team showed a lot of class staying in the game. I think we deserve the draw."

Ching, who replaced McBride in the 60th minute, drove Donovan's layoff under the crossbar from 14 yards for his first international goal. A give-and-go between Cobi Jones, another second-half sub, and Beasley, started the play. Jones, a World Cup veteran, found space down the right flank and crossed the ball in front of goal. The ball deflected off the head of a defender and onto the foot of Donovan, who slid the ball to his right where he found his former Earthquakes teammate.

CHAPTER
4

"On the goal, Cobi made a great cross and I heard Landon say 'leave it,' and the ball hit a defender and went straight to his feet and I think he surprised everyone by passing the ball and I just tried to put it on goal," Ching said. "This is a critical time in my career, and hopefully I will get another opportunity in qualifying."

Landon Donovan [photo: Linda Cuttone]

Ching's goal wiped away what was almost a major upset by the Reggae Boyz. Inspired by a boisterous and partisan home crowd, Jamaica played passionately and for large stretches of the game dominated the heavily favored United States.

After having the better of play in the opening half, Jamaica grabbed the lead in the 49th minute when Ian Goodison lost McBride in front of goal and his bouncing header of Theodore Whitmore's corner kick beat Keller at the top of the goal box.

The Americans woke up and played with more urgency to get the equalizer.

Despite the tie, the U.S. extended its unbeaten streak against Jamaica to 15 games as all four WC qualifiers between had ended in a draw. The other three games were scoreless.

Some three weeks later, on September 4, the U.S. secured a solid 2-0 victory over El Salvador in Foxboro, Mass. It certainly wasn't the prettiest win the U.S. ever recorded in qualifying, but the Americans weren't about to give back the three points they earned. They survived a bizarre encounter that had just about every El Salvadoran on the ground at one time or another with a supposed injury, midfielder Denis Alas being ejected for wearing illegal jewelry and an incredible 12 minutes of stoppage time.

Arena claimed his team never found its rhythm, but the Americans found the back of the net enough to secure three qualifying points with a Wednesday encounter in Panama looming. The win ensured the U.S. (1-0-1, four points) first place in the group.

The goals were scored by Ching (eight-yard header in the fifth minute), his second qualifying goal in as many matches, Donovan (19-yard blast in the 69th minute), whose Earthquakes defeated the New England Revolution, 1-0, in the second game of the double-header before 25,266 spectators at Gillette Stadium.

"It was strange to win the game and feel frustrated after as a team because we couldn't open up and play for 90 minutes," Reyna said. "The game had a little bit of everything. The only thing it lacked was probably flow. That was very frustrating for the players. From the first minute they tried to dive and get us yellow cards. It really ruined the game."

What really ruined the game for the visitors was Alas's 26th-minute ejection as received his second yellow card for wearing contraband jewelry. A day before the match both teams were warned that jewelry would not be tolerated. Several players on the U.S. bench alerted the fourth official to the gold chain around Alas's neck. He threw it toward his bench, but referee Neal Brizan (Trinidad & Tobago) slapped him with his second yellow.

"Maybe he forgot," El Salvador coach Juan Paredes said.

"Nobody expected a red card for this."

Paredes exploded, running onto the field, bumping the referee and getting ejected in the 29th minute. "Everything changed with the call," he said.

Paredes needed to be restrained by team officials and a player. "It was very hard for me to accept that," he said. "I made a mistake. It was the moment."

Reyna commiserated with the Salvadorans. "It was really a bad call," he said. "The player made a genuine mistake. It was a shame. They should have given him a warning and kept him on."

Ching picked up where he left off in the Jamaica draw, heading in a Bobby Convey left-wing cross from eight yards in the fifth minute. Ching's header hit the right post and bounded into the net behind goalkeeper Santos Rivera. "Our early goal essentially ended the game because they weren't going to generate any chances," said Arena, whose team outshot El Salvador, 19-1.

Donovan gave the Americans some much-needed breathing room in the 69th minute, running uncontested from right to left before firing home a 19-yard blast into the lower left corner. It was Donovan's 17th career international score.

"Let's face it, they weathered a big storm," Arena said. "I don't think 2-0 is a fair score. We could have scored more goals. I think we are a little guilty of that. Give El Salvador credit. They played with a lot of heart and did a decent job defensively. We missed the target too much today, as well. We had a few good looks at the goal, and we didn't bury some of our chances."

Any trip to Central America is an adventure for the U.S. National Team, even when it's against a soccer minnow such as Panama, which is better known for producing baseball stars than soccer players. The Americans usually have to battle hostile crowds that have been known to throw batteries, coins and even bags of urine. So, Reyna wasn't taking any chances as the U.S. prepared for its Sept. 8 encounter in Panama City, Panama.

"Expect the worst and anything better we'll take," he said. "That's just how it is."

Reyna had been there before. During qualifying for the 2002

World Cup, Guatemala's Carlos Ruiz (most recently with F.C. Dallas of Major League Soccer) knocked down everything in sight, but never was sanctioned for his ultra-physical play as he scored the tying goal in the waning minutes in a 1-1 draw. A week later, a strange hand ball two minutes into stoppage time gave Costa Rica a controversial penalty kick and a 2-1 win. Arena and Reyna were suspended for two games their post-match conduct and comments.

"We have a lot of players who have experienced a lot of strange environments and decisions, especially on the road," Reyna said. "It always seems to be worse on the road. The referees are against you, the crowd and everything. We expect a very hostile reception in Panama, as we always do in Central America.

"It's up to the experienced guys who have been through it to let the young guys know that it's not going to be easy. The playing field will level off because of the decisions. . . . It's unfortunate a little bit. A combination of the environment and the play acting and all this and with the referees sometimes falling into the trap, it makes the game difficult."

The Americans hadn't fared well in Central America, having accrued only three qualifying victories—all in Honduras—in 14 attempts (3-5-6) since their first trip down there in 1965. Entering this match, they were 5-11-8 overall, including friendlies.

Instead of taking a commercial airline to the match, the U.S. team flew into Panama City on a charter, so they could return home as quickly as possible after the game.

Following a pattern that was established earlier in the year, the U.S. continued to thrive on pulling out ties and wins in the 11th hour. For the second consecutive away match, the U.S. pulled out a dramatic 1-1 draw as Jones struck two minutes into stoppage time.

Jones, a 57th-minute substitute for Clint Mathis, scored from eight yards some 85 seconds into added time to give the U.S. the stunning tie. The tie kept the U.S. (five points) undefeated at 1-0-2 and extended the team's unbeaten streak to 10 games (6-0-4). Panama (four points) was 1-1-1.

It was the fifth time in 2004 the U.S. scored either the equalizing or winning goal in the 88th minute or beyond. "We have a natural attitude of never say die," Jones said. "We're a team that never quits.

CHAPTER 4

We're going to to play ball for 90 minutes. It was a credit to us to come back and get that goal when we're getting outplayed a bit."

With the U.S. in desperate need of a goal, Vanney sent a left-wing cross into the penalty area to Donovan. Donovan's shot went directly to Jones, who beat goalkeeper Donaldo Gonzalez to the far post to silence the estimated enthusiastic crowd of 12,000 and Panama president Martin Torrijeos at Estadio Rommel Fernandez.

"It bounced straight down across the goal," Donovan said of Vanney's cross. "My eyes got big. As I went to shoot it, it hit a little puddle and stopped. It kind of came off the end of my foot and went to Cobi. Things happen for a reason."

Panama, which never had qualified for a World Cup, was on the

Brian McBride
[photo: Linda Cuttone]

165

cusp of a startling upset on the strength of Roberto Brown's 70th-minute goal. Ricardo Phillips, a first-half substitute, made a 45-yard run, going in one-on-one with Keller before firing a shot that the goalkeeper knocked away. The ball was sent back in and hit the right post before Brown scored in a scramble from five yards.

The stadium, already a sea of red with passionate spectators wearing the colors of their team, erupted with smoke bombs and popcorn and drinks flying down from the upper decks.

The match was played under less than optimum conditions. A thunderstorm several miles from the stadium threatened to delay the game, but it abated before kickoff. Still, rain continued throughout the match, making one penalty area waterlogged.

A good three hours prior to kickoff, two radio stations blared loud, deafening, incomprehensible music over loudspeakers for several hundred fans who arrived early. There were only four light towers, which made life miserable for the players, particularly the goalkeepers, and no working scoreboard.

Arena made five changes from the lineup he deployed in the El Salvador win four days prior. He used more veterans in Keller, defenders Eddie Pope, Frankie Hejduk and Vanney and Mathis in favor of Tim Howard (he returned to Manchester United), Cory Gibbs, Steve Cherundolo, Convey and Kerry Zavagnin, respectively.

Panama slowly, but surely, took control of the match in the final 45 minutes. Brown headed a corner kick right to Keller in the 57th minute and defender Carlos Rivera headed another from three yards over the goal. Phillips almost brought the crowd to its feet, firing a hard, 22-yard shot wide right.

In an attempt to revive his team's attack, Arena made three offensive-minded substitutions. He pulled Mathis for Jones in the 57th minute, Casey for McBride in the 62nd minute and Ching for Eddie Lewis in the 77th minute.

While the trio did not immediately make an impact, they came through when the game was on the line. "We wore them down at the end," Arena said. "I thought it would be the other way. The game will be very different in Washington, D.C."

But first, the U.S. faced a golden opportunity to snatch a rare qualifying triumph in Central America.

The U.S. needed four points against host El Salvador on Oct. 9 and visiting Panama on Oct. 13 to reach the final round.

"I don't think we've played at our best up to this point but we're on top of our group," Arena said. "If we can turn a corner here and improve our performance I think we're going to be in good shape. It's a challenge, I don't think people realize that our opponents have been training for a couple weeks and it's very difficult. . . . All players have to be ready to respond and improve on their performances from our last three games."

The Americans would have to accomplish that without two key midfielders missing from the lineup. Reyna (thigh injury) and defensive midfielder Chris Armas (knee operation), who was not fit enough to play at the international level.

GAME FOUR

EL SALVADOR

In 20 of the last 21 qualifiers, Arena had either or both players in the lineup. The only time they both weren't in the starting 11 was in the final 2002 qualifier at Trinidad & Tobago. By then the U.S. had clinched a spot. "It's going to be difficult not having those guys obviously," said veteran defender Eddie Pope. "That's why you have to have a lot of good players on the National Team."

Lo and behold, the U.S. accomplished a rare feat, winning in San Salvador, El Salvador, 2-0, the Americans' fourth win in Central America—ever. The triumph solidified the Americans' hold on first place with a chance to clinch at RFK Stadium in Washington, D.C. four days later. The U.S. (2-0-2, eight points) led the group, followed by Panama (1-1-2, five), Jamaica (1-1-2, five) and El Salvador (1-3-0, three).

"We did well," Arena said. "We took El Salvador's best shot. I think the first half we were a little sloppy in different parts of the field, but I think in the second half we were much more solid. Obviously, we could have scored more goals. You don't win that many games on the road in World Cup qualifying. We finished this round without losing a game on the road so I think that's a big plus for our team."

The last time the U.S. emerged triumphant in Central America was a 2-1 win over Honduras on a late goal by Mathis in March, 2001. The win also ended a dubious American streak as the team finally won a qualifier outside of Honduras. Entering the match the

U.S. had been 0-for-11 (0-5-6) in trying to earn a full three points in Central American qualifying games outside of Honduras, which included a single draw in their only previous qualifying game in El Salvador (a 1-1 tie in 1997).

McBride's game-opening goal—his 26th internationally—came in the 29th minute, after Beasley had tracked down a long ball from Kerry Zavagnin and earned a throw-in on the right side. The PSV Eindhoven midfielder threw the ball in on the wing, where Zavagnin collected it on a run into the box before playing a short pass to McBride.

McBride set himself up for a right-footed shot by sliding across the top of the penalty area with four straight touches as no El Salvador defender closed on him, burying his shot from 16 yards into the upper right corner. It was McBride's seventh goal vs. El Salvador.

"When I received the ball, I just tried to shield it and turn," McBride said. "I faked the shot and the second time I was going to hit it but I faked again and they fell off again and the ball set up for the third time and I struck it pretty well."

The game marked the debut of 20-year-old forward Eddie Johnson, who burst onto the international scene unlike any other American forward prior to him. Only four minutes after making his first appearance as a second-half substitute coming on for McBride, Johnson struck for his first international goal. The goal couldn't have been much easier as he slotted a square ball from Donovan into an empty net after Donovan was sprung by a Beasley pass. Johnson was left unmarked on his goal as the last defender, captain Victor Velasquez, attempted to steal the ball.

"I was lucky. I was in the right place at the right time," Johnson said. "I moved into the box and Landon made a very unselfish play to pass the ball. I just wanted to do well for the team. I wanted to hold the ball up and bring other players into the game."

With Reyna out, Donovan was selected to wear the captain's armband for the U.S. for the first time in his career. "The second highest honor is playing for your country and the highest honor is wearing the (captain's) armband for your country," Donovan said. "It was good because I knew I was going to be ready. It shows that the players have confidence in me and that feels good."

The U.S. would play Panama without defender Cory Gibbs after he picked up his second yellow card. He became the first U.S. player to be suspended due to multiple yellow cards.

Arena was right. It was a very different game in Washington, D.C. as the U.S. booked a spot in the 2005 final round with a rare qualifying laugher, a resounding 6-0 thrashing of Panama. Johnson continued his torrid pace, again coming on a sub and connecting for a second-half hat-trick. Lost in the shuffle was the fact Donovan scored twice as the hosts pounded Panama for five second-half scores.

Johnson's hat-trick was only the eighth in National Team history and the first by a substitute.

"To be qualified in the fifth game of this round is fantastic," Arena said.

The U.S. opened the floodgates in the 21st minute, when Wolff ran onto a long ball down the left side. Wolff crossed it perfectly into the center of the box, where it was met by Donovan who was cutting sideways in front of the goal. Donovan tapped the ball with the outside of his right foot past goalkeeper Donald Gonzalez.

Donovan made it 2-0 in the 57th minute, scoring while tightly marked by two defenders. Zavagnin sent the ball into Donovan, who was flanked by the defenders. As Donovan fell away, he managed to get off a shot that went past Gonzalez and into the net.

Playing in only his third game, Johnson made an immediate impact after entering the game in place of Wolff in the 65th minute. With Carlos Bocanegra running down the far side, Johnson cut in on the opposite side of the play, behind most of the defense. Bocanegra sent a cross through the area that Johnson headed into the far lower corner.

Panama did get off a few shots, but had virtually no serious chances.

It didn't take Johnson much longer to net his second goal. This time, it was Bocanegra sending a cross into the area, where Johnson, set up in virtually the same spot as his first goal, sent a header over Gonzalez.

Johnson added the rare third goal in the 87th minute, sliding onto a ball from Lewis.

"There's a lot to be said for getting into goal scoring positions and sticking the ball in the back of the net," Arena said.

The U.S. closed out the scoring in the 90th minute, as late substitute Oguchi Onyewu headed a pass from Donovan down, the ball glanced off the foot of defender Jose Anthony Torres, catching Gonzalez flat footed.

GAME SIX

JAMAICA

CHAPTER

4

The axiom goes that a tie is just like kissing your sister. For Jamaica on Nov. 17, a draw was more like kissing your chances of reaching the World Cup goodbye. The U.S. made sure of that, playing the spoilers role and holding the Jamaicans to a 1-1 tie in Columbus, Ohio. It was the fifth consecutive qualifying tie played between these two rivals.

The Americans (3-0-3, 12 points), who already had clinched a spot in the final round of six next year, did not need a point. They used essentially a B team lineup, but included veterans Keller, Donovan and McBride.

The Jamaicans (1-1-4, seven), on the other hand, desperately needing a win, deployed their top team and could only solve Keller for one goal—a penalty kick by midfielder and MLS journeyman Andy Williams in the 28th minute. That goal wiped out a 1-0 U.S. advantage on a goal by Johnson in the 15th minute.

Johnson, who became the first player in American history to score goals in his first three qualifiers, joined Alexander Rae as one of only two players with goals in each of his first three caps (Rae's feat was accomplished in three games vs. Mexico in 1937). He also became one of only two players (joining Aldo "Buff" Donelli, two career caps) with five goals in as many as three career games, accomplishing the feat in only 61 minutes.

"He is doing everything well," said Mastroeni, named the man of the match. "He is checking the ball well, holding up well and making great runs. The kid is on top of his game."

The tie ensured Panama (2-2-2, eight) of reaching its first final round. Panama blanked last-place El Salvador (1-4-1, four) at home, 3-0, to clinch a spot.

Besides the U.S. and Panama, Trinidad & Tobago, Costa Rica, Mexico and Guatemala also clinched berths for the next round, which kicked off on Feb. 9, 2005.

"The problem we always have with out MLS players is their layoff," Arena said. "That will be a difficult challenge over the next couple months, to get a group of players ready for February 9. "

The U.S. was forced to play the final 17 minutes a man down after Onyewu was awarded his second yellow card for intentionally handling the ball at midfield.

"I was pleased with our performance," Arena said. "If we could be at fault for anything tonight it was not doing well with our chances, but I thought the opportunity to play some of our young players and the leadership from our veterans like McBride and Keller was an outstanding effort. I can't be more pleased. I would have liked to have the three points, but certainly one point is a fair result. It was a good experience to be in that situation and come out on top."

Johnson connected from 10 yards on the right side to the far post off a Mastroeni feed.

"It was one of those games were I was able to get myself in good positions and I've got great guys around me that can distribute great balls," Johnson said. "As a forward you know you are going to get your chances, and it is a matter of taking your chances when you get them.

"I had two chances before that that I didn't take well, the keeper making a good save on one and the other one I mis-hit. I tried to do something different on the third chance and played the ball to my left foot and was able to get it around him. Just one of those games. It was my first start and I was just happy to be out there."

But Jamaica equalized in the 27th minute after Ramiro Corrales took down Ricardo Fuller in the penalty area. A minute later Williams fired his shot to the upper left corner as Keller dived the other way.

The match also saw the international debut of 18-year-old defender Jonathan Spector. Spector, who performs for Manchester United, replaced Steve Ralston in the 77th minute.

FINAL ROUND

As it turned out, the final round of qualifying in 2005 was bookended by labor talks. It didn't start out optimistic, but it ended up quite well.

Some 56 days before the U.S. took on Trinidad & Tobago in the first game of the 10-match round-round final round on Feb. 9, the Americans' final-round chances of getting off on the right foot were threatened by a labor dispute between U.S. Soccer and the players. Unless it was settled, the Americans faced the possibility of putting together a rag-tag make-shift roster that included young and marginal MLS players and players from its national youth teams.

The players had been performing without a contract since the previous one expired on Dec. 31, 2002.

After hitting a wall in attempts to negotiate with U.S. Soccer, the U.S. National Soccer Team Players' Association said enough was enough and players refused to partake in a December training camp in Carson, Calif. That, in turn, forced U.S. Soccer to cancel the camp and two friendlies at the Home Depot Center.

"The current (U.S. Soccer) approach is part of a longstanding. . . view that the players should not be represented," Mark Levinstein, a Washington-based attorney who represents the men's players association, said on Dec. 15. "The players have been playing for almost two years without a new contract and without any reasonable offer for a new contract. The players association remains hopeful that the federation will soon start to engage in good faith negotiations with the players."

Federation spokesman Jim Moorhouse said U.S. Soccer "notified the players association that if we don't have a deal done (by Feb. 1), we'll pursue other options in the qualifying."

It got complicated from there. The players association viewed a member as any player who has attended at least one full National Team camp, which limits the federation's options of selecting a experienced players for Trinidad. So, theoretically, the team could have very well wound up including then-15-year-old Freddy Adu.

Losing in Trinidad would be considered a disaster for the Americans, who had lost only once there (they had a 3-1-2 record in Port of Spain), especially since a road tie—one point—is considered precious. The U.S. is 10-1-3 lifetime vs. T&T.

"Our requests are all fair," said one U.S. National Team player who asked not to be identified. "The players have all agreed. We absolutely do not want to jeopardize any qualifying game."

But . . .

"The players want to get a contract done and move on," he said.

The players were seeking a higher percentage of the profits from National Team games.

Players were receiving $2,000 for an appearance, $2,500 for a draw and at least $3,150 for a win, although that could be as much as $5,000 if the U.S. defeats a team ranked in FIFA's top 10 or CONCA-CAF rival Mexico. For the top ranked teams, the players are seeking $3,750 per appearance and more than $10,000 for a victory.

Each American player on the team that lost in the quarterfinals to Germany in the 2002 World Cup received a $200,000 bonus.

U.S. Soccer had experienced labor problems before with the National Team. In 1995, the players refused to leave their rooms prior to Copa America in Uruguay unless they were given better terms on their contract. The players also refused to play in a World Cup qualifying warm-up match in Lima, Peru in October, 1996. Then coach Steve Sampson had to scurry around to piece together a make-shift lineup that dropped a 4-1 decision to Peru, one of the poorest results by a U.S. in years.

After a war of words, both sides finally submitted to an agreement on Jan. 21, ending the threat of using replacement players for a World Cup qualifier in Trinidad only 19 days prior to kickoff.

The players agreed to a 38 percent pay increase and promised not to strike in 2005 while the two sides continued to negotiate a new contract.

"We hope this is a good sign," Donovan said. "We hope that with the players back on the field and the coach and the players back to the business of qualifying for the 2006 World Cup, the players can sit down with Federation representatives and put in place a 2003-2006 agreement or perhaps even a 2003-2010 agreement that will benefit the players, the USSF, and the sport of soccer."

Even though the U.S. had owned Trinidad in qualifying (6-0-2) and in other international encounters over the past several decades, T&T was confident it could pull off an upset.

"The guys are quite confident," veteran defender Anton Pierre said as Trinidad's recorded 1-0 and 2-0 wins over Azerbaijan in preparation matches. "I'm quite confident we're going to make history on Feb. 9. Somewhere in life, you're going to do things . . .

and you've got that confidence it's going to happen. No matter what you do it's going to happen. That's how we feel."

Trinidad had never reached the World Cup. The closest it came was 1989, needing only a tie vs. the U.S., which emerged with a 1-0 triumph.

"We are sure and positive that this time we're going to qualify for the World Cup and Germany 2006," Pierre said, "and it starts on Feb. 9."

Each country tries a little gamesmanship and Trinidad was no exception. Instead of playing at Hasely Crawford Stadium, the national stadium, the game would be held at the Queen's Park Oval cricket ground. "It was a good idea," forward Cornell Glen said.

Maybe, maybe not.

Arena played some gamesmanship of his own, not releasing his roster to the media until three days before the match. There were few surprises as he called in 10 European-based players. One player definitely wasn't in the mix—veteran goalkeeper Brad Friedel, 33, a major reason why the U.S. reached the quarterfinals of the 2002 World Cup with his grace under fire and pressure, announced his retirement from international soccer two days prior to the match.

"I have loved every minute of it, but feel now is the right time to end my international career," Friedel said in a statement. "Throughout my career I have been extremely lucky not to have suffered any major injuries. However over the last 18 months or so I have sometimes been left feeling short of full fitness because of the strain of playing for my club and my country and the huge amount of long haul travel involved."

Friedel performed for Blackburn Rovers in the English Premiership.

Like the Panama game in September, the U.S. took a charter flight in and out of Trinidad, not necessarily because they wanted to, but because they had to. The Caribbean island was in the midst of Carnival and hotel rooms and flights were scarce and at a premium because many former residents return home for that annual party.

A day prior to the Wednesday match, a good portion of the 1.3 million people and the estimated one million visitors partied on through Last Lap—Trinidad & Tobago's version of Fat Tuesday—

with endless parades, beautiful women bandying about in revealing attire and steel bands blasting Calypso music.

Through the years, the U.S. had experienced more than its share of gamesmanship, including blaring music outside the team hotel all night and having batteries, coins and even bags of urine thrown at players at games. So, Carnival in all its splendor and raucous all night partying, colorful participants, was not a distraction for the American side, even though their team hotel was close to the celebrations at the Queen's Park Savannah.

"It's nice," Arena said of Carnival. "I thought it was going to be a little more hectic. We had a good night's sleep last night."

Carnival meant taking the good with the bad and the ugly, including scantily clad women wearing colorful attire parade through the street. Three pretty women from the festivities showed up at U.S. practice.

"We're here to distract the players from playing the game," one woman said with a smile.

It didn't work.

They were allowed into the ground, but were kept away from the players.

For the more culturally astute, the Calypso Monarch finals offered some song and dance as The Mighty Chalkdust, captured first place. But on Monday, 32 people were stabbed at the Savannah and there was at least one shooting.

Arena had other things to worry about, making sure his team was ready despite his team's preparation severely hurt by the labor dispute. "I'm as a satisfied as I can be at this point in time," he said. "We can't make up for lost time. Certainly two weeks of preparation for domestic players playing a qualifying game is not enough for me. We can't make any excuses. That's the cards that have been dealt. We have to move on and try to win on Wednesday."

Then there was the field, which was 80 yards wide, five more than the international width, and 120 yards long. The field looked more like crab grass than anything else.

"It's different, that's for sure," Arena said. "I don't think it favors them. . . . It's hard. It's like playing in a parking lot."

Another concern was the late arrival of Keller, who flew in

FINAL ROUND
GAME ONE
TRINIDAD 7
TOBAGO

CHAPTER
4

Monday after his German club, Borussia Moenchengladbach played that Sunday.

"It might be real difficult," Arena said. "Kasey has done it a lot, but he tends to believe it's not a problem. With a field player it would be a lot more difficult. It's still challenging for a keeper."

The pressure, Arena said was on the home team. Trinidad had woefully underachieved through the years.

Trinidad practiced in Tobago for four days to avoid the tumult of Carnival. "We are very aware that the fans have expressed concerns over whether the team can concentrate enough for such a big game at this time of year when all the Carnival madness is taking place," Trinidad captain Angus Eve said. "One thing for sure is that, as a team, we have been through this before and the guys are all psyched up for Wednesday."

Coach Bertille St. Clair pleaded for fans to come and support his team. Some high profile men were expected to attend, including Trinidad president Dr. Maxwell Richards, prime minister Patrick Manning and Brian Lara, considered by many to be the world's greatest cricket player and a close friend of Trinidad international forward-midfielder Dwight Yorke.

Tickets sold for $200 T&T, the equivalent of $33 US, which were expensive for most citizens. Tickets were available at local Kentucky Fried Chicken restaurants. "I hope Trinidad and Tobago recognize how important this is to the country," Bertille was quoted in a local newspaper, *Newsday* (no relation to Long Island's paper). "It could do so much to change the life of the young people."

The U.S. had some unique support of its own—comedian Drew Carey. He flew into Port of Spain on Tuesday, ready to give the U.S. National Team his support. He reportedly told one U.S. soccer official, "I want to be your Jack Nicholson."

Nicholson, of course, is known for being a big time fan of the Los Angeles Lakers. During the match, Carey, who sat in the box of U.S. Soccer president Bob Contiguglia at the Queen's Park Oval cricket ground, spent a couple of hours on Tuesday night with Arena and Contiguglia at a bar at the team hotel, the Trinidad Hilton, entertaining both men with jokes.

All things considered, it was a damn good result. Despite playing with a team that was kept out of training camp until two weeks ago due to a bitter labor dispute and playing in 90-degree heat, the U.S. managed to escape the Queen's Park Oval cricket ground with a 2-1 qualifying victory over Trinidad and three precious road points.

Arena could thank Johnson and veteran Lewis for providing the offensive spark, each scoring a goal, and Keller for supplying the saving graces on several occasions for a tiring American side.

"It's massive. It's so big, especially what was going on around the team," Keller said. "The guys got together with a great victory. We now have to move forward advancing to the World Cup. We took a bit step today."

The Americans' triumph gave them some breathing room before they met archrival Mexico in Mexico City on March 27.

"Obviously it is a great result for the U.S. team," Arena said. "When you write the story of this game, there were a bunch of reasons why we couldn't be successful today. We never agreed with that. I think the way our team pulled together over the last couple of weeks to be ready to play this game under difficult conditions - travel, field conditions, the heat, everything else - it turns out to be a fantastic result."

In fact, the Americans looked more like the home team rather than the visitors the way they attacked in the first half. Trinidad was thwarted by either Keller or being too aggressive and being called for offside.

Johnson found a gaping hole in the Trinidad defense in the 30th minute. Steve Cherundolo sent the ball in from 30 yards on the right side to an unmarked Johnson, who headed the ball into the lower right corner past goalkeeper Shaka Hislop.

"It was one of those situations where I put myself in a good position to score," Johnson said. "I think I caught the keeper off guard.

"Bruce told me that it is only going to get harder. He told me I'm not going to score every game. And (today) it was tougher. It is about taking advantage of the chances you get, because you don't get that many chances. I didn't get many chances tonight, but when I did I took it well."

That made it six goals—that's right—six in only four games as

GAME 2

MEXICO

CHAPTER

4

an international—all World Cup scores. "He's continuing to get better," Arena said.

"It was a very good goal from Eddie. Obviously, we told our players that we had to get that second. That made it easier for us."

After some nifty, quick passing from Johnson to Donovan, Lewis connected off a brilliant 23-yarder in the 54th minute.

Keller made several vital saves. His most important one came in the 53rd minute, when he came out of the net to deny an onrushing Leslie Fitzpatrick from nine yards. "What I tried to do, I would get there the same time he did," Keller said. "You have to time it perfectly."

Glen, who played with the MetroStars and F.C. Dallas (both MLS), came on as a sub to revitalize the Trinidad attack in the 68th minute and the move paid off on Eve's goal in the 89th minute. It was the first goal Trinidad scored against the U.S. in four home qualifiers. "We lost our concentration," Keller said. "We started to get tired."

Played in high heat and humidity, the game definitely had a different atmosphere to it. The U.S. national anthem was played by a steel band while the team faced the U.S. and Trinidad delegations, situated in back of one of the goals, instead of at midfield.

With the sounds of Calypso music reverberating through the ground, the stadium was a sea of red before the match as fans wore mostly the colors of the National Team, although they were seated considerably away from the action partly because of the velodrome that that surrounded the enormous cricket ground.

GAME TWO

MEXICO

Flying high with an unprecedented 31-game unbeaten streak against CONCACAF foes, the U.S. had risen to new heights the past 3 1/2 years. The Americans were preparing to attempt to scale what is considered one of soccer's unattainable peaks—Mount Azteca, better known as Azteca Stadium. They take on the lofty challenge of defeating archrival Mexico in a World Cup qualifier in Mexico City on Easter Sunday, March 27.

Since opening in 1966, conquering the Mexicans at Azteca has been an imposing challenge. They have been virtually invincible with a 25-1-3 qualifying record, losing only to Costa Rica, 2-1, in June, 2001 (In fact, the Mexicans were 54-1-4 in all qualifiers south of the border).

The Mexicans' great advantage didn't come from the anticipated crowd of 100,000, but rather from the altitude (7,200 feet) and
the city's notorious smog.

"Heat will be a bit of a factor," Arena said. "I think it will be in
the 70s or the low 80s on Sunday. I am not exactly sure where it will
be. The biggest factor will be the altitude and the smog. I think the
heat will be less of a factor than it was in Trinidad where it was
horrifically warm. I think we'll be fighting the altitude more than we
will be the heat in Azteca."

Not surprisingly, the U.S. hadn't fared well in Mexico City qualifiers at 0-17-1, while being outscored, 67-12. In fact, the Americans
hadn't scored in Azteca in 396 minutes, or since Perry Van Der Beck's
goal in a 2-1 friendly loss on Oct. 17, 1984.

There are two theories on how to tackle Azteca.

Because the 1997 qualifier was after the MLS season, then
coach Steve Sampson held a two-week training camp in the rarefied
air at Big Bear, Calif. The result: a surprising scoreless tie as the U.S.
was forced to play with 10 men for 57 minutes after a Jeff Agoos red
card. The U.S. won over the crowd, which shouted "Ole!" every time
an American touched the ball. Though his team qualified, Mexican
coach Bora Milutinovic was fired shortly thereafter.

Because the 2001 match was in the middle of the season, Arena
decided to fly in a day prior. The result: a 1-0 loss that was more
lopsided than the score indicated.

With extra preparation time this time around, Arena trained the
team at high altitude in Colorado Springs and played Honduras in
Albuquerque, a 1-0 triumph the previous Saturday.

"I don't think that any of our players will be fully acclimated to
this altitude because there is not enough time," Arena said. "I think
that is also the case with the Mexico players. Let's not kid ourselves,
they don't have players that are necessarily acclimated fully to playing at 7,000 feet. I think that it will be the case for both teams. The
balance for us? I think that I just have to be convinced that the players I put on the field Sunday can perform at their optimal level or
close to it. And, our domestic players do have an advantage because
they are eight or nine days ahead of our players from Europe.

However, our players from Europe getting a full week in at altitude will position themselves to play comfortably in Azteca."

Bolstered by its victory in Trinidad, the U.S. was playing with house money. A loss wouldn't be that devastating. A tie would be great and victory would be incredulous and probably mean the door for Mexican coach Ricardo LaVolpe. The Mexicans faced a must-win situation. They had expected to prevail at Azteca and wanted to avenge a humiliating 2-0 second-round defeat inflicted by the U.S. at the 2002 World Cup.

"We will step on that field Sunday trying to win," Arena said. "I'm not certain that there have been many U.S. teams in the past that really believed that. I don't think I have to convince any of our players that we can win that game and that's the swagger that we do carry into the game. We've had a lot of success. We've done very well since 2002 and I just think that there's a confidence and a momentum our players have when they step on the field each and every game."

Mexico exacted a measure of revenge for its second-round elimination by the United States in the 2002 World Cup by recording a hard-fought 2-1 victory at Azteca.

The Mexicans struck for both their goals within a 90-second span in the opening half before an estimated crowd of 105,000.

Mexico (2-0-0, six points) took the CONCACAF final-round lead with six points as the U.S. dropped to 1-1-0 and three points with Guatemala looming in Birmingham, Ala. on Wednesday.

The Americans still couldn't beat their rivals in Mexico, dropping to 0-22-1 lifetime south of the Rio Grande. They also had a pair of long unbeaten streaks snapped—a 16-game streak against all comers (11-0-5) since a loss in the Netherlands in February, 2004 and a 31-game streak (24-0-7) against CONCACAF foes dating back to a 2-1 home qualifying defeat to Costa Rica in September, 2001.

"Any way you look at it, altitude was a big factor," Arena said. "I believe our players shut down in the last 15 minutes of the first half and it cost us the game. Our goal at halftime was to get a goal back in the first 15 minutes and we did that, and we positioned ourselves to perhaps get a point from the game.

"We were the only team in this competition that had their first two games on the road. If you had asked if I would be happy that we had three points after two games, I would say yes."

The U.S. had surrendered only one goal in its previous eight matches (6-1-1) against Mexico before the fatal two minutes.

"I was surprised by the U.S. defense, how they played as badly as they did today," Mexican defender Carlos Salcido told **Reuters**. "I have seen some of their games and they played so much better before. We had so much more of the ball and were allowed to do so much with it."

Striker Jared Borgetti, who connected for the lone goal in Mexico's 1-0 qualifying victory over the U.S. at Azteca in July, 2001, struck in the 31st minute, heading in a header from Jaime Lozano. Jose Fonseca maneuvered past the defense and left the ball for Lozano, who headed the ball into the center, where Borgetti headed it home from close range.

"When they got the first one in, I think we just died a little," Donovan told **Associated Press**.

Borgetti wound up in the middle of things a little more than a minute later, winning a long ball and heading it to Antonio Naelson, who beat Keller for a two-goal bulge. "That was a really poor goal, one that I'm sure that we'll see two or three times in the next couple of days to try to fix that," Keller said told AP.

Added Lewis, who scored the lone American goal: "We sort of committed our big sin in Mexico City by just dropping off and letting them have the game. We started too tentatively, too conservatively; I think we gave Mexico too much respect."

The Americans tried to make a game of it early in the second half and their efforts paid off with a Lewis score from 12 yards off a Donovan feed in the 59th minute.

The goal broke a 455-minute scoreless streak at Azteca spanning more than 20 years or since Perry Van Der Beck's goal in a 2-1 friendly loss on Oct. 17, 1984.

Donovan, who played so well in the U.S.'s 1-0 friendly win over Mexico in April, 2004, was relatively ineffective in this encounter.

With the game on the line in the final minutes, Arena made several substitutions in an attempt to revitalize the attack. He replaced Mastroeni with Ralston in the 69th minute, Bocanegra with forward Pat Noonan in the 76th minute and defender Cherundolo with McBride in the 83rd minute.

But they really didn't make much difference as Mexico held the ball for long periods of time in the final 15 minutes, forcing corner kick after corner kick.

"We were always taking the initiative," said LaVolpe, who received a congratulatory call from Mexican president Vicente Fox. "For 90 minutes, there was only one team on the field. We weren't lucky enough to make it a blowout."

Beasley was awarded a yellow card in the 37th minute after fouling Mexican captain Rafael Marquez at midfield. It was Beasley's second yellow of the final round of qualifying, meaning he would sit out Wednesday's encounter against Guatemala in Birmingham, Ala.

La Volpe was given his marching orders by referee Rodolfo Sibrian in the 41st minute apparently after criticizing game officials. His assistant coaches, which included former Mexican international and ex-Los Angeles Galaxy and Chicago Fire goalkeeper Jorge Campos ran the team, apparently communicating with the banished LaVolpe via walkie-talkie.

CHAPTER

4

GAME THREE

GUATEMALA

Any thoughts of Sunday's loss in the high altitude of Mexico City damaging the confidence of the U.S. National Team were dispelled as the Americans secured a dominating 2-0 qualifying victory over Guatemala on March 31.

Johnson, who turned 21 the next day, continued his torrid scoring with his eighth international goal in as many matches and Ralston added a second-half score before 31,624 fans at Legion Field in Birmingham, Ala.

The win boosted the U.S. (2-1-0, six points) into second place in the final round behind leaders Mexico (2-0-1, seven), which played Panama (0-1-2, two) to a 1-1 draw in Panama City. Guatemala (four points) fell to 1-1-1. In the other qualifier, host Trinidad & Tobago (0-2-1, one), its World Cup hopes clinging by a thread, managed a scoreless tie with Costa Rica (1-1-1, four).

"It's funny. We played 15 or 16 games without losing," said Donovan, who set up Johnson's 11th-minute goal. "We have one really bad half, a bad five minutes in Mexico against a real good team. All of a sudden we're the worst team in CONCACAF. It makes for some peace and quiet for a week. We needed that."

The Americans dominated in just about every category. "We told our guys that at the end of the game we're going to look at all you guys," Arena said. "You're going to get graded for their performances. Basically on the night, the check is in the column on all 11 positions. We were the better team because we won every battle on the field. We're pleased. After three games, we wanted to have five points. We have six. We're a little bit ahead of the curve right now."

Early on, it seemed the game was played in Guatemala City because it seemed half the fans rooted for the visitors. "There were 110,000 rooting against us the other day," Arena said. "Now we have a real home-field advantage. We cut that number down by about 90,000."

Arena made three changes from Sunday's game, benching defender Gregg Berhalter for Cory Gibbs, subbing the injured Reyna with Ralston and replacing the suspended Beasley (two yellow cards) with Ching.

Despite attacking from the onset, the U.S. could muster only a 1-0 halftime lead on Johnson's 12-yard goal in the 11th minute after missing several close encounters. Donovan took a pass from Mastroeni and flicked a short heel pass to the onrushing Johnson, who took a couple of steps and sent a left-footed, 12-yard shot off the right crossbar and into the net past goalkeeper Richard Trigueno. "He did well to hold the ball," Arena said. "He took a little bit of pressure off of us."

The U.S. easily could have enjoyed a 4-0 halftime advantage, but the Americans couldn't shoot straight. Within a span of three minutes late in the half, Lewis fired a 10-yarder just wide right, Ralston missed from the top of the box wide left and Ching somehow placed an eight-yard volley wide right.

"You go in and you scratch your head," Arena said. "We could have had three goals at halftime. When you have a team like Guatemala who (Carlos) Ruiz who can pull off a play at any time. He might be able to sell a penalty kick, which he sure tried tonight. You never know. We're at fault for keeping them around too long. We took too long to get the second goal."

Ralston atoned for his miss in the 68th minute, scoring his third international goal. Lewis looped a left-wing cross into the penalty area that Johnson, flicked to Ralston. The New England Revolution midfielder then placed a five-yard shot over Trigueno.

Immediately after the match, Donovan boarded a corporate jet of Anschutz Entertainment Group, the L.A. Galaxy owners, so he could fly to Carson, Calif. The Galaxy the next day were going to announce his acquisition after a reported $1.3 million transfer from Bayer Leverkusen (Germany).

"It's been a fun week for me," Donovan sarcastically said. "It's been emotional."

Likewise for the dangerous Ruiz, held in check by defenders Gibbs and Oguchi Onyewu. Hours before the match an unhappy Ruiz discovered he had been traded by the Galaxy to F.C. Dallas for a player allocation that brought Donovan to the west coast club.

The physical Ruiz, who has scored 50 goals in 72 MLS and an equalizer vs. the U.S. in the 2002 qualifying competition, twice banged free kicks into the American defensive wall. "Our center backs were tremendous tonight," Arena said. "Ruiz is a handful. We won that battle."

And for one night the war.

GAME FOUR

COSTA RICA

As Arena has learned during his seven-year tenure, his team can run, but it certainly can't hide from the fervent supporters of its opponents in the U.S. in World Cup qualifiers. This time, however, it might be different. Arena hoped his team has found a safe haven in Salt Lake City, Utah for its World Cup qualifier against Costa Rica on June 3.

More than 32,000 tickets had been sold for the match at Rice-Eccles Stadium, with a possibility of a sellout. "All indications are that it will be a very favorable U.S. crowd," Arena said. "We really believe it's a large contingent of U.S. fans. In all the years I've done this, I don't recall too many games we've had a real, real home-field advantage. If that's the case on Saturday, that will be great because we need an edge."

Similar to what was done to Giants Stadium for the England-Colombia friendly several days prior, the Rice-Eccles artificial turf was covered with grass.

"Hopefully, everything falls into place and it becomes a real advantage for the U.S. team," Arena said.

The U.S. (2-1-0, six points) needed that edge with one of CONCACAF's perennially most difficult teams. And while Costa Rica had its third coach during qualifying in Alexandre Guimaraes, who directed the team in the 2002 World Cup, the Central Americans (1-1-1, four) were still very much alive and could do great damage to the U.S. hopes.

Arena expected Guimaraes to bring back some familiar faces, including Paolo Wanchope. "It's going to be positive for Costa Rica because they're bringing in a very experienced coach who has been through this process before and they're very familiar with the player pool," he said.

CHAPTER

4

Johnson, the team's leading scorer (seven goals in six qualifiers), and Beasley, who had been training on and off this week, were question marks and "day-to-day" with injuries, Arena said.

As it turned out, the U.S. didn't need Johnson. Donovan provided the offense and Keller supplied some timely saves, leading the U.S. to a 3-0 win. Donovan connected for two goals and set up a third by McBride. Keller made several superb second-half stops as the Americans (3-1-0, nine points) solidified their second-place position with a five-point lead over their nearest rival. Group leader Mexico (3-0-1, 10) won at Guatemala (1-2-1, four), 2-0, while Trinidad & Tobago (1-2-1, four) registered a 2-0 home win over Panama (0-2-2, two).

The victory was the first time the U.S. had registered a three-goal win over Costa Rica (1-2-1, four) in 24 matches. In fact, the U.S. had beaten its Central American foes by two or more goals only once—2-0 in Pasadena, Calif. on Feb. 2, 2002.

"I think we're very content with where we are," Donovan said. "We won our two home games and we snuck a win on the road in Trinidad. But you have to remember, it's still early. Last time I think we had 13 points after five games and we thought we were God's gift to the world. We're aware of that and we're more experienced this time."

Keller, 36, stood out and sometimes stood on his head in the second half as he earned his 16th qualifying victory in 28 appearances and his 38th international shutout in his 80-game career. He denied Jafet Soto's point-blank volley in the 47th minute, stopped

Soto's 59th-minute header when he reached behind and slapped the ball off to the side and denied Douglas Sequeira with another great effort in the 69th minute.

"What can I say? Kasey's reactions on the line are fantastic," Arena said. "He's still every bit as quick as he was five years ago. It's nice to see a guy like that who has dedicated himself as an athlete, his fitness is better now than it's probably ever been. I'm just happy that he has the opportunity to be our number one keeper. I know his aspirations are to play in a World Cup so, hopefully, we can make that happen."

Donovan struck for his 20th international goal in the sixth minute, firing home a Beasley feed from the top of the penalty area and past goalkeeper Alvaro Mesen despite Costa Rica having six players in the box before a near-sellout crowd of 40,586.

Donovan doubled the lead in the 62nd minute, knocking in a rebound of a McBride shot from two yards that was saved by Mesen. Donovan's tally was now at six goals and seven assists in 12 qualifying matches for Germany. "Landon did a great job," Arena said. "Obviously the first goal was a tremendous goal, opportunistic on the second goal, which was a big goal at a time where our opponents got after us. The second goal broke their backs."

While he was not credited with an assist, Donovan created the third goal, dribbling down the left side in the 87th minute. He passed to second-half sub Clint Dempsey, whose shot was stopped by Mesen. The rebound, however, went to McBride, who easily put in his 27th international goal from six yards. "The third goal, I think, is great to have because goal differential may be a factor at some point," Arena said.

In what probably was the most ill-advised play of the night, Sequeira was red-carded two minutes into stoppage time for a kicking Cherundolo with his studs up. He wound up with a three-game suspension.

GAME FIVE

PANAMA

There was little doubt the U.S. was playing on all cylinders. For the second consecutive game, the U.S. scored three goals and registered a 3-0 World Cup qualifying victory over Panama in Panama City (where they had struggled for a 1-1 draw nine months earlier) four

CHAPTER

4

days later, a year and a day to the start of the World Cup in Germany.

"We are the first team in this cycle to beat Panama at home," Arena said. "As critical as we are sometimes of our performances, getting a result like that is exceptional. The first goal was big, the second goal was terrific, and then Kasey Keller once again was tremendous. In most game reports, that will go unnoticed, but those three saves were tremendous. Overall, we did what we had to do. The back line played very well and we scored opportunistic goals."

The victory solidified the Americans' hold on second place (4-1-0, 12 points). Mexico (4-0-1, 13), 2-0 winners over Trinidad & Tobago, still was atop the group.

CHAPTER

4

Bocanegra started the scoring in the sixth minute. Donovan sent a corner kick into the penalty area. Bocanegra headed the ball off the crossbar and into the net.

"I just got up and got high on the ball and put it in," Bocanegra said. "It was a big goal, especially in a hostile environment. We knew we had to go and get goals and force them to chase the game. We got really confident after the third goal, but we knew anything could happen."

Donovan made it 2-0 in the 20th minute with his 21st international goal. Ralston crossed the ball into the box. Donovan won the challenge, heading the ball into the bottom left corner of the net. Donovan had collected at least a goal or assist in 12 of 13 qualifiers, a first in U.S. history.

McBride sealed the win in the 40th minute, his 28th international goal and his ninth career qualifying goal, tying him with Stewart for the all-time U.S. lead. McBride recovered the ball at the top of the area and beat goalkeeper Donaldo Gonzalez.

The U.S. received some interesting and good news on the eve of the CONCACAF Gold Cup, the confederation's biennial championship for National Teams, discovering it was ranked sixth in the world by FIFA, its highest rating. While those rankings certainly weren't the last word in seeding teams, they were among the top criteria when FIFA would determined the top eight seeds at the World Cup draw in Leipzig, Germany on Dec. 9. If the U.S. wound up among the elite eight, it meant one less super team to face such as defending champion and top-ranked Brazil, Argentina or Germany.

That could mean the difference between qualifying for the second round or going home early.

If Arena was impressed, he wasn't letting anyone know. "I think anywhere between sixth and 60th is appropriate," he said. "I think they picked a lower number this time. I don't know anything about that stuff, to be honest with you. I know nothing how you seed teams. And I don't really care. I don't know if that helps you, hurts you."

It certainly didn't hurt as the Americans jumped four spots past France, England, Portugal and Spain to move within three points of archrival Mexico.

CHAPTER

4

GAME SIX
TRINIDAD
& TOBAGO

The U.S. welcomed back a familiar face for its Aug. 17 encounter with Trinidad & Tobago in East Hartford, Conn.—Reyna. Reyna, whose English Premiership team, Manchester City, was preparing for its season opener on Saturday, had made only one international appearance to date in 2005, playing the entire way in the 2-1 loss in Mexico on March 27. However, the defense didn't look so solid because Arena was forced to take several more inexperienced players due to recent injuries suffered by Pope and Cherundolo and a suspension of Frankie Hejduk.

When they put together highlights of the U.S.'s Road to Germany, they probably will leave this clunker of a game out of the DVD. The Americans survived themselves, missed scoring opportunities and their inability to solve the defense despite enjoying a one-man advantage for about half the game in their 1-0 victory over T&T. The win—three more precious points—moved the U.S. (5-1-0, 15 points) closer to an unprecedented fifth consecutive Cup appearance.

"We are guilty of perhaps making things difficult for ourselves," said Arena, citing several botched scoring opportunities. "That allowed Trinidad to stay around for 89 minutes."

The U.S. faced a unique situation of clinching with a win over archrival Mexico in the seventh out of 10 games in Columbus, Ohio on Sept. 3. "Fifteen points after six games is as good as it gets," Arena said.

Reyna agreed. "It's a great opportunity for us to play Mexico and clinch it against our big rivals," he said. "I think everyone is looking forward to that already."

Keller, who wasn't severely tested, registered his fourth consecutive qualifying shutout as the Soca Warriors fell to 1-4-1.

It was one of those games in which the Americans' best player of the match—midfielder Bobby Convey—wasn't around at the end, falling victim to a red card after his second yellow in the 88th minute before a Rentscheler Field crowd of 25,488. Convey fouled Silvio Spann. Still, Convey was the midfield sparkplug, creating the lone goal only 91 seconds into the match. John O'Brien fed Convey down the left wing. Convey sent the ball into the penalty area to an onrushing McBride, who slipped the ball past goalkeeper Kelvin Jack from

Eddie Pope defending against Costa Rica's Ronald Gomez

three yards.

It was McBride's 29th international goal and 10th qualifying goal, becoming the all-time leader in the latter category. It also was the second fastest qualifying score in U.S. history. Forward Ante Razov, now with C.D. Chivas USA (MLS), connected 74 seconds into a 2-0 victory over Trinidad on June 20, 2001.

Yet, the U.S. played as though it was content with just one goal and struggled finishing its opportunities.

"We're getting criticized for scoring late goals and for scoring early goals," Arena said. "That's all fair in love and war."

Added Reyna: "We said in the locker room that if we could get the second, it could have been four or five. The longer the game went on and it stayed 1-0, we kind of dropped off a bit."

The U.S. was aided by Dennis Lawrence's red card in the 41st minute for impeding Donovan's progress just outside the penalty area, but couldn't put this one away.

Due to injuries and suspension, Arena was forced to deploy a make-shift backline of Berhalter, Chris Albright, Onyewu and Lewis, a midfielder in his first international appearance at left fullback. Only Onyewu could be considered a regular, but T&T hardly threatened.

GAME SEVEN

MEXICO

Only four days prior to the Mexican clash, Arena had a message for American soccer fans: It was time to put up or shut up. Speaking on a conference call, Arena said that American soccer fans must support the game more, whether it be the National Team or MLS.

The qualifier in Columbus, Ohio was sold out in 20 minutes, but the match would be seen on ESPN Classic and not on the better known ESPN or ESPN2 because the college football season kicked off that weekend.

"I'm happy it is live on an English-speaking channel," Arena said. "I'll be honest with you, it is the job for supporters of soccer in this country to be better supporters of the game. When we demonstrate ratings, we will have an argument for prime time.

"I can see both sides of it. I understand where television is coming from. I understand where supporters are coming from. But the bottom line is television companies don't put these games on as non-profit exercises. And I think it's time that the American public that supports the sport of soccer steps forward and supports our game by watching on television, getting ratings, by attending games in the stands, and by buying soccer products - being good consumers as we see in other sports, whether it's college football, the NBA, what have you. It's time for us to put up or shut up."

Arena wasn't finished. "I think it's critical," he said. "If we want this sport to grow, if we want to truly position ourselves to one day win a World Cup, we need support from the people that follow soccer in the United States."

You could have played this game on the moon and the ongoing rivalry between the two North American sides wouldn't abate one iota.

In fact, the U.S. was on the verge of qualifying for Germany with three games to spare. And accomplishing that rare feat against Mexico would be icing on the cake.

"That would be absolutely a storybook ending," Donovan said. "We're going to do everything we can to make that happen."

Arena wasn't taking anything for granted. "Last time around we were 4-0-1 going into game six in Mexico City and lost there, then lost against Honduras and Costa Rica and we were 4-3-1, so I'm not counting on anything right now and I'm not commenting on anything," he said. "Until you can show me that mathematically we're qualified to go to Germany, I don't have any comment on it. It may go down to game 10 for all I know."

The U.S. certainly could not have picked out a better venue than Columbus Crew Stadium. The Americans were 3-0-3 there (eight goals for, one against), including a stunning 2-0 triumph over Mexico in 29° cold on Feb. 28, 2001.

Mexico hadn't beaten the U.S. in a qualifier on American soil since a 2-1 win in Los Angeles in September, 1972. Since then, the U.S. had a 2-0-2 home qualifying record vs. its rivals.

"The reason I know how special this game is, is on Sunday night, full week before the game, I was already thinking about the game laying in bed," Donovan said. "And I never do that. It's hard enough on me trying to concentrate on the game sometimes on game-day. And I was already thinking about it, what I'm doing to do and how I'm going to play. How it's going to feel when we win. That says it all."

Both teams were confident they were going to win.

"I hope they respect us," Donovan said. "And if they don't, they can keep learning. Sooner or later they have to figure out that we are someone to be reckoned with and that we, right now, deserve to be the best team in this region. We've earned it and we deserve it."

Mexican striker Jared Borgetti, who had been a thorn in the Americans' side in a pair of qualifying wins in Mexico City, threw some trash talk the U.S.'s way. "They always only go for the counter-attack," he told the Mexican newspaper Reforma. "One has to criticize their style of play because it's ugly. We already know how the U.S. plays. They base their soccer on organization and they kick long balls to try to create danger on a counterattack. I don't expect a spectacular game or anything along those lines because the U.S. is going to play a tight game."

Asked if he thought the U.S. was better than his team, Mexico coach Ricardo La Vople told the Mexican newspaper Esto: "Ha. Well they didn't demonstrate it in the last game and in Olympic qualifying they ate up four goals. Besides that there is the last game we played. We've only lost one game and that was a friendly in the 93rd minute off of a header."

Mexico was without three starters. Defender Salvador Carmona and midfielder Aaron Galindo were suspended after testing positive in June for nandrolone. Team captain and midfielder Pavel Pardo was serving a one-game ban for yellow-card accumulation.

The U.S. was without several regulars as well. Defenders Pope and Cherundolo and midfielder O'Brien were sidelined with injuries. Manchester United backup goalkeeper Tim Howard, whose wife was expecting their first child, remained in Manchester, England.

The Americans got back Johnson, who missed the Trinidad win with a toe injury, midfielders Beasley (hamstring) and Mastroeni (sprained ankle) and defender Bocanegra (knee). Johnson hadn't played in qualifying since March and wasn't totally fit.

"I think we need to be patient with Eddie," Arena said. "He's just starting to come back, He's only played a couple of games since his injury in late May, so he's not completely in form at the moment."

But the U.S. was on that Saturday night. In fact, when they're not playing Mexico at Azteca Stadium, the Americans had discovered they have the Mexicans' number.

Actually, it's two numbers—two and zero as in 2-0. That was the score of the U.S. qualifying victory over Mexicans in 2001. That also was the final of the Americans' stunning second-round triumph at the 2002 World Cup.

And not surprisingly, it also was the result of the Sept. 3 qualifier that boosted the U.S. into its unprecedented fifth World Cup in Columbus, again. Goals by Ralston and Beasley early in the second half lifted the U.S. to victory in front of a packed house of 24,685.

"They suck," a gloating Donovan said after a champagne party in the U.S. locker room. "I'm so happy, man. They made it a little bit easier on us. I expected more. After we got the first one, they were never in the game. The only thing sweeter would have been to score. At least for three or four more years they will shut up and can't say anything and I love it."

For the first time since 1934, when it defeated Mexico, 4-2, for the lone spot in the region, the U.S. became the first team from CONCACAF to book a spot in the Cup. "That's fantastic," Arena said.

The U.S. (6-1-0, 18 points) hadn't lost to Mexico (5-1-1, 16) in a home qualifier since 1972 and raised its record at the stadium to 4-0-3. Moreover, the U.S. was unbeaten in seven consecutive home games vs. the Mexicans since 2000, outscoring its foes, 11-0.

As it turned out, the U.S. ended its qualifying quest at the same stadium where it began it in June, 2004, when defeating Grenada, 3-0. This time it took the Americans seven out of 10 games to clinch, as opposed to nine games in 2001.

"It's difficult," said Arena, who directed the U.S. to the 2002 Cup as well. "You look at it and you'll say it's a breeze and it wasn't a breeze. Every game has been difficult, but I think our experiences over the last four years has positioned us to be successful. Our guys know how to win in big games."

So, by dispatching Mexico while qualifying for the World Cup, can the U.S. win the whole thing?

"I mean, let's not get carried away," Donovan said. "We beat

Mexico."

The he made an 180-degree turn. "Sure, why not? Why can't we? Of course we could," he said. "Bruce made a good comment: We qualified and that's great. But let's get better over the next seven months."

After a scoreless first half, the U.S. found a way to break the Mexican defense. "The first half was sluggish," Donovan said. "We didn't play so great. After the halftime, we got a little momentum and we started to get some free kicks in good areas. You knew that if we got a goal, that they would be dead."

The U.S. snapped a scoreless tie in the 53rd minute on Ralston's fourth international goal. Lewis, playing defense again, sent a 35-yard free kick into the penalty area that the tall Onyewu headed off the left post. The ball came to Ralston, who headed it home from point-blank range for his second goal of the qualifying campaign. "It was probably the easiest goal I've ever scored," he said.

Beasley gave the Americans a two-goal advantage in the 58th minute as the PSV Eindhoven midfielder connected from 10 yards. Beasley started it with a short corner kick to Donovan, who played it to Reyna. Reyna then fed Beasley for his 12th international goal.

"We've done that six games in a row," Donovan said. "I don't know if they were sleeping or if their coach wasn't paying attention. They didn't mark Claudio. He said yesterday in training if he makes that pass and goes, they might not follow him. It makes them look stupid, which is good."

At the other end of the field, Onyweu held Borgetti in check. Borgetti was rendered virtually useless by the 23-year-old defender. "Gooch is a great young player," Arena said. "Obviously his physical presence is fantastic. You see a player like Borgetti today and he's bouncing off Gooch for 90 minutes."

Keller, who recorded his fifth consecutive qualifying shutout as his scoreless streak reached 507 minutes, was called on to make one difficult save—a minute into first-half stoppage time after Berhalter fouled Francisco Fonseca 27 yards out. Ramon Morales powered the ensuing free kick toward the left post, but Keller dived to knock it out of bounds for a corner kick.

"We limited them to zero chances, which is great," Reyna said.

"They're a great attacking team. Probably the bigger plus was how well we defended more so than how we attacked."

With his team's mission accomplished, Arena allowed virtually the entire European contingent to return home to train with their European clubs, while recalling MLS players who were allowed to return to their teams for the previous week's matches.

Gone from the team are Keller, Berhalter, Reyna, Beasley and McBride. The Reading duo of Convey and goalkeeper Marcus Hahnemann was all that remained of the Euro-based players for the Guatemala encounter.

Goalkeeper Matt Reis, defenders Chad Marshall and Vanney were recalled from their MLS clubs. Kansas City Wizards defender Nick Garcia was the only new addition to the original training camp roster in Columbus.

"It gives the coach a real chance to look at some other players in games that matter," Berhalter said.

The game was meaningless for the U.S., although Guatemala was still battling for a spot. But for players on the bubble for next year's the 23-man roster, the three remaining matches were vital to make their case. The candidates included the New England Revolution forward Taylor Twellman, Ralston and Dempsey and Reis, among others.

"This is a fantastic opportunity for this group to demonstrate they can perform in this type of environment," said Arena. "Can they win a game where the home team is desperate, the crowd is against them, and the conditions are difficult? Players that can do that are the kind of players that can possibly help your team in a World Cup. It's a great chance for them to prove that."

Guatemala City was hardly a proving ground for the U.S. In only four days, the Americans went from a side that clinched a Cup berth to one that was a spoiler.

They certainly had their chances, but couldn't finish them. They remained unbeaten in eight games (4-0-4) against the Central American side. While the U.S. (6-1-1, 19 points) earned a tie with its sixth consecutive qualifying shutout, the Guatemalans had to leave Mateo Flores Stadium much more frustrated, realizing they had squandered two precious points in their bid to finish third.

The U.S.'s best opportunity came in the 80th minute when a six-yard header from Johnson, a second-half sub, went wide of the near right post. Johnson put his hands on his head, realizing he missed a golden opportunity.

"It was a good ball by Landon, but it's like a kid in a candy store," Johnson told the Associated Press. "I was already thinking about my celebration before I even headed the ball."

The Guatemalans had their best chance in the 90th minute when Edwin Villatoro fired a shot that left the left post. The rebound by Carlos Figueroa sailed over the crossbar.

"Both teams had chances in the second half," Arena said. "I thought our team had a much improved effort in the last 45 minutes. The rule of thumb in qualifying is that if you get a point on the road, you have done well. I'm satisfied with the result. It is always difficult to play on the road, and we made 11 changes to the team that played against Mexico."

GAME NINE
COSTA RICA

It was a good thing that the Oct. 8 qualifier in San Jose, Costa Rica didn't mean much to the U.S. in terms of booking a spot in Germany because the team was forced off schedule thanks to Mother Nature. It was business as usual when the team left its Miami hotel at 2:45 p.m. on Thursday. That all changed when one of the staff members was briefly left behind and the journey quickly became anything but normal.

The charter flight took off for San Jose with an expected arrival time of about 7 p.m. But about an hour out of San Jose, Costa Rica ground control informed the pilots that bad weather in San Jose made landing impossible at the moment. Deciding to head to Panama City to refuel and wait out the storm, the charter touched down about 6:30 p.m.

After three hours, the decision was made to stay in Panama City for the night. But there was one problem. A chicken and egg convention had booked nearly every room in the city. However, with the help of the Intercontinental Hotel in Panama City, the team found accommodations in the jungle resort town of Gamboa, about an hour from the airport.

The U.S. eventually arrived in San Jose, although the less said about the game the better. Carlos Hernandez scored two goals as Costa Rica became the third CONCACAF nation to qualify for World Cup with a 3-0 win over the U.S. at Saprissa Stadium on Oct. 8, The Americans have never won in Costa Rica in eight attempts (0-6-2).

The U.S. left its offense home. The defense didn't fare much better, often looking disorganized in front Howard.

Costa Rica controlled the flow of play for much of the first half, and finally broke through in the 34th minute. Alvaro Saborio got through the defense on a long ball and attemped a point-blank shot on a charging Howard. The rebound found Paulo Wanchope, who finished into an open net.

CHAPTER

4

GAME TEN

PANAMA

It took him 14 games, but Twellman finally scored his first international goal as the U.S. closed out its qualifying campaign with a 2-0 workmanlike victory over Panama at Gillette Stadium in Foxboro, Mass. on Oct. 12.

Martino and Twellman scored their first international goals, Martino in the 53rd minute and Twellman in the 59th minute. Twellman, the MLS scoring champion, ended an extremely long drought for an international striker."It was nice to win the game and to finally contribute, it's nice," Twellman told **ESPN2**. "The first one is always the hardest. My job is to be a target forward and help the team. To score goals is great.

"The first one is always the hardest one. I just wanted to make sure the goalie didn't punch me in the head. He grazed me."

While the offense sputtered in the first half, Howard enjoyed a relatively easy night in goal, except when he faced a penalty kick in the 87th minute after Ching was judged to have handled the ball in the penalty area with his left hand while trying to trap it with his chest. Panamanian legend Julio Dely Valdez took the spot kick,. But after forcing Howard to dive the wrong way, Valdez placed his kick wide of the left post to keep the score at 2-0.

The win gave the U.S. the top spot and it was the first time since the region went to a six-team final qualifying round that the Americans finished first.

"It was nice to finish first, but it was not critical, it was a good accomplishment for our team," said Arena, whose team was level on points with Mexico, but the U.S. had a plus-one goal differential in head-to-head matches with the Mexicans to give the Americans to first place.

LABOR AGREEMENT   As it turned out, there was one other hurdle to overcome—a players. There will be no strikes by the U.S. National Team or lockouts by U.S. Soccer before this World Cup. On. Dec. 19, 2005, U.S. Soccer and the U.S. National Soccer Team Players' Association announced they had reached a five-year collective bargaining agreement that takes them through the 2010 Cup.

"We are pleased to have reached an agreement with the U.S. National Soccer Players' Association on a collective bargaining agreement through the 2010 FIFA World Cup," Contiguglia said in a statement. "We have been confident throughout this process that an amicable agreement would be reached that would positively address the desires of both parties, and that is what we have accomplished together. Our focus now, as it has always been, is to move forward and continue our preparation for the 2006 FIFA World Cup in Germany."

Levinstein, the USSTPA executive director, had similar senti-ments. "The players are pleased that they will continue to prepare for the 2006 World Cup with an agreement in place that benefits both sides," he said in a statement. "We hope this agreement will be the first step in bringing together the millions of individuals and many organizations that support soccer in the United States to work to advance our sport."

While it is unlikely, the U.S. players, as a group, would receive $15.7 million from U.S. Soccer if they won every game en route to the World Cup championship in Germany. That didn't include indi-vidual incentives such as appearance and roster spot bonuses.

Adding in all of the bonuses, each of the twenty-three American players could receive $748,533, if the shares were divided twenty-three ways.

Here were some of the highlights of the agreement obtained from U.S. Soccer:

⊕ As a group, the players will receive a $1.35 million bonus for qualifying for Germany.

⊕ Each player earning a roster spot will receive a $37,500 bonus and an appearance fee of $3,750 per match.

⊕ If the U.S. wins the World Cup, the players, as a group, will receive $3.75 million, $3 million for reaching the final and $500,000 for winning the third-place match.

⊕ In the first round, the players will receive, as a group, $150,000 for every draw and $450,000 for wins. They will receive $2.775 million for reaching the second round, another $2.25 million for advancing to the quarterfinals and another $2.625 million for advancing to the semifinals.

⊕ For the 2010 WC, numbers in most of the above categories will go up by a flat percentage increase to be determined based on the team's performance in Germany. The range of the increase will be from 22.5 percent (elimination in the first round) to 35 percent (winning the World Cup).

⊕ For friendlies, qualifiers and tournaments other than the World Cup, players receive an appearance fee of $3,000 per game.

⊕ For friendlies, players earn bonuses for victories and draws ranging from $750 to $5,250 depending on level of opponent and depending if it is a win or a tie.

⊕ For non-World Cup tournaments, players earn bonuses for triumphs and ties, and in some instances for winning or placing in the tournament. Since each competition is different. Bonuses will vary depending on the level of the foe and significance of the tourney.

⊕ For World Cup qualifiers, players will earn bonuses for wins and draws ranging from $1,350 to $6,000, depending on the level of the opponent.

U. S. Player Profiles
—Meet The U.S. Team

In a perfect world, the U.S. National Team's starting lineup would look something like this:

Kasey Keller in goal, Eddie Lewis or Chris Albright and Oguchi Onyewu, Eddie Pope and Steve Cherundolo and defense, Chris Armas, Claudio Reyna, DaMarcus Beasley and Landon Donovan in the midfield and Brian McBride and Eddie Johnson up top.

So, during the U.S.'s eighteen-game qualifying run, just how many times did coach Bruce Arena have their perfect starting eleven? Not once.

Like it or not, there are injuries, suspensions and players being out of form, whether it is fitness or age catching up to legs that have ran thousands of miles. Yet, saying that, Arena is quite comfortable with his team.

"I think I can come close to naming 23 players today," he said at the WC draw Leipzig, Germany in December 2005. "However, there are a number of issues like there always are. Some players have injuries right now. What are some of the MLS players going to look like coming back from break? And how quickly will they get into form? It's a little bit difficult right now."

The mantra is a simple: Stay healthy. Stay healthy.

The U.S.'s Achilles Heel? Depth. The top 11 to 16 players are solid. But once you get into injuries at key positions, such as holding and defensive midfielder and forward, the depth could wear thin a bit. In fact, Arena has been forced to find healthy bodies for the defensive midfielder roll as several key players went down with injuries.

"If healthy, we're OK," Arena said. "Once we start losing players, we have problems."

In the months leading up the competition, Arena discovered that first hand as midfielders Armas, Reyna and Pablo Mastroeni and defender Albright were sidelined at one time or another.

- ⊕ Armas, who missed the 2002 World Cup with an ACL tear, had worked his way back to top form before he tore another ACL during an MLS playoff game between his Chicago Fire and D.C. United in October. He was expected to be sidelined from five to six months, which would put him back into action in late March or early April, just about when Arena would make his final roster selections.
- ⊕ Reyna (Manchester City, England), the captain of the 2002 WC squad, was sidelined from six to eight weeks after he was diagnosed with a broken right ankle just before New Years.
- ⊕ Mastroeni (Colorado Rapids, MLS) was sidelined seven weeks after partially tearing his left quadriceps during practice at the Home Depot Center in Carson, Calif. on Jan. 9.
- ⊕ Albright (Los Angeles Galaxy, MLS) missed three to five weeks with a torn meniscus on his left knee after suffering the injury during National Team training camp in early January.

GOAL
KEEPERS

The Americans' strength are their goalkeepers. Brad Friedel (Blackburn, England), the squad's best player four years ago, has retired from international soccer, but the U.S. hasn't missed a beat in goal.

Outside of an injury or some other crisis, Keller (Borussia Moenchengladbach, Germany) will start. He has the experience and nerves to handle pressure situations. Keller will be attending his fourth World Cup, but playing in only his second. He was in the nets for the first two opening-round loss at France '98. He was in the running to start in Korea four years later before an injury made Arena's choice much easier.

Marcus Hanhemann (Reading FC) is the No. 2 man with either Tony Meola (MetroStars, MSL) or Tim Howard (Manchester United, England) battling it out for the third spot. It depends on Arena's priorities. In Meola, Arena gets a seasoned keeper (37-years-old) who has been around the World Cup block (starter in 1990 and 1994 and No. 3 in 2002). In Howard, he gets a younger (27) and more athletic keeper. Arena, however, likes to use players who are in form and who are playing regularly. Howard has sat the United bench for most of the English Premiership season behind Dutch international Edwin Van der Sar.

This appeared to be Arena's biggest pre-Cup priority: Finding the right set of defenders. It could depend on which system he felt was most appropriate—a 3-5-2 or 4-4-2.

Cherundolo (Hannover 96, Germany) appears to have the right fullback position locked up, although several players are vying on the left side, including Eddie Lewis (Leeds United, England), who has forged a reputation as a superb crosser at midfield) and MLS all-star Albright, who can play either wing, and Todd Dunivant (Los Angeles), who was quite impressive in his international debut in the winter of 2006. Frankie Hejduk (Columbus Crew, MLS), a veteran of two World Cups can play in the back or midfield on the right side, depending what strategy Arena might deploy.

Onyewu (Standard de Leige, Belgium), a 6-4, 210-lb. defender who manhandled and stifled Mexican Jared Borgetti in the U.S.'s 2-0 Cup berth clinching win over Mexico, is a strong candidate for the central spot. He barely had a dozen caps through the winter, so it would be wise using him with a more experienced player such as Eddie Pope (Real Salt Lake, MLS), who struggled during qualifying to secure his reputation as the best defender in American history, Gregg Berhalter (Energie Cottbus, Germany) or Cory Gibbs (ADO Den Haag, Netherlands).

Carlos Bocanegra (Fulham, England), who also can play an outside position, also are available. Jimmy Conrad (Kansas City Wizards), the MLS 2005 defender of the year, most likely would wind up on the team if players were out of form or injured. Jonathan Spector (Charlton Athletic, England) also has fought his way into the picture as potential backup.

If healthy, Reyna and Mastroeni are the obvious choices in the central holding midfield roles, with Beasley (PSV Eindhoven, Netherlands) or Lewis (if he doesn't wind up on defense) on the left side. Beasley looks like an easy mark due to his size (5-8, 145 lbs; he looks thinner than that). But he has become one tough cookie, being able to thwart dangerous tackles with his speed, quickness and skill and being able to bounce back from a rough takedown.

John O'Brien (ADO Den Haag, Netherlands) is one of the most talented players in American soccer history and one of the key performers in Korea four years ago. However, his history of being injury prone cannot allow Arena to pencil him into any lineup.

Arena is still looking for a right-side starter. Beasley or Donovan can play there. So can Steve Ralston (New England Revolution, MLS), a dangerous crosser, or even Hejduk in a defensive role. Clint Dempsey (New England Revolution, MLS) can play several midfield roles, but may be too young and inexperienced to start. He could come off the bench.

If the injury jinx continues at the defensive/holding slots, then Kerry Zavagnin (Kansas City Wizards, MLS) or Ben Olsen (D.C. United, MLS) could very well find themselves in the mix. While Armas would be a welcome addition, he is considered to be a long shot to make the team, given his age (33), the severity of his injury and the time he would need to return to top form.

CHAPTER

5

FORWARDS

Donovan, who helped the Los Galaxy capture the 2005 MLS Cup after an unsuccessful return and short stint with Bayer Leverkusen (Germany), has the ability to change the course of matches and make life miserable for opposing defenders and midfielders with his precision passes and sharp shooting. He is a major key to the U.S. success. If he enjoys a good Cup, the Americans could go very far. If he doesn't, it could be three and out. Donovan might be most dangerous running at people from the midfield (ask Mexico in the U.S.'s 1-0 win in April, 2004), but might wind up at forward if there is a glut of players in the midfield.

McBride (Fulham, England) was one of the American stars four years ago, and while he is "old" for a World Cup forward (he turns 34 on June 19), Arena still will look for him for goals and leadership.

After that, things are not as certain.

Johnson (Kansas City Wizards, MLS) came on like gangbusters in his first eight international matches, especially in CONCACAF qualifiers, before injuries slowed him down. If healthy, he could be a force, thanks to his speed. But the 22-year-old will have to raise his game a notch or two in the World Cup. After all, Italy and the Czech Republic are not Panama or El Salvador.

Josh Wolff is another fast forward who has an Olympics (Sydney 2000) and a World Cup (2002) under his belt. He is fast and cunning and should be an important role player. Brian Ching (Houston 1836, MLS) grabbed headlines with some goal-scoring heroics during the early days of World Cup qualifying in 2004, but has struggled internationally since.

Taylor Twellman (New England, MLS), on the other hand, has come on strong and gained momentum in recent months. Twellman, the MLS MVP and scoring champion, became only the ninth U.S. player to record an international hat-trick in the 5-0 thrashing of what was essentially Norway B team in Carson, Calif. on Jan. 29, and while the Norway B team is nowhere near the quality of the Italian or Czech sides, confidence is a big deal to strikers, even to someone like Twellman.

Although he hasn't filled the net, Twellman's Revolution team-mate, Pat Noonan, also has impressed Arena with his passing overall performance. Noonan was named to the U.S. roster for its March 1 encounter against Poland in Kaiserslautern, Germany.

And as for the much-hyped Freddy Adu making the squad (he turns 17 on June 2), it is a long shot, barring the teenager enjoying a marvelous spring for D.C. United (if he did play in the World Cup, he would be the youngest performer ever). Adu, who complained about his lack of playing time in the 2005 MLS playoffs with United (and subsequently was suspended by the club), made his international debut in the 80th minute of the scoreless tie with Canada on Jan. 22, 2006. For all the talent and potential that Adu has, he hasn't been a regular for the MLS club in his first two seasons. He needs time to develop.

"It's hard to be on the national team when you're not a regular starter for your club team," Adu told **MLSnet.com** in February, 2006. "I just want to be a regular starter and keep playing games. You get better by playing games and you get better by playing a lot of games and that's what I'm hoping to do. Hopefully I'll make an impression."

United States team (statistics through Feb. 28, 2006)

Chris Albright
Defender
6-foot-1, 185 pounds
Born: Jan. 14, 1979
Hometown: Philadelphia, Pa.
Club team: Los Angeles Galaxy (MLS)
International appearances: 18
Goals: 1

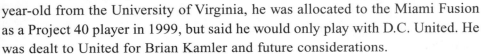

Not only has Albright made the transition from forward to an attacking role, he has made an impact as an outside fullback in MLS and is in the running for a starting spot on the World Cup team.

CHAPTER

5

When Albright joined the league as a 20-year-old from the University of Virginia, he was allocated to the Miami Fusion as a Project 40 player in 1999, but said he would only play with D.C. United. He was dealt to United for Brian Kamler and future considerations.

However, things did not pan out for Albright with United. In fact, his early days were a disaster. He recorded but four goals and two assists in 39 starts over 56 games over three seasons before he was dealt to the L.A. Galaxy in exchange for some MLS SuperDraft picks. Albright's attacking miseries continued, netting only an assist in nine starts over 15 matches during an injury-plagued season. They continued in 2003:three goals, and four assists in 23 games. Coach Sigi Schmid moved him to the backline prior to the 2004 season and he hasn't looked back since. In fact, Albright has excelled on defense, becoming one of the league's top defenders and achieving all-star recognition.

On the international front, Albtight started all four matches for the U.S. Under-20 team at the 1999 FIFA World Youth Championships in 1999, and also started all six U.S. matches at the 2000 Sydney Olympics, recording two goals and an assist.

Albright, who has played on two MLS Cup championship sides (with the Galaxy in 2002 and 2005), made his international debut in a 2-2 tie with Jamaica in Kingston, Jamaica on September 8, 1999. He came on as a substitute in the 78th minute and scored the equalizer minutes later. Ironically, it was his only international goal.

According to the MLS Players Union, Albright earned $97,500 in 2005.

He is married to Leah.

DaMarcus Beasley

Midfielder
5-foot-8, 145 pounds
Born: May 24, 1982
Hometown: Fort Wayne, Ind.
Club team: PSV Eindhoven (Netherlands)
International appearances: 54
Goals: 12

Beasley has three gears—fast, faster and fastest. He has used his speed to ignite the Chicago Fire, and the National Team on two levels—the Under-17 and the full squad in Korea in 2002. Now he utilizes it for PSV Eindhoven (Netherlands), after a reported $2.4 million transfer to the Dutch club. "Once he gets a step on you, he'll get by you," said Fire coach David Sarachan, an assistant coach on the 2002 World Cup team.

Beasley was one of the American revelations in Korea. "Against Korea and Poland, they put faster guys on me," Beasley said. "They knew I had some skill and that I could play, so they wanted to make sure I was put on lockdown."

Beasley has become an impact player for PSV. In his Eredivisie debut, he scored in a 5-2 victory at RBC Roosendaal. In the 2004-05 season, Beasley connected for 10 goals, including four in the Champions League. Through late February, 2006 Beasley had four goals in 18 games for the Dutch First Division leaders (19-3-2 at the time). Beasley bristles when asked about his slight stature. When he gets knocked down, Beasley gets right up again. The best revenge is living well, or in this case, scoring or setting up a goal.

Coaches around Europe have taken notice. After PSV's 1-0 stunner over A.C. Milan in November, 2005, the Italian coach, Carlo Ancelotti praised Beasley. "Beasley and (Jeffersen) Farfan troubled us with their lively play," he said.

Beasley and Landon Donovan are the two most important players on the U.S. National Team. If either player goes down, so will the Americans' hopes of advancing to the second round and beyond.

Beasley earned his first cap against China on January 27, 2001. He scored his first international goal against Korea on January 19, 2002.

He is single.

CHAPTER
5

Gregg Berhalter

Defender
6-foor-1, 175 pounds
Born: Aug. 1, 1973
Hometown: Tenafly, N.J.
Club team: Energie Cottbus (Germany)
International appearances: 42
Goals: 0

He is not one of the flashiest of players and his name might not be mentioned as a possible starter. Yet, Gregg Berhalter has endured and toiled for the National Team for 10 years.

Ironically, Berhalter might be best remembered for his involvement on a pair of vital hand balls—one in qualifying and another in the World Cup itself. In July 2000, he was called for a handball that led to a Costa Rican penalty kick in the waning minutes of a 2-1 qualifying loss in San Jose, Costa Rica, even if he did not intentionally handle the ball.

In the 2002 World Cup quarterfinals, Berhalter fired a shot heading for the back of the German goal that was stopped by the hand of defender Torsten Frings. But the referee did not call a hand ball and Germany managed to hold on to win, 1-0. The Germans eventually reached the championship game, where they fell to Brazil, 2-0. The Americans went home.

Strong on the tackle and good in the air, Berhalter was a high school teammate of Claudio Reyna at St. Benedict's Prep in Newark, N.J. He decided to leave the University of North Carolina a year early to play professionally in the Netherlands. It was a decision he has not regretted. He performed for F.C. Zwolle, Sparta Rotterdam and Cambuur Leeuwarden for over six seasons. Berhalter had several injuries, including torn ankle ligaments, a broken ankle, a back injury, a broken jaw and a broken fifth metatarsal bone in his right foot.

Berhalter, whose brother Jay is deputy executive director of U.S. Soccer, also played for Crystal Palace (England) before signing with Energie Cottbus in August, 2002. He was captain of Cottbus for the 2004-05 season.

He made his international debut in a 2-1 loss to Saudi Arabia on October 19, 1994. He has yet to score a goal.

Berhalter is married to Rosalind and has a son, Sebastian, and a daughter, Santana.

Carlos Bocanegra

Defender
6-foot, 170 pounds
Born: May 25, 1979
Hometown: Alto Loma, Calif.
Club team: Fulham F.C. (England)
International appearances: 38
Goals: 6

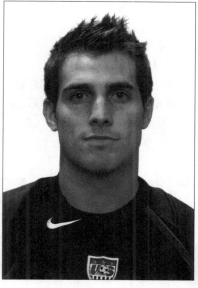

Bocanegra is strong, has deceptive speed and the versatility to play in central defense or the flanks, Taken by the Chicago Fire as the fifth overall pick 2000 MLS SuperDraft after a highly successful career at UCLA, Bocanegra has improved each season. He was named rookie of the year that season, the league's top defender and to the Best XI in 2002 and 2003. Bocanegra moved to the next step—overseas. He joined Fulham F.C. on a free transfer in January 2003, signing a three-year contract with the English Premiership side. Manager Chris Coleman told the club's official website: "I have seen Carlos play and I could see that he has great potential," Fulham coach Chris Coleman said. "He reads the game well and is very skilful and strong which are the prime attributes of a defender. . . . He has a great track record at the international level."

Bocanegra's stay in England has been controversial. He picked up three yellow cards in his first 19 appearances and a red card in only his sixth game. After a bottle had been thrown onto the Craven Cottage field on Feb. 11, 2004, Bocanegra "was guilty of one of the worst tackles of the season - a wild, two-footed lunge on Mark Delaney" in the 75th minute, according to the **Press Association of England**. Villa coach David O'Leary had to be restrained by the referee and fourth official. Through the end of February, 2006 Bocanegra had been behaving with four yellows and no reds this season.

Bocanegra is not just all defense. On Jan. 31, 2006 his injury-time header lifted Fulham to a 1-0 home win against Tottenham Hotspur. Bocanegra played for the red, white and blue for the first time against Korea on December 9, 2001. He scored his first international goal against Canada on January 18, 2003.

He is single.

Steve Cherundolo

Defender
5-foot-6, 145 pounds
Born: Feb. 19, 1979
Hometown: San Diego, Calif.
Club team: Hannover 96 (Germany)
International appearances: 31
Goals: 0

An alternate for the 2002 team, Cherundolo was activated for duty after midfielder Chris Armas and defender Greg Vanney went down with injuries. Ironically, Cher-undolo did not see any action with a bruised knee during a first-round training session. That was after another knee injury knocked him out of the 2000 Sydney Olympics. So you can understand why Cherundolo maybe chomping at the bit to play in the biggest soccer tournament on the planet.

He is coach Bruce Arena's first choice at right fullback—when he's healthy. "There's no reason to believe he won't be starting for us," Arena was quoted by the Washington Post. "Over the last two or three years, he has become a terrific professional and has acquired all the qualities to play that position."

Cherundolo has forged a reputation as an overlapping defender who worked on his upper body to be able to handle the bigger forwards he has to cover week in and week out.

After his sophomore season at the University of Portland, Cherundolo left school to play in Europe. It was a fortuitous decision. He became a regular for Hannover 96, then in the German Second Division. In his seventh season with the club, he's helped the team get promoted into the Bundesliga.

Cherundolo's secret? After his early homesickness, he became fluent in German and learned the city as well. "He knows the city better than some of the locals, and that makes him one of the very popular players," Hannover general manager Ilja Kaenzig told the Post. "He's proud of the city and proud of the shirt."

He made his international debut in a 2-2 tie with Jamaica on September 8, 1999.

Cherundolo is single.

Brian Ching

Forward
6-foot-1, 195 pounds
Born: May 24, 1978
Hometown: Haleiwa, Hawaii
Club team: Houston 1836 (MLS)
International appearances: 15
Goals: 3

Brian Ching, only four years removed from the A-League, has a shot of making the team, even with his sub-par performances during the winter of 2006. He tied for the league scoring lead in 2004 with 12 goals and he scored a pair of key goals for the U.S.'s first two World Cup semifinal round qualifying matches. Ching suddenly has some international recognition. "He's demonstrated that he's about the best goal scorer in MLS, he and (Carlos) Ruiz," U.S. coach Bruce Arena said in September, 2004. In his first international performance, Ching came off the bench to score the equalizing goal in the 89th minute of the 1-1 qualifying draw in Jamaica on Aug. 18, 2004. In his first National Team start on September 4, 2004 he connected for the first goal in the 2-0 win over El Salvador.

On the team's charter flight down to Mexico he ordered milk, a rare order that amused flight attendants. "I don't want to get a big head," Ching said. "Right now I am concentrating taking care of my body and scoring goals."

Ching did not take the traditional route that many National Team players take to the pros, MLS or Europe. He learned the game in Hawaii, becoming the first MLS player drafted from that state. He starred at Gonzaga.

Ching scored 53 seconds into his first game with the Quakes in 2003. On Aug. 19, 2003, he ruptured his right Achilles tendonand missed the rest of the season. He returned in 2004, was named MLS comeback player of the year and to the league's Best XI. "He makes the right runs. He holds the ball. He's strong. He's a great finisher. He works hard defensively. He doesn't have many faults." former San Jose Earthquakes eammate Landon Donovan said.

According to the MLS Players Union, Ching earned $133,000 in 2005. He is married to Charisse.

CHAPTER

5

Jimmy Conrad

6-foot-2, 185 pounds
Defender
Born: Feb. 12, 1977
Hometown: Temple City, Calif.
Club team: Kansas City Wizards (MLS)
International appearances: 12
Goals: 0

Conrad is a longshot to make the team. But if a player or two goes down, Conrad could very well be taken as a back-up insurance. Though he doesn't have much experience internationally, Conrad has proven to be a solid central defender in MLS, where he was named the league's defender of the year in 2005 and a Best XI selection as well.

"All the sudden, people have discovered Jimmy Conrad," Wizards coach Bob Gansler told **USSoccerPlayers.com**. "He's been persistent; he's the kind of guy who comes out every day and says, 'Yep, I'm going to get a little bit better.' And he works at it."

Yet another player from UCLA (member of the Bruins' NCAA Division I national championship side in 1997), Conrad helped the San Diego Flash to the A-League Pacific Division title in 1998. Allocated to the San Jose Earthquakes as a discovery player on Feb. 11, 1997, Conrad eventually became a regular, helping the club to the MLS Cup crown in 2001 after a broken foot forced him to miss the opening six matches of the season.

Conrad was traded to the Kansas City Wizards on MLS SuperDraft day in 2003 and has been a fixture in the lineup since.

He gave many a fan and soccer observer a scare on a hot, muggy August afternoon in 2003, Conrad was taken off the Giants Stadium field after collapsing from heat exhaustion in a game between the Wizards and MetroStars.

Conrad impressed national coach Bruce Arena enough to be called into camp in January, 2005. He earned his first camp in a victory over Cuba in the CONCACAF Gold Cup on July 7, 2005 and played in the U.S.'s 3-0 qualifying loss in Costa Rica on September 7, 2005.

According to the MLS Players Union, Conrad earned $93,750 in 2005.

He is married to Lyndsey.

Bobby Convey

Midfielder
5-foot-8, 150 pounds
Born: May 27, 1983
Hometown: Philadelphia, Pa.
Club team: Reading FC (England)
International appearances: 34
Goals: 1

Convey was the second youngest player (16) to sign an MLS contract at the time in 2000. He became the youngest goalscorer in league history at the time in 2000 and the third youngest player (17 years, 151 days) to receive a cap for the U.S. National Team in a 2-0 win over Mexico October 25, 2000.

Thanks to that early start, Convey—primarily a left-sided player who can perform in the midfield or defense—plays like an experienced hand. He joined D.C. United as a sixteen-year-old in 2000, and is now is a regular at Reading F.C., the tier just below the Premiership in the English soccer leagues. Convey spent five seasons with United before he transferred to Reading for a reported $1.5 million in 2004. Convey was ready to sign with Tottenham in the summer of 2003, but could not obtain a work permit in England.

Through late Februrary 2006, Convey had five goals in 35 games for Reading. He struggled in his first season, but found his form, which included a breakthrough pre-season game against Preston North End in the summer of 2005—having a part in his team's three goals. His confidence was evident in the U.S.'s 1-0 qualifying win over Trinidad & Tobago on Aug. 17. He set up the U.S.'s lone goal, crossing the ball to Brian McBride. "He did well, obviously, creating the first goal," U.S. coach Bruce Arena said. "He had a couple of good chances. Overall, Bobby did well. He and Eddie Lewis created a number of opportunities for us on the left flank, so I was very pleased by their play."

Convey has become more of a hardened player in Europe. "It's not fun any more," he told Soccer America. "In D.C. my first couple of years we had players on the national team, we had perfect training facilities, great fans, everything was great. It was more of a family atmosphere than it is in England."

He is single.

Clint Dempsey

Midfielder
6-foot-1, 170 pounds
Born: March 9, 1983
Hometown: Nacogdoches, Texas
Club team: New England Revolution (MLS)
International appearances: 17
Goals: 3

It certainly has been a whirlwind two years for Clint Dempsey. Since being selected by the Revolution in the first round of the 2004 MLS SuperDraft, Dempsey's star has been on the rise. He quickly became a regular in the New England lineup, collected seven goals and one assist, and earned MLS rookie-of the year honors, despite missing more than a month with a broken jaw. He made his first National Team appearance in a 1-1 draw with Jamaica on November 17, 2004. He was called up by the U.S. National Team and played in the 2-1 World Cup qualifying win over Trinidad & Tobago on February 9, 2005. He scored his first international goal in a 2-1 friendly loss to England on May 28, 2005.

Dempsey's career has been defined by patience, persistence, and even sacrifice. He began playing for a team called the Strikers in kindergarten. Dempsey began to get serious about soccer when he was 10 years-old, trying out for a Dallas Longhorns youth soccer club. A three-hour drive, Dempsey was late for the tryout. However, the coach called him back. He told Dempsey's parents, "If someone is willing to drive three hours, I want to see what kind of player he is." Dempsey earned a spot on the team.

U.S. national coach Bruce Arena has seen a lot of potential in the 6-foot-1, 170-pound Dempsey. "I think he needs to model himself more towards the likes of a Steven Gerrard and a Frank Lampard: two-way midfielders, modern day midfielders who play up and down the field, can attack and defend....very active guys. They use their athleticism and their instincts around the goal to help their team....I think as he's gotten fitter and more experienced he understands how to play that role. Really, those are the qualities he has. He's not experienced enough yet to put a team on his back....he's a guy that's a very good goal scorer out of the midfield and that's the way we line him up."

Landon Donovan

Midfielder
5-foot-8, 148 pounds
Born: March 4, 1982
Hometown: Redlands, Calif.
Club team: Los Angeles Galaxy (MLS Cup)
International appearances: 76
Goals: 25

This is Landon Donovan's time. The Los Angeles Galaxy midfielder certainly has made his mark on the U.S. National Team. Donovan has had a hand in a goal in practically every qualifier he's been in, collecting seven goals and eight assists in 16 appearances.

Donovan's career has been defined by coming up big in games that really matter. At the FIFA Under-17 World Cup in 1999, Donovan scored three times while earning the Golden Ball as the tournament MVP Not surprisingly, he scored a goal in his first international appearance, a 2-0 victory over Mexico on October 25, 2000. The one major knock against Donovan has been his inconsistent and sometimes ordinary performances in the MLS regular season, though he turned it up a notch in the playoffs. Because of his reputation as impact player, Donovan makes the highest salary of all MLS players—$900,000 in 2005, according to the MLS Players Union.

At 24, some people might think he's too young to be an impact player in Germany. But many players have left their mark on the World Cup in their mid-twenties—Carlos Alberto, Zinedine Zidane and Ronaldo, among others. Donovan is just entering his prime, U.S. coach Bruce Arena noticing this, has asked Donovan to take on greater leadership responsibilities, including as team captain on occasion. You could say the 2002 U.S. World Cup team was Claudio Reyna's team. But injuries and age have slowed down the veteran midfielder, forcing him to miss key qualifiers. Reyna might be able to come back and play in qualifiers and World Cup, resuming his role as captain. But his impact most likely will be diminished because his availability has been questionable.

There is little doubt that Donovan is in the process of making the National Team his team. This is his time.

CHAPTER

5

Todd Dunivant

Defender
6-foot, 174 pounds
Born: Dec. 26, 1980
Hometown: Wheat Ridge, Colo.
Club team: Los Angeles Galaxy (MLS)
International appearances: 2
Goals: 0

The professional soccer world discovered Dunivant at the NCAA Division I Final Four in Columbus, Ohio in December 2002. That's when Dunivant's poise and skills stood out for Stanford University. It wasn't until 2003, when the San Jose Earthquakes drafted him that the rest of the soccer world really found out about him.

Dunivant, 25, is an excellent ball-hander. He played every game (32) for the defending champion Galaxy in 2005, collecting two assists. He has one goal and eight assists in 78 matches and 75 starts. He was selected for the U.S.'s international friendly against Poland in Kaiserslautern, Germany on March 1, but a hip flexor forced him out of the match.

If there is one criticism of Dunivant, it is that he has not been physical enough during this three-year MLS career. "People can easily pass him off as being another average player, but he's not," Galaxy coach Steve Sampson told the *Los Angeles Daily News*. "He's a very, very good player who deserved this opportunity (with the national team)....he rarely gets beaten."

Dunivant has shown great potential and poise at the left back spot. In his debut in the 5-0 shellacking of Norway on Jan. 29, 2006, Dunivant set up a pair of goals. He also played 90 minutes in the 3-2 win over Japan on Feb. 10. He did not play in the club's 0-0 draw in the opening leg of their CONCACAF Champions' Cup quarterfinal match vs. Costa Rican side Deportivo Saprissa. because he was diagnosed with a hip injury, A timetable for his return has yet to be determined. As for playing for the U.S. national team, Dunivant told the *L.A. Daily News* "It's been great. You have to think faster and play quicker. You have to raise your game in every aspect."

According to the MLS Players Union, Dunivant earned $59,350 in 2005

Cory Gibbs

Defender
6-foot-3, 178 pounds
Born: Jan. 14, 1980
Hometown: Fort Lauderdale, Fla.
Club team: ADO Den Haag (Netherlands)
International appearances: 17
Goals: 0

Gibbs has forged a reputation as a solid man-marker and someone who is strong in the air. He can play in the middle or on the left side.

Gibbs has bounced around from club to club the past several years. After graduating from Brown University, Gibbs joined St. Pauli F.C. of Hamburg (where the U.S. will be based during the World Cup.) At the age of 21, he became the youngest American to play a full 90 minutes in Germany and to score a goal in the Bundesliga, accomplishing that feat against F.C. Cologne on Nov. 24, 2001.

He became a regular at St. Pauli for 2 1/2 seasons before returning home to the Dallas Burn (now called F.C. Dallas) after the German Second Division club failed to get promoted into the Bundesliga. He played a season there before Feyenoord of the Dutch First Division beckoned and Gibbs transferred there in January, 2005. Things did not work out and Gibbs eventually joined ADO Den Haag (Netherlands), where he is today.

In college, Gibbs led Brown University to the Ivy League crown and to the Elite Eight of the NCAA Division I tournament in 2000, when he was named Ivy League player of the year and a first-team All-American. Gibbs made his international debut in a 2-1 over New Zealand on June 8, 2003.

He is single.

Marcus Hahnemann

Goalkeeper
6-foot-3, 220 pounds
Born: June 15, 1972
Hometown: Seattle, Wash.
Club team: Reading F.C. (England)
International appearances: 6
Goals: 0

Few foreign players have made the impact that Hahnemann has made at Reading F.C. in England. He joined Fulham F.C. on a $130,000 transfer from the Colorado Rapids in May, 1999. Hahnemann was then loaned to Rochdale for five matches and then to Reading. There, he recorded four shutouts in six appearances. eventually joining the club on a free transfer in 2002.

Finally securing the No. 1 spot, he quickly become a fan favorite. After games, Hahnemann throws his jersey into the stands. "I always tend to give to those who have American flags, Hahnemann told *FIFA Magazine*. Hahnemann has a stars and stripes tattoo on his right arm. The tradition started after an English F.A. Cup loss. "A fan screamed 'give me your shirt'," I threw it up, threw my gloves up...the feedback was unbelievable."

"He made one or two early errors the first two months he's been here but since then he's been a rock, an absolute rock," Reading coach Steve Coppell said. As of Feb. 24, Hahnemann had 19 shutouts in 35 games as Reading enjoyed a nine-point lead over second-place Sheffield United with 11 games remaining. If Reading finished first, it will earn an automatic promotion to the English Premiership. "That's everyone's dream, to play in the Premiership," Hahnemann said. "It's what we strive for every day in training. That's your goal. It would be nice to get there. You want to see what you can do against the big boys."

Hahnemann's first international start came in a 1-1 tie with Honduras on November 12, 1994. Then he had to wait another nine years before he got an opportunity to play for the U.S. again—in a 2-1 victory over New Zealand in Richmond, Va. in 2003.

Frankie Hejduk

Defender-midfielder
5-foot-8, 155 pounds
Born: Aug. 5, 1974
Hometown: Cardiff, Calif.Club team:
Columbus Crew (MLS)
International appearances: 71
Goals: 5

Frankie Hejduk proposed to his former wife in knee-keep water while holding a surfboard, which should tell you a lot about him. When the beleaguered U.S. National Team arrived near Nantes for its last first-round match of France '98, Hejduk went to the beach to check out the water—the Atlantic Ocean.

He might have the soul of a surfer, but Hejduk has the heart of a soccer player. There was little question that the Cardiff, California native was the American revelation of the 1998 World Cup. He played with intensity, enthusiasm and eventually was rewarded for those qualities with a three-year contract with Bayer Leverkusen of the Bundeliga. He eventually returned to the states, signing with MLS and the Columbus Crew in 2003.

He gives Coach Bruce Arena some flexibility, playing right fullback or some defensive help as a right midfielder. He started four of five matches in the 2002 WC, serving a one-match suspension due to yellow-card accumulation.

Hejduk has that random personality and sometimes takes unnecessary risks. The U.S. appeared to pay the price for one of his miscues during a 2002 WC qualifier in Costa Rican, when Hejduk knocked down a player in the box late in the match. No foul was whistled, but the referee, in an apparent make-up call, claimed the U.S. handled the ball in the penalty area and awarded the hosts what turned out to be the game-winner.

Hejudk made his international debut in a 3-1 win over El Salvador in August, 1996. In his first international start, on Dec. 21, 1996, Hejduk scored the equalizing goal in a 2-2 draw with Guatemala in a World Cup qualifier.

According to the MLS Players Union, Hejduk earned $191,000 in 2005, the fourth highest paid defender in the league.

He is engaged to Elissa.

Tim Howard

Goalkeeper
6-foot-3, 210 pounds
Born: March 6, 1979
Hometown: North Brunswick, N.J.
Club team: Manchester United (England)
International appearances: 14
Goals: 0

Role models come in all different shapes and sizes. In the sporting world, players are measured by how they deal with pressure and adversity, an how they comport themselves on and off the field. In that regard, Tim Howard is literally on his toes behind Manchester United's defense, and also serves as a striking example of resilience to a number of non-soccer fans. Howard has suffered from Tourette's Syndrome—a neurological disorder characterized by repeated involuntary movements and uncontrollable sounds—for the past fifteen years. Despite that, he became one of the leading goalkeepers in MLS, which led to his going to England. Howard admits he was concerned about revealing his condition, considering the many questions that people would ask. But in spring 2001, after he was handed the MetroStars starting job, he decided to reveal that his story. Nothing happened. The media reported about it in a sensitive matter and no one doubted Howard's ability as a goalkeeper.

Howard enjoyed a fairy tale start with United, performing so well that he became the No. 1 goalkeeper in his first season with the club (2003-04), helping ManU to the F.A. Cup and grabbing individual honors as the best keeper in the country, as voted by his fellow players.

But the next season, Howard made several mistakes in key moments and he wound up on the bench, replaced by as Dutchman Edwin Van der Sar. Howard's dilemma lies in the fact that makes a very good salary but plays in reserve games. Because of his inactivity, Howard has been relegated to the third or perhaps fourth goalkeeper in coach Bruce Arena's pecking order.

Howard made his international debut in a 1-0 over Ecuador on March 10, 2002.

He is married to Laura and they have one child.

Eddie Johnson

Forward
6-foot, 180 pounds
Born: March 31, 1984
Hometown: Palm Coast, Fla.
Club team: Kansas City Wizards (MLS)
International appearances: 12
Goals: 9

Few players have joined the U.S. team with such fanfare and success as Johnson did. Only four minutes after coming on as a substitute in El Salvador on October 9, 2004, Johnson found the back of the net. Only four days later, Johnson again came off the bench and became the first player in U.S. history to secure a hat-trick as a substitute.

MLS thought Johnson was the second coming of Romario and signed him for an incredible salary of $875,000 for the 2005 season, hoping to eventually get a whopping transfer fee. Johnson hardly earned that pay for F.C. Dallas in 2005, scoring only five times in 15 appearances, as he was bothered by a turf toe injury.

In his return to the National Team during the winter of 2006, Johnson played a total of 102 minutes over three international friendlies, suffering a calf injury in 0-0 tie with Canada on January 22, 2006, his first international match since March 30, 2005.

"I think over the next couple of months Eddie should be back in full form and be a player who is challenging, certainly for a spot on the World Cup roster," U.S. coach Bruce Arena said.

On Feb. 13, 2006, Johnson was traded to the Kansas City Wizards. Johnson's attitude has been questioned by some. Ironically, Johnson scored as a sub and celebrated his ninth goal in twelve international appearances, by turning his back toward the crowd in his former home stadium of FC Dallas and snapping his jersey. "I couldn't ask for anything else but to score a goal," he was quoted by **Associated Press**. "It made me feel good about myself. It's kind of a slap back in their face, saying 'Why are you trading me?' "

Kasey Keller

Goalkeeper
Born: Nov. 29, 1969
Hometown: Lacey, Wash.
Club team: Borussia Moenchengladbach Germany
International appearances: 89
Goals: 0

The only way Keller can lose the job is through injury. That's what happened to him just before the 2002 World Cup injuring his elbow only days before the opening match. Brad Friedel played every minute of the five games.With Friedel retiring in February, 2005, the job became Keller's and he has been nothing short of spectacular. He had a 0.56 goals-against average in 2005, while registering eight clean sheets in fourteen games. Keller won Honda Player of the Year as the best American men's soccer player, and the U.S. Soccer male athlete of the year for the third time. "He had an outstanding year and continues to demonstrate why he is such a valuable part of our team," U.S. coach Bruce Arena said.

Since leaving the University of Portland in 1992, Keller has forged a reputation as being one of the top goalkeepers in whatever league he has played in. He has worked the nets for Millwall, Leicester, Tottenham and Rayo Vallecano before settling on Borussia Moenchengladbach in the winter of 2004.

Keller was the backup to Tony Meola at Italia '90, and was *persona non grata* with coach Bora Miltunovic at USA '94. He started twice at France '98 before the unfortunate injury in 2002.

Considered one of the most respected and cerebral American players, Keller has at least one quirk: He doesn't like to talk to the media the day before matches, whether it is a friendly, qualifier or the World Cup itself.

He has 44 shutouts in 89 international appearances, including 19 in WC qualifying matches. Keller made his international debut against Colombia on February 4, 1990. The U.S. tied the Colombians, 1-1, but lost in a marathon penalty-kick shootout, 9-8.

Keller is married to Kristin and they have twins, Chloe and Cameron.

Chris Klein

Midfielder
6-foot-1, 180-pounds
Born: Jan. 4, 1976
Hometown: St. Louis, Mo.
Club team: Real Salt Lake
International appearances: 20
Goals: 5

Probably a longshot to sit the bench in Germany, Klein is making coach Bruce Arena's decision quite difficult, due to his strong play during the winter of 2006. Klein was traded by the Kansas City Wizards to Real Salt Lake for a partial allocation. This seemed to make Klein even more determined to make the team. His shining moment came almost a month later in the 4-0 victory over Guatemala on February 19, 2006, when he scored one goal and set up two others. "It was a good game for us," Klein told the Associated Press. "It was a good game for me personally." That performance certainly got Klein noticed by Arena, who brought in onto the roster for the March 1, 2006 friendly against Poland in Kaiserslautern, Germany after New England Revolution forward Pat Noonan injured his hamstring. "He's got pace, he's got work rate, he scores goals. He can run at people and beat them outside; he can run at people and beat them inside. And defensively, over the years, he's gotten better and better playing both sides of the ball."

After an outstanding University of Indiana career, he was selected by the Wizards at the fourth overall pick in the 1998 MLS draft and managed to play in seventeen games, starting eight. He eventually worked his way into the starting lineup and became one of the more reliable K.C. players Klein has scored 39 goals and set up 45 others in 200 regular-season games over eight MLS seasons. His most important assist came at MLS Cup 2000, when he set up Miklos Molnar's 11th-minute goal in a 1-0 triumph over the Chicago Fire.

Klein made his international debut in a 2-0 friendly win over Mexico on Oct. 25, 2000. He earned $145,250 in 2005, according to the MLS Players Union.

He is married to Angela and they have a son, Carson, and a daughter, Cami.

Eddie Lewis

Midfielder-defender
5-10, 155 pounds
Born: May 17, 1974
Hometown: Cerritos, Calif.
Club team: Leeds United (England)
International appearances: 67
Goals: 8

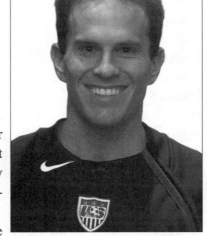

Wherever he winds up playing—defense or midfielder—Lewis will be one of best crossers in the World Cup. He has set up many a teammate through the years with his pinpoint drives.

Lewis, who played for the San Jose Earthquakes, decided to take the plunge on the other side of the Atlantic in February 2000, when he joined Fulham F.C. in a reported $1.9 million deal after being named to the MLS Bext XI in 1999 (four goals, 14 assists).

He was brought in by former coach Paul Bracewell and played reasonably well in the club's final 10 matches that season. However, only two weeks after Lewis joined the team, Bracewell was fired. Former French international Jean Tigana replaced him and Lewis essentially was banished to the bench and reserve matches. He joined Preston North End in November, 2002 for $750,000. Given an opportunity to play, Lewis scored 15 goals in 97 league starts and helped the team gain promotion to the English Premiership. Lewis was only one of two U.S. internationals who helped their clubs reach the Premiership; goalkeeper Brad Friedel being the other.

But Leeds United coach Kevin Blackwell was looking for a left wing and with Lewis out of contract, he was a perfect fit. Lewis joined the club on a free transfer in July, 2005.

Before he signed with Fulham, Lewis had played his entire career—youth, high school and college—in California. He led UCLA in scoring in 1995 with 11 goals and 10 assists. Lewis made his international debut in a 4-1 loss to Peru on October 16, 1996 and scored his first goal in a 2-1 win over Chile on February 21, 1999.

He is married to Marisol and has a daughter, Giselle, and a son James.

Pablo Mastroeni

Midfielder-defender
5-10, 170 pounds
Born: Aug. 26, 1976
Hometown: Phoenix, Ariz.
Club team: Colorado Rapids (MLS)
International appearances: 43
Goals: 0

Mastroeni was given an an opportunity to play a series of World Cup friendlies in the spring of 2002. When a knee injury sidelined Chris Armas, Mastroeni took center stage as defensive midfielder.

He became a key performer and ball winner for the U.S. in the 3-2 upset of Portugal, the 2-0 second-round victory over archrival Mexico and the 1-0 quarterfinal defeat to Germany. He was the only American on the roster who did not participate in the qualifiers. Forging a reputation as someone who is hard on the tackle and who takes no prisoners, Mastroeni has become one of the best defensive midfielders in MLS.

But, in 2004, Mastroeni found himself in a middle of a rather unusual controversy when coach Bruce Arena called in players for an international friendly with Honduras. Colorado Rapids coach Tim Hankinson, however, refused to release Mastroeni for the match, which was a preparation game for the Grenada World Cup qualifying series. Hankinson cited a rule FIFA rule that requires players to be released four days before an international game if they were traveling within the same country.

"It was one of the more difficult things I've had to deal with in my professional career," Mastroeni told the *Rocky Mountain News*. "So, not being able to play for my country was a huge disappointment."

Mastroeni made his international debut in a scoreless draw with Ecuador on June 7, 2001. He earned a team-high $243,000 with the Rapids in 2005, according to the MLS Players Union.

He is married to Kelly, to whom he proposed during a television interview at halftime of a Miami Fusion game.

Brian McBride

Forward
6-1, 170-pounds
Born: June 19, 1972
Hometown: Arlington Heights, Ill.
Club team: Fulham F.C. (England)
International appearances: 90
Goals: 29

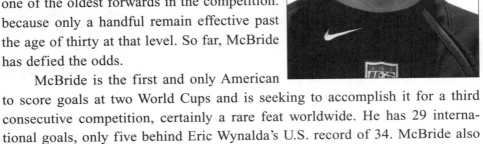

At thirty-four, McBride will most likely be one of the oldest forwards in the competition. because only a handful remain effective past the age of thirty at that level. So far, McBride has defied the odds.

McBride is the first and only American to score goals at two World Cups and is seeking to accomplish it for a third consecutive competition, certainly a rare feat worldwide. He has 29 international goals, only five behind Eric Wynalda's U.S. record of 34. McBride also has played in twenty countries for the U.S.

Even though he never led MLS in scoring, McBride forged a reputation as a fearless, rough-and-tumble front line player. who was unafraid of injuries. He's paid for it on several occasions. In September, 2000, McBride faced a life and death situation when a blood clot was discovered while playing with Preston North End. It was removed and McBride resumed playing.

No one has to remind coach Bruce Arena of McBride's worth. "He's a real forward,' he said. "When he steps on the field you know he is going to give you ninety minutes. I don't know how much more you can ask of him. With his dimensions, obviously he is very good in the air. He's a very good player at holding the ball and pressuring the opponent. He is invaluable."

After flirting with short stints with Preston North End and Everton, McBride finally signed with Fulham in 2004. In his Fulham debut in a 2-1 victory, McBride scored eight minutes after he came on as a substituted, beating fellow national Teammate Kasey Keller on Jan. 31, 2004. He continued to fill the net and has remained with Fulham. McBride made his first international appearance in a 4-1 loss in Honduras on March 25, 1993 and scored his first goal vs. Guatemala in a WC qualifier on Nov. 3, 1996.

He is married to Dina and his two daughters, Ashley and Ella.

CHAPTER
5

Pat Noonan

Forward
Born: Aug. 2, 1980
Hometown: Ballwin, Mo.
Club team: New England Revolution (MLS)
International appearances: 12
Goals: 1

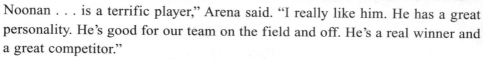

The MetroStars helped Pat Noonan gain confidence and make a name for himself During his 2003 rookie season Noonan scored 10 goals, an incredible seven against the MetroStars.

Noonan's passing and shooting ability are what impressed coach Bruce Arena. "Pat Noonan . . . is a terrific player," Arena said. "I really like him. He has a great personality. He's good for our team on the field and off. He's a real winner and a great competitor."

Arena was impressed with Noonan's performance in the 3-2 win over Japan on Feb. 10, 2006. "Pat had his best game ever for the national team against Japan," he said. "He played well on both sides of the ball. He was involved in one play that set up a goal. He was involved in a bunch of other plays that created goal-scoring opportunities, and, as I said, played well on both sides of the ball."

Noonan was a fixture in the Univeristy of Indiana lineup, starting every game of his four-year career. He called winning the 1999 NCACC Division I championship game his fondest memory.

After he was drafted as the ninth overall pick by New England, Noonan got an opportunity to play in the later part of the 2003 season. Noonan connected for 11 goals and eight assists for 30 points in 2004, sharing the MLS scoring championship with the MetroStars' Amado Guevara, and added eight goals and seven assists in twenty-one appearances in 2005.

Noonan made his first international appearance in a 1-1 tie with Haiti on March 13, 2004. He earned $75,594 in 2005, according to the MLS Players Union.

CHAPTER

5

John O'Brien
Midfielder
Born: Aug. 29, 1977
Hometown: Playa del Rey, Calif.
Club team: ADO Den Haag (Netherlands)
International appearances: 28
Goals: 3

When he's healthy, O'Brien is one of the U.S.'s best players, the key phrase being when he's healthy.

O'Brien has endured a series of ailments through the years, which has kept him out of games for club and country. For example, he played only once in eighteen qualifying matches.

He is left-footed, which is a rare commodity for an American midfielder. Although he has been slowed by injuries, O'Brien has exhibited vision and an ability and desire to move the ball forward and into dangerous scoring positions. When asked about O'Brien in 2005, coach Bruce Arena replied, "He's injured. I think John's an outstanding player. The one good thing: he hasn't been a fixture for us. He won't be noticeably missed by a lot of people except for the coaches and the players who know what a special player he is. And he is outstanding. When he's on the field, he makes us a better team and, not having him, yes, I guess you could say we'll miss him."

In 1997, O'Brien decided to forego a college education and take the plunge with world-renowned Ajax as a youth player. "I made the right decision," he said. "I think of what it would have been like had I stayed and gone to college and stuff like that. I like what I'm doing now for, sure."

O'Brien made his first American appearance in a 3-0 victory over Austria on April 22, 1998. He scored his first goal in the 7-0 qualifying rout of Barbados on August 16, 2000.

Ben Olsen

Midfielder
Born: May 3, 1977
Hometown: Middletown, Pa.
Club team: D.C. United (MLS)
International appearances: 31
Goals: 5

Whether Olsen makes the World Cup team depends on injuries to other members of the team. If the likes of Claudio Reyna and Pablo Mastroeni can't play, then coach Bruce Arena will call on this midfielder. Olsen has proved to be a solid performer in MLS and for the National Team although he has been forced to overcome some injuries himself in recent years.

He can play several positions, including on the right flank and even as a defensive midfielder. After three seasons at the University of Virginia, Olsen decided to turn pro and joined D.C. United as a Project 40 allocation in 1998. It is the only MLS club Olsen has played for, although he had a stint with Nottingham Forest (England) as a loaned player before injuring his ankle (he was forced to undergo four operations during a two-year span).

Olsen played for the U.S. Under-20 team at the FIFA World Youth Championship in 1997, earned U.S. Soccer Young Male Athlete of the Year honors in 1999, while scoring the game-winner in the 2-0 win over Germany in the 1999 FIFA Confederations Cup.

He was a key member of the U.S. Olympic team at the 2000 Sydney Summer Games as the Americans finished a surprising fourth.

Olsen earn $165,000 in 2005, according to the MLS Players Union.

He wore the red, white and blue colors for the first time in a scoreless tie with Australia on November 6, 1998, Bruce Arena's first game as national coach. He scored his first goal in a 2-1 win over Chile on Feb. 21, 1999.

Oguchi Onyewu

Defender
Born: May 13, 1982
Hometown: Olney, Md.
Club team: Standard de Liege (Belgium)
International appearances: 11
Goals: 1

Move over Eddie Pope, there's a new central defender in town and he's not easily bowled over. Oguchi Onyewu has established himself as the U.S.'s dominant defender. Onyewu has proven he can shut down the opposition's top striker and be dangerous on heading free kicks and corner kicks in the penalty area.

Nicknamed Gooch, Onyewu handled American nemesis Jared Borgetti without many problems, keeping him off balance and on the Columbus Crew Stadium grass when push literally came to shove on September 3, 2005.

"Gooch is a great young player," U.S. coach Bruce Arena said. "Obviously his physical presence is fantastic. You see a player like Borgetti today and he's bouncing off Gooch for 90 minutes." Borgetti, who beat Onyewu for a goal in Mexico's 2-1 home win on March 27, 2005, has been a thorn in the U.S. side for years. "We learned a lot from the first game," Onyewu said. "I think we gave the forwards a lot more space in the first game and today we just suffocated them all around the field." Onyewu's said "Now that we've qualified, the most important thing is to play consistently and stay healthy Things have been going pretty well for me the last couple months..."

After playing two seasons at Clemson University Onyewu decided to take a chance at Europe. He signed a four-year contract with F.C. Metz in March 2002, but after a coaching change he was sent to Louviere (Belgium). He was so impressive that the Belgian club exercised its option on Onyweu.

His reward was a return trip to his Belgium club, Standard de Liege. Onyewu earned his first cap in the 6-0 romp over Panama on Oct. 13, 2004.

His first name, Oguchi, means "God fights for me."

He is single.

Eddie Pope

Defender
Born: Dec. 24, 1973
Hometown: High Point, N.C.
Club team: Real Salt Lake (MLS)
International appearances: 77
Goals: 8

Arguably the best defender in U.S. National Team history, Pope is coming near the end of a long and illustrious career. He is the MLS's best defender in its 11-year history. He was voted to the MLS Best XI three times (1997, 2003 and 2004) times and defender of the year in 1997. He played for three MLS Cup champions for D.C. United (1996, 1997 and 1999) and performed in two World Cups (1998 and 2002). He hopes to make it to Germany this June.

"His career with the national team began in 1996," U.S. coach Bruce Arena said. "I was his coach at D.C. United and I remember when we released him for his first camp. At the time he was a talented young central defender who I was quite certain was going to be successful and 10 years later, he's still kicking around. He's had a great career and will potentially be playing in his third World Cup, which is a fantastic achievement for any player in the world."

Pope has led by example. "Eddie's a quiet person," Arena said. "I've known him for a long time. He has a pretty good sense of humor. He takes some time to open up, but he's a guy who really enjoys being part of the national team and the relationships he has with his teammates. As he's closing out his national team career, he enjoys the opportunity to spread some of his wisdom to the younger players. He's been a really good role model for a number of our guys. He's earned a lot of respect."

In 2005, Pope earned $378,948.66, the highest amount for an MLS defender, according to the MLS Players Union. He made his international debut in a 2-0 qualifying win over Trinidad & Tobago on November 10, 1996. He scored his first international goal in a 3-0 victory over Canada in qualifier on March 16, 1997.

He is married to Corina and has a son, Emilio.

Steve Ralston

Midfielder
5-foot-9, 160 pounds
Born: June 14, 1974
Hometown: St. Louis, Mo.
Club team: New England Revolution (MLS)
International appearances: 32
Goals: 4

This is it for Ralston. If he doesn't play in the 2006 World Cup, he never will, given his age. "It's been a long process to get to the national team and be a part of qualifying," he said. "I feel like that this is my last go-around and I want to be a part of it." Ralston has forged a reputation as one of the MLS's best right-sided players, especially when he whips a cross into the penalty area.

But during the January 2006 camp, Ralston suffered a quad injury and wasn't able to make a further impression on coach Bruce Arena. "It's just a shame because he came into camp fitter that I've seen in many years," Arena said.

Ralston's main forte is his crossing ability. Ralston, Arena said, "is probably our most comfortable player in our pool in playing on the right side of the field on the touch line."

Ralston, the MLS's first rookie of the year with the Tampa Bay Mutiny, in 1996, has forged a long career as one of the cleanest players in the league. As a key member of the New England Revolution, Ralson also has become one of the most reliable and durable players in MLS history, having played in more matches (281) and minutes (24,865) than anyone else.

Certainly not too shabby for someone who did not start for his high school soccer team in his senior year and for someone who admittedly had no aspirations to play professional outdoor soccer.

"I might have been a little bit of a late bloomer," Ralston said. "I really improved right after my senior year of high school."

He made his international debut in a 1-0 loss. Peru on January 17, 1997. Ralston earned $156,250 with the Revolution in 2005, according to the MLS Players Union.

He is married to Rachel and has two children.

Claudio Reyna

Midfielder
5-foot-10, 160 pounds
Born: July 20, 1973
Hometown: Springfield, N.J.
Club team: Manchester City (England)
International appearances: 108
Goals: 8

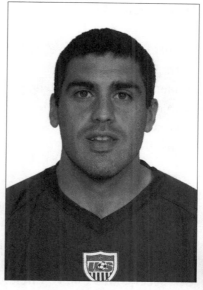

Although he didn't play many qualifying matches, Reyna still is a key to the U.S. success in Germany, given his experience and leadership ability. If he does play, it will be Reyna's fourth association with U.S. World Cup teams. He was picked for the '94 squad, but didn't play a minute due to a hamstring. He performed at France '98 and Korea/Japan '02.

Reyna's career has been punctuated with injuries and his ability and desire to come back and excel for the U.S. His ailments have included groin, hamstring, calf and a torn left knee ACL. He missed six-weeks with a broken ankle suffered while playing for Manchester City right before New Year's 2006.

Coach Bruce Arena hopes Reyna will be available come June. "In the long run Claudio is our captain," he said. "He's one of our better players if not our best player. He brings confidence to our team. He's a leader. That's his role. He can play a variety of positions and he has great experience. When healthy, I think he's invaluable to our team. Whatever role we give him, there's no doubt in my mind that it's a critical role and a very important role.

Reyna has enjoyed a long career in Europe. He first joined Bayer Leverkusen, becoming a starter and vital cog in the Bundesliga side. He also played for Wolfsburg (Germany), Glasgow Rangers (Scotland), Sunderland (England)—for an American-record $5.7 million transfer in December, 2001—and most recently, Manchester City (England) Reyna made his international debut against Norway on January 15, 1994 and scored his first international goal in a 3-0 victory over Moldova on April 20, 1994.

He is married to the Danielle Eagan, a standout player in her own right at the University of North Carolina, a perennial NCAA Division I women's champion. They have two children, Jack and Giovanni.

Jonathan Spector

Defender
6-foot, 180 pounds
Born: March 1, 1986
Hometown: Arlington Heights, Ill.
Club team: Charlton Athletic (England)
International appearances: 3
Goals: 0

If he manages to secure a position for Germany, Spector will be the youngest player on the team. "It is every American soccer players' dream to be able to play for their country and win the World Cup," Spector told **USSoccer.com's** *Center Circle*.

He is a player on the rise, having first signed with famed Manchester United in 2003. His first start was was in a Champions League qualifier against Dinamo Bucharest. Spector only played five times during the 2004-05 season. but in order to develop he needed to play, so ManU loaned him for a season to Charlton Athletic.

Considered a strong and tenacious performer, Spector hasn't played defense for very long. He entered U.S. Soccer Under-17 residency camp at IMG Academy in Bradenton, Fla. in 2002 as a forward. But he was converted to a defender and quickly was noticed by a United scout before signing with the Premiership club a year later. A strong and tenacious performer who is a fine man marker, Spector is also very mobile and has the ability to use both feet.

Spector played his first international match, coming on as a substitute in the 1-1 qualifying tie with Jamaica on November 17, 2004.

He is single.

Taylor Twellman

Forward
5-foot-11, 170 pounds
Born: Feb. 29, 1980
Hometown: St. Louis, Mo.
Club team: New England Revolution (MLS)
International appearances: 16
Goals: 5

For his first 13 international appearances, Twellman couldn't buy a goal. He has regained his form and confidence internationally with four goals in his next two appearances.

"Taylor is a very good player," U.S. coach Bruce Arena said. "Taylor, in our environment, he has struggled to find himself and now he's found himself."

An All-America at the University of Maryland, Twellman went to Europe after his sophomore season and played 40 games with the Munich 1860 reserves in 2000-2001. He was selected by the New England Revolution as the second overall pick of the 2002 MLS SuperDraft. He is a natural goal-scorer, equally dangerous with his feet or head. He led MLS in scoring with 23 goals in 2002, tied for the lead with 15 in 2003 and led the league again with 17 in 2005.98

Twellman was destined to play professional sports. His father Tim played professionally for the Minnesota Kicks, Tulsa Roughnecks and the Chicago Sting (North American Soccer League). His grandfather Jim Delsing played pro baseball and his uncle Jay Delsing is a member of the PGA Tour.

Twellman made his first U.S. appearance in a 2-0 triumph over El Salvador on November 17, 2002. He scored his first goal in the 2-0 victory over Panama in his home field in Foxboro, Mass. on Oct. 12, 2005.

For all his scoring ability Twellman was among the MLS bargains of the year in 2005, earning $131,666, according to the MLS Players Union.

He is married to Lindsay.

Josh Wolff

Forward
5-foot-8, 160 pounds
Born: Feb. 25, 1977
Hometown: Stone Mountain, Ga.
Club team: Kansas City Wizards (MLS)
International appearances: 42
Goals: 9

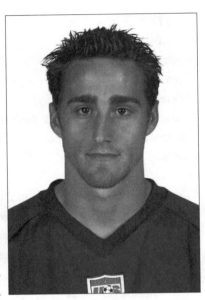

Wolff is fast, quick and cunning. Only the best defenders and injuries have slowed him down through the years

Wolff, a standout performer during the U.S.'s early qualifying run in 2001, has represented the U.S. at three different world championship competitions, including the 1997 FIFA World Youth Championship and the 2000 Olympics. Entering his ninth year in MLS, he started out splitting his first season—1998—with Project 40 and the Chicago Fire After six seasons with the Fire, Wolff was traded to the Kansas City Wizards in 2003.

Staying relatively injury free, Wolff has enjoyed two of his most productive years the past two seasons, connecting for 10 goals in each. He has totaled 53 goals and 33 assists in 145 MLS appearances.

Wolff, easily the U.S.'s outstanding Olympic performer at the 2000 Sydney Summer Games, admitted he might have been acting just a bit when a Japan midfielder was called for tripping him, which set up the equalizing goal in the 90th minute of the quarterfinals. The U.S. went on to win via penalty kicks. "It's part of the game," he said. "My job is to score goals and create goals. Getting PKs creates goals."

He made his international debut in a 2-2 draw with Jamaica on September 8, 1999. He scored his first goal in the 2-0 win over Mexico on October 25, 2000. He earned $420,357.14 in 2005, the fifth highest overall and third most by a forward, according to the MLS Players Union.

Wolff is married to Angela and they have two sons—Tyler David and Owen Michael. Hmmm, there's an English international forward named Michael Owen.

Kerry Zavagnin

Midfielder
5-foot-10, 170 pounds
Born: July 2, 1974
Hometown: Plymouth, Mich.
Club team: Kansas City Wizards (MLS)
International appearances: 19
Goals: 0

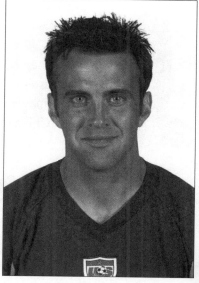

CHAPTER

5

In 1999, Zavagnin voluntarily moved down from MLS to the A-League (the USL First Division). "I made a tough decision to go down to the A-League," Zavagnin said. Some have called it a gamble, or even a potential career suicide. "I was only there for one reason," Zavagnin said. "If I got 25-26 games and accomplished my goal to become a better player, I'd have a better chance of playing regularly in MLS." Incredibly, against all odds, his unorthodox strategy worked as he performed for the now-defunct Lehigh Steam. Today, Zavagnin is one of the top defensive midfielders in the league and in the U.S. National Team pool.

Although Zavagnin has earned a shot at Germany, makeing the team probably will depend on the health of other defensive or holding midfielders. "Kerry, in the beginning, was a player on the alternate list and a little bit in the background to players who play similar positions." U.S. coach Bruce Arena said. Kerry is going to be in there right until the end, when we're looking to finalize our roster."

Zavagnin was the place kicker for his high school football team for three years, earning state honors, before attending and playing soccer for the University of North Carolina. Acquired by the MetroStars for former U.S. international Peter Vermes and a draft pick in 1997, Zavagnin played in a team-high 21 games for rookies. He spent two years there before stepping down a league. In his first year back, Zavagnin helped the Kansas City Wizards capture MLS Cup and helped the team reach the championship game in 2004 as well.

Zavagnin made his international debut in the 2-0 victory over Mexico on Oct. 25, 2000. He earned $120,000 in 2005, according to the MLS Players Union.

He is single.

CHAPTER 5

Would be National Team players and coaches

Chris Armas, midfielder—In 2002, a late injury shelved Armas (66 caps) from the WC. This time around, he tore his ACL at the end of October, 2005. It appeared it would take a miracle for the 33-year-old Chicago Fire all-star to be fit enough to perform in Germany.

Cobi Jones, midfielder—Used during the early stages of qualifying, Jones, who turns 36 on June 16, hasn't been utilized in quite a while. The Los Angeles Galaxy midfielder has 164 caps (and 15 goals), the most of any U.S. player.

Tony Meola, goalkeeper—During the winter of 2006, the 37-year-old Meola said that he was going to be called into national camp in the spring. He played at Italia '90 and USA '94 and was No. 3 at Korea 2002, a position he most likely would assume at Germany 2006.

Santino Quaranta, midfielder—He has lot of potential and was given a nice long look by Arena. But the 21-year-old D.C. United midfielder still needs more seasoning (11 appearances, no goals).

Greg Vanney, defender—Turning 34 on June 11, 2006, and several newcomers at the left fullback position, it appears the F.C. Dallas veteran's chance to play in the World Cup have passed.

Meet the assistant coaches

Glenn Myernick—Nicknamed Mooch, the 51-year-old Myernick is Arena's No. 1 assistant, also having worked under the head coach with the U.S. 1996 Olympic team. Myernick took over the coaching reigns at the CONCACAF Gold Cup in July, 2005, directing the team to the tournament title.

Curt Onalfo—Many people would love to see the 36-year-old Onalfo's frequent flyer mileage as he is the No. 1 scout of the team. He is a cancer survivor, overcoming Hodgkin's Disease (diagnosed in 1993).

CHAPTER 5

Milutin Soskic—goalkeepers coach—An Olympic gold medalist with Yugoslavia (1960), Soskic has served under three U.S. World Cup coaches—Bora Milutinovic (1994), Steve Sampson (1998) and Arena (2002).

Phil Wheddon—goalkeeper coach—One-time goalkeeper of the MetroStars (MLS), Wheddon, who lives in Monroe, Conn. also has been keeper coach for the U.S. women's national side as well.

Pierre Barrieu, fitness coach—He enters his full fourth year as the team's fitness guru after handling that responsibility in the 2002 World Cup.

The U.S. Coach

Are you ready for some more Arena futbol?

Before the 2002 World Cup, there were some concerns from the media that U.S. coach Bruce Arena would not be up to the task of keeping up with international tactics. He laid those worries to rest, manipulating his lineup from game to game with a team that was wracked by injuries and suspensions.

Perhaps his finest moments came in the knockout stages of the tournament, when Arena had less to work with. Without starters Jeff Agoos (injury) and Frankie Hejduk (yellow-card suspension) against CONCACAF archrival Mexico in the second round, Arena deployed a 3-5-2 lineup that exploited the Mexicans' weaknesses. Eddie Lewis, a left midfielder who can send some devastating crosses into the penalty area, hadn't started a World Cup game. Yet, Lewis created the Americans' insurance goal in a stunning 2-0 win. Forward Josh Wolff, another new face in the starting lineup, set up Brian McBride's goal.

Defender Gregg Berhalter and defensive midfielder Pablo Mastroeni also started their first Cup matches as the Americans began their 4-0 qualifying triumph at Barbados.

Arena also was forced to move central midfielder Claudio

Reyna to the right side and he came through with flying colors, making a 40-yard run down the right side to help create McBride's score.

"Change can be good," Arena told *Sports Illustrated*. "I could have done more platooning here, because there's not much of a difference from our top player to our bottom player."

Faced with less than a full complement against highly favored Germany in the quarterfinals, Arena again was forced to mix and match and almost came up with a major upset. The U.S. fell, 1-0, although many observers felt the Americans outplayed their German counterparts and even should have been awarded a penalty kick for a Germany handball in the penalty area.

"The best thing he did was make everyone believe the whole time that they can contribute,' said the U.S.'s No. 3 goalkeeper at the 2002 World Cup, Tony Meola, who played for Arena at the University of Virginia. "Everyone felt they were contributing to the program. And everyone felt like when he was called he'd be ready.

"His biggest quality is his man management skills. He has taken a lot of guys into the system, some guys who may have felt they should have been there before, some guys who never thought they would have gotten a call, and does a pretty good job of having everyone mesh together. It's for sure the best job of man-managing of any coach in U.S. soccer history, in my opinion."

Arena, however, refused to complain about the non-call vs. Germany and offered no excuses.

"I was really proud of our team," he said at the time. "We were a little bit unlucky. If we'd got a break or two we may be in the semifinals of the World Cup."

But he was realistic as well. "It shows the world we can play," Arena added. "If anyone watched the game tonight and thought that the U.S. didn't belong at this stage in the World Cup, I don't think they looked at the game in the right way.

"We've made a lot of progress. We haven't arrived but I think there's a bright future for the game in the United States."

He still might have a tinge of a Brooklyn accent, but don't let that fool you. Arena is one smart cookie who can and has learned. When he took over the coaching reigns in 1998, he knew little about

CHAPTER

6

how the international scene worked. In two World Cup cycles as coach, Arena has learned much about the intracacies of the worldwide game.

Now, he expects surprises when the U.S. ventures into Caribbean and Central American countries for qualifying games. The contest may be played in the middle of nowhere. Local fans and radio stations can make noise outside of the team hotel the night before the game. At the stadium, the team may be harassed with verbal intimidation and even thrown objects.

"The only way you ever learn to be a national team coach is on the job. It's on the job training all the time. I've had enough of these experiences and what happens," Arena said.

Bruce Arena

CHAPTER

6

Arena has forged a reputation as a players' coach. They love and want to play for him. Just ask three players who have been coached by Arena—Meola, midfielder Ben Olsen and Wolff.

Meola played for Arena at the University of Virginia, backstopping the 1989 Division I national championship team. When Meola was called on to become the U.S. National Team's first choice goalkeeper at the age of 20. he played a key role in helping the U.S. secure its first World Cup berth in forty years.

While Arena wanted to win every year, he realized Meola needed to train at a high level and most likely leave school for the 1990 World Cup. During a four-way call between Meola, his mother, U.S Soccer official Sunil Gulati, now the president of the organization, Arena essentially decided the goalkeeper's future.

"Bruce made all of the decisions," Meola said. "He said this was the best thing to do at that point. He told me to go to England. I went to England with John (Harkes) to train before the World Cup. It was completely up to him. Whatever he told me, I would have done."

When he decided to turn pro in 1998 as a junior after three years at Virginia, D.C. United midfielder Ben Olsen needed to stay at the Arena house for four months as he got his feet on the ground. The Arenas—Bruce, his wife, Phyllis, and son, Kenny—welcomed Olsen with open arms.

"I wasn't ready to be on my own," Olsen said. "They take care of people. There's that family. He certainly has it." Olsen admitted that Arena has been difficult to figure out, one of the qualities that has made him a superior coach.

"Your guess is as good as mine about Bruce," he said. "He's a tough guy to kind of figure out. I think that's what makes him such a good coach in the end. It's tough to really read him. It kind of keeps you guessing, keeps you motivated. And that's one of his things as far as being a coach, being a motivator to these guys, (knowing) what makes each player tick and what's going to get him to do a job for Bruce. I think that's one of his best attributes as a coach.

"He's a player's coach. When it's business, it's business with Bruce. When you're playing soccer it's all business. When you're off the field, he gives you that freedom to be yourself and do what you want, as long as it doesn't hamper your ability to help the team. If you deviate from that at all, he's right on it. He'll tell you about it."

In contrast, Wolff knows Arena only from the National Team.

"He keeps the big picture in mind," Wolff said. "When training is difficult and play is not as good, he cracks down on us. And if games are not going that way, he comes down on us and makes his point. He tries to boost us in the right way. I don't think he ever loses his players. He always has them with the right ideas, the right commitment, the desire, whether it's training or games.

"It's important because it's easy to get distracted and lose your focus if it's training or a game. I think he does a good job of keeping everyone in it. The chemistry of the team over the last four years, the last six years, has been a big part of success and I think he creates a positive environment. He's pretty honest with the players. He lets you

CHAPTER 6

know kind of where you sit. If you have a bone to pick with him, he will be the first to sit down and look you right in the eye and tell you how he sees it and the way he feels. As a player, that's all you can ask for. You want some honesty, you want some candor from your coach. And that's clearly what you're going to get from our staff."

One of his friends, C.D. Chivas coach Bob Bradley, once compared him to Dallas Cowboys coach Bill Parcells. "He's got the same sarcastic humor, but what's more important is that he sets a tone for the team," Bradley was quoted by *Sports Illustrated*. "He never gets too caught up in X's and O's, but his teams are always organized well. Bruce lets his players play."

On the left, a young Bruce Arena with Ben Alberto when Bruce played at Nassau Community College

Added Olsen: "He's probably the funniest coach I've ever been coached by. he has a great self-deprecating humor about himself. He definitely knows, when the time's right, to make the team laugh. We're a tough crowd."

As for that sarcastic humor, a day before the World Cup draw in Leipzig on Dec. 9, 2005, Arena met with about 10 American journalists. Asked if he would like to play a top-seeded team such as Brazil early on because favorites usually are slow starters in the tournament, Arena jokingly looked up to the heavens and put his hands together as though he was praying.

"I'd love to play Brazil first," he said with a smile on his face.

The reporters erupted into laughter.

Then he became serious. "I'd rather play them in the final," he said.

He also hasn't been afraid to speak his mind, which sometimes has gotten him into trouble on and off the field.

After a World Cup qualifying loss in Costa Rica, Arena had a run-in with referee Peter Prendergast of Jamaica after protesting a penalty-kick call the Jamaican native made in the waning minutes on July 23, 2000. He was slapped with a three-game suspension (eventually cut down to two matches).

Almost five years to the day in the CONCACAF Gold Cup, Arena wound up in the middle of another incident that ironically involved Predergast. The incident in question occurred in the 59th minute of the U.S.'s 3-2 come-from-behind victory over Honduras in the the semifinals at Giants Stadium in East Rutherford, N.J. on July 21, 2005 as Arena protested a foul call on Chris Armas.

Arena admitted afterwards he used a four letter word. Carlos Batres of Guatemala, the fourth official, apparently felt the language was too strong and alerted Prendergast of Jamaica, who ordered the coach off the field.

"I was baffled at the time," said Arena, who was not allowed to

Arena on the record

U.S. national coach Bruce Arena will never be considered a shrinking violet. The Franklin Square native has an opinion on just about everything. Here's a sampling of what the outspoken Arena has had to say:

On why Major League Soccer must be upgraded with better foreign players, more stadiums and more teams (2004):

"I'm not complaining. When we started this MLS thing, we were walking on egg shells, sort of. We were nervous. It's there now in year nine. We know year ten is going to happen. Hopefully, with the improvement of the facilities and the building of soccer stadiums and the potential of expansion the league will take more of a national presence than they have today. But that league has to get to 16-18 teams, no question about it. It's just

going to have to get better. But it will. It's been pretty much in neutral for a couple of years. They haven't maybe done enough in terms of bringing in some elite players. But I think as the league continues to grow I think we're going to see some of the great players in the world playing in the U.S. Maybe not in the prime of their career, but not in the tail end, either.

"I think that's going to be important because I think people in this country who like soccer—soccer is now a global sport with the satellite dishes today and cable programs they have—everybody sees the top soccer players in the world and they want to see some of them playing in our league. That is something that has to happen to get this league really pushed in the right direction."

coach the team in the final (assistant coach Glenn Myernick did instead—as the U.S. overcame Panama in a penalty-kick shootout to win the title).

"Peter Prendergast is an excellent referee," Arena said. "We get along very well."

"I don't understand the protocol. That decision is made by the fourth official and not by the referee."

Some ten months prior, Arena found himself embroiled in a controversial situation off the field for a number of opinionated and critical remarks he made about Major League Soccer and U.S. Soccer to the New York Times on Sept. 28, 2004.

"In soccer, we don't have any administrators with soccer skills, in terms of knowing the game, and that is the case at U.S. Soccer and MLS," the Times quoted Arena. "We are trying to select venues for qualifying games that give us the best chance to succeed but are compromised when games are put in MLS venues to help the league."

On why he felt the young American soccer players need greater challenges and more opportunities to play and develop:

"People think you're in a lab manufacturing soccer players. What you need to do is just give them opportunities. We have enough kids interested if we give them the right opportunities and continue to give them better competition, they'll blossom and that's no different than any where else in the world. The next real big challenge for MLS is having a development league, having reserve teams, youth teams. It's something that they continue to shy away from, but need to do. Once they do that, we're going to see a lot of players like Landon (Donovan) and DaMarcus (Beasley). We have a number of talented kids between the ages of 14 and 16. But they're never in the right environment to kick them over the top."

On having the U.S.-Mexico qualifier go up against the start of college football in 2005:

"I'm happy, first of all, it is live on an English-speaking channel. I'll be honest with you. I think it's the job of supporters of soccer in this country to be better supporters of the game. Not only U.S. games on television, but MLS games and be better consumers. When we demonstrate ratings, I think we will have an argument for primetime. I can see both sides of it. I understand where television is coming from and I understand where supporters are coming from. But the bottom line is that the television companies don't put these games on as non-profit exercises. I think it's time that the American public that supports the sport of soccer steps forward and supports our game by watching on television and getting ratings, by attending games and

While many observers and media members felt many of his quotes (Note: see the sidebar in this chapter for his other remarks) hit the mark and were not out of order, many MLS and U.S. Soccer officials were furious. One high ranking soccer official wanted Arena fired as coach, according to sources, but that wasn't going to happen because of Arena's excellent track record. Besides, it would have been next to impossible to replace him with a qualified successor.

In his public apology during a media conference call several days later, the usually brash Arena was contrite in his response.

"I have to admit when I read the article, I was truly disappointed in these statements because I believe they can certainly be construed as being very critical of both U.S. Soccer and the MLS," he said. "This was not the spirit, nor the intent for which I participated in this interview.

"I think many of you know, I've worked in the sport of soccer for the last 30 years, and I've tried real hard to try to make soccer

by buying soccer products; being good consumers as we have seen in other sports, whether it's college football, the NBA, what have you. It's time for us to put up or shut up."

More on American soccer supporters:

"I think, without a doubt, the national team program has improved. We see that by our success on the field, rankings, what have you. MLS is getting better. There's no reason why it's not supported at a higher level, in my opinion. We have so many people involved with this sport in this country so we need their support. Again, as I stated, whether it's turning on the television and watching games and helping ratings or actually go to games and support their teams. I think it's critical. If we want this sport to grow, if we want to truly position ourselves to one day win a World Cup, we need support

from the people who follow soccer in the United States. I'm hopeful that it's just going to get better and better. I think the product is good enough at the national team level as well as in our domestic league to get more support."

On developing players to become playmakers:

"I don't have a magic wand where I can create playmakers. Players' qualities and style are developed on a daily and weekly basis with their club teams. A national team coach looks at the qualities of the players he has in his pool and places them on the field in the positions he thinks will best synchronize the whole team. We don't have many players with Claudio's qualities. I think another player that might be comparable is John O'Brien. However, we don't have a whole lot of players like Claudio (Reyna) and I think that's one of more recognizable and respected in this country. And I have to admit at times, the passion and commitment I have for the game tends to cloud my judgment and apparently destroy some of my brain cells as well. For this, I apologize to the people I may have offended.

"I want to be clear about this: I'm very proud and honored to be a part of U.S. Soccer and I'm indebted to the MLS for giving me the opportunity in coaching and three memorable years at D.C. United. Throughout my tenure with U.S. Soccer, the organization has supported both the team and myself. And, let me be clear about this: I support MLS. I think the league has done great things for the sport in our country. I've had the privilege to work with some of its owners—most notably Lamar Hunt, Phil Anschutz and Bob Kraft. These are good people with great vision, commitment and generosity for our sport. Don Garber (MLS commissioner) and his staff, plus the coaches and players of MLS are truly dedicated to the game. I've said this many times—if we're going to move forward and one day be a

the voids on our team. I think there are a couple of young players that perhaps down the road will be able to step up and assume that role, but at the time I think we're a little bit limited in that regard. I think if you look around the world at a variety of national teams that does seem to be a weakness in a lot of the teams. There aren't many players with those kinds of qualities. We're hopeful that as we move forward some of our younger players can emerge in that role."

On the U.S.'s progress in the World Cup:

"Psychologically, it's important for your players to know they can step on the field and win in the World Cup. In 1990, we didn't win any games. In '94, we weren't particularly good but, having said that, we got out of group play—fair enough. Ninety-eight is a disaster (no wins), so think about our players stepping onto the field in 2002. You think they stepped on with a bunch of confidence? For some of them, there was some scar tissue there. This time, at least, we've gotten over the hump psychologically that we can win on a given day."

On MLS scheduling games when the U.S. plays qualifiers (from *New York Times*):

"For the league to play games during World Cup qualifying is insane. It shows a lack of respect for the national team. . . . Ideally, the league should synchronize its schedule with the rest of the world. Next week after I announce my roster, the clubs will complain to me again about calling up their players. We are fighting for our lives in qualifying and they're worried about making the playoffs. People are pulling in opposite directions.

CHAPTER

6

nation capable of winning the World Cup, we're going to be led by our professional league. I really believe that the future of the sport in this country is dependent upon MLS. Therefore, I intend to do everything possible to help make it succeed. Therefore, that is why I am disappointed for the way this article came out. I have no excuses for that, and I just want to apologize to all parties concerned and I appreciate the minute I have to extend my apologies to everyone and thank you."

So, it shouldn't be surprising that Arena has built a wall to hold the media at bay. He doesn't take stupid questions or fools gladly.

However, during a visit to his hometown in Franklin Square, Long Island in June, 2004 Arena let his guard down a bit with some reporters and gave then some insight into himself and background. Arena and the U.S. National Team trained several days on a stopover before they departed for Grenada in the second leg of their World Cup qualifying series (the U.S. had won the opening leg, 3-0).

It started with the bus carrying the U.S. National Team rumbling through on Hempstead Turnpike toward Franklin Square as Arena

Every coach, and I can't blame them, is trying to be successful. And they will call me, every coach. The decision to play games during qualifying is their problem."

On meaningful MLS games (*New York Times*):

"Most of the regular-season games mean nothing. The players are not motivated, and in reality the games don't mean a lot until the last month of the season. And players only get better when they play real games all the time. The league needs to think about a bonus system, going to a single table and reducing the number of teams in the playoffs. It's eight of 10 teams now and I know the league is going to 12 teams, but four in the playoffs would make more sense."

On the expectations of the U.S. winning the World Cup (*New York Times*):

"That's the problem. That's the way people think. It's a product of the environment we live in, that the sporting world is centered around sports we have invented, winning championships and calling ourselves world champions. We actually believe this, and it's pretty comical. There are only a few global sports—soccer, basketball, tennis and golf. Look at how we do. We can't compete in the Ryder Cup, although we think we are the best golfers in the world. We were sixth in the basketball world championships played in our own country and third in the Olympics. People have got to realize that the World Cup is the most challenging sporting competition in the world. And all people can say is that we can't beat told his staff about his boyhood days growing up in the New York City suburban town, his old neighborhood, how he grew up and where he went to school.

A little later that day, he drove through his old neighborhood—past his home, elementary school and high school, a bar and a pizzeria where he worked as a teenager.

The next day he brought his team for the first of three days of practice at the fields where he played his one year of youth soccer—Park Stadium of the N.Y. Hota/Bavarians Soccer Club.

After all, it's not every day the coach of the U.S. National Team—or any National Team, for that matter—brings his team to train on his hometown youth field.

"I'm not here driving around weeping and all but it was really interesting for me to drive here yesterday to see that nothing has changed," a relaxed Arena said while sitting on the blue bleachers at Park Stadium on a warm Tuesday afternoon. "It's remarkable. This place looks exactly the same. I drive down Tulip Avenue to my house and it looks exactly the same. That's what surprises me.

Panama in Panama City. No one gets it. In soccer, every country has experienced players. I'm saying to people. 'Educate yourself now. The boundaries have been extended in global sports, economics and politics.' We have a long way to go."

On the state of the game (*New York Times*):

"In soccer, we don't have any administrators with soccer skills, in terms of knowing the game, and that is the case at U.S. Soccer and M.L.S. We are trying to select venues for qualifying games that give us the best chance to succeed but are compromised when games are put in M.L.S. venues to help the league. Not sure playing El Salvador in Foxboro was the best idea."

On whether the U.S. still has something to prove internationally:

"We still need to earn our way into the elite soccer playing countries in the world. We haven't arrived. We have a long way to go."

On what the U.S. has to do to get there:

"Win games at World Cups. That's the only way you can evaluate where a country is. That is the ultimate competition. It's not friendlies, it's not other competitions, it's the World Cup. So, if you can put together consecutive World Cups where your team competes in a positive fashion, I think it upgrades where your team is at in the eyes and minds of many people."

CHAPTER 6

"I was thinking the Cape Cods (houses) weren't going to be there any more. They're all there. Nothing has changed. The elementary school, the high school, all of that is the same."

Arena admitted he hasn't been back to the island many times since he moved away nearly 30 years ago. "I've been back on a couple of occasions and never good occasions," he said. "Funerals."

He visited the gravesite of and paid his respects to his mother and sister and a college roommate at Holy Rood Cemetery near St. Brigid's Church in Westbury, L.I. and visited his father, who was in a nursing home in the same town. "I'll have a little time to do those things, which I haven't been able to do in a long time," he said.

"This town or Long Island gave me the opportunity to be introduced to the sport at a really late age. But it was something that inspired me. I enjoyed it."

Arena tried football in high school as a ninth-grade quarterback, but he was too small for the sport—5-2 and 100 pounds—so he turned to soccer. There wasn't much organized youth soccer at the time. "You just played because you wanted to play," he said.

At first he was a midfielder, but then an interesting twist of fate happened in the first match of his junior year when the Carey High School goalkeeper hit an opponent and was suspended for the year. Arena was drafted as the goalkeeper. "I played 20 minutes as a midfielder and my career was over," he said before becoming a bit sarcastic. "I could have been the equivalent of (Johan) Cruyff. It never happened."

But something else did. A year later he discovered Hota, then a member of the German-American Soccer League (now called the Cosmopolitan Soccer League), after someone invited him to play for one of the club's youth teams. Hota is a throwback to an earlier era of American soccer, where clubs had a clubhouse, field, and locker room facilities. The club holds its Christmas and Super Bowl parties in the clubhouse.

Its clubhouse is actually a trophy room with dozens of trophies, banners and pictures, reveling in its 84-year history. There are trophies from virtually every conceivable tournament and competition, including the U.S. Open Challenge Cup, Amateur Cup and Cosmopolitan Soccer League, among others. Hota has merged with other clubs through the decades to remain alive and viable.

The Plattduetsche Home Society, which owns an adjacent old-age home and restaurant, gave Hota permission to build tennis courts on its property, which allowed the club some income outside of soccer. Hota donates money to Plattsduetsche every year.

"I lived about a mile away from here," Arena said. "I didn't know Hota existed until someone invited me to play. I remember my first game. The big club played. We both played the Greek Americans and there were probably like 4,000-5,000 people here. Those were the days the (New York) Comsos were the senior team. It opened up a world of soccer that I didn't know.

"I had no clue. It was a very intimidating experience. Interesting."

Arena played a year at Hota. "It was actually shocking to me," he said. "Especially where I was, this whole side of Franklin Square was all Italian and then you came here and all of sudden there were the Greeks, the Germans, the other ethnic groups that we basically didn't come across and didn't know existed in those numbers."

He attended Nassau Community College in Garden City for two years and earned honors as a goalkeeper and a lacrosse player before transferring to Cornell. Ironically, the hotel Arena and the team is staying at—the Long Island Marriott—is adjacent to NCC.

"My junior college team, I've been telling people, it was as good in terms of talent as the teams that I played with at Cornell that made it to the Final Four at Division I," Arena said. "It had a lot of talented players, maybe athletically not the same as the athletes you put on the field in Division I soccer, but certainly more skillful."

He also learned some important lessons from NCC coach Bill Stevenson, whom, Arena said, "created an environment, where you wanted to come out everyday. He wasn't a guy who put a lot of pressure on us, just wanted us to go out and have fun, which I try to do with my teams today."

In fact, Arena shared a secret, crediting another goalkeeper with sparking his interest in the game—former New York Cosmos keeper Shep Messing, currently the MetroStars color announcer.

"This is not known by many, but I think the guy who had the greatest influence on my career was Shep Messing," he said of his

CHAPTER

6

goalkeeper coach at NCC. Messing had taken a year off, transferring from New York University to Harvard. "He really inspired me. I enjoyed listening to his stories and watching him travel with the Olympic team that year."

Arena grew up in simpler times. His parents moved out to Long Island from Brooklyn only a month after he and his twin sister Barbara were born in 1951 (he has two older brothers, Paul and Mike). His house was the first on a street amid potato and tomato farms.

His family was far from being wealthy. His father Vincent was a butcher, his mother Adeline drove a school bus. "But there was never anything we didn't have," he said. "Our view of things those days was pretty simple. Give me a ball, a baseball bat, a glove and I'll be back in about eight or ten hours. We didn't need any of the games, the computers and that kind of stuff.

"I remember my childhood. It was so much fun. Everyday was fun, hanging out with the guys in the neighborhood, playing games. All of that stuff, things that kids today don't do. They jump in the cars with their mothers. They're catered to their activities and all. It was just a whole different world."

Fast forward to the pressure and perhaps the future.

Arena has sloughed off questions on what he plans to do after the World Cup. This is his second go-around and an eight-year tenure as a National Team coach is quite rare in these modern times. A third consecutive try coaching the National Team is not out of the question, but there has been some talk of Arena wanting to coach in Europe someday.

Of course, a club would have to offer him a job first. But if the U.S. survives the opening round in one apiece and reaches the second round (and beyond), it would not be surprising if Arena did get some offers. Probably the best bet would be in England. Don't hold your breath on the English Premiership, at least not first. But the Coca Cola League, which is No. 2 in the English soccer, err, football, pecking order, would be a perfect place to start a new challenge.

But first, let's see how Arena and his Americans fare in Germany.

International Teams—

The History, Qualifying, Players, Coaches, and an Overview

GROUP A—Costa Rica, Ecuador, Germany, Poland

GROUP B—England, Paraguay, Sweden, Trinidad and Tobago

GROUP C—Argentina, Ivory Coast, Netherlands, Serbia and Montenegro

GROUP D—Angola, Iran, Mexico, Portugal

GROUP E—Czech Republic, Ghana, Italy, USA

GROUP F—Australia, Brazil, Croatia, Japan

GROUP G—France, Korea, Switzerland, Togo

GROUP H—Saudi Arabia, Spain, Tunisia, Ukraine

THE "REAL" GROUPS

The World Cup draw divided the thirty-two teams into eight groups of four teams apiece. While those eight groups come out in a neatly tied package, that hardly tells the entire story.

Here's another version that breaks down the countries into nine groups—the contenders, the pretenders, teasers, luck of the draw, on the bubble, unluck of the draw, happy to be there, don't bet the farm and out of Africa.

CONTENDERS

These teams should wind up in the final four.

Brazil—The Brazilians are everyone's favorite, thanks to an endless talent pool. The best team in the world right now, and perhaps on July 9 as well.

England—Many observers seem to tout the English, who find a way to stumble. Who knows? They might surprise the experts.

France—Embarrassed by its first-round elimination in 2002, the French might have learned their lesson. A healthy Zinedine Zidane certainly would help.

Germany—This German team certainly isn't close to the past teams of Franz Beckenbauer, Juergen Klinsmann or Lothar Matthaeus. But it is a team run by Klinsmann, the coach who lives (some claim hides) in Orange County in southern California. Regardless, the Germans must be given the respect of the home team despite the 4-1 debacle of a World Cup warm-up loss in Italy (see Korea and Japan in 2002).

PRETENDERS

These teams could reach the final four if they get a rousing performance or two, or if the ball bounces their way.

Argentina—Another country high on many people's list, but hasn't done anything since finishing second in 1990. South American teams traditionally don't do well in Europe, but after the FIFA Confederations Cup final in 2005 that pitted Brazil and the Argentines, some people are talking about a rematch. That's probably a long shot.

Netherlands—The Dutch have been living off their two runner-ups finishes in 1974 (in Germany) and 1978. They produce some of the most talented players in the world, but usually find a way to submarine their chances. They must play better as a team if they are to do some damage.

Czech Republic—Were the Czechs' Euro 2004 performance an aberration? Does Pavel Nedved have enough gas left in his international tank to work some international magic one last time?

Italy—After two sub-par performances at the 2002 World Cup and Euro 2004, the Italians get this position via reputation. They must prove themselves again.

CHAPTER

7

TEASERS

These teams, at least on paper, look like tantalizing sides. However, when push comes to shove, they perennially underachieve.

Portugal—How ironic Portugal is connected to Spain geographically. There is one slight difference, however, between the two countries. The Portuguese actually have reached the semifinals once in the past 40 years (1966).

Spain—Like clockwork every four years the Spanish tease us with a team that just might go far, and every quadrennial we fall for that premise. Not this year.

These teams wound up in weaker groups thanks to . . . well, the luck of the draw.

Mexico—Being in the same group as Iran and Angola should boost the Mexicans into the second round.

Croatia—Yes, the Croatians have Brazil in their Group F. But they also have Australia and Japan. If they can't get to the second round, they should be embarrassed.

Poland—The Poles should finish ahead of Costa Rica and Ecuador in Group A (which also has Germany).

Switzerland—The Swiss already have proven they can take on France on an equal basis. With Korea and Togo also in Group G, the second round certainly is reachable.

Ukraine—The Ukrainians are fortunate to be in the same group as Tunisia and Saudi Arabia. Heck, the way Spain keeps shooting itself in the foot through the years, they could wind up on top.

These teams could have a great World Cup, but not make it to the second round, given the degree of difficulty of their groups.

United States—The U.S. needs at least a tie from either of its Italy and Czech Republic encounters entering the Ghana match to have a chance of moving on.

Costa Rica—Can the Central Americans duplicate the miracle of Italia '90, when they stunned Sweden and Scotland and reached the second round? It could happen against the likes of Poland and Ecuador (and then there's Germany amongst the four).

Serbia & Montenegro—Here's a rarity: A first-time European qualifier. Being in the Group C of Death, don't expect miracles or many, if any, points.

These teams are in the wrong place at the wrong time.

Sweden—With England and Paraguay in its Group B, it will be a dog fight to reach the second round.

Paraguay—Only two South American teams—Argentina and Brazil—have gone deep when the tournament has been in Europe. Paraguay won't be one of them this time around.

Ecuador—Germany and Poland are the two biggest obstacles for this South American team.

Iran—This is one tough Asian side, but it could be difficult to navigate the Group D waters against the likes of Portugal and Mexico.

Anything more than a tie will be just fine to these nations.

JUST HAPPY
TO BE THERE

Australia—Well, the Aussies certainly have started a unique tradition. They only qualify for the World Cup when Germany hosts it, the last being in 1974.

Trinidad & Tobago—T&T makes its first appearance in the Cup. Don't hold your breath on the Caribbean side getting out in one piece with the likes of England, Sweden and Paraguay around.

If these teams reach the second round, their players should get bonuses for that accomplishment alone.

DON'T BET THE
FARM

Korea—After a fabulous showing and fourth-place finish in 2002, the Koreans will return to their usual struggling ways, especially in Europe.

Japan—After an encouraging showing and second-round finish in 2002, the Japanese will return to their usual struggling ways, especially in Europe.

Saudi Arabia—Good technically, but the Saudis on many occasions lack the physical means teams need to be successful at the World Cup.

Tunisia—This northern African side has been good enough to reach soccer's promised land, but hasn't been good enough to get out of the first round.

In a World Cup rarity, Africa has four countries qualified for the first time. They're not expected to do much, but teams from that continent have a history of surprising (Cameroon, Nigeria and Senegal).

OUT OF AFRICA

Ivory Coast—Very possibily the best of the bunch.

Ghana—Probably the second best from the continent.

Angola—Many players perform in Portugal, but it probably won't be enough in a group that includes Portugal and Mexico.

Togo—With virtually no players performing in Europe or higher leagues, this could be a disaster waiting to happen.

CHAPTER
7

While they may lack the drama of the latter knockout rounds, some opening round matches still have some kick to them. These 11 matches might be worth watching live or on television (in chronological order):

- Portugal vs. Angola (Group D), Cologne on June 11—A confrontation of the former mother country vs. the colony. On paper, Portugal is favored. Many Portuguese fans should be familiar with the Angolan players because many of them play in the Portuguese leagues.
- Australia vs. Japan (Group F), Kaiserslautern on June 12—Well, at least one of these weaker countries from Group F will bring home at least a point from Germany. This match-up is significant for another reason: Australia will join Asia for 2010 WC qualifying and this will be a test to see how the Aussies stack up.
- France vs. Switzerland (Group G), Stuttgart on June 13—A game in which European qualifying opponents tussle in the opening round. It should be a close encounter, given their European qualifying results. They played to a scoreless tie in Paris on March 26, 2005 and then to a 1-1 draw in Berne Switzerland on Oct. 8.
- Germany vs. Poland (Group A), Dortmund on June 14—Another battle of the neighbors. In the seventies and eighties, they were the class of Europe. They didn't meet at the 1972 Munich Olympics, although the Poles earned the gold medal. They did clash at the 1974 World Cup in West Germany as the hosts prevailed in a second-round Group B encounter, 1-0, in Frankfurt (on July 3, 1974) to advance to the championship match. There, the West Germans edged the Netherlands for the title, 2-1. Poland defeated Brazil in the third-place game. They also played to a scoreless tie at the 1978 World Cup in Argentina.
- Saudi Arabia vs. Tunisia (Group H), Munich on June 14—For only the second time in WC history, a pair of Arab sides clash in the opening around. In 1994, the Saudis and Morocco went head-to-head at Giants Stadium in East Rutherford, N.J. The Saudis prevailed, 2-1, producing one of the best goals and one of the most entertaining games of that competition.
- England vs. Trinidad & Tobago (Group B), Nuremburg on June 15—Another battle of the former mother country vs. the colony.

CHAPTER

7

England should win this one handily. But the Caribbean side has several players who perform or who have played in England, so there will be a lot of pride on the line.

⊕ Netherlands vs. Ivory Coast (Group C), Stuttgart on June 16—In what could be the most unusual clash that would pit brother against brother—the Ivory Coast's Bonavneture Kalou could wind up playing against his brother Salomon Kalou, who is trying to obtain Dutch citizenship. Salomon, an Ivory Coast native, has been playing for Feyenoord for the past 2 1/2 years, two years short of the minimum residency requirement for naturalized citizenship. The Dutch have rushed paperwork through the courts so the 20-year-old forward could be a naturalized citizen in time for the World Cup. As The Times of London noted, Salomon Kalou doesn't have any Dutch blood in him. He isn't married to a Dutch wife, have a finacee or a same-sex partner. As this book went to press, Salomon Kalou did not have Dutch citizenship.

⊕ U.S. vs. Italy (Group E), Kaiserslautern on June 17—This WC rivalry goes back to the 1934 competition, when Italy rolled to a 7-1 win. In fact, the Italians used the U.S. as whipping boys in several international competitions through the years, including the 1936 and 1948 Olympic Games. The last time they met at this level was at Italia '90. The Italians prevailed, 1-0, but by the end of the match, the Americans slowed down the pace and managed to turn the crowd on the home team as they whistled their heroes.

⊕ England vs. Sweden (Group B), Cologne on June 20—Besides being a rematch of the 2002 opening round, England coach Sven-Goran Eriksson takes on his native country. And by then, who knows how many chapters of the ongoing English soap opera there will have been written.

⊕ Argentina vs. Netherlands (Group C), Frankfurt on June 21--Because there are so many teams and so many groups in today's World Cup, it is rather rare that two quality sides face one another early on, especially in the Group C, aka "The Group of Death." This is the exception. Just remember their fabulous quarterfinal confrontation at France '98, when a Dennis Bergkamp goal in the waning minutes lifted the Dutch to a dramatic 2-1 triumph.

⊕ Australia vs. Croatia (Group F), Stuttgart on June 22—This will be the battle for Croatian bragging rights. Australia has several players with Croatian heritage on its team and a sizeable population from that Eastern European country living in Melbourne.

England will capture its second World Cup, according to the March 2006 edition of *FourFourTwo*, The British soccer magazine asked the makers of the soccer game Football Manager 2006 to help the publication plot out the entire World Cup.

SOME FANTASY
FOOTBALL

England outlasted Germany in penalty kicks, 4-2, after playing to a 2-2 draw in regulation and extratime. Mike Ballack struck twice for Germany, while Michael Owen and Frank Lampard found the back of the net for England.

As for the U.S., the Americans finished third and out of the Group E money (the top two teams in each group advance to the second round). According to the company and magazine, the Americans tied the Czech Republic, 1-1, lost to Italy, 2-0, and edged past Ghana, 3-2, on Brian McBride's goal five minutes from time. Italy (3-0-0) finished first and the Czechs (1-1-1) moved on thanks to a better goal differential, zero to the U.S.'s minus one.

If you're interested, here's how the tournament turned out:

FIRST ROUND

Group A—Germany 3, Costa Rica 0; Poland 3, Ecuador 0; Germany 2, Poland 0; Costa Rica 2, Ecuador 0; Poland 1, Costa Rica 0;

FANTASY
TOURNAMENT

Germany 3, Ecuador 1.

Group B—England 1, Paraguay 0; Sweden 4, Trinidad & Tobago 2; England 5, Trinidad & Tobago 0; Sweden 3, Paraguay 0; Paraguay 1, Trinidad & Tobago 1; England 3, Sweden 1.

Group C—Ivory Costa 2, Argentina 0; Serbia & Montenegro 1, Netherlands 0; Argentina 3, Serbia & Montenegro 0; Netherlands 3, Ivory Coast 1; Netherlands 2, Argentina 2; Ivory Coast 4, Serbia & Montenegro 2.

Group D—Mexico 2, Iran 0; Portugal 2, Angola 0; Mexico 3, Angola 0; Portugal 2, Iran 0; Iran 3, Angola 1; Portugal 4, Mexico 1.

Group E—U.S. 1, Czech Republic 1, Italy 1, Ghana 0, Italy 2, Ghana 0; Czech Republic 2, Ghana 1; Italy 1, Czech Republic 0; U.S. 3, Ghana 2.

Group F—Australia 2, Japan 0; Brazil 2, Croatia 2; Croatia 3, Japan 1; Brazil 3, Australia 1; Croatia 0, Australia 0; Brazil 2, Japan 0.

Group G—Korea 1, Togo 0; France 2, Switzerland 0; France 3, Korea 1; Togo 3, Switzerland 1; Switzerland 5, Korea 0; France 5, Togo 0.

Group H—Spain 2, Ukraine 0; Tunisia 0, Saudi Arabia 0; Saudi Arabia 2, Ukraine 1; Spain 0, Tunisia 0; Saudi Arabia 2, Spain 2; Ukraine 1, Tunisia 0.

CHAPTER
7

SECOND ROUND

England 3, Poland 1; Ivory Coast 3, Mexico 2; Brazil 2, Czech Republic 0; Spain 2, Switzerland 0; Portugal 1, Netherlands 0; Croatia 1, Italy 0; France 1, Saudi Arabia 0; Germany defeated Sweden (no score printed).

QUARTERFINALS

Germany 2, Portugal 1; Brazil 2, France 0; Spain 3, Croatia 0;

England 0, Ivory Coast 0 (England advances on PKs, 3-0).

SEMIFINALS

Germany 1, Brazil 0; England 4, Spain 1.

THIRD-PLACE MATCH

Brazil 0, Spain 0 (Brazil wins on PKs, 5-4)

Of course, the computer does not take into chance what a particular player's mood is on the day of game, whether he, let's say can't take the pressure or gets a bizarre injury (see Brazil's Ronaldo at the France '98 final) and other factors (such as Germany getting whipped by Italy, 4-1, in an World Cup warm-up on March 1).

In other words, it's fun to play and speculate, but it is far from being the last word.

In case you're wondering, English bookmakers, according to Reuters, made the U.S. 100-1 shots to win it all on the night of World Cup draw on Dec. 9, 2005. That's No. 18 out of 32 teams. Italy was at 8-1, Czech Republic at 20-1 and Ghana at 250-1. Brazil was the favorite to win its sixth world championship at 11-4, followed by England at 13-2.

CHAPTER 7

World Cup 2006 Odds Chart:		
Brazil 11-4	Croatia 50-1	Ghana 250-1
England 13-2	Ukraine 50-1	Korea 300-1
Germany 7-1	Ivory Coast 66-1	Tunisia 300-1
Argentina 8-1	Poland 66-1	Angola 400-1
Italy 8-1	Switzerland 80-1	Togo 400-1
France 10-1	Serbia & Montenegro	Costa Rica 500-1
Spain 12-1	100-1	Iran 500-1
Netherlands 14-1	U.S. 100-1	Saudi Arabia 750-1
Portugal 18-1	Australia 125-1	Trinidad & Tobago
Czech Republic 20-1	Ecuador 125-1	1,000-1
Sweden 28-1	Japan 150-1	
Mexico 40-1	Paraguay 150-1	

The Tournament Schedule

The top two teams in each of the eight groups will qualify for the second round. There will be no wild card teams (which were the four best third-place countries) in contrast to previous World Cups. The rest of the tournament, from second round to quarterfinal to semifinals to the championship match, will be a single-elimination tournament.

For the third consecutive Cup, three points (instead of two) will be awarded for a victory. A draw is still worth one point.

All times listed below are Eastern Standard Time.

Date	Venue	Teams	Time

GROUP A—Costa Rica, Ecuador, Germany, Poland

FIRST ROUND

Date	Venue	Teams	Time
June 9	Munich	GER vs. CRC	18:00
June 9	Gelsenkirchen	POL vs. ECU	21:00
June 14	Dortmund	GER vs. POL	21:00
June 15	Hamburg	ECU vs. CRC	15:00
June 20	Berlin	ECU vs. GER	16:00
June 20	Hanover	CRC vs. POL	16:00

GROUP B—England, Paraguay, Sweden, Trinidad and Tobago

June 10	Frankfurt	ENG vs. PAR	15:00
June 10	Dortmund	TRI vs. SWE	18:00
June 15	Nuremberg	ENG vs. TRI	18:00
June 15	Berlin	SWE vs. PAR	21:00
June 20	Cologne	SWE vs. ENG	21:00
June 20	Kaiserslautern	PAR vs. TRI	21:00

GROUP C—Argentina, Ivory Coast, Netherlands, Serbia and Montenegro

| June 10 | Hamburg | ARG vs. CIV | 21:00 |
| June 11 | Leipzig | SCG vs. NED | 15:00 |

263

GROUP C (*continued*)

June 16	Gelsenkirchen	ARG vs. SCG	15:00
June 16	Stuttgart	NED vs. CIV	18:00
June 21	Frankfurt	NED vs. ARG	21:00
June 21	Munich	CIV vs. SCG	21:00

GROUP D—Angola, Iran, Mexico, Portugal

June 11	Nuremberg	MEX vs. IRN	18:00
June 11	Cologne	ANG vs. POR	21:00
June 16	Hanover	MEX vs. ANG	21:00
June 17	Frankfurt	POR vs. IRN	15:00
June 21	Gelsenkirchen	POR vs. MEX	16:00
June 21	Leipzig	IRN vs. ANG	16:00

GROUP E—Czech Republic, Ghana, Italy, USA

June 12	Hanover	ITA vs. GHA	21:00
June 12	Gelsenkirchen	USA vs. CZE	18:00
June 17	Kaiserslautern	ITA vs. USA	21:00
June 17	Cologne	CZE vs. GHA	18:00
June 22	Hamburg	CZE vs. ITA	16:00
June 22	Nuremberg	GHA vs. USA	16:00

GROUP F—Australia, Brazil, Croatia, Japan

June 13	Berlin	BRA vs. CRO	21:00
June 12	Kaiserslautern	AUS vs. JPN	15:00
June 18	Munich	BRA vs. AUS	18:00
June 18	Nuremberg	JPN vs. CRO	15:00
June 22	Dortmund	JPN vs. BRA	21:00
June 22	Stuttgart	CRO vs. AUS	21:00

GROUP G—France, Korea, Switzerland, Togo

June 13	Stuttgart	FRA vs. SUI	18:00
June 13	Frankfurt	KOR vs. TOG	15:00
June 18	Leipzig	FRA vs. KOR	21:00
June 19	Dortmund	TOG vs. SUI	15:00
June 23	Cologne	TOG vs. FRA	21:00
June 23	Hanover	SUI vs. KOR	21:00

CHAPTER

7

GROUP H—Saudi Arabia, Spain, Tunisia, Ukraine

FIRST ROUND
(*CONTINUED*)

June 14	Leipzig	ESP vs. UKR	15:00
June 14	Munich	TUN vs. KSA	18:00
June 19	Stuttgart	ESP vs. TUN	21:00
June 19	Hamburg	KSA vs. UKR	18:00
June 23	Kaiserslautern	KSA vs. ESP	16:00
June 23	Berlin	UKR vs. TUN	16:00

Date	Time	Locale	Match #	Winner vs Runner-Up	
June 24	11 A.M.	Munich	49	Group A vs.	Group B
June 24	3 P.M.	Leipzig	50	Group C vs.	Group D
June 25	11 A.M.	Stuttgart	51	Group B vs.	Group A
June 25	3 P.M.	Nuremberg	52	Group D vs.	Group C
June 26	11 A.M.	Kaiserslautern	53	Group E vs.	Group F
June 26	3 P.M.	Cologne	54	Group G vs.	Group H
June 27	11 A.M.	Dortmund	55	Group F vs.	Group E
June 27	3 P.M.	Hannover	56	Group H vs.	Group G

SECOND ROUND

Date	Locale	Match #	Winner vs Runner-Up	
June 30	Berlin	57	Game 49 vs.	Game 50
June 30	Hamburg	58	Game 51 vs.	Game 52
July 1	Gelsenkirchen	59	Game 53 vs.	Game 54
July 1	Frankfurt	60	Game 49 vs.	Game 56

QUARTER FINALS

Date	Locale	Match #	Winner vs Runner-Up	
July 4	Dortmund	61	Game 57 vs.	Game 58
July 5	Munich	62	Game 59 vs.	Game 60

SEMIFINALS

CHAPTER
7

Date	Locale	Match #	Winner vs Runner-Up
July 8	Stuttgart	63	Semifinal losers

THIRD PLACE

Date	Locale	Match #	Winner vs Runner-Up
July 9	Berlin	64	Semifinal winners

CHAMPIONSHIP

Checklist of Teams in the World Cup

Angola (ANG)—267	Mexico (MEX)—341
Argentina (ARG)—271	Netherands (NED)—346
Australia (AUS)—276	Paraguay (PAR)—350
Brazil (BRA)—280	Poland (POL)—354
Costa Rica (CRC)—285	Portugal (POR)—358
Croatia (CRO)—289	Saudi Arabia (KSA)—362
Czech Republic (CZE)—293	Serbia and Montenegro
Ecuador (ECU)—298	(SCG)—366
England (ENG)—302	Spain (ESP)—370
France (FRA)—307	Sweden (SWE)—374
Germany (GER)—311	Switzerland (SUI)—378
Ghana (GHA) —316	Togo (TOG) —382
Iran (IRN)—320	Trinidad and Tobago
Italy (ITA)—324	(TRI)—385
Ivory Coast* (CIV)—329	Tunisia (TUN)—389
Japan (JPN)—333	Ukraine (UKR)—392
Korea Republic* (KOR)—337	USA (USA)—396

*Côte d'Ivoire
*South Korea

CHAPTER
7

ANGOLA
Group D

POPULATION: 13,500,000
COLORS: Red shirts, black shorts, red
    socks.
APPEARANCES: First.

None.

In its sixth attempt to qualify for the Cup since 1986, Angola won African Group 4, although the team experienced some tense moments in the preliminary round. The Angolans dropped a 3-1 away decision to lowly Chad, but rebounded with a 2-0 home win, advancing on away goals. After finishing tied with Nigeria with identical 6-1-3 record and 21 points, Angola reached its first World Cup by winning the head-to-head competition. The teams played to a 1-1 draw in Nigeria, but Angola prevailed at home, 1-0.

Team captain and forward Fabrice Akwa scored several key qualifying goals, including the game-winner vs. Nigeria and the lone goal--a header—in the 1-0 win over Rwanda that clinched a spot in Germany. Benfica striker Pedro Mantorras is just coming back from a knee injury, but he can be an impact player if healthy. Midfielder Figueiredo, the team's best free-kick artist, has but 16 international appearances as a 31-year-old, but could emerge as a key performer with his leadership ability and work rate.

Goalkeeper: Goliath (Sagrada Esperanca). João Ricardo Pereira (Moreirense, Portugal), Lama (Petro Atletico). Defenders: Delgado Primero (Agosto), Jamba (AS Aviação), Kai (Santa Clara, Portugal), Jacinto (AS Aviação, Angola), Lebo Lebo (Sagrada Esperanca), Loco (Benfica Luanada), Manuel (AS Aviacao), Marco Airosa (Barreirense (Portugal), Rui Marques (Leeds, England), Yamba Asha (AS Aviacao). Midfielders: Miloy (InterClube), Mendonca (Varzim, Portugal), Figueiredo (Varzim, Portugal), Ze Kalanga (Petro Atletico, Angola). Forwards: Fabrice Akwa (Al Wakra, Qatar), Andre "Titi" Buengo (Clermont Foot, France), Flavio (Al Ahly (Egypt), Love (AS Viascao), Pedro Mantorras (Benfica, Portugal), Maurito (Al Wahda, United Arab Emirates), Santana (Sagrada Esperanca).

PROJECTED
STARTING
LINEUP

Goalkeeper: João Ricardo Pereira (Moreirense, Portugal). Defenders: Delgado (Primero Agosto), Jamba (AS Aviação, Angola), Jacinto (AS Aviação, Angola), Kali (Santa Clara, Portugal), Lebo-Lebo (Sagrada Esperanca). Midfielders: Miloy (InterClube), Mendonca (Varzim, Portugal), Figueiredo (Varzim, Portugal), Ze Kalanga (Petro Atletico, Angola). Forwards: Fabrice Akwa (Qatar, S.C.Qatar), Pedro Mantorras (Benfica, Portugal).

COACH

Luis Oliveira Goncalves, 48, is a national hero after directing Angola to the World Cup for the first time. He should be very familiar with his players after guiding Angola's Under-20 team to the African youth championship and to the second round of the FIFA World Youth Championship, both in 2001. That turned out to be a bountiful year for Goncalves as his club team, InterClube, Luanda's police team, reached the African Cup Winners Cup final. His success led him to the national side in 2003 as Goncalves replaced Brazilian Ismael Kurtz, whose team was stunned by minnows Chad, 3-1, in November, 2003. Called the "miracle man" of Angolan soccer by some, Goncalves was so impressive in transforming the team that some supporters reportedly wanted him to sign a lifetime contract to coach the national team. The Angola Football Association tried to recruit Dunga, who captained Brazil to its 1994 World Cup triumph, to coach the team alongside Goncalves, according to English newspaper, The Independent.

2006
WORLD CUP

Angola is primed for its first appearance in the World Cup. Before qualifying, Angola—the Palancas Negras—the Black Antelopes, a breed of antelopes who are threatened with extinction—had reached the African biennial tournament but twice—South Africa '96 and Burkina Faso '98. This made an astonishing accomplishment even sweeter.

Add the fact that the country has been ravaged by civil war and unrest for the past three decades since it received its independence from Portugal in 1975. So, participating in the world's greatest tournament is seen by some as a potential rallying point to unite the people and to celebrate after the 2002 ceasefire agreement between the Angolan government and the Uniao Nacional para a Independencia Total de Angola (UNITA).

"After 30 years of civil war, to have qualified for the World Cup is a massive boost for our country and our people and our aim in Germany is try and make them happy and proud," coach Luis Oliveira Goncalves told **Reuters**.

Added forward and captain Fabrice Akwa: "We have proved that

Angola is not just about oil, war and poverty."

Angola has stocked its National Team since 1996 with native play-ers and players with Angolan heritage; there are reportedly four million Angolan refugees in Portugal. Originally, then national coach Carlos Alhinho decided to search for professional players who had roots to the African country, even if they had never stepped on Angolan soil. It worked slowly but surely, the Angolan National Team improved.

The less said about the Angolans' performance in the Nations Cup the better. Angola embarrassingly finished third in its group, behind a pair of non-World Cup teams—Cameroon and the Democratic Republic of Congo. The Angolans lost 3-1 to Cameroon and played the Congo to a scoreless draw before edging fourth-place Togo, 3-2. They missed out by one goal to the Congo in goal differential.

"We got four points but we are not happy to miss out on qualifi-cation," Goncalves was quoted by **Reuters**. "We tried with so much effort but we had no luck. We did all we could do but fell short.

"We had a lack of experience on the field but we will prepare well to overcome this at the World Cup. We got some good experience at this tournament. This run has been very good for us. We will try to use this for our World Cup adventure."

In June, however, Angola's opponents will be much more difficult and a greater challenge than its African competition—Portugal, Mexico and Iran.

The Angolans most important World Cup match? Easy. That's against their former colonial masters, Portugal, in Cologne on June 11. They've met twice before in Lisbon and haven't fared too well, getting drubbed 6-0 in 1989 and managing to find the back of the net in a 5-1 pasting in 2001—a game in which Angola had four players red-carded. One expulsion would be devastating with so much at stake this time around.

Goncalves hopes the game will have a different result this time around. "At the World Cup, the two national teams have an obligation to leave a good image," he told *When Saturday Comes* magazine. "Portugal and Angola are almost family, with very strong ties."

Even before a ball was kicked at the Cup, the Angolans suffered a major loss when FIFA suspended fullback Yamba Asha for nine months for drug use. The sentence came down on January 25, 2006, several months after his original ban, which was imposed in November, 2005. Asha, the only Angolan to compete in every match, did not play in the African Nations Cup final because of the suspension.

FIFA has not given details of which drug was involved. Angolan soccer officials said Asha had taken a flu remedy which contained a

ANGOLA

banned substance.

"It's a big blow for a country like ours to lose these players for Germany," Goncalves told **Reuters**. "We know FIFA has its rules and regulations and we abide by them but it is a tough ban. . . . He is a person whose life is football, who earns his living from football and we hope they will understand this."

If one of its warm-up matches is any indication of what is to come, Angola's first stay in the World Cup will be short and sweet. The Africans dropped a 1-0 decision to Korea in Seoul on March 1, 2006, a game in which they struggled without Figueiredo, the team's best midfielder.

Groping for excuses for the loss, Goncalves put his own spin on the match.

"Today we played a very strong side," he said about one of the weakest teams in the 2006 World Cup. "We've just qualified for our first World Cup, but step by step we're improving.

"Today we had two opponents, first Korea and second the snow."

As part of its preparation for the Cup, Angola will play four warm-up matches in Germany this Spring—against Argentina, Australia, Saudi Arabia and Switzerland. The exact dates and venues of the matches hadn't been determined.

Angola is a solid defensive side (only six allowed, the second fewest by an African nation), but is expected to struggle to find the back of the net (their 12 goals scored was the fewest of the five qualified countries from the continent), especially against this opposition, even with the likes of forwards Pedro Mantorras and Akwa, the best bets to score goals. The Africans also could use a top-flight playmaker to control the pace. The likelihood of finding one before June is slim and none.

"Angola will be a very, very strong underdog," LAC radio station's Jose Cunha told **BBC.com**. "We have a lot of ground to gain to compete with these powerful nations. They will play a collective game with strong emphasis on defense and try to spring a few surprises on the counterattack."

An interesting bit of information for all you World Cup history buffs: As Cup debutantes in 2002, Senegal stunned the world and France by winning the tournament opener over the defending champions, 1-0. The African nation went on to reach the quarterfinals before it was ousted by Sweden.

ANGOLA

ARGENTINA
Group C

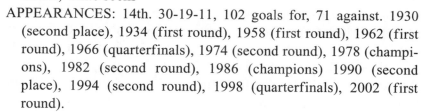

POPULATION: 36,800,000
COLORS: Light blue shirts, black shorts, white socks
APPEARANCES: 14th. 30-19-11, 102 goals for, 71 against. 1930 (second place), 1934 (first round), 1958 (first round), 1962 (first round), 1966 (quarterfinals), 1974 (second round), 1978 (champions), 1982 (second round), 1986 (champions) 1990 (second place), 1994 (second round), 1998 (quarterfinals), 2002 (first round).

The 1978 and 1986 championships were well deserved. While Argentina is considered one of the world powers, the South American side has underachieved since scrapping to a second-place finish at Italia '90, and had the Argentines defeated Germany in 1990, observers agreed it would have set soccer back for years because of the physical, defensive style the team played. The Argentines lost to bitter archrivals Uruguay in the first championship match in 1930, 4-2. It took them thirty-six years before they got past the first round again, losing to England in the quarterfinals in 1966. The Diego Maradona drug scandal at the end of the opening round in USA '94 didn't help. They were eliminated in the second round. They rebounded at France '98, outlasting England in the second round before meeting their ultimate fate in another classic confrontation, a 2-1 last-minute lost to the Netherlands in the quarterfinals. Touted by many as a championship contender in 2002, Argentina fell woefully short, getting ousted in the first round in what many observers considered the Group of Death (England, Sweden and Nigeria).

WORLD CUP HISTORY

Argentina finished second to archrival Brazil in qualifying with a 10-4-4 record, outscoring its opponents, 29-17. The Argentines' clinching certainly was a sweet one, accomplishing the feat against the Brazilians, rolling to a three-goal halftime advantage en route to a 3-1 triumph on June 3, 2005. Hernan Crespo struck twice and Juan Roman Riquelme once.

HOW THEY QUALIFIED

Carlos Tevez and Lionel Messi are two of the most exciting, young-talent to appear on the world scene in years. Messi made headlines for Barcelona after his runs ripped apart Chelsea in the Champions League in February. Tevez's overall imposing performance drew crit-

PLAYERS TO WATCH

ARGENTINA

PLAYERS
TO
WATCH

ical raves during the 2004 Summer Olympics. Hernan Crespo, who hasn't played up to his full potential in club competition, still can be a dangerous striker. Midfielder Juan Roman Riquelme is the playmaker who is good organizer. Defender and team captain Juan Pablo Sorín is considered to be the heart and soul of the side.

PLAYER
POOL

Goalkeeper: Roberto Abbondanzieri (Boca Juniors), Leo Franco (Atletico Madrid, Spain), German Lux (River Plate). Defenders: Roberto Ayala (Valencia, Spain), Nicolas Burdisso (Inter, Italy), Fabricio Coloccini (Deportivo La Coruña, Spain), Gabriel Heinze (Manchester United), Gabriel Milito (Zaragoza, Spain), Diego Placente (Celta Vig, Spain), Clemente Rodriguez (Spartak Moscow, Russia), Gonzalo Rodriguez (Villareal, Spain), Walter Samuel (Inter, Italy), Juan Pablo Sorín (Villarreal, Spain), Javier Zanetti (Inter, Italy). Midfielders: Pablo Aimar (Valencia, Spain), Sebastian Battaglia (Boca Juniors), Esteban Demichelis (Bayern Munich, Germany), Cristian Gonzalez (Inter, Italy), Javier Mascherano (Corinthians, Brazil), Juan Roman Riquelme (Villarreal, Spain), Maximiliano Rodriguez (Atletico Madrid, Spain), Mario Santana (Palermo, Italy). Forwards: Hernan Crespo (Chelsea, England), Cesar Delgado (Cruz Azul, Mexico), Luciano Figueroa (Villareal, Spain), Luciano Galletti (Athletico Madrid), Lionel Messi (Barcelona, Spain), Javier Saviola (Sevilla, Spain), Carlos Tevez (Corinthians, Brazil).

PROJECTED
STARTING
LINEUP

Goalkeeper: Roberto Abbondanzieri (Boca Juniors). Defenders: Roberto Ayala (Valencia, Spain), Fabricio Coloccini (Deportivo La Coruña, Spain), Javier Zanetti (Inter Milan, Italy), Gabriel Heinze (Manchester United, England), Juan Pablo Sorin (Villarreal, Spain). Midfielders Javier Mascherano (Corinthians, Brazil), Cristian Gonzalez (Inter Milan, Italy), Juan Roman Riquelme (Villarreal, Spain). Forwards—Hernan Crespo Chelsea, England), Carlos Tevez (Corinthians, Brazil).

COACH

Jose Pekerman has been coach since September, 2004, when he replaced the quirky Marcelo Bielsa, who suddenly stepped down as coach. Pekerman, 56, certainly paid his dues, although, incredibly, he has never directed a first division team. But he guided the Argentines into the World Cup. "I thank God for having given me the enlightment to select this man," Argentine Football Association president Julio Grondona told *FIFA Magazine*. He directed the Under-20 team to three World Youth Cup victories. In fact, he turned down an offer to coach the National Team in 1998, claiming he did not have enough

ARGENTINA

experience. He was named team manager instead. His philosophy coaching youth teams was a simple one: "You have to go back to the roots, think about the player, give him more freedom," he told *FIFA Magazine*. As a player, Pekerman played with Argentinos Juniors and coached the Colo Colo youth team (Chile). For a while, early in his career, Pekerman dropped out of soccer and scrambled just to make ends meet, taking jobs as a taxi driver, barman or as an assistant in a pharmacy. "My thoughts are not guided by money," he was quoted by FIFA Magazine. "There are more important things than that." Pekerman was the only coach who failed to attend the 2006 World Cup draw due to the death of his father and a hand injury, a FIFA spokesman said.

There are some great expectations of Argentina in Germany. But then again, we have said that at the last three World Cups.

2006 WORLD CUP

So, which Argentina team are we going to see in June? Will it be the team that grossly underachieved in Japan in 2002 and was embarrassed with a first-round elimination? Or will it be the team that reached the final of the FIFA Confederations Cup in Germany before losing to Brazil, 4-1, in the summer of 2005. It's probably somewhere in-between, although the team's supporters are hopeful for something big.

During a rather perplexing three-week period in 2005, the mercurial Argentines showed how inconsistent they can be against their bitter South American rivals—Brazil.

On June 21, Argentina was on top of the world, not only besting Brazil, 3-1, to become the first South American side to qualify for the Cup, but embarrassing their archrivals as well, as they were working on all cylinders, from front to back. The Argentines tallied on their first three shots. Hernan Crespo struck only four minutes into the match. Roque Junior added a goal in the 18th minute and Crespo connected again in the 40th minute. The result was never in doubt.

La Nacion certainly was impressed. "World Cup qualification was secured in proud and stirring fashion—and at the expense of the world champions no less," the newspaper said. "If one day, Argentina needs an advertisement for all that's good about its football, then it need look no further than the video of the first half of this game. It was irresistible, almost impeccable stuff."

You could say the same thing about the FIFA Confederations Cup final—the competition was considered a dress rehearsal for the World Cup—in Frankfurt, Germany on June 29. The Brazilians ripped through the Argentines as though they were butter en route to a spectacular 4-1 triumph.

Using some humor to make its point, the Argentine sports daily

Olé printed on its front page: "Error. For technical reasons this page cannot be printed. Apologies for any inconvenience, see you all tomorrow."

Of course, the newspaper printed the facts inside, paying tribute to their victors. "Congratulations. At times we even found ourselves wanting to applaud Brazil," the newspaper said.

"Like any fan, I wonder how we can go from being the best in the world to the worst in 21 days," coach Jose Pekerman told *FIFA Magazine*. "But in my position, I have to stay analytical, and I think that this defies logic and consistency."

It will be intriguing to see if Pekerman has learned from his predecessor's mistakes in 2002. That's when Marcelo Bielsa decided to start then 33-year-old Argentine legend Gabriel (Batigol) Batistuta over 26-year-old Hernan Crespo, who was in his scoring prime. Bielsa refused to play them together. It was a major mistake that cost Argentina a place in the second round and beyond. Batistuta connected but once in three games.

This time around it is Crespo (he turns 31 during the Cup) who is the veteran with some young, talented turks as such Lionel Messi (he turns 19 during the Cup) and Carlos Tevez (22), the best player at the 2004 Olympics, ready to showcase their skills and magic. Messi awed the British media when he stared for Barcelona in the Champions League in February. Tevez, also known as Carlitos, ripped defenses apart with his amazing shifty moves and outstanding vision to score and set up teammates during the Summer Games. He was the leading scorer and the lone goal-scorer in the 1-0 gold-medal triumph over Paraguay. Playing for Corinthians in Brazil after a record $18 million transfer, Tevez was 2005 named South American player of the year.

But in March, Pekerman received some not so encouraging news about both budding stars. Messi was to be sidelined at least a month after tearing a muscle in his right thigh, during the second leg of Barcelona's Champions League first knockout game against Chelsea. Barcelona team doctors described the injury as "significant but not serious," but it was the second muscle tear Messi suffered within a month.

Tevez injured his right knee while playing for Corinthians (Brazil) in a Copa Libertadores game against Tigres (Mexico). Tevez was injured in the the 78th minute, when he earned a yellow card for a foul before he fell to the ground in pain.

"It's too early to say anything about Carlito's injury, but I can reveal that he won't be playing in next Sunday's big game against Sao Paulo," a worried Corinthians coach Antonio Lopes said.

Pekerman has shaken things up from 2002, adding a youthful blend to the current team. He has an old pro, Roberto Abbondanzieri, 33, in goal, and a defense led by captain Juan Pablo Sorín, who is still in his prime. The gifted Juan Roman Riquelme is a good organizer and has superb vision and a lethal right foot. But he might lack the pace against the top teams if Argentine moves beyond the first round.

When on its game, Argentina's one-touch, quick passing has been known to open up opposing defenses.

Sorín told *FIFA Magazine* that the team's style is different under Pekerman. "Before the pace used to be much faster and more intensive," he said. "Now the pace is slower and we focus on the build-up more just as we did during the last Copa America in 2004 when Bielsa was in charge. We change tactics more often to surprise the opponent and make our game less predictable."

Some observers have claimed that the South American side's weakness is that there is too much pressure for the players to perform well and that it lacks a more mature captain who can assume control of the team during tough times.

Former Argentine defender Oscar Ruggeri, a member of the 1986 world championship team, had a theory "They say that the Argentine player throws himself to the ground and wastes time and that the balls disappear when they're winning," said in a radio interview. "But at international level, these little things can help you win the match and get through to the next round and we have to work on them.. . . . We have to slow the Europeans down."

But it might be psychological as well. Veteran goalkeeper Jonny Walker of the Columbus Crew summed up the rivalry between Brazil (five world titles) and Argentina (two) perfectly, "One thinks they're the best, the other knows they're the best."

"The Argentines think they're the best. . . .The people in the stadium—there is a crazy environment. People are throwing things at you. . . .Brazilians know they're the best. They're going to go out there and create a festive environment. . . ."

Argentine fans might not want to hear this. But being stuck in the same group—many called it the Group of Death—as the Netherlands, Serbia & Montenegro and Ivory Coast, it is possible the South American team might not get out of the first round of a World Cup for the second consecutive time. A sobering thought: The last time that rare occurrence happened was at the 1958 and 1962 competitions.

ARGENTINA

AUSTRALIA
Group F

POPULATION: 19.7 million

COLORS: Gold shirts with green trim, green shorts with gold trim and gold socks

APPEARANCES: Second. 0-2-1, no goals for, five against. 1974 (first round).

WORLD CUP HISTORY

Australia opened the 1974 tournament with a 2-0 loss to East Germany, followed by a 3-0 defeat by West Germany. The Aussies managed a point—a scoreless draw with unheralded Chile—and they still are looking for their first World Cup goal.

HOW THEY QUALIFIED

After coming close in the playoff round four previous times, Australia made sure the fifth was a charm. The Socceroos were Oceania champions, having beaten the Solomon Islands, 7-0 at home and 2-1 away. In a special playoff against Uruguay, South America's fifth-ranked team, the teams swapped 1-0 home wins. It came down to a shootout in which Australia prevailed, 4-2, on Nov. 16, 2005. It was called the greatest night in Australia soccer history as 82,000 fans packed Telstra Stadium in Syndey and were joined by a record 3.4 million television viewers. Substitute John Aloisi converted the game-winner PK after goalkeeper Mark Schwarzer stopped shots by Dario Rodriguez and Marcelo Zalayeta. Marco Bresciano had drawn Australia even in this total goals series in the 34th minute.

PLAYERS TO WATCH

When he decided against playing for Croatia, team captain and forward Mark Viduka became a vital part of the team under former coach Frank Farina. The Middlesbrough (England) player is known for his shooting accuracy, although his international production has not belied that (six goals in thirty-one appearances). Midfielder Mark Bresciano, the first Australian to succeed in Italy's Serie A with Parma, is the side's playmaker. Left-sided attacking midfielder Harry Kewell, after several injuries and poor play for Leeds (England) has worked himself into better form, enjoying a rousing performance in the Uruguay playoff.

PLAYER POOL

Goalkeeper: Ante Covic (Hammarby, Sweden), Zeljko Kalac (Milan, Italy), Mark Schwarzer Middlesbrough (England). Defenders: Stephen Laybutt (Gent, Belgium), Stan Lazaridis (Birmingham, England), Ljubo Milicevic (Thun, Swizterland), Craig Moore

(Newcastle, England), Lucas Neill (Blackburn Rovers, England), Tony Popovic (Crystal Palace, England), Michael Thwaite (National, Romania), Tony Vidmar (Cardiff City, England), Scott Chipperfield (FC Basel, Switzerland). Midfielders: Marco Bresciano (Parma, Italy), Alex Brosque (Queensland Roar), Tim Cahill (Everton, England), Jason Culina (PSV Eindhoven, Netherlands), Ahmad Elrich (Fulham, England), Brett Emerton (Blackburn, England), Vince Grella Parma (Italy), Harry Kewell (Liverpool, England), Josip Skoko (Wigan, England), Mike Sterjovski (Basle, Switzerland), Luke Wilkshire (Bristol City, England). Forwards: Paul Agostino (1860 Munich), John Aloisi (Alaves, Spain), Joel Griffiths (Neuchatel Xamax, Switzerland), Ante Milicic (Newcastle United, Australia), Archie Thompson (Melbourne Victory), Mark Viduka (Middlesbrough, England).

PLAYER POOL

Goalkeeper: Mark Schwarzer Middlesbrough (England). Defenders: D Lucas Neill (Blackburn Rovers, England), Tony Popovic (Crystal Palace, England), Tony Vidmar (Cardiff City, England), Scott Chipperfield (FC Basel, Switzerland). Midfielders: Vince Grella Parma (Italy), Harry Kewell (Liverpool, England), Jason Culina (PSV Eindhoven, Netherlands), Marco Bresciano (Parma, Italy), Tim Cahill (Everton, England). Forwards: John Aloisi (Alaves, Spain), Mark Viduka (Middlesbrough, England).

PROJECTED STARTING LINEUP

Bora Mulitinovic, who has directed five different countries (including the U.S.) in as many World Cups, has forged a reputation as a miracle worker. Traditionally his teams have overachieved. While he has not coached teams in as many World Cups, Dutchman Guus Hiddink has done Bora two better. He has guided teams into the semifinals the last two competitions—the Netherlands (1998) and surprising Korea (2002), where he is a national hero. Whether he can do the same with Australia remains to be seen. But Hiddink brings to the side an excellent soccer resume and background. Hiddink, had aspirations of becoming a farmer before he turned to soccer, performed with the Washington Diplomats and San Jose Earthquakes in the old North American Soccer League. He coached at Real Madrid and has had two stints at PSV Eindhoven (Netherlands), whom he took to the 2005 Champions League semifinals. He replaced Frank Farina as coach prior to the Uruguay showdown and will be able to give full attention to Australia after the Dutch season ends on April 16, 2006. He is a stickler for details. "I am always critical," he said after a 5-0 friendly win over Jamaica in England in 2005. "Even now I am looking to some point of criticism. I am

COACH

AUSTRALIA

always looking at details. There are little details, but I am sharp at that." Hiddink has been linked to the Russian national job after the Cup, but both sides have denied that any deal had been finalized.

2006 WORLD CUP

Like clockwork, once every thirty-two years. Australia qualifies for the World Cup when it is hosted in Germany. The Socceroos first accomplished that feat in 1974. Now, more than a generation later after great frustration while being on the World Cup doorstep for three consecutive tournaments, Australia is back in. The Socceroos' next challenge is getting out of the group. Brazil is a gimme and Croatia should be a difficult side to crack—although the Australians' June 22 confrontation with the European side will be a crucial one for several reasons. The winner most likely will book in the second round—against the winner of Group E— and there's a certain sibling rivalry with Croatia, considering Australia has a huge Croatian population. "We're obviously not going there believing we're destined to lose," Hiddink told **Agence-France Presse**. "We're only just in the top 50 in the world ranking, but we're always capable of springing a surprise, and we're determined. "

Hiddink promised that the Socceroos won't just be on the defensive as they will use a possession game to take the game to their foes. "This is not a team to lean back and rely on just one or two counterattacks each half," he said.

"When you have the spirit of this team on the pitch you might have a chance to win," he said. "They never give up. They go for 90 minutes at high pace. It's very important to go for 90 minutes with a huge mental force. It's quite an achievement already to be in the World Cup."

Hiddink possesses the ability to inspire players and use the players' strengths to the best of their abilities. He did it with Korea, but he trained the team on a daily basis for six months before the tournament. Six weeks is better than nothing, but Korea was co-host of the 2002 tournament with Japan.

Playing in Europe, however, should not be as big a problem for the Socceroos as one might think. Most of the key players perform there. For international friendlies, Hiddink continued the tradition started by former coach Frank Farina by holding them on the continent. Hiddink likes to use a 3-5-2 formation with Tim Cahill (seven qualifying goals in Oceania competition), Harry Kewell and Marco Bresciano in the midfield and Mark Viduka and John Aloisi up front.

Australia must overcome an aging defense, something that could catch up to the team later in the first round, and a thin bench from which to choose, which could pose a problem against an attacking

AUSTRALIA

side such as Brazil. Hiddink said. "It's tough finding the right tactics against them, as they have unbelievable individual class, and they can wrap up a match at any moment."

Just qualifying for the World Cup was considered a major accomplishment for Australia, after it was sent home after playoff elimination in the 1986, 1994, 1998 and 2002 competitions. The Aussies were ousted by Scotland (1986), Argentina (1994), Iran (1998) and Uruguay (2002).

⊕ In 1986, Scotland won the first leg in Glasgow, 2-0, and played to a scoreless tie in Melbourne two weeks later.

⊕ In 1994, Gabriel Batistuta's goal lifted the Argentines to a 1-0 home victory, to capture the final spot for USA '94.

⊕ In 1998, Iran gave Australia the most excruciating defeat in playoff history. After playing to a 1-1 draw in Tehran in the total goals series. Iran struck twice in the final 14 minutes to pull off an amazing 2-2 tie before 80,000 in Melbourne. The series ended up at 3-3, Iran scored more away goals (two to one).

⊕ In 2002, Uruguay prevailed in the aggregate goals series, 3-1, dropping the first leg, 1-0, rebounded in the second leg in Montevideo, 3-0. Australia's arrival at Montevideo airport turned into an ugly scene as angry Uruguayan supporters reportedly jostled and abused the Australian players.

Hiddink and Australia have to hope that their 2006 German experience comes nowhere near what transpired thirty-two years ago.

⊕ In 1974, the game that saw two countries make their World Cup debut, the Aussies fell to East Germany, 2-0. Incidentally, East Germany upset eventual-champion West Germany, 1-0, several days later.

⊕ Taking on the host West Germans in Hamburg on June 18, Australia actually played well, but still lost 3-0.

⊕ The Aussies did come home with a point at Olympic Stadium in Berlin on June 22, even if it was a 0-0 tie with Chile. The game was played in a torrential rain. Midfielder Raymond Richards was red-carded in the 83rd minute for time-wasting. As it turned out, Richards stayed on the field for five minutes after he was booked. A linesman discovered the error and pointed it out to Jafar Namdar of Iran, who ordered Richards off the pitch.

Incidentally, Australia is not scheduled to play in Hamburg or Berlin in the opening round, having matches set for Kaiserslautern, Munich and Stuttgart.

AUSTRALIA

BRAZIL
Group F

POPULATION: 165,000,000
COLORS: Yellow shirts, blue shorts,
 white socks
APPEARANCES: 18th (every World Cup). 60-13-14. 190 goals for,
 82 against. 1930 (first round), 1934 (first round), 1938 (third
 place), 1950 (second place), 1954 (quarterfinals), 1958 (champion), 1962 (champion), 1966 (first round), 1970 (champion),
 1974 (fourth place), 1978 (third place), 1982 (second round), 1986
 (quarterfinals), 1990 (second round), 1994 (champion), 1998
 (second place), 2002 (champion).

WORLD CUP
HISTORY

Brazil is synonymous with World Cup success and glory, having participated in every tournament and having captured an unprecedented five World Cups, highlighted by three world championships in four attempts from 1958-1970. Pelé led three marvelously talented teams dripping with flair and artistry that won in 1958, 1962 and 1970. Until winning it back in 1994, however, the Brazilians struggled as a hard luck team. They compiled a solid 17-5-5 record, but advanced past the quarterfinals only once in five competitions. Under the guidance of coach Carlos Alberto Parreira, who took a more pragmatic approach in 1994, the Brazilians won their first World Cup crown in twenty-four years. They disappointed their supporters at France '98, taking a backseat to the host French in the championship match, 3-0, as a less-than-fit Ronaldo played poorly. In 2002, Brazil became only the second country to win out of its hemisphere—the South American side first accomplished that feat in Sweden in 1958—with its penta—fifth title—as Ronaldo completed a self-resurrection of global proportions by striking twice in a 2-0 final triumph over Germany.

HOW THEY
QUALIFIED

Brazil (9-2-7, 34) finished tied for the South American lead with Argentina (10-4-4) with 34 points apiece, but was crowned champs thanks to goal differential (18 to 12). The Brazilians booked a trip to Germany in a 5-0 thrashing of Chile on Sept. 5, 2005. "It was a magical evening for the team, and for me," said Adriano, who finished with a hat-trick.

PLAYERS TO
WATCH

Overshadowed by Ronaldo and Rivaldo in 2002, Ronaldinho demonstrated he was the best player in the world while starring for

BRAZIL

Barcelona in 2005. If his club performance follows him north to Germany, then watch out. Adriano and Robinho wowed fans and foes in Europe with their scoring exploits in the latest generation of high-powered strikers. With all that young talent, you would think it would be difficult for an aging Ronaldo (he might be 29, but the condition of his knees is probably closer to 40) to find some quality time. But Parreira realizes Ronaldo is only two WC goals away from tying the all-time record of 14, set by West Germany's Gerd Mueller. Cafu, the right fullback and captain, set a record by playing in his third consecutive championship game in 2002.

Goalkeepers: Dida (A.C. Milan, Italy), Heurelho Gomes (PSV Eindhoven, Netherlands), Julio Cesar (Inter, Italy). Defenders: Alex Rodrigo (PSV Eindhoven, Netherlands), Cafu (A.C. Milan, Italy), Cicinho (Real Madrid, Spain), Gilberto (Hertha Berlin, Germany), Gustavo Nery (Corinthians), Juan (Bayer Leverkusen, Germany), Lucio (Bayern Munich, Germany), Luisao (Benfica, Portugal), Maicon (Monaco, France), Roberto Carlos (Real Madrid, Spain), Roque Junior (Bayer Leverkusen, Germany). Midfielders: Alex (Fenerbahce, Turkey), Edmilson (Barcelona, Spain), Emerson Ferreira (Juventus, Italy), Gilberto Silva (Arsenal, England), Julio Baptista (Real Madrid, Spain), Juhinho Pernambucano (Lyon, France), Kaka (A.C. Milan, Italy), Renato (Sevilla, Spain), Ricardinho (Santos), Ronaldinho (Barcelona, Spain), Ze Roberto (Bayern Munich, Germany). Forwards: Adriano (Inter, Italy), Fred (Lyon, France), Ricardo Oliveira (Betis, Spain), Robinho (Real Madrid, Spain), Ronaldo (Real Madrid, Spain).

Goalkeeper: Dida (A.C. Milan, Italy). Defenders: Cafu (A.C. Milan, Italy), Juan (Bayer Leverkusen, Germany), Lucio (Bayern Munich, Germany), Roberto Carlos (Real Madrid, Spain). Midfielders: Emerson Ferreira (Juventus, Italy), Ze Roberto (Bayern Munich, Germany), Kaka (A.C. Milan, Italy), Ronaldinho (Barcelona, Spain). Forwards: Adriano (Inter, Italy), Ronaldo (Real Madrid, Spain).

Carlos Alberto Parreira is attempting to accomplish what only one man has done before—win multiple World Cups. Italy's Vittorio Pozzo did it back-to-back in 1934 (as hosts) and 1938. If Parreira accomplishes that feat, he will have done it twice away from home, having guided Brazil to the USA '94 crown. Parreira had a brief career in the Brazilian Second Division and turned to coaching in his early 20s. His first international coaching position was with Ghana at the 1968 African Nations Cup. He has directed four different teams

BRAZIL

in the World Cup—Kuwait (1982), United Arab Emirates (1990), Brazil (1994) and Saudi Arabia (1998). He coached the MetroStars in the 1997 MLS season, but Parreira left before completing his two-year, $1.2 million contract because the Saudis dangled an offer he certainly couldn't refuse: six months of work coaching their World Cup team for a reported $3 million. He took the offer. The Saudis dropped their first two matches and helped Alberto make history once again as he became the first coach to be fired in the middle of the competition. Having directed Brazil under ridiculously intense pressure in 1994 made Parreira a perfect candidate to take over the Brazilian coaching reigns again. "I'd be lying if I told you I didn't feel the pressure," he said. "The thing is you are more prepared to face it. You are more experienced. That's life. . . . ."

2006 WORLD CUP

It seems that just about everyone has already anointed Brazil as World Cup champions. There's just one slight problem. The Brazilians haven't played a game yet. Yes, they are an imposing side with the likes of Ronaldinho, Robinho, Adriano, and Ronaldo having the ability to make some magic with the ball and make opposing defenders quake in their boots. They were a feared and entertaining side during the 2005 FIFA Confederations Cup, romping past archrival Argentina in the final, 4-1. The Argentines had rolled over Brazil in a South American qualifier three weeks prior.

But as we all know, with apologies to those modern computer games, all World Cups and athletic events are decided on the field, not off it. Besides, the Brazilians have a history of disappointing themselves and their followers when they are the favorites.

Cases in point:

⊕ As hosts of the 1950 tournament, Brazil was favored to take its first world championship. They remained that way throughout the competition—until the bizarre final round robin. Needing only a draw against Uruguay to clinch the title, the Brazilians didn't protect the lead or a tie and wound up losing to their South American rivals, 2-1.

⊕ They were favorites entering the 1982 World Cup in Spain, but could never really get their act together. They were ousted by Italy and a red-hot Paolo Rossi in the second-round group stage in a fantastic back-and-forth encounter, 3-2.

⊕ In 1998, most assumed Brazil was thinking of a victory samba at Le Stade de France. That was before Ronaldo suffered from convulsions from painkillers and the French pulled off one of the biggest upsets of the ages with a 3-0 stunner.

In contrast, under severe criticism by its own media and supporters, Brazil wasn't considered the favorite at USA '94. But thanks to coach Carlos Alberto Parreira's pragmatic approach, they prevailed, overcoming Italy in a penalty-kick shootout at the Rose Bowl.

⊕ "In 1970, 1994 and 2002, we started the tournament discredited and with people questioning us," Parreira told *World Soccer*. "Now, it's time for us to start as favorites and win the title as favorites."

As good as that 1994 team was, boasting the likes of Dunga the Destroyer, the ageless Romario and the elusive Bebeto, this version of the team might even be better.

⊕ "The current generation is spectacular, perhaps the best ever," TV Globo's Flavio Orro told **www.BBC.com**. "If Ronaldo hasn't worn himself out during the season, he can really put on a show. He can become their top scorer in World Cup play and equal Pelé by winning his third. I'm backing him and Brazil to pull it off."

During qualifying, Parreira tried to down play how good Brazil really was. After vanquishing Venezuela on Oct. 12, Parreira said he would keep his dangerous lineup, selecting four players from Robinho, Ronaldo, Ronaldinho, Kaka and Adriano.

The Brazilian media liked to call them the "Magic Quartet." But not Parreira. "The word magic is not part of our vocabulary," he told **Reuters**. "We're not getting involved in this sort of talk. I want to hear words like efficiency, productivity, winning well, sweat, perspiration and talent."

Don't worry—Parreira isn't having an inferiority complex. He realizes how good his team is. After all, this team is the reigning world champions, Copa America champs and FIFA Confederations Cup titlists.

How confident are the Brazilians of advancing out of the opening round? They already have booked a castle as their base for the second round. They will play their second-round match in Dortmund if they win Group F. So, they decided to stay at the Schlosshotel Lerbach located in Bergisch Gladbach between Cologne and Leverkusen. The confederation said that it had set up an alternative near Kaiserslautern, where Brazil would play if the team finished second in a group that includes Croatia, Japan and Australia.

Brazil has so much talent that it could field a B team that could go far in the tournament and probably a competitive C team as well. That meant Parreira will have to sit out talented performers such as Robinho if everyone—i.e. Ronaldo—is healthy.

In fact, seven months prior to the Cup, Parreira apparently settled on his lineup Dida in goal, Cafu, Juan, Lucio, Roberto Carlos on

BRAZIL

defense, Emerson, Ze Roberto, Kaka, Ronaldinho in the midfield and Adriano and Ronaldo up front in a 4-4-2 formation that has a pair of holding midfielders.

If there is a weakness, it is the defense. As talented as the outside fullbacks are—captain Cafu (36) and Roberto Carlos (33)—they are getting a bit long in the tooth. In fact, the backline has difficulty with long balls sent into the penalty area and the top two goalkeepers, Dida and Julio Cesar, are prone to lapses.

Under new FIFA rules, Brazil became the first defending champion forced to qualify for the next World Cup. Parreira certainly didn't like it one bit. Brazil, like the nine other South American countries, was forced to play a marathon, 18-game schedule over two an a half years to determine four definite spots. The fifth-place finisher, Uruguay, had to take on the Oceania winner, Australia, in a playoff.

Parreira couldn't believe his own continental confederation would force countries to torture themselves through the twenty-seven-month process, especially when a country's best players had to take a roundtrip from Europe to participate in qualifiers.

"This kind of competition doesn't help us at all," he said in January, 2005 before Brazil played Ecuador in a qualifier. "They're going to stay four months away from me. They just come two days before to put them in the right motivation and focus. That's the big challenge. . . .The solution is to go back to the old way—two groups of five. But now the small countries, they like playing because they play 18 games. But it is not good for the big teams like Brazil, Argentina and Paraguay."

We are in the midst of Brazil's second great run. If the South Americans win the final in Berlin on July 9, that would mean victories in three of four World Cups (1994, 2002 and 2006), with an appearance in the fourth final (1998). No team has accomplished that, not even the fabulous Pelé teams.

Brazil is the only South American country to win a World Cup title in Europe (Sweden in 1958). But in the other seven tournaments in Europe, the Brazilians are 21-11-4 and have reached the Final Four four times (third place in 1938, fourth place in 1974, fourth place in 1982 and runners-up in 1998).

COSTA RICA

Group A

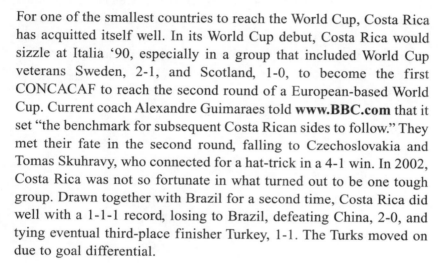

POPULATION: 3,800,000

COLORS: Red shirts, black shorts, white socks

APPEARANCES: 3rd. 3-3-1. 9 goals for, 12 goals against. 1990 (second round), 2002 (first round).

For one of the smallest countries to reach the World Cup, Costa Rica has acquitted itself well. In its World Cup debut, Costa Rica would sizzle at Italia '90, especially in a group that included World Cup veterans Sweden, 2-1, and Scotland, 1-0, to become the first CONCACAF to reach the second round of a European-based World Cup. Current coach Alexandre Guimaraes told **www.BBC.com** that it set "the benchmark for subsequent Costa Rican sides to follow." They met their fate in the second round, falling to Czechoslovakia and Tomas Skuhravy, who connected for a hat-trick in a 4-1 win. In 2002, Costa Rica was not so fortunate in what turned out to be one tough group. Drawn together with Brazil for a second time, Costa Rica did well with a 1-1-1 record, losing to Brazil, defeating China, 2-0, and tying eventual third-place finisher Turkey, 1-1. The Turks moved on due to goal differential.

WORLD CUP HISTORY

Costa Rica almost didn't make it out of the CONCACAF second round when it barely got past a plucky Cuba side via the away goals rule after a pair of embarrassing ties. After a change of two coaches, the Costa Ricans found themselves. Despite not being able to beat Honduras in the semifinal round, they managed to advance to the final six with a 3-2-1 mark. Costa Rica took third in the final CONCACAF qualifying group with a 5-4-1 record and 16 points behind the U.S. and Mexico. The Costa Ricans clinched a berth behind a 3-0 home victory over the Americans on October 8, 2005 as Carlos Hernandez scored twice and Paulo Wanchope once.

HOW THEY QUALIFIED

Paulo Wanchope, the country's all-time leading scorer (43 goals) must get a couple of goals for the Ticos to make any kind of impact in Germany. The versatile Gilberto Martinez, must raise his game to organize the defense. The midfield schemer is Walter Centeno, 31, who is best known for scoring against Real Madrid for AEK Athens (Greece) in a Champions League match.

PLAYERS TO WATCH

COSTA RICA

PLAYER POOL

Goalkeepers: Wardy Alfavro (Alajuelense), Alvaro Mesen (Herediano), Jose Francisco Porras (Saprissa). Defenders: Gabriel Badilla (Saprissa), Try Benneth (Saprissa), Carlos Castro (Alajuelense), Jervis Drummond (Saprissa), Leonardo Gonzalez (Herediano), Luis Marin (Alajuelense), Gilberto Martinez (Brescia, Italy), Roy Myrie (Alajuelense), Douglas Sequeira (Real Salt Lake, U.S.), Michael Umana (formerly with Los Angeles Galaxy, U.S.), Harold Wallace (Alajuelense), Mauricio Wright (Herediano). Midfielders: Cristian Bolanos (Saprissa), Walter Centeno (Saprissa), Danny Fonseca (Cartagines), Carlos Hernandez (Alajuelense), Jose Luis Lopez (Saprissa), Wilmer Lopez (Alajuelense), Alonso Solis (Saprissa), Mauricio Solis (Comunicaciones, Guatemala), Jafet Soto (Herediano). Forwards: Minor Diaz (Alajuelsense), Ronald Gomez (Saprissa), Froylan Ledezma (Alajuelense), Bryan Ruiz (Alajuelense), Alvaro Saborio (Saprissa), Paulo Wanchope (Al Gharafa, Qatar).

PROJECTED
STARTING
LINEUP

Goalkeeper: Jose Francisco Porras (Saprissa). Defenders: Jervis Drummond (Saprissa), Leonardo Gonzalez (Herediano), Luis Marin (Alajuelense), Gilberto Martinez (Brescia, Italy), Harold Wallace (Alajuelense). Midfielders: Walter Centeno (Saprissa), Mauricio Solis (Comunicaciones, Guatemala), Jafet Soto (Herediano). Forwards: Ronald Gomez (Saprissa), Paulo Wanchope (Al Gharafa, Qatar).

COACH

Alexandre Guimaraes directed Costa Rica into the 2002 World Cup, left the National Team in November, 2002, but returned in 2004 when the federation fired former U.S. national coach Steve Sampson after some poor results. In his first game as national coach after several matches as an assistant, Guimaraes had one tough challenge as Costa Rica took on Guatemala in a special qualifier playoff during 2002. The Costa Ricans won and advanced to the final. Born in Rio de Janeiro, Guimareaes became a Costa Rican citizen at age eleven. He starred at Saprissa, helping the club to three titles (1982, 1988 and 1989) while scoring ninety-five goals in 377 games. He also played at Italia '90 with the National Team before he went into coaching with stints at Belen, Herediano and Saprissa and Comunicaciones (Guatemala). As a coach, he is considered an excellent tactician who has preached team ethics over the individual.

2006
WORLD CUP

Costa Rica will find itself under the international spotlight and close scrutiny come June 9, 2006, when the Central Americans meet the host Germans in the World Cup opener in Munich. Can the Costa

COSTA RICA

Ricans emulate World Cup minnows such as Cameroon (1990) or Senegal (2002) and pull off an opening surprise?

"It's great to be kicking off a World Cup," forward Ronald Gomez told **FIFAWorldCup.com**. "At the end of the day, the first and last games are the ones that most people see. This honor should motivate us even more as we face up to the challenge of this group."

What makes the Ticos' World Cup success so sweet is that most of the players perform for domestic clubs. Only a handful of players toil outside the counry; and only one in Europe—defender Gilberto Martinez (Brescia, Italy). The others are defenders Douglas Sequeira (Chivas USA, Major League Soccer) and Michael Unama (Los Angeles Galaxy, MLS), midfielder Mauricio Solis (Comunicaciones, Guatemala), who performed in MLS, and forward Paulo Wanchope (Al Gharafa, Qatar).

As it turns out, three Costa Rican First Division clubs dominate the player pool. Alajuelense and Saprissa lead the way with virtually their entire starting lineup with 10 players apiece. In the modern World Cup, it is almost mandatory that a National Team's best players perform in Europe.

Costa Rica used a lot of coaches during qualifying. "Our main problem was having to adapt under different coaches," Gomez said. "The problems started in 2002 when Guimaraes left. We went through several different coaches and a whole host of new players. . . .It's a sign that you haven't found the right blend. Guimaraes returned to the helm and was able to steer us back on course. He made us into a team again, the wins started coming and we qualified."

For the third consecutive World Cup, the Ticos have found themselves in a difficult group. Instead of whining about its predicament, the Central American side will find away to negotiate its way to the second round.

Even with Germany showing weaknesses and problems in its embarrassing 4-1 loss to Italy on March 1, 2006, the hosts still have to be given high respect due to their World Cup history—three championships—and the fact that home teams traditionally fare well. The Costa Ricans must find a way to overcome Poland and Ecuador to duplicate their success in Italy in 1990.

Costa Rica has its work cut out for the team, if its World Cup warm-ups is any indication. Despite being dominated by Korea in a game in Oakland, Calif. on February 11, 2006, the Central Americans managed to walk away with a 1-0 win on a 39th-minute penalty kick by Alvaro Saborio.

The Ticos like to attack with some flair. Their weakness is defending. The backline is not very good in the air and has a history of giving opponents some room.

Still, there is optimism. "There's no doubt that this team is good enough to make it through the group phase, reach the next round and then strive towards one of the biggest achievements in our history," said Gomez, who added that the Ticos have "a good mix of players with experience of playing abroad and at the World Cup, and a handful of promising youngsters. . . . It's difficult to get noticed in Costa Rica, but the World Cup will be an ideal opportunity. . . .We're going to surprise a few people."

"We have to plan well, prepare ourselves down to the last detail and learn our tactics inside out to be able to emulate the team of 1990," Gomez told **www.FIFAWorldCup.com**.

Gomez, 31, scored twice at the 2002 competition, connecting against Brazil and China. He is one of the team's most experienced players, having performed in Spain, Guatemala, Greece, Kuwait and Mexico.

"We'll try to recreate the spirit of 2002, but hopefully we can get a bit more luck," he said. "In 1990, I think Costa Rica's game lacked depth - they got good results but without playing half as much football as we did in 2002. In my opinion, it was better to have lost 5-2 to Brazil than just to have sat back and not won a corner."

During qualifying, Costa Rica lost a reserve forward in Whayne Wilson, who died in June, four days after he was in a car accident. He was 29 and started a pair of qualifiers before the car crash.

Regardless what transpires in Germany, the tournament will be the international swan song for the 29-year-old Wanchope, who says he will retire afterward. "There are several good and young players vying for a place and I have to leave the road open for them," he said on his personal website. "My time in the national team will come to an end after the World Cup Germany 2006."

Wanchope, who plays for Q-League champion Al Gharafa in Qatar, has been his country's main man through the years, connecting for 43 international goals, the most in Costa Rican history. "I cannot imagine the day of my last match," he said. "It will be difficult to take in the retirement from the 'Tricolor.' "

Costa Rica enjoyed one of the best debuts of any team playing outside of its hemisphere in World Cup history, finishing with a 2-2 record and reaching the second round at Italia '90. Mexico became the second team to accomplish that feat at France '98.

CROATIA
Group F

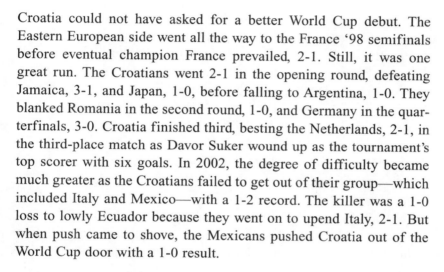

POPULATION: 4,300,000
COLORS: Checkered red and white
  shirts, white shorts, white socks
APPEARANCES: 3rd 6-4-0. 13 goals for, eight against. 1998 (third
  place), 2002 (first round).

WORLD CUP HISTORY

Croatia could not have asked for a better World Cup debut. The Eastern European side went all the way to the France '98 semifinals before eventual champion France prevailed, 2-1. Still, it was one great run. The Croatians went 2-1 in the opening round, defeating Jamaica, 3-1, and Japan, 1-0, before falling to Argentina, 1-0. They blanked Romania in the second round, 1-0, and Germany in the quarterfinals, 3-0. Croatia finished third, besting the Netherlands, 2-1, in the third-place match as Davor Suker wound up as the tournament's top scorer with six goals. In 2002, the degree of difficulty became much greater as the Croatians failed to get out of their group—which included Italy and Mexico—with a 1-2 record. The killer was a 1-0 loss to lowly Ecuador because they went on to upend Italy, 2-1. But when push came to shove, the Mexicans pushed Croatia out of the World Cup door with a 1-0 result.

HOW THEY QUALIFIED

Croatia finished atop of European Group 8 with a 7-0-3 record and 24 points. The Croatians tied Sweden for the top spot, but was crowned champs by the virtue of beating the Swedes twice—by 1-0 scores on goals by Dario Srna. In fact, it was his penalty kick in the 1-0 home win on October 8, 2005, that clinched a World Cup berth for Croatia in Zagreb. City celebrations were punctuated with fireworks, a rare display at any qualifier. "I knew I had support from the whole team, the whole stadium, the whole nation," Srna told **Reuters**. "I just knew I would score and take us to Germany."

PLAYERS TO WATCH

Midfielder Dario Srna and forward Dado Prso each led the team with five qualifying scores and each had eight international goals entering the winter. But they have different ways and styles in accomplishing that feat. Srna, 24, a speedy right midfielder who plays professionally for Shakhtar (Ukraine) is considered the engine of the side who is a solid defensive player as well. World Soccer said that Srna's passing and free kicks were "Beckham-esque." Prso, 31, is the team's main man up front. He excels in the air and keeps possession well. A

CROATIA

late bloomer for a European international—Prso made his National Team debut at 27 on the orders of Croatian Football Federation president Vlatko Markovic. He plays for Rangers (Scotland). A member of the starting 11 since France '98, midfielder Igor Tudor has switched positions from a central defender to a holding midfielder since Zlatko Kranjcar took over as coach in 2004. Captain and midfielder Niko Kovac, 34, is an influential figure due to his experience.

PLAYER POOL

Goalkeepers: Tomislav Butina (Club Brugge, Belgium), Joey Didulica (Austrian Wien, Austria), Stipe Pletikosa (Hajduk Split), Vedran Runje (Standard Liege, Belgium). Defenders: Ivan Bosniak (Dinamo Zagreb), Robert Kovac (Juventus, Italy), Ivica Krizanac (Zenit, Russia), Danijel Pranjic (Heerenveen, Netherlands), Goran Sablic (Kiev Dynamo, Ukraine), Anthony Seric (Panathinaikos, Greece), Dario Simic (A.C. Milan, Italy), Josip Simunic (Hertha Berlin, Germany), Mario Tokic (Austrian Wien, Austria) Stjepan Tomas (Galatasaray, Turkey). Midfielders: Marko Babic (Bayer Leverkusen, Germany), Mario Bazina (Grazer AK, Austria), Niko Kovac (Hertha Berlin, Germany), Niko Kranjcar (Hajduk Split), Ivan Leko (Club Brugge, Belgium), Jerko Leko (Kiev Dynamo, Russia), Darijo Srna (Shakhtar, Ukraine), Igor Tudor (Siena, Italy), Jurica Vranjes (Werder Bremen, Germany), Davor Vugrienec (Rijeka). Forwards: Bosko Balaban (Club Brugge, Belgium), Sahsa Bjelanovic (Ascoli, Italy), Eduardo Da Silva (Dinamo Zagreb), Ivan Klasnic (Werder Bremen, Germany), Ivica Olic (CSKA Moscow, Russia), Dado Prso (Rangers, Scotland).

PROJECTED
STARTING
LINEUP

Goalkeepers: Tomislav Butina (Club Brugge, Belgium). Defenders: Robert Kovac (Juventus, Italy), Stjepan Tomas (Galatasaray, Turkey), Josip Simunic (Hertha, Berlin, Germany). Midfielders: Igor Tudor (Siena, Italy), Niko Kovac (Hertha Berlin, Germany), Marko Babic (Bayer Leverkusen, Germany), Darijo Srna (Shakhtar, Ukraine), Niko Kranjcar (Hajduk Split). Forwards: Dado Prso (Rangers, Scotland), Bosko Balaban (Club Brugge, Belgium).

COACH

Zlatko Kranjcar replaced the conservative Otto Baric after Croatia failed to get out of their group at Euro 2004. Born on November 15, 1956, Kranjcar (pronounced CRUNCH-ar) is a very popular sports figure in Croatia having made 556 league appearances for Dinamo Zagreb, and scoring 98 times, as well as playing 11 times and scoring three goals for Yugoslavia before the break-up of that country. He also played for Rapid Vienna and reached the 1985 European Cup

CROATIA

Winners Cup final. As coach of Dinamo, Kranjcar's teams won the double league and cup competition twice and another league championship with F.C. Zagreb. He also coached at FC Linz, SV Wienerfeld and NK Rijeka. His son, midfielder Niko Kranjcar, is a member of the National Team, although some Croatian soccer observers felt that the younger one hasn't lived up to his promising start as a teenager.

2006
WORLD CUP

The pressure is on a new generation of Croatian players. Gifted and talented players such as Robert Prosinecki and Davor Suker have moved on internationally and have stepped aside or are close to calling it quits with their club teams.

Can these men be expected to take Croatia to the next level, or at least to the second round in Germany? They're good and show promise, but are they in the class of their predecessors?

Croatia's group includes defending champion and overwhelming favorite Brazil, which probably will finish undefeated, and pair of teams expected to struggle to make the second round—Japan and Australia. "A good result for Croatia would be to qualify from the group stage." *Sportske Novosti* editor Antun Samovojska told **www.BBC.com**. In other words, Croatia probably is good enough to reach the second round. But after that, who knows?

"Our greatest strength is our team work," coach Zlatko Kranjcar said. "We have a solid team, which can play well tactically and can also look for a result. We can be optimistic about the World Cup."

A big reason why Kranjcar is optimistic is his defense, which the team believes is among the best in the world. The Croatians recorded six shutouts (a pair of 1-0 victories over Sweden) in 10 qualifying encounters and surrendered but five goals. They allowed only an opponent to find the net on multiple occasions in one game (Bulgaria in a 2-2 draw in an early qualifier).

While they outscored their opposition in qualifying, 21-5, there has been concerns that if Croatia allows an early first goal, the team would struggle in attempting to equalize. Some of those doubts were relieved on March 1, 2006, when the Croatians rallied from a one-goal deficit to stun Argentina, 3-2, in a World Cup warm-up in sub-freezing conditions in Basel, Switzerland. While their defense wasn't at top effiency against the South Americans, the Croatians' attack certainly was, especially under urgent conditions. After forward Ivan Klasnic gave the Eastern Europeans the lead, they found themselves on the wrong end of a 2-1 score. But they bounced back with second-half goals by Darijo Srna and Dario Simic.

"We already showed in our qualifying campaign that we have some

CROATIA

very good individual players and we have proven it again with this performance against one of the World Cup favorites," Kranjcar told **Reuters**. "I know this will increase expectations back home, but I don't think that will cause us any problems. In fact, I am sure it will give us even more confidence for the World Cup."

Prso is one gritty performer. He played in the World Cup-berth clinching win over Sweden despite an ailing knee. He reportedly needed to have his swollen knee drained the morning of the encounter and still was named man of the match. "When I woke up I thought I would not make it, but the doctors did their thing," Prso told the Croatian daily newspaper *Jutarnji*. "I clenched my teeth and went to play and it turned out fantastic."

One advantage for Croatia is that five players from its pool perform in the German Bundesliga. As it turns out, two players should feel quite comfortable when the Croatians take on Brazil in their Cup opener in Berlin on June 13th as defender Josip Simunic and midfielder Niko Kovac both play for Hertha Berlin.

One of Croatia's more intriguing side stories is the father-son relationship of coach Zlatko Kranjcar and midfielder Niko, who is on the team. When he was 16-years-old old, Niko was hailed as the next great Croatian player, being compared in some quarters to French great Zinedine Zidane. He helped Croatia take third place in the 2001 European Under-16 championships, helping them qualify for the FIFA World U-17 event, where he scored two goals. While he has turned into a decent player for Dinamo Zagreb, Niko has yet to fulfill his promise. Niko, 21, has plenty of skill and vision, but lacks the proper movement to turn him into a star. Some of it could be the fact that he sometimes is a bit overweight, some coaches and observers claim. He wants to play for Barcelona, but probably is not ready just yet to take a giant step to such a giant club.

Zlatko sounds more like a typical father than a coach in the matter, blaming other coaches for his son's lack of progress. But former Croatian national coach Tomislav Ivic, the most respected coach in the country, did not agree. "His father is partly to blame for his physical condition," he said. "If Niko was my son, I would put him in order."

It certainly will be interesting to see if any of this simmering controversy will spill over into the World Cup in June.

For World Cup history buffs: Croatia went further than any other first-time Cup team since Italy won the whole thing as hosts of the second tournament in 1934.

CROATIA

CZECH REPUBLIC
Group E

POPULATION: 10,290,000
COLORS: Red shirts, white shorts, blue socks
APPEARANCES: 1st. Important note: Czechoslovakia appeared in eight World Cups, with an 11-14-5 record, 44 goals for, 45 against 1934 (second place), 1938 (first round), 1954 (first round), 1958 (first round), 1962 (second place), 1970 (first round), 1982 (first round), 1990 (quarterfinals).

WORLD CUP HISTORY

This is the first time the Czech Republic has qualified for the World Cup. However, as Czechoslovakia, the Eastern European country made eight visits to soccer's promised land. It may be a well-kept secret, but the Czechs finished second in the World Cup twice, including an incredible off-continent and off-hemisphere run in 1962, when the Czechs lost to Brazil in the final in Chile, 3-1. Actually, the Czechs—they were led by midfielder Josef Masopust—were a mediocre 1-1-1 in the opening round and even had a negative goal differential. They started with a 1-0 victory over Spain, played Brazil to a scoreless tie and lost to Mexico, 3-1. But they edged Hungary, 1-0, in the quarterfinals and Yugoslavia in the semifinals, 3-1. Interestingly, the Czechs finished at a zero goal differential in that competition, scoring seven and allowing seven goals. The last time Czechoslovakia participated was in 1990, when it finished second in its group with a 5-1 trouncing of the U.S. (playing in its first World Cup match in 40 years), a 1-0 victory over Austria and a 2-0 loss to Italy. The Czechs stopped surprise side Costa Rica with a solid 4-1 second-round win, but were eliminated in the quarterfinals by eventual world champions Germany, 1-0. Oldirch Nejedly is the Czechs' all-time World Cup goal-scorer with seven goals.

The Czechs finished second to the Netherlands in European Group 1 with a 9-3-0 record and 27 points, qualifying for the playoffs. They then defeated Norway in the total goals series, 1-0 and 1-0, on November 12 and 16. Tomas Rosicky scored in the second game. "This is the peak of my career," coach Karel Brueckner told **Reuters** before his players picked him up and carried him on the field. "We showed our character tonight, I'm proud of how they played."

HOW THEY QUALIFIED

Coaxed out of international retirement to boost the Czechs into the

PLAYERS TO WATCH

CZECH REPUBLIC

PLAYERS TO
WATCH

World Cup, midfielder Pavel Nedved, 33, the 2003 European player of the year, brought a unique mental toughness to the team. As good as he is, Nedved is injury prone. Petr Cech is arguably the world's best goalkeeper and the 2005 Czech player of the year at 23, a baby in international keeper years, has risen to the occasion. Forward Milan Baros is a prolific scorer (26 goals in 45 matches entering the winter). His partner in crime up front, Jan Koller (40 goals in 66 matches) is recovering from a knee injury and his status for the Cup is unknown.

PLAYER POOL

Goalkeepers: Petr Cech (Chelsea, England), Jaromir Blazek (Sparta Prague), Antonin Kinsky (Saturn, Russia). Defenders: Rene Bolf (Auxerre, France), Tomas Hubschman (Shakhtar Donetsk, Ukraine), Marek Jankulovski (A.C. Milan, Italy), Martin Jiranek (Spartak Moscow, Russia), Pavel Mares (Zenit St. Petersburg, Russia), Zdenek Pospech (Sparta Prague), David Rozehnal (Paris St-Germain, France), Tomas Ujfalusi (Fiorentina, Italy), Tomas Zapotocny (Slovan Liberec). Midfielders: Tomas Galasek (Ajax, Netherlands), David Jarolim (Hamburg, Germany), Jiri Jarosik (Birmingham, England), David Kobylik (Bielefeld, Germany), Radoslav Kovac (Spartak Moscow, Russia), Pavel Nedved (Juventus, Italy), Karel Poborsky (Ceske Budejovice), Jan Polak (Nuremberg, Germany), Jaroslav Plasil (Monaco, France), Tomas Rosicky (Dortmund, Germany), Tomas Sivok (Sparta Prague), Rudolf Skacel (Hearts, Scotland), Roman Tyce (1860 Munich, Germany), Stepan Vachousek (Austria Wien, Austria). Forwards: Milan Baros (Aston Villa, England), Marek Heinz (Galatasaray, Turkey), Tomas Jun (Besiktas, Turkey), Jan Koller (Dortmund, Germany), Vratilsav Lokvenc (Salzburg, Austria), Vaclav Sverkos (Hertha Berlin, Germany), Vladimir Smicer (Bordeaux, France), Jiri Stajner (Hannover, Germany).

PROJECTED
STARTING
LINEUP

Goalkeepers: Petr Cech (Chelsea, England). Defenders: Marek Jankulovski (AC Milan, Italy), David Rozehnal (Paris SG, France), Tomas Ujfalusi (Fiorentina, Italy).Midfielders: Jan Polak (Nuremberg, Germany), Pavel Nedved (Juventus, Italy), Jan Polak (Nuremberg, Germany), Tomas Rosicky (Dortmund, Germany), Vladimir Smicer (Bordeaux, France). Forwards: Milan Baros (Aston Villa), Jan Koller (Dortmund, Germany).

COACH

Back home in the Czech Republic, Karel Bruckner is known as "Kleki Petra," a nickname taken from an American Indian chief from a novel. At 66 and with age creases on his face and grey hair,

CZECH REPUBLIC

Bruckner certainly looks like a wise old chief having directed the Czech Republic to the World Cup. His actions certainly fit the bill as a brilliant tactician. The oldest head coach in the finals, Bruckner is expected to retire from coaching after the World Cup. Bruckner has forged a reputation as an astute coach who understands the modern game. He directed the Czech Republic Under-23 team in the 2000 Summer Games in Sydney and the full national side to the Euro 2004 semifinals in Portugal (on a reported annual salary of only $110,000). Bruckner's coaching career began in 1973 at Sigma Olomouc, with whom he has had four spells in charge. Despite his long career, Bruckner has won only one championship—the Slovakia Cup in 1985 with Bratislava. During his younger days as a coach, Bruckner reportedly was obsessed over tactics and formations. He would draw various systems on pieces of paper while staying up late into the night. There is a good reason—Bruckner is considered a superb chess player. According to **www.BBC.com**, Bruckner devised this strategy in the eighties: He had two players take a free kick, but they collided. While his foes looked on in disbelief, a third player then fired home a goal. His best known piece of strategy came at Euro 2004. His team trailing the Netherlands, 2-0, Bruckner pulled defender Zdenek Grygera for Vladimir Smicer. Another forward, Marek Heinz, was inserted later on. The Czechs rallied for a rather improbable 3-2 victory as Smicer connected for the game-winner in the 88th minute. Even Dutch coach Dick Advocaat admitted he had been outcoached.

Big things are expected of the Czech Republic, ranked second in the world in FIFA's poll. Think of this interesting scenario: If Brazil wins Group F and the Czechs finish second in their group, there will be a titanic match-up of the defending world champions and No. 1 ranked team in the world (according to the FIFA poll) against the No. 2 team in that very poll—in the second round of all places.

"Czech teams have always preferred to be underdogs," Czech journalist Petr Nosalek told **www.BBC.com**. "This time it's different, we now have the best football generation ever. (Coach Karel) Bruckner is strong enough to do something big. You can't pretend the number two in the FIFA world ranking is not a co-favorite for the next World Cup."

The Czechs will be the United States's first opponent and test at Germany 2006 as they tussle in Gelsenkirchen on June 12. Even a tie against this loaded side would be considered a great victory for the Americans.

Bruckner coached many of the players on the Czech under-21

2006
WORLD CUP

CZECH REPUBLIC

team that finished second in the 2000 Euro championships, garnering their respect. Among National Team regulars were Milan Baros, Zdenek Grygera, Marek Heinz, Marek Jankulovski and Tomas Ujfalusi. These veterans of an older generation will be playing with younger, but experienced players.

Although he was out of international soccer for 14 months—Nedved had retired—the Juventus midfielder had a galvanizing effect on the team after he returned. Nedved, who had 17 goals in 85 international appearances heading into the winter, is a natural leader and it certainly doesn't hurt that he can pass and score goals as well. Nedved, 33, is far from a one-man show in the midfield. Tomas Rosicky, 25, nicknamed "Dumpling" after his favorite food,, scored seven qualifying goals, including the game-winner in the playoffs. Team captain Tomas Galasek, 33, is a solid defensive midfielder. And there's 34-year-old veteran Karel Poborsky (111 caps) waiting in the wings.

If key players are healthy, the attack is first class. Baros is only 25, yet he already has 26 goals in 45 international appearances. Jan Koller, 33, also is a handful (40 goals in 66 matches, including a team-high nine qualifying scores). Koller's availability, however, still was a question mark this spring. He tore a cruciate ligament in September and faced six months of rehabilitation. "Koller is a key member of our team and our system iss quite dependent on him," Bruckner was quoted by *World Soccer*. "He's not only a formidable attacking force but also valuable in other areas, even. I believe he'll recover from his knee injury in time. Whether he's in form or not, I need Koller in the lineup."

If there's a weakness, it is inconsistency on the backline in front of Petr Cech, already a world class goalkeeper at 24. In fact, Cech was named the Czech 2005 player of the year. Cech helped Chelsea to its first English League title in 50 years, while setting two Premiership records: a 1,025-minute goalless streak and 24 shutouts.

It will be interesting to see how Bruckner will rest his veteran players in such a grueling, month-long tournament when being over 30 can catch up to players and teams. Bruckner coached against the U.S. at the 2000 Olympics. At the World Cup draw in Leipzig, Germany on Dec. 9, 2005, Bruckner admitted that he knew very little or nothing about the U.S. national team. That's surprising. His team played the U.S. Under-23 side to a 2-2 draw during the opening round. He walked away from that match quite impressed with the Americans and told this author after that Olympic confrontation: "They are a wonderful team. We were defending all night. They managed to get through all of our defensive formations no matter what we did." Bruckner did say he expected the U.S. to "be a very strong team," in the World Cup in June.

It looks like the Czechs are perfectly positioned for Germany as eight players from their player pool perform in the Bundesliga.

The Czechs led 1-0 in both World Cup finals in which they have participated, only to lose on second-half goals to Italy (1934) and Brazil (1962).

REPLAY IT AGAIN, SAM
(originally appeared in *Soccer Week*)

The Americans' 5-1 loss to the Czechs exposed their every weakness to the world: They're slow. They lacked a physical presence. And they showed their inexperience in the way of soccer savvy. They were outshot, 23-7. They gave up two goals off corner kicks, and another from the penalty spot. They also had a player ejected. One of the few bright spots was Paul Caligiuri, who scored a goal for the U.S. in the World Cup on June 10, 1990 game.

Believe it or not, it could have been worse, much worse. The Czechs seemingly fired at will at the U.S. goal and Meola had to save a penalty kick in the 89th minute to save any further embarrassment before 32,226 at Estadio Communale in Florence. In other words, it was a game to forget.

The Czechs did little damage early, probing the American defense for soft spots and weaknesses in the early going. Finally, in the 25th minute, the Czechs went into high gear when midfielder Lubos Kubik raced through the U.S. midfield, passed defender John Stollmeyer on the left side and crossed the ball to Skuhravy, who surged into the penalty area to beat goalkeeper Tony Meola from just about the penalty spot.

They continued to attack, and the U.S. continued to make mistakes. Steve Trittschuh's inability to clear the ball in the penalty area led to the second goal. Mike Windischmann, the sweeper, got possession of the ball and then lost it to Ivan Hasek, whom he tripped while reaching for the ball. On the ensuing penalty kick, Meola guessed correctly, but Michel Bilek still powered it into the upper corner for a two-goal advantage.

It went from bad to worse. In the 51st minute, Hasek headed home Frantisek Straka's corner kick from yards while U.S. defenders played statues, standing around and watching. Two minutes later, midfielder Eric Wynalda was given a red card for retaliating against midfielder Lubomir Moracik, who had stepped on his foot, and became the first U.S. player to be ejected from a World Cup match. "It's called paying your dues", Coach Bob Gansler said. "Eric got baited. No. 11 stepped on his foot and he pushed back. And a lot of times the first foul is not seen. It's a matter of inexperience."

Despite playing a man down, Caligiuri raced down the right wing, eluded a couple of defenders, and pulled goalkeeper Jan Stejskal out of the net to score from 12 yards in the 61st minute. "

The Czechs were not finished. Skuhravy headed in his second goal, this time from three yards in the 79th minute, and substitute Milan Luhovy closed out the scoring in the 92nd minute, two minutes into injury time. Sandwiched between those two goals, was a penalty kick awarded after midfielder John Harkes tripped a player in the box.

Again Bilek took the kick, trying to embarrass the U.S. by blooping it into the upper right corner. Again, Meola guessed correctly, this time catching it in mid-air. "I had a feeling he was going to try to beat me with something tricky," Meola said.

Several minutes later, referee Kurt Roethlisberger of Switzerland mercifully whistled an end to the rout. "The most frustrating thing is we made all the odds makers look like kings," Meola said. "This team doesn't deserve that."

CZECH REPUBLIC

ECUADOR
Group A

POPULATION: 12,000,000
COLORS: Yellow shirts, blue shorts, red socks
APPEARANCES: 2nd. 2002 (first round).1-2-0. Two goals for, four against.

WORLD CUP HISTORY

Talk about baptism by fire. Ecuador's very first World Cup match was against Italy, allowing a pair of goals in the first half hour and settling for a 2-0 defeat. The South Americans dropped a 2-1 decision to Mexico (Agustin Delgado scored Ecuador's first World Cup goal) before becoming a spoiler and eliminating Croatia—semifinalists at France '98, with a 1-0 win. Midfielder Edison Mendez, who is in the mix for this year's competition, scored the winner in the 48th minute.

HOW THEY QUALIFIED

Ecuador finished third in South American qualifying with a rather ordinary 8-6-4 mark and 28 points, but since the top four teams automatically clinched a spot in Germany, it didn't matter what the record was. The Ecuadoreans managed to defeat SA powers Brazil and Argentina at home, no mean feat anywhere. Ecuador clinched a berth in a scoreless draw with Uruguay in an ill-tempered match in Quito with a game to spare on October 8, 2005. In the game prior in La Paz, Bolivia on September 3, 2005 Ecuador wound up on the brink of qualifying after a 2-1 victory over Bolivia as Agustin Delgado connected twice.

PLAYERS TO WATCH

One of the veterans coach Luis Fernando Suarez did not dump was 31-year-old central defender Ivan Hurtado (127 international appearances), who has participated in an incredible 57 qualifiers. Moreover, he is a leader—team captain and calm when the pressure is on—and organizes the backline. Versatile midfielder Edison Mendez, who is expected to be the fulcrum of the attack in the middle, can also play on the outside. Forward Agustin Delgado is the country's all-time scorer (29 goals in 67 appearances through the winter). But will he be able to fill the net come June? He has fallen out with his Ecuadorean club, Barcelona (of Guayaquil) and his fitness certainly will be in question. He has had to overcome back problems as well.

PLAYER POOL

Goalkeepers: Damian Lanza (Deportivo Cuenca) Cristian Mora (LDU Quite), Edwin Villafuerte (Deportivo Quito). Defenders: Paul

ECUADOR

PLAYER POOL

Ambrossi (LDU Quito), Renan Calle (Aucas), Jairo Campos (LDU Quito), Jose Cortez (Aucas), Erick de Jesus (El Nacional), Ulises de la Cruz (Aston Villa, England), Giovanny Espinosa (LDU Quito), Ericson George (Barcelona), Jorge Guagua (El Nacional), Ivan Hurtado (Al Arabi), Neicer Reasco (LDU Quito). Midfielders: Marlon Ayovi (Deportivo Quito), Walter Ayovi (Barcelona), Segundo Castillo (El Nacional), Cristian Lara (El Nacional), Marlon Ayovi (Deportivo Quito), Patricio Urrutia (LDU Quito), Edison Mendez (LDU Quito), Antonio Valencia (Recreativo Huelva, Spain). Forwards: Jhonny Baldeon (Barcelona), Felipe Caicedo (Basel, Switzerland), Cristian Benitez (El Nacional), Felix Borja (El Nacional), Agustin Delgado (LDU Quito), Ivan Kaviedes (Argentinos Juniors, Argentina), Roberto Mina (F.C. Dallas, U.S.), Franklin Salas (LDU Quito), Carlos Tenorio (Al Sadd, Qatar).

PROJECTED STARTING LINEUP

Goalkeeper: Christian Mora (LDU Quito). Defenders: Ulises de la Cruz (Aston Villa, England), Ivan Hurtado (Al Arabi, Qatar), Giovany Espinoza (LDU Quito) Marlon Ayov (Sociedad Deportivo). Midfielders: Neicer Reasco (LDU Quito), Paul Ambrossi (LDU Quito), Antonio Valencia (Recreativo de Huelva, Spain), Edwin Tenorio (Barcelona SC, Ecuador), Edison Mendez (LDU Quito). Forward: Agustin Delgado (LDU Quito).

COACH

Ecuador must have a thing for Colombian national coaches, having used three through the years. Most recently in 2002, Colombian Hernan Dario Gomez guided the team into its first cup. This time around another Colombian, Luis Fernando Suarez, 46, who took over the coaching reins after the 2004 Copa America debacle. He rebuilt the team, bringing in new players and getting rid of several older players (midfielder Alex Aguinaga and his 109 caps retired of his own volition the year prior.) Suarez, who had been coaching the Ecudorean First Division club Aucas de Quito when he was tapped for the national post, won the Libertadores Cup as a player with Atletico Nacional (Colombia) in 1989.

2006 WORLD CUP

Four years older and hopefully wiser, Ecuador enters its second consecutive World Cup a much more confident side, having gained much experience in 2002. But that doesn't necessarily make life any easier for the South Americans, who must traverse difficult Group A territory against host Germany, Poland, which is playing on its home continent, and a hungry Costa Rican side. "

We have the chance to show the progress we have made," coach Luis Fernando Suarez told *World Soccer*. "We have the raw mater-

ECUADOR

ial—well-motivated players with technical and tactical qualities—and we're in a group that gives us the possibility of getting through to the second round. Logic makes Germany clear favorites, but we have a chance of finishing in front of the others."

On one hand, only a handful of Ecuadorian players perform in Europe. That could come back to hurt the South Americans against the more experienced Germans and Poles. On the other, nine players from the player pool perform back home for Liga Deportiva Universitaria (LDU) de Quito. So, there is more continuity in that regard.

There is also the lack of home-field advantage in Germany. Ecuador finished unbeaten at home in qualifying, thanks to Quito's high altitude (9,350). With no such advantage in Germany, you might say the playing field will be leveled.

Pin-pointing Ecuador's strengths are easy.

Ivan Hurtado, the 31-year-old veteran central defender, who is the pillar of the backline with his vast experience. Continue with central defender Giovany Espinoza, who was the only South American player to participate in all 18 qualifying matches, is the glue to the defense in the air and might have to work overtime in trying to compensate for his teammates' weaknesses off the ground. Midfielder Edison Mendes, who scored Ecuador's only goal in the 1-0 upset of Croatia in 2002, has great vision and is the engine of the midfield. He also is known for his booming, long-range shots and free kicks.

Hopefully, Ecuador finishes in more ways than one with forward Agustin Delgado, who will be in fighting form but needs proper fitness for the World Cup in the wake of his suspension last year. Delgado was suspended by his Ecuadorian club, Barcelona, for indiscipline until his contract finishes at the end of the year. Delgado was banned after he was seen in a disco with a teammate only hours after a 1-0 loss to Olmedo in November, 2005. "He doesn't feel anything for this shirt, that's why he's going to play in the B team," club president Isidro Romero said. "It's incredible for a player who's an idol of the national team, because this idol hasn't been up to standard in the local championship." Delgado, who had scored 29 goals in 67 international matches through the winter, was Ecuador's co-top scorer with Edison Mendez (five goals apiece) in qualifying thanks to a powerful shot and his superb heading ability. nicknamed Tin, Delgado has fought injuries—primarily back ailments—the past four years, so being in top shape for Germany is a must if Ecuador wants to get out of its group.

The South Americans have moved away from the short passing

game and use the wings more. "Nowadays, any side can complicate matters by packing the midfield with battlers," Suarez told *World Soccer*. "A good team is one that attacks and defends well down the flanks."

Ecuador's weaknesses stand out as well: the defense is inconsistent, especially on crosses, air balls and overall performances. For example, after securing a place in Germany, the team had a pair of embarrassing results in friendlies, losing to Poland, 3-0, in Spain and Barcelona of Guayaquil (Ecuador), 4-1.

Suarez admitted he wouldn't want to play foes who are "dangerous in the air and play a type of football against which Ecuador (doesn't) have much experience."

But there is optimism in some quarters. "We may still be a young side in terms of participating on the big stage, but now we've qualified in fine style for the second time running," Sandra Lopez told **www.BBC.com**. "We've been face to face with the mighty Brazil and Argentina and beaten both at home. Si se puede - yes, we can do it."

For World Cup history buffs: Outside of Brazil and Argentina, South American teams have compiled a 9-19-13 record (46 goals for, 66 against) in European based World Cups. So Ecuador certainly has its work cut out for itself.

ECUADOR

ENGLAND
Group B

POPULATION: 48,500,000

COLORS: White shirts, blue shorts, white socks

APPEARANCES: 12th. 22-13-15, 68 goals for, 45 against. 1950 (first round), 1954 (quarterfinals), 1958 (first round), 1962 (quarterfinals), 1966 (champions), 1970 (quarterfinals), 1982 (second round), 1986 (quarterfinals), 1990 (fourth place), 1998 (second round), 2002 (quarterfinals).

WORLD CUP HISTORY

For the country that claims to have invented soccer, England's journey through the world's greatest sporting spectacle has been a rocky one. The English were surprised by the United States, 1-0, in their first Cup appearance in 1950 (which is considered their low point) and won the entire thing at home in 1966. Geoff Hurst was one of the heroes of the '66 triumph, which was decided by a controversial goal (Hurst's shot caromed off the crossbar onto the goal line or over it, depending if you were German or English). In between and since then, their results have been sporadic. Until the fourth-place finish at Italia '90, England had not reached a final four except for 1966. England's hopes were squelched by Brazil in the 2002 quarterfinals, losing 2-1, though they had a man advantage for 30 minutes of the second half after Ronaldinho was red-carded.

HOW THEY QUALIFIED

England finished atop European Group eight with an 8-1-1 record and 25 points, one more point than Poland. The English clinched a spot behind a 2-1 victory over the Poles on October 12, 2005. Frank Lampard scored off an acrobatic volley eight minutes from time after Polish substitute Tomasz Frankowski equalized only seconds into the second half. Michael Owen tallied England's first goal.

PLAYERS TO WATCH

Midfielder David Beckham is overrated and overhyped, but still has plenty of magic left in that skilled right foot of his, whether it is crossing the ball from the right wing into the penalty area or bending one of his patented free kicks past the defensive wall and goalkeeper for a goal. Frank Lampard, the only player to have participated in all 10 qualifiers, is a rock in the midfield as is Steven Gerard. Forward Michael Owen is coming back from a broken bone in his foot and is needed at top scoring form (to rebound from a disappointing 2002 World Cup) if England is serious about its title aspirations. Forward

Wayne Rooney, 20, is already making an impact, although he is a hothead and could get into yellow-card peril if he doesn't sit on his emotions during the heat of the game.

Goalkeepers: David James (Manchester City), Chris Kirkland (West Bromwich), Paul Robinson (Tottenham). Defenders: Wayne Bridge (Fulham; Chelsea loan), Sol Campbell (Arsenal), Jamie Carragher (Liverpool), Ashley Cole (Arsenal), Rio Fernando (Manchester United), Ledley King (Tottenham), Garry Neville (Manchester United), Phil Neville (Everton), John Terry (Chelsea), Jonathan Woodgate (Real Madrid, Spain), Luke Young (Charlton). Midfielders: David Beckham (Real Madrid, Spain), Michael Carrrick (Tottenham), Joe Cole (Chelsea), Stewart Downing (Middlesbrough), Kieron Dyer (Newcastle United), Steven Gerrard (Liverpool), Owen Hargreaves (Bayern Munich, Germany), Jermaine Jenas (Tottenham), Frank Lampard (Chelsea), Scott Park (Newcastle United), Shaun Wright-Phillips (Chelsea). Forwards: Peter Crouch (Liverpool), Jermain Defoe (Tottenham), Michael Owen (Newcastle United), Wayne Rooney (Manchester United), Darius Vassell (Manchester City).

PLAYER POOL

Goalkeeper: Paul Robinson (Tottenham). Defenders: Gary Neville (Manchester United), John Terry (Chelsea), Rio Ferndinad (Manchester United), Ashley Cole (Arsenal). Midfielders: David Beckham (Real Madrid, Spain), Steven Gerrard (Liverpool), Frank Lampard (Chelsea), Joe Cole (Chelsea). Forwards: Michael Owen (Newcastle United), Wayne Rooney (Manchester United).

PROJECTED STARTING LINEUP

Sven-Goran Eriksson's five-year tenure as coach of England has been followed by one controversy after another. Even when he was hired in January of 2001, xenophobic fans protested that the team didn't need to be guided by a foreign coach (Eriksson is Swedish). There is no question Eriksson is a good coach, it's his personal life that seems to get in the headlines all of the time. In the fall of 2004, Eriksson was embroiled in a personal controversy because of an affair with the former secretary of the English F.A. The tabloids, which always put the National Team and top club sides under scrutiny, put Eriksson through the wringer and under the microscope. "I don't know if you learn to cope with it," he said. "When it happened to me the first time, you have to take a decision by yourself. You give in to pressure or you go on fighting or don't care about it. I chose the second one because I will not quit the job because of the tabloid press. I would quit this job because of football results. Because the other way I

COACH

ENGLAND

would give in to the tabloid press. I don't want to do that. I'm too stubborn for that." In January, 2006, his usually strong bond with his players was severely tested after he gave some indiscreet comments about Michael Owen, Rio Ferdinand and captain David Beckham to an undercover tabloid newspaper reporter dressed as a wealthy sheikh (we can't make this stuff up) on a yacht in the harbor of Dubai, United Arab Emirates (a country that made major headlines in the United States a little later for some other reasons). Although his contract was to run to 2008, Eriksson told the "sheikh:" "After five and a half years . . . it is a long time to be England's manager. Anyhow, if I win the World Cup, I will leave, goodbye." The Football Association beat him to the punch. Eriksson, who earns a reported $4.8 million a year after taxes, will be shown the door after the Cup. You just have to wonder how many other skeletons Eriksson might have in his closets. Born on February 5, 1948, Eriksson has coached club teams to titles in Sweden, Portugal and Italy. He also captured the UEFA Cup championship with IFK Gothenberg. His trustworthy assistant, Tord Grip, has helped Eriksson considerably with tactics and scouting.

2006
WORLD CUP

A popular television show running for years on British television called The Dream Team, chronicles the escapades of a fictional soccer club team in England call Harchester United and the sometimes steamy, controversial, comedic life of the players and team management. The English National Team seems to be living a real-life version of the TV show. Without naming names, consider these plots and sub plots:

The big star of the team, a nice chap with a whiny voice, but over-hyped and overrated, is arguably the best known player in the world and is married to a former pop star and supposedly had an affair with his nanny; the team's coach has an affair with the Football Association secretary, who sells her story to one of the British tabloids; the coach then reveals his inner-most thoughts about the game to a stranger—a tabloid newsman posing as a sheikh. The coach is forced to resign before his contract is up—but is allowed to coach the team in the World Cup—essentially becoming a lame-duck coach—while a search is started for a successor (who could be named before the competition begins).

The team, when it does play, is fairly successful, but makes major international headlines and puts its qualifying chances in jeopardy when it loses to Northern Ireland for the first time in 33 years. And of course, the national media, particularly the newspapers, blow most of these events out of proportion. They are very happy to build up an

ENGLAND

individual, just to set him up for a major take down. And so it goes. Sound familiar? It should. Welcome to the English National Team, the best soap opera (or is it the worst?) in all of international soccer.

Despite all these distractions, England still is considered in many quarters to have a decent shot of winning it all. Forty years ago, in 1966, England won its first World Cup championship. Since then, England has been disappointing, falling short of all expectations.

While no team is only one man, a healthy and in-form Michael Owen would go a long, long way. He has just turned 26, in the prime of his career for a striker (remember, Owen made his World Cup debut in spectacular fashion at France '98 eight years ago, although it seems he has been around forever). Owen broke a metatarsal in his right foot in late December, 2005 in a collision with goalkeeper Paul Robinson, who managed to take out defender Wayne Bridge (injured ankle ligaments) in England's 3-2 World Cup warm-up win over Uruguay on March 1. Owen swore he would be back as soon as possible as he continued an incredible team jinx with broken metatarsals by key players such as David Beckham and Gary Neville (2002) and Wayne Rooney, whose fabulous Euro 2004 performance ended prematurely with the same exact injury.

Rooney, 20, the youngest player to make his England debut (at the age of 17) is the striker of the present and future. He has so much potential to do some serious damage, but his temperament is his greatest liability. You wonder if he will wind up serving a yellow-card suspension (two cautions in separate matches) in Germany.

Of course, there's always the option of using 6-foot-7 Liverpool forward Terry Crouch as the ultimate target player in front of the opposition's net.

The well paid and much-maligned Beckham still can be a force in games, especially thanks to his swirling crosses into the box and his specialty—free kicks. But Beckham might not be the most influential midfielder because Eriksson has a few hard workers and talents who can change the course of matches—Frank Lampard and Steven Gerrard, although questions abound as to whether these two stars can play on the same team.

"Of course they can," Eriksson told the *Times of London*. "But if we want to have one sitting midfield player then we have to find one. This is one area which we are going to look at because maybe you need it at some stage in the World Cup."

The bigger headache, however, could come on defense and in goal. Once the bastion of strength for the English national side, finding a competent goalkeeper has become a major challenge. The English Premiership is partially to blame because it employs some of the best

ENGLAND

keepers in the world, leaving many British keepers out in the cold, whether it is on the bench or in a lower division, where they can't develop and hone their skills. Instead of getting the likes of Gordon Banks and Peter Shilton, who were very consistent, we get David Seaman, who misjudged Ronaldinho's free kick that turned out to be the deciding goal in the 2002 quarterfinals.

The best of the lot this time around is Robinson, who plies his trade for Tottenham Hotspur. To give you an idea of the quality of keepers, one of Robinson's backups, David James, earned the nickname "Calamity James" for all his mishaps and misadventures in goal. He has improved in recent years.

Questions abound on the backline. Manchester United star defender Rio Ferdinand served an eight-month suspension for forgetting to take a drug test. So there is always that specter of a drug test or his refusal to take one that might derail his travel plans. Arsenal's usually stable Sol Campbell, who went AWOL for a while this past winter, had to be told by Eriksson that he needed to be in top shape or be forced to watch the World Cup on TV.

Of course, if Eriksson wanted to add some tragic comedy to the team, he could select the often injured defender Jonathan Woodgate to the final 23. Woodgate, who had been sidelined more than a year due to injuries, endured an own goal and a red card in his Real Madrid debut in Santiago Bernabeu on September 22, 2005. Woodgate put one into his own net in the 25th minute and was given his marching orders for his second yellow card in the 62nd minute. Real prevailed over Athletic Bilbao, 3-1.

England does have one booster in its corner to win it all—Pelé, of all people. "Two teams from England, Italy or Brazil will be in the final," he said. "But if I have to name a team to win, I name Brazil. . . . England (has) a chance to be in the final. I have seen almost every one of their games during the last two years, and they have improved a lot. . . . Italy, Brazil and England have been the best teams during the last two years."

FRANCE
Group G

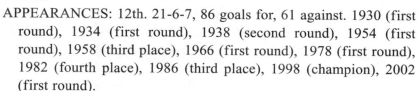

POPULATION: 58,600,000

COLORS: Blue shirt, white shorts, red shots

APPEARANCES: 12th. 21-6-7, 86 goals for, 61 against. 1930 (first round), 1934 (first round), 1938 (second round), 1954 (first round), 1958 (third place), 1966 (first round), 1978 (first round), 1982 (fourth place), 1986 (third place), 1998 (champion), 2002 (first round).

WORLD CUP HISTORY

France has experienced four memorable World Cups and one it would rather forget. In 1958, behind the stellar passing of midfield general Raymond Kopa and the superb finishing skills of Just Fontaine (a World Cup record thirteen goals), the French reached the semifinals before succumbing to eventual champion Brazil. Under the guidance of midfield maestro Michel Platini and a generation of talented stars, again they reached the Final Four in 1982 and 1986. They were robbed in a bittersweet semifinal elimination (via penalty kicks) by Germany. With the core of the team more than 30 years of age four years later, the French baked in the Mexican sun and settled for third place in 1986. Combining a stellar backline, an outstanding midfield and the best player in the world at that time, Zinedine Zidane and an opportunistic attack, the French finally captured their coveted prize in 1998. But in 2002 tired from a long European season and with several key injuries, the French became the first defending champion not to win at least at match and score a goal in the next World Cup, going 0-2-1 in Korea.

HOW THEY QUALIFIED

France went undefeated (5-0-5, 20 points) and captured the European Group 4. But that didn't mean the French didn't struggle. They did mightily—playing to a pair of draws each with Switzerland and Israel, who finished with 18 points apiece. The French cruised to a 4-1 victory over Cyprus to clinch a spot in Germany on October 12, 2005 as Zinedine Zidane, Sylvain Wiltord and Vikash Dhorasoo connected in the first half and substitute Ludovic Giuly added a fourth late in the match.

PLAYERS TO WATCH

You have to start with team captain Zidedine Zidane, the biggest hero of France '98. But for all his skills, vision and experience, can someone who turns 34 during the Cup be an impact player? When healthy

FRANCE

and in form, the tandem of Thierry Henry and David Trezeguet up front is arguably the most dangerous in the world. Many observers consider Claude Makelele is the best defensive midfielder in the world.

PLAYER POOL

Goalkeepers: Fabien Barthez (Marseille), Gregory Coupet (Lyon), Michael Landreau (Nantes). Defenders: Eric Abidal (Lyon), Jean-Alian Boumsong (Newcastle, England), Patrice Evra (Manchester United, England), William Gallas (Chelsea, England), Gael Givet (Monaco), Bernard Mendy (Paris Saint-German), Anthony Reveillere (Lyon), Willy Sagnol (Bayern Munich, Germany), Sebastian Squillaci (Monaco), Lilian Thuram (Juventus, Italy), Jonathan Zebina (Juventus, Italy). Midfielders: Vikash Dhorasoo (Paris St-Germain), Alou Diarra (lens), Ludovic Giuly (Barcelona, Spain), Sidney Govou (Lyon), Claude Makelele (Chelsea, England), Florent Malouda (Lyon), Camel Meriem (Monaco), Jerome Rothen (Paris St-Germain), Patrick Vieira (Juventus, Italy), Zinedine Zidane (Real Madrid, Spain). Forwards: Nicolas Anelka (Fenerbachce, Turkey), Djibril Cisse (Liverpool, England), Thierry Henry (Arsenal), Louis Saha (Manchester United, England), David Trezeguet (Juventus, Italy), Sylvain Wiltord (Lyon).

PROJECTED
STARTING
LINEUP

Goalkeeper: Fabien Barthez (Marseille). Defenders: Antoine Reveillere (Lyon), Lilian Thuram (Juventus, Italy), Jean-Alain Boumsong (Newcastle United, England), William Gallas Chelsea (England). Midfielders: Vikash Dhorasoo (Paris St. Germain), Claude Makelele (Chelsea, England), Patrick Vieira (Juventus, taly), Zinedine Zidane (Real Madrid Spain). Forwards: Thierry Henry (Arsenal, England), David Trezeguet (Juventus, Italy).

COACH

Raymond Domenech succeeded Jacques Santini after Euro 2004. He was the French Under-21 coach for 11 years and reportedly is an amateur dramatics enthusiast and has a passion for astrology. Born on January 24, 1952, Domenech played eight times for the French National Team, his first appearance against the Republic of Ireland in a 1-1 draw on May 19, 1973. One of his appearances was as starter in France's 6-0 drubbing of the U.S. at Giants Stadium in 1979. A Lyon, native, he performed for several French League teams, including Olympique Lyonnais (1970-1977), RC Strasbourgh (1977-81), Paris St-Germain (1981-82), Bordeaux (1982-84), and FC Mulhouse (1984-88). He coached FC Mulhouse from 1985-88 as well and at Olympique Lyonnais from 1988-93, directing the club to the French Second Division championship in 1989. Domenech became national

FRANCE

technical director on July 1, 1993. He directed the French U-20 side to the quarterfinals of the 2001 FIFA world championships.

What exactly will we see from this French team in Germany? Will it be the last hurrah or the twilight of the soccer gods? Time is running out on a talented generation of players that includes the great Zinedine Zidane, who had to come out of international retirement along with defender Lilian Thuram and midfielder Claude Makelele to give a lackluster French attack some bite to help the team into the World Cup. Zidane, who turns 34 during the Cup (June 23), played only four games, but that was the perfect tonic for a team that under-achieved and struggled during qualifying.

2006
WORLD CUP

"The World Cup is not an important objective, it's the greatest objective," Zidane told the daily sports newspaper *L'Equipe.* "We'll go to Germany to win the World Cup. We are not going to play a World Cup just for the pleasure of taking part. I don't know if we'll win it but we can make it, I'd stake my life on it. . . . I'm 33, I'll be 34 in Germany. When one has won the World Cup and lost it four years later, winning it back is a magnificent and imperious obligation. If we are at 150 percent on D-Day, I don't see which country could trouble us—apart from Brazil, obviously—because they are the fearsome team—they have always been."

Six of the eleven projected starters will be 30 or older in June. They are goalkeeper Barthez (turns 34 during the Cup), defender Thuram (34), midfielders Vikash Dhorasoo (32), Claude Makelele (33), Patrick Vieira (turns 30) and Zidane (turns 34). That could especially hurt in the midfield, which has to do most of the running for this team.

The team has serious doubters, even at home. "They won't do any better than quarterfinals," French author Xavier Rivoire told **www.BBC.com**. "The team is too old. Young players like Franck Ribery cannot break into the squad. Germany will be the twilight for the dinosaurs of the golden generation."

It would be surprising if the French don't get out of the first round in one piece. Their most difficult foe is neighbor and qualifying group rival Switzerland, but they have weak opponents in Korea and Togo, which should present few problems. Of course, the same was said about World Cup debutantes Senegal in 2002, and the Africans pulled off a major 1-0 upset in the Cup opener.

If Barthez is in goal, the defense, led by Thuram, will have to work extra hard to make sure he doesn't produce one or two of his patented blunders. It's amazing that a keeper with a history of making big mistakes is still a member of the National Team pool.

FRANCE

Makelele and Vieira bring excellent reputations as holding midfielders and are expected to form a viable partnership. The 1998 championship side was not geared around forwards doing the bulk of the scoring. This team is, so the pressure is on Henry Thierry (31 goals in 76 games) and David Trezeguet (31 goals in 61) to produce. They did en route to France capturing the Euro 2000 title. Due to injuries and ineffectiveness, the 28-year-old strikers combined for only three goals in nine total qualifying appearances, a far cry from their club reputations. Thierry had two qualifying scores and Trezeguet had but one. You have to wonder if both or neither are producing at the World Cup whether coach Raymond Domench will replace one of them with younger legs. Someone such as 24-year-old Djibril Cisse, who led France with four qualifying goals.

One of Domenech's most anticipated decisions will be the announcement of the No. 1 goalkeeper. Gregory Coupet and Barthez, who backstopped the champions at France '98, split the qualifying duties, the former seeing action in six games, the latter in four. Domenech, however, has delayed his announcement until May. Barthez, 34, played 75 internationals for France through the winter, although he wound up getting a multiple game suspension for spitting at a referee while playing for Marseille in a friendly in Morocco in Febuary, 2006. Coupet, who plays for French champions Lyon and has 18 caps, took over for Barthez during his qualifying suspension. "We will make our move during the preparation session scheduled in May. Bruno Martini (assistant coach) is still to work on this matter and I need his advice to make up my mind," Domenech told **Reuters**. "There is no use making a decision now as it would leave the number two waiting for the number one to die to take the position. There's no doubt it's going to be a tough choice. . . ."

If the 2-1 home loss on March 1, 2006 to non-qualifier Slovakia is any indication, the French could be in for a short stay in Germany. It was the French's first international loss in 17 games—or since it was eliminated from the Euro 2004 quarterfinals. The media termed the French performance "clumsy." Add a comeback 3-2 win over Costa Rica in Martinique in November, 2005, and scoreless tie with struggling Germany, and there had to be concerns. Well, maybe to many people, but not to Domenech and his players. "This is the kind of game that helps you prepare for the future," he said. "I'm certain that this match was good for us." Henry put his spin on it. "This is only our first defeat for 17 matches and we can't say it's deserved," he said. "We must not start mulling things over."

France became the first country to capture the European Championship (2000) as defending World Cup champions (1998).

GERMANY
Group A

POPULATION: 82,100,000
COLORS: White shirts, black shorts, white socks
APPEARANCES: 16th. 50-17-18. 176 goals for, 106 against. 1934 (third place), 1938 (first round), 1954 (champions), 1968 (fourth place), 1962 (quarterfinals), 1966 (second place), 1970 (second-round group), 1974 (champions), 1978 (second-round group), 1982 (second place), 1986 (second place), 1990 (champions), 1994 (quarterfinals), 1998 (second round), 2002 (second place).

Between 1966 and 1990, no team had a better record than Germany, which reached the championship game in 1966, 1974, 1982, 1986 and 1990 and came away victorious in 1974 and 1990. In 1954, the West Germans stunned heavily favored Hungary in the championship match, 3-2, after losing an earlier encounter in the first round, 8-3. In 1974, behind "Der Kaiser," Franz Beckenbauer (he's head of the 2006 World Cup Organizing Committee), the Germans defeated the Netherlands, 2-1, to capture the Cup at home. And in 1990, under the direction of coach Beckenbauer, they emerged as the best team in a rather mediocre tournament, edging Argentina, 1-0 in the championship match. The 1994 competition wasn't kind to the Germans, who lost a 1-0 lead in a quarterfinal encounter with surprising Bulgaria. The Bulgarians struck twice late in the match en route to a 2-1 upset. In 1998, however, the Germans proved to be closer to mere mortals. They managed to reach the second round, where they were dispatched by another surprise side, Croatia, 3-0. The German rode the stellar goalkeeping of Oliver Kahn, the skills of Michael Ballack, some gritty play and even some luck (that non-handball call against the U.S. in the quarterfinals) to win all of their knockout round games by 1-0 scores to reach the championship game before Brazil prevailed, 2-0, in the first World Cup encounter ever between those two powerhouse nations.

WORLD CUP HISTORY

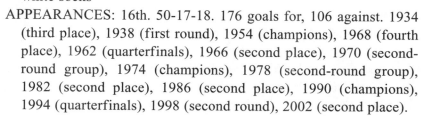

GERMANY

Germany received an automatic berth as hosts.

HOW THEY QUALIFIED

Without a doubt, midfielder Michael Ballack is this team's best player. That's why Chelsea has pursued the Bayern Munich star. Ballack, however, doesn't have the leadership impact of a Franz Beckenbauer or even a Lothar Matthaeus. And as good as he is, he'll need a little help from his German friends if they want to go far in

PLAYERS TO WATCH

PLAYERS TO
WATCH

this competition. Assuming Coach Klinsmann gives him the nod over Jens Lehmann, Oliver Kahn can be one intimidating goalkeeper when the game is on the line. Just ask any forward or midfielder who tried to score on him at the 2002 World Cup. Forward Lukas Podolski, who turns 21 on June 4, 2006, is Germany's great young hope (10 goals in 20 internationals through the winter), thanks to his great acceleration, strength and hard shot. Of course, he has never been forced to do it at such a high level with so much on the line.

PLAYER POOL

Goalkeepers: Timo Hildebrand (VfB Stuttgart), Oliver Kahn (Bayern Munich), Jens Lehmann (Arsenal, England). Defenders: Arne Friedrich (Hertha Berlin), Manuel Friedrich (Mainz), Robert Huth (Chelsea, England), Marcell Jansen (Borussia Moenchengladbach), Philipp Lahm (Bayern Munich), Per Mertesacker (Hannover), Christoph Metzelder (Borussia Dortmund), Patrick Owomoyela (Werder Bremen). Midfielders: Michael Ballack (Bayern Munich), Tim Borowski (Werder Bremen), Sebastian Deisler (Bayern Munich), Fabian Ernst (Schalke), Torsten Frings (Werder Bremen), Sebastian Kehl (Borussia Dortmund), Bernd Schneider (Bayer Leverkusen), Bastian Schweinsteiger (Bayern Munich). Forwards: Gerald Asamoah (Schalke), Mike Hanke (Wolfsburg), Miroslav Klose (Werder Bremen), Lukas Podolski (Cologne).

PROJECTED
STARTING
LINEUP

Goalkeeper: Oliver Kahn (Bayern Munich). Defenders: Arne Friedrich (Hertha Berlin), Robert Huth (Chelsea, England), Marcell Jansen (Borussia Moenchengladbach), Per Mertesacker (Hannover). Midfielders: Michael Ballack (Bayern Munich), Sebastian Deisler (Bayern Munich), Torsten Frings (Werder Bremen), Bastian Schweinsteiger (Bayern Munich). Forwards: Miroslav Klose (Werder Bremen), Lukas Podolski (Cologne).

COACH

One of German's all-time greats and a member of the 1990 World Cup championship team, Juergen Klinsmann took on the greatest challenge of his career in 2004 to coach the German team, replacing Rudi Voeller on July 26, 2004 although he had no actual coaching experience. Whether that will come back to haunt him and the German Football Federation, it remains to be seen. No one, however, can dispute Klinsmann's hall of fame playing career. He scored 47 goals in 108 international appearances, winning a bronze medal in the 1988 Summer Olympics. He starred in three World Cups, playing a key role in Germany's 1990 championship team. Born on July 30, 1964, Klinsmann retired from international play after the 1998 World Cup. He also performed for the Euro 96 champions as well. At the club level, Klinsmann played for VfB Stuttgart and Bayern Munich in Germany, AS Monaco in France, Inter and Sampdoria in Italy, and twice at Tottenham Hotspur in England. Even though he had no pro coaching experience when he was hired, Klinsmann has demonstrated he can be a leader, an influential one at that. But sometimes he can be obstinate, very obstinate—i.e. refusing to live in Germany fulltime in the months before the World Cup while commuting from southern California. The jury is still out—we will know by July 9—if that decision was good or bad for the German team or for Klinsmann, for that matter. He's also been vice president of a sports marketing consultancy company based in the U.S.

The March 2, 2006 headline in *Kicker* said it all: DESASTER!

2006 WORLD CUP

Even in German, most English speaking soccer fans know what the meant: an embarrassing 4-1 debacle to Italy had transpired the previous night in Florence. "Mamma mia we're bad!" the Germany's biggest-selling daily *Bild* said on its front page. "Only 99 days to the World Cup and our national team is playing worse than ever before. If we play like that at the World Cup we'll be obliterated."

With exactly 100 days to the kickoff of the World Cup, no one was expecting that result. And that from a country that has a work ethic in the international end of the sport that is second to none.

"We are all very disappointed," coach Juergen Klinsmann said. "It was a lesson for us above all in the first half. But it's over now and we cannot escape it. We have to face the criticism."

But Klinsmann didn't. He flew-or better yet-ran across the Atlantic to take refuge in his southern California home in Orange County. Adding fuel to the controversy was that Klinsmann conveniently missed a World Cup workshop for all 32 coaches in Dusseldorf several days after the game, taking refuge in the United States. "It's incredible that he's not here,"said German soccer great Franz Beckenbauer, the president of Germany's World Cup organizing committee. "As host country you have to be here. Nearly all the coaches are here. Carlos Alberto Parreira came from Brazil, Sven-Goran Eriksson came from England, but our head coach is not here. He should have been here. This is an obligatory meeting and he does not have all that many meetings that are obligatory. I don't want to say anything more about it because the more I think about it, the more drastic my choice of words will become."

They were drastic enough, considering Beckenbauer, a long-time backer of the coach, also criticized Klinsmann's performance as coach and the lack of progress made by the team. "At the beginning it worked out very well and Klinsmann was able to change a few

GERMANY

things but now there's not much left of all that," he said. "We are back where we were a few years ago and time is running out." To which Klinsmann retorted in the *Bild* newspaper: "I was in Germany for three of the last five weeks after the Bundesliga started up after the winter break. I've got my plan with everything necessary for the World Cup preparations. I've seen matches almost every weekend this winter, but I'm not someone who puts himself in the forefront."

Trying to squeeze as much as he can out of his talent has been Klinsmann's challenge. "I believe, like the rest of the country, that the national team is a catastrophe," former German international and current Bayern Munich general manager Uli Hoeness told **www.BBC.com** before the Florence flop.

Beyond fans and soccer officials, Klinsmann has found himself under intense scrutiny, including by politicians. "It would be good if Herr Klinsmann would come before the sport committee and explain what his concept is and how Germany can win the World Cup," Norbert Barthle, a member of Chancellor Angela Merkel's CDU, told **Reuters**. "The match against Italy was gruesome and we wonder that can be fixed by the summer. The federal government is the biggest sponsor of the World Cup. In light of that, I'd like to get a few answers from him."

Added Reinhold Hemker, a deputy on the sport committee: "I'd like to hear from Juergen Klinsmann how he plans to create a secure foundation for the team. Klinsmann has good players but there are too many uncertainties. He should start saying clearly who he is counting on."

"I still believe that it works perfectly," an unapologetic Klinsmann told reporters of his commuting between Southern California and Germany. That controversial decision could backfire on Klinsmann if Germany is eliminated early. Germany has become accustomed to going deep in the tournament. The World Cup needs the host country to be around to keep the domestic interest level at a high level.

Against lightweights such as Costa Rica and Ecuador (Poland is the only true test), Germany should get through the first round without too much trouble. "It could have been worse," Klinsmann said. "The draw gives us every possibility."

It's in the latter rounds in which the Germans will get their most severe test against the best in the world. Sure, playing at home will get them a boost or two. They run into the likes of talented sides such as England and Sweden in the second round, Argentina and the Netherlands in the quarterfinals and either the Czech Republic, Italy or France during the ultimate crunch time?

Oliver Kahn, who had such a dominating performance in 2002 and was named the Golden Ball winner—MVP in American terms—by the media, is a question mark in goal. His form and health over the past several years has been questionable, opening the door for Arsenal goalkeeper Jens Lehmann to grab the top spot. Klinsmann, however, has been alternating both players in the net. As of March, he hadn't given any indication which one he would choose to be in goal for the World Cup opener against Costa Rica in Munich come June 9.

Of course, the brash Kahn had other ideas. "The national team coach told me again recently that I was the number one and would remain the No. 1 as long as I kept performing well," he told *Kicker*.

Klinsmann has implemented a "fast-paced, attacking and very aggressive" style which has helped, but hindered the defense. The Germans paid for that dearly with a relatively inexperienced defense that allowed 11 goals in five games in the 2005 FIFA Confederations Cup hosted by Germany.

A lot of responsibility and pressure will fall on the shoulders of Michael Ballack, who should have some World Cup fire in him after missing the 2002 championship game due to a pair of yellow cards. Whether he has the fortitude and strength to take this team on his back in the mold of Franz Beckenbauer. Chelsea's billionaire owner Roman Abramovich and coach Jose Mourinho certainly don't, as they made a push to sign Ballack before the World Cup began in the spring of 2006. Fortunately for Ballack, he has some help in the midfield with Bastien Schweinsteiger and Sebastien Deisler in a platoon that could be the strength of the team.

The scoring responsibilities will fall to Miroslav Klose, who connected for four of his team-high five goals at the 2002 competition against Saudi Arabia, and 20-year-old Lukas Podolski, who has gotten off to a fast interntional start (10 goals in 20 matches). Podolski, who plays for struggling Colgone in the Bundesliga, is best suited for a position just behind the forward line thanks to his powerful shot and acceleration. He has an attitude, however, and he hasn't scored much for his club team this season.

"It is a possibility that I might remain the national coach after the World Cup," he was quoted in *Kicker* in March. Of course, all that could become moot if the Germans continue their struggling ways come June.

For World Cup history buffs: The Germans failed to reach the semifinals of two consecutive World Cups (1994 and 1998), rebounding with a final appearance in 2002. As it turned out, it was the first time Germany and Brazil had ever met in a World Cup match, even though they boasted eight world championships between them.

GERMANY

GHANA
Group E

POPULATION: 20,500,000.
COLORS: White shirts, white shorts,
   white socks
APPEARANCES: 1st.

WORLD CUP HISTORY

None.

HOW THEY QUALIFIED

After dropping a 1-0 decision to Burkina Faso in the first game of African Group 2, Ghana rebounded and beat South Africa in both encounters and finished atop the group at 6-1-3 with 21 points, ahead of the Democrat Republic of the Congo and South Africa, the 2010 World Cup hosts. In fact, Ghana beat the embarrassed South Africans twice, 3-0 and 2-0. The clincher came in a 4-0 triumph at the Cape Verde Islands on October 8, 2006. Frimpong Asamoah gave Ghana all the scoring it needed in the fifth minute as Sulley Muntari, Asamoah Gyan and Godwin Attram added goals.

PLAYERS TO WATCH

Midfielder Michael Essien, who signed with Chelsea in a record $43 million transfer (for an African) from Lyon, is a major impact player at the age of 23. He scored three qualifying goals, making every one count. The man who makes this team go is midfielder and captain Stephen Appiah, who at only 25, has played for three Serie A clubs in Italy.

PLAYER POOL

Goalkeepers: Sammy Adjei (Moadan Sport Ashdod, Israel), George Owu (AshantiGold), Philemon McCarthy (Feyenoord, Ghana). Defenders: Yakubu Abubakari (Vitesse Arnhem), Issah Ahmed (Asante Kotoko), Aziz Ansah (Asante Kotoko), Francis Dickoh (FC Nordsjaelland, Denmark), Daniel Edusei (Egaleo, Greece), Samuel Osei Kuffour (Roma, Italy), Emmanuel Pappoe (Hapoel Kfar Sava, Israel), John Painstil (Hapoel Tel Aviv, Israel), John Mensah (Cremonese, Italy). Midfielders: Stephen Appiah (Fenerbache, Turkey), Godwin Attram (Al Shabab, Saudi Arabia), Haminu Dramani (Red Star Belgrade, Serbia & Montenegro), Michael Essien (Chelsea, England), Laryea Kingston (Krylya Sovietov Samara, Russia), Hamza Mohammed (Real Tamale United, Ghana), Sulley Muntari (Udinese, Italy). Forwards: Matthew Amoah (Borussia Dortmund, Germany), Asamoah Gyan (Modena, Italy), Joetex Frimpong (Enyimba, Nigeria), Prince Tagoe (Hearts of Oak).

GHANA

Goalkeeper: Sammy Adjei (Mohadon Sports Ashdod, Israel). Defenders: John Mensah (Cremonese, Italy), John Pantsil Ashdod (Tel Aviv, Israel), Sammy Kuffour (AS Roma, Italy), Emmanuel Pappoe (Ashdod Tel Aviv, Israel). Midfielders: Sulley Ali Muntari (Udinese, Italy), Michael Essien (Chelsea, England), Stephen Appiah (Fenerbahce, Turkey), Kingston Laryea (Krylya Sovietov Samara, Russia). Forwards: Matthew Amoah (Borussia Dortmund, Germany), Asamoah Gyan (Modena, Italy)

PROJECTED STARTING LINEUP

Sometimes it pays to wait to get the big payoff. Consider the case of Ratomir Dujkovic, for example. The Serbian native has bounced around the coaching ranks for years trying to make a name for himself and trying to transfer one of soccer's minnows into a World Cup team. He guided the National Teams of Venezuela and Myanmar (formerly Burma) before landing with Rwanda. There, he directed the surprising side into the 2004 Nations Cup over Ghana. Impressed, Ghana soccer officials signed the 60-year-old Dujkovic and he took a country that has had so much promise and several well-known stars, yet failed to qualify for the World Cup, usually due to poor management off the field. As for his three predecessors, German Ralf Zumdick started the merry-go-round as he left and became an assistant coach at Hamburg in December, 2003. Portuguese native Mariano Barretto was there for nine months before he quit to join Maritimo in Portugal. Sam Arday ran the show as a caretaker coach for one qualifier before Dujkovic took over in December, 2004. As it turned out, Durkovic could have become history himself in February, 2006 because some fans wanted his head after a disappointing showing in the African Nations Cup. How quickly some people forget. "I know the Ghanaians are frustrated, but he was the first ever coach to guide Ghana to the World Cup finals," midfielder Michael Essien said.

COACH

How many times have soccer's experts and observers put Ghana on the World Cup pedestal, only to be severely disappointed with the reality of the results? They're too numerous to mention. Ghana became the first country to win the African Nations Cup four times. Africans won the FIFA Under-17 World Cup, not once, but twice (although age cheating revelations in later years tainted the championships). They boasted some of the best and most exciting players in Africa, if not the world in the fabulous Abedi Pele and Anthony Yeboah. But when push came to shove for the grand prize—a trip to the World Cup, the western African country—always fell short of reaching soccer's promised land—until the 2006 World Cup.

2006 WORLD CUP

GHANA

Despite having four coaching changes and obvious continuity problems—i.e. lineup changes—Ghana finally made it. "I didn't care much for all this talk about Ghana having never made it to the World Cup before," coach Ratomir Dujkovic told *FIFA Magazine*. "I was not interested in what happened before. I just knew deep down we would be in Germany." When Ghana became one of five African sides to qualify for the World Cup, Dujkovic likened it to the country receiving its independence from the United Kingdom in 1957. "This is the crowning of my career," he said. "I am very happy. We are very proud to be in this competition. We are not coming to participate. We are coming to compete."

Dujkovic was realistic about his team's chances, but he has to be hopeful as well. "I believe [Ghana] and USA will do their best to surprise for one of the first or second positions," he said. "We are happy to be there. But of course, it will be so very difficult for us because we are new. I always said, with 11 boys anything can happen."

Instead of dominating at the 2006 African Nations Cups as they did in the past, the Ghanaians were eliminated in the first round, but the team had an excuse—Michael "The Bison" Essien didn't play due to an ankle injury. Ghana finished out of the money, losing to Nigeria, 1-0, rebounding with a 1-0 win over Senegal and eliminated in a 2-1 defeat to Zimbabwe. Only 23, Essien could wind up on that same pedestal as Pele and Yeboah—with one big exception—he will have played in a World Cup. Essein signed with Chelsea in a record $43 million transfer (for an African) from Lyon in 2005. He is a handful to stop.

So, it shouldn't be surprising that the team relies on him a lot, which, of course can be good or bad, depending which way you look it. On the plus side, if Essien has a dominating match, he'll carry the Black Stars on his shoulders. If he is injured or has a sub-par game, Ghana could be in trouble.

Before the tournament, Dujkovic said the absence of the injured Essien and Sulley Muntari and Asamoah Gyan would severely weaken his team. "We cannot expect too much without these players, them not being here is a big problem for us," he told **Reuters**. He was correct.

But the Black Stars have a few other players who can play, as well. Nicknamed Tornado, captain and midfielder Stephen Appiah is the engine of this team as a two- way player. He has scored 10 international goals in 38 appearances, excellent for someone who is an accomplished ball-winner as well. Only 25-years-old, Appiah already has eight seasons of top-flight experience with the likes of Udinese,

GHANA

Parma, Brescia and Juventus in Italy's Serie A and Fenerbahce of Turkey, for which he currently performs.

Veteran defender Sammy Kuffour, apparently has ironed out his problems with Dujkovic; he was restored to the team after a two-year absence when the team qualified. Kuffour, a clever and fast defender who performs for Borussia Dortmund (Germany), will bring plenty of big game experience to a back line that could use some.

"The only famous player we have are Appiah and Essien," midfielder Matthew Amoah told Calcio Italia magazine. "The rest of the guys are relatively unknown. But we are a strong group. We work for each other. We are one, like family and that is the secret of our success."

One player Dujkovic shouldn't count on Germany midfielder Laryea Kingston, who was suspended four games for fighting with Senegal's Habib Beye in a 1-0 victory at the Nations Cup in January.

In a group that includes the Czech Republic, second in FIFA's rankings through March 15, 2006, No. 5 United States, and No. 12 Italy, it will be difficult to move on. But Ghana certainly has its backers.

"They will not win the World Cup, and, while they could qualify for the second round, I can't see them getting beyond that," African soccer journalist Durosimi Thomas told **www.BBC.com**.

At one point Ghana had considered going after D.C. United's much-heralded Freddy Adu, who turns 17 on June 2.

Ghana twice tried to coax Adu to join its national side. If Adu had changed his mind, Ghana team spokesman Ranford Abbey said his team would welcome him with open arms. "Why not? Why not?" he said. "We love him. He's Ghanaian. He's a talented player." But Ghana was forced to give up the dream on January 22, 2006, when Adu made his first international appearance for the U.S., coming in for Eddie Johnson in the 81st minute of the scoreless draw with Canada. In fact, Adu became the youngest male player to play for the U.S. at 16 years, 234 days old.

For World Cup history buffs: Despite its glorious history and talented players, Ghana had to wait years before it qualified for the Cup. Nine African teams made it there before the Ghanaians did— Algeria, Cameroon, Egypt, Morocco, Nigeria, Senegal, South Africa, Tunisia and Zaire.

GHANA

IRAN
Group D

POPULATION: 62,800,000
COLORS: White shirts, white shorts, white socks
APPEARANCES: Third. 1-4-1. Four goals for, 12 against. 1978 (first round), 1998 (first round).

WORLD CUP HISTORY

Iran's World Cup visits have been short and sweet—and memorable as well. In 1978, the Iranians finished last in their group in Argentina. They dropped a 3-0 decision to the Netherlands, tied Scotland, 1-1, and lost to Peru, 4-1. One of their goal-scorers, Iraj Danaifard, eventually played for the Tulsa Roughnecks of the old North American Soccer League. In 1998, Team Melli dropped a 1-0 decision to Yugoslavia, edged the U.S., 2-1, and was eliminated via a 2-0 loss to Germany.

HOW THEY QUALIFIED

Iran finished second behind Japan (5-1-0, 15 points) in Asian Group B of the third qualifying stage with a 4-1-1 record and 13 points The top three teams in the two groups qualified with the fourth-place team, Bahrain, moving onto a special playoff with CONCACAF's fourth-place side, Trinidad & Tobago. On June 8, 2005, Iran became the second team to qualify for the World Cup (Japan was the first earlier that day) behind a 1-0 triumph over Bahrain in Tehran with one game to spare. Defender Mohammad Nosrati, who has but three international goals, scored off a header in the 47th minute. "I had a dream last night about scoring a goal," Nosrati told **Reuters**. "With God's help, we won. We played very well and deserved to win." The victory touched off a vociferous celebration as hundreds or thousands of fans spilled onto the Tehran streets, setting off firecrackers, blowing whistles and waving national flags while fireworks lit up the skies.

PLAYERS TO WATCH

At 36, forward Ali Daei (107 goals in 143 matches) will be one of the oldest field players in the Cup, if not the oldest. Some observers feel he is past his prime, but Iran is more concerned about the leadership and experience he brings to the team. He scored a team-high nine qualifying goals. Midfielder Ali Karimi, the 2004 Asian player of the year, is an expert dribbler and the creative force of the team. Midfielder Mehdi Mahdavikia, who scored the game-winner in Iran's win over the U.S. at France '98, is better known for his right-wing crosses than goals (11 in 89 appearances).

Goalkeepers: Ebrahim Mirzapour (Foolad Khuzestan), Mehdi Vaezi (Paykan Tehran), Hassan Roudbarian (Pas Tehran), Mehdi Rahmati (Fajr Sepasi Shiraz), Vahid Taleblou (Esteghlal Tehran). Defenders: Mehdi Amirabadi (Esteghlal), Ali Ansarian (Pirouzi), Yahya Golmohammadi (Saba Battery), Rahman Rezaei (Messina, Italy), Hossein Kaebi (Foolad FC) Mohammad Nosrati (Pas), Sattar Zare (Bargh Shiraz, Iran). Midfielders: Mehdi Mahdavikia (Hamburg, Germany), Javad Nekounam (Al-Wahda, United Arab Emirates), Ferydoon Zandi (Kaiserslautern, Germany), Moharram Navidkia (VfL Bochum, Germany), Mohammad Alavi (Foolad FC, Iran), Mojtaba Jabbari (Esteghlal, Iran), Andranik Teymourian (Abu Moslem), Mehrzad Madanchi (Persepolis), Mehdi Rajabzadeh (Zob Ahan), Hamed Kavianpour (Pirouzi), Javad Kazemian (Perspolis), Eman Mobali (Al Shabab, United Arab Emirates), Ali Reza Vahedi-Nikrakht (Esteghial). Forwards: Vahid Hashemian (Hannover 96, Germany), Ali Daei (Saba Battery), Ali Karimi (Bayern Munich,Germany), Arash Borhani (Pas), Siavash Akbarpour (Esteghlal), Rasoul Khatibi (Sepahan), Mehdi Rajabzadeh (Zob-Ahan).

Goalkeeper: Ebrahim Mirzapour Foolad Khuzestan (Iran). Defenders: Yahya GolMohammadi (Saba Battery), Rahman Rezaei (FC Messina, Italy), Mohammad Nosrati (Pas Tehran, Iran), Sattar Zare Bargh (Shiraz, Iran). Midfielders: Hosein Kaebi (Foolad Khuzestan), Javad Nekounam (Pas Tehran, Iran), Ferydoon Zandi (FC Kaiserslautern, Germany), Mehdi Mahdavikia (Hamburg SV, Germany). Forwards: Ali Karimi (Bayern Munich,Germany), Ali Daei (Saba Battery)

Croatian Branko Ivankovic, the former assistant coach of this side, took over for fellow countryman Miroslav Blazevic when Iran missed out on the 2002 Cup after the Republic of Ireland stopped their quest in a special playoff. He then guided the team to the Asian Games championship and to a third-place finish at the Asian Cup in 2004. Ivankovic was on shaky ground during qualifying after the team had some sub-par performances. Born on February 28, 1954, Ivankovic holds a doctorate in physical education. After coaching several Croatian club teams, Ivankovic first assisted Miroslav Blazevic guide Croatia to a third-place finish at France '98. He coached Hannover 96 for a short time in the 1999-2000 season before returning to the Croatian national side as an assistant to Mirko Jozic during the 2002 World Cup qualifying run. He then hooked up with Blazevic again as an assistant with Iran and after an unsuccessful attempt to reach the

IRAN

2002 competition, Blazevic left and Ivankovic eventually was appointed head coach on January 29, 2002.

2006
WORLD CUP

Iran already is in a difficult enough group with Portugal and Mexico as the favorites to move, and Angola as the probable weak sister of the group. Veteran forward Ali Daei felt that his Asian side will be a team to be reckoned with in June.

"After this victory nobody will consider us a second-rate team," he said after Iran secured a berth in 2005. "We're going to the World Cup with the aim of reaching the second round."

Many observers felt that this Iran team is the best the country has produced. "Well, I couldn't tell you if this is true," coach Branko Ivankovic told **www.FIFAWorldCup.com**. "But I must say that I am delighted with my team, who have done a great job so far. In my 26 matches in charge we have lost one, drawn four and won 21. Winning makes people happy. This team has made people happy."

Iran's hopes at success in the World Cup, hinge on the legs of a quartet of players currently playing in the German Bundesliga, which is perfect preparation for this tournament—Ali Karimi (Bayern Munich), 27, Mehdi Mahdavikia (Hamburg), 28, Ferydoon Zandi (Kaiserslautern), 27, and Vahid Hashemian (Hannover 96), 29. The star of the group is Karimi was named the Asian Player of the Year in 2004. Nicknamed "The Wizard of Tehran," he has been a mainstay on Bayern Munich's front line this season, stepping in when Michael Ballack was sidelined with a hamstring injury. He's scored three times this season. Beyond the quartet, Iran is essentially a young side with 15 players on its roster are between 21 and 25.

The incomparable Daei, opened the door for the other players to perform in the Bundesliga when he played for Arminia Bielefeld and Bayern Munich years ago. He has scored many international goals (107—in 143 games). Daei always plays with "responsibility, zest and motivation" Ivankovic told **www.FIFAWorldCup.com**. But Daei's real worth to this particular team comes from his experience and leadership abilities as team captain. "The country is rich in home-grown talent and I believe that some players could develop into stars if we give them the chance," Ivankovic said. "The injection of new blood into the team has made Iran stronger and I have seen players mature incredibly over the past three years."

Controversy seems to follow this team around. On March 26, 2005, at least five fans reportedly were killed after a crush following Iran's 2-1 victory over Japan in Tehran. The problems began when the estimated crowd of 100,000 tried to leave Azadi (Freedom) Stadium after the match. No other details were available. Four days later,

IRAN

several ugly scenes marred Iran's 2-0 victory over North Korea in Pyongyang. The referee and assistant referees could not leave the field for a good 20 minutes as angry Korean fans threw bottles, rocks and chairs, yes chairs, in frustration with the defeat at Kim Il-sung Stadium. Soliders and police had to be called in to restore order. They apparently were incited by Nam Song-chol's red card for shoving Syrian referee Mohamed Kousa, forcing the game to be held up for five minutes as fans hurled bottles on the track that surrounded the pitch.

The fans, however, weren't finished as thousands of them prevented Iranian players from boarding their team bus. Riot police were needed to push back the crowd so the team could leave the stadium two hours after the final whistle. "The atmosphere on the pitch and outside the pitch was not a sports atmosphere," Ivankovic was quoted by **Reuters**. "It is very disappointing when you feel your life is not safe. My players tried to get to the bus after the game but it was not possible—it was a very dangerous situation."

American soccer fans might remember the Iran National Team from France '98. The Iranians defeated the U.S. 2-1, in the second opening-round match for both sides on June 24, 1998. The Iranian players walked with their heads held high, being able to secure a win and three points, while the U.S, shaking theirs, wondered what had happened. The Americans became the third national side to be eliminated after two losses in that World Cup.

From the game, Iran got some international bragging rights, beating the U.S. at something. Given today's political overtones, a 2006 clash on the field probably would not be well advised. But they're in two entirely different groups and it would take several miracles fpr them to meet

IRAN

ITALY
Group E

POPULATION: 58,000,000

COLORS: Blue shirts, white shorts, blue socks

APPEARANCES: 16th. 39-14-17. 110 goals for, 67 against. 1934 (champions), 1938 (champions), 1950 (first round), 1954 (first round), 1962 (first round), 1966 (first round), 1970 (second place), 1974 (first round), 1976 ((second round), 1982 (champion), 1986 (second round), 1990 (third place), 1994 (second place), 1998 (quarterfinals), 2002 (second round).

WORLD CUP HISTORY

Italy was the first country to win back-to-back titles and was the second to capture the championship three times. After Brazil and perhaps Germany, no other country has experienced a more glorious World Cup history. Fans will remember Italy's amazing run to the 1982 title—the Italians were 14-1 long shots before the competition began—behind the scoring feats of Paolo Rossi. After a disappointing performance in Mexico in 1986, the Italians, behind an unlikely hero in Salvatore Schillaci, rebound with a third-place finish at home four years later. In 1994, Italy, despite injuries and several suspensions, put together a second-place finish, losing to Brazil in the penalty-kick shootout. For many countries, that would have been sufficient. But we're talking about Italy where nothing less than a championship is accepted. In France four years later, the Italians were eliminated in the quarterfinals by eventual-champion France. In 2002, Italy crashed out of the tournament in controversial style in the second round due to refereeing blunders in a 2-1 extra-time loss to co-host Korea. The Italians finished 1-2-1, their second worst Cup record ever only to the 1-2 records each from the 1954 and 1966 tournaments.

HOW THEY QUALIFIED

Italy (7-1-2, 23 points) captured European Group 5 quite handily, by five points over second- place Norway. But don't let that wide margin deceive you. It was an easy group. Norway did not win in the play-offs and Scotland, which has never gotten out of the first round of a World Cup, Slovenia, Belarus and Moldova—they had a collective record of 9-18-13—don't exactly make their opponents quake in their boots. The Italians clinched a spot with a 1-0 victory over Slovenia on October 8, 2005 as Cristian Zaccardo scored the lone goal.

PLAYERS TO WATCH

The best defender in Italy and arguably the best in the world, 29-year-

324

old Alessandro Nesta is simply irreplaceable. He is superb in the air or on the ground. He has great vision and can run with the best of them. What more do you want from a central defender? Italian soccer officials have their fingers crossed that forward Francesco Totti, rehabilitating from a fractured fibula, will be in form come June. He can create goals or score them, although his critics claim he disappears when push comes to shove. Forward Luca Toni has come into his own as a force to be reckoned with on Fiorentina, although there are worries he could be shut down in a competition such as the World Cup. Goalkeeper Gianluigi Buffon, considered in many quarters to be the best in the world, returned to the Juventus lineup in mid-season after missing the first half of the Serie A season with a shoulder injury. His form could come into question.

Goalkeeper: Gianluigi Buffon (Juventus, Italy) Morgan De Sanctis (Udinese), Angelo Peruzzi (Lazio). Defenders: Andreas Barazglia (Palermo), Girogio Chiellini (Juventus), Marco Materazzi (Inter), Gianluca Zambrotta (Juventus, Italy), Alessandro Nesta (AC Milan, Italy), Fabio Cannavaro (Juventus, Italy), Fabio Grosso (Palermo, Italy), Massimo Oddo (Lazio), Cristian Zaccardo (Palermo), Gianluca Zambrotta (Juventus). Midfielders: Gennaro Gattuso (AC Milan, Italy), Andrea Pirlo (AC Milan, Italy), Mauro Camoranesi (Juventus, Italy), Francesco Totti (AS Roma, Italy), Massimino Ambrosoni (A.C. Milan), Simone Barone (Palermo), Manuel Blasi (Juventus), Danielle De Rossi (Roma), Aimar Diana (Sampdoria), Stefano Fiore (Fiorentina), Gennaro Gattuso (A.C. Milan), Simone Perrotta (Roma). Forwards: Luca Toni (Fiorentina, Italy), Alberto Gilardino (AC Milan, Italy), Antonio Cassano (Real Madrid, Spain), Alessandro Del Perio (Juventus), Vincenzo Iaquinta (Udinese), Filippo Inzaghi (A.C. Milan), Francesco Totti (Roma), Christian Vieri (Monaco, France).

Goalkeeper: Gianluigi Buffon (Juventus, Italy). Defenders: Gianluca Zambrotta (Juventus, Italy), Alessandro Nesta (AC Milan, Italy), Fabio Cannavaro (Juventus, Italy), Fabio Grosso (Palermo, Italy). Midfielders: Gennaro Gattuso (AC Milan, Italy), Andrea Pirlo (AC Milan, Italy), Mauro Camoranesi (Juventus, Italy), Francesco Totti (AS Roma, Italy). Forwards: Luca Toni (Fiorentina, Italy), Alberto Gilardino (AC Milan, Italy).

One of the most successful and respected coaches in Serie A, it was only natural that Marcello Lippi would become national coach some day. He earned five Serie A titles, one Italian Cup, four Italian Super

Cups and a Champions League crown (1996) with Juventus from 1995 to 2003 (with a break from 1999 to 2001 when he coached at Inter). He also guided Juventus to the 2003 final, falling to Italian rival A.C. Milan on penalty kicks. He has many of the traits you want in a coach. He can be tough, he is an excellent tactician, he is not afraid to experiment, and he can be flexible when the time comes. "Everyone should feel like they're on the bubble," he said. "That's why I won't replace (Francesco) Totti. Whoever I would have called up would feel like a backup, and here there are no (backups)." Born April 11, 1948, Lippi played professionally for Savona, Sampdoria, and Pistoiese before becoming a youth coach with Sampdoria in 1982. He eventually became a head coach at A.C. Cesena before moving on to Lucchese, Atalanta, and Napoli. After Italy's failed endeavor at Euro 2004, Lippi was named the new coach, replacing Giovanni Trapattoni and signing a two-year contract on July 16, 2004. Lippi has been thinking of retirement so he could be with his grandson more. He hinted that he could go into his parents business and start a bakery.

2006
WORLD CUP

World Cup reputations are forged over decades of success and failure. It may take years to reverse a positive or negative trend. Italy's recent struggles are such example. It has won three World Cup titles, but if you delve into the details, even that impressive number could be a bit misleading. Two of those championships came in the days before the World Cup was the World Cup—as we know it—in 1934 and 1938. Their last title was won in 1982—a fantastic and memorable romp through Spain—but that was a generation ago. In this what-have-you-done-for-me-lately world, just what has Italy accomplished in recent World Cups? Since 1994, when an overachieving Italian side reached the final only to be beaten by Roberto Baggio's wayward penalty kick in the shootout finale with champions Brazil, Italy has been bounced in the quarterfinals and second round by the host countries in the past two World Cups, respectively, not exactly an advertisement for world power status.

It won't be easy with the likes of the second-ranked Czech Republic, the fifth-ranked United States and a hungry Ghana side with which to contend in Group E. That's not to say the 12th-ranked Italians are just another pile of spaghetti. When the Azzurri play up to their potential with their steel curtain defense, they can be among the best in the world, but it seems something happens to them in the latter rounds.

"Italy might not have won anything in 24 years but have still had some good performances," coach Marcello Lippi told **Agence-**

ITALY

France Presse. Take what transpired in Florence, Italy on March 1, 2006, when the Azzurri were given a big psychological boost when they destroyed and embarrassed World Cup host Germany, 4-1, in a warm-up match.

But Lippi, however, warned about becoming overconfident. "You have to keep this result in perspective and not to judge Germany on that performance," he told **Agence-France Presse**. "There isn't such a big difference in goals between us and Germany. Everything went our way in that match, while the Germans couldn't get anything right. We have to wait for other occasions to see clearer. At the World Cup Germany will be at home and could be more efficient." Lippi has a lot of weapons-both offensive and defensive-at his disposal. That might be his biggest challenge-selecting the right players to play together, not necessarily the best individual ones.

Group E is one tough group. The Czech Republic is second in the world in FIFA's March 2006 rankings, while the U.S. was fifth. Ghana, which boasts Michael Essien, is a solid African side.

"We respect all our rivals but we don't fear anyone in particular," Lippi said. "We have to focus on our strengths and possibilities because we have the potential to take on any of our opponents." Italy traditionally has an airtight defense and this team is no different, except that Lippi indicated he will let the Azzurri open up its attack from its traditionally conservative "catenaccio" defensive game. He has the firepower and creativity to do so, at least on paper.

The defense is strong with the likes of central defenders Alessandro Nesta and Fabio Cannavaro playing in his third Cup. He missed the 2-1 loss to Korea in 2002 because of a suspension. "In all honesty, I don't see any great Italian defenders right now," former Italian international Pietro Vierchowod told *Calcio Italia* magazine. "If you take away the likes of Nesta and Cannavaro then I struggle to come up with any names. I think we can genuinely call it a real crisis It's odd because Italy has always been the kingdom of defenders." Mauro Camoranesi and Gianluca Zambrotta, who can play either side, are expected to be deployed on the flanks in a 4-4-2 formation. Lippi hopes Buffon can regain his winning form by June after missing the first half of the Italian Serie A season with a shoulder injury.

Whether Italy can regain past glory and some pride probably will rest on the feet of their midfielders, and especially their strikers. Assuming he's healthy, Francesco Totti will work with A.C. Milan teammates Gennaro Gattuso and Andrea Pirlo in the midfield. Luca Toni has emerged as the new scoring star and World Cup hope. He connected for a team-high four qualifying goals, most of them key strikes. Some Italian supporters fear that Toni could be stifled by

ITALY

superior competition. He has enjoyed a dominant and impressive season for Fiorentina. Lippi probably will pair Alberto Gilardino with Toni.

For Totti, on the other hand, the expectations are much more. He was to be sidelined from two to three months after fracturing his left fibula and strained ligaments in his left ankle in Roma's 1-0 win over Empoli on February 19, 2006. Totti said that he would play in the World Cup if he was completely healed. "The whole world hopes Totti will play in the World Cup," Lippi said, "except the U.S., the Czech Republic and Ghana."

The roles of former National Team and World Cup heroes Alessandro Del Piero and Christian Vieri are uncertain. Lippi said he considers the 32-year-old Vieri one of Italy's top forwards, but he isn't so sure about the 31-year-old Del Piero. "Some players are certain, others a bit less so," Lippi said. "To be honest, (Del Piero) is not among those that are certain."

For you World Cup history buffs: Italy did not participate in two tournaments. The first in 1930 in Uruguay, in which many European teams did not want to take a two-week boat ride across the Atlantic— and in 1958, due to the Italians' short-sidedness. FIFA referee Istvan Zsolt of Hungary could not fly out of Heathrow Airport near London due to the fog. The Italians refused to use a local game official, so the game became a friendly, but it unturned into an "unfriendly" (vicious tackling in a match that was called "The Battle of Belfast") ending in a 2-2 tie. Had that result stuck, Italy would have qualified. The match was played with Zsolt in the middle a month later on Jan. 15, 1958 with Northern Ireland securing a berth in the finals, thanks to a 2-1 upset win.

ITALY

IVORY COAST
Group C

POPULATION: 17,000,000
COLORS: Orange shirts, white shorts,
  green socks
APPEARANCES: First.

None.

Ivory Coast won African Group 3 with a 7-2-1 record and 22 points over two other countries that have participated in previous World Cups—Cameroon (6-1-3, 21) and Egypt (5-3-2, 17). It certainly wasn't easy. With their hopes seemingly dashed after dropping a 3-2 decision to Cameroon in September 2005, the Elephants needed some help and luck to reach the World Cup. They recorded a 3-1 victory over the Sudan as Aruna Dindane struck twice within a 22-minute span in the second half and Kanga Akale added a goal before their foes scored late in the match. Ivory Coast was helped by Cameroon playing Egypt to a 1-1.

Striker Didier Drogba is an obvious choice as the main man up front (nine qualifying goals), as an inspirational leader and as high-powered player on Chelsea's English Premiership champions. Defender Kolo Toure, who performs for Chelsea rival Arsenal, has been a calming force in the back that has seen things get out of control. Midfielder Didier Zokora is the engine of the team.

Goalkeeper: Boubacar Barry Beveren (Belgium), Gerard Gnanhouan (Montpellier, France), Jean-Jaques Tizie (Esperance, Tunisia). Defenders: Kolo Toure (Arsenal, England). Blaise Kouassi (Troyes, France), Didier Zokora (St. Etienne, France), Abdoulaye Djire (Beveren, Belgium), Arthur Boka (Strasbourg, France), Issoumailia (Toulouse, France), Cyril Domoraud (Creteil, Frnace), Emmanuel Eboue (Arsenal, England), Seydou Kante (Beveren, Belgium), Blaise Kouassi (Troyes, France), Abdoulaye Meite (Marseille, France), Marc Zoro (Messina, Italy). Midfielders: Gilles Yapi Yapo (Nantes, France) Almamy Doumbia (Melfi, Italy), Siaka Tiene (St. Etienne, France), Arouna Konm (PSV Eindhoven, Netherlands), Kanga Akale (Auxerre, France), Guy Demel (Hamburg, Germany), Abdoulaye Djire (Beveren, Belgium), Emerse Fae (Nantes, France), Christian Manfredini (Lazio, Italy), romaric N'Dri (Le Mans, France), Marco

Ne (Beveren, Belgium), Yaya toure (Olympiakos, Greece), Didier Zokora (St. Etienne, France). Forwards: Bonaventure Kalou (Paris St. Germain, France), Didier Drogba (Chelsea, England), Aruna Dindane (Lens, France), Kader Keita (Lille, France), Arouna Kone (PSV Eindhoven, Netherlands), Bakary Kone (Nice, France), Kandia Traore (Le Havre, France), Bonaventure Kalou.

Goalkeeper: Boubacar Barry Beveren (Belgium). Defenders: Kolo Toure (Arsenal, England). Blaise Kouassi (Troyes, France), Didier Zokora (St. Etienne, France), Abdoulaye Djire (Beveren, Belgium). Midfielders: Gilles Yapi Yapo (Nantes, France) Almamy Doumbia (Melfi, Italy), Siaka Tiene (St. Etienne, France), Arouna Konm (PSV Eindhoven, Netherlands). Forwards: Aruna Dindane (Paris St. Germain, France), Didier Drogba (Chelsea, England).

Frenchman Henri Michel has made a career coaching African teams. The Ivory Coast is his fourth team, after directing Cameroon (1994 World Cup), Morocco (1998) and Tunisia (2002). He quit the North African team after only 67 days in protest after the Tunisian Football Federation fired Frenchman Albert Rust. He also coached the United Arab Emirates from 2000-01. Michel's greatest success came with France, directing the French to the 1984 Olympic gold medal and the National Team to a third-place finish at Mexico '86. Born on October 29, 1947, Michel played midfield for Aix and Nantes and made fifty-eight appearances for the national side, including playing in the 1978 World Cup. He began his coaching career with Paris St. Germain and Al-Nasr. He replaced countryman Robert Nouzaret, who resigned in March 2004. "I'm very proud to have taken over this Cote d'Ivoire team," Michel said several months later. "It's a fine side, with so much potential that I won't understand it if we don't qualify for the World Cup. It's a very exciting challenge." He is a bit shy of the spotlight. Michel did not attend the presidential gala after qualifying. "The players, who are the real heroes, must be allowed to enjoy this moment with the people of Cote d'Ivoire," he explained on French television. "They have earned the right." Michel has been under intense criticism and scrutiny by the Ivory Coast media and fans, who do not always comprehend his tactics and team selections. Some Ivory Coast Football Federation officials reportedly harbor the same feelings.

Imagine a country, any country, considering dropping out of the World Cup after it has qualified. Ivory Coast did just that in February, 2006 when the Ivorian Football Federation president Jacques

Anouma said that the team would not participate in the games in Germany if there was no peace in that war-torn country. Ivory Coast—known officially by FIFA as Cote d'Ivoire—has been split in half since 2002. Rebels hold the northern part, while the government controls the south. Even the players have seen themselves as a unifying force. After Ivory Coast's 3-1 win over the Sudan booked a spot in Germany, captain Didier Drogba, while kneeling in the locker room, led the team in a prayer for peace. "Ivorians we beg your forgiveness. Let us come together and put this war behind us," Drogba reportedly said.

After returning home victorious from the Sudan, the players were honored by Ivory Coast president Laurent Gbagbo, who awarded them the equivalent of knighthood. Each player who performed in the qualifiers and the coaching staff received a villa worth 30 million African francs. "On 4 September we lost (to Cameroon) and no-one gave these boys a chance," Gbagbo said. "But they have shown that they are winners. I want to promote a successful Cote d'Ivoire. I offer these young men up as an example which must be followed."

The players have hoped that they could lead by example. Drogba and defender Kolo Toure play for top English Premiership teams Chelsea and Arsenal, and they both live in London. Yet, they come from opposite corners of Ivory Coast. Drogba hails from a poor Catholic section of Abidjan, the capital. He and his family left when he was five. Toure, on the other hand, is a Muslim and the son of an army officer who lived in the northern part of the country until he was 20. "Our National team has brought people together," Toure told The *Sunday Times of London*. "When we qualified for the World Cup, Didier spoke to the people and told them we need to be together. He said "Kolo is from the north and I'm from the south. But look, we're friends and we work together for our country. Our team has different cultures, languages and religions to it, yet we come together and we win."

As good and as well balanced as Ivory Coast is-it is considered the best of the five African sides-it still might not be able to get to the second round. That's because the team finds itself in this Cup's Group of Death: the Netherlands, Argentina and Serbia & Montenegro. "We may be up against it, but we will give it our best shot," defender Cyril Domoraud was quoted by *World Soccer*. "If Ivory Coast can get out of the group, I can see them getting all the way to the final," German World Cup Organizing Committee president Franz Beckenbauer said.

The star of the show is Drogba, who joined Chelsea in July 2004 for a $45 million transfer from Marseille (France), the second largest in English soccer history. Drogba scored a team-best nine qualifying

IVORY COAST

goals, including two critical goals in a key victory over Egypt. He also managed to find the back of the net to give the Elephants the lead in a 1-1 international friendly draw with Italy in November, 2005 and forced the Italians' vaunted defense to work overtime. "We have played against a team with valuable players," Italy coach Marcello Lippi told the **Press Association**. "Drogba is an outstanding player. . . . It was important for us to get to know this new football reality that is the Ivory Coast." Inter defender Marco Materazzi, who covered Drogba, realized what he was in for it early in the match. "When you find yourself facing players like him (Drogba), it means that you are playing at the highest level and this is a good thing," he said.

Other players to watch include 24-year-old Toure, whose experience playing with Arsenal has been invaluable in terms of shoring up the shaky backline. His younger brother Yaya Toure (Olympiakos, Greece) patrols the midfield along with Didier Zokora, who was nicknamed Maestro by his teammates. *World Soccer* said that Zokora has the potential to be Africa's next great holding midfielder. In contrast to several other Germany-bound sides, the Elephants acquitted themselves quite well in the African Nations Cup in the winter of 2006, earning second place honors to host Egypt, which outlasted Ivory Coast after 120 scoreless minutes and a 4-2 penalty-kick tiebreaker in the final.

Including the civil war, this team has been through more than enough personal tragedy. Aruna Dindane, Drogba's strike partner who scored two of his seven qualifying goals in the clinching win over the Sudan, missed a good chunk of the African Nations Cup after the sudden death of one of his twin daughters in January, 2006. He was forced to leave the team for two weeks. Two years prior, assistant coach and Mama Ouattara, also head coach of the youth team, died in Paris on June 12, 2004 due to an apparent heart attack at the age 54.

JAPAN
Group F

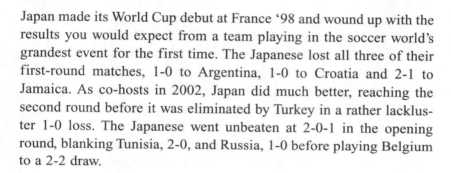

POPULATION: 127,200,000
COLORS: Blue shirt, white shorts, blue socks
APPEARANCES: Third. 2-4-1. 6 goals for, 7 against. 1998 (first round), 2002 (second round).

Japan made its World Cup debut at France '98 and wound up with the results you would expect from a team playing in the soccer world's grandest event for the first time. The Japanese lost all three of their first-round matches, 1-0 to Argentina, 1-0 to Croatia and 2-1 to Jamaica. As co-hosts in 2002, Japan did much better, reaching the second round before it was eliminated by Turkey in a rather lackluster 1-0 loss. The Japanese went unbeaten at 2-0-1 in the opening round, blanking Tunisia, 2-0, and Russia, 1-0 before playing Belgium to a 2-2 draw.

WORLD CUP HISTORY

Japan won its Asian preliminary group with a 6-0-0 mark and finished atop Group B (5-1-0, 15 points). With the exception of host country Germany (which received an automatic berth when they got the World Cup bid in 2000), the Japanese became the first country to win a berth with a 2-0 victory over North Korea in Bangkok, Thailand. Atsushi Yanagisawa and Masashi Oguro scored in the second half. The match was played behind closed doors.

HOW THEY QUALIFIED

The two best players perform overseas. Shinji Ono (Feyenoord, Netherlands) is considered to be one of the team's best all-round players and a leader. But the real star of the side is midfielder Hidetoshi Nakata (Bolton, England), who is considered the best player of his generation. Central defender and captain Tsueyasu Miyamoto has skill and excellent vision.

PLAYERS TO WATCH

Goalkeepers: Yoshikatsu Kawaguchi (Jubilo Iwata), Takashi Shimoda (Sanfrecce Hiroshima), Ryota Tsuzuki (Urawa Reds). Defenders: Makoto Tanaka (Jubilo Iwata), Tsuneyasu Miyamoto (Gamba Osaka), Alex (Urawa Reds), Yuji Nakazawa (Yokohama F. Marinos), Koji Nakata (FC Basel, Switzerland), Keisuke Tsuboi (Urawa Reds), Akira Kaji (Gamba Osaka), Yuichi Komano (Sanfrecce Hiroshima). Teruyuki Moniwa (FC Tokyo). Midfielders: Takashi Fukunishi (Jubilo Iwata), Hidetoshi Nakata (Bolton Wanderers, England),

PLAYER POOL

JAPAN

333

Shunsuke Nakamura (Celtic Glasgow, Scotland), Mitsuo Ogasawara (Kashima Antlers), Junichi Inamoto (West Bromwich Albion, England), Shinji Ono (Urawa Reds), Yasuhito Endo (Gamba Osaka), Daisuke Matsui (Le Mans, France). Forwards: Tatsuhiko Kubo (Yokohama F. Marinos), Atsushi Yanagisawa (FC Messina, Italy) Naohiro Takahara (Hamburger SV, Germany), Masashi Oguro (Grenoble, France).

PROJECTED STARTING LINEUP

Goalkeeper: Yoshikatsu Kawaguchi (Jubilo Iwata). Defenders: Yuuji Nakazawa (Yokohama F. Marinos), Tsuneyasu Miyamoto (Gamba Osaka,), Akira Kaji (FC Tokyo), Alex (Urawa Reds). Midfielders: Hidetoshi Nakata (Bolton Wanderers (England), Shunsuke Nakamura (Celtic, Scotland), Mitsuo Ogasawara (Kashima Antlers), Shinji Ono (Urawa Reds). Forwards: Naohiro Takahara (Hamburg SV, Germany). Masashi Oguro (Gamba Osaka).

COACH

Brazilian-born Zico replaced Philippe Troussier as coach in July 2002 and after a slow start and despite some rumors that he would quit, moved the team in the right direction. He received a rather unusual offer to play with Garforth Town, an English non-league team, and remain as Japanese coach, although there have been a number of fans calling for his head. He's probably happy he did, guiding the team to the Kirin Cup and Asian Cup in 2004 and of course, to a berth in the World Cup in 2005. Zico, born March 3, 1953, enjoyed a marvelous career, being named one of the world's best 125 players by Pelé. Zico played most of it with Flamengo in his native country, scoring 508 goals in 731 matches. He went on to play for Udinese (Italy) and Kashima Antlers (Japan)—becoming an icon with the latter club—before turning to coaching with the Antlers. For all competitions, including the Brazil Masters team, Zico has scored an amazing 826 goals in 1,180 games. He also played for the Brazilian National Team (66 goals in 88 appearances) and in three World Cups (1978, 1982 and 1986). Zico has said that he will retire from coaching after the World Cup.

2006 WORLD CUP

Like it or not, Japan is not being given much of a chance to get out of Group F in one piece, and for good reason. With defending champion Brazil the overwhelming favorites to win the World Cup and a solid Croatia side, it will be difficult becoming one of the two teams to reach the second round. Of course, coach Zico would love to extract a point—a tie from his native country, Brazil—as he did during the 2005 FIFA Confederations Cup.

Despite becoming the first team to clinch a World Cup berth on the

JAPAN

field, there are still doubts as to whether the Japanese improved from the 2002 competition, when they went an impressive 2-1-1, to take on the world's powers. However, that was at home on the other side of the world where there were more upsets than usual. The 2006 tournament returns to European soil, where many off-continent teams, including Asian sides, have struggled mightily in the past. In qualifying for this upcoming tournament, several observers claim that Japan was lucky to get last-minute goals in victories over Oman and North Korea, which will never be confused with World Cup powers.

Even those back home have their doubts of the team advancing. "They've not really improved since (Philippe) Troussier's reign," *Japan Times* sportswriter James Mulligan told **www.BBC.com**. "Japan's chances depend on strikers Takahara and Yanagisawa weighing in with the goals. If the draw's kind, put your money on a dramatic qualification from the group stages and a gallant loss in the second round. That should satisfy the Japanese."

After playing eventual champion Brazil to a 1-1 tie, Zico proclaimed: "We showed our ability and potential in the Confederations Cup and we are now at the top level in the world." That might have been a rallying or psychological ploy. Since then, Zico has seen the team and he doesn't exactly like what he has seen, especially in the 3-2 loss to the U.S. in which the Japanese were forced to try to overcome a three-goal deficit. If the team has a glaring weakness, it's that the players get frustrated when they fall behind. "There were a lot of mistakes against the U.S. and we definitely can't afford to do the same thing," Zico told **Reuters** before Japan took on Finland. "I've told the players they need to be stronger mentally because this is a game we want to win."

Japan might be considered the best Asian team, but the World Cup is an entirely different matter. So, Zico has his work cut out for him, trying to improve the standard of the team. He did so immediately by putting together a pair of Gamba Osakda teammates—Tsuneyasu Miyamoto and Yuji Nakazawa—at central defense during qualifying to make a solid defense better. The Japanese will win or lose games due to their midfield. Hidetoshi Nakata, Shinji Ono, Shunsuke Nakamura and Junichi Inamoto and Mitsuo Ogasawara, a free-kick expert, form one of the best in the world.

Nakata, in his 12th season as a professional at twenty-nine, has combined vision and skill to become the best Japanese player of his generation. He has played for three Italian Serie A clubs and helped Japan upset Brazil at the 1996 Olympics and led the team to the Asia Cup in 2000 and 2004.

Nakamura has physical attributes in his game, which is rare for a

JAPAN

Japanese player. He has played for Celtic in the Scottish Premier League and in Italy.

They'll be looking for forward Masashi Oguro, to demonstrate his knack for scoring goals. For Gamba Osaka in the J-League, he led the league in scoring in 2004 with 20 goals in 30 matches and helped the club capture the championship. But if Oguro is off his game or marked out of it, Japan could be in for a long day.

Zico's other challenge stems from FIFA's recent decision not to allow more than one person to enter the technical zone during World Cup matches. Zico claimed that would interfere with communicating with his players because his interpreter, Kunihiro Suzuki—with whom he has been working since he came to Japan more than 10 years ago—would not be allowed. "I don't understand why FIFA made such a decision to hinder our performance," Zico said. The Asian Football Confederation has allowed a second person in the zone. The Japan Football Association had asked FIFA to allow both Zico and his interpreter into the zone, but the request was rejected.

Given that the world of soccer truly never has a beginning or an end with all the club and international competitions going on simultaneously. Only months after securing a spot in Germany, the Japanese had to start qualifying for another tournament—the 2008 Asian Cup.

They kicked off their defense of the championship with a 6-0 rout of India behind five second-half goals on February 23, 2006. Striker Tatsuhiko Kubo scored twice and Ono added a goal. "It's always important to score the first goal but it took the team some time to find any rhythm," Ono said. "We played a lot better in the second half and we got the start we wanted." Perhaps trying to qualify for another competition will stoke Japan's competitive fires.

Even though the 2006 World Cup is on the other side of the world, economists have predicted that the event could bring the Japanese economy $4 billion in television sales, tourism and other spin-off economic activities. That figure would increase to $4.8 billion if the team reached the semifinals or final.

For World Cup history buffs: Japanese soccer fans might be the cleanest in the world. Stadium officials during France '98 were surprised to find the Japanese fans' seats cleaner after the game than before.

JAPAN

KOREA
Group G

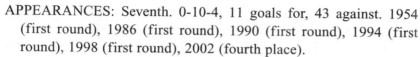

POPULATION: 49.000,000

COLORS:Red shirts, red shorts, red socks

APPEARANCES: Seventh. 0-10-4, 11 goals for, 43 against. 1954 (first round), 1986 (first round), 1990 (first round), 1994 (first round), 1998 (first round), 2002 (fourth place).

Korea (Republic of South Korea) is the first Asian team to reach six consecutive World Cups and seven overall. But the Koreans have struggled when they reach the final round. In their World Cup debut in 1954, the Koreans were drubbed by Hungary, 9-0, and Turkey, 7-0. In 1986, Korea tied Bulgaria, 1-1 and lost two other matches by one goal. In 1994, the gritty Koreans rallied for a pair of goals in the waning minutes to tie Spain, 2-2, played Bolivia to a scoreless draw, and gave Germany some headaches, rallying from a three-goal deficit to lose, 3-2. The victory drought continued in France with Korea going 0-2-1, losing to Mexico, 3-1, to the Netherlands, 5-0, and playing to a 1-1 draw with Belgium. As co-hosts with Japan, it was an entirely different story in 2002. The Koreans went undefeated in their group. During the knockout rounds, they were just as equally difficult to beat. The Koreans started out with a 2-0 win over Poland, continued with a 1-1 draw with the U.S. and wound up undefeated in group play with a 1-0 shutout of Portugal. Korea eliminated favored Italy in the second round in extratime, 2-1, and bounced Spain by winning a penalty-kick tie-breaker, 5-3, after playing to a nil-nil draw. The hosts finally came down to earth with a 1-0 semifinal loss to Germany and a 3-2 defeat to Turkey in the third-place match.

WORLD CUP HISTORY

Korea finished second to Saudi Arabia (4-0-2, 14 points) in Asian Group A with a disappointing 3-2-1 mark and 10 points. The Koreans did it in style, cruising to a 4-0 victory over Kuwait in Friendship and Peace Stadium in Kuwait City, Kuwait on June 8, 2005. Park Chu-Young, Lee Dong-gook, Chung Kyung-Ho and Park Ji-Sung tallied for Korea.

HOW THEY QUALIFIED

Forward Ahn Jung-Hwan, 30, scored only once in nine qualifiers, but his experience and leadership to this team has proven to be invaluable. The team's leading scorer, Lee Dong-Gook (five goals in eight games), usually found the back of the net when it was most needed.

PLAYERS TO WATCH

KOREA

Midfielder Park Ji-Sung has become better known with several impressive performances since his transfer from PSV Eindhoven to Manchester United. Veteran defender Choi Jin-Cheul is expected to lead and organize the backline in the wake of several international retirements.

PLAYER POOL

Goalkeepers: Lee Woon-Jae (Suwon Samsung), Cho Jun-Ho (Jeju United), Kim Young-Kwang (Chunnam Dragons). Defenders: Lee Young-Pyo (Tottenham), Kim Sang-Shik (Seongnam Ilhwa), Cho Won-Hee (Suwon Samsung), Kim Young-Chul (Seongnam Ilhwa, You Kyoung-Youl (Ulsan Hyundai), Kim Dong-Jin (FC Seoul), Choi Jin-Cheul (Chonbuk Hyundai). Midfielders: Park Ji-Sung (Manchester United, England), Kim Nam-Il (Suwon Samsung), Lee Ho Ulsan (Hyundai), Jang Hack-Yong (Seongnam Ilhwa), Baek Ji-Hoon (FC Seoul), Lee Eul-Yong (Trabzonspor, Turkey), Kim Do-Heon (Seongnam Ilhwa). Forwards: Ahn Jung-Hwan (MSV Duisburg), Seol Ki-Hyun (Anderlecht Wolves), Choi Yong-Soo (FC Seoul), Cha Du-Ri (Eintracht Frankfurt),Choi Tae-Uk (Shimizu S-Pulse), ChoJae-Jin (Shimizu S-Pulse), Jung Jo-Gook (F.C. Seoul), Lee Chun-Soo (Ulsan Hyundai), Chung Kyung-Ho (Gwangju Sangmu), Park Chu-Young (F.C. Seoul), Lee Dong-Gook (Pohang Steelers).

PROJECTED
STARTING
LINEUP

Not available.

COACH

Dick Advocaat, who directed the Netherlands to a quarterfinal finish at USA '94, was named Korea coach on September 14, 2005, replacing countryman Jo Bonfrere, who had resigned a month prior because of poor results. Bonfrere had been under increased fire despite qualifying Korea. "That's the reason I took the job," Advocaat said. "Because of the challenge." He forged a reputation as a hard-working and temperamental midfielder for several club teams, including O Den Haag, Roda J.C., Sparta Rotterdam, and F.C. Utrecht in the Netherlands and Chicago Sting in the North American Soccer League. Born on September 27, 1947, Advocaat turned to coaching at Haarlem and S.V.V. and went on to coach the Glasgow Rangers (Scotland), PSV Eindhoven, the Netherlands again (at Euro 2004), Borussia Moenchengladbach (Germany) and the United Arab Emirates, from whom he resigned to take over Korea. A disciple of the late, great Rinus Michels, Advocaat was nicknamed the "Little General." Michels was called "The General." Advocaat guided the Dutch to the 2004 semifinals, but he was criticized by the media for his controversial tactics, such as using aging midfielder Paul Bosvelt in place of fan favorite Arjen Robben. He eventually was forced to resign on July 6, 2004 after some death threats.

Advocaat told **Reuters**: "Of course, there is one big difference this time around. The Koreans won't be hosts, but rather in Europe, where they have never won a match. We won't be at home this time so that is a disadvantage. . . . With full support from fans and the players we can do a good job. Definitely, let's try to do what Guus (Hiddink) did."

Korea has found itself in Group G with France, Switzerland and first-timer Togo. France and Switzerland were neck-to-neck in the same European qualifying group, so the Koreans will have to hope for some kind of miracle or upset to advance.

Hiddink might have spoiled the Koreans because they went through coaches fast and furiously. After only 15 months on the job in April 2004, Portuguese coach Humberto Coelho, who directed Portugal to the Euro 2000 semifinals, had a mutual parting of the ways with the Korean Football Federation. He was replaced by Park sung-Hwa, who was a caretaker coach for 66 days before he resigned following a 2-0 victory over Vietnam. Park reportedly felt he had fulfilled his duties. Bonfrere became the next coach and he lasted until August, 2005.

Korea doesn't necessarily have one big player who has been head and shoulders over the rest of the squad. Rather, a series of players and teamwork have been a major reason behind its success.

Defender Choi Jin-Cheul is expected to be the anchor of the backline after a spate of international retirements in recent years, which included former Los Angeles Galaxy defender Hong Myung-Bo.

Defender Lee Young-Pyo, who has made 81 international appearances, the most of any current player, also is expected to be a key figure in the back. Goalkeeper Lee Woon-Jae had allowed only 82 goals in 92 international appearances through the beginning of March, 2006.

Korea's one major weakness is having a striker or midfielder who can put the ball in the net on a fairly regular basis. Lee Dong-Gook, who led the side with five qualifying goals, has scored 21 international goals in 55 appearances.

Forward Ahn Jung-Hwan (MSV Duisburg), who was bounced by Seria A side after his goal eliminated Italy in 2002, is also a dangerous player.

2006
WORLD CUP

KOREA

Korea has enjoyed some recent success against World Cup-bound sides. In October 2005, Korea defeated Iran, 1-0 and played Sweden to a 2-2 draw. On November 16, 2005, the Koreans blanked Serbia & Montenegro, 2-0, in Seoul. On March 1, 2006, the Koreans bested Angola, 1-0, on a goal by Park Ji-Sung at the Seoul World Cup Stadium in Seoul, Korea.

"I think the first half was very good, the way we played in difficult circumstances," Advocaat told a post-match news conference, referring to the sub-freezing conditions. "The pitch was very difficult . . . but the way we played, passing, moving, defensively (was) excellent. Only one problem, we just scored one goal."

Added Advocaat: "We have a team that likes to work, that likes to run and is a danger to every team in the world."

For World Cup history buffs: Asian teams have never fared well in the World Cup, compiling a 4-31-8 mark before the 2002 competition, in which Asian teams finished at 6-9-3. The breakdown from 2002: Korea (4-2-1), Japan (2-1-2), China (0-3-0), Saudi Arabia (0-3-0).

KOREA

MEXICO
Group D

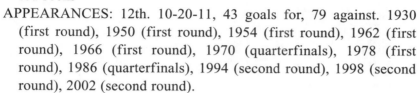

POPULATION: 105,000,000

COLORS: Green shirts, white shorts, red socks

APPEARANCES: 12th. 10-20-11, 43 goals for, 79 against. 1930 (first round), 1950 (first round), 1954 (first round), 1962 (first round), 1966 (first round), 1970 (quarterfinals), 1978 (first round), 1986 (quarterfinals), 1994 (second round), 1998 (second round), 2002 (second round).

WORLD CUP HISTORY

Despite dominating CONCACAF for more than half a century, Mexico hasn't done well at the highest levels of the world stage. The Mexicans were winless in their first thirteen matches (0-12-1), which including a World Cup record nine-game losing streak in the process before they finally defeated Czechoslovakia, 3-1, in 1962. In fact, Mexico's shining moments came on home turf, reaching the quarter-finals in both Cups they have hosted—in 1970 and 1986, with records of 2-1-1 and 3-0-2, respectively. In 1994, the Mexicans reached the second round, where they were eliminated in penalty kicks by Bulgaria. For the first time in their history, the Mexicans qualified for the second round of a European-based World Cup. But again they stumbled, losing a 1-0 lead and eventually the game to a never-say-side German side, 2-1.

HOW THEY QUALIFIED

Mexico (7-2-1, 22 points) finished second to the United States in the CONCACAF final round, although both teams had the same amount of points. The Americans, however, got the nod by winning the head-to-head competition between the two sides in total goals, 2-1. After dispatching Dominica with relative ease, the Mexicans took first place in its semifinal group with a 6-0-0 mark. They booked their ticket to Germany by rolling to a 5-0 victory over Panama on September 8, 2005.

PLAYERS TO WATCH

Jared Borgetti, who scored 14 qualifying goals and 37 internation-ally, is the go-to man up front. Jose Fonseca, his strike partner, did not fare too badly, either, connecting for 10 goals. As of March 2006, it appeared Cuauhtemoc Blanco was not in coach Ricardo LaVolpe's plans, even though he has been one of the most dangerous strikers in Mexican history. Captain and defender Rafael Marquez, who plays just in front of his defense, is a world-class defender for Mexico and

MEXICO

Barcelona, helping the latter capture the Spanish La Liga crown. Attack-minded midfielder Jaime Lozano, 26, came into his own during qualifying with 11 goals. Goalkeeper Oswaldo Sanchez played very well during qualifying and is said to be at the best form of his career.

PLAYER POOL

Goalkeepers: Oswaldo Sanchez (Guadalajara/Chivas), Moises Munoz (Morelia/Monarcas). Defenders: Jose Castro (America), Joel Huiqui (Cruz Azul). Rafael Marquez (Barcelona, Spain), Ricardo Osorio (Cruz Azul/Cementeros), Mario Perez (Nexcaxa), Francisco Rodriguez (Guadalajara/Chivas), Carlos Salcido (Guadalajara/Chivas), Mario Mendez (Toluca/Diablos), Franciso Rodriguez (Guadalajara), Ricardo Osorio (Cruz Azul/Cementeros). Midfielders: Andreas Guardado (Atlas) Gonzalo Pineda (UNAM/Pumas), Pavel Pardo (America/Aguilas), Oscar Rojas (America/Aguilas), Gerardo Torrado (Cruz Azul/Cementeros), Ramon Morales (Guadalajara/Chivas), Antonio "Zinha" Naelson (Toluca/Diablos), Luis Perez (Monterrey/Rayados), Gerardo Galindo (UNAM/Pumas). Forwards: Cuauhtemoc Blanco (America), Guillermo Franco (Villareal, Spain), Alberto Medina (Guadalajara/Chivas), Jose Fonseca (Cruz Azul/Cementeros), Jared Borgetti (Bolton, England), Omar Bravo (Guadalajara/Chivas).

PROJECTED
STARTING
LINEUP

Goalkeeper: Oswaldo Sanchez (Guadalajara/Chivas). Defenders: Rafael Marquez (Barcelona, Spain), Francisco Rodriguez (Guadalajara/Chivas), Carlos Salcido (Guadalajara/Chivas). Midfielders: Pavel Pardo (America/Aguilas), Gonzalo Pineda (UNAM/Pumas), Antonio "Zinha" Naelson (Toluca/Diablos), Luis Perez (Monterrey), Gerardo Torrado (Cruz Azul/Cementeros). Forwards: Jared Borgetti (Bolton, England) Jose Fonseca (Cruz Azul/Cementeros).

COACH

An Argentine native, born on February 6, 1952,Ricardo LaVolpe is a rarity when it comes to the Mexican National Team. He is a foreigner who was selected to direct the side in 2002. LaVolpe guarded the nets for Club Atletico Banfield and San Lorenzo in Argentina and for Atlante and Oaxtepec in Mexico. He also was a reserve goalkeeper when Argentina won the 1978 World Cup. LaVolpe has coached several Mexican clubs over the years, including Puebla, Atlante, Guadalajara, Queretaro, America, Atlas and Toluca, winning the title in 1992. He has clashed with the media, club owners and even club coach Hugo Sanchez. Many of his detractors do not like his explosive temperament and gruff personality. During Mexico's 1-0 win over the

MEXICO

U.S. at Azteca Stadium on March 27, 2005, LaVolpe was expelled from the bench after criticizing game officials.

At one time, Mexico was the class and scourge of CONCACAF. During the last decade or so, the Mexicans have been forced to deal with a rising new kid on the block—the United States—as well as a few other countries that have begun to hold their own against them, including Costa Rica and even Trinidad & Tobago. Even though they hold most of their qualifiers in the rarefied air at Azteca Stadium in Mexico City (7,200 feet high)—where opponents eventually wear down because they are unaccustomed to the lack of oxygen—the era of Mexican dominance is history.

2006
WORLD CUP

When put on a neutral playing field, the Mexicans got their heads handed to them by the U.S., which registered a stunning 2-0 triumph in Korea at the 2002 World Cup. During qualifying, the Tricolores prevailed over the Americans at home, 1-0, but fell in Columbus, Ohio, 2-0.

After the latter game, coach Ricardo LaVolpe threw a pot shot the U.S.'s way. "Here, everyone's interested in baseball and American football and many people didn't even know that a soccer match was being played today," he said. "So it's easy for them, because they aren't playing under any pressure. My mother, my grandmother or my great grandmother could play on a team like that."

With LaVolpe's temperament, it should not be at all surprising that problems and controversies had arisen on the road to Germany. A key player who had been left off the team challenged and criticized the coach; two players were suspended for testing positive for banned drugs; and, the coach has gotten into the act by making some controversial statements.

Defenders Salvador Carmona and Aaron Galindo of Cruz Azul tested positive for a derivative of the banned steroid nandrolone during the 2005 Confederations Cup in Germany, but were allowed to continue playing. The duo helped Mexico squeeze past Japan, 2-1, and blank eventual champions Brazil, 1-0. Finally they were sent home and suspended by the Mexican Football Federation but by then, the damage had been done.

Initially, the federation said the two players had been kicked off the team due to indiscipline. The way the ederation had handled the situation caused ripples, creating even more controversy and it almost cost Federation president Alberto de la Torre his job, as well as LaVolpe's position as coach of the national team. LaVolpe got into the act by telling the media it was none of its business on whether the players broke doping rules. Later, LaVolpe was forced to apologize

MEXICO

for comments he made about Cruz Azul, the home club to both players.

It was a mess. Dr. Nicolas Zarur, chairman of the Mexican federation's medical committee, was banned for two years and del la Torre received a reprimand and $15,500 fine. Team doctor Jose Luis Serrano also was fined $3,850 and reprimanded by FIFA's disciplinary committee. The federation was fined $580,000 by FIFA for mishandling the entire incident

But wait, there was more controversy. Former Mexican international and Real Madrid star Hugo Sanchez, ripped into LaVolpe. "Let the owners of the clubs have no doubt that Hugo Sanchez should be the coach of the national team," he said.

Forward Cuauhtemoc Blanco, a long-time National Team team player, found himself in LaVolpe's doghouse after he pulled out of playing at the Confederations Cup, claiming he needed a rest. Blanco was left out of the team's next qualifier against Costa Rica on August 17, 2005. Several days after the competition was finished, Blanco said he was ready to play. "I'm ready when the coach needs me," he said. "The World Cup is coming and I will have to work 100 percent to get a place." LaVolpe ignored him, which made Blanco bristle. "If he picks me, fine, and if he doesn't, it's the same to me. He doesn't have big enough trousers to pick me. It's as simple as that."

When asked about Blanco's status in October, LaVolpe sounded like he was giving mixed signals, saying one thing and doing the exact opposite. "I consider him an important player," LaVolpe said. "If he is in top form, and we all know he will be, he will be there. He does not need minutes. People want to see Cuauhtemoc Blanco, but I would tell them that I need to know who would play in his place and that is why I am trying out different players." It will be interesting to see how Mexico will feel about LaVolpe not including the 32-year-old Blanco in his team come June.

Even when embroiled in controversy, the Mexican side is capable of playing good soccer. They managed to stun eventual champion Brazil, 1-0, to finish fourth in the tournament. The Tricolores made Argentina sweat in the quarterfinals, but fell in the penalty-kick shootout. They pushed host Germany to the limit in the third-place match before losing, 4-3.

Only weeks after that competition, the Mexicans jumped back into competitive soccer with the CONCACAF Gold Cup. The Tricolores did not fare as well as it was eliminated in the quarterfinals, 2-1, on a late fluke goal by guest team Colombia. In an unrelated age-group tournament that demonstrated the country's promise, Mexico captured the FIFA Under-17 World Cup, the nation's first international trophy, blanking Brazil, 3-0 in Peru on October 2, 2005.

Thirty-two year-old Jared Borgetti is the most dangerous man up top. He became Mexico's all-time leading goal-scorer by connecting for his 37th international goal in a 2-0 victory over Costa Rica on August 17, 2005. He had been tied with Carlos Hermosillo and Luis Hernandez. His 14 qualifying goals not only led his country, but CONCACAF as well. He became the first Mexican player to join an English Premiership club when he signed with Bolton on August 4, 2005 for a $1.7 million transfer fee.

Taking a page out of the U.S. and other countries' books, the Tricolores even have a naturalized citizen in the starting lineup— Brazilian-born Antonio Naelson, also known as Zinha, had so impressed LaVolpe with his creative talent that the coach suggested he apply for Mexican citizenship. He did and is now an important member of the team.

The bulk of Mexico's side comes from its Primera Division of Futbol Liga Mexicana. They're able to attract and keep the top Mexican players from going overseas because they are paid quite handsomely back home.

For World Cup history buffs: Mexico has won only once in twelve Cup matches played in Europe. That was in 1998, when the Mexicans downed South Korea, 3-1. The Mexicans have a 1-6-5 record in Euro matches, being outscored, 12-26.

MEXICO

NETHERLANDS
Group C

POPULATION: 16,000,000
COLORS: Orange shirts, white shorts, orange socks
APPEARANCES: Eighth. 11-8-6 record, 43 goals for, 29 against. 1934 (first round), 1938 (first round), 1974 (second place), 1978 (second place), 1990 (second round), 1994 (quarterfinals), 1998 (fourth place).

WORLD CUP HISTORY

The Dutch are one of the most unlucky World cup countries of all-time, twice finishing second with two of the most talented and entertaining sides to play in the tournament. Those teams boasted a world-class player at virtually every position, including Johan Cruyff, Rudi Krol, Robbie Resenbrink and Johnny Rep, among others. In 1974, they were undefeated at 5-0-1 before losing to Germany, the host national, in the final, 2-1. Without the great Cruyff in 1978, the Dutch reached the final in Argentina, only to fall again, this time in extra time, 3-1. In what was considered one of the best World Cup encounters ever, the Dutch rallied from a 2-0 deficit against Brazil in the second half of their 1994 quarterfinal, but the South Americans scored to register a 3-2 victory. In 1998, the Dutch enjoyed their third best Cup showing. They defeated Argentina on a brilliant and dramatic late goal by Dennis Bergkamp, 2-1, but were eliminated by Brazil in the semifinals via a penalty-kick shootout.

HOW THEY QUALIFIED

The Netherlands (10-0-2, 32 points), third in the FIFA world rankings, captured a tough European Group 1, leaving the No. 2-rated Czech Republic (9-3-0, 27) five points behind. The Dutch clinched a Cup spot with a 2-0 triumph over the Czechs on October 8, 2005 as Rafael Van der Vaart and Barry Opdam found the back of the net. Goalkeeper Edwin Van der Sar made sure the foes didn't as he denied Tomas Rosicky an early penalty kick in the Dutch side's first win on Czech soil, in Prague.

PLAYERS TO WATCH

When healthy and in form, forward Ruud Van Nistelrooy is one of the world's best. He scored seven qualifying goals and had 25 goals in 47 international matches. Goalkeeper and captain Edwin Van der Sar, who has kept Tim Howard on the bench at Manchester United, knows how to keep his cool under pressure and has produced several key saves during qualifying. The versatile Phillip Cocu excels at midfielder, but can play central defense as well.

NETHERLANDS

346

Goalkeepers: Edwin Van der Sar (Manchester United, England), Maarten Stekelenburg (Ajax), Henk Timmer (AZ Alkmaar). Defenders: Khalid Boulahrouz (Hamburger SV, Germany), Wilfred Bouma (Aston Villa, England), Gio Van Bronckhorst (Barcelona, Spain), Tim de Cler (AZ Alkmaar), Johnny Heitinga (Ajax), Nigel de Jong (Hamburger SV, Germany), Jan Kromkamp (Liverpool, England), Joris Mathijsen (AZ Alkmaar), Mario Melchiot (Birmingham City, England), Barry Opdam (AZ Alkmaar), Ron Vlaar (Feyenoord). Midfielders: Mark Van Bommel (Barcelona, Spain), Phillip Cocu (PSV Eindhoven), Edgar Davids (Tottenham Hotspur, England), Denny Landzaat (AZ Alkmaar), Hedwiges Maduro (Ajax), Andy Van der Meyde (Everton, England), Wesley Sneijder (Ajax Amsterdam), Rafael Van der Vaart (Hamburger SV, Germany). Forwards: Ryan Babel (Ajax), Dirk Kuyt (Feyenoord), Roy Makaay (Bayern Munich, Germany), Ruud Van Nistelrooy (Manchester United, England), Robin Van Persie (Arsenal, England), Arjen Robben (Chelsea, England), Jan Vennegoor of Hesselink (PSV Eindhoven).

Goalkeeper: Edwin Van der Sar (Manchester United, England). Defenders: Jan Kromkamp (Liverpool, England), Khalid Boulahrouz (Hamburg SV, Germany), Barry Opdam (AZ Alkmaar), GioVanni Van Bronckhorst (Barcelona, Spain). Midfielders: Philip Cocu (PSV Eindhoven), Mark Van Bommel (Barcelona, Spain), Rafael Van der Vaart (Hamburg SV, Germany). Forwards: Arjen Robben (Chelsea, England), Dirk Kuyt (Feyenoord), Ruud Van Nistelrooy (Manchester United, England).

His fabulous career cut short by a severe ankle injury, Marco Van Basten eventually turned to coaching. The three-time European player of the year played with Elinkwijk and Ajax in his native Netherlands, but forged his international reputation with the legendary A.C. Milan teams of the late eighties and early nineties. Born on October 31, 1964, Van Basten, called "San Marco" and "The Swan of Utrehct," scored 276 goals. Perhaps his best and most memorable goal was his volley in the Euro '88 final triumph over the Soviet Union. He officially retired in 1995. Though he said he would never go into management, he couldn't stay away from the game. Starting out as an assistant coach with Ajax's second team in 2003-04, he was named Dutch coach on July 29, 2004. Van Basten said he would select players only on the merits of their performance. He stuck with his word, although he certainly shook things up by not calling such well-known players as Clarence Seedorf and Patrick

NETHERLANDS

Kluivert onto the team and by benching Edgar Davids, who had forged a reputation as the best all-around defensive midfielder on the planet. It worked, as the Dutch team has been rejuvenated, qualifiying for Germany 2006.

The Dutch team has to be admired for finishing second in successive World cups. There may be the feeling that there were perfect opportunities missed that probably won't come the team's away again.

The Dutch seem to find ways to lose:

⊕ In 1978, the incomparable Johan Cruyff refused to play with the National Team in Argentina. That move most likely cost the Dutch the title because Cruyff still was in his prime.

⊕ In 1990, a major squabble with the coach, Thijs Libregts, left the squad in disarray several months before the competition. The Dutch did not win a game in the tournament, despite the presence of the great Marco Van Basten, Ruud Gullit and Frank Rijkaard. They were eliminated in the second round by rival West Germany, 2-1. Several players blamed the poor performance on Libregts' conservative tactics. He was fired by the Dutch Football Federation upon the urging of the players.

⊕ In 1994, Gullit, who regained most of his outstanding ability and agility after four knee operations, quit the team only weeks before the World Cup kickoff, leaving a gaping hole in the midfield. Not surprisingly, the Netherlands struggled in the opening round, losing to Belgium before being eliminated by Brazil in the quarterfinals, 3-2, in a game for the ages.

⊕ In 1998, the Dutch finished fourth and lived up to their potential. They lost a shootout to Brazil before losing to Croatia, 2-1, in the third-place match. Even with all the talent that is available, the Netherlands still finished out of the money in Korea-Japan 2002.

Coach Marco Van Basten is trying to change that cycle and mentality by bringing young, promising talent that don't necessarily play for Ajax, PVS Eindhoven and Feyenoord, the three Dutch clubs that comprise the backbone of the national side. Instead, Van Basten has "discovered" such "unknowns" as Barry Opdam, Khalid Boulahrouz and Dirk Kuyt, who scored three key qualifying goals.

On the other hand, the writing might be on the wall for Tottenham Hotspur's Edgar Davids, considered the best defensive midfielder by many in the world. Left off the team for the March 1, 2006 World Cup warm-up against Ecuador. Davids was also ignored for an international friendly vs. Italy in November, 2005. "We watched Davids several times but he didn't convince us and so he did not make the squad," Van Basten said.

There are still some key players left over from Dick Advocaat's failed regime, including midfielder Philip Cocu—considered an excellent defender—and Edwin Van der Sar. During qualifying, it was Van der Sar who saved the team with several spectacular saves. He allowed only three goals in 12 games—a miniscule 0.25 goals-against average.

The Dutch are expected to be a formidable side. Striker Ruud Van Nistelrooy has been the mainstay of the attack the past five years as he has enjoyed an incredible strike rate of more than a goal every other international match (25 goals in 47 appearances). But speculation emerged that his position could be in jeopardy after Kuyt, one of those "unknowns" scored the lone goal in the Netherlands' 1-0 win over Ecuador in Amsterdam on March 2. "Kuyt did well and played with a lot of movement so the central striker position is getting busy, even though he should have handled his chances with more efficiency," Van Basten said. "He left a good impression today and we will take that into consideration."

The other key player up front is Arjen Robben, who also left PSV Eindhoven for the big bucks—$22 million transfer fee in 2004—and competition of the English Premiership with Chelsea. Robben's forte is his speed and skills. However, Robben has to avoid diving and indiscipline that has led to a pair of red cards.

The Dutch are grouped together with Argentina, Serbia & Montenegro and Ivory Coast, which has been termed this World Cup's "Group of Death." Yet, Van Basten did not seem fazed with the stiff competition. In fact, he welcomed the challenge. "It isn't the 'Group of Death' " he told *World Soccer*. "It's an interesting group."

For World Cup history buffs: The Netherlands is one of two countries that has finished second in successive World Cups--in 1974 and 1978. the other nation is West Germany, which accomplished the feat in 1982 and 1986.

NETHERLANDS

PARAGUAY
Group B

POPULATION: 6,000,000
COLORS: Red and white striped shirts,
white shorts, blue socks
APPEARANCES: 7th. 5-7-7, 25 goals for, 34 against. 1930 (first round), 1950 (first round), 1958 (first round), 1986 (second round), 1998 (second round), 2002 (second round).

WORLD CUP HISTORY

It has usually been first round and out for Paraguay; now, it's become the second round and out. The South Americans finally reached the second round of the 1986 World Cup behind a pair of former New York Cosmos—Julio Cesar Romero and Roberto Cabanas. The Paraguayans edged Iraq, 1-0, tied host Mexico, 1-1 and tied Belgium, 2-2, before losing to England and Gary Lineker in the second round, 3-0. In fact, the South Americans managed to reach the second round despite playing two draws in group play (scoreless ties with Bulgaria and Spain) and a 3-1 win over Nigeria. They held out as long as they could against eventual champion France in the second round, losing on a "golden goal," 2-1. In 2002, Paraguay had its first-round unbeaten streak snapped in a 3-1 loss to group champ Spain, but managed to move on to the next round behind a 1-1-1 mark and a second-place finish. Germany showed the Paraguayans the exit door in a 1-0 win in the second round.

HOW THEY QUALIFIED

Paraguay (8-6-4, 28 points) finished fourth in the South American group with a mediocre record for a World Cup-bound team. The Paraguayans clinched their third consecutive berth thanks to a 1-0 victory over host Venezuela on October 8, 2005. Nelson Haedo scored the game's lone goal in the 65th minute.

PLAYERS TO WATCH

Midfielder Carlos Paredes has shown he can do it all, whether it is leading the attack or tackling the ball away from the opposition. Captain and veteran defender Carlos Gamarra, who recently made his 100th international appearance, is such a skillful defender that he did not commit a foul at France '98. Only 22, Nelson Valdez is considered one of the most promising talents in South America, thanks to his speed and skill.

PLAYER POOL

Goalkeepers: Justo Villar (Newell's Old Boys, Argentina), Derlis Gomez (Sportivo Luqueno), Diego Barreto. Defenders: Denis Caniza

(Cruz Azul, Mexico), Julio Cesar Caceres (River Plate, Argentina), Carlos Gamarra (Palmeiras, Brazil), Delio Toledo (Real Zaragoza, Sapin), Paulo Da Silva (Toluca, Mexico), Juan DanielCaceres (Estudiantes, Argentina), Jorge Nunez (Estudiantes, Argentina). Midfielders: Edgar Barreto (NEC Nijmegen, Netherlands), Roberto Acuna (Deportivo La Coruna, Spain), Carlos Paredes (Reggina, Italy), J Dos Santos (Bayern Munich, Germany), Cristian Riveros (Libertad), D Gavilan (Newell's Old Boys, Argentina), W. Fretes (Cerro Porteno, Uruguay). Forwards: Nelson Valdez (Werder Bremen, Germany), Cesar Ramirez (Flamengo, Brazil), Jose Saturnino Cardozo (Toluca, Mexico), Salvador Cabanas (Jaguares, Mexico), Nelson Valdez (Werder Bremen, Germany), Roque Santa Cruz.

PROJECTED STARTING LINEUP

Goalkeeper: Justo Villar (Newell's Old Boys, Argentina). Defenders: Jorge Nunez (Estudiantes La Plata, Argentina), Carlos Gamarra (Palmeiras, Brazil), Julio Cesar Caceres (River Plate, Argentina), Edgar Barreto (NEC Nijmegen, Netherlands), Denis Caniza (Cruz Azul, Mexico). Midfielders: Roberto Acuna (Deportivo La Coruna, Spain), Carlos Paredes Reggina (Italy), Salvador CabaÃ"as (Jaguares de Chiapas, Mexico). Forwards: Nelson Valdez (Werder Bremen, Germany), Nelson Cuevas (Pachuca, Mexico).

COACH

He may be a Uruguayan by birth, but Anibal Ruiz is an adoptive Paraguayan. Like many South American coaches, Ruiz has lived a gypsy existence on the continent and even in the Caribbean, bouncing from club team to club team and sometimes directing national teams. He hooked up with Paraguay in 2002 and guided the team to its third successive World Cup berth, an unprecedented feat in the country's soccer history. He was appointed caretaker coach in 2002, replacing the controversial Italian, Cesare Maldini. Asked by **www.FIFAWorldCup.com** if he was surprised that he was named permanent coach, Ruiz responded: "Not really, but it was hugely satisfying nonetheless. We took it as just reward for all our hard work over the past few years. A coach thinks like a footballer: first he dreams of playing in the top division, then of being capped by his country. As far as we were concerned, our dream was to manage this team. You can imagine how surprised we were when we got the news by telephone. We were over the moon." When push came to shove and Paraguay had to play Uruguay, Ruiz knew where his bread was buttered and where his heart lay. "I love my country but I have a professional job to do," he said. "I have a great deal of affection for Paraguay. I only coached twice in Uruguay, in 1981 and in 1988. Let's

PARAGUAY

say I want Paraguay to beat Uruguay by playing some great football!"

Bora Milutinovic, who has coached five different countries in as many World Cups since 1986, likes to tell this story about the balancing act called coaching: "You have a blanket. You pull it toward your face to keep the top part of your body warm. You notice your feet are exposed and cold, so you pull it back down. But now you don't have enough blanket near your face and you're getting cold up top." That little story can describe the slight transition that Paraguay has gone through in recent years. The Paraguayans are much improved on the attack, but are not as strong as they once were on defense. Against the likes of England and Sweden in Group B, the South Americans will have to be at their best to stop their opponents from finding the back of the net.

Coach Anibal Ruiz has done a fine job of blending veteran players with young ones, but it remains to be seen how and if that will affect the defense, which was the corner stone of the 1998 and 2002 sides. Ruiz feels one generation is passing the torch to another. "Absolutely. We have to be watchful during this transition period and proceed progressively and carefully if we are to be successful," he told **www.FIFAWorldCup.com**. "We have great respect for what the experienced players have achieved for Paraguay. In football, it is not age that counts but how you perform on the pitch. It is also important to give the youngsters a chance."

Gone is goalkeeper Jose Luis Chilavert, who retired in 2004. The flamboyant keeper, who didn't know a free kick or penalty kick he didn't like taking, forged a reputation as the most prolific goalkeeper of his generation and one who seemingly always wound up in the middle of controversy. In his place is Justo Villar (Newell's Old Boys, Argentina), who is decent but lacks the presence of Chilavert.

Carlos Gamarra, 35, has the experience and vision. El Colorado, as he is nicknamed, isn't afraid to go in for the tackle and his superb skills and timing have allowed him not to be booked as many times as one would think. Moreover, Gamarra lacks a partner in the back to compensate for his fading speed.

Paraguay would love to give its opponents a full Nelson from its front line. In other words, the South American side would love to see forwards Nelson Valdez and Nelson Cuevas score some goals in Germany. That would probably go a long way in its group, which includes England and Sweden and World Cup newcomer Trinidad & Tobago. Valdez is considered to be one of the top rising young talents from South America. If Valdez enjoys a dominant opening round and puts a couple past the opposing goalkeeper, Paraguay could be seeing the second round for the third time in a row. He is only twenty-two and just coming into his prime. He was passed over for the 2004 Olympics, in which Paraguay captured a silver medal to Argentina's gold. Morever, he was called to the team for Copa America 2004. While he didn't score, Valdez still helped produce goals.

When healthy, the versatile Roque Santa Cruz, a forward, is one of Paraguay's most dangerous players. He has been slowed down by injuries and his availability for Germany could be in doubt. "Santa Cruz is a key player for Paraguay," Ruiz said. "He's technically gifted and a good header of the ball. And you can play him in a number of positions, as a striker or midfielder."

Gamarra is optimistic that Paraguay will forge ahead again. "I can assure you that Paraguay will qualify for the next round," he said.

Without the defense of 1998 and 2002, keeping the opponents' scores down and within reach, it certainly will be a challenge.

For World Cup history buffs: Excluding Argentina, Brazil and Uruguay, the other South American teams have a combined 16-25-15 record in 20 appearances, meaning the Paraguayans once again will have their work cut out for them.

PARAGUAY

POLAND
Group A

POPULATION: 39,000,000
COLORS: White shirts, white shorts,
  white socks
APPEARANCES: Seventh. 14-9-5. 42 goals for, 36 against. 1938
  (first round), 1974 (third place), 1978 (second round), 1982 (third
  place), 1986 (second round), 2002 (first round).

WORLD CUP HISTORY

All things considered, Poland has enjoyed a storied history in its previous six appearances. In 1938, in their first Cup appearance, the Poles were knocked out in the opening round, losing to Brazil, 6-5. In one of the more intriguing encounters in Cup history, both teams boasted players who scored four goals apiece. Ernst Willimowski scored his quartet for Poland, Leonidas da Silva countered for Brazil. Poland had to wait thirty-six years for its next appearance, but it was worth the wait. During a ten-year span in which the country captured silver and gold medals at the Summer Olympics and reached the World Cup semifinals, the Poles finished third in 1974 and again in 1978 behind the likes of Grzegorz Lato, Kaz Deyna and Zbigniew Boniek.

HOW THEY QUALIFIED

Poland finished second to England with an 8-2-0 record and 24 points in European Group 6. The Poles didn't even play when they qualified as either the best second-place team in the entire European field, thanks to results from other Euro groups on October 8, 2005.

PLAYERS TO WATCH

Jerzy Dudek has demonstrated he is quite capable of producing big saves and stopping penalty kicks, which he did for Liverpool in its incredible Champions League final comeback in May 2005. But Artur Boruc might start in his place because Dudek lost the top spot at Liverpool. Tomasz Frankowski and Maciej Zurawski, a pair of speedy forwards, finished with seven goals apiece in qualifying.

PLAYER POOL

Goalkeepers: Jerzy Dudek (Liverpool, England), Artur Boruc (Celtic, Scotland), Wojciech Kowalewski (Spartak Moscow, Russia), Tomasz Kuszczak. Defenders: Marcin Adamski (SK Rapid Wien, Austria), Marcin Baszczynski (Wisla Krakow), Jacek Bak (Al Rayan), Bartosz Bosacki (Lech Poznan), Mariusz Jop (F.C. Moscow, Russia), Tomasz Klos (Wilsa, Krakow), Marcin Kus, Tomasz Rzasa (ADO Den Haag, Netherlands), Michal Zewlakow (Olympiacos,

POLAND

Greece). Midfielders: Piotr Giza (Cracovia Krakow), Damian Gorawski (F.C. Moscow, Russia), Kamil Kosowski (Southampton F.C.), Jacek Krzynowek (Bayer Leverkusen, Germany), Mariusz Lewandowski (F.C. Shakhtar), Sebastian Mila (Austria Wien, Austria), Arkadiusz Radomski (Austria Wien, Austria), Euzebiusz Smolarek (Borussia Dortmund, Germany), Radoslaw Sobolewski (Wisla Krakow), Miroslaw Szymkowiak (Trabzonspor, Turkey), Maciej Scherfchen, Marcin Zajac (Groclin). Forwards: Tomasz Frankowski (Wolverhampton, England), Andrzej Niedzielan (NEC Nigmegen, Netherlands), Grzegorz Rasiak (Southampton, England), Lukasz Sosin, Maciej Zurawski (Celtic, Scotland).

PROJECTED STARTING LINEUP

Goalkeeper: Artur Boruc (Celtic, Scotland). Defender: Michal Zewlakow (Anderlecht, Belgium), Tomasz Klos (Wisla Krakow), Mariusz Jop (FC Moscow, Russia), Marcin Baszczynsk (Wisla Krakow). Midfielders: Radoslaw Sobolewski (Wisla Krakow, Poland), Jacek Krzynowek (Bayer Leverkusen, Germany), Kamil Kosowski (Southampton, England), Miroslaw Szymkowiak (Trabzonspor, Turkey). Forwards: Tomasz Frankowski (Elche, Spain), Maciej Zurawski (Celtic, Scotland).

COACH

A former Polish international, Pawel Jenas took over the coaching reins on December 20, 2002. Janas started his pro career with Wlókniarz Pabianice, playing there from 1965-73. He represented Poland 53 times and was a member of the 1982 side that finish third in the 1982 World Cup. Born March 4, 1953, Janas turned to coaching as an assistant at Legia Warsaw in 1988, then helped Wladyslaw Stachurski direct the Polish youth team from 1990-1992 and was assistant Olympic coach at the 1992 Summer Olympics as Poland won a silver medal. He joined Legia Warsaw as an assistant coach later that year. He finally became a head coach in 1994 at Legia, his team twice winning the Polish league and Polish Cup and advancing to the Champions League quarterfinals in 1996. He went back to the Polish Under-23 from 1996-99 and was vice president and manager of Amica Wrokni until he took over the national reigns. His first match was a scoreless tie vs. Croatia on February 13, 2003. Despite enjoying success, Janas was heavily criticized for some of his player selections. Grzegorz Raskia has been a favorite of his at forward, although his critics claim there are better players than him.

POLAND

When Poland lines up against Ecuador on June 9 (the B game on opening day), there is a good chance that one of its best players won't be in the lineup, namely goalkeeper Jerzy Dudek, who lost his number one position at European champions Liverpool to Jose Reina of Spain. This was hard for Dudek to take. He was one of the heroes of the Reds' amazing comeback in the match against A.C. Milan. Liverpool rallied from a 3-0 halftime deficit to tie it in regulation and win in the penalty kick shootout, where Dudek stood out. Liverpool coach Rafael Benitez told Dudek that he wanted the 32-year-old goalkeeper to remain with the team unless Reina was benched by injury of loss of form, according to the Polish newspaper *Gazeta Wyborcza*.

"I told him that solution does not interest me," Dudek told the newspaper. "I don't want to be counting on an injury to a colleague and that he places me in a tough situation. I played most of Poland's matches in qualifying for the World Cup but if I don't play for my club I could wind up not going to the finals. For me this would be a disaster." Dudek asked to be traded, but the team has not complied.

His former understudy on Poland, Artur Boruc, acquitted himself well when he stepped in for the injured Dudek in Poland's final qualifiers in September and October, 2005. Many members of the media believe that Boruc, who tends goal for Celtic in Scotland will wind up between the posts. Boruc, 26, has been at the right place at the right time. He transferred from Legia Warsaw to Celtic on loan in 2005. But he wound up as the top choice after Scotland international David Marshall surrendered nine goals in two games. Boruc took over and never gave up his spot, allowing about a goal a match as his transfer to Celtic became permanent.

In fact, goal might not be the only position in which a talented player might not start. Midfielder-forward Ebi Smolarek, one of the leading goalscorers in the German Bundesliga in the 2005-06 season, might come off the bench, thanks to his exceptional ability to go one-on-one with opposing defenders. He earned the dubious nickname "The Hasch Bomber" when he tested positive for hashish during a stint with Feyenoord (Netherlands).

The Poles can get the job done. Their defense has a reputation as being slow, but their fast forwards Tomasz Frankowski and Maciej Zurawski more than make up for it as their partnership up front produced seven goals each during qualifying.

As for getting the job done, the Poles certainly didn't do it against the U.S. in a World Cup warm-up in Kaiserslautern, Germany on March 1, 2006, as the Americans walked out of the stadium with a 1-0 victory in a snow-driven game. Coach Pawel Janas praised the

Americans, who scored an opportunistic goal off a Poland error. "They were the better team," Poland coach Pawel Janas said. "They deserved to win."

Janas, clawing for excuses, claimed the snow helped the U.S. more. "The snow didn't help," he said. "We had it in our faces. They had in their backs. Maybe it helped them a little bit."

U.S. coach Bruce Arena noted that the American-based players had been training in the warmer weather of California for seven weeks. "I don't think the snow was that much of an advantage," he said.

Poland has done quite well internationally. The Poles' glory days spanned a decade a generation or so ago. They captured the 1972 Olympic gold medal and the silver in 1976. They finished third in the 1974 and 1982 World Cups.

The Poles were hopeful of adding another player to their World Cup team—Argentine-born midfielder Mauro Cantoro, who had applied for Polish citizenship. Cantoro has forged a reputation as the Polish First Division's best central midfielder, standing out as the holding midfielder in Wisla Krakow's three championship teams.

Janas also was considering Christoph Dabrowski, who has joint Polish-German nationality. Dabrowski, 28, who has performed for the German B National Team, plays for Hannover 96 in the Bundesliga.

Let's face it. The Poles have lacked a world-class playmaker since the late Kaz Deyna (he played for the San Diego Sockers in the old North American Soccer League) and Zbigniew Boniek for the two third-place World Cup sides.

Poland has a history of using naturalized citizens. Nigerian-born Emmanuel Olisadebe became the top qualifying scorer in Europe for the 2002 World Cup, helping Poland to qualify. But he has been plagued by injuries the past several years.

For World Cup history buffs: Poland has one of the best winning percentages in World Cup history at 58.9 percent with a 14-9-5 record.

POLAND

PORTUGAL
Group D

POPULATION: 10,100,000
COLORS: Red shirts, green shorts, red
   socks
APPEARANCES: 4th. 7-5-0, 25 goals for, 16 against. 1966 (third
   place), 1986 (first round), 2002 (first round).

WORLD CUP HISTORY

It's a short one—with one memorable tournament. Making their Cup debut in 1966, the Portuguese were the outside sensations, finishing third as the fabulous Eusebio led the way with a tournament-high nine goals. Portugal rolled through its opening group, defeating Hungary, 3-1, Bulgaria, 3-0, and defending champion Brazil, 3-1, The Portuguese rallied from a 3-0 deficit against a surprised North Korea side en route to a 5-3 triumph in the quarterfinals as Eusebio scored four goals and set up a fifth. They met their match in eventual champion England, 2-1, in the semifinals, before rebounding for a 2-1 victory over the Soviet Union for third place. Portugal had to wait sixteen years before securing another World Cup berth, defeating England, 1-0, but dropping a 1-0 decision to Poland and a 3-0 result to Morocco. Again the Portuguese had to wait some sixteen years before yet another Cup appearance. The U.S. stunned them in their group opener, grabbing a three-goal advantage en route to a 3-2 victory. They trounced Poland, 4-0, but lost to host South Korea, 1-0 to finish at 1-2.

HOW THEY QUALIFIED

Portugal finished atop European Group 3 with a 9-3-0 record and 27 points. They Portuguese scored an incredible 35 goals, tying the Czech Republic for the Euro lead. The Portuguese, who played little Liechtenstein to a 2-2 tie in 2004, clinched a spot with a 2-1 victory in 2005. After falling to a 1-0 halftime deficit, the Portuguese rallied in the second half behind goals by Pauleta and Nuno Gomes. Luis Figo missed a penalty kick.

PLAYERS TO WATCH

Forward Pauleta, who struck for a European-best eleven goals, is the go-to guy up front. Captain and midfielder Luis Figo, who came out of international retirement to help the team qualify, still has moments of grandeur. Cristiano Ronaldo is the heir apparent to Figo as he can dazzle the crowd and opponents at any juncture during the match.

PLAYER POOL

Goalkeepers: Ricardo Pereira (Sporting), Quim Silva (Benfica), Paulo Santos (Sporting Braga). Defenders: Ricardo Carvalho

PLAYER POOL

(Chelsea, England), Marco Caneira (Sporting), Miguel Monteiro (Valencia, Spain), Fernando Meira (VfB Stuttgart, Germany), Nuno Valente (Everton, England). Midfielders: Joao Alves (Sporting Lisbon), Costinha (Dynamo Moscow, Russia), Frechaut (Dynamo Moscow, Russia), Armando Petit (Benfica), Tiago Mendes (Olympique Lyon, France), Deco (Barcelona, Spain), Maniche Ribeiro (Chelsea, England), Cristiano Ronaldo (Manchester United, England), Luis Boa Morte (Fulham, England), Luis Figo (Inter Milan, Italy). Forwards: Cristiano Ronaldo (Manchester United, England), Helder Postiga (Saint Etienne, France), Ricardo Quaresma (Porto), Pauleta (Paris St Germain, France), Nuno Gomes (Benfica), Helder Postiga (FC Porto).

PROJECTED STARTING LINEUP

Goalkeeper: Ricardo (Sporting Lisbon, Portugal). Defenders: Nuno Valente (Everton, England), Ricardo Carvalho (Chelsea, England), Paulo Ferreira (Chelsea, England). Midfielders: Maniche (Chelsea, England), Petit (Benfica), Deco (FC Barcelona, Spain), Cristiano Ronaldo (Manchester United, England), Luis Figo (Inter Milan, Italy). Forward: Pauleta (Paris St. Germain, France).

COACH

After directing Brazil to the 2002 World Cup title, Luiz Felipe Scolari could have written his ticket to whatever national team he wanted to coach. Scolari signed on as Portuguese national coach. Big Phil, as he is known, has let it be known that he is serious about the England job when Sven-Goran Eriksson leaves, after the World Cup. "He will stay until the World Cup," Portuguese Football Association president Gilberto Madail told Reuters, "but if it was up to me, he would stay beyond that." Scolari had been Brazil's most successful club coach over the past decade, guiding two clubs Gremino (1995) and Palmeiras (1999) to the Libertadores Cup (South America's version of the European Champions League). Scolari, fifty-seven years old, a pragmatic man who stresses organization and defense, had forged a reputation as a disciplinarian—of using strong-arm tactics against opponents rather than doing something pretty with the feet. Asked by the *Sunday Telegraph* if the beautiful game was dead, Scolari replied, "Yes, for me it's a piece of history. When I have the conditions to play futebol-arte, when I'm winning, when I have qualification guaranteed, when I have got everything right, when it's a friendly and we can afford to lose—then I'll let them play futebol-arte. But in competition the very definition of the word means we have to compete. We have to win. And if we have to win by force and organization, well, forget futebol-arte. To me, it's something from the fifties, something lyrical, something Utopian. We don't have it any more. I don't play this way."

PORTUGAL

It's now or never for Portugal. A fantastic generation of Portuguese players face their last hurrah for international glory in Germany.

In 1989 and 1991, Portugal captured back-to-back Under-20 World Cup championships under former MetroStars coach Carlos Queiroz in Major League Soccer. Many international soccer observers expected Portugal to emerge as a power in the 90's, although the country's coming out party was delayed until a few years ago when the Portuguese reached the semifinals of Euro 2000 and advanced to their very first World Cup since 1986 in 2002. Whether this golden generation's time has passed, it remains to be seen.

Which Portuguese team will show up in Germany? Will it be the side that was stunned by the U.S. in its opening match of the 2002 World Cup, 3-2, and an eventual first-round exit? Or, will it be the team that reached the finals of Euro 2004 before falling to champion Greece for the second time in the competition. Coach Luiz Felipe Scolari hoped that Portugal learned some valuable lessons after the first-round elimination. "I have a good team. I have a lot of respect for our adversaries, but once we know who we're playing against and what the groups are you can make some projections,' said Scolari."

"When Portugal drew the United States, Poland and South Korea in 2002, everyone thought it was easy and look what happened," he told Brazilian television. "If we get this idea into our heads, then we don't even need to go to the World Cup. Mexico beat Brazil at the Confederations Cup, the Angola match has that extra ingredient because of the political aspect and Iran can play very good football."

There's plenty of talent on this team. Whether Scolari can lasso all the personalities and turn it into a force to be reckoned with, will have to wait until June"We must reach the quarterfinals at the very least," Pauleta told **www.FIFAWorldCup.com**. "We are determined to prove that we're one of the eight best teams in the world. However, before we start thinking about that, we need to concentrate on the first match, as that will be the key to whether we have a good or bad tournament."

The most influential figure is captain and midfielder Luis Figo, 33, Portugal's most capped player who came out of international retirement to help the team. He was 2001 FIFA player of the year and still has all the tools you want in a midfielder—playmaking skills, vision, a deadly shot and leadership—even if his pace isn't the same as before.

Pauleta, 29, is Portugal's all-time scorer (42 goals), surpassing the great Eusebio during qualifying. The striker finish with a Euro-best 11 goals. However, Pauleta has a reputation for missing easy opportunities and not playing up to his potential in big tournaments. While he did have a hat-trick in a victory over Poland in 2002, the perception lingers that he didn't do enough in Portugal's two losses. The man known as the "Azorean Hurricane" was blanked at Euro 2004.

"He's a genuine, old-fashioned goal-scorer," Portugal teammate Nuno Gomes said. "He occupies the space between the two central defenders and just loves to get on the end of attacking moves. His game is all about being one step ahead of defenders and being clinical in front of goal."

Cristiano Ronaldo, Figo's heir apparent who plays for Manchester United, needs to have a superior Cup if this team wants to go deep in the tournament.

The Portuguese's weakness is in goal. Vitor Baia, for so many years the No. 1 keeper (he had a disastrous first half vs. the U.S. in 2002), is out of favor as Quin (Benfica) and Ricardo (Sporting Lisbon) are battling it out for the top spot.

Portugal suffered a crippling blow in its World Cup preparations when Deportivo Coruna central defender Jorge Andrade learned in March 2006 that he would miss six months due to knee surgery after severing the patellar tendon in his left knee during Deportivo's 3-2 loss at Barcelona. "His injury is terrible news," Scolari was quoted in sports daily newspaper *AS*. "If he wants, he can still accompany us in Germany because he is still part of the team."

Andrade joined Deportivo teammate Juan Carlos Valeron of Spain on the international sidelines after the Spaniard tore the cruciate ligament in is left knee in January, 2006.

"I think Portugal will be in the top eight teams in Germany," *Publico newspaper's* Luis Octavio Costa told **www.bbc.com**. "They are more prepared for competition than at Euro 2004 and the coach understands his players better."

Portugal has been known to play up or down to its opponents. In a four-day stretch during qualifying, the Portuguese went from hell to heaven. They stumbled to an embarrassing 2-2 draw with lowly Liechtenstein on October 9, 2004. The result was so humiliating that the country's media severely criticized the team. But four days later Portugal rolled to a 7-1 thrashing of Russia. It turned into the worst loss for Russia since the demise of the Soviet Union.

PORTUGAL

SAUDI ARABIA
Group H

POPULATION:25,000,000
COLORS: Green shirts, white shorts,
  green socks
APPEARANCES: 4th. 2-7-1, 7 goals for, 25 against. 1994 (second
  round), 1998 (first round), 2002 (first round).

WORLD CUP
HISTORY

Saudi Arabia made the world stand up and take notice with a sterling debut at USA '94. The Saudis finished the opening round with a surprising 2-1 record, stunning heavily favored Belgium, 1-0, on a goal by Saeed Owairan, losing to the Netherlands, 2-1, but defeating Arab rival Morocco, 2-1. They were eliminated in the second round, falling to Sweden, 3-1. In 1998, the Saudis struggled, dropping two opening-round matches—1-0 to Denmark and 4-0 to France—before playing South Africa to a 2-2 draw. In fact, their performance was so distressing that coach Carlos Alberto Parreira—yes, the same Parreira who guided Brazil to its fourth world championship four years prior and the 2006 coach—was fired after two matches.

HOW THEY
QUALIFIED

Saudi Arabia captured its Asian Group 1 crown with a 4-0-2 record over second-place South Korea, Uzbekistan and Kuwait. The Saudis clinched a spot by defeating Uzbekistan, 3-0, in Riyadh, Saudi Arabia on June 8, 2005. Team captain Sami Al-Jaber scored twice. Saad Al-Harthi, who replaced Jaber in the 68th minute, added another goal.

PLAYERS TO
WATCH

Captain and forward Sami Al-Jaber is a legend in his own country, having played half his life—he's 34-years-old—with the National Team, scoring in his first international match in 1990. Goalkeeper Mohammed Al-Daeyea, who has played in three World Cups, is back in the picture with a new coach. He could very well replace Mabrouk Zaid, considered one of the best keepers in Asia. Central defender Hamad Al Montashari leads one tough defensive back four as the Saudis surrendered only one goal in six qualifiers.

PLAYER POOL

Goalkeepers: Mohammed Al-Daeyea, Hasan Al-Otaibi, Mabrouk Zaid. Defenders: Ahmed Al-Bahri, Ahmed Dukhi Al-Dosari, Osama Al-Harbi, Abdulaziz Al-Khathran, Hamad Al-Montashari, Zaid Al-Mowalad, Naif Al-Qadi, Khaled Al-Thaker, Hussain Sulaimani, Redha Tukar. Midfielders: Manaf Abushgeer, Bandar Al-Dosari,

Khamis Owairan Al-Dosari, Taiseer Al-Jassam, Saud Al-Khariri, Mohammed Al-Shlhoub, Nawaf Al-Temyat, Saad Al-Zahrani, Mohammad Haidar, Mohammed Noor. Forwards: Mohammed Saad Al-Anbar, Saad Al-Harthi, Sami Al-Jaber, Talal Al-Meshal, Marzouq Al-Otaibi, Yasser Al-Qahtani, Naji Majrashi.

Goalkeeper: Mohammed Al-Daeyea. Defenders: Taiseer al-Jassam (Al-Ahli), Hamad al-Montashari (Al-Ittihad), Redha Fallatha (Al-Ittihad, Ahmed al-Bahri (Al-Ittihad). Midfielders: aud al-Khariri (Al-Ittihad), Mohammad Noor (Al-Ittihad (Saudi Arabia), Nawaf al-Temyat (Al-Hilal (Saudi Arabia), Mohammad Al-Shalhoub (Al-Hilal). Forwards: Yasser Al-Qahtani (Al-Hilal), Sami Al-Jaber (Al-Hilal).

PROJECTED STARTING LINEUP

Brazilian Marcos Paqueta was named Saudi coach on January 9, 2006, replacing the fired Gabriel Calderon, who had guided the team to qualification. A one-time Argentine international, Calderon was given the boot on December 21, 2005. He was under intense criticism by the Saudi media after the team's sub-par performance at the West Asian Games—two losses to Iraq and one to Iran. He was also criticized for the many changes to his staff and for the World Cup training schedule, Six days prior, Saudi Football Federation head Prince Nawaf Bin Faisal claimed Calderon's job was not in jeopardy. As it turned out, it was. "We also wanted to know the wisdom behind holding a training camp for two weeks before the finals without playing a single friendly match during the camp," Prince Faisal said. Calderon had replaced Gerard van der Lem after a poor showing at the 2004 Asian Cup. Paqueta directed Al Hilal to the Saudi league and cup title and had helped Brazil to win the Under-20 and U-17 world titles in 2003.

COACH

No team qualifying for the World Cup the past four times has gone through as many coaches as Saudi Arabia has. En route to USA '94, the Saudis used three coaches—Brazilian Jose Candido, Dutchman Leo Beenhakker and Argentine Jorge Solari. For France '98, the Saudis had deployed nine coaches in the previous three years, finally settling on Brazilian Carlos Alberto Parreira, who replaced German Otto Pfister, who had taken over for Tigo Viganda. For the 2002 competition in Korea and Japan, Saudi native Nasser Al-Joher was named two matches into the final round as he replaced Yugoslav Slobodan Santrac. It shouldn't be surprising that the Saudis made yet another switch after qualifying for Germany.

A new coach means a new philosophy and sometimes new players,

2006 WORLD CUP

SAUDI ARABIA

which was the case this time around. "Every coach in the world lives under pressure 24 hours a day and you can't escape from that," said Brazilian Marcos Paqueta, who took over the coaching reins in December, 2005. "But I don't think it's that bad. Pressure just motivates me. It's like a fuel that I transform into positive energy for myself."

Paqueta decided to bring in veteran goalkeeper Mohammed Al Deayea, who had made more appearances (179) than any other male player in the world (U.S. women's international midfielder Kristine Lilly had 306 and counting as of March, 2006). The thirty-three year old Al Deayea was inserted into the lineup for a pair of friendlies and performed quite well—in a 1-1 tie with Finland in January, 2006 and a 3-0 loss to Portugal on March 1. The 6-foot, 4-inch Al Deayea had all but been forgotten under the Calderon regime, appearing in only three games over three years. Mabrouk Zaid had played in all six qualifiers in 2005.

Paqueta will rely on forward Sami Al-Jaber, who has devoted half his life playing for the National Team. He came out of retirement to score twice in the qualifying clinching win over Uzketistan. Forward Yasser al-Qahtani is expected to partner with Al-Jaber. He is a perfect complement. At twenty-three, he is younger, unpredictable and quick.

After showing so much promise in its first World Cup appearance in 1994, Saudi Arabia has stumbled in the past two tournaments. In 1998, the Saudis made World Cup history midway through the tournament by firing coach Carlos Alberto Parreira. In 2002, the Saudis lost all three matches in Japan. They were outscored, 12-0, winding up on the wrong end of an 8-0 triumph by eventual finalist Germany in the opening round.

Nicknamed al-Sogour (the Falcons) or al-Akhdar (the Green), the Saudis are a team with excellent technical skills but lacking physical presence. They will face difficulties trying to reach the second round with the likes of Spain and the Ukraine in Group H. Tunisia is the other team.

Virtually any country that has apsirations of going beyond the first round has its roster dominated by players who perform regularly in Europe. The Saudis, however, only have a pair of players who have played with Euro clubs—Al-Jaber and Fahd Al Ghashayan. "Arab players have quality and good technique but they lack greater involvement at the international level," Paqueta was quoted by **www.FIFAWorldCup.com**. "They need to make that change so that they value themselves a little, increase their self-esteem and see that they have a chance and can take on any team in the world on an equal basis. My job is to try to emphasise this. Arab football is on the rise. We have new players, such as Al Ittihad and full-back Hamad Al Montashari, who was voted the best player in Asia. This all leads me to believe that we can do better. As a matter of fact, I think it's great that everyone considers Saudi Arabia to be outsiders in the competition." Paqueta then laughed. "That's how we can surprise people," he added.

For World Cup history buffs: Before Saudi Arabia recorded two victories at USA '94, Asian teams had won only one match at previous World Cups. They are 10-41-10 entering this World Cup, having gone 6-9-3 in 2002.

SAUDI ARABIA

SERBIA & MONTENEGRO
Group c

POPULATION: 11,000,000
COLORS: Blue shirts, white shorts, red
  socks
APPEARANCES: 1st—as Serbia & Montenegro.

**WORLD CUP
HISTORY**

Officially, there is none. But under the previous name of the country, Yugoslavia, that nation made nine appearances.

The Slavs became the first and only European team to reach the Final Four in the very first World Cup in 1930, defeating Brazil, 2-1, and Bolivia, 4-1, before it was drubbed by eventual-champion and host Uruguay in the semifinals, 6-1. In 1962, the Yugoslavians also reached the semifinals before losing to Czechoslovakia, 3-1, and wound up finishing fourth. They rolled to a 9-0 win over Zaire when Germany last hosted the tournament in 1974. Their best recent over-all performance occurred at Italia '90, when they outplayed Argentina in a scoreless quarterfinal confrontation before they were eliminated via a penalty-kick shootout, 3-2. In their most recent appearance at France '98, Yugoslavia finished with a 2-1 opening round record, defeating the U.S. and Iran by 1-0 shutouts and tying Germany, 2-2 before losing to the Netherlands in the second round, 2-1.

**HOW THEY
QUALIFIED**

Serbia & Montenegro surprisingly finished atop European Group 7 (with a 6-0-4 record, 22 points) over second-place Spain (5-0-5, 20), outscoring its opposition, 16-1. The country qualified with a 1-0 victory over Bosnia-Herzegovina on a Mateja Kezman goal in Belgrade on October 12, 2005. In some respects, the result was a loss for Serbia & Montenegro as FIFA fined Serbia & Montenegro $28,000 and ordered the National Team to play one home game in an empty stadium due to crowd trouble. Rival supporters pelted each other with flares and seats. There is lingering hostility from the ethnic war between the Serbs and Muslims in the early 1990s.

**PLAYERS TO
WATCH**

Forward Mateja Kezman of Atletico Madrid (Spain) connected for several key goals during qualifying. That included the important tying goal in the 1-1 tie in Spain and the game-winner in the 1-0 win over Bosnia, which clinched a spot. Captain and defender Mladen Krstajic, who performs for Schalke O4 (Germany), anchors one of the toughest defenses in the world.

Goalkeepers: Dragoslav Jevric (Anakaraspor), Oliver Kovacevic (CSKA Sofia), Vladimir Stojkovic. Defenders: Dusan Basta (Red Star Belgrade), Ivica Dragutinovic (Sevilla, Spain), Marko Basa (Le Mans, France), Nemanja Vidic (Manchester United, England), Mladen Krstajic (Schalke 04, Germany), Milivoje Cirkovic (Partizan Belgrade). Nenad Djordjevic (Partizan Belgrade), Ivica Dragutinovic (Standard Luuttich), Goran Gavrancic (Dynamo Kiev, Ukraine), Mladen Krstajic (Schalke 04, Germany), Aleksandar Lukovic. Midfielders: Dejan Stankovic (Inter, Italy), Igor Duljaj (Shaktar Donetsk), Predrag Djordjevic (Olympiakos Piraeus, Greece), Ognjen Koroman (Portsmouth, England), Sasa Ilic (Galatasaray, Turkey), Albert Nadj (Partizan Belgrade), Danijel Ljuboja (VFB Stuttgart, Germany), Dragan Mladenovic (Real Sociedad, Spain), Ognjen Koroman (Krylia Sowjetow Samara), Simon Vukcevic (Partizan Belgrade). Forwards: Mateja Kezman (Atletico Madrid, Spain), Nikola Zigic (Red Star Belgrade), Savo Milosevic (Osasuna, Spain), Mirko Vucinic (Lecce, Italy), Nenad Jestrovic (Anderlecht, Belgium).

PLAYER POOL

Goalkeeper: Dragoslav Jevric (Anakaraspor). Defenders: Mladen Krstajic (Schalke 04, Germany), Memanja Vidic (Manchester United, England), Nenad Djordjevic (Partizan Belgrade), Goran Gavrancic (Dyanmo Kiev, Ukraine). Midfielders: Sasa Ilic (Galatasaray, Turkey), Igor Duljaj (Shaktar Donetsk), Dragan Mladenovic (Real Sociedad, Spain), Ognjen Koroman (Portsmouth, England). Forwards: Nikola Zigic (Red Star, Belgrade), Mateja Kezman (Atletico Madrid, Spain).

PROJECTED STARTING LINEUP

This is Ilija Petkovic's second stint with a national team from the area, having directed the Yugoslavian National Team for two months in 2001 after he was an assistant coach to Slobdoan Santrac at France '98. At 60, Petkovic will be one of the oldest coaches at Germany 2006. He replaced Dejan Savicevic, who served from 2002-03. Petkovic, who scored six goals and appeared 43 times for Yugoslavia from 1968-74, played against Brazil in the opening game of the 1974 World Cup in Frankfurt, Germany. He played most of his career with OFK Beograd Belgrade in the old Yugoslavian First Division, appearing in more than 500 matches in 15 years. He also played with Troyes in France. Petkovic began his coaching career with OFK Beograd prior to directing Servette to the Swiss championship and coaching in Greece.

COACH

SERBIA & MONTENEGRO

The line in the Belgrade newspaper *Blic* on December 10, 2005 was as incredulous as it was funny. "Heidi Klum has sent us to hell," the newspaper said. *Blic* was referring to World Cup draw TV host Heidi Klum and Serbia & Montenegro's World Cup opponents in Group C—also know as the Group of Death—Argentina, the Netherlands and Ivory Coast.

"Many people are talking about our group being the hardest one of the whole tournament, but this is nothing for me to worry about," coach Ilija Petkovic said.

Petkovic added in an interview with **FIFAWorldCup.com**:

"I am not worried about anything, least of all the pressure. We know where we're playing, we know who we're playing, we know that the world is watching us. Our players are very experienced from club level and they will take that and implement it on the next level. Nobody expected us to be there so we cannot lose, we can only win."

The Serbians certainly have their work cut out for themselves. But Petkovic certainly is confident in his team.

"There's this 'One for all and all for one' feeling and a massive desire to represent our country on the world stage," he told **FIFAWorldCup.com**. "We want to show everybody that Serbia and Montenegro is still 'alive' on the map."

It is sometimes difficult to size up Serbia & Montenegro. In fact the European side might be one of the intriguing contradictions in this World Cup.

Officially, Serbia will be participating in its first World Cup. But before the eventual break-up and renaming of Serbia & Montenegro several years ago, the country competed as Yugoslavia in nine World Cups. Yugoslavia renamed itself in 2003. Serbia & Montenegro will be playing in its first World Cup under that name.

Yugoslavia was known for its veteran players and attacking players. Serbia & Montenegro qualified for Germany behind its younger contingent and has forged a reputation as being a stingy defensive side.

If Serbia does go through to the second round in what just about every soccer observer has called the "Group of Death" (Argentina, the Netherlands and Ivory Coast are the other teams), it probably will be because of its defense.

The team allowed only one goal in 12 qualifiers and that was in a 1-1 tie with Spain. Before that, the Serbians reeled off an impressive seven successive shutouts.

The team will have to play its first match against the Netherlands in Leipzig on June 11 without suspended defender Nemenja Vidic. In January, 2006, Vidic moved from Spartak Moscow to Manchester

United on a $12 million transfer. "Good defenders win you things and this lad is really natural and athletic," United coach Sir Alex Ferguson was quoted on the English Premiership team's TV channel.

The key man up front is forward Mateja Kezman of Atletico Madrid (Spain), who connected for several important qualifying goals. That included the equalizer in the 1-1 tie with Spain and the game-winner in the 1-0 victory over Bosnia, which clinched a spot.

Team captain and defender Mladen Krstajic, who performs for Schalke O4 (Germany), anchors one tough backline. "No, we are not defensive," Petkovic said. "We have our tactics and a strong defense is an important aspect, but we have very good midfielders and forwards, too. I firmly believe that we will prove this in Germany. Defending is not the main part of our mentality—attacking is. But if we get results this way, I do not want to change anything."

If they don't get out of the opening round, the Serbs might want to blame it on inexperience and a midfield that hasn't displayed much flair or creativity. "They didn't lose a game in the qualifiers and only conceded one goal in a group with Spain and Belgium," **BBC Belgrade** correspondent Matt Prodger was quoted on his organization's website. "They're underdogs with good recent form. Supporters point to a solid squad, lacking in big names, but consistent in performance. In as much as a national team reflects a nation's character, however, be prepared for surprises."

For World Cup history buffs: Even though Yugoslavia was a European side, its two best finishes came off-continent—the semifinals in the very first tournament in Uruguay in 1930 and fourth place in Chile in 1962. In fact, the National team has a better record in South America—7-5—than playing on the continent—9-8-8.

SERBIA & MONTENEGRO

SPAIN
Group H

POPULATION: 40,200,000

COLORS: Red shirts, blue shorts, blue socks

APPEARANCES: 12th. 19-14-12, 71 goals for, 453 against. 1934 (second round), 1950 (fourth place in round-robin final round), 1962 (first round), 1966 (first round), 1978 (first round), 1982 (second round), 1986 (quarterfinals), 1990 (second round), 1994 (quarterfinals), 1998 (first round), 2002 (quarterfinals).

WORLD CUP HISTORY

Except for a fourth-place finish in 1950 in Brazil, Spain has had a history of teasing its supporters. The Spanish are good enough to qualify and sometimes good enough to get out of the first round, but have rarely made an impact when it really counted. After a rather discouraging result when they hosted the 1982 Cup—a second-round elimination—one Spanish newspaper refused to publish the team's lineup. Spain reached the quarterfinals at USA '94, but lost to Italy on Roberto Baggio's goal with three minutes left in a 2-1 loss. Spain embarrassed itself at France '98, failing to get out of the opening round. The side might have pulled off its greatest tease in the 2002 competition as the Spaniards finished undefeated at 3-0-2, but were eliminated in the quarterfinals. Spain swept through its opening round group at 3-0 and squeaked past Ireland in the second round via penalty kicks. But, they wound up on the other side of the PKs in the quarterfinals, losing to host South Korea via penalties, 5-3.

HOW THEY QUALIFIED

Spain (5-0-5, 20 points) finished second to Serbia & Montenegro (6-0-4, 20) in European Group 7. The Spaniards got past Slovakia in the playoffs. Luis Garcia struck for a hat-trick in a 5-1 triumph in the first leg on November 12, 2005.

PLAYERS TO WATCH

Real Madrid striker Raul, the greatest goal-scorer in European Champions League history, hasn't enjoyed the same success in the World Cup. He suffered a severe knee injury in November, 2005. How long and how well he recovers could make the difference between success or failure in Germany. As it turned out, it was not Raul who led Spain in goals during qualifying. Forward Fernando Torres, 21, with seven goals, did. Goalkeeper Iker Casillas is considered top class and defender Carles Puyol one of Europe's best.

PLAYER POOL

Goalkeepers: Iker Casillas (Real Madrid), Pepe Reina (Liverpool), Victor Valdes (Barcelona). Defenders: Antonio Lopez (Atletico Madrid), Pablo Ibanez (Atletico Madrid), Oleguer (Barcelona), Carles Puyol (Barcelona), Juanito (Real Betis), Asier del Horno (Chelsea), Joan Capdevila (Deportivo Coruna), Ivan Helguera (Real Madrid), Michel Salgado (Real Madrid), Sergio Ramos (Real Madrid), Carlos Marchena (Valencia) Midfielders: Cesc Fabregas (Arsenal), Jose Antonio Reyes (Arsenal), Andres Iniesta (Barcelona), Xavi (Barcelona), Joaquin (Real Betis), Pedro Munitis (Deportivo Coruna), Juan Carlos Valeron (Deportivo Coruna), Ivan de la Pena (Espanyol), Luis Garcia (Liverpool), Xabi Alonso (Liverpool), Guti (Real Madrid), David Albelda (Valencia), Ruben Baraja (Valencia), Vicente (Valencia), Marcos Senna (Villarreal). Forwards: Fernando Torres (Atletico Madrid), Fernando Morientes (Liverpool), Raul (Real Madrid), David Villa (Valencia).

PROJECTED STARTING LINEUP

Goalkeeper: Iker Casillas (Real Madrid). Defenders: Defenders: Michel Salgado (Real Madrid), Carles Puyol (Barcelona), Pablo Ibanez (Atletico Madrid), Asier del Horno (Chelsea, England). Midfielders: Xabi Alonso (Liverpool), Xavi (Barcelona), Vicente Valencia. Forwards: Raul (Real Madrid), Fernando Morientes (Liverpool, England), Fernando Torres (Atletico Madrid).

COACH

Luis Aragones took over as coach in July, 2004—he had turned down a previous offer—after Spain endured a poor Euro 2004 under the guidance of Inaki Saez. Born during the Spanish Civil War on July 28, 1938, Aragones has always been a colorful character of the game, as a player and a coach. He is referred to in many newspapers by his first name alone. He played for several clubs, including Real Betis, Oviedo and Recreativo before joining Atletico Madrid for a decade in 1964. He led La Liga—the Spanish First Division—in scoring in 1969-70, gaining the nickname "Zapatones"—big boots—while becoming a free-kick specialist. After retiring from the game, he coached Atletico Madrid while the club was owned by the late Jesus Gil, who changed coaches more than some people change underwear. Aragones had a couple of stints as coach—he gained another nickname there as "The Wise Man of Hortaleza." After illness forced Aragones from the game for a while, he went on to coach Barcelona, Sevilla, Valencia, Espanyol, Real Betis, Real Oviedo and Real Mallorca.

SPAIN

In 11 appearances in soccer's promised land, Spain has never reached the semifinals. Given that the country boasts one of the best leagues in Europe, with not one, but two mega-clubs that enjoy a successful history, the failings are mind-boggling. Despite its World Cup struggles in the past, the Spaniards were still selected as one of the eight seeded slots, but this year's team could very well be headed toward some familiar territory.

One problem with these great expectations has been the success of Spanish First Division sides in European competition, notably Real Madrid and Barcelona. While these teams traditionally vie for the Spanish title and go deep into the Champions League, many of the key players on both teams are of foreign ancestry.

As one of the eight seeded teams, Spain should have a relatively easy time in Group H against the likes of the Ukraine, Saudi Arabia and Tunisia. If the Spaniards can't find their way to the second round with that relative easy path, coach Luis Aragones should resign right after the referee blows his final whistle of the June 23 match with Saudi Arabia.

Even with the uneven success of the national side—Spain failed to get out of the first round at Euro 2004—Aragones is optimistic. "We know we are capable of beating any team and are close to being among the top sides," Aragones told **Reuters** on March 1, 2006, when his team pulled off a 3-2 comeback in an international friendly with Ivory Coast. Spain rallied twice as Real Betis defender Juanito scored on a header with five minute remaining. "We believe we are very close to where we want to be for the World Cup."

Arsenal's 18-year-old midfielder Cesc Fabregas made his international debut in the match. Forward David Villa said the teenager had dazzled everyone. "I was pleased with my performance and I hope I have done enough to prove to the coach that I can continue on the squad," Fabregas said.

Spain might need the likes of Fabregas to excel because its top scorer, Raul, was sidelined for several months with a partial cruciate ligament tear in his left knee in November, 2005. Raul, who should be in the prime of his career—he turns 29 on June 27— suffered the injury when he misfired a shot during Real Madrid's 3-0 home loss to Barcelona. He was hopeful of a quick comeback even though Real team physicians said the striker had to follow a conservative treatment program. "There was a moment in which I thought I would be out for a very long time," Raul told reporters at a news conference. "That still may happen, but the probability is that I will be back in a much shorter period. At the moment there are no dates set, and it might take three or four months to see how the knee responds, but I can see myself helping Real win a trophy and then playing in the World Cup."

Raul wasn't the only key performer struck by the knee injury jinx. Midefielder Xavi, 25, tore the anterior cruciate ligament in his right knee during training in December, 2005 and was considered a long-shot for Germany. "It's a great shame and a big setback,"Aragones told **Reuters.**

Aragones, incidentally, wound up in the middle of a controversy, making some unwanted worldwide headlines himself. In 2004, a Spanish TV crew caught Aragones trying to motivate Arsenal's Jose Antonio Reyes during a National Team training session. Aragones referred to French international Thierry Henry, Reyes' Arsenal team-mate, using language that was interpreted as offensive and racist. When the footage was shown in England, the media was surprised there wasn't a demand for Aragones to resign. As it turned out, Spain hosted England in an international friendly at Real Madrid's home, Santiago Bernabeu Stadium, as the hosts prevailed. But the fans and soccer were the real losers that day as Spanish supporters made "monkey chants" every time a black English player touched the ball.

Spain's traditional No. 1 weakness is in goal. Keepers have made blunders that cost Spain in the Olympics (all the way back to the 1920 Summer Games) and World Cups. For example, Andoni Zubizarreta, a four-time World Cup performer, literally handed a 3-2 result to underdog Nigeria at France '98 by fumbling the ball away on two occasions. Santiago Canizares became the last victim stepping on the broken glass from a bottle of cologne he dropped in the bathroom several weeks before the kickoff of the 2002 World Cup. In his place stepped Real Madrid's Iker Casillas, who performed admirably well and is still the No. 1 keeper.

The team enjoyed an 18-game unbeaten run through the winter of 2006, having last lost on June 6, 2003.

"I'm not very confident about the national team," Canal Nou TV's Paco Lloret was quoted by **www.BBC.com**. "They are good players but never can reach the semifinals. Although Spain will be with the best teams in the draw, I don't expect a successful World Cup."

Spain has thrown the theory of home-hemisphere advantage out of the window. In its five appearances in European-based World Cups, the Spaniards are unfortunately 6-7-5. In fact, they have one of the worst records for a host country, going 1-2-2 in 1982.

SPAIN

SWEDEN
Group B

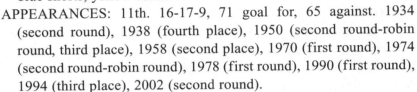

POPULATION: 9,000,000
COLORS: Yellow and blue shirts,
  blue shorts, yellow socks.
APPEARANCES: 11th. 16-17-9, 71 goal for, 65 against. 1934 (second round), 1938 (fourth place), 1950 (second round-robin round, third place), 1958 (second place), 1970 (first round), 1974 (second round-robin round), 1978 (first round), 1990 (first round), 1994 (third place), 2002 (second round).

WORLD CUP
HISTORY

Most countries would love to have the World Cup history that Sweden has. The Swedes have never won the coveted trophy, but they finished in fourth place in 1938, third in 1950, second to a Brazil-led Pelé side in 1958 and third at USA '94. They also captured the Olympic gold medal in 1948 and the bronze in 1952. Their best performance came as the hosts in 1958, when they finished second to Brazil, losing 5-2 in the final. The Swedes were the surprise side of the 1994 World Cup, finishing third with a 3-1-3 mark. They were eliminated in the semifinals by Brazil, 1-0, although the game was much more one-sided for the winners than the final score indicated. In 2002, the Swedes won that competition's "Group of Death" (England, Nigeria and Argentina were the other teams) and reached the second round, falling to Senegal in extratime, 2-1.

HOW THEY
QUALIFIED

Sweden (8-2-0, 24 points) finished second to Croatia (7-0-3, 24) in European Group 8 as one of the top two runners-up (which received automatic qualification). The Swedes qualified with a 3-1 victory over Iceland on Oct. 12, overcoming a one-goal deficit. Zlatan Ibrahimovic, Henrik Larsson and Kim Kallstrom connected for the winners.

PLAYERS TO
WATCH

Strikers Zlatan Ibahimovic and Henrik Larsson give Sweden a unique one-two punch. Goalkeeper Andreas Isaksson was very sharp during qualifying. Team captain and defender Olaf Mellberg might not have the same speed as he had during his prime, but his vision, experience and leadership abilities are vital to the backline's success.

PLAYER POOL

Goalkeepers: Eddie Gustafsson, Andreas Isaksson (Rennes, France). Defenders: Christoffer Andersson, Mikael Dorsin, Erik Edman

(Rennes, France), Petter Hansson, Teddy Lucic (BK Hacken), Olaf Mellberg (Aston Villa, England), Alexander Oststlund (Feyenoord, Netherlands). Midfielders: Niclas Alexandersson, Daniel Andersson, Kim Kallstrom, Tobias Linderoth (F.C. Copenhagen, Denmark), Freddie Ljungberg (Arsenal, England), Mikael Nilsson, Anders Svensson (Elsfborg), Christian Wilhelmsson (Anderlecht, Belgium). Forwards: Marcus Allback, Johan Elmander, Zlatan Ibrahimovic (Juventus Italy), Mattias Jonson, Henrik Larsson (Barcelona, Spain), Markus Rosenberg.

PROJECTED STARTING LINEUP

Goalkeeper: Andreas Isaksson (Rennes, France). Defenders: Olaf Mellberg (Aston Villa, England), Teddy Lucic (BK Hacken), Erik Edman (Rennes, France), Alexander Oststlund (Feyenoord, Netherlands). Midfielders: Christian Wilhelmsson (Anderlecht, Belgium), Tobias Linderoth (FC Copenhagen, Denmark) Anders Svensson (Elfsborg), Freddie Ljungberg (Arsenal, England). Forwards: Zlatan Ibrahimovic (Juventus, Italy), Henrik Larsson (Barcelona, Spain).

COACH

Lars Lagerback, who split the 2002 coaching responsibilities with Tommy Soderberg, was named sole coach after Euro 2004. They had served together at the 2002 World Cup. Lagerback joined the National Team's coaching staff in 1997 as an assistant to Soderberg, who left the national side to take over as Sweden Under-21 national coach. Born on July 16, 1948, Lagerback is a superb analyst. He labored in Sweden's lower pro leagues before he turned to coaching. He was Soderberg's assistant, but shared head coaching responsibilities after Sweden's excellent qualifying run to Euro 2000. On December 13, 2005, Lagerback had extended his contract until after the Euro 2008.

2006 WORLD CUP

For a country that doesn't have a high-powered professional soccer league, Sweden has done relatively well over the years. The players have overcome this potential obstacle by playing for highly competitive European sides. Just take a look at the probable starting lineup that is listed in the team profile. Forwards Zlatan Ibahimovic and Henrik Larsson perform for Juventus (Italy) and Barcelona (Spain), respectively. Midfielder Freddie Ljungberg toils for Arsenal in the English Premiership. Defenders Olaf Mellberg, the team captain, plays for Aston Villa (England) and Alexander Ostlund for Feyenoord (Netherlands).

SWEDEN

If the Swedes can get out of their group of England, Paraguay and Trinidad & Tobago, there's no telling what damage they might do later on in the tournament.

For years, Sweden was known as a tough defensive side. These days it will take one to stop Sweden's attack.

The Swedes have an imposing one-two strike force up front. Larsson, who fills the net for Barcelona, scored one of the most memorable goals in Euro 2004. Zlatan Ibrahimovic who performs for Juventus (Italy), combines skill and strength as one of the most feared and respected strikers around.

Few players are as dynamic or bring so much energy to the field as this 24-year-old. While he has a temper, Ibrahimovic uses his energy on the field, turning routine plays into spectacular goals. He is also a winner. He helping Ajax to the Dutch First Division crowns in 2002 and 2004 and Juventus to Italy's Serie A title in 2005. Juventus was so impressed that the club paid a $19 million transfer fee for him in 2004.

"Zlatan is the future," French international and Juventus teammate David Trezeguet told **www.FIFAWorldCup.com**. "He's a player with extraordinary potential who has acclimatized rapidly to Juve. When I play with him, I stay in the center and let him roam around the flanks. We complement each other well, actually."

England coach and Swedish native Sven-Goran Eriksson quoted by **www.SI.com**: "If Zlatan Ibrahimovic goes on like he does at the moment, he will be the best in the world."

Larsson led the Scottish Premier League in scoring for two seasons while with Celtic, but has been plagued by injuries at Barcelona. When healthy, however, he is a handful to cover. He recently was voted Sweden's best player of the past 50 years.

At 28, Ljungberg might not be the same midfield player he was several years ago, but he certainly gets the job done as he still has the knack of finding open space and scoring key goals. He is is just happy to be alive and playing since he a cancer scare in May 2005. Ljungberg complained about a mystery hip ailment and after tests, was given the all-clear by the doctors to play. As it turned out, Ljungberg had a nerve problem that was corrected by surgery.

"I was frightened," Ljungberg told the *Sun*. "I was tested but nobody seemed to know what was wrong with me." He had a shooting pain in his hip. "First of all we thought it was an old injury," he was quoted by the *Mirror*. "But they didn't find anything wrong, even though when I had an ultrasound test it was all really swollen. Then they realized the glands in the hip had caused it by swelling up but still didn't know why I had the infection.

"So I had a lot of different tests because they had to find the reason why I was in so much pain. I had to have tests for cancer and other diseases - as you can guess it wasn't much fun."

Defensively, the Swedes can be very stingy, surrendering only four goals during qualifying. The backline is led by team captain Olaf Mellberg who has been known to get a yellow card or two on occasion. Teddy Lucic teams with Mellberg to clog up the middle.

If their March World Cup warm-up loss in Dublin, Ireland was any indication, then the Swedes will be three and out come June. Remember, Ireland did not qualify for the tournament and it was Sweden's last match before coach Lars Lagerback will choose his World Cup team. He said it was one of the worst games played during his coaching tenure.

"It seems like we're not focused," Lagerback told **Reuters**. "We make too many mistakes. We're not playing like a team."

Mellberg agreed. "We did nothing well today," he said. "It's another friendly in which we didn't reach our normal level. . . . Hopefully, we can pull ourselves together and step up our game when it really matters."

Sweden's opening-round match against England on June 20 will be important: the game is a rematch of the 1-1 draw between the two teams in the 2002 World Cup; these are the top two teams of the group; and, the English coach is Swedish, which certainly brings the rivarly to another level. A victory probably will mean advancement to the second round and perhaps the group title. A loss will certainly make things more difficult for the Swedes.

For World Cup history buffs: In its first three Cup appearances, Sweden finished fourth, third and second, a record not many countries could duplicate.

SWEDEN

SWITZERLAND
Group G

POPULATION: 7,500,000

COLORS: Red shirts, white shorts, red socks.

APPEARANCES: 8th. 6-13-3 record, 33 goals, 51 goals against. 1934 (quarterfinals), 1938 (quarterfinals), 1950 (first round), 1954 (second round), 1962 (first round), 1966 (first round), 1994 (second round).

WORLD CUP HISTORY

The Swiss had some glorious moments in the early years of the Cup, participating in four of the first five tournaments, hosting the 1954 competition and reaching the quarterfinals twice. But, as time went on, they found it more difficult to reach the finals. In 1966, the Swiss were ousted in the first round, losing to West Germany, Spain and Argentina. At USA '94, Switzerland managed to reach the second round on the strength of a 1-1-1 record. The Swiss drew with the U.S., 1-1, rolled over Romania, 4-1, and lost to Colombia, 2-0. Spain dispatched them in the second round, 3-0.

HOW THEY QUALIFIED

Even though it finished undefeated (4-0-6, 14 points) in European Group 4, Switzerland finished second, winding up in a playoff with Turkey. After winning at home, 2-0, on November 12, 2005, the Swiss dropped a 4-2 decision in Istanbul four days later in a match marred by violence after the final whistle. While the goal aggregate was deadlocked at 4-4, the Swiss advanced because the away goals rule counts them double. Marco Streller scored six minutes from time to make the score 4-2. In what is a rarity and certainly a first, the Swiss qualified without defeating a team that had a winning record. They beat Cyprus (1-8-1) and the Faroe Islands (0-9-1) twice apiece. They tied France, Israel and the Republic of Ireland in each of their two games against them.

PLAYERS TO WATCH

Forward Alexander Frei, 26, one of the leading scorers in the French League last season (22 goals in 40 games), connected for seven goals in 10 qualifiers. The Swiss will be relying on Frei for the bulk of the scoring load if they are to do anything. Left fullback Ludovic Magnin's specialty is set pieces that set up goals. Defender Philiippe Senderos, 21, who performs for Arsenal, could be a star of the future. Veterans Raphael Wicky and captain Johann Vogel bring leadership to the midfield.

SWITZERLAND

Goalkeepers: Pascal Zuberbahler (FC Basel, Switzerland), Eldin Jakupovic, Fabio Coltorti. Defenders: Phillip Degen (Borussia Dortmund, Germany), Philippe Senderos (Arsenal, England), Patrick Mueller (Lyon, France), Ludovic Magnin (VfB Stuttgart, Germany), Stephane Henchoz, Johan Djourou, Stephane Grichting (Auxerre, France), Boris Smiljanic. Midfielders: Tranquillo Barnetta (Bayer Leverkusen, Germany), Johann Vogel (AC Milan, Italy), Raphael Wicky (Hamburg SV, Germany), Ricardo Cabanas (FC Cologne, Germany), Hakan Yakin (VfB Stuttgart, Germany), Christoph Spycher, Ludovic Magnin (Werder Bremen, Germany), Benjamin Huggel (Basel), Johan Vonlanthen (PSV Eindhoven, Netherlands), Valon Behrami, Blerim Dzemaili. Forwards: Daniel Gygax (Lille, France), Alexander Frei Rennes (France), Marco Streller, Mauro Lustrinelli.

Defenders: Phillip Degen Borussia Dortmund (Germany), Philippe Senderos (Arsenal, England), Patrick Mueller (Lyon, France), Ludovic Magnin (VfB Stuttgart, Germany). Midfielders: Tranquillo Barnetta (Bayer Leverkusen, Germany), Johann Vogel (A.C. Milan, Italy), Raphael Wicky (Hamburg SV, Germany), Ricardo Cabanas FC Cologne (Germany). Forwards: Daniel Gygax (Lille, France), Alexander Frei Rennes (France).

Jakob "Kobi" Kuhn has coached the team since June, 2001, the first Swiss coach of the country's national side in a dozen years. Born on April 15, 1948, Kuhn made 63 international appearances for Switzerland while playing most of his club ball with F.C. Zurich. He took over the reigns of the Swiss Under-21 team after he retired. Guiding the Swiss into Euro 2004 and the 2006 World Cup, Kuhn is a big hero in his home country. His best skill is communication, and he has the courage to shake things up when needed. "He has been of crucial importance, not only in helping us qualify for the World Cup but also in building up Swiss football in recent years," forward Alexander Frei told *FIFA Magazine*. "After his success with the U-21 National Team, he has now taken the senior side to Euro 2004 and the 2006 World Cup. Having been a great player, Kuhn is now a great coach, too. He has never shied away from making difficult decisions regarding players. His secret is the extraordinary way he manages people."

SWITZERLAND

Back after an absence of 12 years, Switzerland certainly has a number of motivations to do well at Germany 2006. One of course, is the pride involved in playing as well as possible, especially when the World Cup is hosted by your neighbor. The other is about moving ahead toward Euro 2008, which the Swiss will co-host with Austria.

That Switzerland reached the World Cup certainly was no mistake. It is the product of an ongoing program that has developed the youth structure in the country at an accelerated rate. The plan is the brainchild of Swiss technical director Hansruedi Hasler, who started planting the seeds for success in 1995.

The key to the plan was the appointment of professional coaches at the youth level and the implementation of a clearly defined system of play. The system includes an attacking and polished passing game "with all eyes on the initial pass launching attacks from defense," Hasler told *FIFA* Magazine. "You can play a variety of ways, but you have to stick to a fundamental system and then polish it off," he added. It was worked—spectacularly.

The fruits of the program helped the Swiss capture the U-17 Euro title in 2002 and to reach the semifinals of the U-21 Euro championship that same year, opening up the door to qualify for Euro 2004 and reach the FIFA World Youth Championship for the first time.

"I'm so happy that the training scheme has been so well received," Hasler said.

The program has worked so well, bringing in a new generation of players. In fact, only one player is more than thirty-years-old, a rarity for a European side—6-foot-6, 221-pound goalkeeper Pascal Zuberbahler at thirty-five years old. That is considered prime time for international keepers.

Coach Jakob Kuhn helped matters by moving aside a number of international veterans such as team captain Ciriaco Sforza so members of the younger generation could get a chance. The new generation includes the promising and talented defender Philippe Senderos, midfielders Tranquillo Barnetta and Valon Behrami and forward Daniel Gygax, though this World Cup might come a bit too soon for the Swiss.

With such a young team, Switzerland probably will be a team that will mature in two to four years time. Booking a spot in Germany was a surprise.

"It wasn't entirely expected," forward Alexander Frei was quoted by *FIFA* Magazine. "But, before the qualifiers started, we knew that Switzerland could play good football and we would be using the campaign to prepare for Euro 2008, which will be co-host with Austria. We deserved to qualify for the World Cup in Germany because we made it out of a strong group. Swiss football has taken a step forwards."

Switzerland will play France in Stuttgart on June 13. Other Group G opponents include South Korea and Togo.

"You can be sure that this Swiss team will play with plenty of soul and enthusiasm," Frei said. "Our team is still developing and we will not be at our best until we host Euro 2008. Even so, we will go to Germany full of ambition. We can get further than the last 16."

Switzerland isn't accustomed to winning and qualifying for the World Cup. "The Swiss expect to lose every time they play a half-decent side and have a bit of an inferiority complex." Geneva-based journalist Pete Sanderson told **www.BBC.com**. "But when they qualified, the population celebrated wildly, and came out of their shells for first time in ages."

Frei explained one of the keys to Switzerland's success. "We have a powerful team spirit," he told *FIFA Magazine*. "We don't air problems in the media. And we are fairly relaxed when we play because there are always three or four youngsters in the team who are not overwhelmed by the pressure on us to win. Over eight of ten matches, the younger members of the squad have proved that they can keep up with the pace of the game at the international level."

The day Switzerland booked a spot to Germany wasn't exactly the right way to celebrate reaching the World Cup for the first time in twelve years. According to the **Associated Press**, this is what transpired in the post-match brawl in the players' tunnel:

The Swiss players left the field under a hail of missles and objects thrown from the stands. Swiss midfielder Benjamin Huggel kicked Turkish assistant coach Mehmet Ozdilek in the back of the legs. Turkey's Alpay Ozalan tried to kick Huggel in retaliation, but instead made contact with another Swiss player in front of him. Huggel then grabbed Alpay around the neck and fell to the ground, with the other players, coaches and security guards piling on.

Fines and suspensions were handed out, Huggel getting the worst of it—a six-game suspension that starts in the World Cup.

For World Cup history buffs: Switzerland endured one of the longest losing streaks and winless streaks in World Cup history. The Swiss snapped a seven-game losing streak dating back to a 4-1 victory over Italy in the 1954 Cup with a 1-1 draw with the USA in 1994. They ended their eight-match winless streak the next game, a 4-1 win over Romania.

SWITZERLAND

TOGO
Group G

POPULATION: 5,500,000
COLORS: Yellow/green shirts, green/white shorts, white/red socks
APPEARANCES: 1st.

WORLD CUP HISTORY

None.

HOW THEY QUALIFIED

After a slow start, Togo captured African Group 1 with a 7-1-2 record and 23 points over Senegal, Zambia, Congo, Mali and Liberia. The Togolese clinched a berth by edging the Congo, 3-2, in Brazzaville, the Congo on October 8, 2005. Emmanuel Adebayor, Ma Diafar and Kader connected for the winners. Thousands of people in the capital of Lome poured into the streets to celebrate, during which there was a power blackout that lasted for hours.

PLAYERS TO WATCH

Thanks to his quickness and speed, forward Emmanuel Adebayor, 24, led all African players in scoring (11 goals). Captain Abalo Dosseh is the anchor of the backline. Goalkeeper Kossi Agassa's nickname is "Magic Hands," which should tell you something about his goal-saving ability.

PLAYER POOL

Goalkeepers: Ouro Tchanirou, Kossi Agassa (F.C. Metz, France), Safiou Salifou. Defenders: Jean-Paul Yaovi Abalo (Dunkerque, France), Eric Akoto (Admira Wacker Madling, Austria), Mohama Zanzan Atte-Oudeyi (Lokeren, Belgium), Emmanuel Mathias (Esperance, Tunisia), Abdoul Moumouni, Dare Nibombe, Massamasso Tchangai (Benevento Calcio). Midfielders: Komlan Amewou, Yao Aziawonou (Young Boys Bern), Thomas Dossevi (Valenciennes), Komlan Eninful, Alessandro Farias, Ali Kaddafi, Koffi Kossi, Abdul Mamah, Sherif Toure Mamam, Souleymane Mamam (Manchester United—England, on loan at Royal Antwerp—Belgium), Lantame Ouadja, Djima Oyawole, Alaixis Romao (Louhans-Cuiseaux, France), Tadjou Salou, Robert Souliemdane, Sherif Toure (F.C. Metz, France), Junior Senaya (Juventus Zurich, Switzerland), Yao Aziawonou (Young Boys Bern, Switzerland). Forwards: Sheyi Emmanuel Adebayor (Arsenal, England), Abdel Coubadja, Mohamed Kader Coubadja (FC Sochaux, France), Guyazou Kassim, Adekamni Olufade, Abdou-Nassirou Ouro-Akpo, Moustapha Salifou.

TOGO

Goalkeeper: Kossi Agassa (FC Metz, France). Defenders: Eric Akoto (VfB Admira Wacker Madling, Austria) Jean-Paul Abalo (Dunkerque, France), Mohama Zanzan Atte-Oudeyi (Lokeren, Belgium), Emmanuel Mathias (Esperance, Tunisia). Midfielders: Junior Senaya (Juventus Zurich, Switzerland), Yao Aziawonou (Young Boys Bern, Switzerland), Sherif Toure (FC Metz, France), Alaixis Romao (Louhans-Cuiseaux, France). Forwards: Mohamed Kader Coubadja (FC Sochaux, France), Emmanuel Adebayor (Arsenal, England).

PROJECTED STARTING LINEUP

German Otto Pfister is the third coach since the start of qualifying. He replaced Nigerian Stephen Keshi on Feb. 22, 2006. Keshi, 43, had guided Togo into the World Cup, but was severely criticized after Togo lost all three its opening-round matches at the 2006 African Nations Cup and had a major row with striker Emmanuel Sheyi Adebayor. Pfister has coached six African National Teams—Rwanda, Upper Volta (now Burkina Faso), Senegal, the Ivory Coast, Zaire (now the Democratic Republic of Congo) and Ghana—and clubs in Tunisia and Egypt. Pfister, 68, knows the feeling of being replaced as a coach of a national team he had guided into the Cup. The same thing happened 1997 when he took over as Saudi Arabia coach for Tigo Vingada during qualifying in October 1997, before eventually stepping down as coach weeks later. Pfister signed a short-term contract with Togo, which could be extended if "the results are good," said Togolese Football Federation president Commander Rock Gnassingbe. The way the Togolese Football Federation handled the transition was questionable and contradictory at best. Keshi's firing was announced on Togo National Television, although Gnassingbe denied it. Keshi, who had been named 2005 African coach of the year a week prior, told *BBC Sports* that he was still coach. "I have not been told by anyone at the Togolese football federation that I have lost my job and I remain in Togo to honor my contractual obligations to them." But two days later federation secretary general Espoir Assogbavi told the **BBC** that the press reports were accurate.

COACH

Of the seven World Cup newcomers, many observers are not giving Togo much of a chance of winning a game. That's because the Africans deploy a young side and the quality and experience of the opposition—France, Switzerland Korea—might be too much for the team to overcome.

Nicknamed "*Les Eperviers*"—the Sparrow Hawks—the Togolese can only pray that their first venture into big-time international soccer doesn't repeat their past history. That came at the FIFA Under-

2006 WORLD CUP

TOGO

20 World Cup in Chile in 1987, when the Togolese had three players red-carded in their first two matches.

Togo has an extremely young team. The average age of the players who participated in the qualifiers were 22 years, four months, the youngest of all the 32 qualifiers. Its oldest player is 31-year-old defender Jean-Paul Abalo.

Expect a lot of athleticism and enthusiasm in their game. They lack international experience and with that fear and nerves will work against them. Togo has a reputation for being slow starters.

If Togo is to pull off an upset or even make a game interesting, it must play a tight defensive game and have someone score an opportunistic goal. That second responsibility likely will fall at the feet of 6-foot-3 Emmanuel Adebayor, a 21-year-old striker who has combined raw talent with speed and quickness to become a scoring terror. Adebayor, who performs for Arsenal (England), led all Africans with 11 qualifying goals. As good and promising as he is, Adebayor is a bit undisciplined. He missed a number of practices with Monaco (France) and wound up being booted off the team. Arsenal quickly gobbled him up.

Team captain and defender Jean-Paul Abalo has nearly 70 international appearances, including four stints at the African Nations Cup (the 2006 competition included). Abalo performed for a decade at S.C. Amiens (France) before moving to Dunkerque (France) earlier this season.

"We have good players and we have a chance to show that in our first World Cup appearance," defender Eric Akoto told **www.FIFAWorldCup.com**. "Look, nobody expected Senegal to get to the quarterfinals of the last World Cup finals, so there is no reason why we can't achieve the same kind of result."

Coach Otto Pfister said that he will select players for the Cup who are playing regularly. "There are at least seven or eight regulars who will be the backbone of the side," he told **Radio France International** African sports program.

"It's a new challenge for me, but I have plenty of experience in African football," Pfister said. "I'm not expecting a lot of problems."

For World Cup history buffs: Ten countries went 0-3 in their initial Cups—El Salvador (1970), Haiti (1974), Zaire (1974), New Zealand (1982), Canada (1986), Iraq (1986), United Arab Emirates (1990), Greece (1994), Slovenia (2002) and China (2002).

TRINIDAD & TOBAGO
Group B

POPULATION: 1.3 million
COLORS: Red shirt with black
    sleeves, red shorts, white socks
APPEARANCES: 1st.

None.

Trinidad & Tobago had the longest road to Germany, playing 20 matches. The Soca Warriors did not compile a sterling record—11-7-2—but they could care less because they finally reached soccer's promised land. They clinched a spot by besting Bahrain (Asia) in an aggregate goals series, tying at home, 1-1, on November 12, 2005, and winning in Bahrain, 1-0, on a Dennis Lawrence goal four days later. The Trinidadians worked their way into a position to qualify by finishing fourth in the CONCACAF final round with a 4-5-1 record.

After playing pro soccer for more than half his life, 34-year-old midfielder-forward Dwight Yorke finally gets an opportunity to play on the world's biggest stage. He isn't the same player who starred for Manchester United and the English Premiership, but still has his moments. Forward Stern John, who once terrorized opposing defenders while playing for the Columbus Crew (MLS), is the team's main scoring threat, combining power and speed.

Goalkeepers: Shaka Hislop (West Ham, England), Clayton Ince (Coventry City, England), Tony Warner (Fulham, England). Defenders: Ian Gray (CL Financial San Juan Jabloteh), Marvin Andrews (Glasgow Rangers, Scotland), Dennis Lawrence (Wrexham), Avery John (New England Revolution, U.S.), Anthony Noreiga (Kansas City Wizards, U.S.), Nigel Henry (unattached). Midfielders: Christopher Birchall (Port Vale, England), Aurtis Whitley (Cl Financial San Juan Jabloteh), Silvio Spann (unattached), Kevon Neaves (University of South Florida), Carlos Edwards (Luton Town, England), Ricky Shakes (Swindon Town, England), Densill Theobold (Falkirk, Scotland), Dwight Yorke (Sydney F.C. Australia).Forwards: Russell Latapy (Falkirk, Scotland), Stern John (Coventry City, England), Kenwyne Jones (Southampton, England), Collin Samuel (Dundee United, Scotland).

PROJECTED
STARTING
LINEUP

Goalkeeper: Shaka Hislop (West Ham United, England). Defenders: Ian Gray (CL Financial San Juan Jabloteh), Marvin Andrews (Rangers, Scotland), Avery John (New England Revolution, U.S.), Dennis Lawrence (Wrexham, England). Midfielders: Christopher Birchall (Port Vale, England), Densill Theobold (Falkirk, Scotland), Russell Latapy (Falkirk, Scotland), Dwight Yorke (Sydney F.C., Australia). Forwards: Carlos Edwards Wrexham (England), Stern John (Coventry City, England).

COACH

Dutchman Leo Beenhakker has been around the international soccer at the club and national team level. He has coached a number of top-flight clubs during his thirty-three years as a coach: six clubs in the Netherlands—Ajax, Feyenoord, Go Ahead Eagles, S.C. Cambuur, F.C. Volendam, Vitesse; two in Spain—Real Madrid and Real Zaragoza; two in Mexico—Chivas de Guadalajara, Club America; and one each in Switzerland (Grasshopper) and Turkey (Istanbulspor A.S.). He also directed the Dutch and Saudi Arabian National Teams, at the 1990 and 1994 World Cups, respectively. While guiding Real Madrid to three titles in the late eighties, Beenhakker earned the nickname "Don Leo." Born on August 2, 1942, Beenhakker was named Trinidad & Tobago coach on April 1, 2005, replacing Bertille St. Clair. "Leo Beenhakker came and what he did was make us actually believe that we can do it and that none of the other sides are any better," defender Dennis Lawrence told **www.FIFAWorldCup.com**. "Obviously he has got so much experience and I have realised there are a lot of things I can learn from him. He gives us the freedom to express ourselves on the pitch. He is a confident manager and his confidence rubs off on the players." Beenhakker has become famous for the line: "I'm getting so tired of this . . . "

2006
WORLD CUP

The country's soccer fans suffered until the Soca Warriors qualified for Germany 2006, becoming the smallest country to reach the World Cup and only the second English-speaking Caribbean country to accomplish the feat (Jamaica was the other in 1998).

Trinidad faces a formidable task of trying to overcome World Cup veterans England, Sweden and Paraguay. Just getting a point would be considered a major accomplishment for the Soca Warriors. "You take it from me that Trinidad & Tobago is not going to Germany to become numbers," said Trinidad Football Federation consultant Warner, a controversial figure during his tenure as a FIFA vice president. "We are not going to Germany to be beaten by Tom, Dick or Harry. We are going to Germany to light up the country with our culture, our music, our talents, our steel band. We are going to show

TRINIDAD & TOBAGO

our cuisine. Most importantly, on the field of play, we shall perform in a most clever way."

Veteran midfielder-forward Dwight Yorke agreed. "We don't plan to go there and be just another team," he said. "We can progress. This team has already made a lot of progress and we can go a lot further. We aim to go there and to be counted."

T&T never reached its potential under coach Bertille St. Clair. he fueded with the Trinidad media for several months. The papers claimed St. Clair was "by far teh most media unfriendly" coach in the past 16 years. in its November 25, 2005 editions, The Express printed a quote from St. Clair after he was asked a question about T&T's disappointing performance in its 2-1 victory over St. Vincent Grenadines. This is the exact quote from the Express:

"I the most successful coach all yuh ever had in all yuh life. All yuh bring foreigner, all yuh bring them from all over, andwhen they do wrong, all yuh bawl, yeah, yeah. They bawl meh down because I from Tabago. I carry all yuh to the Gold Cup, the Under-16 win thing, the U-13 win. But because I from Tobago, I know it. I know the cry...the papers go write it tomorrow. But I don't care. I know where I going when I leave here. But doh worry 'bout the firing, that ain't have nothing to do with it, ah go through that already."

Since the 1970 qualifying competion, Trinidad had attempted to reach the World Cup 10 times and 10 times the country failed. Their closest encounter was in 1989. Most T&T football supporters agree that their Strike Force-which they were called then-would never have a better opportunity to reach the Cup.

Even with such dangerous players as forwards Yorke and Jerren Nixon, Trinidad fell short of its potential inits attemtps at the 1994, 1998, and 2002 World Cup

Dutch coach Leo Beenhakker started to turn thigs around. he took over on April Fool's Day, 2005 and demonstrated that he certainly wasn't fooling around as Trinidad became the smallest country ever-1.3 million population-to reach the World Cup. Warner said that Beenhakker "has been simply a magician. We have to repect him. we have to thank him for what he has done. We have given coach Beenhakker total control. He has been told he has all the funding he needs."

The clinching game certainly wasn't without it's slip-ups and dramatic points, Trinidad's 1-0 victory over host Bahrain showed that the Caribbean side had some fortitude. In the late going Dennis Lawrence, a lanky 6-foot-7 defender, headed in the lone goal in a 1-0 victory.

While nowhere near the same player of ten and even five years "

Yorke certainly still has moments after he was persuaded by St. Clair to come out of retirement. Playing more of a laid-back forward or attacking midfielder role, Yorke 34, proved he still has some magic left in his feet. For example, the team captain scored both goals in a 2-0 win over Iceland on March 1, 2006. "That's why we invited him," Beenhakker told **Agence-France Press**. "He's a good player. I know that some people are talking about his age and stuff like that, but so long as he's fit he's a great player, not only in an individual way but for the team. He's a great help to me. I can give him a message and he can translate it on to the pitch."

The victory over Iceland on British soil was a confidence builder.

"Players are coming back to train with us from all over the world and we are having just three or four days together," Beenhakker said. "They all come from different football cultures and play in different leagues so sometimes it is hard for them to adapt quickly to the way we want them to play. I think a lot of people will be surprised at what we will be able to do at the World Cup. This is a very good squad of players." Stern John, who in 1999 led Major League Soccer with 26 goals will be the striker the team will rely upon up front. He certainly got some decent target practice during qualifying, connecting a team-best twelve times.

Russell Latapy, 37, first decided to retire from international soccer, then came back as a player-coach, which is quite rare at a World Cup.

It won't be easy against the likes of England, Sweden and Paraguay. "Our dream is to surprise these opponents," Beenhakker told the *Hamburger Abendblatt*. "In football two and two don't always add up to four. Sometimes five. No one can be sure, not even the big sides. In football you always have a chance. It's that simple." Trinidad once was a colony of England, so just getting a point would be considered quite an accomplishment. "The general consensus in Trinidad is: It doesn't matter what else we do, the main thing is to beat England," he said. "After our qualification we had three months of carnival. If we don't lose against England we could well have carnival for a whole year."

For World Cup history buffs: Trinidad & Tobago is only the fifth Caribbean country to reach the World Cup. Its predecessors include Cuba (1938), Dutch East Indies (1938), Haiti (1974) and Jamaica (1998), who have compiled a 2-7-1 record, scoring ten goals and allowing forty-one.

TUNISIA
Group H

POPULATION: 10 million
COLORS: Red shirts, white shorts, red
    socks
APPEARANCES: 4th. 1-5-3. 5 goals for, 11 against. 1978 (first
    round), 1998 (first round), 2002 (first round).

Other than qualifying for the second round, Tunisia could not have
asked for a better World Cup debut in 1978. The North Africans
stunned Mexico, 3-1, in their very first match, dropped a 1-0 decision
to Poland and played West Germany to a scoreless tie. It wasn't
enough to advance, but it was quite a start. The less said about the
next two tournaments, the better. At France '98, the Tunisians wound
up 0-2-1, losing to England, 2-0, and Colombia, 1-0, before tying
Romania, 1-1. In Japan in 2002, it was more of the same. The Les
Aigles de Carthage (The Eagles of Carthage) lost to Russia, 2-0,
played Belgium to a 1-1 draw, and were beaten by Japan, 2-0. Tunisia
is winless in its last eight World Cup matches.

Tunisia captured Africa Group 5 with a 6-1-3 record and 21 points.
The North Africans clinched a berth in a 2-2 draw with unbeaten
Morocco (5-0-5, 20) in Tunis on October 8, 2005 as Talal El-
Karkouri, who had tallied for the winners earlier, scored an own goal
for the Moroccans to draw Tunisia even. Jose Clayton converted a
penalty kick to tie the game at 1-1. Tunisia joined Nigeria and
Cameroon as the only African side to qualify for three consecutive
World Cups. Perhaps *Le Temps* newspaper best summed up the
match: "Enduring suffering brought us this victory. This match was
one of the most pathetic and difficult in the history of our national
team. We were twice eliminated but we twice turned the situation
around with incredible mental strength."

Forward Silva dos Santos, struck six times during qualifying, including four in the 7-0 triumph over Malawi, and is the best finisher.
Midfield playmaker Riadh Bouazizi, 32, is known for his take-no-
prisoners tackles and often-injured defender Hatem Trabelsi, who
performs for Ajax (Netherlands) is a solid player on the backline.

Goalkeepers: Ali Boumnijel, Khaled Fadhel, Adel Nefzi, Hamdi
Kasraoui. Defenders: Khaled Badra, Essam Merdassi, Karim Haggui,

Hatem Trabelsi, Riadh Bouazizi, Radhi Jaidi, David Jemmali, Anis Ayari, Jose Clayton, Alaeddine Yahia, Karim Saidi. Midfielders: Sofiene Melliti, Ziad Jaziri, Hamed Namouchi, Kaies Ghodbane, Jawher Mnari, Adel Chedli, Selim Benachour, Karim Essediri. Forwards: Chaouky Ben Saada, Haykel Gmamdia, Silva dos Santos, Essam Gomaa, Amine Letaiif.

PROJECTED STARTING LINEUP

Goalkeeper: Ali Boumnijel (Club Africain). Defenders: Hatem Trabelsi (Ajax Amsterdam, Netherlands), Karim Hagui (Strasbourg, France), Radhi Jaidi (Bolton Wanderers, England), Jose Clayton (Qatar SC, Qatar). Midfielders: Hamed Namouchi (Rangers, Scotland), Riadh Bouazizi (Kayserispor, Turkey), Adel Chedli (Nuremberg, Germany), Khais Ghodbane (Konyaspor, Turkey). Forwards: Ziad Jaziri (Troyes, France), Silva dos Santos (Toulouse, France).

COACH

It's incredible how quickly some people can go from being a bum to a hero. In 2002, Roger Lemerre was considered a pariah in his native land. Because defending champion France was eliminated in the opening round of the World Cup after failing to win a game or score a goal, Lemerre was subsequently fired. In 2004, Lemerre directed Tunisia to the African Nations Cup crown and was hailed as the savior of Tunisian soccer. In 2006, Lemerre has guided the side into the World Cup. Lemerre played 414 games for Sedan, Nantes, Nancy and Lens in the French First Division and six international matches as a defender for the French before turning to coaching. He directed several club sides, including Red Star of Paris, Lens, Paris F.C., F.C. Strasbourg and Esperance (Tunisia). He then joined the French F.A. and coached France's military team to the military world championship before taking over the reins of the full national side. An assistant to Aime Jacquet when the hosts captured France '98, Lemerre guided Les Blues to the Euro 2000 title and then to the FIFA Confederations Cup in 2001.

2006 WORLD CUP

Coach Roger Lemerre felt his side can surprise someone come June. "We proved at the Confederations Cup that we can play excellent football. Tunisia can perform at a consistently high level and we are not far behind the top countries," he told **Agence-France Presse**.

The key to the Tunisians success? Lemerre said the team plays a European style of soccer. "Discipline—tactically and mentally—are very important for us," Lemerre told **www.FIFAWorldCup.com**.

Lemerre is expected to use more defensive, than attacking

midfielders to keep the score low and the North Africans in the game. The influence of French soccer on Tunisia is immense. High profile clubs such as Esperance, Club Africain, Etoile du Sahel and Club Sportif Sfaxien set up training centers and hired experienced French coaches. "There is a lot of French influence in Tunisian football," Lemerre said. "Many former Tunisian managers and youth coaches learned their trade in France."

Known as Les Aigles de Carthage (The Eagles of Carthage), the Tunisian players received a minimum $100,000 after they qualified. Of the five African sides that qualified for Germany, the Tunisians had the second best showing to Ivory Coast, which lost to champion and host Egypt in the 2006 African National Cup final. Tunisia was ousted by Nigeria in a 16 penalty-kick shootout, 6-5, after playing to a 1-1 tie in regulation and extratime.

If the Tunisians need to convert penalties for any reason in June, they could be in trouble because two of their best players missed key penalty shots against the Nigerians. Riadh Bouazizi missed his during the tie-breaker and Jose Clayton's regulation time attempt was saved by goalkeeper Vincent Enyeama.

The engine of the team is midfielder Bouazizi, who is a solid ball-winner and who can direct the attack as well. He has been called an extension of Lemerre. Defender Jose Clayton and forward Silva dos Santos, naturalized citizens from Brazil, must perform out of their skin for Tunisia to have any chance of suriving to play another day. Dos Santos will have to shoulder the burden as a dangerous forward, after his impressive haul (12 goals) during qualifying.

Khaled Badra, who captained Tunisia to the 2004 African Nations Cup title, will anchor the backine along with often-injured defender Hatem Trabelsi. The 6-foot-4, 200-lb. Radhi Jaidi is another solid man in the back.

For World Cup history buffs: After waiting twenty years to qualify a second time for the World Cup, Tunisia now has reached the final thirty-two for the third time in a row.

TUNISIA

UKRAINE
Group H

POPULATION: 43,000,000
COLORS: Yellow/blue shirts, yellow/blue shorts, yellow/blue socks

WORLD CUP HISTORY

APPEARANCES: 1st.

None.

HOW THEY QUALIFIED

The Ukraine became the first European team to qualify for the World Cup, clinching a spot on the strength of a 1-1 draw with Georgia in Tbilisi, Georgia on September 3, 2005. The tie and the fact that Turkey played Denmark to a 2-2 draw helped the Ukrainians (7-1-4, 25 points) capture the Europe Group 2 title. What made it more rewarding was that the Ukraine overcame 2002 World Cup teams Turkey and Denmark and Euro 2004 champion Greece. The Ukrainians celebrated the next day, pouring Soviet champagne over the players, who danced around in a circle celebrating in Kiev. "It is impossible to put into words the feeling and excitement about the result we have already achieved," goalkeeper Oleskander Shovkovsky told **Reuters**. "We have achieved the goal that other generations of Ukrainian footballers only dreamt of."

PLAYERS TO WATCH

Forward Andriy Shevchenko is one of the best players in the world.

PLAYER POOL

Goalkeepers: Oleskander Shovkovsky (Dynamo Kiev), Vitaly Reva (Dynamo Kiev), Vyacheslav Kernozenko (Dnipro Dnipropetrovsk). Defenders: Andriy Nesmachny (Dynamo Kiev), Serhiy Matyukhin (Dnipro), Oleksander Radchenko (Dnipro Dnipropetrovsk), Volodymyr Zezersky (Dnipro Dnipropetrovsk), Andriy Rusol (Dnipro Dnipropetrovsk). Midfielders: Ruslan Bydenko (Dnipro Dnipropetrovsk), Serhiy Nazarenko (Dnipro Dnipropetrovsk), Oleksander Rykun (Dnipro Dnipropetrovsk), Ruslan Rotan (Dnipro Dnipropetrovsk), Andriy Husyn (Krylya Sovietov), Anatoly Tymoshchuk (Shakhtar Donetsk), Maksim Biletsky (Saturn Ramenskoye), Oleh Husev (Dynamo Kiev). Forwards: Andriy Shevchenko (A.C. Milan, Italy), Andriy Vorobei (Shakhtar Donetsk), Oleksiy Belyk (Shakhtar Donetsk), Oleksander Kosyrin (Chernomorets Odessa), Andriy Voronin (Bayer Leverkusen, Germany).

UKRAINE

Goalkeeper: Oleskander Shovkovski (Dynamo Kiev). Defenders: Andriy Rusol (Dnipro Dnipropetrovsk), Andriy Nesmachny (Dynamo Kiev), Vladimir Yezersky (Dnipro Dnipropetrovsk). Midfielders: Anatoly Tymoshchuk (Shakhtar Donetsk), Ruslan Rotan (Dynamo Kiev), Andriy Husin (Krylya Sovietov Samara, Russia), Oleh Husev (Dynamo Kiev). Forwards: Andriy Voronin (Bayer Leverkusen, Germany), Andriy Shevchenko (A.C. Milan, Italy), Andriy Vorobei (Shak
htar Donetsk).

PROJECTED
STARTING
LINEUP

Former Soviet Union international and Ukraine native Oleg Blokhin has been coach since October, 2003, replacing former Soviet international Leonid Buryak, who was fired due to poor results. "Blokhin was disliked by many during his playing days simply because of his uncompromising character and he hasn't been able to shake off this perception later on," a source close to the Ukrainian Football Federation told **Reuters**. "But despite all that, he definitely brought a breath of fresh air into Ukrainian football." Named 1975 European player of the year, Blokhin scored 39 goals in 109 international appearances for the Soviets. He resigned as Ukraine coach on March 25, 2005, claiming he could not combine his job as a Ukrainian parliament member with coaching the national team. But the Appeal Court in Kiev, ruled that he could do both jobs. The Ukrainian constitution bars deputies from holding other jobs. But Bolkhin has received no financial gain from coaching. "I would like to thank the court for its objective and fair ruling in my case," Blokhin was quoted by **Reuters**. Born on November 15, 1952, Blokhin, the Soviet Union's national championship all-time goal leader (211) and appearance leader (432), led Dynamo Kiev to the Cup Winners Cup titles in 1975 and 1986, and to the Russian championship eight times. He performed for Russia in the 1982 and 1986 World Cups and at Euro '88 and became the first Soviet player to play abroad in 1988 with Vorwaerts Steyr (Austria), moving on to Aris (Greece). Blokhin coached Olympiakos, PAOK and Ionikos in Greece. He was elected to Ukraine's parliament—Verkhovna Rada—in 2002.

COACH

UKRAINE

With all due apologies to that classic television show, Newhart, coach Oleg Blokhin might introduce his front line this way: "This is my striker Andriy, and this is my other striker Andriy, and this is yet my other striker Andriy." No, Blokhin doesn't repeat himself too often. His three front men are all named Andriy. That's Andriy Voronin from Bayer Leverkusen (Germany), Andriy Vorobei from Shakhtar Donetsk (Ukraine) and Andriy Shevchenko of A.C. Milan (Italy).

2006
WORLD CUP

Undoubutedly the star of the three Andriys is Shevchenko, whose reputation precedes him as one of the most dangerous strikers in the world. Shevchenko is the entire package. He can run fast. He has great vision. His skills on the ball are amazing, especially in tight quarters. And his strength and shot are formidable. Put them all together and you have an incredible scoring machine.

Shevchenko, 29, the 2004 European football player of the year, has scored 28 goals in 63 international appearances through the winter of 2006. He also had tallied 19 times in his first 22 matches for A.C. Milan during the 2005-06 season.

But it goes to show that even having one of the best players in the world doesn't necessarily mean a country is a shoo-in for any tournament. Remember, the Ukraine failed to reach the last four major tournaments—the 1998 and 2002 World Cups and Euro 2000 and 2004.

"There is no point in building an entire team around Andriy Shevchenko," Blokhin told **Reuters**. "This team needs backbone and Shevchenko can only put the finishing touches on it. We simply don't have enough players. There are, for instance, no proper right-sided defenders."

While it is difficult to portray soccer as a one-man show, the Ukraine's notoriety and attack, like it or not, might be the closest thing to it. Not too many people outside of the country know of anyone else but Shevchenko, who can change the course of a game with one well-timed strike of his foot.

There are a number of able-bodied performers, such as midfielder Ruslan Rotan, who scored several important qualifying goals, including the lone one in the vital 1-1 tie with Denmark.

Blokhin likes to use a 4-2-1-1-2 formation. That starts with four defenders, two holding midfielders in front of them, an attacking midfielder, a deep-lying forward and two strikers.

There are, however, some question marks. The midfield could very well buckle against quality sides. Goalkeeper Olexander Shovkovsky missed two months of Dynamo Kiev's season with a broken collarbone after colliding with an opponent during a club friendly against FK Moscow. Shovkovsky, who played every minute of the Ukraine's 12 qualifiers, needed to get himself back in form for June or risk leaving the team without an experienced international goalkeeper.

Bolkhin is a disciplinarian and refuses to take anything from players who don't follow the rules. For example, midfielder Oleksander Rykun failed to stick to a training regime. Blokhin dumped Rykun from the team along with his three Dnipro teammates after they returned drunk and missed the curfew.

In November, 2004, three players—Alexander Zotov, Viacheslav

Checher and Serhiy Zakarlyuka—were sent home for reporting for duty to the National Team in the middle of the night. They were supposed to show up at 5 p.m., but arrived at 2 a.m.

Outside of a total collapse, the Ukraine should be able to reach the second round with seeded Spain and the weaker Saudi Arabia and Tunisia in Group H. After that, it could be anyone's guess.

"At this moment, we are simply not prepared to win the world championship," Blokhin said. "But we will not be whipping boys."

For World Cup history buffs: The Ukraine became the first former member of the Soviet Union (other than Russia) to qualify for the World Cup on its own in 2006.

UKRAINE

UNITED STATES
Group E

POPULATION: 290,000,000

COLORS: Blue shirts, blue shorts, white socks

WORLD CUP HISTORY

APPEARANCES: 8th. 6-14-2. 25 goals for, 45 against. 1930 (semi-finals), 1934 (first round), 1950 (first round), 1990 (first round), 1994 (second round), 1998 (first round), 2002 (quarterfinals).

HOW THEY QUALIFIED

For a country that has played in only seven World Cups and waited forty years between appearances, the U.S. has a surprisingly rich history. In the very first tournament in 1930, the Americans, nick-named the "Shot-putters" by the French because of the size of their players, reached the semifinals before Argentina rolled to a 6-1 victory. In 1950, the U.S. lost two of its opening-round matches, but pulled off the upset of the ages, a 1-0 stunner over England. In 1994, the Americans again surprised another superior team, upending Colombia, 2-1. Despite having a man advantage for the second half of its second-round match with Brazil, the U.S. hardly attacked and was eliminated, 1-0. The less said about France '98 the better, as the U.S. finished a dismal last among the thirty-two countries. The 2002 competition in Japan/Korea, however, was another story entirely. The Americans jolted Portugal, 3-2, rolling to a three-goal advantage in the first round, beat up CONCACAF archrival Mexico, 2-0, in the second round, and lost to eventual runner-up Germany, 1-0, in the quarterfinals, knowing that a botched hand-ball call by the referee could have changed the course of the match.

The U.S. finished atop the final CONCACAF group with a 7-2-1 record and 22 points. The Americans also went 3-0-3 in the semifinal round and defeated Grenada in the second-round, total goals series, 6-2. They clinched a spot behind a 2-0 victory over Mexico on September 3, 2005 as Steve Ralston and DaMarcus Beasley scored.

PLAYERS TO WATCH

Kasey Keller is one of the best in the world in goal. Midfielder-forward Landon Donovan has a history of rising to the occasion in important matches. DaMarcus Beasley might look fragile, but he is one tough hombre. A healthy Claudio Reyna is needed to be the midfield traffic cop. Forward Brian McBride, who has scored goals in two consecutive Cups, will try to make it three in a row.

UNITED STATES

Goalkeepers: Marcus Hahnemann (Reading, England), Tim Howard (Manchester United, England), Kasey Keller (Borussia Moenchengladbach, Germany). Defenders: Chris Albright (Los Angeles Galaxy), Gregg Berthalter (Energie Cottbus, Germany), Carlos Bocanegra (Fulham, England), Steve Cherundolo (Hannover 96, Germany), Jimmy Conrad (Kansas City Wizards), Cory Gibbs (ADO Den Haag, Netherlands), Frank Hejduk (Columbus Crew), Oguchi Onyewu (Standard de Liege, Belgium), Eddie Pope (Real Salt Lake), Jonathan Spector (Charlton Atheltic, on loan from Manchester United, England). Midfielders: DaMarcus Beasley (PSV Eindhoven, Netherlands), Bobby Convey (Reading, England), Clint Dempsey (New England Revolution), Landon Donovan (Los Angeles Galaxy), Eddie Lewis (Leeds United, England), Pablo Mastroeni (Colorado Rapids), John O'Brien (ADO Den Haag, Netherlands), Ben Olsen (D.C. United), Steve Ralston (New England Revolution), Claudio Reyna (Manchester City, England), Kerry Zavagnin (Kansas City Wizards). Forwards: Brian Ching (Houston Dynamo), Eddie Johnson (Kansas City Wizards), Brian McBride (Fulham, England), Taylor Twellman (New England Revolution), Josh Wolff (Kansas City Wizards).

Assuming key players are healthy (yes, we know that's a longshot): Goalkeeper: Kasey Keller. Defenders: Steve Cherundolo, Oguchi Onyweu, Eddie Pope, Eddie Lewis. Midfielders: DaMarcus Beasley, Pablo Mastroeni, Claudio Reyna, John O'Brien. Forwards: Landon Donovan, Brian McBride.

For a detailed look at Bruce Arena, see chapter 6.

It is possible for the U.S. to play well, very well, in fact, and not make the second round. Here's one possible scenario: The U.S. loses to the Czech Republic, 1-0. The Americans rebound with in a 1-1 tie with the traditionally slow starting Italians and then defeat Ghana, 2-0. That's a 1-1-1 record and in some groups with weaker teams, that would allow the U.S. to go through. But this time that might not be the case if aggregate goals determine who moves on and who goes home.

If the U.S. does manage to advance to the second round, it would be a bigger deal than what the Americans pulled off in Korea, given the quality of their group and where the World Cup is being played. The 2002 competition was held on the other side of the world—in Asia for the first time. Teams and players took longer to adapt to the time change—some didn't at all. This Cup is in Europe, where

European teams traditionally do well.

The U.S., which traditionally has struggled in Europe, has never won a World Cup match on the continent. The Americans are 0-7 (yes, not even a draw). That doesn't mean it can't happen this time, but it demonstrates how difficult it has been.

Reaching the second round would mean a probable match-up with defending world champion Brazil.

But we're getting a bit ahead of ourselves. For the U.S., its opening-round mission is clear and simple. The Americans must finish first or second in Group E. There are no wildcard berths. Third place in Germany is an early ticket home. Second place means a match-up against the winner of Group F, most likely defending champion Brazil. Most teams—sane teams—would rather avoid the Brazilians and play either Croatia, Australia or Japan. In other words, there is very little room for error against the Czech Republic, Italy and Ghana.

To accomplish that feat, every American player must be at the top of his game in each match and be healthy. Moreover, five key players have to overachieve and dominate:

- ⊕ Kasey Keller. The veteran goalkeeper has to have a World Cup similar to that of Brad Friedel in 2002. Translated: Making big saves, playing a near perfect game and saving a penalty kick or two.
- ⊕ Landon Donovan. He's probably better playing at midfield running at people, but Arena might have to deploy him depending on who's healthy or fit. Donovan, at forward, has risen to the occasion for important encounters. He definitely has turned it on in the MLS playoffs as opposed to the regular season. Likewise in World Cup qualifiers and the 2002 competition.
- ⊕ DaMarcus Beasley. He hadn't been playing regularly for PSV Eindhoven in the Netherlands during the winter of 2006, which could affect his form entering into the May training camp. He has to rediscover that in time for June. When at top form, Beasley's devastating and dazzling runs can rip open a defense.
- ⊕ Claudio Reyna—Ankle and shoulder injuries have slowed down Reyna's progress. On March 22, 2006, Manchester City announced that Reyna had been sidelined for three 0weeks due to a separated shoulder. Assuming he stays away from injuries, Reyna will be needed in the midfield, controlling traffic with his vision, skill and experience, especially during crunch time.
- ⊕ Brian McBride. He's the U.S.'s best chance to score up front.

Fearless and determined, McBride, who turns 34 on June 19, 2006, might not be able to last a full 90 minutes every game at the international level any more (the U.S. plays three games in 10 days). It will be interesting to see how Arena uses this veteran forward, in terms of resting him late in matches. It will probably be a game-by-game decision.

As a team, what does the U.S. have to do to have a reasonable chance to reach the second round? The team not only has to play soccer, but SOKA as well. Here are four vital points:

S for stay healthy—After the starting 11, there is a drop in depth, especially on the backline.

O for overachieve—Every player must perform up to his potential and then some. The Americans cannot afford lackluster performances from anyone.

K for keep scores close—Probably the only way the U.S. will reach the second round will be through goal differential. That means every goal counts—on both sides of the field. It also means that if U.S. loses to either the Czech Republic or Italy, it cannot be by more than one goal.

A for Avoid getting beaten on the wings—The Americans' Achilles Heel was discovered during qualifying. Teams with speed, such as Costa Rica, attacked frequently and effectively on the right and left flanks. Avoiding this will be more of a challenge against difficult opposition.

A quick synopsis of the opponents:

⊕ Czech Republic—If everyone is healthy and fit, the Czechs, No. 2 in the FIFA world rankings, pose the most difficult challenge to the Americans. Peter Cech is a world-class goalkeeper. Jan Koller (knee injury) is a scoring machine. Forward Milan Baros is an equally prolific scorer. Peter Nedved might be getting on in years, but is still a midfield maestro as he competes in his final international tournament. And coach Karel Bruckner is considered a master tactician. The June 12 match-up in Gelsenkirchen certainly will be a challenge for coach BruceArena to match wits and strategy against someone who is among the world's best.

⊕ Italy—Their reputation tarnished a bit due to lackluster results at the 2002 World Cup and Euro 2004, the Italians are expected to be a hungry side wanting to rectify recent history as quickly as possible. The U.S. should not take the Italians lightly when they meet in Kaiserslautern on June 17. They are still a dangerous side and a new attacking wrinkle behind the likes of Francesco Totti (recovering from a fractured fibula) and Luca Toni. Their defense might not look to be as imposing as in the past—Alessandro Nesta is considered one of the best in the world—but it should not be underrated.

⊕ Ghana—Assuming the U.S. earns at least a point in the first two matches, a win against this African side will be a must in Nuremberg on June 22. Nowhere near as strong as the two European teams, Ghana's athleticism will pose a threat. Midfielder Michael Essien is among the world's best midfielders, though the quality around him drops off precipitously.

The U.S. has a handful of international warm-up matches from which to prepare—vs. Jamaica in Cary, NC on April 11; vs. Morocco in Nashville on May 23; vs. Venezuela in Cleveland on May 26 and vs. Lativa in East Hartford, CT on May 28. Training camp is to begin in Cary, NC. on May 9.

Two games played in Germany in March are a reminder of how fragile and precious goals and points will be in Germany.

On March 1, 2006, the U.S. edged Poland in Kaiserslatuern, 1-0, on a Clint Dempsey goal. Just as importantly, the U.S. wanted to plant the seeds for a home-field advantage in this southern German city. The Americans will play Italy there on June 17 and it certainly doesn't hurt that the Ramstein Air Force base, home to some 50,000 American soldiers and their families, is close by. Because March 1 was the only FIFA sanctioned playing date before the World Cup, the U.S. wanted to make the most of its opportunity by bringing in a team that combined its European and MLS players.

The March 22 match vs. Germany in Dortmund did not give Arena that luxury. The Americans lost, 4-1, and discovered how it felt to get their nose bloodied and pride hurt. "It is important to see this entire group together at least one time before we name our roster," he said before the Poland game.

Defender Steve Cherundolo, who plays for Hannover 96 of the Bundesliga, saw the match as a perfect barometer for the team. "Our record in Europe is not very good," he said. "These are the type of games we need to win if we want to be successful at the World Cup, which is a great way to measure where we're at as a National Team."

The defeat tied for the most goals and largest losing margin since Arena's tenure as coach started in 1998. The Americans were whipped by Germany almost four years to the day, 4-2, and lost in in Costa Rica, 3-0, in October, 2005, after they had qualified.

"It's just as important as their kick in the ass against Italy," U.S. goalkeeper Keller said. "It's as important to us as well that we're not going to walk into the World Cup thinking "Ah, we beat Norway five-nil and we beat Japan in some games and we're great and we're untouchable.' Now you've learned aagainst a tought team in the country where the World Cup is being held...Wake up. I's a reality check for some guys. That's a good thing this time, that is dosen't happen June 12."

Due to injuries and club commitmeant, Arena was unable to deploy anything close to resembling his starting 11 and it showed especialy in the second half. Among the missing were Donovan (right calf strain) and Beasly (club commitments), McBride (club commitments) and defenders Oguchi Onyewu (club commitments) and Eddie Pope (injuries). Only three players in the line-up were likely to start against the Czech Republic on June 12-Cherundolo, midfielder Pablo Mastroeni and Keller.

"We've worked real hard to build out team to where it is today, and to not prepare properly to play a game of that magnitude is a mistake, and I accept the full resposibility for that," Arena said. "If I felt that it wasn't the right time for us to play that gmae, I should have been a little bit strong in saying this is not the right time to play."

As the Poland National Team was putting the finishing touches to its practice two days prior, a helicopter swept into the area and hoverd above the F.C. Kaiserslautern practice field. As the Polish team departed for its team bus, four bulky men dressed in black, giving strangers an evil eye walked into the field entrance and walked around the pitch. Minutes later, the U.S. National team marched into the field for its 4 p.m. practice. That's what you can see of the secu-rity. What happens behind the scenes is something U.S. Soccer offi-cials won't talk about.

"I belive the security is not an issue," Arena said "I belive we have tremendous confidence in the German government about the security going well. It won't be a factor." Like it or not, it is a fact of life with the U.S. team.

The U.S. has played three World Cups in Europe-1934 (Italy), 1990 (Italy) and 1998 (France) without a point to show for its efforts in seven games.

UNITED STATES

Stadiums—Are the World Cup
stadiums ready or not?

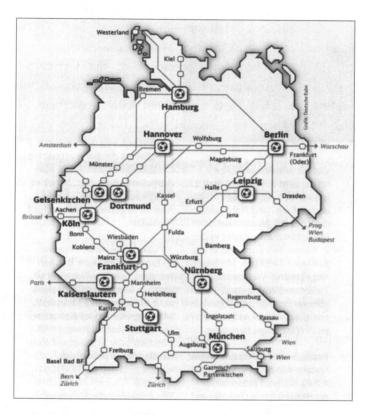

Depending on your point of view, the dozen World Cup stadiums were in terrific shape only five months before the event's kick-off or needed further upgrades for safety reasons.

Despite $1.8 billion being spent to renovate these days, the Stiftung Warentest group, a consumer group, released a report claiming that some of the stadiums lacked adequate fire safety measures and escape routes. Olympic Stadium in Berlin, site of the July 9 final, and three other stadiums were "substantially" unsafe. Eight other stadiums were called "clearly" unsafe.

For example, the Gelsenkirchen and Leipzig stadiums had substantial safety shortcomings, the group reported. It was from mostly a lack of sufficient escape routes that could result in a crush of spectators should panic break out. The group cited stairs that were too steep and obstructions in escape routes among key problems.

Fritz Walter Stadi in Kaiserslautern had entrances that were be too narrow for firefighters, the report claimed.

All but one stadium—in Leipzig—host German League matches from August through May.

Franz Beckenbauer, president of the Germany World Cup Organizing Committee, criticized the study. "The Stiftung Warentest might know what it's talking about with face creams, olive oil and vacuum cleaners, so it should stick to them," he was quoted in the Bild. "Frankly, I've had enough of these know-it-alls who are trying to make themselves important and profit from the World Cup."

The organizing committee also was critical of the report, claiming it had created a false impression that "a lack of safety exists that would require immediate intervention."

"The safety of Bundesliga spectators during the regularly scheduled matches is in no way in danger and, consequently, that goes for the World Cup as well," spokesman Gerd Graus said.

Interior minister Wolfgang Schaeble said the government would examine the group's claims. "Everything that is recognized as a problem will be taken seriously and handled as such," vice chancellor and labor minister Franz Muentefering added.

While not safety issues, there were some other problems identified as well from practical use.

Fritz Walter Stadion was closed for a few days in December, 2005 so supports could be put in place after a large crack appeared in the east stand that forced the cancellation of a Bundesliga match. During the FIFA Confederations Cup in June and at another Bundesliga match during that same year, rain poured through the roof at Commerzbank Arena in Frankfurt as massive amounts of water fell onto the field, hindering play.

CHAPTER
8

"This (the stadium problems) is trivial," Beckenbauer said. "It's being played up because people are getting very excited."

Then there was the issue of fan violence. On Dec. 4, fans interrupted a Second Division match in Dresden, firing flares and throwing other objects onto the field. Two players were hit by objects at Bundesliga matches a day prior.

Beckenbauer felt these problems were more for the German league than the World Cup. "We have to watch these matters. It is possible that the Bundesliga needs to step up security at some games," he said. "As soon as a door starts squeaking, people blame it on the World Cup. People are beginning to attribute this behavior to the World Cup. I don't see a link to it."

Only time will tell.

In an effort to be fair, German World Cup organizing officials tried to spread around the number of games so few, if any, cities would be left out in the cold. Each venue will host a minimum of five matches. That came out to four first-round encounters and at least one game in the knockout rounds (round of 16, also known as the second round, quarterfinals, semifinals, third-place match and final).

Berlin, site of the July 9 final, Munich (host of the June 9 Cup opener), Stuttgart and Dortmund have six dates apiece. The remaining eight venues—Frankfurt, Gelsenkirchen, Hamburg, Hannover, Kaiserslautern, Cologne, Leipzig and Nuremberg—get five games apiece.

CHAPTER

8

Berlin

CHAPTER 8

More than $290 million was poured in to renovate the same Olympic Stadium (also known as Olympiastadion) where Jesse Owens embarrassed Hitler during the 1936 Olympic Games by winning four gold medals.

Prior to the World Cup, the stadium's capacity was 66,021. But due to restrictive views and security purposes, the stadium will hold 56,358 for first-round matches, 56,316 for the quarterfinal and 55,562 for the championship game. A match between home-team Hertha Berlin and Besiktas (Turkey) inaugurated the stadium on Aug. 1, 2005, with Germany hosting world champion Brazil in a rematch of the 2002 World Cup final in an international friendly a month later.

One of the biggest improvements of the stadium is that more people are protected from the rain. Olympic Stadium also has hosted the German Cup final since 1985.

Berlin, the former Germany capital which gained notoriety as the focal point of and tensions in East-West relations during the Cold War due to the Berlin Wall, has a population of 3.39 million people, the largest city in the country.

Cologne

SCHEDULE

When Muengersdorfer stadium was first opened during the glory days of F.C. Cologne in 1975, it was the first and only German stadium with a roof. Some three decades later, the stadium has been renovated and modernized for the sum of $143 million.

Now called the Rhein Energie stadium, the structure was renovated and open for business over a two-year period as four stands were demolished and replaced, as was a running track. That meant spectators would be closer to the action. The new version of the stadium opened with an international friendly on March 31, 2004.

Before the World Cup, the stadium held 46,120. For first-round games, it will fit in some 35,926 spectators and 35,580 for its second-round encounter.

The Pope has held Mass at the stadium, which also has rocked to the music of the Rolling Stones.

JUNE 11
ANGOLA VS. PORTUGAL

JUNE 17
CZECH REPUBLIC VS.
GHANA

JUNE 20
SWEDEN VS. ENGLAND

JUNE 23
TOGO VS. FRANCE

JUNE 26
SECOND ROUND

CHAPTER
8

CHAPTER
8

Dortmund

Home to Borussia Dortmund of the Bundesliga, the Westfalenstadion was built for the 1974 World Cup. It needed only $67 million for refurbishment and modernization, one of the lowest costs of the World Cup stadiums.

The South Stand terraces, which is standing room for some 25,000 enthusiastic Dortmund fans, was transformed into an all-seating area for the Cup.

For the competition, it will have a capacity of 50,768 for the group-stage matches, 50,276 for the second round and 49,876 for the semifinals. The stadium can hold up to 65,982. Dortmund has a population of 590,000.

When team officials wanted to build a new stadium in the 1960's, more than 50,000 cubic meters of earth was removed. But it was not without some drama. A total of thirty-four bombs left over from World War II needed to be defused. But the finished product was hardly a bomb. When then West Germany coach Helmut Schoen first saw the stadium, he said that "there's only one football stadium better than this in the whole world, the Azteca (Stadium) in Mexico City."

Frankfurt

Called the Waldstation when it was built in 1922, the Commerzbank Stadium has been transformed into a modern stadium for a price tag of $152 million. Reconstruction began in the middle of 2002 and was finished in time for the 2005 FIFA Confederations Cup, which hosted the final between Brazil and Argentina.

Home to Eintracht Frankfurt, the stadium certainly won't set any World Cup attendance records. Its capacity is 48,132. But for the Cup, first-round games will only hold 38,427 and its quarterfinal will be less than that at 37,925.

Commerzbank Stadium boasts the world's retractable temporary roof, which was not at 100 percent efficiency during the Confederations Cup, a dress rehearsal for the World Cup. Heavy rain ripped the canopy as water poured down on photographers during the championship match.

It wasn't the first time rain grabbed the headlines at the stadium. There was the water-logged semifinal between eventual champion West Germany and Poland in 1974. The stadium also hosted the heavyweight bout between Muhammad Ali and Karl Mildenberger bout in 1966. Frankfurt has a population of 650,000.

JUNE 10
ENGLAND VS. PARAGUAY

JUNE 13
KOREA VS. TOGO

JUNE 17
PORTUGAL VS. IRAN

JUNE 21
NETHERLANDS VS. ARGENTINA

JULY 1
QUARTERFINAL

CHAPTER
8

CHAPTER
8

Gelsenkirchen

Regardless what it has been known as during its five-year history—the Veltins Arena (the current name), SchalkeArena and AufArena—all will agree that this stadium is as modern as it comes.

Veltins Arena, which was completed for $230 million in 2001, boasts a retractable roof that can open or close in only 20 minutes. It is host to exhibitions and concerts without a problem. The Arena is home to Schalke 04.

The new stadium has a smaller capacity than Park Stadion, but Schalke's fans have a number of modern conveniences, including the elimination of using cash at the stadium as fans utilize a chip and pin card. So, it shouldn't be surprising that UEFA, European soccer's governing body, gave Veltins Arena a six-star rating, a first. It normally can hold 53,804, although its first-round capacity will be cut to 43,920 and its quarterfinal size will be further diminished to 43,574. Gellsenkirchen has a population of 278,000.

Another reason why the stadium was so attractive: the project was financed privately—the public did not have to pay a cent.

Hamburg

This bustling northern port city of 1.7 million will be the home to the U.S. National Team. But by the luck of the draw, the U.S. won't play any of its group encounters in Hamburg.

JUNE 10

ARGENTINA VS. IVORY COAST

The Americans will miss out on one modern stadium that was built on the grounds of the old Volksparkstadion, beginning in March 1998. Now called AOL Arena, the stadium was the first of the 12 World Cup structures ready for use—at SV Hamburg's first Champions League match against Juventus in 2000. Hamburg, incidentally, is the only club in the 42-year history of the Bundesliga that has stayed in the top flight of the league.

JUNE 15

ECUADOR VS. COSTA RICA

JUNE 19

SAUDI ARABIA VS. UKRAINE

JUNE 22

CZECH REPUBLIC VS. ITALY

CHAPTER

8

There doesn't seem to be a bad seat in the house. According to spectators who sat in the upper deck, the view of the field was magnificent.

JUNE 30

QUARTERFINAL

AOL Arena can hold 51,055. But like the other World Cup venues, its capacity will be greatly reduced to 40,918 for the opening round and 40,442 for the quarterfinal.

CHAPTER 8

Hannover

Here's a rarity: The reconstruction of the Nieder-sachsen-stadion was completed early—it seems all we hear these days is about building being behind schedule—in December 2004. Built in 1954, the stadium has been home to Hannover 96 of the Bundesliga since 1959. The new stadium was used for the first time at the FIFA Confederations Cup in 2005.

Renovated for $77 million, the AWD Stadium will be one of the smallest capacity found at the Cup. It can hold as much as 44,652, but will have room for 34,311 spectators for the opening round matches and 33,965 for the second round.

The stadium hosted games for the 1974 World Cup and the 1988 European Championships.

Sections of the stadium's roof overhangs the field—according to Fuller's Fans Guide to German Stadiums, it seems to hover over the ground. But thanks to an ultra-violet permeable foil, the field can receive enough sunlight.

Hannover, capital of the state of Lower Saxony, is home to 525,000 people.

Kaiserslautern

Fritz Walter Stadion, named after Germany's World Cup championship captain from the 1954 competition, has been around since 1920.

Reconstruction of the stadium, which cost $58 million (relatively small change when compared to some of the others), was completed in November, 2005. Revamping it, however, was not without problems. Due to structural headaches in reconstructing the East End, Kaiserslautern could not host any games in the 2005 FIFA Confederations Cup. The ground is home to F.C. Kaiserslautern.

The stadium, which is the closest to the city center than any of the 11 other grounds, can hold as much as 43,450 fans, but like the other World Cup venues, it will be downsized due to sight lines and security purposes. So, the stadium's capacity will be 37,084 for first-round matches and 36,392 for its second-round game.

Kaiserslautern is the smallest of the 12 Cup cities, with a population of 100,000.

JUNE 12
AUSTRALIA VS. JAPAN

JUNE 17
ITALY VS. U.S.

JUNE 20
PARAGUAY VS. TRINIDAD & TOBAGO

JUNE 23
SAUDI ARABIA VS. SPAIN

JUNE 26
SECOND ROUND

CHAPTER
8

Leipzig

CHAPTER 8

Leipzig is the only city in the former East Germany that will host World Cup games. The Leipzig Zentralstadion, was built within the walls of the old Zentralstadion at a cost of $109 million.

The stadium is state-of-the-art, but there is no professional team to play in it. F.C. Leipzig once was among East Germany's top teams, but after joining the Bundesliga in 1993, it found it could not keep up with the big boys and eventually declared bankruptcy in 2004. A new club, Lokomotiv Leipzig, has started playing in the 11th division in the German soccer pecking order, at another stadium.

The old stadium, build in 1956 during Communist rule, held 100,000 spectators and was the home to many of East Germany's international matches.

The new stadium's capacity is 44,199, although it will hold only 34,384 for the first round and 34,038 for the second round.

Entering the stadium is unique. Fans must go through turnstiles, then walk up a flight of stairs and then down a flight to get into the structure.

414

Munich

Munich will wind up in the international spotlight again on June 9 as it hosts the Cup opener between Germany and Costa Rica. Instead of using Olympic Stadium, officials decided a new stadium was in order. Olympic Stadium was showing its age and the fans' sight lines weren't the best. A track separating spectators from the players and field, greatly hindered game atmosphere.

So, $338 million later, a new stadium—the Allianz Arena was completed on time and under budget in April 2005. It is home to both TSV 1860 Munich and F.C. Bayern Munich, who evenly divided the construction costs (the first Bundesliga goal, incidentally, was scored by England international Owen Hargreaves in Bayern Munich's 3-0 win over Borussia Moenchengladbach).

The Allianz Arena will be one of the larger stadiums at the Cup. It will hold 52,782 spectators for its group stage matches, 52,636 for the second round and 52,090 for the semifinal, although its actual capacity is 66,016.

The headquarters for the international media center during the competition, Munich has a population of 1.3 million.

SCHEDULE

JUNE 9
GERMANY VS. COSTA RICA

JUNE 14
TUNISIA VS. SAUDI ARABIA

JUNE 18
BRAZIL VS. AUSTRALIA

JUNE 21
IVORY COAST VS. SERBIA & MONTENEGRO

JUNE 24
SECOND ROUND

JULY 5
SEMIFINAL

CHAPTER
8

CHAPTER
8

Nuremberg

Unlike most of the other World Cup stadiums, the Frankenstadion has not undergone a complete transformation or had a new structure built on its site. Yet, despite the refurbishment and the addition of 5,000 seats, fans say it still retains its old atmosphere. In fact, Frankenstadion is one of three stadiums that will have a track around the field (Berlin and Stuttgart are the others).

The structure was renovated for $68 million as it was completed in April 2005. Originally built as Municipal Stadium in 1928, the stadium was renovated in 1991 and was renamed Frankenstadion. The home to F.C. Nuremberg, the stadium hosted three matches at the 2005 FIFA Confederations Cup.

The smallest of all the grounds, Frankenstadion can hold as much as 41,926 for Bundesliga matches. But its capacity will be severely cut to 32,341 for its four first-round matches and to 31,995 for its second-round game.

Like it or not, Nuremberg is probably better known to the general public as the venue for the trials of Nazi war criminals after World War II. The city has a population of almost a half-million (490,000).

Stuttgart

Revamped for "only" $62 million, Gottlieb-Daimler-Stadion hardly looks like the 77,000-capacity structure it was a decade ago. Built in 1933 for the German gymnastics festival, Neckar Stadium was an open bowl. A number of improvements, including a new roof and 44 executive boxes upgraded it to World Cup standards.

The stadium's capacity has been reduced from 53,200 for VfB Stuttgart's Bundesliga matches to 39,030 for first-round encounters to 38,884 to second-round games and to 38,538 for the third-place match.

The stadium has been the site of many sporting events, including Germany's first international soccer match after World War II (103,000 spectators squeezed into the ground to watch the Germans edge Switzerland in 1950), the 1974 World Cup, the European Athletic Championship in 1986, the 1988 European Cup final and the venue of the first unified German National Team (after the fall of East Germany), a 4-0 triumph over Switzerland in 1991. German coach Juergen Klinsmann made his final appearance as a player there as well in May, 1999.

Stuttgart is home to 590,000 German citizens.

SCHEDULE

SCHEDULE

JUNE 13
FRANCE VS. SWITZERLAND

JUNE 16
NETHERLANDS VS. IVORY COAST

JUNE 19
SPAIN VS. TUNISIA

JUNE 22
CROATIA VS. AUSTRALIA

JUNE 25
SECOND ROUND

JULY 8
THIRD-PLACE MATCH

CHAPTER

8

Soccer Stars—
the Best and the Brightest

Michel Plantini, France (right) against Hungary, WC 1986

The World Cup has always been a showcase of the planet's greatest talent. Presenting forty-five players and four coaches who distinguished themselves in the world's greatest sporting spectacle:

GOALKEEPER

Banks, Gordon England (1966, 1970)—He starred for the 1966 champions, giving up only three goals in six matches, including two in the final victory over West Germany. The Germans managed to neutralize Banks four years later, but not before he produced what many consider the greatest save in World Cup history, denying Pelé a goal in a 1–0 defeat over Brazil in Mexico in 1970. Pelé headed the ball toward the corner of the net and Banks, standing at the far post, miraculously knocked the ball out of harm's way with one hand. Banks, born December 30, 1937, performed for Chesterfield, Leicester City, and Stoke City in the English League and for Morton in Scotland. After an automobile accident cost him his right eye, Banks completed his playing career with the Fort Lauderdale Strikers of the North American Soccer League from 1977–78.

Teofilio (Nene) Cubillas, Peru

GOALKEEPERS

Gilmar   Brazil (1958, 1962)—He is the only goalkeeper to have played on two winning World Cup sides. Gilmar and Brazil allowed four goals in six matches in Sweden in 1958 and five goals in six games in Chile in 1962. Gilmar's World Cup record is 10–0–2. Born on August 22, 1930, Gilmar performed for the Corinthians and Santos in his native country from 1951 to 1969. He made ninety-three appearances for the Brazilian National Team.

Kahn, Oliver   Germany (2002)—Not many goalkeepers single handedly have kept their team alive in the World Cup. But Kahn did so in 2002. In fact, Kahn's performance was so stellar that Germany reached the finals, allowing only one goal—in a 1-1 first-round draw with Ireland. However, the Bayern Munich goalkeeper proved to be rather mortal in the final, surrendering a pair of goals to Ronaldo as Brazil won, 2-0. Yet, Kahn, known as King Kahn partially due to his hulking presence (6-3, 194-lbs.) has proven to be one of the most intimidating keepers around. A bench-warmer at the 1994 and 1998 Cups, Kahn took over the top spot in Germany soon afterward. He certainly had put his time in, playing some 500 Bundesliga matches with Karlsruhe and Bayern Munich and setting a league record of 736 consecutive scoreless minutes in 1999. A year later he was voted as the German player of the year and selected the best keeper in Europe. Kahn, who was born on June 15, 1969, manned the nets in Bayern's heart-breaking loss to Manchester United in the 1999 Champions League final. But he gained a measure of revenge by becoming the penalty-kick hero of the 2001 championship match.

Maier, Sepp   West Germany (1970, 1974)—Maier anchored Germany's world championship team in 1974. Maier had a thing about streaks. The acrobatic keeper set a World Cup record for keeping the opposition off the scoresheet (475 minutes) that was eventually broken by Italy's Walter Zenga in 1990, and he played an incredible 442 successive West German First Division matches from 1966 to 1979 with Bayern Munich. Maier, who was born on February 28, 1944, was also voted West German Footballer of the Year on three occasions. He made ninety-five international appearances.

CHAPTER
9

Zoff, Dino Italy (1974, 1978, 1982)—The book on Zoff in his later years was that he could be beaten by long shots, although it was a long shot to put a goal past this crafty veteran. Between September, 1972 and June, 1974, he went 1,145 minutes without allowing a goal. Born on February 28, 1942, Zoff was forty years old when Italy captured its third World Cup in 1982. He was magnificent in the nets, becoming the oldest captain on a World Cup championship team. Zoff, who starred for Mantova, Napoli and Juventus, made 112 appearances for his country. He later coached Juventus to the UEFA Cup in 1990 and directed Lazio.

Johan Cruyff, Netherlands

DEFENDER

Alberto, Carlos (1970) —Trivia question: Which position did Alberto play when Brazil took home its third World Cup title? Would you believe right fullback? That's right—the Brazilian captain, who was better known as a sweeper during his heyday with the New York Cosmos, patrolled the right side for the 1970 champions. He helped steady a defense that wasn't worked very much because Brazil controlled the ball for long periods of time. Alberto scored only one World Cup goal—the exclamation point of the tournament—the final goal in the 4–1 championship win over Italy. Born on June 17, 1944, Alberto also played on four North American Soccer League champion teams with the Cosmos, and did a year's stint with the California Surf in 1981. Alberto, whose son Carlos Alexandre was a defender for Fluminense, played in seventy-three international matches.

Beckenbauer, Franz West Germany (1966, 1970, 1974)—Before his accomplishments as a coach, in which he reached the final twice and captured one title (1990), Beckenbauer was the mainstay of the great West German machine a generation ago. That team finished second to England in the controversial 1966 final, made it to the Final Four in Mexico ("The Kaiser" played despite a painful shoulder injury) and captured the crown in 1974. Beckenbauer, who revolutionized the sweeper position by attacking from the back, also captained West Germany to the European Championship in

CHAPTER
9

DEFENDER

Garrincha, Brazil

1972 and sparked Bayern Munich to the European Cup titles in 1974–76. Beckenbauer, who was born September 11, 1945, starred for the New York Cosmos from 1977–80 and again in 1983, before returning to his homeland to finish his career with Hamburg. He made 103 international appearances.

Breitner, Paul West Germany (1974, 1978, 1982)—It was easy to get lost in the shuffle on a team that included Franz Beckenbauer and Gerd Mueller, but Breitner established himself domestically with Bayern Munich and internationally with the West German national side. Breitner is considered one of the most inventive fullbacks of modern times, excelling for the 1974 world champions with a powerful shot. Born on September 5, 1951, Breitner also performed for Real Madrid (Spain) and Eintracht Frankfurt. Breitner, who has written a controversial column for a German newspaper, often clashed politically with Beckenbauer because of his Maoist views. He scored ten goals in forty-eight international appearances, including goals in the 1974 and 1982 championship matches.

Facchetti, Giacinto Italy (1966, 1970, 1974)—Although he never played on a championship team—he was Italy's captain in the 1970 final against Brazil—the 6-foot, 3-inch Facchetti made his mark in international soccer as an attacking defender, usually from the stopper position. In fact, Franz Beckenbauer drew his inspiration from Facchetti. Born on July 18, 1942, Facchetti was the cornerstone of the Inter attack for many years. He scored three goals in ninety-four appearances.

Krol, Ruud Netherlands (1974, 1978)—He could do it all in the backfield as a standout on the flanks and as a central defender on a Dutch team that finished second twice. He was the captain of the 1978 squad. He is fluent in German, English and Italian. Born on March 24, 1949, Krol played for Ajax, Vancouver Whitecaps (NASL), Napoli (Italy) and Cannes (France). He scored twice in eighty-three appearances for the Netherlands.

CHAPTER
9

Matthaeus, Lothar Germany (1982, 1986, 1990, 1994, 1998)—He scored only four goals in twenty-five World Cup appearances, but Lothar Matthaeus's true value to Germany was his leadership ability and organizational skills on the

DEFENDER

field. As the number one midfielder, he captained the Germans to the 1990 World Championship. He later returned as a central defender to help Germany reach the second round at France '98. Born on March 21, 1961, Matthaeus set World Cup records for most tournaments by a field player (non-goalkeeper) with five and most games with twenty-five. Matthaeus starred for Moenchengladbach (Germany), Bayern Munich (Germany) and Inter Milan (Italy) for most of his career. He finished his playing career with the New York/New Jersey MetroStars in the 2000 Major League Soccer season.

Bobby Moore, England

Moore, Bobby   England (1962, 1966, 1970)—Moore, who died of cancer in February, 1993 at the age of fifty-one, was a member of three consecutive World Cup teams, anchoring the defense on the 1966 championship side. The former England captain completed a unique hat trick when he climbed the famous steps at Wembley to collect the World Cup trophy. As West Ham captain in 1964, he took the same route to lift the F.A. Cup and a year later, he picked up the European Cup. Born April 12, 1941, Moore played the central defender position unemotionally. Moore, who was named the outstanding player of the 1966 World Cup, had 106 caps.

Passarella, Daniel   Argentina (1978, 1982, 1986)—He was captain of Argentina's 1978 championship squad, the rock of a solid defense and the initiator of many of the Argentineans' attacks. He also moved up into attacking position, scoring three career World Cup goals. Passarella, born on May 25, 1953, played for River Plate, Fiorentina (Italy) and Inter (Italy). He scored twenty-four goals in sixty-nine international appearances.

Santos, Djalma   Brazil (1954, 1958, 1962, 1966)—It's almost an oxymoron—a Brazilian defender among World Cup greats? Aren't the Brazilians more famous for their attacking abilities? They sure are, but Santos contributed to four World Cup teams and two world champions as a superb overlapping right fullback. Born on February 27, 1929, Santos starred for Portuguesa, Palmeiras and Atletico Parana in Brazil. Santos, who had 101 caps, was known for his quick tackling.

CHAPTER
9

DEFENDER

Bobby Charlton, England

Santos, Nilton Brazil (1958, 1962, 1966)—Santos, no relation to Djalma Santos, played both ends of the field equally well. Whether it was keeping his cool during a foe's offensive onslaught or overlapping from his left fullback position, Santos was an impact player. In the 1958 final against Sweden, for example, Santos shut down the home team's top threat, Kurt Hamrin. He played twenty-two years for Botafogo until his retirement in 1970. Born on May 16, 1927, Santos scored three goals in seventy-five appearances for Brazil.

MIDFILEDERS

Bozsik, Jozsef Hungary (1954, 1958)—Considered the greatest midfielder Hungary has produced, Bozsik was a member of the Magic Magyars of the fifties. He usually set up the legendary Ferenc Puskas and Sandor Kocsis. Born on November 22, 1925, he starred for Kispest and Honved. He scored eleven goals in 100 international appearances.

Charlton, Bobby England (1962, 1966, 1970)—A classy man on and off the field. He was a forward in the 1962 tournament and returned as a creative force in England's quest for the trophy four years later. Charlton, one of the survivors of the horrific Manchester United plane crash in Munich in 1958, had 106 caps for England. Former England international Jimmy Greaves called his one-time teammate a "Nureyev on grass." Born on October 11, 1937, Charlton scored a record forty-nine goals for England. He is now a spokesman for MasterCard, a World Cup sponsor.

Cruyff, Johan Netherlands (1974)—Though he participated in only one World Cup, Cruyff, nicknamed El Flaco—The Thin Man—made his presence felt in West Germany, masterfully guiding the Dutch to a second-place finish. He did not play on the 1978 squad that also finished second, although observers felt if he had, the Dutch would have been champions. Born on April 25, 1947, Cruyff led Ajax to the European Cup crown three times before joining Barcelona and the Los Angeles Aztecs and Washington Diplomats (NASL). He scored thirty-three goals in forty-eight international matches. Cruyff coached champion Barcelona of the Spanish First Division.

Didi, Brazil (1954, 1958, 1962)—Another member of those great Brazilian champi-

MIDFIELDER

onship teams, Didi was the midfield architect of the 1958 and 1962 squads. The midfielder, whose full name is Waldir Pereira Didi, helped originate the boomerang free kicks, which were called the folha seca (dry leaf). When he wasn't distributing the ball to Pelé, Didi managed to score twenty-four goals in seventy-two international appearances. Born on October 8, 1928, he was injured and nearly had his right leg amputated when he was fourteen. Didi starred for Fluminese, Real Madrid (Spain), Valencia (Spain) and Botafogo. He was also a coach, first with Peru at the 1970 World Cup and later with Saudi Arabia.

Diego Maradona, Argentina

Gerson, Brazil (1966, 1970)—After a rather impressive performance in one start in the 1966 World Cup in England, Gerson—whose full name is Gerson de Oliveira Nunes—was the midfield schemer for the world champions four years later in Mexico. Gerson, who played for Flamengo and Botafogo, was not a particularly big fan of practice and reportedly smoked forty cigarettes a day. Born in 1941, Gerson made eighty-four international appearances for Brazil.

Kempes, Mario   Argentina (1974, 1978, 1982)—The 1978 World Cup was a showcase for Kempes, who connected for six goals in seven matches, including a goal in the 3–1 triumph over the Netherlands in the final. Known for his flowing hair, Kempes was equally effective at midfield or forward. Born on July 15, 1954, Kempes played for Rosario Central, Valencia (Spain), River Plate and Sankt Polten (Austria). He scored twenty goals in forty-two international appearances.

Maradona, Diego   Argentina (1982, 1986, 1990, 1994)—No player has dominated a World Cup from start to finish as Maradona did in 1986, when the Argentineans won their second title in three tries. He had a hand, or more appropriately, a head or a foot in eleven of Argentina's fourteen goals, including setting up the game-winner to Jorge Burruchaga with only minutes left. There were, however, two goals Maradona is best known for, and they both came in the same game, a 2–1 win over England in the quarterfinals, a testimony to his chicanery and brilliance. While leaping for an airball, Maradona "accidentally" punched the ball into the net. Incredibly the

CHAPTER

9

MIDFIELDER

Josef Masopust,
Czechoslovakia

goal stood. As though he was making amends for his sin, several minutes later Maradona embarked on a sixty-yard jaunt that will be difficult to duplicate. He meandered through six English players before sliding the ball past goalkeeper Peter Shilton. Maradona 9 was a hard act to follow. He performed at Italia '90 with an injured ankle and did not score a goal. He found the back of the net at the 1994 competition, but several days later he was banned from the World Cup and then from soccer for fifteen months after he failed a drug test. The tests revealed that Maradona had taken a drug cocktail of banned stimulants (he had lost twenty-six pounds over several weeks before the Cup). Maradona had a history of drug abuse, having been suspended from the sport in 1991. Born on October 30, 1960, Maradona, who has retired and unretired six times, has played most recently for Boca Juniors in his native country.

Masopust, Josef   Czechoslovakia (1962)—He was the key to the Czech attack in the team's second-place finish to Brazil in Chile. His only goal came in the final—the first goal of what turned into a 3–1 Brazilian win. Still, he was named Europe's Footballer of the Year in 1962. Born on February 9, 1931, Masopust played for Teplice, Dukla Prague, which was the Czech Army team, and Royal Molenbeek (Belgium). He scored ten times in sixty-three international matches.

Platini, Michel France (1978, 1982, 1986)—Platini actually distinguished himself more in European and club competitions, thanks to his vision and skills. He guided France to a third-place finish in 1982 after the French blew a 3–1 lead to West Germany in extratime in the semifinals. Born on June 21, 1955, Platini played in the 1976 Olympics in Montreal, and starred for Nancy, St. Etienne and Juventus (Italy). Platini, who mastered the free kick, scored the lone goal for Juventus in the team's victory over Liverpool in the 1985 European Cup final in Brussels, Belgium, the same game that saw thirty-nine Italian fans die in pregame rioting against English supporters. He scored forty-one goals in seventy-two international appearances. Most recently, Platini coached the French to a rather disappointing finish at the 1992 European Championship. He resigned

MIDFIELDER

almost immediately after the competition, and became head of the French World Cup Organizing Committee for 1998.

Gerd Mueller, West Germany

Neeskens, Johan Netherlands (1974, 1978)— Neeskens was one of the driving forces behind the Dutch team's two consecutive second-place finishes (only West Germany has duplicated that feat, in 1982 and 1986). Neeskens scored the first goal off a penalty kick in the 1974 final against the West Germans. Neeskens, who began his professional career with Ajax, also played for Barcelona (Spain) and the New York Cosmos (NASL). Born September 15, 1951, Neeskens scored seventeen goals in forty-nine appearances for the Netherlands.

Schiaffino, Juan Uruguay (1950, 1954)—He was a frail-looking player who could dominate the game with his dribbling and passing. Schiaffino—nicknamed Pepe—scored the tying goal in the 1950 World Cup final, which Uruguay eventually won over Brazil, 2–1. He finished the competition with five goals. Born on July 28, 1925, Schiaffino performed for Penarol and A.C. Milan (Italy), leading the club to three league championships and the 1958 European Cup crown, and AS Roma (Italy). He made forty-five international appearances for Uruguay and four for Italy, before the rule was established limiting players to playing for one country.

Walter, Fritz West Germany (1954, 1958)—How great might his career have been if not for World War II? Still, it wasn't too bad as Walter, behind his exceptional vision and technical skill, captained the 1954 world champions, scoring twice in the 6–1 semifinal win over Austria. His international career got off to a rousing start in July, 1940, as Walter scored three goals in a 9–3 romp over Romania. He did not play with the National Team from 1942 through 1951 because of the war. Born on October 31, 1920, Walter played for Kaiserslautern. He scored thirty-three goals in sixty-one international matches.

Zito, Brazil (1958, 1962)—Zito, whose full name was Jose Eli de Miranda, helped make Brazil's offense-minded 4–2–4 formation click en route to a pair of world championships, behind his imaginative passing and tackling

CHAPTER

9

FORWARD

ability. Born on March 8, 1932, Zito played with Pelé at Santos and on Brazilian title teams in 1959 and 1963. He scored three goals in forty-five international matches.

FORWARD

Jose Leandro Andrade, Uruguay

Andrade, Jose Leandro Uruguay (1930)—He was among the first World Cup stars, setting up several goals behind his exceptional sklls and keen sense of position-ing for the champions in the very first competition. After starring on Uruguay's gold-medal winning teams at the 1924 and 1928 Olympics, Andrade retired from international soccer. He was coaxed out of retirement for the 1930 World Cup. Born on November 20, 1901, he performed for Bellavista, Nacional, Penarol, Atalanta and the Wanderers. His nephew, Victor Rodriguez Andrade, was a member of the second Uruguayan side to win a World Cup—in 1950. Andrade made forty-three international appearances. He died in 1954.

Cubillas, Teofilo (Nene) Peru, (1970, 1978, 1982)—Considered Peru's finest player ever, Cubillas is the only player to have scored five goals in two separate World Cups—five in 1970 and five more in 1978—thanks to an explosive shot. He is tied for sixth on the career scoring list. He played another three matches in the 1982 competition, but failed to score. Born March 8, 1949, Cubillas starred for Alianza and for the Fort Lauderdale Strikers (NASL) from 1979 to 1983. In fact, Cubillas settled in South Florida, playing for amateur teams and helping the growth of the game in his new home. He scored thirty-eight goals in eighty-eight international appearances.

Da Silva, Leonidas Brazil (1934, 1938)—Legend has it that Da Silva wanted to play without his cleats against Poland in the 1938 World Cup because the field was too muddy. The referee would not allow this and Da Silva went out and scored four goals—three in the opening half—in a 6–5 Brazilian victory. Nicknamed the Black Diamond, Da Silva's specialty was the bicycle kick. Born November 11, 1913, he must have been the original free agent as he played for eight clubs during his nineteen-year career. The seemingly endless list includes Sao Cristovao, F.C. Sun America, Bomsucesso, Penarol (Uruguay), Vasco da Gama,

CHAPTER 9

FORWARD

Flamengo, Boca Juniors (Argentina) and Sao Paulo. He scored twenty-two goals in nineteen international matches.

Eusebio, Portugal

Eusebio, Portugal (1966)—Another one of those one-Cup wonders, but again, what a Cup! Eusebio struck for nine goals in Portugal's first appearance. His most memorable performance came in the quarterfinals against an upstart North Korean side that had stunned and eliminated Italy, 1–0, and had taken a 3–0 lead over the Portuguese. But Eusebio took things into his own hands and scored four goals—including two penalty kicks—in an amazing 5–3 comeback victory. Born January 25, 1942, in Mozambique, Eusebio starred for Benfica (313 goals in 291 games) before crossing the Atlantic to lead the Toronto Metros-Coratia to the 1976 NASL title. He also performed for the Boston Minutemen and Las Vegas Quicksilvers. Eusebio, whose full name is Eusebio da Silva Ferreira, had forty-one goals in sixty-four international matches.

Fontaine, Juste France (1958)—He played in only one World Cup, but it was an

THE JUSTE FONTAINE FILE

It may be years before someone scores ten goals in a World Cup, let alone thirteen. So the record of French striker, **Juste Fontaine**, could remain for a very, very long time. In fact, only one player has scored more goals in World Cup competition than Fontaine—West Germany's marksman Gerd Mueller, who has fourteen.

Fontaine scored his goals in six matches for France in the 1958 World Cup, his only appearance in the competition.

All told, Fontaine, who was only twenty-four years old at the time, scored in all six games he played. Seven of his goals were scored in the first half, six in the second. He had two goals in the final four minutes of a match. He scored two or more goals four times. Fontaine scored eight times with his right foot, four times with his left and once with his head. Raymond Kopa helped to create five of the goals.

CHAPTER

9

FORWARD

unforgettable performance by Fontaine, who scored a record thirteen goals as the French finished third in Sweden. He had a hat trick in his World Cup debut in a 7–3 win over Paraguay, two in a 3–2 loss to Yugoslavia and another in a 2–1 victory over Scotland, all in the opening round. Fontaine, who benefited from his rapport with French midfield general Raymond Kopa, connected for two goals in a 4–0 quarterfinal triumph over Northern Ireland and one in a 5–2 defeat of Brazil. He scored four goals in the third-place match, a 6–3 victory over West Germany. Born on August 18, 1933, in Morocco, Fontaine played for USM Casablanca (Morocco), Nice, Reims and the French Army. In early 1961, at age twenty-eight, his career as a prolific scorer ended prematurely with a second fracture of his left leg. He finished with one of the best goals-per-game average in international history, connecting for thirty in twenty-one appearances.

Garrincha, Brazil (1958, 1962, 1966)—His left leg was shorter than his right because of a birth defect, but the man known as The Little Bird was a big man when it came to the World Cup, standing out on two championship teams. While Pelé received many of the international accolades, Garrincha was known to tear a defense apart with his incredible runs and skills down the wing. After his teammates begged the coach to play him in Sweden in 1958, Garrincha did not disappoint, creating Brazil's first two goals in the championship match. He scored five World Cup goals. Born Manoel dos Santos Francisco on October 28,

---

A quick breakdown of Fontaine's brilliance:

GAME I

FRANCE 7,
PARAGUAY 3

June 8—Fontaine started it (and eventually finished it) with a hat trick. Rumor has it that Fontaine forgot his playing shoes and borrowed a teammate's. After he converted the hat trick, Fontaine refused to return those shoes to their owner.

⊕ Goal 1—24th minute—With Paraguay enjoying a 1–0 lead, Roger Piantoni found an open Fontaine, who beat the defense with a right-footed shot. "As the keeper wasn't coming out, I just kicked the ball very hard," Fontaine was quoted in the January, 1998, edition of *Goal* magazine.

⊕ Goal 2—30th minute—A virtual duplicate of the first goal, although it was Raymond Kopa (the man who picked the U.S.'s ball out of the bowl during the 1998 World Cup draw) who was the playmaker and started a counterattack that broke a 1–1 tie with a right-footer from fifteen yards. "I accelerated through three defenders and shot from the right," Fontaine said.

CHAPTER 9

FORWARD

Jairzinho (second from left), Brazil

1933, Garrincha bounced around with several clubs, including Botafogo, Corinthians, Flamengo, Bangu, Portuguesa Santista and Olaria. He scored twelve goals in forty-one international appearances. He died in January, 1983 at the age of forty-nine.

⊕ Goal 3—66th minute—After another set-up by Piantoni, Fontaine fired a shot that Paraguayan goalkeeper Ramon Mageregger stopped, but left the rebound for Fontaine, who made it 5–3 with his left foot.

June 11—This was a heartbreaker as Yugoslavia scored in the final minute, only minutes after Fontaine equalized.
⊕ Goal 4—4th minute—Piantoni set up Fontaine, who called it "quite simply an unstoppable goal," from his left foot for a 1–0 advantage.
⊕ Goal 5—86th minute—Perhaps the most dramatic goal he had scored, Fontaine worked himself ahead of the Yugoslav defense and faked out goalkeeper Vladimir Beara with a right-footed shot to tie the match at 2–2.

June 15—One goal was enough this time. It was the game winner.
⊕ Goal 6—45th minute—Taking a pass from Robert Jonquet, Fontaine broke through a pair of defenders and scored from the

GAME 2
YUGOSLAVIA 3,
FRANCE 2

CHAPTER 9

GAME 3
FRANCE 2,
SCOTLAND 1

FORWARD

Jairzinho, Brazil (1966, 1970, 1974)—He proved to be a worthy successor to Garrincha, thanks to his speed and uncanny shooting ability. In Mexico in 1970, he became the only player to score in every World Cup match, including the final. Born Jair Ventura Filho in 1944, he played for Botafogo, Olympique Marseille (France) and for clubs in Venezuela and Bolivia. He had eighty caps for Brazil.

Kocsis, Sandor   Hungary (1954)—Kocsis, who was called The Man With The Golden Head, led the 1954 World Cup with eleven goals, including a couple of headers in overtime in Hungary's 4–2 semifinal victory over Uruguay. His seven hat tricks tied him with Pelé at the top of the international list. A member of the magnificent Magical Magyars of the fifties, Kocsis scored seventy-five goals for Hungary. Born September 21, 1928, Kocsis led the Hungarian League in scoring on three occasions, playing with Honved and as a member of Hungary's 1952 gold-medal winning team. He also performed with Young Boys Berne (Switzerland) and Barcelona (Spain). He played sixty-eight international matches. He died in 1978.

right side with his right foot for a 2–1 lead that France never relinquished.

GAME 4
FRANCE 4,
NORTHERN
IRELAND 0
QUARTERFINAL

June 19—He struck within an eight-minute span in the second half that turned a close game into a rout.

⊕ Goal 7—56th minute—He headed home a right-wing cross by Armand Penverne, his only header of the tournament to raise France's lead to 2–0.

⊕ Goal 8—64th minute—On a throw-in by Kopa, Fontaine said he pretended that he would kick with his right foot, only to score with his left to give the French some breathing room.

GAME 5
BRAZIL 5,
FRANCE 2
SEMIFINAL

June 24—While Fontaine could only find the back of the net once, this was a game for a 17-year-old named Pelé, who struck three times within a twenty-minute span in the second half.

⊕ Goal 9—8th minute—It was the first goal the Brazilian had allowed in the competition. Goalkeeper Gilmar tackled Fontaine, who regained his balance and shot with his left foot into an empty net that tied the match at 1–1.

CHAPTER
9

FORWARD

Juste Fontaine, France

June 28—This was one of the great performances in Cup history, the only time a player had scored four goals in a Final Four match.

⊕ Goal 10—16th minute—The hard-working Kopa passed the ball to Fontaine, who said, "I only had to help the ball into the back of the net." He called the goal off his right foot, which gave France a 1–0 bulge, "by far the easiest of the thirteen goals."

⊕ Goal 11—36th minute—This one was scored during a scramble after a corner kick. French defender Andre Lerond kicked the ball into a pack and Fontaine, with his right foot, managed to place the ball through "a forest of German legs" for a 3–1 advantage.

⊕ Goal 12—78th minute—Fontaine faked a pass to Maryan Wisnieski on the right side, which allowed him to race in on the goal by himself to score another right-footer for a 5–2 lead.

⊕ Goal 13—89th minute—With the score out of hand and German goalkeeper Kwiatkowski losing interest, Fontaine completed his amazing run, forcing the keeper to come out of the goal and scoring with his right foot with twenty seconds remaining.

GAME 6

FRANCE 6,
GERMANY 3
THIRD-PLACE

CHAPTER
9

FORWARD

Meazza, Giuseppe Italy (1934, 1938)—The brilliant, elusive forward starred for the Italians' back-to-back champion teams, captaining the 1938 side. He scored twice in 1934 and once in 1938. Born on August 23, 1910, Meazza played for Ambrosiana, A.C. Milan, Juventus, Atalanta and Inter Milan, collecting 261 goals in 443 league matches. Stadio Meazza, home of both Milan sides, was named after him. He scored thirty-three goals in fifty-three international appearances. He died in 1979.

Mueller, Gerd West Germany (1970, 1974)—Just the mention of his nickname—Der Bomber—would make opponents quake in their cleats. And why not? He finished with a career record fourteen goals over two tournaments. In Mexico in 1970, Mueller led everyone with ten goals, including consecutive hat tricks, which earned him European Footballer of the Year honors. He also led the continent twice in scoring to capture the Golden Boot. Mueller, who eventually went on to play for the Fort Lauderdale Strikers (North American Soccer League), did not look like a classic striker—many clubs thought he was too short and too stocky. Tell that to opposing goalkeepers. He finished with 628 goals. Born November 3, 1945, Mueller scored a German record sixty-eight times in only sixty-two appearances.

Pelé, Brazil (1958, 1962, 1970)—The man who was born on October 23, 1940 as Edson Arantes do Nascimento is the only player to have performed for three

---

THE PELÉ FILE

There is no question that Pelé is the greatest soccer player. His performance in the World Cup underscores that:

*He is the only player to have played on three World Cup champions.

*He scored twelve goals in fourteen matches, making him third on the all-time list behind Germany's Gerd Mueller, who scored fourteen goals in two Cup appearances and France's Juste Fontaine, who recorded thirteen goals in only one Cup.

*Brazil was 8–0 whenever Pelé scored a goal and was 12–1–1 when he was in the lineup. The only blemishes were a scoreless tie with Czechoslovakia in 1962 and a 3–1 loss to Portugal in 1966.

*Pelé played in all of Brazil's matches only once—in 1970.

A breakdown of the World Cup goals he has scored:

1958 (Sweden)

June 15 (opening round)—Brazil 2, Soviet Union 0 (no goals)
June 19 (quarterfinals)—Brazil 1, Wales 0 (one goal)

FORWARD

Pelé, Brazil

June 24 (semifinals)—Brazil 5, France 2 (three goals)
June 29 (final)—Brazil 5, Sweden 2 (two goals)

1962 (Chile)
May 30 (opening round)—Brazil 2, Mexico 0 (one goal)
June 2 (opening round)—Brazil 0, Czechoslovakia (no goals)
June 12 (opening round)—Brazil 2, Bulgaria 0 (one goal)
June 19 (opening round)—Portugal 3, Brazil 1

1970 (Mexico)
June 3 (opening round)—Brazil 4, Czechoslovakia 1 (one goal)
June 7 (opening round)--Brazil 1, England 0 (no goals)
June 10 (opening round)--Brazil 3, Romania 2 (two goals)
June 14 (quarterfinals)--Brazil 4, Peru 2 (no goals)
June 17 (semifinals)--Brazil 3, Uruguay 1 (no goals)
June 21 (final)--Brazil 4, Italy 1 (one goal)

CHAPTER
9

FORWARD

Dino Zoff, Italy

world champions. He is considered the greatest player to have played the game because of his prolific scoring ability, artistry leading up to the goal and ability to set up his teammates. Pelé, who stole the spotlight when he strolled onto the international stage with a sterling performance as a 17-year-old in Sweden in 1958, scored twelve goals in fourteen matches for Brazil. Although he missed most of the 1962 tournament in Chile (scoring once in two games) because of an injury and was butchered for most of the 1966 competition in England (one goal in two games), Pelé bounced back with a brilliant individual performance in the 1970 Cup in Mexico (four goals in six matches). He played nineteen years for Santos, then joined the New York Cosmos (NASL) in a multi-million dollar deal for three years starting in 1975. Pelé finished his career with 1,281 goals in 1,363 matches. He scored ninety-seven times in 111 international appearances. Although he performed for three champions, Pelé participated in only one qualifying series because Brazil automatically qualified twice as the defending champion. His qualifying appearance occurred in 1969, for the 1970 World Cup in Mexico. The Black Pearl played in six matches during that run, scoring as many goals, as Brazil defeated Colombia, Venezuela and Paraguay, outscoring its foes, 23–2. Pelé was not the top scorer for the Brazilians—Tosato was, connecting for ten goals.

Romario, Brazil (1990, 1994)—Months before the 2002 World Cup, many Brazilian fans clamored for the return of Romario to the National Team. But his age at the time—thirty-six—probably would have limited his effectiveness and made it a long shot for him to recapture his past glory. Supporters obviously remember his contributions to Brazil's 1994 world championship team. A lethal finisher, Romario scored a team-high five goals in seven matches, failing to find the back of the net only against the U.S. and Italy in the final. Born Romario de Douza Faria on January 29, 1966, Romario always had a nose for the goal no matter where he performed. He relied on quickness and an ability to get behind

FORWARD

defenders and bring long passes under control. Two years after the World Cup, he scored sixty-three goals in one year, demonstrating that someone in his thirties could still be a valuable player. Romario, who played for Barcelona (Spain), PSV Eindhoven (Netherlands) and Flamengo and Vasco da Gama (Brazil), was a member of the 1990 and 1994 Cup teams, but injuries limited him to only one game in 1990.

Puskas, Ferenc Hungary, Spain (1954, 1962)—Was there ever a player with a better left foot than Puskas? The Galloping Major, as English fans dubbed him, was a vital part of the Magical Magyars of the fifties. He helped Hungary reach the final of the 1954 World Cup in Switzerland, only to see his side lose, 3–2. Puskas might be partly to blame for the defeat because he had insisted on playing although he was not fully recovered from an ankle injury. He had four goals in that tournament. After defecting to Spain because of the Hungarian Revolution in 1956, Puskas went on to star for Real Madrid (242 goals in 269 matches), played for Spain in the 1962 World Cup, and for the Vancouver Royals (National Professional Soccer League). Born April 2, 1927, Puskas scored eighty-five goals in eighty-four international matches.

Ferenc Puskas, Hungary, Spain

Rivelino, Roberto Brazil (1970, 1974, 1978)—He scored three times for the 1970 champions, then captained a pair of teams that fell short in the next two tournaments. Rivelino, who had one of the strongest shots around, also scored another three goals in 1974. Born on January 1, 1946, Rivelino performed for the Corinthinians, Sao Paulo, Fluminese and Hillal Al Riyad

CHAPTER
9

FORWARD

(Saudi Arabia). He scored twenty-five goals in ninety-six international appearances.

Ronaldo (1998, 2002) Not many players have experienced the highest of highs and the lowest of lows in the World Cup. In 1998, a twenty-one-year-old Ronaldo was forced to miss the game due to convulsions. Stunned by the developments, favored Brazil sleep-walked through the game, losing to France, 3-0. In 2002, in an on-the-field resurrection of the highest soccer order, Ronaldo scored eight goals—including both of Brazil's in its 2-0 victory over Germany in the final—the most since Gerd Mueller connected for 10 goals in 1970. Ronaldo, born on Sept. 22, 1976, said that the 2006 World Cup would be his last—at the age of 29. Compared to Pele because both players

Guillermo Stabile, Argentina

performed for Brazil when they were 17, Ronaldo is a completely different player. While Pele could bedevil a defense with his magnificent runs and passes, Ronaldo has been more of a pure goalscorer using his powerful runs in the open field. Ronaldo, who has played for PSV Eindhoven (Netherlands), Barcelona (Spain) and Inter Milan (Italy), has performed with Real Madrid (Spain) since he signed a $55 million contract in August, 2002. With three more goals, Ronaldo is poised to become the all-time leading World Cup goalscorer. He has tied Pele for third place on the all-time list (12), behind only Mueller (14) and France's Just Fontaine (13).

Rossi, Paolo Italy (1978, 1982)—If you want to get technical, Rossi's contribution to World Cup folklore lasted only three games in 1982. But what a memorable three games. After sitting out for two years due to his involvement in a game-fixing scandal, Rossi caught fire in a quarterfinal round match against favored Brazil, in which he scored all of Italy's goals in a 3–2 victory. He scored both goals in the 2–0 semifinal triumph over Poland and the first in the 3–1 championship victory over West Germany. Incredibly, Rossi did not play a minute in 1986, and Italy subsequently was given the boot in the second round by France. Born on September 23, 1956, Rossi played in the Italian First Division for Como, Vicenza, Perugia, Juventus, Milan and Verona. He scored twenty goals in forty-eight international games.

CHAPTER 9

FORWARD

Stabile, Guillermo   Argentina (1930)—Stabile was a prolific goal scorer, even though he was not included on the Argentinean squad until captain Ferreira was not available. He made sure he was not taken out of the lineup, registering the first hat trick in World Cup history in a 6–3 victory over Mexico. Stabile was the tournament's leading scorer with eight goals. Born on January 17, 1906, Stabile played for Huracan, Genoa (Italy), Napoli (Italy) and Red Star Paris (France). He made thirty-one international appearances.

Helmut Schoen, West Germany

COACH

Behind every successful team there is a coach, or manager, as they say in the rest of the world

Beckenbauer, Franz West Germany (1986, 1990)—He was the first and only player to have both captained a championship team (1974) and coached a team to the world title (1990). His finest coaching job, ironically, was in 1986, when the West Germans finished second to the more talented Argentina, losing in the final with five minutes left, 3–2. Beckenbauer moved players in and out of the lineup just to reach the final.

Bilardo, Carlos   Argentina (1986, 1990)—There was no question Bilardo had an easy task in 1986 because he had the greatest player on the planet on his side. In Italy four years later, Diego Maradona was not himself, and Bilardo had to juggle twenty players in his lineup because of injuries and suspensions. Argentina probably used mirrors to get into the final, a game in which they did not deserve to be.

Pozzo, Vittorio Italy (1934, 1938)—He is the only man to coach a country to consecutive World Cup titles. Cynics will claim that Pozzo directed the Italian squad during a time when the World Cup lacked much of the luster that goes with it today, but try winning successive championships at the international level. Italy was 65–15–17 during Pozzo's reign. Pozzo, incidentally, helped form the Torino Club, studied in England and directed Italy in the 1936 Olympics. He died on December 21, 1968.

CHAPTER

9

Schoen, Helmut   West Germany (1966, 1970, 1974, 1978)—Just keeping a job for one World Cup is difficult enough. Schoen coached the West Germans to the 1966 final against host England, to the semifinals in Mexico in 1970 and finally to the world championship in 1974. Born on September 15, 1915, Schoen made sixteen international appearances as a player.

CHAPTER

9

Matches

—the Most Memorable, the Most Forgettable

The best thing about the World Cup is the memories it has generated, the outstanding performances, the beautiful goals and the unforgettable matches. With that in mind, here is a list of the top fifteen games together with the eleven ones to forget if you can—they will be remembered as long as the sport is played.

Franz Beckenbauer clearing the ball

THE MOST MEMORABLE

United States 1, England 0

June 29, 1950

Belo Horizonte, Brazil

Has there been a more stunning result in World Cup history? When the score appeared on the wire services, editors thought it was a mistake, that a one had been dropped off the English score. Some fifty-two years later, however, it is considered by many experts to be the greatest victory in U.S. soccer history, if not the greatest upset in World Cup history.

"There never has been an upset of that measure," U.S. defender Harry Keough said.

The American team was made up of European immigrants and a handful of native-born citizens, and was considered to be a heavy underdog.

"We went into the game hoping to keep the score down," U.S. goalkeeper Frank Borghi said.

The English pounded away at the American goal, but could not score. The game's only goal was scored by Haitian native Joe Gaetjens, who headed home a long pass by Walter Bahr in the 37th minute. Not surprisingly, some critics and embittered English fans claimed the ball hit Gaetjens rather than the forward hitting the ball. But the goal stood.

As it turned out, Gaetjens was not a U.S. citizen at the time—he had a Haitian passport. Under current World Cup rules, Gaetjens would not have been eligible to play for the U.S.

"We shouldn't have played," said the late Joe Maca, who was a U.S. resident but a Belgian citizen. "At that time they didn't ask any questions. Now in order to play for a national team, you have to be full-fledged citizen. If we hadn't beaten England, no one would have said anything. "It was like the Yankees losing to an amateur team."

West Germany 3, France 3

(Germany advanced on penalty kicks, 5–4)

July 8, 1982

Barcelona, Spain

Someone had to lose in what perhaps was the greatest World Cup game played—if you counted the drama, the quality of both teams, and what was at stake: a place in the finals.

"Surely, it was the craziest match I ever played," said West German star Karl-Heinz Rummenigge, one of the heroes.

The Germans connected in the 18th minute on Pierre Littbarski's goal but the French equalized on Michel Platini's penalty kick in the 27th minute after Dominique Rocheteau was held back by Bernd

Chapter Ten: **Matches**

Forester. He kissed the ball—soccer's version of the French kiss—placed it down and then booted it past goalkeeper Toni Schumacher.

The game remained tied until twelve minutes into the second half when a controversial play changed the course of the match. French substitute Francois Battiston raced into the German end and fired a shot that missed the net by inches. Still in stride, Battiston was leveled by Schumacher. Battiston was replaced by Christian Lopez, and Schumacher remained in the game, although many observers felt that the goalkeeper should have been red-carded. Others claimed the collision wasn't intentional. The Germans were able to play at even strength into extratime.

If this had been sudden death, the match would have been over after Marius Tresor scored off a volley for France two minutes into the first extra period. Teammate and midfielder Alain Giresse connected several minutes later and the French seemingly had a commanding 3–1 advantage.

There were twenty-two minutes remaining, plenty of time for a German miracle. The thrust toward victory began in the first extra time when Rummenigge, who did not start because of a leg injury, was inserted into the match after France's first extra-time goal.

It worked. Rummenigge cut the margin to a goal in the 102nd minute and Klaus Fischer equalized in the 107th minute, so, for the first time in the World Cup, a match—a semifinal—would be decided by penalty kicks.

Giresse led off for France, and he put his attempt through, as did Manfred Kaltz. Manuel Amoros and Paul Breitner converted theirs

England's Geoff Hurst fires in the third goal against West Germany in what is considered the most controversial goal in soccer (England 4, West Germany 2; July 30, 1966).

443

for a 2–2 tie, but the French took a 3–2 lead as Rocheteau connected and Uli Stielike shot straight at goalkeeper Jean-Luc Ettori. France was in the driver's seat, but Didier Six missed his attempt and Littbarski scored for a 3–3 tie. Platini and Rummenigge made it 4–4 to force sudden death. Schumacher saved Jean-Luc Bossis's attempt but Horst Hrubesch calmly put his shot into the back of the net and the Germans survived an incredible match.

"We had the luck immediately to score the second goal," Rummenigge said. "Secondly, I think we never have lost important games against the French National Team. Combined with that, we were physically better prepared than the French team."

England 4, West Germany 2
July 30, 1966
London, England

Traditionally, World Cup finals have rarely lived up to the hype of the entire tournament. But the British and West Germans threw away the script in an incredible see-saw match that included dramatic comebacks and controversy.

Helmut Haller lifted the West Germans to a 1–0 edge thirteen minutes the match, but Geoff Hurst tied it with the first of his three goals in the 19th minute. Martin Peters gave the hosts a 2–1 lead in the 78th minute off an Alan Ball corner kick. Hurst fired a shot that was cleared by the defense, but the ball rolled to Peters.

The score remained that way until the final minute. Jack Charlton fouled Siegfried Held. Lothar Emmerich's ensuing free kick rebounded to Wolfgang Weber, who beat goalkeeper Gordon Banks to the far post for a 2–2 tie with fifteen seconds remaining in regulation.

It was a disheartening goal for the English. Before they entered the pitch at the start of the first extratime, English coach Alf Ramsey told his team: "You've beaten them once this afternoon. Now go out and do it again."

Hurst made sure of it, scoring what proved to be a controversial goal when his shot bounded off the crossbar into the goal.

The Germans claimed it wasn't a goal, but linesman Tofik Bakhramov, of the Soviet Union, ruled the ball had crossed the line and the goal stood.

"I believe the goal was in," Hurst said in 1993. "When you played in the final, you believed the goal was in . . . I don't think anyone has proved the goal didn't cross the line. It is one of the most controversial moments in world sports. It is still talked about today."

Hurst connected for his third goal in the waning minutes to become the first and only player to have scored three goals in a World Cup championship game.

North Korea 1, Italy 0
July 19, 1966
Middlesbrough, England
and

Joe Gaetjens' header passes English goalkeeper Bert Williams to score the lone goal in one of the biggest upsets in soccer history (U.S. 1, England 0; June 29, 1950).

Portugal 5, North Korea 3

July 23, 1966

Liverpool, England

Another David vs. Goliath encounter.

The entertaining North Koreans ran circles around the heavily favored Italians. Their efforts and hard work paid off in the 43rd minute, when Pak Seung-zin beat Giovanni Rivera on a clearance and headed the ball toward the goal. Pak Doo Ik got the ball at the edge of the area and scored from fifteen yards for what turned out to be the only goal of the game.

The Italians returned home disgraced and were pelted with vegetables at the Rome airport.

The North Koreans? They had to wait twenty-four hours before discovering if they had qualified for the quarterfinals—thanks to the Soviet Union's 2–1 win over Chile—where they met heavily favored Portugal. Twenty-four minutes into quarter finals, it appeared the North Koreans were headed toward yet another upset, holding a 3–0 advantage. But the great Eusebio picked this day to score four goals, in the 27th, 42nd, 55th and 58th minutes—two via penalty kicks— Jose Augusto added a fifth goal—to lead a stirring comeback en route to a 5–3 Portuguese victory.

North Korea has never been heard from again in serious international soccer.

England 3, Cameroon 2

July 1, 1990

Naples, Italy

Cameroon, the saviors and darlings of Italia '90, came close to pulling off a stunning result. In a World Cup devoid of goals and memorable moments, this match stood out. It had a little bit of everything—a flair for the dramatic, heroics, lead changes and even goals in a tournament starved for excitement.

Two of the goals were by striker Gary Lineker—the last a penalty kick in the first extratime period—and they put England into the semifinals for only the second time.

"We pulled it out of the fire," England Coach Bobby Robson said.

Cameroon had enjoyed a 2–1 lead in the hard-fought match with seven minutes remaining in regulation in front of 55,205 at Stadio San Paolo as its not-so-secret weapon, 38-year-old substitute Roger Milla (four goals), set up goals by Emmanuel Kunde and Eugene Ebwelle. "At one time I thought we were on the plane home," Robson said.

It was up to Lineker to pull his teammates off that plane, even though he was in the midst of a miserable World Cup, having injured a toe by kicking a Dutch player earlier in the tournament.

In the 83rd minute, Lineker was tripped in the penalty area by defender Benjamin Massing. He converted his kick, beating goalkeeper Thomas N'Kono to the lower right for a 2–2 tie.

As time was running out in the first extra period, Lineker broke in alone on N'Kono, who tripped him for another penalty. This time the striker placed the ball into the middle while N'Kono dived to his right.

Uruguay 2, Brazil 1

July 16, 1950

Rio de Janeiro, Brazil

This is just another example of a soccer team counting its soccer trophies and winners' medals before they are handed out.

As hosts of the 1950 World Cup, Brazil was considered the overwhelming favorite—1–10 by the oddsmakers—to capture its first world championship. The 1950 World Cup, the first since 1938, had an unusual set up. Instead of having a planned game, four teams were placed in a final-round group—Brazil, Uruguay, Sweden and Spain.

As it turned out, the two leading point-getters, Brazil and Uruguay, played in the final match. The hosts led with a 2–0–0 mark and four points and needed only a tie, while the Uruguayans (1–0–1; 3 points) needed a victory.

A World Cup-record crowd of 199,854 packed newly built Maracana Stadium (the world's largest) for one big celebration party. There was one roadblock—Uruguay, the first champions in 1930, had other ideas.

The Brazilians went out and attacked, but could not penetrate Uruguay's solid defense in the scoreless first half. Only two minutes into the second half, Friaca scored off an Ademir feed for a 1–0 lead.

Instead of playing more defense—coach Flavio Costa had ordered Jair to drop back on defense, but the instructions never reached him—Brazil continued to attack.

Uruguay leveled the score in the 66th minute as Alcide Elgardo Ghiggia connected off a pass from captain Obdulio Varela. With the Brazilian defense expecting Ghiggia to center another pass, the right winger ran toward the goal and beat goalkeeper Moacyr Barbosa to the near post.

The Brazilian fans took the loss hard, crying in the stadium and on the streets of Rio.

Brazil 3, Netherlands 2

July 9, 1994

Dallas, Texas

This match got better as it went on. Even though it was a score-less tie at halftime it seemed that both teams would break out in the second half at the Cotton Bowl. And they did, scoring five goals in twenty-nine minutes, including a dramatic and marvelous game-winner by Brazilian defender Branco, who was only playing because teammate Leonardo was suspended for the rest of the World Cup. (His elbow had fractured the skull of U.S. midfielder Tab Ramos in a 1-0 second-round win.)

The Brazilians grabbed a 2-0 advantage behind goals by Romario (52nd minute) and Bebeto (63rd)—a controversial goal the Dutch claimed was offside (the ball floated over the head of Romario, who appeared to be in an offside position) that Bebeto celebrated with his famous cradle rock with teammates, commemorating the birth of his child.

"Everybody could see it was offside," Dutch coach Dick Advocaat said. "This shouldn't happen at such a level."

The Dutch, however, refused to give up. They equalized as Dennis Bergkamp (64th) and Aron Winter (77th) found the back of the net.

Finally, Branco fired home a brilliant twenty-five-yard free kick in the 81st minute to break the score. Brazil managed to hold on to win a game for the ages.

An interesting footnote: Branco went on to play for the New

Chapter Ten: **Matches**

York/New Jersey MetroStars during the 1997 Major Lague Soccer season. While he was dangerous in free-kick situations—he scored a marvelous goal off a low line drive from a free kick against the Dallas Burn in the U.S. Open Cup quarterfinals—his conduct in other situations was disastrous. Branco was red-carded a league-record three times in eleven games, including a spitting incident involving U.S. international defender Mike Lapper in a vital game late in the season.

Czech goalkeeper Karel Burket is about to save a Brazilian shot during the replay of the "Battle of Bordeaux," (Brazil 1, Czechoslovakia 1; June 12, 1938).

Netherlands 2, Argentina 1
July 4, 1998
Marseille, France

An exhilirated Dennis Bergkamp laid on his back outside of the Argentine penalty area with his hands stretched toward the heavens as though he was thanking the great soccer god in the sky.

He could have been giving thanks to teammate Frank DeBoer as well, it was DeBoer's precision, 50-yard pass that set up Bergkamp on the winning goal with thirty-two seconds remaining on July 4 to give the Dutch a 2-1 triumph in this July 4 firecracker of a quarterfinal.

In the 12th minute, Bergkamp's diving header set up Patrick Kluivert's goal. But the Argentines tied it six minutes later as Claudio Lopez converted a two-man break from twelve yards. He celebrated by pulling up his jersey to reveal an undershirt that read, "*Felize*

Cumple Viejo"—Happy Birthday Father.

After a furious start, the game slowed down. The Argentines seemingly had an advantage when Dutch defender Arthur Numan was red-carded in the 77th minute. But playmaking midfielder Ariel Ortega, wearing Diego Maradona's famed No. 10 (which must have explained his utter brilliance and occassional madness), was ejected for head-butting goalkepeer Edwin Van Der Sar in the penalty area eleven minutes later. Silent since his assist, Bergkamp trapped DeBoer's on-target cross, took a couple of steps around defenders and placed a twelve yard shot past goalkeeper Carlos Roa on the right side.

Argentina 2, England 2
(Argentina advances on penalties, 4-3)
June 30, 1998
St. Etienne, France

In their first Cup encounter since Diego Maradona's "Hand of God" goal in 1986, it came down to the quick hands of goalkeeper Carlos Roa, who made a pair of saves in the penalty-kick shootout in a second-round confrontation in St. Etienne, France on June 30, 1998.

Roa stopped midfielder Paul Ince and dived to his left to deny David Batty to clinch the shootout win, 4-3, after playing a one hundred twenty minute nail-biter that ended in a 2-2 draw.

The loud and passionate crowd at Le Stade de Geoffroy-Guichard was rewarded with one of the most entertaining and intense matches of France '98, which had plenty of heroics and plot twists. "Our never-ending battle was finally rewarded," said midfielder Juan Sebastian Veron, who converted one of the penalties and scored a goal in regulation.

After the teams traded dubious penalty kicks (Gabriel Batistuta for the Argentines in the sixth minute Alan Shearer for the English in the 10th minute), this confrontation got interesting.

First, 18-year-old Michael Owen's incredible fifty yard jaunt through the Argentine defense in the 16th minute created one of the great goals of World Cup history.

Owen used his speed several times. He first to accelerated away from Argentine defenders to catch up to David Beckham's finely placed chip pass from one end of the center circle to the other as he headed toward the left wing. Owen used his vision, suddenly cutting to his right just before the penalty area to make space for himself. He then used his strength to ward off a challenge by defender Jose Chamot at the top of the box before combining his skill and poise to calmly fire a right-footed shot from ten yards into the left corner past a confused Roa.

The Argentines drew even on instructions from coach Daniel Passarella regardingon a twenty-two yard free kick thirty-eight seconds into stoppage time at the end of the first half. Instead of taking the kick, Batistuta ran over the ball and Veron shuffled it to Javier Zanetti at the edge of England's five-man wall. Zanetti fired home a ten yard shot for a 2-2 tie.

The game took a decided turn against England early in the second half as midfielder David Beckham kicked Diego Simeone while he was on the ground. Simeone supposedly saw stars, Beckham red— as in a red card. The English were forced to play the rest of the way a man down. After the Cup Simeone admitted that he added some uncalled for acting in his fall to the ground to secure the card.

West Germany 2, Netherlands 1

June 24, 1990

Milan, Italy

In a second round encounter as intense as any World Cup championship match, the West Germans outlasted the Dutch, 2-1. Neither team stopped running causing confrontation. In the 21st minute, Dutch defender Frank Rijkaard was given a yellow card for tripping forward Rudi Voeller, who received a yellow himself for arguing that his opponent deserved more punishment. On the ensuing free kick, Voeller ran into Dutch goalkeeper Hans Van Breukelen. Rijkaard came over and spat at Voeller and both were ejected by referee Juan Loustau of Argentina.

The Germans scored in the 49th minute as Juergen Klinsmann put in a left-wing cross by midfielder Guido Buchwald from twelve yards, and Buchwald created the second goal with six minutes remaining, setting up defender Andreas Brehme, who scored from

World Cup Soccer: Germany 2006

the top right of the area. The Dutch came back in the 88th minute on Ronald Koeman's penalty kick.

"Today was just not a football match between two countries," Klinsmann said. "This is one of the best matches I ever played in my life."

Italy 3, Brazil 2
July 5, 1982
Barcelona, Spain

It might be more accurate to say it was Paolo Rossi 3, Brazil 2, because the Italian striker put on one of the greater individual scoring displays in World Cup history. Every time the Brazilians came within striking distance of Italy, destiny's darlings of the tournament, Rossi would come back with a goal of his own.

Rossi, who had just returned from a two-year ban because of his involvement in a game-fixing scandal, began his amazing run of six goals in the final three matches. Rossi first struck, five minutes into the game, heading in Antonio Carbrini's cross in front of 44,000 spectators at Sarria Stadium.

For the Brazilians, who had come from behind to defeat the Soviet Union and Scotland, it was business as usual. They tallied in the 12th minute as Socrates scored on a great individual effort off a Zico feed.

Though a defensive mistake by Brazil allowed Rossi to score again in the 25th minute, Falcao tied the score in the 68th minute. Seven minutes later, Rossi hit his third goal after Junior did not clear a corner kick.

France 1, Brazil 1
(France advanced on penalty kicks, 4-3)
June 21, 1986
Guadalajara, Mexico

It was a game for the ages as two talented and skillful opponents slugged it out for 120 minutes in the mid-day Mexican heat before the match was decided by penalties.

Brazil grabbed a 1–0 lead in the 18th minute, when Careca con-

nected from fifteen yards, but the French equalized with four minutes remaining in the half on a goal by the great Michel Platini. He scored off fine passes by Alain Giresse and Dominique Rocheteau to get past Brazilian goalkeeper Carlos, who allowed his first goal in 401 minutes.

The second half featured end-to-end action, but no goals. Zico, who replaced Muller in the 70th minute, had a grand opportunity to put the Brazilians in front with a penalty kick in the 74th minute, but goalkeeper Joel Bats saved the attempt.

Then came the drama of penalties. Socrates missed his kick and Yannick Stopyra made his to give France the lead. Brazil's Alemao and Manuel Amoros traded kicks. The Brazilians drew even when Zico converted his kick and France's Bruno Bellone fired his try off the post. Platini missed his attempt as did Julio Cesar for Brazil. Luis Fernandez ended this madness, converting his kick to win the tie-breaker, 4–3, and the French went into the semifinals against West Germany, setting up a rematch of the 1982 semifinal

Germany's Forster could deny Bossis his goal (West Germany 3, France 3; Germany advanced on penalty kicks, 5–4; July 8, 1982).

Brazil 6, Poland 5

June 5, 1938

Strasbourg, France

There were tons of goals and plenty of drama in this encounter, including two outstanding individual performances. Leonidas da Silva of Brazil known simply as Leonidas, and Ernst Willimowski of Poland, each scored four goals, the only time in which two players have each scored four times in the same World Cup match.

By halftime, Leonidas, who was nicknamed the "Black Diamond", had connected for a hat trick to give the Brazilians a seemingly safe 3–1 lead at Stade de la Meinau. In the second half, the Polish midfield took over as Willimowski connected three times forcing the teams to enter extratime tied at 4-4. (Berjum Peracio also scored for Brazil.

Leonidas and Willimowski each scored a goal in overtime. But surprisingly, the game-winner did not come from either player: midfielder Romeo settled this wild affair by scoring three minutes into extratime.

As it turned out, this was not the highest scoring match in World Cup history. Austria and Switzerland combined for twelve goals—a 7–5 Austrian victory—in the 1954 quarterfinals.

U.S. 2, Colombia 1
June 22, 1994
Pasadena, California

Just call this the day the U.S. National Team came of age. The Colombians were many observers' favorites to go far in the tournament, perhaps even winning it all. The Americans? They weren't even supposed to get out of the opening round, much less pull off an upset or two.

The U.S. had other things in mind. In the 35th minute, U.S. midfielder John Harkes powered a left-wing cross toward Ernie Stewart that Colombian defender Andres Escobar tried to clear out of harm's way, but misdirected into his own net.

The American players wound up playing the game of their lives that night at the Rose Bowl, denying the Colombians serious penetration in their defensive zone. Stewart gave the U.S. some breathing room at 2-0, turning a lead pass by Tab Ramos into a goal in the 52nd minute before Adolfo Valencia cut the lead in half in the waning minutes. U.S. defender Marcelo Balboa, who cleared a shot off the line by Colombian forward Antony De Avila (who played with the New

York/New Jersey MetroStars in 1996 and 1997) that bounced off American midfielder Mike Sorber, almost scored on a spectacular bicycle kick with minutes remaining in the match. When referee Fabio Baldas—who caused the game to be delayed for several minutes early on after he changed from a silver-grayish shirt to a purple one so he wouldn't be confused with the denim blue and white worn by the U.S.—signalled the game was over, many of the American players grabbed flags and ran around the stadium in patriotic fervor. The U.S. National Team went on to qualify for the second round, losing to eventual champion Brazil, 1-0, on July 4. The humiliated Colombians were eliminated after three games and went home in disgrace. Escobar's fate turned out to be a tragic one. On July 2, he was gunned down outside a nightclub in Medellin, Colombia.

FORGETTABLE GAMES

It seems for every great game there are a dozen clunkers. In fact, here are examples of eleven games World Cup officials and fans would rather not remember.

Hungary 4, Brazil 2
June 27, 1954
Berne, Switzerland

The game appropriately is called the Battle of Berne; and everyone thought the Swiss were neutral. Think again when it comes to World Cup soccer.

This might have been the most disgraceful World Cup game ever played. There were forty-two free kicks, which meant there were a minimum of forty-two fouls called (no telling how many fouls were not whistled because of the advantage rule), three ejections, two penalty kicks and a locker room fight in a quarterfinal match played before a crowd of 40,000 at Wankdorf Stadium.

The game started to unravel in the opening minutes as Hungarian defender Gyula Lorant was slapped with a yellow card by referee Arthur Ellis of England. Lorant, who laughed at Ellis's decision, was fortunate he was not given another yellow card for dissent, which would have meant his dismissal.

The Brazilians were off their game because of the wet field conditions, and it showed early on as Nandor Hidegkuti scored in the fourth minute. His shorts were ripped from his body. Hidegkuti turned playmaker four minutes later, setting up Sandor Kocsis's header.

The 2–0 deficit sparked Brazil to find its game in a match that saw both sides tackling aggressively. Brazilian Indio felt the brunt of it in the 18th minute, as he was hammered in the penalty area, which set up a penalty kick by defender Djalma Santos to slice the lead to 2–1. The score stayed that way until the second half when Ellis awarded Hungary a questionable penalty kick after Kocsis and Santos collided in the penalty area. Hungary was expecting a free kick, but was surprised when Ellis awarded a penalty. Mihaly Lantos converted for a 3–1 advantage.

The Brazilians were furious at the decision, and the game got out of hand. Julinho cut the margin to 3–2, but tempers flared as Nilton Santos and Jozsef Bozsik fought and were ejected. They needed police to escort them off the field.

With four minutes remaining, Brazil's Humberto was given his marching orders for kicking Lorant. With one minute left, Kocsis headed in a Zoltan Czibor cross for the final goal.

The game was over, but the battle continued on the way to the locker room. One story had the Brazilians hiding and attacking the Hungarians in the tunnel to the locker rooms. Another had the great Hungarian captain Ferenc Puskas, who did not play because of an injury, throwing a bottle at the Brazilians as they came off the field. Regardless of how it began, a bloodbath ensued as bottles and soccer cleats were swung in anger. Hungary's Gustav Sebes had his cheek was cut open and Ellis was escorted to his locker room by armed guards in the World Cup's lowest moment.

West Germany 1, Austria 0
June 25, 1982
Gijon, Spain

Of course, not every bad match included an ugly scenario. Some were downright boring, others suspicious.

While no one can prove that it was collusion, a 1–0 result in favor of West Germany was what each country needed to reach the second round at the expense of Algeria.

Horst Hrubesch headed home a Pierre Littbarski cross in the 10th minute and then both sides simply quit playing. Much of the game was played in the midfield before a disappointed crowd of 41,000 at El Molinon Stadium. French coach Michel Hildalgo, scouted the match, but did not take a note. He did suggest, however, that both teams be awarded the Nobel Peace Prize for their unaggressive play.

One West German fan was so disgusted with his country's performance that he set fire to the German flag in the stands. Algerian fans, who claimed the match was fixed, booed and heckled both sides. In what might have been the most aggressive action associated with the match, Algeria protested to FIFA that the game was fixed and called for both countries to be disqualified. FIFA turned it down.

Former New York Cosmos and West German World Cup star and coach Franz Beckenbauer could not believe what he had seen.

"Later many people asked me whether there had been a previous deal on the score," Beckenbauer wrote in his book, *World Cup Espana 82*. "I know this was not the case. But of course there exists in soccer something of a tacit agreement that comes about in the course of the game. What remains is an unpleasant memory. This was not a game worthy of the World Cup and it has done great harm to the prestige of German soccer."

Italian Humberto Maschio suffered a broken nose in the Battle of Santiago after Leonel Sanchez punched him (Chile 2, Italy 0; June 2, 1962).

Chile 2, Italy 0

June 2, 1962

Santiago, Chile

This confrontation—named the Battle of Santiago—started to boil over well before these two teams met. Italian journalists fired things up at the outset by criticizing the Chilean living and playing conditions. The story made it back to Chile, which was bent on revenge. The game was televised live worldwide, and attended by 66,057 at Estadio Nacional. Only eight minutes into the rough game, Giorgio Ferrini was ejected for retaliating after being kicked from behind by Chilean striker Honorino Landa. Referee Ken Aston of England red-carded Ferrini, but he refused to leave the field. Ferrini finally left ten minutes later, but not before FIFA officials and police were called in.

Some five minutes before the half, Italian Humberto Maschio took Leonel Sanchez down on a bad foul. Sanchez then broke Maschio's nose with a left hook that would have done Muhammad Ali proud. Everyone in the stadium, plus the TV audience, saw the punch—everyone but Aston, whose back was turned, and the two linesmen. Sanchez never was ejected (years later in newspapers accounts of the incident, Sanchez proudly described the punch) and even set up Chile's first goal, by Banda Ramirez in the 74th minute. Sanchez Toro scored two minutes from time.

Another Italian, Mario David, was ejected for tackling Sanchez around the neck.

Not surprisingly, Aston needed a police escort off the field, and never officiated another World Cup match.

Brazil 1, Czechoslovakia 1
June 12, 1938
Bordeaux, France

Before there was Santiago and before there was Berne, there was Bordeaux, as in the Battle of Bordeaux.

The body count included a broken leg, a broken arm, a stomach injury and three ejections in a match that was chosen as the show-piece of the opening of Parc de Lescure, Bordeaux's new stadium.

Only moments into the game, Brazil's Zeze Procopio kicked Czech forward Oldrich Nejedly for no apparent reason, and subsequently was given his marching orders by referee Paul Van Hertzka of Hungary in the quarterfinal match in front of 25,000 spectators.

There was some soccer played, too, as Leonidas da Silva connected for the Brazilians in the 30th minute. It looked as though the teams would escape the half without any further incidents when Jan

Riha and Brazil's Machado were sent off for fighting.

The Czechs got an opportunity to equalize in the 64th minute when defender Domingos—the father of 1950 Brazilian World Cup star Ademir—was called for a handball in the penalty area. Nejedly, who was still standing—he eventually left the match with a broken leg—converted the penalty.

Amid more rough stuff later on, Czech goalkeeper Frantisek Planicka had his arm broken.

The rematch—the Brazilians used nine new players, the Czechs six—had no such incidents in what was a 2–1 victory for Brazil.

Argentina 1, France 0

July 15, 1930

Montevideo, Uruguay

Actually, it was nothing the players did that made this match forgettable. Blame it on an overzealous and miscalculating referee named Almeida Rego.

Late in the second half, the Argentines enjoyed a 1–0 lead with the French threatening to score when Rego suddenly whistled the game was finished. The French rightfully protested, claiming there were six minutes left. As mounted police entered the field to restore order, Rego talked with his linesman, and it was decided there were six minutes remaining. The game was restarted, but Argentine mid-fielder Cierro fainted. The Argentines held on for the victory, but it was not without repercussions.

The Uruguayans, who attended the match, claimed that France should have won. The Argentineans, arch-enemies of Uruguay on the soccer field, complained about the game to the World Cup Organizing Committee and threatened to pull out of the Cup. The Argentineans did reach the championship match, only to lose to Uruguay, 4–2.

West Germany 1, Argentina 0

July 8, 1990

Rome, Italy

In a match hardly befitting a final, the West Germans managed to score a goal and defeat the defending champion Argentineans, 1–0.

It was a disgraceful game as the Germans came to play soccer, but most of the time were unsuccessful at it. The Argentineans came to play something, but it wasn't soccer. Argentina somehow made it to the final using mirrors, a record twenty players and an ailing Diego Maradona, who would have rather complained than play the game.

Defender Andreas Brehme converted the lone goal—a penalty kick in the 84th minute—before 73,603 fans and a worldwide TV audience estimated at 1.5 billion. They deserved better.

"It wasn't a very good final," German coach Franz Beckenbauer said. "It was just too bad the Argentines didn't participate in the game. They wanted to destroy."

Argentina acutally got within striking distance of the German goal in the 38th minute when Guido Buchwald tripped midfielder Jose Basualdo twenty yards from the net on the right side. Maradona's free kick sailed over the goal and goalkeeper Bodo Illgner, who touched the ball only once, when a teammate passed it back.

The Argentineans did get a piece of soccer history. Referee Edgardo Codesal of Mexico red-carded Pedro Monzon and Gustavo Dezotti, the first players to be sent off in a World Cup final in the 65th and 87th minutes, respectively.

The bitterly disappointed Argentineans continued to argue with Codesal after the final whistle. Argentina's coach, Carlos Bilardo, had to run onto the field to pull his players away from the referee.

The game ended disgracefully, with the Argentineans complaining to the game officials and crying.

Brazil 2, Bulgaria 0

July 12, 1966
Liverpool, England

Bulgarian midfielder Zhechev is not a name etched in World Cup lore. He holds the distinction of finding a way to stop the marvelous Pelé—injure him. He did so in the opening half, but not before Pelé fired in a free kick to become the first player to score in three consecutive tournaments. Pelé, who at twenty-five was in his prime, was taken down brutally in the first half by Zhechev. "Pelé won't finish the World Cup," a French journalist was quoted in *The Sunday Times History of the World Cup*. "It's amazing he hasn't gone mad."

Brazil and Pelé were never the same, failing to reach the next round. Without Pelé, Brazil went down to Hungary three days later, 3–1. And even with the Great One in the lineup, Brazil was not its former self, losing to Portugal, 3–1, on July 19.

France 4, Kuwait 1

June 21, 1982

Valladolid, Spain

How often does a referee reverse his decision and take a goal away from a team after the opposition complains? In the World Cup, fortunately, it does not happen very often, but it occurred in this first-round match.

With France enjoying a 3–1 lead with fifteen minutes remaining, Soviet referee Miroslav Stupar awarded the French a goal when Alain Giresse scored from in close as the Kuwaiti defenders did not move.

The Kuwaitis claimed they had heard a whistle and stopped. Prince Fahid, the Kuwaiti Football Association president, walked from the stands onto the field—which usually meant automatic expulsion—to protest and argue the decision. Kuwait appeared ready to walk off the field, but Stupar did a 180-degree turn on his original decision, upsetting the French.

By the time the matter had been settled, the match had been held up for eight minutes in front of 30,034 at Nuevo Estadio Jose Zorrilla.

The French got a measure of revenge and the goal back in the final minute as Maxime Bossis scored.

And, oh yes, FIFA slapped Kuwait with a $12,000 fine, which had to be loose change for Fahid, one of the world's richest men.

Argentina 3, Chile 1

July 22, 1930

Montevideo, Uruguay

Before there was even the Battle of Bordeaux, there was the under-publicized mini-battle of Montevideo between these two South American neighbors in the very first World Cup.

Guillermo Stabile had scored twice for the Argentineans in the opening half and Asgorga Subiabre scored for Chile before a crowd of 1,000 at Centenary Stadium. Several minutes before halftime, however, a fight broke out between the teams. It got so ugly that police had to come onto the field to separate the brawlers.

Incredibly, the second half was free from incident as both teams played soccer. Mario Evaristo closed out the scoring for the winners.

Brazil 1, Sweden 1

June 3, 1978

Mar del Plata, Argentina

When it a goal not a goal? When it is scored after time has elapsed. Referee Clive Thomas of Wales whistled the end of the match while Zico's corner kick that eventually went into the net was in the air. It cost Brazil a goal, a win, Group 3 title and quite possibly a chance to reach the championship match. Thomas Sjoberg had given the Swedes the lead in the 37th minute, but Reinaldo equalized with a goal in injury time in the opening half before a crowd of 38,000 at Estadio Mar del Plata.

That was it for scoring, although the Brazilians disagreed. As time was running out, Zico lifted a corner kick into the net, although Thomas had blown his whistle to signify the end of the match only a split second before the ball had crossed the line.

Not surprisingly, the game ended in confusion as Thomas was pelted by coins from upset fans.

Had Brazil won, it would have received two points instead of one for the draw. The Brazilians would have finished first in their group instead of Austria and been put in Group A instead of Group B in the final eight teams' quest of reaching the championship match. In other words, Brazil would have vied for the spot along with Italy, Germany and the Netherlands.

In Group B, along with Peru, Poland and Argentina, Brazil lost out on goal differential to Argentina (plus eight to plus five) for the right to qualify for the final. In their final Group B game, the Brazilians defeated Poland, 3-1, on June 21. The Argentineans, playing later in the day, knew what they had to do—score four goals and win by three goals (since then, FIFA has made sure teams playing their final game in a group kick off at the same time).

To make matters a bit suspicous, the Peruvian goalkeeper, Arencibia Quiroga, was born in Argentina.

Chapter Ten: **Matches**

One Brazilian sportswriter wrote, "If Brazil had won 50-0 against Poland, Argentina would have won 52-0."

Over the past twenty years, there have been allegations that Peru had agreed to some sort of deal with the Argentineans in allowing the hosts to score so many goals, but nothing was ever proved.

Brazil 0, Italy 0

(Brazil was awarded the title on penalty kicks, 3-2)

July 17, 1994

Pasadena (Rose Bowl), California

It just wasn't fair. After a highly memorable and scintillating World Cup, the championship game turned out to be a bust. The game was anticlimactic, even if Brazil became the first team to win the World Cup four times, its first championship since 1970.

"I'm glad our team is number one again," said Brazilian coach Carlos Alberto Parreira, who will direct Saudi Arabia at France '98. "Our mission has been accomplished."

Both teams, especially the Italians, were tired. Brazil tried to attack; Italy tried to hang on. When the Brazilians tried to attack, they could not find the back of the net. Part of that was due to the fine play of defenders Paolo Maldini and Franco Baresi, the sweeper, who was hobbled by a knee injury, and also by the fact Italy packed the back with as many as eight players before a crowd of 94,194.

The two countries battled and cramped up through 120 minutes of scoreless soccer, ninety minutes in regulation and another thirty in extratime, before sport's most unthinkable way to decide a match—the penalty-kick tie-breaker—was required.

Brazilian goalkeeper Claudio Taffarel, unemployed during the World Cup after competing a stint with Reggiana (Italy), had had to make only twelve saves in six games entering the match. Ironically, he wound up saving the tie-breaker. "There's a lot of luck involved," he said. "Penalty kicks are like a lottery and nobody likes to arrive at a penalty-kick decision."

"We had such great confidence that losing through penalties never crossed our minds," said Bebeto, who was set to take Brazil's fifth kick, if necessary.

It wasn't. Baresi, a surprise starter after sitting out most of the tournament with a knee injury suffered in the 1–0 first-round victory over Norway, took the first kick and blasted it into the stands. Brazil's Marcio Santos returned the favor seconds later as goalkeeper Gianluca Pagliuca blocked his attempt.

Demetrio Albertini nailed one into the upper right corner and Romario equalized, barely hitting the left post. Alberico Evani fired one into the middle of the net with Taffarel diving to his right, but Branco slotted his try into the lower right corner for a 2–2 tie. Daniele Massaro, hero of A.C. Milan's European Cup triumph over Barcelona and Romario only two months earlier, had his attempt blocked by Taffarel. Dunga, the Brazilian captain, powered his shot to the right side for a 3–2 advantage.

Up stepped Roberto Baggio, who carried Italy into the final with five goals in three games, but had been doubtful for the match because of a hamstring injury. The tired superstar sailed his attempt into the stands, incredibly ending the match on an anticlimactic note.

Brazilian players took a victory lap around the entire field. During a special ceremony, the FIFA World Cup trophy was handed to Dunga, and the party really began.

Germany 2, Cameroon 0

June 11, 2002

Shizuoka, Japan

In a perfect world, referees are supposed to be invisible men. We're not supposed to see that they are doing their job because they should fit so seamlessly into the match. There are unfortunate occasions, however, in which game officials not only decide a match, but just about become the story of the game. Take, for example, what transpired at Shizuoka Stadium.

Referee Antonio Lopez of Spain became a human version of a traffic light this misty night, handing out a record 16 cards—14 yellows and two reds. Each team was awarded eight cards, including one red card.

Lopez ruined the flow of the match because some of those yellow were just plain fouls and should not have been booted. Fortunately, it did not alter the game in that the better team prevailed that night—Germany in a 2-0 victory over Cameroon.

Incredibly, neither coach complained about the excessive book-ings, at least not publicly, in which had to be one of the most embar-rassing, if not the most embarrassing, and disgraceful performances by a referee in a World Cup match.

The game began innocently enough. In fact, there were no cards given in the opening seven minutes. But Cameroon's Marc-Vivien Foe—who would die of heart failure while playing a match at the FIFA Confederation Cup in Lyon, France a year later—was awarded the first yellow in the eighth minute. A minute later, Carsten Jancker got one for Germany.

A whole 20 minutes went by before Lopez booked Germany's Dietmar Hamann in the 29th minute and then teammate Michael Ballack two minutes later.

Once Lopez began, he couldn't stop.

A German player would foul a Cameroonian and Lopez had his yellow out immediately. On the other side of the field, a Cameroon player would foul a German and the same scenario occurred.

Carsten Ramelow saw his first yellow in the 37th minute before getting a second card—and a expulsion from the match three minutes later, fouling Samuel Eto'o twice in succession, which forced the Germans to play a man down. German captain and goalkeeper Oliver Kahn was slapped with a yellow card in the 42nd minute along with Rigobert Song of Cameroon. Bill Tchato was booked in the 44th minute.

Halftime gave everyone, including the trigger-happy Lopez a respite. But he picked up where he left off 11th minute into the sec-ond half, when he carded Cameroon's Geremi. Teammate Salomon Olembe was slapped with a yellow in the 58th minute, followed by Patrick Suffo, another Cameroonian, two minutes later. Christian Ziege (72nd minute) and Torsten Frings (74th minute) of Germany were booked in succession before Lopez finished off with a pair of Cameroon players. Suffo not only saw yellow, but he saw red in the 77th minute and Lauren was yellow-carded in the 81st minute.

Despite Lopez's breakdown, Germany managed to survive. A man down, the Germans scored in the 50th minute on Marco Bode's score. With the sides evened up, Miroslav Klose added an insurance tally in the 79th minute.

"Prior to the game there was great skepticism by the German people and the media on whether we could be successful in the World Cup," defender Christoph Metzelder said. "Tonight we demonstrated that we can do anything."

At halftime the Germans moved a midfielder back as a fourth defender and replaced forward Jancker with Marco Bode, who had played but six minutes in the Cup until then. But five minutes into the second half, Miroslav Klose found Bode on a quick pass and Bode beat goalkeeper Boukar Alioum from 12 yards on his first touch of the match. After Suffo saw red in the 77th minute, Germany took advantage. Klose celebrated his 24th birthday two days late by scoring his tournament-high fifth goal—all on headers—off a right-wing cross by Michael Ballack in the 79th minute.

"We went into the match as favorites, but we couldn't deal with that," German coach Rudi Voeller said. "But strangely enough, when we went a man down we played good football."

Cameroon coach Winfried Schaeffer warned his team how dangerous the Germans could be. "I told my players they had to work more because 10 players on the field instead of 11 tend to grow wings as they say," he said. "Cameroon did it at the Olympics. It is something that happens in the head."

The win, however, came at a great cost to the Germans, who captured the Group E title. They were forced to play Paraguay in Seogwipo, South Korea without three starters—Ramelow, who was red carded, and two players who picked up their second yellow card of the tournament—defender Ziege and midfielder Hamann (Germany managed to overcome the South Americans, 1-0).

Amazing Facts—World Cup Trivia

It will be intriguing to see if "Jeopardy!" will add a category or two about Korea/Japan 2002, in honor of the World Cup. If the game show doesn't, there is still plenty to talk about, and you don't have to put your response in the form of a question.

There's a First Time for Everything

First game: Mexico vs. France in Montevideo, Uruguay, on July 13, 1930. France won, 4–1.

First goal: By Lucien Laurent of France in the first half.

First multiple-goal game: By Andre Maschinot of France, as he scored twice in the opener.

First hat trick: By Guillermo Stabile of Argentina in a 6–3 victory over Mexico on July 19, 1930.

First penalty kick: By Mexico's Manuel Rocquetas Rosas in the 38th minute of Argentina's 6–3 win in 1930.

First penalty kick miss: By Argentina's Fernando Paternoster in the 6–3 triumph over Mexico.

First tie: Italy 1, Spain 1 on May 31, 1934, in Florence, Italy.

First replay: Italy edged Spain, 1–0, on June 1, 1934, after the first tie.

First scoreless tie: Brazil 0, England 0 on June 11, 1958, in Stockholm, Sweden.

First own goal: By Ernst Loertscher for Switzerland vs. Germany on June 4, 1938, in Paris.

First yellow card: In Mexico's scoreless tie with the Soviet Union on May 31, 1970.

First red card: Chile's Carlos Caszely for kicking West Germany's Berti Vogts (who coached Germany in the 1998 Cup) in the 67th minute in the Germans' 1–0 win over Chile on June 14, 1970.

First ejection: Peru captain Mario de las Casas by Chilean referee Alberto Warken in a 3–1 loss to Romania on July 14, 1930.

First substitute: The Soviet Union's Albert Shesterniev was replaced by Anatoly Pusatch at halftime in the 1970 opener, a scoreless tie with host Mexico on May 31.

First player to replace a substitute: Mexico's Juan Basaguren, who replaced Salgado Lopez, who had replaced Garcia Borja in a 3–0 first-round victory over El Salvador on June 7, 1970.

First player to score as a substitute: Mexico's Basaguren scored in the 83rd minute of that same game.

First substitution of a goalkeeper: Romania's Steve Adamache had to come out after an injury in the 29th minute of a 3–2 loss to Brazil on June 10, 1970. He was replaced by Necula Raducanu.

First injury: To French goalkeeper Alex Thepot, who had to be replaced in his country's 4–1 1930 opening victory ten minutes into the match after a Mexican player kicked him in the jaw. Augustin Chantrel, a midfielder, replaced him.

First player to score an extratime (overtime) goal: Austria's Anton Schall, who tallied against France to break a 1–1 tie on May 27, 1934 en route to a 3–2 triumph. A number of observers felt Schall was offside. Years later, he agreed he probably was.

First player to score an extratime goal in a World Cup championship game: Italy's Angelo Schiavo, who scored against Czechoslovakia in the 95th minute of the 1934 final in a 2–1 win.

First final: Uruguay vs. Argentina on July 30, 1930 in Montevideo. Uruguay won, 4–2.

First televised game: Yugoslavia vs. France in Lausanne, Switzerland, on June 16, 1954.

First time a goal was scored a minute or less into a match: By Emile Veinante of France, who scored forty seconds into the game of his country's 3–1 victory over Belgium on June 5, 1938, in Paris.

First time penalty-kick tie-breakers were used: In 1982 as West Germany took on France. The teams were tied after extratime, 3–3, but Germany prevailed in the tie-breaker, 5–4.

First time a final was decided by a shootout: West Germany 1, Argentina 0 on July 8, 1990.

First World Cup mascot: World Cup Willie at the 1966 cup in England. It was a lion-like boy.

The teams that participated in the first World Cup (13): Argentina, Brazil, Uruguay, Paraguay, United States, France, Mexico, Chile, Yugoslavia, Bolivia, Romania, Peru and Belgium.

First time a non-European or non-American country played: Egypt in 1934.

First time two CONCACAF countries qualified for the second round: In 1994, when the U.S. and Mexico accomplished that feat. In fact, CONCACAF teams had reached the second round or beyond only five times before—the U.S. (1930), Cuba (1938), Mexico (1970 and 1986, when it hosted the cup), and Costa Rica (1990).

First time a player scored and was red-carded in the same match: Brazilian forward Garrincha, who accomplished that rare feat in the 1962 semifinals (he was, however, allowed to play in the championship match). It happened a second time during France '98— South Korea's Ha Seok-Ju duplicated the feat in a 3-1 loss to Mexico on June 13, 1998.

Countries participating for the first time at Korea/Japan 2002: China, Ecuador, Senegal, Slovenia.

First time a player scored for two separate countries in World Cup finals:

Robert Prosinecki. He scored for Yugoslavia against the United Arab Emirates at Italia '90 and then for newly created Croatia vs. Jamaica at France '98.

First time a coach was fired during a World Cup: Carlos Alberto Parreira by Saudi Arabia after it was eliminated after the second match of the three-game, first-round at France '98 on June 18. As it turned out, Tunisia and South Korea quickly followed suit. Henri Kasperczak was dismissed by the African country after two defeats in two games on June 20, and Cha Bum-Kun was given his walking papers by Korea after two losses in as many games on June 22.

First time a team scored two goals in an official World Cup opening match: Brazil, which found the back of the net twice in a 2-1 victory over Scotland at France '98. Every opening match ended either 1-0 or in a scoreless draw since FIFA decided to have one official opener in 1954.

The United States, Mexico and Costa Rica, which won their opening games in 2002, the first time CONCACAF teams started 3-0 at any World Cup.

Fast, Faster, Fastest

The fastest goal in World Cup history: Turkey forward Hakan Sukur made his first goal of the 2002 Cup a memorable one. He found the back of the net only 11 seconds into his team's 3-2 win over Korea in the third-place match. The record was held by England's Bryan Robson, who connected after only twenty-seven seconds of a 3-1 victory over France on June 16, 1982, exactly forty-four years to the day that Olle Nyberg of Sweden struck after thirty seconds against Hungary in the 1938 World Cup. The fourth fastest goal was scored by Bernard Lacombe of France, thirty-one seconds into a 2-1 loss to Italy on June 2, 1978.

Fastest substitution: Italy's Mauro Bellugi was replaced by Antonello Cuccureddu six minutes into a 1–0 triumph over Argentina on June 10, 1978.

Fastest red card: Bolivian midfielder Marco Etcheverry entered the 1994 World Cup opener in the 79th minute in place of Luis Ramallo. Three minutes later, he was red-carded for fouling German captain Lothar Matthaeus from behind in what turned into a 1–0 victory for the Europeans on June 17, 1994.

The Only Time

The only occasion four teams from the British Isles qualified: 1958, when England, Scotland, Northern Ireland and Wales made it to the final sixteen.

The only time a host country had to qualify: Italy, in 1934.

The only players who have participated in the World Cup before and after World War II: Switzerland's Alfred Bickel and Sweden's Erik Nilsson played

Italian captian, Giesseppe Meazza and French
captain, Etienne Mattler before Italy's 3-1 win.

in the 1938 and 1950 tournaments.

The only time a player scored in consecutive World Cup championship games: Vava, who accomplished the feat in 1958 and 1962.

The only player to have participated in five World Cups: Mexican goalkeeper Antonio Carbajal played in 1950, 1954, 1958, 1962, and 1966.

The only time two countries met twice in the same World Cup (other than replays): West Germany vs. Hungary in 1954. Hungary won the first matchup, 8–3, when the Germans rested six regulars. They met again in the final, with the Germans at full strength and emerging victorious, 3–2.

The only time a player recorded a hat trick in a championship game: By Geoff Hurst for England in a 4–2 victory over West Germany on July 30, 1966, at Wembley Stadium in London.

The only countries to lose back-to-back finals: The Netherlands and West Germany. The former lost to the host countries, West Germany and Argentina in 1974 and 1978, respectively, the latter to Italy and Argentina, in 1982 and 1986, respectively.

The only players to have scored in two World Cup championship matches: Brazil's Vava and Pelé and West Germany's Paul Breitner are the only three players who have accomplished that feat. Vava is the only player to have done it in two consecutive finals—1958 and 1962—while Pelé scored in 1958 and 1970, and Breitner in 1974 and 1982.

The only player to have scored five or more goals in two World Cups: Peru's Teofilo Cubillas scored five goals in each of the 1970 and 1978 tournaments.

The only time the scoring champion never played after the opening round: That happened in 1994, when Russia's Oleg Salenko performed in only three matches. Russia was eliminated in the first round, so Salenko could not add to his total of six goals. Even though Bulgaria's Hristo Stoichkov also finished with six goals, Salenko was declared scoring champion because he had played in fewer games (three to Stoichkov's seven).

The only player to score five goals in a game: Salenko, who found the back of the net against Cameroon in Russia's final match of the 1994 cup, a 6–1 victory.

The only team to win out of its hemisphere: Brazil won in Sweden in 1958.

The only brothers to play for a champion: Fritz and Otmar Walter of West Germany in 1954, and Jack and Bobby Charlton of England in 1966.

The only father and son combination: Domingus Da Guia of Brazil played in the 1938 Cup and his son, Ademir Da Guia, performed in the 1974 event. Interesting note: There was an uncle-nephew combination. In 1930, Jose Andrade competed for Uruguay. Twenty years later, his nephew, Rodrigeuz Andrade, played for the World Cup champions.

The only times a player with a hat trick played on a losing team: Poland's Ernst Willimowski, who scored four goals in his side's 6–5 loss to Brazil in the opening round on June 5, 1938, and Igor Belanov in the Soviet Union's 4–3 loss to Spain in the second round on June 15, 1986.

The only time brothers have coached in the World Cup: Zeze Moreira coached Brazil in 1954 and brother Aimore directed the team in 1962.

The only time brothers were a goalkeeping tandem on the same team: Viktor and Vyacheslav Chanov for the Soviet Union in the 1982 World Cup.

The only time a country won its group with a negative goal differential: Cameroon (2–1–0), which captured Group B at Italia '90. The Africans scored three goals and allowed five for a negative goal differential of two, after a 4–0 loss to the Soviet Union. As it turned out, they finished with the worst differential of their group. Romania (1–1–1) was at plus one, Argentina (1–1–1) at plus one and the Soviet Union (1–2) was even.

The only four players who have played for two countries in the World Cup: Luis Monti (Argentina in 1930 and Italy in 1934), Ferenc Puskas (Hungary in

1954 and Spain in 1962), Jose Santamaria (Uruguay in 1954 and Spain in 1962), and Jose Mazzola (Brazil in 1958 and Italy in 1962). The rules have been changed since then, limiting players to one country, but there are exceptions. Midfielder Robert Prosinecki, who performed for Yugoslavia in the 1990 World Cup—before the nation's breakup and international sanctions that changed the soccer landscape—will be allowed to play for Croatia.

The only player to play for two countries in a championship game: Luis Monti, who performed for his native Argentina in a losing effort to Uruguay 1930 and for champion Italy in 1934.

The only player who scored for both teams: The Netherlands' Ernie Brandts, who kicked the ball into his own net while crashing into his goalkeeper, Pieter Schrijvers, who was carried off on a stretcher. Brandts made amends for his miscue, equalizing on a twenty-yard free kick five minutes into the second half as the Dutch went on to record a 2–1 victory over Italy.

The only country to have participated in every World Cup: Brazil, which will make it eighteen in 2006.

The only player to have been ejected in two World Cups: Cameroon defender Rigobert Song was red-carded in both 1994 (vs. Brazil) and 1998 (vs. Chile).

It's Never Happened—Yet

No player has captained a championship team twice, but two came close. West Germany's Karl-Heinz Rummenigge did it twice as a loser in the final—1982 and 1986. Argentina's Diego Maradona was the captain of the 1986 champions and the 1990 runners-up.

Olympian Feats

Only eight players can claim the accomplishment of being Olympic and World Cup champions. Jose Nasazzi, Jose Leonadro Andrade, Hector Scarone and Pedro Cea from Uruguay's 1924 and 1928 Olympic gold-medal winning teams and the 1930 World Cup champions, and Alvaro Gestidio in 1928 and 1930. Italy's Alfredo Foni, Pietro Rava and Ugo Locatelli played for the 1936 Olympic titlists and the 1938 World Cup champions.

There have been twenty-seven players who have played in an Olympic and World Cup final: Jose Nasazzi, Jose Leandro Andrade, Hector Scarone and Pedro Cea played for Uruguay in the 1924 and 1928 Olympics, and the 1930 World Cup. Fellow countryman Alvaro Gestidio did the same in 1928 and 1930; Italy's Alfredo Foni, Pierto Rava and Ugo Locatelli played in the 1936 Olympic title match and for the 1938 World Cup title; Argentina's Fernando Paternoster, Juan Evaristo, Luis Monti and Manuel Ferreira played in the 1928 Olympics and the 1930 World Cup (Monti also played for Italy in the 1934 World Cup final); Sweden's Nils Liedhold and Gunnar Gren played in the 1948 Olympics and the 1958 World Cup final; Hungary's Gyula Groscis, Jeno Buzansky, Mihaly Lantos, Jozsef Bozsik, Gyula Lorany, Jozsef Zakarias, Zoltan Czibor, Sandor Kocsis, Nandor Hidegkuti and Ferenc Puskas won the gold in 1952 and were runners-up to Germany in 1954; and Brazil's Claudio Taffarel, Bebeto and Romario took home silver medals in the 1988 Olympics and were on the World Cup champions team in 1994.

Only three players have scored in Olympic and World Cup finals: Uruguay's Pedro Cea, who did it in the 1924 Olympics and 1930 World Cup, and Hungary's Ferenc Puskas and teammate Zoltan Czibor, who accomplished the feat at the 1952 Olympics and the 1954 World Cup. Romario scored for Brazil in the 1988 gold-medal match, but could not duplicate his performance at USA '94.

Four stadiums have hosted Olympic and World Cup championship matches: Wembley Stadium, London, England (1948 Olympics and 1966 World Cup), Olympic Stadium, Munich, Germany (1972 Olympics and 1974 World Cup), Azteca Stadium, Mexico City, Mexico (1968 Olympics and 1970 and 1986 World Cups), and the Rose Bowl (1984 Olympics and 1994 World Cup).

Brotherly Love

There have been several sets of brothers who have performed in the Cup. Perhaps the best known were Bobby and Jack Charlton, starters and key players on England's world championship side in 1966. Fritz and Otmar Walter starred for West Germany, the 1954 champs. They each scored a goal in the 6–1 semifinal victory over Austria. Then there were the Van der Kerkhof twins—Rene and Willy—of second-place Netherlands in 1978. Ironically, they each scored in the 83rd minute against West Germany (Rene) and Austria (Willy) in second-round group matches.

The first brother combination was Fernando and Manuel Rosas of Mexico, who played in the very first World Cup match against France on July 13, 1930. Other brother combinations include: Juan and Mario Evaristo (Argentina, 1930), Zlatko and Zeljko Cajkovski (Yugoslavia, 1950), Albert and Robert Koerner (Austria, 1954), Antonio and Francesco Lopez (Paraguay, 1950), Anatoliy and Viktor Ivanov (Soviet Union, 1958), Piotyr and Emil Kozlicek (Austria, 1958) and John and Mel Charles (Wales, 1958).

It's Not Always Fair

These four countries finished undefeated in the World Cup, but for some reason, they did not advance to the next round:

Scotland In 1974, the Scots compiled a 1–0–2 record and outscored their opposition, 3–1, but did not qualify for the second round because the country Scotland was tied with—Brazil—had a better goal differential (3 goals for, 0 against).

Brazil In 1978, the South Americans recorded a 3–0–3 mark, but could not make it into the semifinals.

Paraguay's Romero gives England's Gary Lineker a little push.

They tied Argentina for first place in that group with a 2–0–1 record, but the Argentines had the better goal differential (8 to Brazil's 5).

Cameroon In 1982, Cameroon had not lost a first-round game, but did not advance. Italy did not win a game, but reached the second round. They were in the same group and finished with the same records (0–0–3), but Italy scored two goals in its first-round games, Cameroon one.

England And again in 1982, England recorded an impressive 3–0–2 mark, only to be sent packing after the second round. The English tied both their second-round matches, finishing second to West Germany in Group B.

For the Ages

The youngest player to participate in a World Cup: Northern Ireland's Norman Whiteside, who was seventeen years, forty-two days old, when he played in the 1982 World Cup. Pelé was the youngest player to perform in a championship game as a 17-year-old in 1958. He was seventeen years, 237 days old. Incidentally, striker Ronaldo was seventeen years, 235 days old when Brazil played its first game at USA '94. However, Ronaldo never saw a minute of playing time.

The oldest player: Forward Roger Milla, the hero of Cameroon's amazing run in the 1990 competition, was forty-two years old when he played for his country, coming on as a substitute in the second half of a 6–1 loss to Russia on June 28, 1994.

The oldest goalkeeper: Northern Ireland goalkeeper Pat Jennings, who was forty-one years old when he played in his final match against Brazil in the 1986 World Cup.

The oldest player on a championship team: Italy's Dino Zoff, who, at 40, was the goalkeeper of the 1982 Cup-winning team.

The oldest player to score at a World Cup: Cameroon's Roger Milla, 38, who connected four times at Italia '90.

Medicine Men

Players who were banned because of drug use: Haiti's Ernst Jean-Joseph (for taking a stimulant containing phenylmetrazin) in 1974, Scotland's Willie Johnston (stimulants) in 1978 and Argentina's Diego Maradona (for his famous cocktail of stimulants) in 1994. Drug testing began at the 1966 World Cup.

Illegal drugs were found in the system of Spanish player Ramon Caldere at the 1986 cup, but he was not banned from playing because the team doctor mistakenly gave him the drugs. The Spanish Soccer Federation was fined $13,000 for the incident.

The Money Game and Other Incentives

In 1982, Kuwaiti players could have earned $200,000 each if the team reached the second round. It didn't.

In 1990, Khalid Ismail Mubarak scored the United Arab Emirates' first World Cup goal ever in its 5–1 loss to West Germany on June 9. He received a Rolls Royce for his feat.

In 1990, the Royal Dutch Soccer Federation said it would pay bonuses of $65,220 to each player if the Netherlands won the title (it didn't). That prompted the team's three leading players—Ruud Gullit, Marco van Basten and Frank Rijkaard—to offer their bonuses to their teammates. Gullit called them "the lowest players' bonuses around." There's more. Italian players would have received $370,000 apiece if they had won. Each Belgian player had been promised $105,000 and the United Arab Emirates players, technically amateur, received $135,000 each from President Sheik Zayed bin Sultan Ali Nahyan just for qualifying. Businessmen and rulers of the seven emirates (states) also gave the players and coaches a number of gifts.

And then there's Egypt, which would pay $600 a victory and $300 for a tie. **In 1998, it looked like the coaches were cashing in.** Brazil's Carlos Alberto Parreira was to receive $2.5 million for a year's work coaching the Saudi Arabian National Team, according to reliable sources, although reports had him getting as much as $3 million. Bora Milutinovic, who was fired as Mexican coach in November, 1997 despite guiding the team to the Cup, received a $100,000 bonus for coaching Nigeria, a tax-free salary of $35,000 a month (from January to July, 1998), and a series of bonuses depending on how well the team fares in France ($50,000 bonus if Nigeria reaches the second round, $75,000 if it makes the quarterfinals, another $75,000 if it finishes third, $150,000 is its reaches the final and $250,000 for winning the World Cup).

Odds and Ends

Pelé, not surprisingly, has played for three champions. Ten other players have taken the victory lap twice. They are Giovanni Ferrari (Italy, 1934, 1938), Giuseppe Meazza (Italy, 1934, 1938), Didi (Brazil, 1958, 1962), Garrincha (Brazil, 1958, 1962) Gilmar do Santos Neves (Brazil, 1958, 1962), Djalma Santos (Brazil, 1958, 1962), Nilton Santos (Brazil, 1958, 1962), Vava (Brazil, 1958, 1962), Mario Zagallo (Brazil, 1958, 1962), Zito (Brazil, 1958, 1962).

Cesar Zavala just might have had the hardest shot at the 1986 World Cup. The Paraguayan midfielder fired the ball barely over the crossbar midway through the first half of a 1–1 opening-round draw with Mexico. The power of the shot deflated the ball, which was replaced.

The best performance by a substitute was by Hungary's Laszlo Kiss, who scored three goals after coming on in the second half of his country's 10–1 romp over El Salvador in 1982.

The most unusual souvenir of all-time at a World Cup had to be the official World Cup '82 bagpipes, which were sold in Gio and La Coruna in Spain.

Scalpers in Valencia, Spain, made a killing for the Spain-Honduras match in 1982. They sold nine dollar tickets for $100. Then there were forty-two would-be scalpers in Seville, who were arrested trying to sell 1,060 tickets for the Scotland-Soviet Union match.

Brazilian coach Tele Santana lost six and a half pounds because of his team's tough workouts in the heat (more than ninety degrees) in 1982.

Algeria enjoyed a memorable Independence Day celebration at the 1982 World Cup. On the 20th anniversary of the country's birth—June 16—Algeria jolted West Germany, pulling off a 2–1 upset.

When Czechoslovakia gained the 1934 championship match, the squad was made up of eleven players from only two teams—Sparta and Slavia. No other finalist has had such a small club representation.

Before qualifying in USA '94, Bolivia advanced to the World Cup on two occasions, doing so without playing a qualifier. The 1930 tournament was by invitation only, and the Bolivians' road to Uruguay in 1950 was after Argentina dropped out.

John Charles, who scored for Wales in its 1–1 tie with Hungary in 1958, arrived in Sweden only a day before that match after the Italian Football Federation gave him a last-minute permission to released from commitments to Juventus.

The most frequent surname in the World Cup is Gonzales or Gonzalez; there have been fourteen players. Lopez is next with eleven.

Poland's Leslaw Cmikiewicz made six appearances for his country as a substitute in the 1974 World Cup. Cmikiewicz played all of 102 minutes. His longest stint was thirty-three minutes vs. Yugoslavia. He replaced Robert Gadocha (vs. Argentina), Zygmunt Maszcyzk (vs. Haiti) and Andrzej Szarmach (vs. Italy) in the opening round, Szarmach (vs. Yugoslavia) and Henryk Kasperczak (vs. Germany) in the second round, and Kasperczak (vs. Brazil) in the third-place match. The only match he did not appear in was a second-round encounter vs. Sweden.

Brazil used only twelve players—a record—in six matches in its march to the championship in 1962. Had Pelé not been injured—he was replaced by Amarildo in the second game—the Brazilians would have used an unchanged lineup.

Perhaps the most interesting save not made by a goalkeeper in a World Cup came after the 1994 competition. Los Angeles taxi driver Juan Blanco found the victory medal, family passports and $60,000 of Brazilian goalkeeper Claudio Taffarel after he had mistakenly left them in the backseat of the cab a couple of days after the Cup.

Senegal midfielder Salif Diao produced an interesting hat-trick in a 1-1 draw with Denmark in 2002. His foul caused a penalty kick, scored Senegal's lone goal and then was red carded in a 1-1 tie with Denmark.

Cameroon striker Samuel Eto'o kept the media waiting for nearly three

U.S team celebrating Ernie Stewart's game winning goal over Columbia 3-1 in 1994.

hours because he was unable to give a urine sample to FIFA doping control after he scored the lone goal in the 1-0 first-round victory over Saudi Arabia in 2002. Senegal midfielder Khaililou Fadiga was charged with stealing a necklace worth $250 from a Korean jewerly store in Daegu several days before the start of the 2002 Cup. Fadiga called it a "stupid joke," which was part of a prank involving teammates. Fadiga, 27, returned the necklace and charges were dropped.

Of Coaches and Kings

The king who would be coach was Romanian King Carol II. For the very first World Cup in 1930, Carol made sure his country was represented in Uruguay. Originally, the invitation was rejected because the Romanian players could not get three months off from work to take the roundtrip boatride and stay in South America. Carol intervened, making sure each player would have his job—at full pay—when he returned. Romania was eliminated after only two matches. In 1940, Carol was overthrown and he fled to South America, where he was remembered as the "football-mad" king.

The most successful coach has been Vittorio Pozzo of Italy, who directed championship teams in 1934 and 1938. He is the only coach to have guided teams to a pair of World Cup crowns. Honorable mention goes to West Germany's Helmut Schoen, who directed his country to a second-place finish in 1966, a third-place finish in 1970 and the title in 1974.

The most successful player-coaches were Brazil's Mario Zagallo and West Germany's Franz Beckenbauer, who are the only men to have played on and coached World Cup championship squads. Zagallo played for the 1958 and 1962 champions and guided Brazil to the 1970 crown. Beckenbauer played in the 1966 final and for the 1974 champions, and directed Germany to a final appearance in 1986 and to the title in 1990.

Have coaching license, will travel :Carlos Alberto Parreira and Bora Milutinovic are the only men to have coached four different countries in a World Cup. Parreira, a Brazilian, guided Kuwait in 1982, the United Arab Emirates in 1990, Brazil to the world championship in 1994, and Saudi Arabia in 1998. Milutinovic, a Yugoslav, guided Mexico to a quarterfinal finish in 1986, first-time qualifier Costa Rica into the second round in 1990, the U.S. to a second-round finish in 1994, and Nigeria to the second round in 1998. This year, barring a major calamity or firing, Bora, who directed China's fortunes during qualifying, will become the first man to coach teams in five different countries. Two other men—Rudolf Vytlacil and Blagjoe Vidinic—have coached two different countries in a World Cup. Vytlacil, a Czech, coached his native country in 1962, when it finished a surprising second to Brazil in Chile, and guided Bulgaria four years later. Vidinic, a Yugoslav, directed Morocco in 1970 and Zaire in 1974.

Paraguayan coach Cayetano Re became the first coach to be thrown out of a World Cup match, getting tossed in the waning minutes of a 2–2 opening-round tie with Belgium in 1986. He was standing too close to the field.

Uruguyan coach Omar Borras became the first coach to coach from the stands in Cup history. He was not allowed to sit on the bench for his team's 1–0 second-round loss to Argentina on June 16, 1986. He called French referee Joel Quiniou "a murderer" after a scoreless tie with Scotland.

Some Shirt Tales

The trading of shirts at athletic competitions, most common in soccer, probably began during the 1954 World Cup in Switzerland, according to Professor Julio Mazzei, confidant of Pelé and former coach of the New York Cosmos. "Since then it has become a tradition," Mazzei said. "Some players start collecting special shirts from special idols, such as Pelé ."

In the 1986 World Cup, however, FIFA had a rule prohibiting the trading of shirts because the organization did not want players to bare their chests on the field, but several players traded shirts anyway.

Some interesting shirt tales:

- The first time numbers were used on shirts was in the 1938 competition in France.

- Brazilian star Tostao gave his shirt and World Cup medal to the surgeon in Houston who had performed two operations on a detached retina in his eye before the 1970 tournament.

- Early in the second half of Uruguay's 1–1 tie with West Germany in the 1986 cup, referee Vojtech Christov of Czechoslovakia noticed that teammates Jose Batista and Miguel Bossio were wearing each other's jerseys. He had the Uruguayan players switch shirts on the field. He could have given each a yellow card for being out of uniform.

- After France dropped a 2–0 decision to West Germany in the 1986 World Cup, French players Michel Platini and Jean Tigana, instead of trading shirts with the victors, threw their jerseys into the stands in Jalisco Stadium in Guadalajara, thanking fans for their support.

- At the same competition, Portuguese players threatened to wear their shirts inside out if their World Cup bonuses were not doubled from $2,000 a match.

- And then there were Guadalajaran prostitutes, who, after Brazil's 1–0 victory over Spain in 1986, wore yellow shirts—Brazil's color—to celebrate the victory and attract joyful customers.

- Croatia's Ivica Olic had trouble getting his shirt back on after celebrating a goal against Italy in a first-round loss in 2002. He celebrated by showing his undershirt, which had a picture of his newborn child. Olic, however, had to wait on the sidelines while team officials had to cut the lining off from his shirt before he could re-enter the game.

- And while it didn't have anything to do with actual play, there was a clever credit card commercial that had just about everyone in the world trading shirts. Hopefully, it returns for the 2006 competition.

What's in a Name?

The most appropriate name in World Cup history must belong to South Korean goalkeeper Oh Yun-Kyo, who participated in the 1986. That's oh, as in zero, or a shutout.

Early in the second half of England's 3–0 second-round victory over Paraguay in 1986, Gary Andrew Stevens replaced Peter Reid at midfield. There was nothing unusual about that, except that there was a Gary Stevens in the lineup already for the English—defender Gary Michael Stevens—which drove several radio and television announcers crazy.

Is it Roger Milla or Roger Miller? Actually it's both. The Cameroon star changed his name to Milla to sound more African.

The players with the shortest names were Paraguay's Cayetano Re in 1958 and Argentina's Francisco Sa in 1974.

Even though players have the same first name, it doesn't mean they are spelled the same way. Take, for example, Sweden goalkeeper Thomas Ravelli and forward Tomas Brolin in the 1994 World Cup.

Then there was Argentine Julio Olarticoechea. Try to pronounce that. ESPN announcers called him Julio. He just might have had the most intimidating name at the 1986 cup.

Incredible But True

After Hungary lost to Italy in the 1938 final in Paris, Hungarian goalkeeper Antal Szabo said: "I have never felt so proud in my life." Say what? "We may have lost the match, but we have saved eleven lives. The Italian players received a telegram from Rome before the game which read, 'Win or die!' Now they can go home as heroes." The telegram reportedly came from Mussolini.

Sometimes celebrating can be hazardous to your health. After Uruguayan Juan Hohberg scored the tying goal in the 87th minute against Hungary in the 1954 semifinals, his teammates jumped on him and knocked him out. He did recover and hit the post with a shot in overtime, but Hungary registered a 4–2 victory.

After Italy was bounced by North Korea, 1–0, fans at the airport in Rome pelted the team with vegetables. Italian fans were more into psychological warfare in 1986. When the team arrived at Rome airport after elimination, the Italians were welcomed with the sign, "Italy Vomits on You."

Oops

In the 1934 World Cup championship game, Italy's Raimondo Orsi scored a brilliant goal against Czechoslovakia: He curled a shot into the goal. The day after, Orsi attempted to repeat the feat more than twenty times for photographers in a posed situation, but could not do it.

As he scored a penalty kick in Italy's 2–1 semifinal victory over Brazil in

1938, captain Peppino Meazza lost his shorts, torn earlier in the match, and they fell to the ground. His teammates gathered around him as a new pair was produced.

As he left his locker room for a match against Brazil in 1950, Yugoslav midfielder Rajko Mitic walked into an iron girder and knocked himself out at Maracana Stadium. His ten teammates walked out onto the field and tried to walk back to the locker room to delay the kickoff, but referee Mervyn Griffiths of Wales demanded they start the match on time. By the time Mitic, who was heavily bandaged, returned, the Yugoslavians had a 1–0 deficit. Brazil went on to win, 2–0.

Mexican goalkeepers proved to be a superstitious lot at the 1966 cup. Ignacio Calderon knelt underneath the

Salvatore "Toto" Schillaci, top gun, 1990

crossbar before two matches and Antonio Carbajal kissed both goal posts for luck. It must have worked because Mexico played Uruguay to a scoreless tie.

They almost began the World Cup without the proper field markings in the 1974 World Cup in West Germany, of all places. After a spectacular opening ceremony before Brazil and Yugoslavia tussled, officials had to quickly put in the corner and center flags while the referee delayed the start of the match.

During Italy's 1–1 draw with Peru in 1982, West German referee Walter Eschweiler ran into a Peruvian player, was knocked on his back and lost his whistle in the process.

After he allowed a goal in a 1–1 draw with Honduras in 1982, Spanish goalkeeper Luis Arconada later was roughed up by a Valencia policeman who mistook him for a burglar.

A computer in the Soviet Union predicted that Brazil would win the 1982 World Cup, defeating West Germany in the final, 1–0. The computer was half-right. Brazil did not reach the semifinals, but the West Germans did lose in the finals to Italy, 3–1.

CHAPTER
11

During the 1986 World Cup in Mexico, a soft drink commerical showed that Mexican star Hugo Sanchez converted a penalty kick. In real life, Sanchez missed an important penalty in the final moments of the 1–1 first-round tie with Paraguay, much to the amusement of his critics. He was twenty years old at the time, but there was no excuse for what happened to Belgian Enzo Scifo in a 2–2 opening-round draw with Paraguay in 1986. He apparently had scored a goal off a free kick for a 3–1 advantage late in the match—or so he thought. It was nullified because the call actually was an indirect free kick. Another player had to touch the ball before it went into the net.

The same thing happened to Bulgarian midfielder-forward Hritso Stoichkov in the 1994 World Cup. He thought he had scored a goal off a goal kick against Nigeria. But it was disallowed because it was an indirect free kick.

Iraqi defender Barmeer Shaker was given a one-year suspension from international matches by FIFA for spitting at the referee during a 2–1 first-round defeat to Belgium in 1986.

English midfielder Ray Wilkins threw the ball at referee Gabriel Gonzalez (Paraguay) during a 0–0 draw with Morocco in 1986. He was given a red card and a two-game suspension by FIFA.

Forward Branko Segota showed up late for Canada in the 1986 World Cup because his visa had expired.

Uruguayan defender Jose Batista was hit with the fastest red card in cup history. He was ejected only fifty-three seconds into a scoreless draw with Scotland in the opening round of the 1986 cup.

Gianluca Vialli experienced one of the most embarrassing matches in Italy's 1–0 victory over the United States in 1990, registering a unique hat trick. He missed a penalty kick, had a goal called back because of an offside call and looked terrible when he attempted and missed a bicycle kick in the penalty area.

At Italia '90, Japanese journalists Juzuru Saito and Isoyama Katsuni were attacked by English hooligans while filming fans on the street near the main railroad station in Cagliari, Sardinia. Saito sustained a cut eyebrow when he was hit by a rock and Katsuni received severe chest bruises from a beating.

Alain Lammortain, a 26-year-old Belgian, was mistaken as a hooligan and was attacked by youths in Latina, about thirty miles south of Rome at the 1990 World Cup.

German midfielder Stefan Effenberg received the most embarrassing and humiliating of departures when he was sent home early by coach Berti Vogts after he gave the finger to a fan in Dallas in 1994.

The most unusual wager of that World Cup occurred in Albania, where an unidentified man who was short of cash was so confident that Argentina would beat Bulgaria in the opening round that he put up his wife. Bulgaria prevailed, 2–0. The man's wife disappeared with the winner and the man complained to police.

And how's this for enjoying ecstasy and agony at virtually the same time? Spanish midfielder Jose Luis Caminero became a hero by scoring two goals within minutes midway through the second half of a 3–1 first-round victory over Bolivia on June 27, 1994, but turned into a potenial goat for the next game in the second round against Switzerland. He received his second yellow card in the 90th minute, meaning he would miss that game.

It's Not Always a Grand Old Flag

During West Germany's controversial and lackluster 1–0 victory over Austria in 1982, which qualified both countries for the second round, Algerian fans burned West German flags in protest of the less-than-exhuberant performances by both sides.

Four years after the Falkland Wars, Argentine fans burned English flags during the quarterfinal confrontation between the two teams at the 1986 World Cup.

All Creatures Great and Small

During France's 1–0 victory over Canada in 1986, an overzealous French fan threw a rooster—the national team's symbol—onto the field. The rooster was removed by the referee.

A dog ran onto the field in Peru's scoreless tie with Cameroon in the 1982 cup. The dog was on the field for several minutes. Finally, the game was held up to clear out the pooch.

And speaking of animals, the all-time best mascot had to be Kuwait's live camel at the 1982 cup.

The Spanish National Team adopted a dog in 2002 to make sure he wouldn't become dog meat in Korea's dog market.

World Cup Trends
Can You Trust a Forward Over 30

S o, who will be the scoring stars of this World Cup?

Well, if you go by history—the seventeen previous World Cups—count on the likes of Brazilian rising stars Adriano (24), Kaka (24) and Robinho (22), England's Michael Owen (24), if he has recovered from his broken foot in time, or even Argentina's Lionel Messi, who turns 19 midway through the Cup, or Carlos Tevez, the star of the Argentine's Olympic gold-medal winners at the Athens Games in 2004, to make an impact and fill the net.

Several of them will be 25 or around that age this June. Why is 25 the magic number? That is the average age of the World Cup scoring champion. Well, it's actually 24.72, but the number was rounded up to the nearest whole digit.

"This is a young man's tournament," U.S. coach Bruce Arena said four years ago. "This isn't for wise old veterans."

Size might not matter in the World Cup, but age certainly does. The younger a midfielder or forward is, the better chance he will score a goal or score many goals.

This has been documented by extensive research. The research was broken into two categories: World Cup scoring champions and players scoring goals under and over the age of 30. From 1954 to 1994, a span of eleven World Cups, the tournament's leading scorer was either 24 or 25 years-old.

Thierry Henry, France's striker, *par excellence*

That impressive list included France's Just Fontaine (24), who connected for a Cup record 13 goals in 1958, Portugal's Eusebio (24), who scored nine goals in 1966, Germany's Gerd Mueller (24), who found the back of the net 10 times in 1970, Italy's Paolo Rossi (25), the hero of the 1982 World Cup with six goals, England's Gary Lineker (25), who collected six goals in 1986, and most recently, Ronaldo (25), who struck for a tournament-best eight goals in 2002.

The oldest scoring champion was Croatian striker Davor Suker, who connected for six goals at France '98 at the age of 30. Until Suker performed that feat, Italy's Angelo Schiavio (28) was the oldest player to lead the World Cup in scoring, in 1934.

In another telling statistic, it was discovered that 75.1 percent of the goals scored in the 68-year history of the World Cup have been tallied by players 29-years-old or less. Since (and including when) Lucien Laurent found the back of the net for France in the very first World Cup match in 1930, 1916 goals have been scored.

According to this research, 1,264 of 1,681 goals scored were by players who were 29 or under. A total of 235 goals could not be verified because of age discrepancies. Regardless, there definitely is a trend here.

The average age of goalscorer was 27.1 for the 2002 competition.

It even goes beyond scoring goals. Players such as Diego Maradona (25 when he led Argentina to the 1986 title), Daniel Passarella (25 when he captained Argentina to the 1978 crown), Bobby Moore (25 when he captained England to the 1966 championship) and Carlos Alberto (26 when he captained Brazil in 1970) were all in their prime at the time.

As for the great Pelé, he was 17 and 21 when Brazil won in 1958 and 1962, respectively, and 29 when the South Americans emerged victorious in 1970. He was on the other side of 30.

"In this particular area of the game, you need a striker who has strength, power and speed, which you tend to lose a little with time," said Brazilian coach Carlos Alberto Parreira, who directed Brazil to the USA '94 title.

"In defenders and goalkeepers you see players who are 34, 35 even 37. They need more experience. They don't have to run that much to accelerate that much. But in the box, no way (for) players over thirty-two, unless they play like Romario, just standing there."

Of course, there are exceptions to the rule. Cameroon's Roger Milla scored four key goals in the 1990 World Cup as a spry thirty-eight-year-old, but that was as a second-half super sub, not as a starter.

Peru's Nene Cubillas, now a TV commentator, knows a thing or two about scoring goals. He is the only player to score five goals in two separate World Cups, performing the feat as a twenty-one-year-old in 1970 and a twenty-nine-year-old in 1978. He was blanked in three games at Spain '82, when he was thirty-three.

"When you are younger, you come with all your power," Cubillas said. "You try hard, you work for 90 minutes. Older players, they are more experienced. They don't try to run that much. They try to keep. . .their position. But the young go and back and forth and back and forth."

Current Tunisia coach Roger Lemerre, who directed France to the European Championship in 2000 and who guided the French to their disastrous first-round elimination in Korea in 2002, felt experience was an important ingredient in the equation.

"As you get older, obviously you are not going to be as strong as when you are younger," he said. "But as you get older obviously you are a smarter player. So the young players might not have the savvy of an older player, but that's compensated by their speed. It's a balance.

"There is a saying in France: 'The strong takes over the weak

The Young Inherit The Scoring Championships		
Year Player (Country) Goals / Age	Year Player (Country) Goals / Age	
1930 Guillermo Stabile (Argentina) 8	24	1966 Eusebio (Portugal) 9	24	
1934 Angelo Schiavio (Italy) 4	28	1970 Gerd Mueller (Germany) 10	24	
Oldrich Nejedly (Czechoslovakia) 4	24	1974 Grzegorz Lato (Poland) 7	24	
Edmund Conen (Germany) 4	19	1978 Mario Kempes (Argentina) 6	24	
1938 Leonidas da Silva (Brazil) 8	24	1982 Paolo Rossi (Italy) 6	25	
1950 Ademir (Brazil) 9	27	1986 Gary Lineker (England) 6	25	
1954 Sandor Kocsis (Hungary) 11	25	1990 Salvatore Schillaci (Italy) 6	25	
1958 Just Fontaine (France) 13	24	1994 Oleg Salenko (Russia) 6	24	
1962 Drazen Jerkovic (Yugoslavia) 5 25	1998 Davor Suker (Croatia) 6	30	

ones.' The speed takes over strength. But intelligence takes over everybody. You cannot disassociate one from another. But once in a while you have a younger player who is very talent, very smart."

While players might be in fabulous shape and in their physical prime in their teen years, Aime Jacquet, who guided France to the World Cup crown in 1998, said that players in their mid-twenties excel for several reasons.

"That's normal because in that age group under 30 they are very confident," he said. "They also have a lot of years of playing under their belt as they have a better feeling for the game, compared to a seventeen- or eighteen-year-old player. They're more mature players and have a better feel for the game at twenty-eight-years-old than a seventeen-year-old."

Some coaches, however, learned the hard way. Take the case of what happened to Argentina in 2002. Coach Marcelo Bielsa, considered a master tactician (he guided the Argentines to the 2004 Olympic gold medal prior to resigning) decided to start 33-year-old Gabriel Batitusta instead of twenty-six-year-old Hernan Crespo, who was in his prime. Batitusta, revered in his homeland, had several chances and scored in a 1-0 victory over Nigeria, but was not much of a factor in the two remaining first-round matches. Crespo was relegated to a reserve role and Argentina was relegated to an embarrassing first-round elimination.

DOES FOREIGN
AID HELP?

Of the thirty-two countries in the 2002 World Cup, eight—that's one quarter of the teams—were guided by coaches from other countries.

In 2006, a record number of countries will have foreign coaches at the helm. Chances that one of the eight coaches taking the victory lap around Olympiastadion in Berlin come July 9, 2006? None, if you go by history. Each of the previous seventeen World Cup champions was coached by a native son.

Of the forty-seven foreign coaches who have worked the last fourteen World Cups (back to 1950), only four teams have reached the Final Four and only three others have reached the quarterfinals. Generally, "Third World" soccer nations will tap a foreign to bring a team to the next level.

The most likely candidates come from Brazil, Yugoslavia,

France and Germany. It's no great embarrassment. Even the U.S. has used non-natives as head coaches in the past, the most recent being Bora Milutinovic, who directed the Americans into the second round at USA '94. In fact, Bora coached his fifth different country in the 2002 World Cup—China (as this book went to press, Bora hadn't found a team. However, he was named Costa Rica coach some three months before the 1990 kickoff, so anything is possible at the eleventh hour).

Bora's best finish? He brought Mexico to the quarterfinals in 1986, when the hosts succumbed to Germany in penalty kicks. Costa Rica's achievement of reaching the second round as World Cup debutantes playing across the Atlantic Ocean in Europe was considered a remarkable accomplishment as Bora coached that side as well. Bora's other team got out of the first round in one apiece—Nigeria (1998).

Bora's worst finish? By China in 2002. The Chinese lost all their matches in their World Cup debut.

⊕ George Raynor. The Englishman certainly had the magic touch with Sweden. He guided the Swedes to an Olympic gold medal in 1948, a fourth-place finish in the 1950 World Cup (2-3) and runners-up (4-1-1) to a fabulous Brazilian side in 1958.

⊕ Otto Gloria. The Brazilian was blessed to have such a talented player as Eusebio on his Portugal side (5-1), which finished third in the 1996 competition in England.

⊕ Guus Hiddink. The Dutch native guided Korea, which had never won a World Cup match in five previous tries, to a surprising fourth-place finish and a 3-2-2 record (buoyed by its enthusiastic supporters, Korea was 3-0-2 before losing its final two matches, in the semifinals and third-place match).

⊕ Jack Charlton. The Englishman coached Ireland (0-1-4) to the 1990 quarterfinals without the team winning a match before it lost to Italy, 1-0. Four years later at USA '94, Charlton got Ireland to overachieve (1-2-1) again, but was eliminated by the Netherlands in the second round.

⊕ Valeri Nepomniachi. This Soviet Union coach transformed Cameroon (3-2) into the darlings of the 1990 competition when the Africans upended defending champion Argentina in the opener, 1-

THE BEST
COACHING
JOBS BY
FOREIGNERS:

491

0, and took England to extratime in the quarterfinals, 3-2.

- ⊕ Waldir "Didi" Pereira. Didi, who played for Brazilian championship sides in 1958 and 1962, managed to get Peru (2-2) to the quarterfinals in 1970, where it lost to eventual champion Brazil.

- ⊕ Sven-Goran Eriksson. A controversial choice for the land that invented the game, the Swede directed England (2-1-2) into the 2002 quarterfinals before dropping a 2-1 decision to eventual champion Brazil. This time around, however, there are greater expectations for Eriksson and England.

- ⊕ Bruno Metsu. As coach of World Cup debutantes Senegal, this Frenchman and his team overcame overwhelming odds, upending France in the 2002 opener, 1-0, and reaching the quarterfinals before losing to another surprise side, Turkey, 1-0.

- ⊕ Bora Milutinovic. He directed undefeated Mexico (3-0-2) to the quarterfinals in 1986 before the hosts were eliminated by eventual runner-up Germany via a penalty-kick shootout after playing to a scoreless tie. Bora is the only foreign coach to finish a World Cup with an unbeaten record (remember, PK shootout losses officially go down as ties in the knockout rounds).

- ⊕ Jose Faria. The Brazilian native guided Morocco (1-1-2) into the second round in 1986, losing to runners-up West Germany, 1-0.

- ⊕ Sepp Piontek. The German directed Denmark to a 3-0 mark in the opening round in 1986 before the Danes (3-1) were thrashed by Spain, 5-1, in the second round.

- ⊕ Clemens Westerhof. The Dutch coach led Nigeria (2-2) in to the second round, but the Africans could not come up with the big defensive play when they needed it in a frustrating 2-1 extratime defeat to eventual runner-up Italy in 1994.

- ⊕ Jorge Solari. The Argentine coached Saudi Arabia (2-2) into the 1994 second round, where it lost to Sweden, 3-1.

- ⊕ Ray Hodgson. Another Englishman guided Switzerland (1-2-1) into the second round at USA '94, where it was ousted by Spain, 3-1.

- ⊕ Philippe Troussier. The Frenchman guided Japan (2-1-1) into the second round as the co-hosts went out of the 2002 competition with a whimper and not a bang, falling meekly to Turkey in the second round, 1-0.

- ⊕ Cesare Maldini. The father of Italian great and international defender Paolo Maldini helped Paraguay (1-2-1) reach the 2002 second round before Germany eliminated the South Americans, 1-0.

As for this year's crop of foreign coaches, Brazil leads the way with three, followed by the Netherlands and France with two apiece. Because there are not many foreigners—14—directing teams this time around, the odds are in their favor that their teams will accomplish something, perhaps to go as far as the quarterfinal or semifinals.

This year's crop (and their citizenship):

Australia—	Guus Hiddink (Netherlands)
Ecuador—	Luis Suarez (Colombia)
England—	Sven-Goran Eriksson (Sweden)
Ghana—	Ratomir Dujkovic (Serbia and Montenegro)
Iran—	Branko Ivankovic (Croatia)
Ivory Coast—	Michel Henri (France)
Japan—	Zico (Brazil)
Korea—	Dick Advocaat (Netherlands)
Mexico—	Ricardo LaVolpe (Argentina)
Paraguay—	Anibal Ruiz (Uruguay)
Portugal—	Luiz Felipe Scolari (Brazil)
Saudi Arabia—	Marcos Cesar Paqueta (Brazil)
Togo—	Stephen Keshi (Nigeria)
Tunisia—	Roger Lemere (France)

SOME
TRENDY
FACTS AND
FIGURES

More than anything else, the World Cup is about history. For example, only seven countries have paraded around with the World cup trophy in the 16 previous tournaments. History will be made in South Korea and Japan with the first World Cup stadium with a foot that will have a retractable grass field.

Saying that, here are a few tidbits that will help you understand the hows and whys of the world's greatest sporting spectacle.

IT PAYS TO
SCORE
FIRST

How important is scoring first? Well, teams that score first have registered a 418-87-97 mark, which is a healthy 77.4 percent winning percentage, or just about four out of five games. When a team scores first, it can begin to dictate a match. As the opposition gets antsy and starts to push up, the team in the lead has the option to counterattack and add to its total. It certainly doesn't happen that way all of the time, but it is a familiar scenario.

IT PAYS TO
WIN EARLY

CHAPTER
12

ABERRATIONS?

How important is winning your first match at a World Cup? If you plan on advancing to the second round it is virtually a must. Since group play was instituted for the first round in 1950, countries that win their first match have moved onto the next round 81.1 percent of the time (73-17). Teams that have lost their opening games have gotten out of the first round only 18.8 percent of the time (19-82). And if you tie, you have more than a fighting chance—62.5 percent (45-27) of playing in the second round.

The unlucky seventeen teams that won their first game but for some reason were eliminated in the opening round were Yugoslavia (1950), Uruguay ((1962), Argentina (1962), Brazil (1966), Italy (1966), Belgium (1970), Scotland (1974), Italy (1974), Tunisia (1978), Algeria (1982), Hungary (1982), Scotland (1982), Portugal (1986) and Norway (1994), Costa Rica (2002), Argentina (2002) and Russia (2002).

The fortunate nineteen nations that lost their opening game, but reached the second round and beyond were Yugoslavia (1962); England (1962); Hungary (1966); North Korea (1966); Argentina (1974); West Germany (1982), which reached the championship game before falling to Italy, 3-1; Argentina (1982); France (1982); Soviet Union (1982); Belgium (1986), which finished fourth; Spain (1986); England (1986); Argentina (1990), which lost in the championship game to Germany, 1-0; Yugoslavia (1990); Bulgaria (1994), which finished fourth; Mexico (1994); Italy (1994), which lost in the championship game to Brazil via penalty kicks; Saudi Arabia (1994): and Turkey (2002), which finished third. No team has lost its first match and won the World Cup.

FIRST-ROUND LOSSES	SECOND-ROUND LOSSES
1954--England 2, Switzerland 0	1994--Brazil 1, U.S. 0
1962--West Germany 2, Chile 0	1938--Italy 3, France 1
1974--East Germany 1,	1982--West Germany 2, Spain 1
West Germany 0	**QUARTERFINALS LOSSES**
1978--Italy 1, Argentina 0	1954--Austria 7, Switzerland 5
1982--Northern Ireland 1, Spain 0	**SEMIFINALS LOSSES**
1994--Romania 1, U.S. 0	1962--Brazil 4, Chile 2
	FINAL LOSSES
The seven latter round losses:	1950--Uruguay 2, Brazil 1
	1958 --Brazil 5, Sweden 2

In fact, thirteen of those fortunate nineteen countries advanced thanks to a wildcard berths at the 1982, 1986, 1990 and 1994 Cups. Since there won't be any wildcard team in 2006, it will be just about mandatory to win and survive and play at least another day.

Except for a handful of exceptions, teams that had their leading scorer with at least three goals have reached the semifinals sixty-three out of a possible sixty-eight times.

The four exceptions: Austria (1934), Uruguay (1950), which had four players who scored one goal apiece, France in 1986 (Jean-Pierre Papin, Yannick Stoprya and Michel Platini had two goals apiece), Argentina in 1990 (Claudio Caniggia finished with a team-best two goals) and Korea in 2002 (Jung Hwan Ahn, who had two goals).

Every champion has had a player who scored at least four goals, until France broke the rule in 1998. Thierry Henry scored three goals to lead France to the world championship.

How difficult is it for one player to dominate the scoring these days? Until Ronaldo accomplished the feat with eight goals in 2002, no player had scored more than six goals in a single World Cup since Grzegorz Lato hit the back of the net seven times for Poland in the competition in 1974. That's was a span of seven World Cups.

It depends on whether he will play at all, but if Italy's Christian Vieri can score one goal, he will join an elite group of players who have scored ten or more goals. Vieri struck five times at France '98 and on four occasions at Korea/Japan 2002. Ten players are in that club—Gerd Mueller (West Germany) 14; Just Fontaine (France) 13; Pelé (Brazil) 12; Ronaldo (Brazil) 12; Sandor Kocsis (Hungary) 11; Juergen Klinsmann (Germany) 11; Uwe Rahn (West Germany) 10; Nene Cubillas (Peru) 10; Grzegorz Lato (Poland) 10, and Gary Lineker (England) 10.

Don't expect the opening match between Germany and Costa Rica in Munich to break any scoring records if history is a guide. There have been only nine goals scored in the last 10 openers—three in Brazil's 2-1 win over Scotland in 1998. There have been four scoreless draws, four 1-0 results and a 1-1 tie.

There are many reasons why some countries pray to avoid others in the opening round. The primary reason is because those teams don't lose very often. Take, for example, Brazil. The South

IT PAYS
TO HAVE

CHAPTER
12

GOALSCORERS

THE BARRIER,
PART I

THE BARRIER,
PART II

FOR OPENERS

FIRST-ROUND
WONDERS

495

American side has lost but five times in the opening round in 17 appearances. The Brazilians have compiled 31-5-9 mark since 1930. As scary as those numbers are, here is the most frightening one of the bunch. Since the Brazilians were bounced from the opening round in 1966, they have lost but once—a meaningless 2-1 defeat to Norway in 1998 (Brazil already had won its group). They're a sparking 21-1-5 during that span, outscoring their opposition by an astounding 96-30 margin.

Germany isn't that far behind at 24-5-12. Argentina is next at 21-10-6, while Italy is pretty decent at 19-9-12.

It shouldn't be all that surprising that those four countries have combined for thirteen world championships.

FOR OPENERS
AND CLOSERS

Six teams have played in the opening and championship matches of the same tournament—champion Italy (1934), Brazil (1950), Sweden (1958), Chile (1962), champion England (1966) and Argentina (1990).

DEBUTANTES

Don't expect much from first-timers Angola, Ivory Coast, Togo, Ghana, Serbia and Montenegro and Trinidad & Tobago. The Czech Republic technically is making its World Cup debut, but it has a number of key players from the old Czechoslovakia teams and has been ranked as high as No. 2 in the world. Thus, it wouldn't be fair to call the Czech Republic a debutante. Countries participating in the World Cup for the first time just don't fare well.

Since 1934 (it would be unfair and unwise to count 1930 because all thirteen teams were making their World Cup debuts), teams performing in the tournament for the first time have compiled a 41-80-28 record. The four newcomers in 1998—Japan, Iran, South Africa and South Korea combined for a 1-9-2 mark, the lone victory being Jamaica's win over Japan. In 2002, the four new kids on the block—Senegal, Ecuador, Slovenia and China—combined for a 3-9-2 record, which was helped by the Africans—two victories.

BEST FIRST-
TIME PERFOR-
MANCE

The best first-time performance? It depends.

In 1934, Italy, as host won the World Cup with a 4-0-1 record, outscoring its foes, 12-3. But since the tournament was so young at the time—it was after all, the second World Cup—teams with decent or even outstanding records were bound to happen because a consistent qualifying process was virtually non-existent and many top teams still refrained from competing.

In modern times, Portugal probably enjoyed the most memorable Cup debut finishing with a perfect 3-0-0 first-round mark and 5-1 overall in 1966. The Portuguese reached the semifinals before losing to eventual-champion England, 2-1. They finished third, defeating the Soviet Union, 2-1, in the third-place match.

Denmark is a close second in first-round performances, rolling to a perfect 3-0-0 in 1986 before the Danes were dismantled by Spain in the second round, 5-1.

More recently, Croatia could not have asked for a better debut in 1998. The Croatians went 2-1-0 in the opening round, losing to Argentina, 1-0. They finally met their match in the semifinals, losing to France, 2-1, but rebounded for a 2-1 win over the Netherlands for third-place honors.

Costa Rica deserves mention because as a CONCACAF country playing in Europe, they were given no chance to survive. The Central Americans, however, finished with a 2-1 first-round mark, stunning Cup veterans Sweden and Scotland, but losing to Brazil at Italia '90. They met their match in the second round, losing to a bigger and more physical Czechoslovakian side, 4-1.

And Senegal certainly deserves mention as well. Playing under the scrutiny of the opening match in 2002, the African side stunned defending champion France, 1-0—and the rest of the world, for that matter—in the Cup opener in Korea. Senegal went on to finish second in its group to Denmark with a 1-0-2 record. The Senegalese squeaked past Sweden in extratime, 2-1, in the second round, before Turkey turned the table on the Africans with a 1-0 extratime quarterfinal triumph.

The worst performance? Ten countries went 0-3 in their initial Cups—El Salvador (1970), Haiti (1974), Zaire (1974), New Zealand (1982), Canada (1986), Iraq (1986), United Arab Emirates (1990), Greece (1994), Slovenia (2002) and China (2002).

BRAZIL BY THE NUMBERS

The Brazilians have used 210 players in 17 World Cups, fifty-nine who have scored. Brazil twice ran the table in the Cup, 6-0-0 in 1970 and a perfect 7-0-0 in 2002. It's worst competition? The Brazilians were eliminated after only one game in 1934, losing to Spain, 3-1. In more modern times, they were 1-2-0 and did not get out of the first round—with Pelé—in 1966.

Goalkeeper Claudio Taffarel and midfielder Dunga have made the most appearances—18 apiece—in the 1990, 1994 and 1998 competitions. Pelé and Ronaldo each have scored the most goals (12) of any Brazilian. They are followed by Leonidas, Ademir, Vava and Jairzinho, who have nine apiece.

CHAPTER

12

HOME
COOKING
IN THE
OPENING
ROUND

Much has been written about how well home teams fared. Here's taking it another step: How host countries perform in the opening and latter rounds. Hosts have lost only six times in the first round en route to a 31-6-10 record. In the second round and beyond, they're pretty close with a 25-10-6 record. Ironically, three of the losses came in the 2002 tournament as Turkey managed to beat both hosts.

The six first-round losses:
1954—England 2, Switzerland 0
1962—West Germany 2, Chile 0
1974—East Germany 1, West Germany 0
1978—Italy 1, Argentina 0
1982—Northern Ireland 1, Spain 0
1994—Romania 1, U.S. 0

The ten latter round loses:
1938—Italy 3, France 1 (second round)
1950—Uruguay 2, Brazil 1 (final)
1954—Austria 7, Switzerland 5 (quarterfinals)
1958—Brazil 5, Sweden 2 (final)
1962—Brazil 4, Chile 2 (semifinals)
1982—West Germany 2, Spain 1 (second round group)
1994—Brazil 1, U.S. 0 (second round)
2002—Germany 1, Korea 0 (semifinals)
2002—Turkey 3, Korea 2 (third-place match)
2002—Turkey 1, Japan 0 (second round)

Two elimination matches officially go down as a draw because the team was eliminated via a penalty-kick tie-breaker. That occurred in 1986, when West Germany prevailed over host Mexico in penalties, 4-1, after playing to a scoreless tie, and in 1990 when Argentina survived host Italy, in penalties, 4-3, after a 1-1 draw.

Four teams have lost two matches at home (one in the opening round, the other in the second round or beyond)—Switzerland (1954), Chile (1962), Spain (1982) and the U.S. (1994).

Six nations have won the World Cup on their own soil—Uruguay (1930), Italy (1934), England (1966), West Germany (1974), Argentina (1978) and France (1998).

Only Brazil has managed to win out of its hemisphere—Sweden in 1958 and in Korea/Japan in 2002. In fact, Brazil is among only two countries who have successfully defended its title. The Brazilians won in 1958 and in Chile in 1962. Italy captured titles at home in 1934 and in France in 1938.

So, what impact does a country winning all its three first-round matches have? A big one. Counting the 1930 competition (which had opening round group play), and since the World Cup went to group play in 1950, 10 teams—slightly more than half of the 18 teams who have swept through their opening-round games have reached at least the semifinals.

Three have won championships—Brazil (1970), France (1998) and Brazil again (2002). Argentina (1930) lost to Uruguay in the very first championship game. Portugal (1966) finished third, as did West Germany (1970), Poland (1974) and Italy (1990). Spain (1950) and Italy (1978) took fourth place.

But it wasn't always a happy ending or close to one. The first countries to run the table in the first round and come up way short were England (1982) and Brazil (1982), who were eliminated in their respective second round groups. The Brazilians, who have more perfect opening rounds (five), than any other country, were ousted in the 1986 quarterfinals, losing to France in a penalty-kick shootout, and to archrival Argentina in 1990, in a 1-0 second-round defeat. After a promising first round in its Cup debut, Denmark was thrashed by Spain, 5-1, in the second round. Argentina got off to a strong start in 1998, but the Netherlands sent the South American side packing with a dramatic 2-1 quarterfinal triumph. Spain, perennial disappointments, got its supporters' hopes way high in 2002, sweeping through the first round before it was sent home by Korea, shootout-winners in the quarterfinals.

CHAPTER

12

HOME

HEMISPHERE

ADVANTAGE

THREE AND IN

It must be noted that in the flawed 1954 tournament, three teams did finish unbeaten and untied—Hungary, which went on to lose to Germany, 3-2, in the final, and Austria, which was dismantled in the semifinals by Germany, 6-1, and Uruguay, who also was eliminated in the semis, 4-2 decision by the Hungarians.

According to the theory of sports relativity, for every winner there is a loser. In the World Cup, for every champion there is a last-place team. Mexico has finished last more times—three—than any other team in the 17 previous Cups. In fact, CONCACAF teams have wound up in the World Cup basement nine times. The roll call, bottoms up style: Mexico (1930), U.S. (1934), Netherlands Antilles (1938), Bolivia (1950), South Korea (1954), Mexico (1958), Switzerland (1962), Switzerland (1966), El Salvador (1970), Zaire (1974), Mexico (1978), El Salvador (1982), Canada (1986), United Arab Emirates (1990), Greece (1994), U.S. (1998) and Saudi Arabia (2002). Switzerland is the only country to finish last in back-to-back World Cups. Please note that the 1930 and 1950 tournaments had 13 teams each and the 1938 competition had 15. The 1934 and 1954-78 competitions had 16 teams, 1982-1994 had 24 countries. 1998 and 2002 had 32 nations.

Bibliography

1992 Information Please Almanac

1993 Information Please Almanac—America's Soccer Heritage, by Sam Foulds, Associated Press

BBC.com

BigAppleSoccer.com

Bobby Robson's Year at Barcelona, by Jeff King

CBS SportsLine (CBS Sportsline.com) Complete Book of Soccer/Hockey, Times Books

Complete Book of the Olympics, The, by David Wallechinsky

Daily Telegraph

Dizionario Del Calcio, a publication of La Gazzetta dello Sport

Encyclopedia of World Soccer, The, by Richard Henshaw

Encyklopedia Pitkarskich Mistrzostw Swiata, by Andrzej Gowarzewski

ENYSoccer.com

European Football Yearbook, 1991-92, The edited by Mike Hammond

European Football Yearbook, 1992-93, The edited by Mike Hammond

European Football Yearbook, The, 1996-97, edited by Mike Hammond

European Football Yearbook, 1997-98, The, edited by Mike Hammond

FIFA.com

FIFA News

FIFA Technical Report of the 1984 Olympics

FIFA Technical Report of the 1992 Olympics

FIFA Technical Report of the 1996 Olympics

FIFA Magazine

FIFA World Cup-Spain '82 (official report)

FIFA World Cup-Mexico '86 (official report)

FIFA World Cup-Italia '90 (official report)

FIFA World Cup-USA '94 (official report)

FIFA World Cup-France '98 (official report)

FIFA World Cup-Korea/Japan 2002 (official report)

FIFAWorldCup.com

FourFourTwo magazine

France Football magazine

Bibliography

Goal magazine

Guardian, The

Guinness Book of Olympic Facts and Feats, The, by Stan Greenberg

History of the World Cup, The, by Brian Glanville

International Herald Tribune

Italia â ˜90 information service

Jack Rollin's Complete World Cup Guide (1982), by Jack Rollins

Le Guide Du Football â ˜98

Los Angeles Times

Major League Soccer media guides, 1996 and 1997

Match of the Day magazine

Mexico â ˜86 information service

NASL, A Complete Record of the North American Soccer League, by Colin Jose

New York Daily News

New York Post

New York Times

Newsday

Olympic media guide (soccer), 1996

Onze magazine

Playfair World Cup, Mexico 1986, edited by Peter Dunk

Playing in Europe 1993-94 Reuters

Rochester Democrat and Chronicle

Rothman Presents World Cup 1982, by John Morgan and David Emery

SI.com

Simplest Game, The, by Paul Gardner

Soccer America

Soccer Digest Spain 1982, by Phil Soar and Richard Widdows

Soccer International

Soccer Magazine

Soccer New York

Soccer Tribe, The, by Desmond Morris

Soccer Week

Sporting News, The

Sunday Times (of London), The

Sunday Telegraph, The

Times (of London), The

Total Football magazine

U.S. Soccer 1993 Media Guide U.S. Soccer 1997 Media Guide U.S. Soccer 1998 Media Guide U.S. Soccer 2005 Media Guide U.S. Soccer 2006 Media Guide

U.S. Soccer vs. The World, by Tony Cirino

Ultimate Encyclopedia of European Soccer, The by Keir Radnedge

Ultimate Encyclopedia of Soccer, The by Keir Radnedge

United Press International USA TODAY

Washington Post, The

World Cup, 1930-90, The by John Robinson

World Cup, 1930-90, Sixty Glorious Years of Soccer's Premier Event, The by Jack Rollin

World Cup 1930-82, The by Jimmy Greaves

World Cup 86, by Philip Evans

World Cup, A Complete Record 1930-90, The by Ian Morrison

World Cup Espana â ˜82, by Franz Beckenbauer

World Cup media guide 1998

World Cup, The by Walt Chyzowych World Cup USA â ˜94 media guides of the competing countries

World Soccer magazine

Acknowledgments

As I've said a number of times prior, one person might write a book, but it is far from a one-man now.

To kick off my personal quadrennial acknowledgment marathon, once again a big thank you to Britt Bell, the publisher and editor at Moyer Bell. Twelve years ago he had the bold vision to publish the first edition of World Cup Soccer and in 2006 as he still has the resolve and ongoing vision to put out a fourth incarnation of the work. He also showed extreme patience with a writer who had an overloaded work schedule (especially with MetroStars/Red Bulls stories and scoops that needed to be researched and written during crunch time). Then there's Peter Sawyer and his colleagues at the Fifi Oscard Agency who once again made sure all the i's were dotted and the t's were crossed on the contract and who dispensed some important legal advice now and then.

A number of communications directors and public directors again came through big time on short notice. The long list starts with U.S. Soccer and Jim Moorhouse, Mike Kammarman, Neil Buethe, David Applegate and Elizabeth Sanchez, whose warp-speed turnaround time on getting information to me and pictures to Moyer Bell made life bearable when push came to shove. It continues with Steve Torres of CONCACAF, who pointed me in the right direction on a number of confederation-related matters. There's also Dan Courtemanche, Simon Borg, Marisabel Munoz, Will Kuhns and German Sferra of the Major League Soccer communications department, Rick Lawless, Phil Green and Patrick Mulrenin at MLSnet.com, and Matt Chmura and Eric Tosi of the current Red Bulls (formerly MetroStars) communications department and Nick DiBenedetto, formerly of the MLS team who was a great help early on.

Across the Atlantic, a big tip of my hat to Andreas Herren, Marius Schneider and Andreas Werz at FIFA and Keith Cooper of the German World Cup Organizing Committee for their ongoing assistance.

At ESPN.com, Jen Chang and Bob Wickwire have given yours

truly an a golden opportunity to broaden my horizons by allowing me to write columns and stories for their website about two World Cups (2002 and 2006) and one Olympics (2004).

I certainly cannot convey enough gratitude to the classy Youri Djorkaeff, with the help of Tosi, for conjuring up a magnificent Foreword that captured the true spirit of what it is like to actually win the coveted World Cup. I couldn't write or say those words any better myself. I should point out that in the Foreword, the humble Djorkaeff talks about a corner kick that led to France's second goal against Brazil in the 1998 final triumph. He did not mention it was he who originated the play.

A thank you for the staff at award-winning BigApple-Soccer.com (selected as best news website for 2005 by the Press Club of Long Island) for helping me directly and indirectly on this project. That includes my associate editor Dylan Butler, my business partner in what I unashamedly consider the best soccer website in the United States, Charlie Cuttone, and his wife, Linda Cuttone, who is also our photo editor and who contributed some photos to this book.

It certainly would not be fitting if I didn't include my inspiration among my peers and some talented writers who have written extensively about the beautiful game: Brian Glanville (*The Times of London, World Soccer*), Rob Hughes (*International Herald Tribune*), Simon Kuper (freelance writer, author), Patrick Barclay (*The Telegraph*) and Keir Radnedge (*World Soccer*) from across the pond, and Paul Gardner (*Soccer America*), Grahame Jones (*Los Angeles*), Steve Goff (*Washington Post*), Frank Dell'Apa (*Boston Globe*), Kelly Whiteside (*USA Today*), Jeff Bradley (*ESPN The Magazine*) Grant Wahl (*Sports Illustrated*), George Vecsey (*New York Times*) Ridge Mahoney and Mike Woitalla (both *Soccer America*) and Filip Bondy (*New York Daily News*).

And finally, but certainly not least, to a group of fantastic people who have put up with my crazy and seemingly always chaotic schedule: Judy, Alan, Jill, Debbie, Rob, Jacob, Rachel, and of course, Jennie.

COLOPHON

Michael Lewis is one of the pre-eminent soccer writers in the United States. He has covered five World Cups (1986, 1990, 1994, 1998 and 2002) and five Olympics. He has been the soccer columnist for the *New York Daily News* since 1988 and is editor and co-founder of the award-winning BigApple-Soccer.com. He also has written for *USA Today*, CNNSI.com and ESPN.com. Lewis, the author of six books, has won fifty-five writing awards. He lives in Coram, New York.

The text was set in Times New Roman, a typeface designed by Stanley Morison (1889-1967). This face designed for The Times of London was the result of a criticism Morison made to the management of The Times complaining of the paper's typography. They asked him to improve it. Working for the Monotype Corporation, Morison designed a face based on Granjon, and delivered it for use beginning in 1932. It has since become one of the most widely used faces and often copied because of its readability.

World Cup Soccer was composed by Rhode Island Book Composition, Kingston, RI. The book was printed by Data Reproduction, Auburn Hills, Michigan on acid-free paper.

Date	Venue	Teams	Time
GROUP A—Costa Rica, Ecuador, Germany, Poland			
June 9	Munich	GER vs. CRC	18:00
June 9	Gelsenkirchen	POL vs. ECU	21:00
June 14	Dortmund	GER vs. POL	21:00
June 15	Hamburg	ECU vs. CRC	15:00
June 20	Berlin	ECU vs. GER	16:00
June 20	Hanover	CRC vs. POL	16:00
GROUP B—England, Paraguay, Sweden, Trinidad and Tobago			
June 10	Frankfurt	ENG vs. PAR	15:00
June 10	Dortmund	TRI vs. SWE	18:00
June 15	Nuremberg	ENG vs. TRI	18:00
June 15	Berlin	SWE vs. PAR	21:00
June 20	Cologne	SWE vs. ENG	21:00
June 20	Kaiserslautern	PAR vs. TRI	21:00
GROUP C—Argentina, Ivory Coast, Netherlands, Serbia/Montenegro			
June 10	Hamburg	ARG vs. CIV	21:00
June 11	Leipzig	SCG vs. NED	15:00
June 16	Gelsenkirchen	ARG vs. SCG	15:00
June 16	Stuttgart	NED vs. CIV	18:00
June 21	Frankfurt	NED vs. ARG	21:00
June 21	Munich	CIV vs. SCG	21:00
GROUP D—Angola, Iran, Mexico, Portugal			
June 11	Nuremberg	MEX vs. IRN	18:00
June 11	Cologne	ANG vs. POR	21:00
June 16	Hanover	MEX vs. ANG	21:00
June 17	Frankfurt	POR vs. IRN	15:00
June 21	Gelsenkirchen	POR vs. MEX	16:00
June 21	Leipzig	IRN vs. ANG	16:00
GROUP E—Czech Republic, Ghana, Italy, USA			
June 12	Hanover	ITA vs. GHA	21:00
June 12	Gelsenkirchen	USA vs. CZE	18:00
June 17	Kaiserslautern	ITA vs. USA	21:00
June 17	Cologne	CZE vs. GHA	18:00
June 22	Hamburg	CZE vs. ITA	16:00
June 22	Nuremberg	GHA vs. USA	16:00
GROUP F—Australia, Brazil, Croatia, Japan			
June 13	Berlin	BRA vs. CRO	21:00
June 12	Kaiserslautern	AUS vs. JPN	15:00
June 18	Munich	BRA vs. AUS	18:00
June 18	Nuremberg	JPN vs. CRO	15:00
June 22	Dortmund	JPN vs. BRA	21:00
June 22	Stuttgart	CRO vs. AUS	21:00
GROUP G—France, Korea, Switzerland, Togo			
June 13	Stuttgart	FRA vs. SUI	18:00
June 13	Frankfurt	KOR vs. TOG	15:00
June 18	Leipzig	FRA vs. KOR	21:00
June 19	Dortmund	TOG vs. SUI	15:00
June 23	Cologne	TOG vs. FRA	21:00
June 23	Hanover	SUI vs. KOR	21:00
GROUP H—Saudi Arabia, Spain, Tunisia, Ukraine			
June 14	Leipzig	ESP vs. UKR	15:00
June 14	Munich	TUN vs. KSA	18:00
June 19	Stuttgart	ESP vs. TUN	21:00
June 19	Hamburg	KSA vs. UKR	18:00
June 23	Kaiserslautern	KSA vs. ESP	16:00
June 23	Berlin	UKR vs. TUN	16:00

Date	Time	Venue	Match	Winner vs Runner-U
Second Round				
June 24	11 A.M.	Munich	49	Group A vs. Grou
June 24	3 P.M.	Leipzig	50	Group C vs. Grou
June 25	11 A.M.	Stuttgart	51	Group B vs. Grou
June 25	3 P.M.	Nuremberg	52	Group D vs. Grou
June 26	11 A.M.	Kaiserslautern	53	Group E vs. Grou
June 26	3 P.M.	Cologne	54	Group G vs. Grou
June 27	11 A.M.	Dortmund	55	Group F vs. Grou
June 27	3 P.M.	Hannover	56	Group H vs. Grou
Quarter Final				
June 30		Berlin	57	Game 49 vs. Game
June 30		Hamburg	58	Game 51 vs. Game
July 1		Gelsenkirchen	59	Game 53 vs. Game
July 1		Frankfurt	60	Game 55 vs. Game
Semi Finals				
July 4		Dortmund	61	Game 57 vs. Game
July 5		Munich	62	Game 59 vs. Game
Third Place Final				
July 8		Stuttgart	63	Semifinal losers
Championship				
July 9		Berlin	64	Semifinal winners

TEAMS   page

TEAMS page #	TEAMS page #
Angola (ANG)—267	Mexico (MEX)—341
Argentina (ARG)—271	Netherands (NED)—346
Australia (AUS)—276	Paraguay (PAR)—350
Brazil (BRA)—280	Poland (POL)—354
Costa Rica (CRC)—285	Portugal (POR)—358
Croatia (CRO)—289	Saudi Arabia (KSA)—362
Czech Republic (CZE)—293	Serbia and Montenegro
Ecuador (ECU)—298	(SCG)—366
England (ENG)—302	Spain (ESP)—370
France (FRA)—307	Sweden (SWE)—374
Germany (GER)—311	Switzerland (SUI)—378
Ghana (GHA)—316	Togo (TOG)—382
Iran (IRN)—320	Trinidad and Tobago (TRI)
Italy (ITA)—324	385
Ivory Coast (CIV)—329	Tunisia (TUN)—389
Japan (JPN)—333	Ukraine (UKR)—392
Korea Republic (KOR)—337	USA (USA)—396

GROUPS—Team

GROUP A—Costa Rica, Ecuador, Germany, Poland

GROUP B—England, Paraguay, Sweden, Trinidad and Tobago

GROUP C—Argentina, Ivory Coast, Netherlands, Serbia/Montene

GROUP D—Angola, Iran, Mexico, Portugal

GROUP E—Czech Republic, Ghana, Italy, USA

GROUP F—Australia, Brazil, Croatia, Japan

GROUP G—France, Korea, Switzerland, Togo

GROUP H—Saudi Arabia, Spain, Tunisia, Ukraine